ARTIFICIAL INTELLIGENCE
THEORY AND PRACTICE

ARTIFICIAL INTELLIGENCE
THEORY AND PRACTICE

THOMAS DEAN
BROWN UNIVERSITY

JAMES ALLEN
UNIVERSITY OF ROCHESTER

YIANNIS ALOIMONOS
UNIVERSITY OF MARYLAND

ADDISON-WESLEY PUBLISHING COMPANY

MENLO PARK, CALIFORNIA
READING, MASSACHUSETTS • NEW YORK • DON MILLS, ONTARIO
WOKINGHAM, U.K. • AMSTERDAM • BONN • SYDNEY
SINGAPORE • TOKYO • MADRID • SAN JUAN

Acquisitions Editor: J. Carter Shanklin
Executive Editor: Daniel Joraanstad
Editorial Assistant: Melissa Standen
Marketing Manager: Mary Tudor
Production Manager: Gwen Larson
Senior Production Editor: Judith Hibbard
Text Design Director: Michele Carter
Text Design: Art Ogawa
Cover Art Director: Yvo Riezebos
Cover Designer: Ison Design
Senior Photo Editor: Cecilia Mills
Manufacturing Coordinator: Janet Weaver
Composition: Electronic Technical Publishing Services Co.
Copyeditor: Robert Fiske/Vocabula Communications Co.
Proofreader: Joanne McClintock

Cover image: Wassily Kandinsky, "Swinging" 1925. Tate Gallery, London/Art Resource, NY. ©1995 Artists Rights Society, New York/ADAGP, Paris

Many of the designations used by manufacturers and sellers to distinguish their products are claimed as trademarks. Where those designations appear in this book, and Benjamin/Cummings was aware of a trademark claim, the designations have been printed in initial caps or all caps.

The programs and applications presented in this book have been included for their instructional value. They have been tested with care but are not guaranteed for any particular purpose. The publisher does not offer any warranties or representations, nor does it accept any liabilities with respect to the programs or applications.

Microsoft is a registered trademark of Microsoft Corporation.

Library of Congress Cataloging-in-Publication Data
Dean, Thomas L., 1950–
    Artificial intelligence: theory and practice / Thomas Dean, James
Allen, John Aloimonos.
        p. cm.
    Includes bibliographical references and index.
    ISBN 0-8053-2547-6
    1. Artificial intelligence. I. Allen, James, 1950–
II. Aloimonos, John. III. Title
Q335.D4 1995
006.3–dc20   94-32625
                                                                           CIP

ISBN 0-8053-2547-6

    2 3 4 5 6 7 8 9 10-DOC-98 97 96 95

Addison-Wesley Publishing Company
2725 Sand Hill Road
Menlo Park, CA 94025

CONTENTS

PREFACE

This book is designed to introduce students to a set of theoretical and computational techniques that serve as a foundation for the study of artificial intelligence (AI). The presentation is aimed at students with a background in computer science at about the sophomore or junior level in college. The emphasis is on algorithms and theoretical machinery for building and analyzing AI systems. Traditional symbolic AI techniques such as deductive inference, game-tree search, and natural language parsing are covered, as are hybrid approaches such as those employed in neural networks, probabilistic inference, and machine vision. The coverage is broad, with selected topics explored in greater depth but with no attempt to exhaustively survey the entire field.

Representation

The book focuses on the importance of representation in the core chapters dealing with logic, search, and learning. It incorporates a more formal treatment of AI than is found in most introductory textbooks. This formal treatment is reflected in the attention given to syntax and semantics in logic and in the material concerning the computational complexity of AI algorithms.

The material on learning draws on recent unifying work in computational learning theory to explain a variety of techniques from decision trees to neural networks.

The book provides a consistent pedagogic example of AI in the real world through examples focusing on AI systems corresponding to robots and software automation "softbots." A wide range of other examples are also introduced to characterize both the potential and the variety of AI applications. The chapters on natural language processing, planning, uncertainty, and vision supply a state-of-the-art perspective unifying existing approaches and summarizing challenging areas for future research.

This book is not meant as an exhaustive survey of AI techniques. Subjects such as qualitative reasoning about physical systems and analogical reasoning are only briefly touched on in this text. Other subjects are given much more attention in this book than in traditional texts. Learning, planning, and probabilistic reasoning are treated in some depth, reflecting their increased importance in the field. The chapter on vision (Chapter 9, Image Understanding) is substantial in its coverage of topics to reflect the importance of perception in understanding intelligence and building artifacts that interact with the world in useful and interesting ways.

Theory and Practice

Although the text emphasizes theoretical foundations, practical problems involved with the implementation of AI algorithms are addressed in every chapter. A self-contained introduction to symbolic programming in Common Lisp is provided to encourage students to perform computational experiments. Lisp code is given for many of the important algorithms described in the text; however, the text is designed so that the student can ignore Lisp and implementation issues altogether if he or she chooses. The code uses a carefully chosen subset of Common Lisp to teach algorithmic issues in AI. In contrast, other texts use AI algorithms to teach Lisp programming techniques.

All the algorithms in the text are described in English prose and pseudo code. In the case of algorithms that are also given in Lisp, most of the time the code appears in a Lisp Implementation appendix at the end of the chapter, but on some occasions it appears in the main body of the chapter. Code appears in the main body when it is considered particularly important that the student explore the underlying issues empirically. With most of the Lisp code relegated to appendices, instructors are free to choose the areas they want to emphasize empirically. The tight coupling between the descriptions of algorithms in the text and the accompanying Lisp code makes it easy for students to experiment, without the bother of using two texts with different perspectives and algorithmic approaches.

We use Lisp instead of Prolog because Lisp is closest in structure to languages such as Pascal and C that students are likely to be familiar with. We use Lisp instead of Pascal or C because the list processing and symbolic manipulation routines available in Lisp allow for elegant implementations of important algorithms that can be compactly listed. Note, however, that a library of C++ code is available (see the section on "Supplements") that mirrors the Common Lisp treatment in the text function for function and algorithm for algorithm.

To the Student

Preface material is usually aimed at instructors who are thinking of adopting a text for a course. Generally, students cut straight to the first chapter or the table of contents to get some idea of what the book is about. This book is designed to teach students about the theory and practice of building computer programs that perform interesting and useful tasks. With the exception of some diversions in the introductory chapter, we leave the philosophical conundrums to the philosophers and focus on techniques, algorithms, and analytical tools that we believe students will find useful in building sophisticated (even *intelligent*) computer programs.

The book describes precise problems, analyzes them from a computational perspective, and specifies efficient algorithms for their solution where possible. Along the way, we provide the necessary logic, computer science, and mathematics for you to understand the important issues and ultimately develop your own solutions and propose your own problems. Our hope is that you will find the techniques and ideas in this book useful, whether you pursue a career in engineering, computer science, business management, or any other area that requires you to think in terms of computational processes that have to interact with a complex and changing world.

To the Instructor

The core material in the book is in the first five chapters covering basic introductory and motivational material, symbolic programming for courses interested in implementation, representation and logic, search, and learning. Within these core chapters, instructors have considerable flexibility regarding what to include and how much time to spend on particular topics.

The choice of topics and allocation of lecture time will depend on the background of the students taking the course. Often students have a reasonable background in boolean logic from a previous course in computer science, engineering, or mathematics, in which case the chapter on representation and logic can move along rather quickly. Search issues are generally familiar to computer science students, and the basic blind-search methods, including depth-first and breadth-first search, should take very little time.

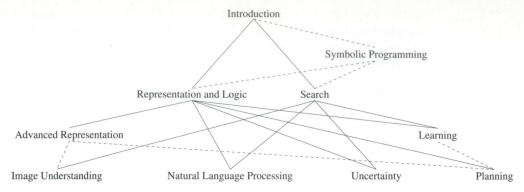

Figure 1   This graph illustrates some of the dependencies and connections among the chapters in this text. A solid line indicates a strong dependency between two chapters, and a dashed line indicates a connection or conditional dependency between two chapters that an instructor may wish to consider.

We recommend spending a significant amount of time on learning since the area is reasonably mature, the issues dramatically illustrate the role of representation and search, and students are generally fascinated with the prospect of building systems that learn.

Representation appears before search in the order of chapters because representation is the more fundamental idea as far as AI is concerned. We emphasize logic because it enables students to think precisely about representation. Pedagogically, there are situations that merit covering search before representation; if you are teaching Lisp and this is the students' first exposure to Lisp and symbolic programming, consider covering the search chapter first because the examples of search procedures provide a somewhat easier introduction to Lisp programming issues. With the exception of the section on discrimination networks at the end of the search chapter, the representation and search chapters can be covered in either order.

Figure 1 illustrates some of the dependencies and connections among the chapters in this text. A solid line indicates that one chapter should be covered before another chapter in order to fully understand all the material. A dashed line indicates a connection between two chapters that an instructor may wish to emphasize or a conditional dependency that an instructor may wish to account for. For example, the section on spatial representation and robot navigation in Chapter 6 (Advanced Representation) can be used to motivate and set the stage for topics covered in Chapter 9 (Image Understanding). All the chapters are conditionally dependent on Chapter 2 (Symbolic Programming) if implementation issues are to be covered and the students require instruction in symbolic programming methods. Additional information regarding chapter dependencies and synergies as well as suggestions for course syllabi are available in the Instructors Resource Guide (see the section on "Supplements").

Supplements

Source supplemental materials for this book are available via anonymous FTP from aw.com in the subdirectory aw/dean. The supplemental materials for the book include the following items:

- Instructor's Guide and Solutions Manual—contain notes on each chapter, solutions to selected exercises, additional exercises for the Lisp (Chapter 2) and vision (Chapter 9) chapters, and sample exams with answers. This guide is available only on a $3\frac{1}{2}$" disk from the publisher (ISBN 32548-4).

- Selected figures—selected figures in encapsulated PostScript format are available for overhead transparencies.

- Source code—the sample source code contained in the text is available in both Lisp and C++ implementations. Other implementations may be available (for example, the Scheme dialect of Lisp); check the README file in bc/dean for current status and recent developments.

To obtain the supplemental materials, FTP to bc.aw.com as follows:

```
% ftp aw.com
```

and log on as anonymous. Use your electronic mail address as your password and connect to the directory for this book by typing

```
% cd aw/dean
```

Before retrieving supplements, it is a good idea to look at the README file to see if changes have been made since this book went to press. You can retrieve this file by typing

```
% get README
```

Type quit to exit FTP and read the README file. (Although you could read the file online, it is courteous not to load the FTP server while you are just reading.) Then log back on when you are ready to download the files that you want. Using FTP to retrieve archived files can get complicated. The README file will give you some additional advice, but you may find it helpful to consult your favorite UNIX guide or local artwork wizard.

Thanks

We benefited from the efforts of many previous authors in organizing the material covered in this text and figuring out how to present the material to students. In particular, we would like to acknowledge the texts by Charniak and McDermott [1985], Nilsson [1980], and Winston [1979] that provided our first introductions to AI. We are also indebted to Davis [1990], Genesereth and Nilsson [1987], Ginsberg [1993], and Winston [1992], whose books we consulted while writing this text.

A lot of friends and colleagues contributed to this book by providing feedback to the authors during crucial times during its writing. In particular, we would like to thank the following people:

Mark Boddy	Robert Goldman	Bart Selman
Chris Brown	Steve Hanks	Jude Shavlik
Jack Breese	Eric Horvitz	Yoav Shoham
Eugene Charniak	Leslie Kaelbling	Mike Shwe
Ernie Davis	Paris Kanellakis	Austin Tate
Mark Drummond	Richard Korf	Prasad Tadepalli
Charles Dyer	Tom Mitchell	Dan Weld
Nort Fowler	Ann Nicholson	Mike Wellman

The production and editorial help from Addison-Wesley Publishing Company was exceptional. We would like to thank Carter Shanklin, the Acquisitions Editor for Computer Science at Addison-Wesley, for shepherding us through the entire process. Judith Hibbard, the Senior Production Editor, Melissa Standen, the Editorial Assistant, and Ari Davidow, the Technical Production Assistant, were amazingly helpful at all the right times. We would also like to thank Sara Larson from the University of Maryland at College Park, who helped with the vision chapter, and Mary Andrade and Dawn Nichols from Brown University, who provided invaluable assistance in keeping track of the many drafts and handling the extensive correspondence that was required.

A large number of students also provided feedback while we were writing the text, far too many to list, but the following deserve special mention:

Scott Baetz	Michael Littman
Ted Camus	Mike Perkowitz
Lloyd Greenwald	Kostadis Roussos
Shieu-Hong Lin	Smith Surasmith

A special thanks goes to Jon Monsarrat for his unflagging enthusiasm for the project and for the many hours he spent hacking UNIX, PostScript, and LaTeX. Finally, each of us would like to thank our respective spouses and loved ones for being supportive when it was needed most.

Thomas Dean
James Allen
Yiannis Aloimonos

About the Authors

Thomas Dean is a Professor in the Computer Science Department at Brown University. His general research interests include temporal and spatial reasoning, planning, robotics, learning, and probabilistic inference. Professor Dean's recent work has led to the design and implementation of a temporal database system for applications involving mobile robots and factory automation. He is on the executive council and is a Fellow of the American Association for Artificial Intelligence (AAAI). He served as the program co-chair for the 1991 National Conference on Artificial Intelligence. Professor Dean was also a recipient of the NSF Presidential Young Investigator Award (1989–1994).

James Allen is the John H. Dessaurer Professor of Computer Science at the University of Rochester. He is a fellow of the AAAI and was a recipient of the NSF Presidential Young Investigator Award (1985–1989). In addition, Professor Allen was the Editor-in-Chief of *Computational Linguistics* from 1983 to 1993.

Yiannis Aloimonos is an Associate Professor at the Computer Science Department and the Institute for Advanced Computer Studies of the University of Maryland. He also heads the Computer Vision Laboratory of the Center for Automation Research. His research interests include computer vision and the integration of perception, reasoning, and action. He is a recipient of the NSF Presidential Young Investigator Award (1990–1995).

This book is dedicated to Jo

CHAPTER ▮

INTRODUCTION

Artificial intelligence (AI) is the design and study of computer programs that behave intelligently. These programs are constructed to perform as would a human or an animal whose behavior we consider intelligent. AI computer programs schedule airlines and control factories. They also perform more mundane tasks like cleaning floors and delivering mail.

Some tasks that you may consider difficult are easy to program, and others that you take for granted are quite difficult. AI researchers have written programs to control nuclear power plants and diagnose problems in complicated electronic devices. However, it has proved to be more difficult to write programs that can reliably recognize faces or clean your house without terrorizing your cat and destroying your furniture.

AI is concerned with programs that respond flexibly in situations that were not specifically anticipated by the programmer. A house-cleaning robot should distinguish between a scrap of tin foil and a diamond ring, and it should be able to cope if you rearrange the furniture. A face recognition program should be able to identify the same person with a different hat or hair cut. We measure intelligence in humans by observing how people solve problems and respond in novel situations. We evaluate computer programs in much the same way.

In this chapter, we provide examples of AI theory and practice. We consider what it might mean for a program to exhibit intelligence. We also describe some of the issues involved in constructing theories of behavior in which computation plays an important role. We begin our discussion by considering an application for which intelligent machines are ideally suited.

Robot Explorers

Space explorations to Mars have brought us closer to understanding the large features of the red planet. The first probe to reach Mars orbit, in 1971, returned beautiful pictures of Martian craters and channels. The mission revealed complex canyon systems and enormous volcanos. Evidence of running water millions of years ago was discovered, and Mars was found to have a thin atmosphere. The surface of Mars has also been studied. Actually touching down on the planet's surface, the Viking spacecraft sent back pictures of a pink sky and great expanses of red sand and rocks. They took soil samples to search for microscopic traces of life and listened carefully for earthquakes. Of course, this information has led to more questions; the surface of Mars remains a mystery.

Unfortunately, the spacecraft that landed on Mars were not designed for travel on the planet's surface, so they sat immobile, gathering data from their immediate surroundings. There is not much they could do in one place. A better way to explore Mars would certainly be to send people there. Visiting astronauts could drive over the surface, making surveys of several remote sites and performing experiments. They could make quick decisions about where to explore and adapt to any changes in plan.

Humans, however, cost a great deal to transport to outer space. Astronauts need room to move around in and numerous facilities not only for survival, but also for comfort, since a trip to Mars would last several years. Morever, the ship landing on Mars would need to be much heavier and more complex because it would need to be able to return the crew to Earth. Because of these considerations, there will probably be no manned mission to any planet in the near future. Instead, we will send machines (see Figure 1.1). A machine can spend years in space with few amenities and need not be returned to Earth.

A machine to explore Mars would need some of the same capabilities as a human astronaut. Such a machine or *robot* would have to perceive its surroundings, navigate on the Martian surface, respond to events as they occur, and decide what to do next. Some of the decision making could be carried out by humans on Earth, but delays in communication will require the robot to perform autonomously for significant periods. What sort of capabilities would a robot explorer need? To what extent can we give a machine humanlike capacities for perception and decision making? These are some of the questions addressed by artificial intelligence.

Artificial intelligence is like physics, chemistry, and biology in that each of these fields has applied and theoretical sides. But these fields differ in that artificial intelligence is the study of human-made machines, not the

Figure 1.1 The camera image on the left was taken by NASA's Viking 1 Orbiter spacecraft while searching for a landing site for the Viking 2 Lander. The speckled appearance of the image is due to missing data, caused by problems in transmitting the image data from Mars to Earth. The photograph on right shows a prototype mobile robot designed by researchers at NASA's Jet Propulsion Laboratory for exploring the Martian surface. Both photos courtesy of Jet Propulsion Laboratory.

study of natural phenomena. The scope of AI is limited not by nature but by imagination and the fundamental limitations of computing machinery. Some examples of artificial intelligence in practice and theory will help illustrate the different aspects of the field.

1.1 Artificial Intelligence in Practice

Artificial intelligence systems serve a wide variety of practical purposes. There are programs that generate investment strategies by predicting trends in the stock market, diagnose patient illnesses suggesting treatment, and control assembly robots in factories. Many people who work in AI consider themselves to be engineers, focusing on building practical tools. These tools, called *AI systems*, are used to plan routes for airlines, build cars in factories, and play master-level chess. Our robot for exploring Mars would be controlled by an AI system.

How does a robot like our Mars explorer see its environment? How does it decide what actions to take? Given two or more possibly conflicting goals, how does it balance their priorities? How would the rover know to stop and examine an entirely unexpected quartz formation? More generally, how do we design a system versatile enough to adapt to its environment yet rigid enough to be encoded in a computer program?

▲ AI IN PRACTICE

NASA Mission to Explore Mars

The next NASA mission to Mars is planned to use rovers based on "Rocky," a robot designed by the Jet Propulsion Laboratory. It has an all-metal chassis, to withstand the cold temperature of Mars, and a special suspension, made for travel on sandy, rocky terrain. Rocky was designed to be light and small (only 2 feet long), so it can be transported easily. However, it will carry a small computer, some cameras, and a spectrometer to analyze rocks.

Because communication to Mars at light speed takes 40 minutes, the robot needs to be able to drive itself for short distances. Rocky will be controlled remotely from Earth by a pilot who will see the Martian terrain through Rocky's stereo cameras. When the pilot chooses a path for Rocky to follow, our Mars explorer follows the path until some obstacle is encountered. Then Rocky tries to go around the obstacle. If at some point the rover gets stuck, it calls Earth for instructions.

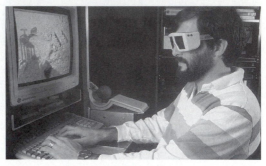

Both photos © Guy Spangenberg

Examples of Artificial Intelligence Systems

Artificial intelligence is the basis for a host of other practical systems. Some of these systems already exist, and some are being designed for the future.

Language translation systems   There are now artificial intelligence translators that you can speak to and have them print transcripts of what you say in foreign languages. The most advanced systems can answer questions based on the information in the text and produce useful summaries.

Air traffic control systems   The skies over our airports are becoming crowded as air travel becomes more popular. Tracking thousands of flights, personnel, and maintenance schedules is a difficult job for humans. Computers help by scheduling the arrival and departure of flights to maximize passenger safety and minimize delays.

Supervisory systems   As large office buildings and shopping malls become more complex, we need systems to control public services. A supervisory AI system controls elevators, power, and climate conditions. It also manages security and safety inspections and directs visitors to their destinations.

Automated personal assistants   It is now possible to build AI systems to actively guide you in using computer networks. They can search through bulletin boards and filter your mail so that you read only the most important and interesting items. They can help you find information, buy products and services, and locate people through the electronic networks. This kind of AI system is called a *softbot,* for *soft*ware ro*bot.* Softbots are disembodied robots, computer programs that move about in networks of computers.

Intelligent highways   Traffic congestion is a growing problem on our major highways. But doubling the size of our road system would be expensive in the countryside and impossible in cities where space is limited. Instead, efforts are now underway to build AI systems that optimize the usage of existing highways by broadcasting traffic warnings, redirecting vehicles to alternative streets, and controlling the speed and spacing of vehicles. In the future, your car will plan the route to your destination in coordination with the automated highway managers.

Robots for hazardous conditions   Toxic waste cleanup, especially in the nuclear industry, will become increasingly important in the coming years. There are also important applications in biohazard handling in hospitals; underground mining; and underwater mining, salvage, construction, and agriculture. Robots can also handle nonhazardous tasks that are unpleasant or tedious, such as garbage collection or harvesting crops.

All these programs require skills we normally associate with natural intelligence. Autonomous robots have to solve problems and respond correctly in new, unanticipated situations. Language translation systems must apply general, common-sense knowledge in order to answer questions, which can be worded in a variety of ways. Air traffic controllers and supervisory systems have to make complicated decisions under time pressure. Softbots should improve their searches by learning from experience and adapt to the needs of their user. Figuring out how to implement these skills is a large part of what applied AI is all about.

1.2 Artificial Intelligence Theory

Artificial intelligence is more than an engineering discipline; it is also a subject of scientific investigation. Researchers construct theories about what AI programs are capable of and test them with mathematical analyses or experiments. What adaptations are possible for systems that learn from experience? How can systems change in response to new information? What kind of training should a learning program receive? Scientists in AI are developing general computational theories to answer these questions and others.

Theories are subjected to examination analytically by developing mathematical abstractions and proving theorems. They are also studied empirically by developing programs, running experiments, and analyzing the results—much as a psychologist might conduct experiments on human

▲ AI IN PRACTICE

Theory and Practice in Learning

Professor Q. has been asked to help design a robot to carry mail for the Feral Express overnight package delivery company. This robot will be given priority mail to deliver in downtown Providence, Rhode Island, in the middle of the business day. She is designing the navigation system that computes a route for the robot to follow in delivering a package.

The problem has a straightforward solution that is easy to implement: *Read the address on the package, use a map of the city to find the shortest route from the Feral Express depot to the address, and then follow the path.* However, this solution fails to account for changes in traffic conditions, road construction, and other information that is not available on a static map of the city.

Professor Q. has developed a learning algorithm that continually adapts its strategy for finding routes to account for new information regarding malfunctioning traffic lights, road construction, and traffic congestion. She is trying to prove that under certain assumptions her learning algorithm is the best possible.

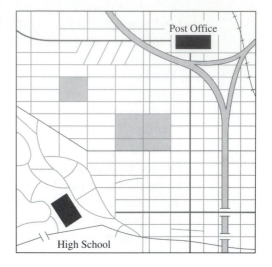

subjects. The behavior of complex AI systems is difficult to predict. Often researchers are surprised by the behavior of the systems that they build.

Examples of Artificial Intelligence Theory

Here are some examples of results that have important consequences for theoretical research in artificial intelligence. The descriptions are simplified somewhat to avoid introducing new terminology. We revisit these results in later chapters after we have provided the necessary background.

Inferring structure from motion in machine vision   Machine vision is concerned with interpreting the information contained in electronic camera images. Researchers have shown that there is an upper bound on the information that must be extracted from a series of camera images in order to answer questions about the structure and motion of an object captured in those images. (Ullman [1981] showed that, given three distinct views of four points on a rigid object, the structure and motion of the object compatible with the three views are uniquely determined.)

Finding consistent hypotheses in learning   In concept learning, a system is given a set of examples of a target concept and asked to find a hypothesis describing the concept that is consistent with examples it has seen so far. For some classes of concepts, finding a consistent hypothesis can be done efficiently. (Valiant [1984] showed that finding a hypothesis that is consistent with a set of examples of a concept that can be described by a conjunction of simple features can be done in polynomial time.)

Probabilistic inference in diagnostic reasoning   In medical diagnosis, networks involving probabilities are used to infer the most likely disease from a patient's symptoms. It has been shown that the calculations required for such inferences are computationally complex. (Exact calculation of probabilities for network probability models is NP-complete [Cooper, 1987], and certain types of approximate calculations are NP-hard [Dagum and Luby, 1993].)

Search in automated planning   In planning for robots or factories, it is desirable that an algorithm never consider the same plan twice and that the algorithm always find a solution to a planning problem if one exists. Such algorithms have been found for particular classes of planning problems. (McAllester and Rosenblitt [1991] provide an algorithm for finding a plan represented as a partially ordered set of actions. This algorithm never considers the same plan twice and always finds a solution if one exists.)

Parsing sentences in language understanding   Parsing reveals the structure of sentences and is an important step in automated language understanding. The context-free languages represent a special class of languages. It has been shown that the problem of parsing sentences from a context-free language is computationally easy. Although most natural languages are not context free, they can often be closely approximated by a context-free language. (Parsing context-free languages can be done in time proportional to the cube of the length of the sentence [Earley, 1970] even though the number of parses is often exponential in the length of the sentence [Church and Patil, 1982].)

The theoretical results described here were motivated by particular problems encountered in AI applications. Theoretical results are cast in abstract terms, and their immediate impact on practical applications is sometimes hard to quantify. As in any theoretical discipline, the theoreticians are limited by their mathematical tools, and so there is a constant effort to improve these tools so that the theoretical results can more directly guide practitioners.

1.3   Identifying and Measuring Intelligence

An intelligent system can respond to its environment in a variety of ways. Such a system can explore its surroundings, manipulate objects, or seek communion with other intelligent systems. Whatever the response, the system

▲ AI IN PRACTICE

Intelligence Test for Computers

Alan Turing, a pioneer in the theory of computation, once proposed an intelligence test for computer programs [Turing, 1950]. In one variant of the *Turing test*, a human judge is allowed to interrogate a program though some sort of an interface such as a video terminal. If the program can fool the human into believing that it is another human responding rather than a computer, then the program is judged intelligent. You can imagine variants of this test in which you manipulate a robot's environment to see how the robot responds and judge the robot as intelligent or not depending on whether the robot responds in accord with how a human might in the same situation.

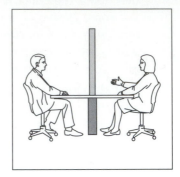

is usually governed by some directive or *goal*. A robot in a factory might be governed by the goal of keeping all the assembly machines in the factory supplied with parts. A goal might be supplied by a supervisor, or a goal might arise out of the system's evaluation of its situation. For example, a factory manager might tell a robot what to do, or the robot might decide for itself to proceed directly to the nearest charging unit before its batteries reach dangerous levels. We are particularly concerned with how an intelligent system might infer appropriate goals and then construct courses of action, called *plans*, to pursue in attempting to achieve those goals. This process, often called *planning*, is a particular case of automated problem solving, an important subfield of AI.

Some people believe that humans are the ultimate problem solvers. Humans build highway systems to solve their transportation problems, and automated farms and factories to solve their food and durable goods production problems. People often judge one another based on the ability to solve problems. Traditionally, intelligence is, in part, a measure of problem-solving skills. It seems natural then to measure the performance of a system that purports to possess "artificial intelligence" in terms of its ability to solve problems.

It is quite possible, however, that robots and softbots will exhibit a very different sort of intelligence than humans. Computer programs may even surpass humans in some tasks that humans now believe only they can accomplish. In search of a less biased arbiter for what constitutes intelligence, many researchers employ engineering criteria to judge their progress in building systems. For instance, if you wish to build a robot to deliver mail, then you judge the robot's performance on the basis of its skill in maneuvering in an office environment and its accuracy and speed in routing mail to its intended destination. Similarly, if you are interested in evaluating the performance of a softbot that searches in a computer network to retrieve information, then you measure the speed with which the information is retrieved. In this text, we avoid the sticky philosophical issues concerning whether or not it is possible to write programs that are intelligent. Where appropriate, we apply engineering criteria to analyze the performance of a program or compare its performance with that of a human who is expert at the same task. Machine intelligence will not appear suddenly on the scene. Instead, machines will steadily become more complicated as we learn to improve their abilities to perceive and reason about their environment.

1.4   Computational Theories of Behavior

Ultimately, we are interested in building systems that manifest interesting and useful behavior. To that end, we are interested in computational theories that serve to explain and realize such behavior. A robot behavior might correspond to avoiding obstacles in negotiating office corridors or learning to distinguish recyclable containers from other items found in the garbage. At times, we may find it useful to consider abstract behaviors in order to speak generally about a particular class of algorithmic tasks. For example, we might be interested in algorithms that learn the structure of a labeled graph from a random walk along the edges of that graph. The abstract behavior realized by such algorithms might be concretely applied to a robot learning about its surroundings. A *computational theory* for a given behavior consists of a well-defined computational goal and an information-processing description of the target behavior in terms of inputs, outputs, and algorithms for transforming the one into the other [Marr, 1982]. An example of a well-defined computational goal in machine vision is to produce a line drawing representing the visible edges of a solid, polyhedral object as rendered in a gray-level image of that object generated by a video camera (see Figure 1.2, page 10).

Central to a computational theory is the formal system or set of mathematical conventions by which we make explicit the entities or types of information that play a role in the theory. The entities in a theory of machine vision might be the pixels in the image generated by a video camera or the line segments in a line drawing of a polyhedral object. Such a formal system is usually referred to as a *representation*.

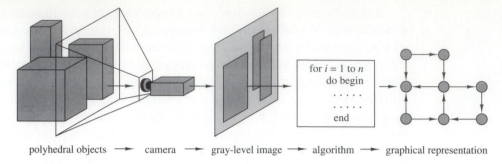

polyhedral objects → camera → gray-level image → algorithm → graphical representation

Figure 1.2   Schematic description of a computational theory concerned with processing camera images to produce graphical representations of polyhedral objects

Representation

The notion of a representation is rather general, and hence, somewhat elusive. A road map, a computer-aided-design (CAD) model for a product, and an integrated circuit layout are all examples of descriptions of complex objects employing different representations.

The conventions used to construct and interpret road maps constitute a representation in the sense that we use the term in this text. The road map shown in Figure 1.3a describes some but not all aspects of a particular system of roads and highways.

In a reasonably accurate road map, the distances between cities measured along highways are roughly proportional to the distances between the actual cities measured along the actual highways. There are, however, practical limits in describing a system of roads. For instance, most road maps do not include the exit and entrance ramps where one highway meets another.

Another approach is to describe a system of roads and highways as a graph in which the vertices correspond to cities and the edges to numbers identifying thoroughfares (see Figure 1.3b). Or we could use a table of shortest distances between cities (see Figure 1.3c). Which description is most appropriate depends on the task at hand and the routines available for making use of the information encoded in a given description.

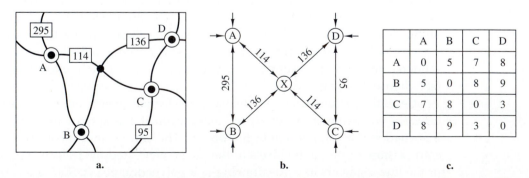

Figure 1.3   Alternative representations for a system of roads

Some researchers prefer to separate the syntactic aspects of a representation from the semantical and computational aspects. We prefer not to make such a distinction. In order to compare different representations, we need to attach meaning to the formal specification and state clearly how the formal descriptions are to be mechanically manipulated.

Syntax and Semantics

Representation involves three components that stand in a particular relationship to one another. We can express this relationship as a simple formula.

$$\text{representation} = \text{notation} + \text{denotation} + \text{computation}$$

As shown, a representation requires appropriate notational conventions for writing things down. This component corresponds to the graphical conventions for displaying highways and cities in the road-map example. We often use the term *syntax* to refer to the notational conventions associated with a given representation. The syntax specifies the objects of discourse and a language for relating them to one another.

Second, a representation requires the meaning (or denotation) of the objects and relations specified in the syntax. In the road-map example, the denotation corresponds to the interpretation of the marks on a road map as actual cities and highways. We often use the term *semantics* to refer to the denotational conventions associated with a given representation.

Finally, a representation includes a computational model specifying how the objects and relations are manipulated in accord with the semantical conventions.

The distinction between syntax and semantics is rather subtle and may take a little getting used to. For the moment, assume that the role of syntax is to determine whether or not a given expression is well formed in the sense that it obeys certain rules for the formation of expressions. The role of semantics is to assign to each well-formed expression either True or False. Consider the sentence "New York is the closest city to Boston." Syntactically, this sentence is well formed; it obeys the English grammatical rules for sentence formation. However, semantically, it is not at all clear what this sentence means because it is not clear what the individual words mean. What determines a "city": size, population, tax revenue? What determines "closest": air miles, highway miles, travel time?

To establish the meaning of individual words, we need conventions for connecting words to entities in the world. The real world is pretty complicated and so instead of connecting words to the world, we connect words to some suitable abstraction of the world. At first, it may not seem like we are making progress. We start with an abstraction, the syntax used to establish the legal entities in our representation, and then to make sense of this abstraction we connect it with another abstraction used to establish the meaning of entities in our representation. Wasn't one abstraction enough? Perhaps, but the semantic abstraction is more basic, and hence, helps us justify operations that manipulate the syntax of our representation.

You might ask why we are concerned with semantics. Why don't we just write programs for robots and measure our success by the robot's performance? The answer from an engineering point of view is that complex systems require the combined efforts of many contributors. If an engineer is to use a component designed by someone else, the engineer needs a clear specification of the behavior of that component. From a scientific point of view, careful attention to semantics allows us to be precise about the capabilities of the systems we build. Then using appropriate computational analyses, we can ultimately understand what is possible and what is not.

1.5   Automated Reasoning

In the following chapters, we explore a number of techniques for *automated reasoning*. Automated reasoning is defined as any computation that takes as input some representation encoding knowledge about the world and provides as output conclusions based on that knowledge. We will be particularly interested in the role that representation plays in automated reasoning. Consider the following example using a representation that should be familiar to many of you.

The engineering students in Sigma Phi Gamma Omega have built a magnetic vertical accelerator (see Figure 1.4). They want to test their accelerator by seeing how high it can propel a grand piano. Being good engineers, they decide to build a model to try to predict the outcome of their experiment. As a representation for specifying their model, they use the differential and integral calculus.

Newton's second law of motion states that the product of an object's mass and the acceleration of its center of mass are proportional to the force acting on the object. Let x be a function that depends on time (t) and denotes

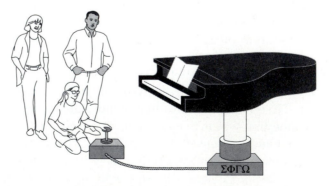

Figure 1.4   The students of Sigma Phi Gamma Omega prepare to launch a grand piano in the interest of furthering science

the position of the center of mass of the piano as measured from some fixed point along a line perpendicular to the Sigma Phi Gamma Omega parking lot and intersecting the propulsion arm of the magnetic vertical accelerator. Let M be the mass of the piano and F be the force acting on the piano in the direction of travel. The following differential equation:

$$M\frac{d^2x}{dt^2} = F \tag{1.1}$$

is called the equation of motion of the piano. This equation is syntactically well formed by the conventions of the differential calculus. You may be more familiar with syntactic variants such as $M\ddot{x} = F$ or $Ma = F$ that are typically found in physics textbooks.

Equation 1.1 corresponds to very general knowledge about the behavior of objects acted on by forces. If we know something about a specific object, say a piano, and the forces acting on the object, then we can use this equation to make predictions about the motion of the object, but to do so we need some additional machinery.

Inference and Symbolic Manipulation

The students have determined that the velocity of the piano as it leaves the accelerator will be $\frac{dx(0)}{dt} = v_0$. Given an initial position $x(0) = 0$, if we integrate Equation 1.1 twice and make appropriate substitutions for the constants of integration, we obtain the following formula:

$$x(t) = -\frac{1}{2}gt^2 + v_0t \tag{1.2}$$

where g is the acceleration due to gravity near the surface of the earth. This equation describes the position of the piano at $t > 0$ given the initial conditions and assuming that the piano is propelled upward at time $t = 0$. We obtained Equation 1.2 by manipulating Equation 1.1 according to the rules of calculus. By performing additional manipulations involving Equation 1.2, we can predict the maximum height ($v_0^2/2g$) reached by the piano and the time it takes the piano to fall back to the surface of the parking lot ($2v_0/g$).

Our knowledge of physics tells us how to represent the problem in mathematical terms, and our knowledge of calculus tells us how to manipulate the symbols to make a prediction on the basis of knowledge about the initial conditions. The manipulations correspond to a form of *inference*; from knowledge of general physical principles, mathematics, and the initial conditions, the students are able to infer answers to specific questions about the behavior of the piano. The role of inference in automated reasoning is important, and we will return to this idea frequently in this text. Programs already exist that can solve simple differential equations of the sort described. Automating the process of formulating word problems in terms of differential equations is somewhat more complicated, but programs that do this sort of thing also exist in the AI literature.

There are other representations suitable for automated reasoning. One such representation that we look at in this text involves first-order predicate logic.

Representing Common-Sense Knowledge

Consider the following bit of common-sense knowledge. If a person is currently at home, and getting to work requires driving, and this person always drives at or under the legal speed limit, then for that person to transport himself or herself from home to work will take at least the distance along the route from home to work divided by the maximum legal speed limit posted along that route. Now suppose that we are told that John is at home and has to drive 25 miles to get to work and always obeys the 50-mile-per-hour speed limit. From this information, we can conclude that it will take John at least a half hour to get to work. To arrive at this conclusion, we employed two rules of inference that are part of first-order predicate logic.

First, given a statement that applies to any person, the rule of inference called *universal instantiation* allows us to apply the statement to any particular person, in this case, John. Second, given a statement of the form "if *antecedent condition* then *consequent conclusion*," the rule of inference called *modus ponens* allows us to conclude the consequent conclusion if we can establish the antecedent conditions. In first-order predicate logic, modus ponens and universal instantiation are like the rules for integration, differentiation, and algebraic manipulation in calculus.

In order to automate this sort of common-sense reasoning, we would have to provide a precise syntax for encoding knowledge in the first-order predicate logic. In addition, we would have to write programs that manipulate such encodings in accord with rules of inference like modusponens.

As we set out to explore various representations, it should be noted that the knowledge that we encode in first-order predicate logic or in the integral and differential calculus serves only as an approximation to the actual laws governing behavior in the real world. In many cases, it is impossible to write down all the conditions necessary to warrant a given conclusion and even if we were able to write down all such conditions, there would probably be too many of them to manage. Recognizing this, we have to design systems that can make use of approximations to expedite inference while being prepared to deal with the consequences of drawing conclusions that turn out to be wrong.

Combinatorial Problems and Search

Many of the computational problems in AI are combinatorial. Combinatorial problems involve making many separate decisions that tend to depend on one another in complicated ways. There are generally a great many possible combinations of decisions, most of which do not lead to solutions. In automated reasoning, there are decisions about which symbolic manipulations or rules of inference to apply and decisions about which formulas to apply them to.

Because combinatorial problems abound in AI, there is a great deal of interest in developing both general- and special-purpose techniques to *search* in the space of possible combinations for those that satisfy particular criteria. An algorithm that finds a path between two nodes given a graph of the sort shown in Figure 1.3 is an example of a general-purpose search technique. A computer program that uses lots of specialized knowledge about genetics to find matches in a genetics database is an example of a special-purpose search technique.

Representation and search are closely related. For instance, it is easier to find a path between two cities using the graphical representation shown in Figure 1.3b than it is using a bit-map representation such as that shown in Figure 1.3a. The representation in Figure 1.3a can be used to construct the representation in Figure 1.3b but at some computational cost. Issues involving representation and search are common in AI and will come up often in this text.

Complexity and Expressivity

We are interested in developing "efficient" algorithms for symbolic reasoning. Usually, we are satisfied if the procedures we write perform a total number of steps determined by some low-order polynomial function of the size of the inputs. In this text, we assume that you have at least heard about asymptotic complexity and *big-O* notation. For instance, you might know that you can compute the minimum of a list of n integers with $O(n)$ comparisons or sort the list using $O(n \log n)$ comparisons. Problems such as sorting, shortest path, minimum-cost spanning tree are all said to be easy because they can be computed with a small (polynomial in the size of the problem description) number of basic steps.

Plenty of problems are not easy. The best known exact solutions to the general traveling salesperson problem require an exponential number of steps. The yes-or-no version of this problem[1] is said to be in the class of *NP-complete* problems [Garey and Johnson, 1979].

---

[1]The classical formulation of the traveling salesperson problem as a yes-or-no decision problem is as follows: Given a positive integer K and a complete graph whose vertices represent cities and whose edges represent routes between cities labeled with the distance between adjacent cities, determine if there exists a tour of length at most K corresponding to a sequence of vertices and edges that visits each city. Given that the yes-or-no problem is hard, the corresponding optimization problem (find the minimum length tour) is hard.

In the following chapters, we will be faced with other problems in the class of NP-complete problems. NP-completeness does not mean that we should despair. For some problems, we can find approximations that suffice for particular applications. In the case of the traveling salesperson problem, we may be able to find a tour that is within a small factor of the minimum tour. For other problems, it might be acceptable to find a good solution with high probability. It may be that most of the time we can find a tour that is not too long. Algorithm complexity will figure prominently in our discussion of representation issues.

Expressiveness concerns what you can or cannot represent in a given representation without regard to computation. First-order predicate logic will allow you to represent just about anything you care to represent. Along with increased expressivity, however, often comes some disadvantages. There is no algorithm that is guaranteed to terminate in a finite number of steps for determining whether a given statement follows from some set of other statements encoded in the first-order predicate logic. There are times when it will seem reasonable to sacrifice expressivity in order to ensure that our algorithms do not run indefinitely or take an inordinate amount of time to return a result. Tradeoffs of this sort involving expressivity and complexity will surface time and again in the following chapters.

1.6   How This Book Is Organized

AI is a diverse and rapidly evolving field emphasizing a wide range of techniques and applications. We cannot hope to survey the entire field in this text. Instead of an exhaustive survey, we investigate a range of well-established techniques and attempt to tie them together by emphasizing representational issues. Representation plays an important foundational role in this text. Throughout the following chapters, you will be exposed to representations that facilitate different sorts of problem solving. The theme of intelligent robots will also recur often as a source of motivation for the techniques we will be investigating.

We begin our exploration of AI in Chapter 2 by focusing on computation and start with *Lisp*, a language that is probably new to you but is less different from other representations we will consider. We hope to convince you that some part of what you have been doing all along involves representation and that much of what you know about programming will carry over to designing good representations.

There is an important aspect of AI that we certainly do not want to get lost in the details; AI is an exciting field to work in. There is a lot of satisfaction to be had in building a robot that roams around an office, or a vision system that recognizes faces, or a natural language system that answers questions that you type to it. A lot of the fun for students starting out in AI comes from experimenting with systems, testing limitations, and trying out alternatives. We believe this so strongly that we have made programming in Lisp an integral part of this text. You can learn about AI using this text without learning to program in Lisp; however, it is our experience that students learn more if they are encouraged to experiment by writing and modifying programs that implement computational theories. It is our hope that the experience gained in writing AI programs will provide students with an appreciation of the theory that is meant to guide building systems.

Chapter 3 provides an introduction to logic and theorem proving as a basis for representation. This chapter considers the syntax and semantics of propositional and first-order predicate logic. Computational issues are considered in the context of automated theorem proving, and machinery is developed for building expert systems.

Many computational problems in AI can be described in terms of search. Chapter 4 describes basic search algorithms along with simple analyses of their computational complexity. Algorithms are described that can take advantage of specialized knowledge about a domain to expedite search. This chapter looks at optimization in terms of search and explores optimization techniques that involve simulating physical processes. Chapter 4 also establishes the connection between search and the storage and retrieval of information.

The connections between learning and search are many. When we search our knowledge and find useful information, we can store that information in such a way that it is easier to find the next time we need it; this constitutes a simple form of learning. When we are trying to learn a concept from examples, it often becomes necessary to search in a space of possible concepts. Chapter 5 provides a general framework for learning and then considers several specific techniques ranging from specialized graph search to neural networks.

Chapter 6 takes up where Chapter 3 left off by considering specialized representations for time, space, and knowledge. Since time, space, and knowledge play such an important role in our understanding of the world, it makes sense to consider representations that facilitate reasoning about these basic modalities. These specialized representations provide a basis for structuring information so that it can be efficiently stored and retrieved.

Chapter 7 introduces the notion of state-space search, establishing a close connection between planning and search and providing a general framework for planning and problem solving. Issues of efficiency and incomplete information are addressed by exploring new representations for plans. We reemphasize the close connection between learning and search as we explore an approach to adapting existing plans for future use called explanation-based generalization.

Chapter 8 addresses the problem of representing and reasoning about uncertainty. Problems in diagnosis and planning are addressed using a network representation for probabilistic models. As with earlier representations, the computational problems that arise in reasoning with such probabilistic models are discussed and tradeoffs are considered.

Machine vision and natural language understanding are two major subfields of AI. Chapter 9 provides an introduction to the basic problems and solution methods in machine vision. Chapter 10 addresses the problems involved in processing natural language input and generating natural language output. Both machine vision and natural language understanding are referred to as AI-complete problems in that they appear to be as hard as any problems in AI, and given a comprehensive solution to either machine vision or natural language understanding, solving any other problem in AI would be straightforward. It is fitting that we end the text by addressing two of the most demanding and exciting areas of AI.

Our primary objectives in this text are twofold. First, we describe a variety of computational techniques that have proved useful in designing machines that exhibit interesting behavior that we believe are on the path toward useful AI systems. Second, we focus on representation as a means of exploring the computational prerequisites for building AI systems.

This text describes only a small but representative sample of what has been done to date and an even smaller portion of what needs to be done before we can understand intelligence in any real sense or build sophisticated robots of the sort encountered in popular fiction. By the end of this text, you should have more questions than you started with; if not, then we have failed to convey the magnitude of the problems that we are attempting to address.

▼ Summary

AI is concerned with the design and analysis of computer programs that behave intelligently. This chapter motivates the study of artificial intelligence by sampling a wide range of applications from robots for exploring the planets to automated personal assistants for navigating in the world of networked computer systems. We largely ignore the thorny philosophical issues concerning the identification and measurement of intelligence and take an engineering stance to measuring the performance of AI systems.

AI researchers develop computational theories that begin with well-defined computational goals and that provide information-processing descriptions of target behaviors in terms of inputs, outputs, and algorithms. Representation is central to such information-processing descriptions. Representation is concerned with developing notations, establishing the meaning of those notations, and providing computational methods for using those notations to solve problems. Examples of representations include road maps and computer-aided-design models. We take representation to be the most important issue in developing AI systems.

Automated reasoning is defined as any computation that takes as input some representation encoding knowledge about the world and provides as output conclusions based on that knowledge. The differential and integral calculus and first-order predicate logic are examples of representations that can be used for automated reasoning. Automated reasoning systems employ inference and symbolic manipulation to draw new conclusions from existing knowledge.

Most automated reasoning problems involve making large numbers of decisions that combine with one another in a complicated fashion. Often an AI system has to search through many combinations in order to find one that solves a particular problem. Building efficient search algorithms is one aspect of designing representations to solve problems.

The chapters of this book are meant to address the important issues in building useful representations. We use the programming language Lisp to provide examples of AI programs that the reader can experiment with. AI research involves a blend of theory and practice. By experimenting with Lisp programs, you should gain a greater appreciation of the need for theory and a better understanding of where additional theory is needed. The last two chapters of this book deal with machine vision and natural language processing, two of the most challenging problems facing AI.

Background

At the end of each chapter in this book, we provide references for readers wanting to pursue topics covered in the chapter. Readers interested in the history of AI should start with McCorduck [1979]. For interesting philosophical discussions concerning intelligence in machines, see the collection edited by Haugeland [1985].

Fischler and Firschein [1987] provide a high-level overview of AI with an emphasis on representation and machine vision intended for a general audience. There are several excellent AI textbooks besides this one. For further reading and a different perspective on the field, we recommend Charniak and McDermott [1985], Rich and Knight [1991], Winston [1992], and Ginsberg [1993]. For more advanced subjects, the texts by Davis [1990] and Genesereth and Nilsson [1987] are first rate. Our discussion of computational theories borrows from Marr's approach to machine vision [1982].

For more about autonomous robots, you might start with the science fiction of Isaac Asimov. Asimov is mainly concerned with robots of the distant future, but his stories provide interesting predictions about the social consequences of machine intelligence.

AI research is published in a number of journals. The journal *Artificial Intelligence* is perhaps the best known and most widely read journal devoted to AI. *Cognitive Science, Computational Intelligence,* and the *IEEE Transactions on Pattern Analysis and Machine Intelligence* also publish AI research. *Robotics and Automation* and *Robotics*

Research are journals that focus primarily on robotics. The *AI Magazine*, published by the *American Association for Artificial Intelligence*, is a good source of surveys and news about the field.

Other sources of information on AI are the two major AI conferences and their published proceedings. The *International Joint Conference on Artificial Intelligence* is held every other year and is often referred to by its initials (IJCAI) in citations. The *National Conference on Artificial Intelligence* is held every year in the United States unless IJCAI is being held in the United States that year. Both of these conferences publish proceedings that are widely distributed and provide a good indication of the active areas of research in the field. The National Conference on Artificial Intelligence is often called AAAI since it is run by the American Association for Artificial Intelligence.

■ Exercises

1.1 Design a variant of the Turing test in which the person administering the test gets to set up challenges using an action video game and then watch the screen as the program being tested responds to each challenge. The criterion for passing the test should be based entirely on the program's actions in meeting the challenges. In particular, this variant would not test the program's language skills. Discuss how this variant compares with the original version of the test.

1.2 Suppose that you wish to build a program that, given a starting location and a destination, returns a set of directions to follow in getting from the start to the destination. You are provided with a map of the region of interest. Describe how you would encode the relevant information in the map in terms of data structures that your program could make use of in generating directions. Think about how the program could be extended to provide instructions that account for failures in observation. For instance, the directions might indicate to follow Route 114 five miles until you see the sign for Route 136, but then also state that if you see a large red barn with a cow painted on the side, then you have gone too far.

1.3 Sketch the design of a computer program that solves simple physics word problems. For instance, the program should be able to answer questions concerning the trajectory of objects falling near the surface of the earth or objects sliding on a frictionless surface. Contrast the knowledge required to solve such word problems with the knowledge required to perform simple juggling tricks or play a game of billiards.

1.4 If an AI system is just a computer program, then a system that learns from experience must correspond to a program that modifies itself. In almost any programming language, you can write procedures that modify themselves. Describe how to do this in your favorite programming language. Write a procedure that modifies its source code so that each time the program is compiled and subsequently run the program will behave differently. Compare such esoteric, self-modifying procedures with more conventional procedures that modify their behavior by, say, updating a file of information.

1.5 In the following, we assume that semantics is concerned with assigning True or False to well-formed expressions. Consider the meaning of the expression "it's raining." Sometimes we may wish to assign it True and sometimes False; it will depend on the circumstances. A *model* roughly corresponds to a possible set of circumstances and assigns every expression True or False. It may be that what we assign one expression will depend on what we assign others. For instance, we would expect "it's raining" to be assigned True in every model that assigns True to both "if it's Saturday then it's raining" and "it's Saturday."

Consider the following syntactic conventions. Let C be a set of constant symbols, {one,two,three,four,small-num,big-num}, and R be a set of relation symbols, {$=$, $<$, $\neq$, $\nless$}. We define a set of legal formulas of the form $(c\ r\ c')$, where $c, c' \in C$ and $r \in R$. Describe a set of models for these legal formulas in accord with your understanding of the integers. Restrict your attention to a finite domain corresponding to the integers 1 through 10. Write a program that given a set of formulas called *facts* and a formula called a *query* returns True, just in case the query is assigned True in all those models in which every one of the facts is assigned True.

CHAPTER 2

SYMBOLIC PROGRAMMING

Fred is sure that his landlord has violated the city building ordinance requiring that the ceiling in all apartment buildings be no less than 2.5 meters in height. Fred is exactly 2 meters tall and, if he stands on a stack of three 10-centimeter-thick wooden blocks, his head just touches the ceiling of his apartment. Using this information, he can compute the height of the ceiling by evaluating the expression $(2.0 + (3 \times 0.10))$ to obtain the result 2.3.

Fred can easily calculate this result in his head, by using a calculator, or by writing a simple program. We are interested in building systems that can construct an expression such as this one from general knowledge and then evaluate it to arrive at a conclusion. Indeed, our goal is even more ambitious since we are interested in building systems that, faced with the problem of measuring the height of the ceiling, would propose a scheme such as the one outlined to obtain a measurement by using objects of known measurement.

2.0, 3, and 0.10 correspond to *symbols* and are generally used to represent numbers. Numbers have properties (e.g., odd or even), relationships (e.g., equal or greater than), and methods of combination (e.g., plus and times) that can also be represented as symbols and used to construct *symbolic expressions* such as (3×0.10). In *symbolic programming*, we create symbols and symbolic expressions, pass them around as the arguments to procedures, and manipulate them to infer new expressions.

▲ AI in Practice

Symbolic Programs for Playing Chess

A game of chess can be analyzed by a symbolic program. Each chess piece is represented by a symbol, and the rules governing legal moves are represented by symbolic expressions. We might represent the four knights by symbols, black_knight1, black_knight2, white_knight1, white_knight2, and a legal move for a knight might be represented by the expression (sequence (forward 2) (right 1)).

We could also create symbolic abstractions for standard chess positions that would allow a program to reason about moving groups of pieces. In the diagram, black is employing a King's_indian_defense and white has pressed the attack by pawn_storming the Queen's side where there is an opening. A chess program for black could employ a rule for pawn_storming an opening. This rule lets the program infer that black is going to lose the Queen's side, but a pawn storm on the open King's side would turn the game in black's favor. If it can then infer king_in_check, then closing the attack will result in checkmate.

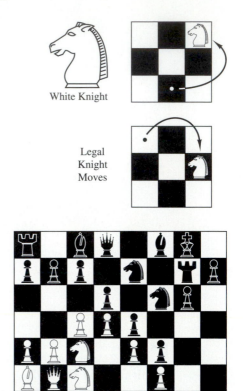

White Knight

Legal Knight Moves

Symbols can be used to reason about things other than numbers. For instance, we can represent Fred by the symbol fred and the three blocks by the symbols, block1, block2, and block3. We can define properties, relationships, and methods of combination for our symbols as we need them. For instance, the expression (height fred) might be used to represent Fred's height, and (on block1 block2) the relationship corresponding to one block being located on top of another block. Given the expressions (on block1 block2) and (on block2 block3), we might infer another relationship (stack block1 block2 block3) corresponding to three blocks forming a stack of blocks.

Throughout this text, we describe programs written in a programming language called Lisp (for *list processing* language) that was designed for symbolic programming. Lisp includes a large set of routines for manipulating symbols and symbolic expressions. Lisp also provides support that frees the programmer from a lot of low-level details. Because the syntax of Lisp is simple, it is easy to learn and write programs in.

In this chapter, we assume that you already know how to program in at least one programming language. We begin with a robot programming problem to motivate the use of symbols and symbolic expressions. We return to this example at the end of the chapter and produce Lisp code to solve the problem using what we have learned in the earlier sections. The details of Lisp are presented in stages starting with the basic syntax and an introduction to using some of the interactive tools available in Lisp. These tools make it easy to experiment with Lisp. We cover recursion and iteration as well as other techniques that you should have some familiarity with from learning other programming languages. We cover techniques for creating and manipulating lists in some detail since they provide the basis for manipulating symbolic expressions. We provide simple (but sufficient for our purposes) machinery for data abstraction (structured data types).

From a practical perspective, we spend embarrassingly little time on input and output, debugging, and modularity, which are absolutely necessary in writing complicated programs. This is not a comprehensive introduction to Lisp; we confine our attention to a subset sufficient to provide students with access to programs that instantiate concepts and encourage student experimentation. As you read through these pages, you should write lots of small Lisp programs and experiment with variations on the examples you see printed in the text. Whenever possible, sit down in front of a computer running Lisp and make use of the interactive tools to experiment. The chapter concludes with an extended example.

2.1   Rule-Based Reactive System Example

A company is developing a control system for a robot that delivers mail in office buildings. They have already written a high-level planning system that tells the robot which corridors to use in navigating from one office to another. We are interested in another part of the control system that enables the robot to actually negotiate the corridors and open spaces of buildings without running into things. When the robot moves down a corridor, it must avoid people and boxes in its way. This simple behavior can be produced by a *rule-based reactive system*. The system is *rule based* because it uses a set of rules represented as symbolic expressions to determine what to do next. The system is *reactive* because it responds more-or-less directly to changes in the environment indicated by the robot's sensors. We begin by introducing symbols that are used to represent sensors and controls.

Representing Sensors and Sensor Values as Symbols

The robot has six sensors that detect whether obstacles are nearby but do not indicate the shape of the obstacles or describe their positions in detail. If an obstacle is detected, then its position is reported as being either near to the robot, away from the robot, or far away from the robot. These rough, qualitative distinctions are sufficient for the robot to navigate without hitting obstacles.

Six sensors provide information about obstacles in the area around the robot. The sensors are arranged to provide more information about what is in front of the robot to assist in navigation and obstacle avoidance. The symbols forward, jright, jleft, right, left, and rear are used to represent the six sensors. Each sensor is responsible for reporting on the presence of obstacles in a fixed region about the robot, returning one of the values near, away, or far. Figure 2.1a shows the arrangement of the sensors, and Figure 2.1b depicts the robot in a corridor of an office building with a water cooler partially blocking its way.

In addition to the sensors, there are two control parameters that determine the behavior of the robot. By adjusting these parameters, our reactive, rule-based program tells the robot how to move. The speed of the robot is represented by the symbol speed and can be assigned one of three values, zero, slow, or fast. The direction that the robot is pointed in is represented by the symbol turn, which can be assigned one of the values, left, straight, and right.

In the following sections, we introduce techniques that will enable us to represent rules as symbolic expressions and implement procedures that use these rules to control the robot. We return to this example at the end

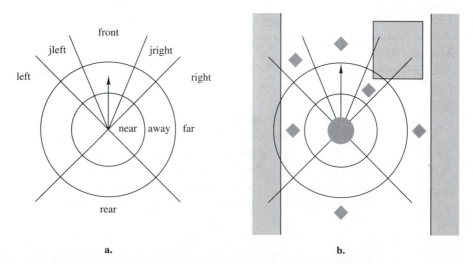

Figure 2.1   Obstacle detection sensors for a mobile robot

of the chapter and provide Lisp code implementing a simple rule-based reactive system.

2.2 Introduction to Lisp

Lisp is similar in many respects to other languages such as Pascal and C that allow you to define procedures and call those procedures from within other procedures. Lisp is different in that it has a simpler syntax, is less restrictive in terms of explicit data typing requirements, and offers a great many built-in procedures and much support for interactive program development. Generally, when programmers talk about Pascal, they are referring to the syntactic conventions for specifying Pascal programs and the compiler and associated tools for generating executable code. When programmers talk about Lisp, they are referring to the syntactic conventions for specifying Lisp programs plus an associated *programming environment* that includes a large set of built-in procedures and a diverse suite of tools for compiling, debugging, and interacting with Lisp programs.

Programming Language Requirements

We begin our introduction to Lisp by considering what we want and need from a programming language. Certainly we want all the standard data types (e.g., numbers, strings, and pointers) and operations on such data types (e.g., addition, multiplication, concatenation, and pointer following). In addition, we need flow of control constructs to facilitate sequencing, conditional branching, and procedure invocation. The means of reading and writing from files and standard devices such as terminals will be useful for any real applications. Finally, it will help in writing complicated programs if there are methods for structuring programs (e.g., subroutines and modules) and facilities for creating new control constructs and abstract data types.

Common Lisp

There are many dialects of Lisp. In this text, we use a dialect called *Common Lisp*. We choose Common Lisp rather than one of the more elegant dialects of Lisp because Common Lisp has become a commonly accepted standard. We restrict our attention to a subset of Common Lisp and, as a result, much of what we say applies to other dialects as well. The particular subset of Common Lisp we have chosen includes all the functionality required for the examples and exercises in this text and provides a good basis for learning more about Lisp. To help you use this subset, we have included at the end of the book an index of general symbolic programming terms and Lisp notation, including function names, special forms, and special characters; the general terms are repeated in the general index, but the Lisp notation is not.

Lists and Lisp Syntax

The syntax of Lisp is relatively simple. It is so simple, in fact, that Lisp can seem structureless to programmers used to languages with greater syntactic restrictions. In Lisp, programs and data are represented as lists, where a list is represented by an open parenthesis followed by zero or more *expressions* and a closing parenthesis.

An expression corresponds to any Lisp object (e.g., a number or string), or (inductively) a list comprising zero or more expressions. For instance, (), (1), and (1 (2)) are all lists, the first being called the empty (or *null*) list. The list (1) consists of one expression, the number 1. The list (1 (2)) consists of two expressions, the number 1 and the list (2). With a few caveats that we consider shortly, every expression corresponds to a syntactically well-formed Lisp program.

Lists provide an abstraction of pointers that simplifies a wide variety of programming tasks. If you are not comfortable with pointers, then relax; Lisp lists do not require you to explicitly manipulate pointers.

Lisp also has numbers (integer and floating point) and strings (represented in the conventional manner between double quotes, "string") and a variety of other primitive data types, but the ease with which programmers can manipulate lists in Lisp is one of its most attractive features.

Symbols

Another important data type in Lisp is the *symbol*. A symbol looks a lot like a string, but it is not set off with double quotes. For our purposes, symbols are constructed from alphanumeric characters (e.g., sym and sym14), possibly with embedded hyphens or underscores (e.g., sym-one and sym_two). In Lisp, numbers are not of type symbol, and so every Lisp symbol must include at least one character that is not a number or decimal point.[1] Generally, case does not matter (e.g., foo is the same symbol as FOO or Foo). Lists can and often do contain symbols. For instance, (foo bar (baz)) is a list consisting of three expressions, foo, bar, and (baz).

Programs and Documentation

A Lisp program consists of a sequence of Lisp expressions. In this book, we present Lisp programs by displaying formatted Lisp expressions in figures or interspersed with the text describing the expressions. More often than not, you will compose and store Lisp programs in files. Typically, a Lisp program

---

[1]The complete story is more complicated. For instance, 0E0 is a representation for floating-point zero (the E stands for exponent), whereas 0H0 is a symbol. We will not be using floating-point numbers with exponent specifications in this text. See Steele [1990] if you are interested in a complete description of symbols and floating-point numbers.

```
;; This comment appears just prior to an expression.
(defun square (x)
  ;; Comments can also appear inside an expression.
  (* x x ))   ;; Comments can appear to the right of an expression.


;; Comments can run for as many lines as are needed
;; in order to adequately document an expression.
(defun cube (x)
  (* x x x)) ;; The expression to the right is ignored! (+ x x x)
```

Figure 2.2   Examples of comments as they might appear in a file

stored in a file consists of a sequence of Lisp expressions interspersed with *comments* that provide documentation for the program.

Comments are set off by specific punctuation so that compilers and other tools can distinguish programs from documentation. The semicolon (;) is the standard comment character. Characters on the same line to the right of a semicolon are ignored by Lisp tools that read files. We typically use two semicolons (;;) to distinguish comments from other uses of the semicolon for punctuation purposes. In the book, we also display comments in italics to make the documentation stand out further from programs. Figure 2.2 provides some examples of comments as they might appear in a file containing a Lisp program. If you have access to the code that was written to accompany this text, then you will have many examples of well-documented Lisp code.

2.3 Interacting with Lisp

To make any further progress, you will have to learn more about the semantics of Lisp. In a more traditional language, this would mean learning about compiling, linking, and executing programs. In our discussion of Lisp, we focus on a Lisp program called eval that serves to interpret or *eval*uate other Lisp programs. Eval behaves much as a compiler does in other programming languages; the fact that eval can incrementally compile Lisp programs without complicated linking considerably simplifies experimenting with Lisp code. Common Lisp supports other forms of compilation besides those implemented by eval, but we do not consider them in this text.

The Lisp Interpreter

Conveniently, most implementations of Lisp provide an interactive program that allows the user to type Lisp expressions to a terminal interface to be evaluated by eval. This interactive program is called a *read-eval-print loop* because it reads an expression from the terminal, evaluates the expression, and then prints the result of the evaluation to the terminal along with a prompt asking for another expression. We make use of this interactive program (called the *interpreter*) in the following presentation and suggest that, if possible, you follow along at a terminal performing experiments of your own. Consult a local Lisp hacker to find out how to invoke the interpreter and how to recover from the inevitable errors that will occur. Don't be afraid to experiment; the interpreter is designed to facilitate exploration.

When a Lisp interpreter starts up, it generally prints out a message indicating the version number, restrictions on copying, and a variety of other information that you can safely ignore at this stage. When it is finished with its greeting, it displays a prompt indicating that you can begin typing. The interpreter is expecting a complete expression. If you type such an expression followed by a carriage return, the interpreter reads it, evaluates it, and prints out the result. For instance, in Lisp, strings and numbers evaluate to themselves.

```
> "string"
"string"
> 3.14
3.14
```

Symbols and other expressions are a different matter. If you just type a random symbol to the interpreter, you will probably get an error. Note that the particular interpreter used here displays all symbols using uppercase letters only; this is the default mode in many Lisp implementations.

```
> sym
Error: The symbol SYM has no global value
```

Later, we say exactly what it means for a symbol to have a global value and how to set that value; for now, it is enough to know that some symbols do have global values. In particular, the symbols t and nil, which are the default Lisp boolean values, evaluate to themselves. In Lisp, t corresponds to the boolean True, and nil corresponds to the boolean False. Nil and the empty list () are equivalent symbols in a sense that will be explained later in this chapter.

```
> t
t
> nil
nil
```

Nested lists are often the most difficult expressions to enter since correctly typing a list requires that the parentheses balance, a feat that many fledgling Lisp hackers find difficult to accomplish. We left out the many errors and false starts that occurred as we generated the interactions recorded here. We will not persist in giving you advice about how to interact with your interpreter, except to suggest once again that you consult a manual or local expert regarding your implementation of Lisp. You may find that your local Lisp system includes utilities for balancing parentheses, controlling indentation, and a variety of other aids that will make your experience more productive and less frustrating.

2.4 Functions in Lisp

If the expression typed to the interpreter is not a string, number, symbol, or other primitive object, then it had better be a list. If it is a list, then it had better be either a *special form* or an expression corresponding to the invocation of a function. We use the terms *function* and *procedure* interchangeably in this text. Special forms include conditionals and other flow of control constructs that are treated specially by Lisp.

  We assume that functions are stored in a single global table that maps symbols to functions. This need not be the case in Common Lisp, but making this assumption avoids a number of what we consider peripheral issues. Eval makes use of another Lisp program called apply to handle function invocations. Apply takes two arguments, a function and a list of zero or more arguments. Eval and apply work together as follows:

1 Eval takes the list corresponding to the function invocation and extracts the first element of the list and the list of arguments corresponding to the remaining elements of the list.

2 If the first element of the list is not a symbol or the symbol is not associated with a function in the global table, then eval signals an error; otherwise, Eval passes the function associated with the symbol and the list of arguments to apply.

3 Apply uses eval to evaluate the list of arguments in left-to-right order.

4 Apply extracts the definition associated with the function. If the number of formal parameters associated with the definition differs from the number of arguments, then apply signals an error.

5 Apply substitutes the results from step 3 for the formal parameters in a copy of the function definition and sends the resulting expressions to eval to be evaluated.

The preceding description is called the *substitution model* for function invocation. In the substitution model, a function is invoked by substituting values for the formal parameters in a copy of the function's definition and then evaluating the resulting expressions. Now that we know how Lisp handles function invocations, we need some functions to invoke.

Function Invocation

Common Lisp has a lot of built-in functions. You can scan through a reference manual (e.g., Steele [1990]) to get some idea of the range of functions, but most if not all the functions found in other widely used programming languages are also available in Common Lisp in some form or another. For arithmetic, Common Lisp includes functions for addition (+), subtraction (-), multiplication (*), and division (/) involving one or more arguments. These functions can generally be counted on to behave reasonably given any mixture of integer or floating-point arguments. Here is an example

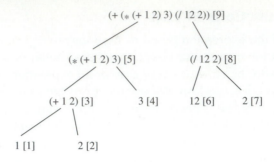

Figure 2.3 Order of evaluation in nested function invocation

adding three numbers and another example subtracting 2 and 1 from 4.

```
> (+ 3 4 5)
12
> (- 4 2 1)
1
```

In evaluating a list corresponding to a function invocation, the arguments are evaluated (recursively) in left-to-right order. In nested function invocations, this evaluation strategy results in the innermost arguments being evaluated first. Figure 2.3 shows the tree of evaluations that results from the following invocation; the order of evaluation for subexpressions is indicated by the integers in square brackets:

```
> (+ (* (+ 1 2) 3) (/ 12 2))
15
```

By appropriately indenting subexpressions, we can make this tree of evaluations explicit.

```
> (+ (* (+ 1
         2)
      3)
    (/ 12
       2))
15
```

Lisp syntax does not enforce a discipline for making explicit the structure in programs. Indenting is the method of choice for displaying structure in programs.

Procedural Abstraction

Functions are defined using a special form defun that takes a symbol as the name for the function, a list of symbols corresponding to the formal parameters of the function, and a definition consisting of one or more expressions. Defun installs the definition in the global table under the specified name. Function definitions allow us to specify abstract procedures. For instance, (* 3 3) computes the square of the number 3. The following use of

```
;; Hypotenuse takes two arguments corresponding
;; to the length of the two legs of a right triangle and
;; returns the length of the hypotenuse of the triangle.
(defun hypotenuse (a b)
    ;; Sqrt is a built-in function that
    ;; computes the square root of a number.
    (sqrt (+ (square a)
             (square b))))


;; Square computes the square of its single argument.
(defun square (x)
    (* x x))
```

Figure 2.4   Function definitions as they might appear in a file

defun defines a procedure for computing the square of any number:

```
> (defun square (x) (* x x))
SQUARE
> (square 3)
9
```

When eval encounters the expression (square 3), it determines that the expression is a function invocation and sends square and the list of arguments (3) off to apply. Apply looks up the definition for square in the global table. In this case, the definition is (* x x). Apply uses eval to evaluate the single argument to obtain 3, which it substitutes for x in (* x x) to obtain (* 3 3), which is sent to eval for evaluation.

Figure 2.4 lists two function definitions as they might appear in a file accompanied with documentation in the form of comments. Note that hypotenuse refers to square before the definition of square appears in the file. Function definitions can appear in a file in any order as long as they appear before they are actually invoked.

Conditional Statements

Lisp supports a form of the familiar if statement for flow of control. A Lisp if statement is of the form (if *test conditional alternate*), where the final *alternate* expression is optional. When eval encounters an if statement, the *test* expression is evaluated immediately.

In Lisp, any expression can serve as a test. If the expression returns nil (or equivalently ()), then the test is said to fail; otherwise, it is said to succeed. For instance, the Lisp predicates =, >, <, >=, and <= enable us to test numerical relationships. Numberp tests if its only argument is a number, and symbolp tests for symbols. In an if statement, the *conditional* expression is evaluated only if the test succeeds, and the *alternate* expression is evaluated only if the test fails.

The function next-odd-number returns the next odd integer following the integer specified as its only argument. Next-odd-number uses evenp to test if its only argument is even. There is also a function oddp that tests for odd numbers.

```
> (defun next-odd-number (n)
    (if (evenp n)
        (+ n 1)
        (+ n 2)))
NEXT-ODD-NUMBER
> (next-odd-number 1)
3
```

We can construct more complicated tests using the boolean operators or, and, and not.

```
> (or (oddp 2) (and (not (oddp 4)) (evenp 6)))
T
```

The operator not returns t if its only argument evaluates to nil and returns nil otherwise. The operator and takes any number of arguments and returns the value of its last argument if all the arguments evaluate to non-nil and returns nil otherwise. The operator or takes any number of arguments and returns the value of the first argument that evaluates to non-nil or nil if no arguments evaluate to non-nil.

Lisp also supports a more general conditional statement. A cond statement is of the form (cond *clauses*), where a clause is of the form (*test body*), in which the body consists of zero or more expressions. A cond statement is evaluated by evaluating the test of each of its clauses in turn until some test succeeds. When that happens, the expressions in the body of that clause are evaluated in sequence, and the value of the last expression is returned as the value of the cond. If the clause has no expressions in its body, then the value of the test is returned. If no test succeeds, then the cond returns nil.

Here we define a predicate primep that tests if a number less than 49 is prime. Primep uses a Lisp print function princ to signal when it has been given a number outside its range. The function princ evaluates its single argument, prints the resulting value, and then returns that value. Primep also uses the Lisp modulus function mod to determine if a number is divisible by 2, 3, or 5.

```
> (defun primep (n)
    (cond ((>= n 49) (princ "Can't count that high.") nil)
          ((or (= n 2) (= n 3) (= n 5)) t)
          ((or (= (mod n 2) 0)
               (= (mod n 3) 0)
               (= (mod n 5) 0)) nil)
          (t t)))
```

```
> (primep 32)
NIL
> (primep 37)
T
> (primep 76)
Can't count that high.
NIL
```

In the function primep, t (a symbol that evaluates to itself) plays the role of a test that always succeeds. Some consider it bad form to write a cond statement for which no test succeeds, and hence, you will often see cond statements whose last clause is of the form (t *body*).

Recursive Functions

A recursive problem-solving method reduces the problem it is given to one or more simpler problems and then applies itself to solve the simpler problems. It breaks the problem down again, and again, until the pieces of the problem can be solved easily without further reduction. We can define functions that behave in a similar manner.

Many of the functions described in this text are defined recursively. A *recursive function* is one in which the function is invoked (recursively) in the body of its definition. In the recursive invocation, the function is generally applied to some reduction of the original arguments. Each recursive invocation reduces the problem still further until some criterion, called the *base-case* criterion, is satisfied.

The function raise takes two arguments, a number of any type and a nonnegative integer n, and returns the number raised to the nth power. A recursive definition is provided here.

```
> (defun raise (x n)
    (if (= n 0)
        1
      (* x (raise x (- n 1))))))
RAISE
> (raise 3 3)
27
```

The base-case criterion (terminating condition) for the recursion is the case of $n = 0$; any number raised to the 0 power is 1. If $n \neq 0$, then we multiply x times the result of calling raise with arguments x and (- n 1).

We present many examples of recursive functions in the following pages. We also introduce a number of iterative constructs that will serve in cases in which recursion is clumsy.

Evaluating Functions in Files

Now that you can write functions, you will probably want to store some of them in files so that you do not have to repeatedly type them to the

Lisp interpreter. A Lisp program is just a sequence of Lisp expressions. Executing a Lisp program consists of evaluating the expressions in the program in the order that they appear in the sequence. If you write a set of expressions in a file, then you can execute it by *loading* it from the Lisp interpreter. Loading is done by evaluating an expression of the form (load *file-specification*), where *file-specification* is an expression that evaluates to a string indicating a file.

The exact form of the file specification will depend on your particular implementation of Common Lisp and local operating system. Generally, however, if you start Common Lisp in a directory in which a file program.lisp resides, then evaluating (load "program.lisp") will serve to load that file and evaluate the expressions found in it. You can also embed load statements in files to establish dependencies between files. For instance, if program.lisp depends on the definitions in functions.lisp, then you might place a statement (load "functions.lisp") somewhere in program.lisp.

2.5   Environments, Symbols, and Scope

In the preceding discussion, we never introduced the notion of assignment. In fact, we never even mentioned the word *variable*. We allowed substitution for formal parameters in function definitions, but you could not "set" a formal parameter. It is true that defun allowed us to assign function definitions to symbols, but we could have avoided defun by introducing unnamed functions, a feature that we discuss in the next section. The symbols other than function names were constants like t or nil. The subset of Lisp presented so far is basically *pure Lisp*, Lisp with functions, constants, and boolean operators, but no assignment. In the following, we add assignment and variables to Lisp, and in so doing, we make explicit some of the ways in which Lisp uses memory.

Assigning Values to Symbols

There really is no difference between variables and symbols in Lisp, and we use the terms interchangeably. Symbols have *values* that can be changed. Symbols in Lisp correspond to call-by-value variables in languages that have such variables. We can set or change the value of symbols by using the special form setq (for *set* equal).

```
> (setq sym 2)
2
> sym
2
> (setq sym 3)
3
> sym
3
```

Setq takes a minimum of two arguments; the first must be a symbol and is not evaluated, and the second can be any expression and is evaluated.

```
> (setq new sym)
3
> new
3
```

Setq can be used to set the value of several symbols at once, as in the expression (setq new 1 old 0).

When eval encounters a symbol, it looks up the symbol's value in a structure that behaves like a table; if there is no entry in the table, then it reports an error. The structure is called an *environment* and eval has to figure out the appropriate environment to look in. In the preceding examples, eval looks up symbol values in the *global environment*. Later on, we consider how additional environments are created and referenced by eval.

In Common Lisp, a symbol can have a value that is used when the symbol appears as an argument of a function and a definition that is used when the symbol appears as the first element of a list interpreted as a function invocation.[2]

Eval and Apply Revisited

At this point, we reconsider the operation of eval and apply taking into account symbols and environments. Eval takes a single argument corresponding to an expression. In addition, eval is given an environment, initially the global environment. Here is the pseudo code for eval.

1. If the expression is a number or a string, then return the expression.
2. If the expression is a symbol, then look up its value in the environment.
3. If the expression is a special form, then handle it accordingly.
4. If the expression is a list and not a special form, then send the function associated with the symbol corresponding to the first item in the list and the arguments corresponding to the rest of the items in the list to apply.

In the previous section, we described apply using a substitution model; now we provide an alternative model in terms of environments. Apply takes a function and a list of expressions corresponding to arguments. Each function has associated with it the environment that was in place at the time the function was defined. In many cases, the associated environment is just the global environment, but there are exceptions that we will get to shortly. Apply uses the environment associated with a given function to create a new

---

[2]Not all modern dialects of Lisp make this distinction between functions and arguments. For example, there is a dialect of Lisp called Scheme [Abelson and Sussman, 1985], in which each symbol has a single value resulting in a very clean and conceptually simple implementation.

environment in which to evaluate the definition of the function. We describe exactly how environments are created from other environments in the section on structured environments. Like eval, apply is also given an environment.

1. Look up the definition of the function.
2. Use eval to evaluate each argument in the environment.
3. Create a new environment in which each formal parameter in the definition has the value of the corresponding item in the list of arguments. This new environment is created using the environment associated with the function and *not* the environment given to apply.
4. Use eval to evaluate the definition in the new environment.

It should be noted that both eval and apply correspond to functions that can be invoked in Lisp programs. We describe apply in later sections. The use of eval in Lisp code is complicated by the fact that eval, like most Lisp functions, evaluates its arguments. If this seems circular, that's because it is. In the preceding discussion, we ignore the first level of evaluation and just consider what eval does if the first level of evaluation were to result in a particular expression. We suggest that you be careful in using eval in writing programs; it is only rarely necessary.

Structured Environments

An environment allocates storage for symbol values. You can think of the global environment as just a large table. Whenever you setq a new symbol, memory is set aside in the global environment to point to the value of that symbol. The environments created during function application and in evaluating certain special forms have a more complicated structure. In general, an environment is a linked list of tables. A new environment is created from an existing environment by creating a new table and having it point to the existing *parent* environment. The new environment points to this newly created table that allocates storage for specific symbols. In the case of a function definition, space is allocated in the table for the formal parameters. To determine the value of a symbol in an environment, eval first looks in the table pointed to by the environment. If there is no entry for the symbol in that table, then eval looks in the parent environment, and so on until it reaches the global environment. You can change the (local) value of a symbol in an environment without changing its value in the global environment.

```
> (setq x 2)
2
> (defun local (x)
    (setq x (+ x 1))
    (* x x))
```

```
LOCAL
> (local (+ x 1))
16
> x
2
```

Figure 2.5 shows the environments that exist at different stages during the execution of (local (+ x 1)). The global environment is shaded in Figure 2.5.

Generally speaking, setting the value of symbols in the global environment is frowned on. One of the main reasons for this attitude is that global variables are often difficult to track down in large pieces of code; widely scattered global variables can make large programs difficult to understand.

```
> (defun global (x)
    (setq sym (+ x 1))
    (* sym sym))
GLOBAL
> (global 1)
4
> sym
2
```

Local Variables

You do not have to introduce a symbol as a formal parameter in order to use it as a local variable. The special form let can also be used to produce a new environment. Using let, you can introduce a local variable and later setq it to a specific value, or you can set it at the same time you introduce it. The general form is (let *variable-specifications body*), where *variable-specifications* is a list of zero or more expressions each corresponding to a variable or an expression of the form *(variable initial-value-expression)*, and *body* consists of one or more expressions. In evaluating such a form, Lisp assigns each variable the value of the corresponding initial value expression if such an expression exists and nil otherwise. These assignments are carried out in parallel so that you cannot refer to one variable in the initial value expression of another. There is a variant of let called let* that assigns local variables sequentially so that you can refer to one variable in the initial

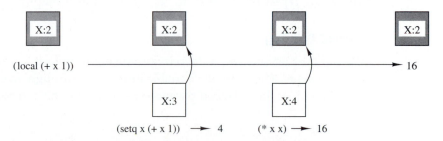

Figure 2.5   Environments created during function invocation

value expression of another variable appearing later in the list of variable specifications.

In the following, we illustrate both styles of setting local variables in the definition of a simple linear interpolation function that takes two points on a line in terms of their x and y coordinates and returns the y coordinate of a third point given its x coordinate.[3]

```
> (defun interpolate (x1 y1 x2 y2 x3)
    (if (= x1 x2)
        y1
        (let ((m (/ (- y2 y1) (- x2 x1)))
              (b y1)
              (x (- x3 x1)))
          (+ (* m x) b))))
INTERPOLATE
> (interpolate 1 1 5 5 4)
4
> (interpolate 1 3 4 3 2)
3
```

Note the use of the if statement to avoid dividing by zero.

The following function provides another illustration of the use of let, this time using a cond statement. Read is a function of no arguments that reads an expression from the standard input (usually a terminal), and random is a function that takes a single argument corresponding to a positive number *n* and returns a number of the same type—in this case an integer—between zero (inclusive) and *n* (exclusive). In the case of *n* being an integer, the possible results appear with the (approximate) frequency $1/n$.

```
> (defun guess ()
    (princ "Guess an integer from 0 to 9: ")
    (let ((response (read)) (number (random 10)))
      (cond ((> response number) (princ "Too high!"))
            ((< response number) (princ "Too low!"))
            (t (princ "Lucky guess!")))))
GUESS
> (guess)
Guess an integer from 0 to 9: 3
Too low!
```

The 3 was typed by the user in response to the prompt.

Lexical Scoping

We can nest let statements thereby producing more complicated structured environments. The *scope* of a variable introduced through an environment is determined by the balanced parentheses enclosing the corresponding let or

---

[3]In many cases (present example included), local variables are not strictly necessary. However, if skillfully employed, local variables help enhance readability.

defun. For this reason, such variables are often referred to as *lexical* (or *static*) variables, and the rule for determining their scope as *lexical scoping*. Many dialects of Lisp also support *dynamic* variables whose scope is determined at evaluation time. Lexical scoping has the advantage that code relying entirely on lexically scoped variables tends to be easier for programmers to understand and compilers to produce efficient code for. In this text, a variable is either global or local, and if it is local, then it has lexical scoping.

In the following code fragment, we use the Lisp print function princ to illustrate lexical variable scoping. Recall that princ evaluates its only argument, prints the result, and then returns the result as the value of the print statement.

```
> (let ((x 1))
    (let ((x 2))
      (let ((x 3))
        (princ x))
      (princ x))
    (princ x))
321
1
```

The first line following the let statement is the result of the three princ invocations; the second line is the value returned by the let statement, which is the value of the last princ statement. Figure 2.6 shows the environments that exist at different stages during the execution of the code.

Let statements allow us to build complicated structured environments. From what we have observed so far, each time a function is invoked, evaluation begins in a new environment with a new table allocating storage for

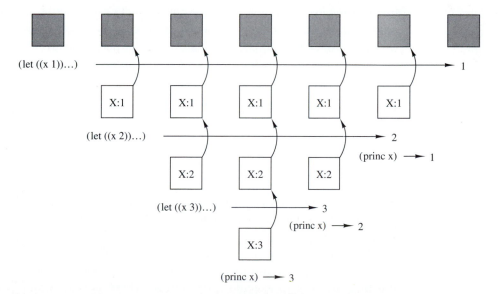

Figure 2.6 Environments created using nested let statements

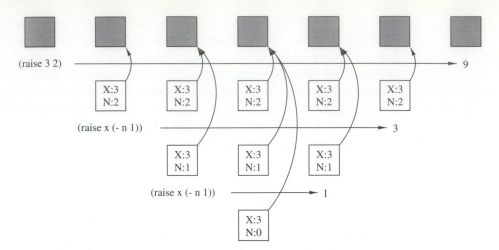

Figure 2.7 Environments created during recursive function invocation

the formal parameters and pointing to the global environment. Without let, all environments would consist of a table pointing to the global environment. As an example involving recursive functions, Figure 2.7 shows the environments that exist at different stages during the execution of (raise 3 2). In the next section, we consider more sophisticated ways of using environments.

2.6 More on Functions

The methods that we have introduced so far for defining and using functions have limitations. For instance, a function cannot recall anything from prior invocations except by using global variables. Every function has to have a name. Functions cannot create new functions, pass functions as arguments, or make use of functions other than those defined by defun. In this section, we show how Lisp enables us to overcome these limitations.

Functions with Local State

It is often useful to associate data (or *state*) with a particular function or set of functions. One way of doing this is to create one or more global variables and setq them to appropriate values. As noted earlier, however, this use of global variables is generally frowned on by purists. As an alternative, we might create an enclosing environment for the function or set of functions that introduces variables local to the environment that refer to the local state.

The time during which an environment exists is called its *extent*. So far, the extent of the environments we have talked about is brief, usually just the time it takes to execute a procedure. There is one notable exception. The extent of the global environment is the entire time the Lisp process is running. Whenever a Lisp object is created that is capable of making references to symbols, that object maintains a pointer to its immediate environment so that references can be made with respect to that environment. As long as that object exists, its associated environment exists. So far, the only objects we have encountered that are capable of making variable references are functions, but shortly we will learn how to create other such objects.

All the functions we have considered until now have as their associated environment the global environment, but we can easily define functions with different environments. The following (novelty) function, squarelast, uses local state to remember the number corresponding to the value of its single argument the last time it was invoked and returns the square of that number. Squarelast is always one step behind the user.

```
> (let (x (y 1))
    (defun squarelast (z)
      (setq x y) (setq y z) (* x x)))
SQUARELAST
> (squarelast 2)
1
> (squarelast 3)
4
```

Lambda and Functions as Arguments

Named functions defined with defun are not the only Lisp objects capable of referencing variables. Lisp also allows us to create unnamed functions called *lambda functions*. The expression (function (lambda *arguments body*)) evaluates to a function defined with the formal parameters in *arguments* and the definition supplied in *body*. Function does not evaluate its single argument; it expects either a list whose first element is lambda or a symbol defined as a function (e.g., (function square)). Function has a handy abbreviation. Common Lisp allows you to write #´*expression* as an abbreviation for (function *expression*). In Common Lisp, you cannot call such a function simply by having it appear as the first element of a list (as you can in the Scheme dialect), but rather, you have to funcall or apply it.

Funcall takes as its first argument an expression that evaluates to a function and as many additional arguments as the function corresponding to the first argument has arguments of its own (e.g., (funcall #´square 3)). Apply is similar except that it takes only two arguments, the second must evaluate to a list of the arguments to be supplied to the function corresponding to the first argument. Since we do not as yet know how to construct expressions that evaluate to lists, we hold off on examples using apply. Here is a simple example illustrating function and funcall.

```
> (funcall #´(lambda (x) (* x x)) 3)
9
```

Both named and lambda functions are often passed around as variables and in lists to be passed as arguments to funcall.

```
> (defun decreasingp (x y f)
    (if (> (funcall f x) (funcall f y)) t nil))
DECREASINGP
> (decreasingp 1 2 #´(lambda (x) (* x x)))
NIL
> (setq reciprocal #´(lambda (x) (/ 1 x)))
#<Interpreted-Function (LAMBDA (X) (/ 1 X)) 104BB75>
> (decreasingp 1 2 reciprocal)
T
```

Lambda functions can also have associated state.

```
> (let ((x 0))
    (setq counter #´(lambda () (setq x (+ x 1)))))
#<Interpreted-Function (LAMBDA () (SETQ X (+ X 1))) 104BB76>
> (funcall counter)
1
> (funcall counter)
2
```

If we were to set the symbol counter to something new, then the environment created here would cease to exist, thereby terminating its extent.

2.7 List Processing

So far lists have appeared only as the representation for programs. In Lisp, both programs and data can be represented as lists. We use lists to build abstract data types and to serve as the primary abstraction of Lisp storage.

Suspending Evaluation Using Quote

Contradictory as it might sound, a symbol does not have to have a value in order to be valuable for symbolic manipulation purposes. In order to refer to a symbol (rather than its value), it is often useful to get eval to suspend evaluation. This is done in Lisp with the quote function. Quote is used so often in Lisp that there is a convenient abbreviation; ´*expression* is an abbreviation for (quote *expression*). Quote causes eval to suspend evaluation on any expression.

```
> (quote sym)
SYM
> ´sym
SYM
> ´(first second third)
(FIRST SECOND THIRD)
```

Using quote, we can construct lists of symbols if we know what those symbols are in advance. Using list, we can build lists more flexibly under program control.

Building and Accessing Elements in Lists

The function list provides a convenient method of constructing lists. List takes any number of arguments and returns a list of their values.

```
> (list 1 2 3 4)
(1 2 3 4)
> (list 1 (list 2 (list 3)))
(1 (2 (3)))
```

The function first allows us to access the first element of a list. Second, third, fourth, fifth, sixth, seventh, eighth, ninth, and tenth are also defined in many dialects of Lisp to access the second, third, fourth, fifth, sixth, seventh, eighth, ninth, and tenth elements of a list. More generally, (nth *i l*) allows us to access the *i*th element of the list *l*. Note that nth is zero based, so the first element of *l* is (nth 0 *l*), second (nth 1 *l*), and so on.

```
> (setq four (list 1 2 3 4))
(1 2 3 4)
> (list (first four) (second four) (nth 2 four))
(1 2 3)
> (rest four)
(2 3 4)
```

We take lists apart using first and rest and we put them back together using cons (for *cons*tructor), which takes two arguments.

```
> (setq first 1)
1
> (setq rest (list 2 3 4))
(2 3 4)
> (cons first rest)
(1 2 3 4)
```

For many applications, the second argument to cons is a list, but it need not be so.

Lists in Memory

Cons constructs what is called a *dotted pair* for reasons that will soon become apparent; construction involves allocating storage for two *pointers* that refer to the values of the two arguments.

```
> (setq x (cons 1 2))
(1 . 2)
> (setq y (cons 1 (cons 2 ())))
(1 2)
```

The structures in memory corresponding to dotted pairs are called *cons cells* and are depicted graphically as joined boxes with pointers. Pointers to nil are depicted by a slash through the corresponding box. Figure 2.8 (page 46) shows the structures that result from evaluating the preceding expressions.

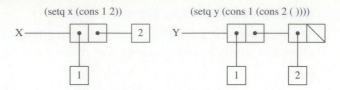

Figure 2.8   List structures in memory

In reading other books about Lisp, you may encounter the functions car and cdr. First and rest are the preferred, mnemonic names for car and cdr. The names car and cdr can be traced to the machine architecture of the computer that Lisp was first designed to run on.

```
> (car x)
1
> (cdr y)
(2)
> (car (cdr y))
2
```

One reason that some programmers retain the archaic car and cdr is the related but very convenient abbreviations for nested cars and cdrs. In many dialects of Lisp, short sequences of cars and cdrs (usually up to four) (e.g., (car (cdr (car *expression*)))) are abbreviated by functions of the form c[a|d]*r (e.g., (cadar *expression*)). If these functions are not available in your dialect, you should find it easy to define them.

You do not really need to know about the structure of memory to program in Lisp. If you want to modify the list that a symbol points to, then you can construct a new list and setq the symbol to be the new list. This strategy can result in considerable time spent in copying large lists and some rather tedious bookkeeping. For instance, the new list might look almost identical to the old list with perhaps one or two small differences, and you will be forced to reconstruct most of the old list. In addition, if two symbols point to the same list or one symbol points to a subexpression of the list that another symbol points to, then you will have to make appropriate changes. By directly modifying the contents of memory, we can avoid a lot of unnecessary copying and bookkeeping.

Modifying List Structures in Memory

Lisp allows you to modify existing list structures by changing the contents of memory. Setf takes a location in memory (such as provided by a symbol reference or by first and rest invocations) and an expression, and changes what is stored at that location to be the value of the expression. Setf is said to *destructively* modify its first argument.

```
> (setq x (list 1 (list 2)))
(1 (2))
```

```
> (setf (first (first (rest x))) 1)
1
> x
(1 (1))
```

Setf is more general than setq, but the latter is often still used as a form of documentation to indicate that a symbol is being set rather than some more complicated memory modification. Be careful with setf; employed carelessly, it can often be the cause of subtle bugs in programs. Setf allows us to build circular list structures that are very useful for representation purposes; you do, however, have to be somewhat careful in displaying such structures.

```
> (setf (first (rest x)) x)
(1 (1 (1 (1 (1 (1 (1 (1 (1 (1 (1 ...
```

The interpreter's response to this invocation had to be interrupted or it would have continued printing indefinitely. Figure 2.9 displays the resulting structure graphically. Common Lisp has print procedures that perform a more reasonable job of printing circular list structures.

Alternative Parameter-Passing Conventions

Lisp passes parameters using call by value, as illustrated by the following exchange with the interpreter:

```
> (defun foo (x) (setq x 0))
FOO
> (let ((x 1)) (foo x) (princ x))
1
```

We can easily simulate other parameter-passing conventions using pointers and setf. The following illustrates how to simulate call-by-reference parameter passing:

```
> (defun bar (x) (setf (first x) 0))
BAR
> (let ((x (list 1))) (bar x) (princ (first x)))
0
```

However, there is no way in Lisp to achieve call by reference for symbols.

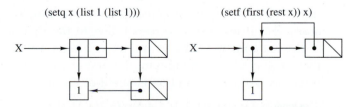

Figure 2.9 Modifying list structures in memory

Predicates on Lists

Lisp has a variety of boolean predicates for performing tests on lists. Listp tests for lists, consp tests for dotted pairs, null for the empty list nil (or ()). To compare list structures, there are eq and equal. Eq determines if its two arguments point to the same location in memory. Nil and () are eq. Equal determines if its two arguments are structurally similar.

```
> (setq sym 'foo)
FOO
> (eq sym 'foo)
T
> (setq sym (list 'foo))
(FOO)
> (eq sym (list 'foo))
NIL
> (setq new sym)
(FOO)
> (eq new sym)
T
> (equal sym (list 'foo))
T
```

Built-In List Manipulation Functions

Other functions that operate on lists include append, which takes zero or more arguments that evaluate to lists and returns a new list that consists of all the elements in those lists, and nconc, which is similar to append except that it destructively modifies all its arguments but the last.

```
> (setq x '(1 2) y '(3 4))
(3 4)
> (append x y)
(1 2 3 4)
> x
(1 2)
> (nconc x y)
(1 2 3 4)
> x
(1 2 3 4)
```

Reverse takes a list and returns a new list that consists of the elements of the old list arranged in reverse order. Member is a particularly useful Lisp function that takes two arguments corresponding to an arbitrary Lisp object and a list. If the object corresponding to the first argument is an element of the list corresponding to the second, then member returns that portion of the list (its *tail*) beginning with the first element of the list that is eq to that object. If the object is not an element of the list, member returns nil.

```
> (member 5 (append '(1 2 3) '(4 5) '(6 7 8)))
(5 6 7 8)
```

Optional Arguments

Many Common Lisp functions take optional arguments corresponding to functions that are introduced with keywords. Keywords appear in argument lists as symbols whose first character is a colon (e.g., :test). For instance, we mentioned that member uses eq to check for objects in a list; if instead of writing (member *x l*), we write (member *x l* :test #´equal), then member will use equal as a test instead of eq. We can also specify a lambda function as a test.

```
> (member ´(2) ´((1) (2) (3)))
NIL
> (member ´(2) ´((1) (2) (3)) :test #´equal)
((2) (3))
> (member ´(1 2) ´((0 4) (1 3))
        :test #´(lambda (x y) (eq (first x)
                                  (first y))))
((1 3))
```

List-Processing Examples

Using our new list-processing machinery, we now define a function insert that takes two arguments: a pair of numbers (e.g., (1 2)) and a list of pairs of numbers (e.g., ((1 2)(2 4)(4 8))). We assume that the list of pairs is sorted by the size of the first number in each pair with smaller numbers appearing earlier in the list. The list of pairs represents samples in the form of a pair of numbers, x and $f(x)$, of a scalar function f of one variable. There is no need to include two pairs with the same first element; if the pairs all come from the same function and two pairs have the same (=) first element, then the second elements will also be the same and the pairs will be equal. Insert creates a new sorted list that includes the pair corresponding to the first argument. It does so by pulling the list apart with first and rest and putting it back together with cons, adding the new pair if necessary.

```
> (defun insert (new pairs)
    (cond ((null pairs) (cons new ()))
          ((= (first new) (first (first pairs))) pairs)
          ((< (first new) (first (first pairs))) (cons new pairs))
          (t (cons (first pairs) (insert new (rest pairs))))))
INSERT
> (insert ´(3 4) ´((1 2) (2 4) (5 6)))
((1 2) (2 4) (3 4) (5 6))
> (insert ´(1 2) (insert ´(3 4) ()))
((1 2) (3 4))
```

Insert applies itself recursively to the rest of the list corresponding to its second argument until that list is nil. It is also often useful to recurse on both the first and the rest of arguments corresponding to complex nested list structures. The following function recurses on both the first and rest of a list to test for the appearance of a given symbol:

```
> (defun search (symbol expression)
    (cond ((null expression) nil)
          ((symbolp expression) (eq expression symbol))
          (t (or (search symbol (first expression))
                 (search symbol (rest expression))))))
SEARCH
> (search 'fred '(student (name fred) (year junior)))
T
```

We now define a function that given a number and a list of pairs of numbers returns nil if the number is greater than the greatest of the first elements of the pairs or less than the least of them. If there exists a pair whose first element is = to the number, then the function returns a list consisting of the existing pair with the = first element (e.g., ((1 2))). Otherwise, the function returns a pair consisting of the two consecutive existing pairs such that the first element of the first pair is less than the number and the first element of the second pair is greater than the number (e.g., ((1 2) (3 6))).

```
> (defun nearest-pairs (x pairs)
    (cond ((null pairs) nil)
          ((= x (first (first pairs)))
           (list (first pairs)))
          ((or (< x (first (first pairs)))
               (null (rest pairs))) ())
          ((< x (first (second pairs)))
           (list (first pairs) (second pairs)))
          (t (nearest-pairs x (rest pairs)))))
NEAREST-PAIRS
> (setq pairs '((1 2) (2 4) (5 6)))
((1 2) (2 4) (5 6))
> (nearest-pairs 2 pairs)
((2 4))
> (nearest-pairs 3 pairs)
((2 4) (5 6))
```

As an example using local state, we define two functions that keep track of data and make estimates. Remember remembers pairs of numbers of the form $(x \ f(x))$ for a function f. When asked for an estimate of $f(x)$ for a particular value of x, estimate returns a warning if x is outside the range of its data, returns $f(x)$ if it has stored a pair $(x \ f(x))$, or invokes the linear interpolation function described earlier. Figure 2.10 lists the code for the two functions.

```
> (remember 1 1)
((1 1))
> (remember 2 3)
```

```
((1 1) (2 3))
> (remember 3 3)
((1 1) (2 3) (3 3))
> (estimate 2.4)
3
> (estimate 1.2)
1.4
```

Data Abstraction

Using cons and list, you can build arbitrary data structures, reference them with first and rest, and modify them with setf. However, complicated data structures so implemented tend to result in impenetrable code. In keeping with standard programming practice, most programmers design *data abstractions* that hide the details of how data structures are implemented. This allows one or more programmers to use an abstraction without worrying about the implementation or caring that the implementation might change without their knowledge.

Suppose that we are writing programs that involve the manipulation of labeled binary trees. Rather than manipulating binary trees using primitives like cons, first, and rest, we design a data abstraction using functions that we define and have mnemonic names. Figure 2.11 (page 52) lists functions defining an abstract data type for labeled binary trees with operations for creating, testing, accessing, and modifying instances of this data type.

To make it easier to read code involving abstract data types, we use a few simple conventions in defining abstract data types. Suppose that we want to implement an abstract data type called TYPE. The function for constructing an instance of TYPE would be called make-TYPE. The function for testing if an arbitrary Lisp object is an instance of TYPE would be called

```
;; Keep track of the data in a local state variable.
(let ((data ()))
  ;; Add new data to the existing data set.
  (defun remember (x y)
    (setq data (insert (list x y) data)))
  ;; Make an estimate on the basis of the data.
  (defun estimate (x)
    (let ((pairs (nearest-pairs x data)))
      (cond ((null pairs) "Outside range!")
            ((null (rest pairs)) (second (first pairs)))
            (t (interpolate (first (first pairs))
                            (second (first pairs))
                            (first (second pairs))
                            (second (second pairs)) x))))))
```

Figure 2.10   Functions for remembering data and making estimates

```
;; Create an instance of a labeled binary tree.
(defun make-TREE (label left right)
  (list 'labeled-binary-tree label left right))

;; Determine if an object is a labeled binary tree.
(defun is-TREE (x)
  (and (listp x) (eq (first x) 'labeled-binary-tree)))

;; Return the label of a labeled binary tree.
(defun TREE-label (tree) (second tree))

;; Return the left branch of a labeled binary tree.
(defun TREE-left (tree) (third tree))

;; Return the right branch of a labeled binary tree.
(defun TREE-right (tree) (fourth tree))

;; Set the label of a labeled binary tree.
(defun set-TREE-label (tree value)
  (setf (second tree) value))
```

Figure 2.11   Abstract data type for labeled binary trees

is-TYPE. If the data type allows access to some internal structure called slot, then the accessor function would be called TYPE-slot. If the internal structure identified by slot is modifiable, then the function for making modifications would be called set-TYPE-slot. Though Lisp generally does not care whether symbols are in uppercase or lowercase, in displaying Lisp code, we use uppercase letters to indicate abstract data types with everything else in lowercase. These conventions constitute a simple programming discipline that makes Lisp code easier to understand.

Having created a data abstraction, we can now forget about the details and write programs using the abstraction. Figure 2.12 lists a function that modifies the labels in a labeled binary tree. TREE-sub makes use of progn, a Lisp construct for collecting a sequence of expressions into a single form. Eval evaluates each of the expressions in a progn form in turn, returning the value of the last one.

```
;; Substitute new for old in tree.
(defun TREE-sub (tree old new)
  ;; Don't bother unless it really is a tree.
  (if (is-TREE tree)
    ;; Make the substitution if required.
    (progn (if (eq old (TREE-label tree))
             (set-TREE-label tree new))
           ;; Recurse on the left and right branches.
           (TREE-sub (TREE-left tree) old new)
           (TREE-sub (TREE-right tree) old new))))
```

Figure 2.12   Program for changing the labels in a binary tree

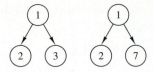

Figure 2.13   Labeled binary tree before and after label substitution

Here is an example creating a labeled binary tree and then using TREE-sub to make label substitutions.

```
> (setq tree (make-TREE 1 (make-TREE 2 () ())
                          (make-TREE 3 () ())))
(LABELED-BINARY-TREE 1 (LABELED-BINARY-TREE 2 NIL NIL)
                       (LABELED-BINARY-TREE 3 NIL NIL))
> (TREE-sub tree 3 7)
NIL
> tree
(LABELED-BINARY-TREE 1 (LABELED-BINARY-TREE 2 NIL NIL)
                       (LABELED-BINARY-TREE 7 NIL NIL))
```

Figure 2.13 depicts the instances of the abstract data types created by these invocations and the change that results from the label substitution.

This chapter provides only a glimpse of the procedural and data abstraction capabilities that Lisp has to offer. Common Lisp and its extensions include a wide variety of techniques for structuring large programs and managing complex data types. Lisp provides a wonderful environment for experimenting with languages that support abstraction. To note just one area in which Lisp has had an impact, a great deal of research on object-oriented programming was carried out using Lisp. Today, a number of packages provide a basis for object-oriented programming within Common Lisp.

2.8   Iterative Constructs

By stressing recursion in the previous sections, we are not trying to discourage the use of other forms of iteration in Lisp programming. Rather, we are anticipating the material on logic and logic programming in which recursive specification is the most natural means of representation. Common Lisp provides a variety of constructs for iteration and, in the following, we describe some of the constructs that we make use of in later chapters.

Mapping Functions to Arguments

Often it is useful to apply the same operations to all members of a list. Lisp provides for this with a variety of *mapping* constructs. Mapcar applies its first argument to successive cross sections of lists and returns a list of the results.

Here is a compact way to compute the sum of two vectors represented as lists of numbers.

```
> (mapcar #'+ '(1 2 3) '(4 5 6))
(5 7 9)
```

Lambda functions are often created just to be passed to other functions. For instance, you might wish to compute the maximum of the corresponding entries in two lists.

```
> (mapcar #'(lambda (x y)
              (if (> x y) x y))
            '(2 7 5) '(1 9 4))
(2 9 5)
```

Mapc is like mapcar except that it does not do anything with the results; mapc is used only for its side effects. Mapcan is like mapcar except that it appends the results using nconc.

```
> (mapcan #'(lambda (x)
              (if (numberp x) (list x) nil))
            '(1 2 nil 3 4 nil 5 6 7 nil 8 9))
(1 2 3 4 5 6 7 8 9)
```

Reduce takes a function corresponding to a binary operation and a list and combines the elements of the list using the binary operation. Here are two examples illustrating reduce.

```
> (reduce #'+ `(1 2 3))
6
> (reduce #'(lambda (v w) (mapcar #'+ v w))
            '((1 0 0) (0 1 0) (0 0 1)))
(1 1 1)
```

The first example computes the sum of a list of numbers. The second example computes the sum of a list of vectors. Note that we could have used (apply #'+ '(1 2 3)) as an alternative in the first case.

General Iteration

The do construct is one of the most widely used iterative constructs in Common Lisp. The general form is (do *index-variable-specifications* (*end-test result*) *body*), where *index-variable-specifications* is a list of items of the form (*step-variable initial-value step-value*), *end-test* is any expression, and *result* and *body* consist of one or more expressions. The step value or the step value and the initial value can be left out of an index-variable specification; in the latter case, you need not enclose the step variable in parentheses. Upon entering the do, each step variable gets its initial value or nil if no initial value is provided. On each subsequent loop through the do, each step variable gets its step value or remains unchanged if no step value is provided. The step variable assignments are carried out in parallel.[4] On each loop, after the step variables are assigned, the end test is evaluated. If the end test returns non-nil, the result expressions are evaluated in order returning the value of the last one; otherwise, the expressions in the body are evaluated in order. Here is a simple example of a do loop computing 9! and printing out the numbers 1 through 9 as a side effect.

```
> (do ((i 1 (+ i 1))
       (j 1 (* j i)))
      ((= i 10) j)
      (princ i))
123456789
362880
```

Here is an example of how a do loop might substitute for an expression involving a mapping function.

```
> (setq list '(1 2 3 4))
(1 2 3 4)
> (do ((args list (rest args))
       (results nil (cons (oddp (first args)) results)))
      ((null args) (reverse results)))
(T NIL T NIL)
> (mapcar #'oddp list)
(T NIL T NIL)
```

In this particular case, the mapcar expression is more concise, but there are plenty of occasions in which the do loop will serve more appropriately than a mapping function.

Simple Iteration

There are other iterative constructs corresponding to special cases of do that represent common patterns of use and are often convenient. Dolist is generally invoked using the form (dolist (*var expr result*) *body*), where *var* is a symbol repeatedly bound to the elements of the list that results from evaluating *expr*, *body* is evaluated once for each element of the list, and *result* is an optional form that is evaluated and returned as the value of the dolist after the last time the *body* is evaluated. If no *result* is provided, then dolist returns nil. Note that *expr* is evaluated only once before entering the body of the loop for the first time, and changing the values of variables in *expr* does not change the number of times that the *body* is evaluated and is not considered good practice. Dotimes is generally invoked using the form (dotimes (*var expr result*) *body*), where in this case *var* is bound to the integers from zero up to (but not including) the integer resulting from evaluating *expr*. Note that it is dangerous to set the value of *var* in the *body*. Here are

---

[4]A variant construct do* is identical to do except that variable assignments are carried out sequentially.

some examples illustrating these iterative constructs.

```
> (dolist (x '(a b c)) (princ x))
ABC
NIL
> (dotimes (i 10 i) (princ i))
0123456789
10
```

In the following chapters, we make use of mapping functions, recursion, and these iterative constructs to illustrate different styles of programming. There is no one way to write the programs listed in this text, and you should experiment to find a coding style that you feel comfortable with.

2.9   Monitoring and Debugging Programs

For the most part, debugging a Lisp program is no different from debugging any other program. If your code fails to behave as expected, then start debugging by checking for the most common errors, such as misspelled function names, unbalanced parentheses, wrong number of arguments to a function, inappropriate arguments, or using a variable before it is set.

Most modern implementations of Lisp provide elaborate debugging tools, but discussion of these tools is outside the scope of this text. In the following, we consider some simple tools and techniques that are available in all implementations of Common Lisp and that should suffice for the exercises in this text.

To print out information while your code is running, you can use either princ or a somewhat more sophisticated print utility called format described at the end of this section. One of the simplest debugging aids is to liberally add print statements throughout your code to track changes in the value of variables.

Tracing and Stepping Through Programs

Using the Common Lisp trace utility, you can keep track of when and with what arguments certain functions are called. The following script illustrates how to trace two of the functions defined earlier in this chapter:

```
> (trace raise square)
(RAISE SQUARE)
> (square (raise 2 2))
1 Enter RAISE 2 2
| 2 Enter RAISE 2 1
|   3 Enter RAISE 2 0
|   3 Exit RAISE 1
| 2 Exit RAISE 2
1 Exit RAISE 4
1 Enter SQUARE 4
1 Exit SQUARE 16
16
```

We can also turn off tracing on one or more functions using untrace.

```
> (untrace raise)
(RAISE)
> (square (raise 2 2))
1 Enter SQUARE 4
1 Exit SQUARE 16
16
```

Sometimes tracing does not provide enough information or provides more than we want. In such cases, it is often useful to single-step though the evaluation of a program. The step utility allows just this. The details of step, like the details of trace, will depend on the particular implementation of Common Lisp, but the following script will give you some idea of what is available:

```
> (setq n 3)
3
> (step (square n))
  (SQUARE N) -> :h
     :n    Evaluate current expression in step mode.
     :s    Evaluate current expression without stepping.
     :x    Finish evaluation, but turn Stepper off.
     :p    Print current expression.
     :b    Enter the Debugger.
     :q    Exit to Top Level.
     :h    Print this text.
  (SQUARE N) -> :n
    (FUNCTION SQUARE) -> :n
    #<Interpreted-Function (NAMED-LAMBDA SQUARE (X)
                             (BLOCK SQUARE (* X X))) 100DCD6>
    N = 3
    (BLOCK SQUARE (* X X)) -> :n
      (* X X) -> :n
        (FUNCTION *) -> :n
        #<Compiled-Function * 4ABA76>
        X = 3
        X = 3
```

In this script, :h and :n were typed by the user in response to the -> prompt.

It is nearly impossible to write a program that evaluates without error. Whenever an error occurs, you will enter the debugger, some confusing information will be displayed, and you will see an alternative prompt. Usually typing something like ? or help will give you a list of options that will enable you to continue from the error or give you some idea of what caused the error.

Errors and debugging are inevitable in programming. Take some time to familiarize yourself with the debugging tools available with your implementation of Common Lisp.

Formatted Output

We have already seen one function, princ, for generating formatted output from programs. Using princ and another function terpri, which takes no arguments and results in a line feed, you can handle most of your output needs. Less primitive alternatives are available in Common Lisp, however, and we briefly describe one of them.

Format is a complicated printing and formatting utility. The expression (format *destination string arguments*) is a common way of invoking format, where *string* generally includes embedded directives that control tabbing, line feeds, and the printing of *arguments*. Directives are specified by the tilde character (˜) followed by one or more additional characters. The following examples illustrate just a few of the ways that format can be used:

```
> (format nil "˜D is an integer; ˜A is a symbol" 17 'foo)
"17 is an integer; FOO is a symbol"
> (format nil "˜4,2F is a real number" 1.23456)
"1.23 is a real number"
> (let ((x 6) (y 1.2))
    (format nil "˜D times ˜4,2F is ˜4,2F" x y (* x y)))
"6 times 1.20 is 7.20"
> (format nil "Here˜%is a line break.")
"Here
is a line break."
```

The directive ˜4,2F is used to print a fixed-format, floating-point number with a minimum display width of four characters, including the decimal point and two digits after the decimal point. The directive ˜A is used to print an arbitrary object just as it would be printed by princ. If the destination is nil, then format returns the formatted string; otherwise, format returns nil and sends the string to the specified destination. If the destination is t, then format prints to the *standard output*, which is generally the terminal or display device that the Lisp interpreter is using.

Common Lisp provides a variety of other printing routines for handling errors and interacting with the interpreter. We mention one that may prove useful in dealing with the Lisp interpreter. By executing (setq *print-pretty* t), deeply nested list structures will appear much more readable.

2.10   Rule-Based Reactive System Revisited

At the beginning of this chapter, we described an example application that used rules to control the behavior of a delivery robot. We introduced symbols for representing sensors and possible sensor values, and for representing control parameters and their possible values. We now have the necessary machinery to describe rules and the procedures necessary to employ those rules to control the robot. We begin with a data abstraction that is used to represent possible reports on the values of sensors and control parameters.

```
(defun make-TUPLE (param value) (list param value))
(defun TUPLE-param (tuple) (first tuple))
(defun TUPLE-value (tuple) (second tuple))
```

For example, (forward near) corresponds to a report that the forward sensor has the value of near.

The same sensor will report different values at different times. To keep track of the time of a report, we associate with each report an integer referred to as a *time stamp*. The following data abstraction is used for time-stamped sensor and parameter reports:

```
(defun make-REPORT (tuple stamp) (list tuple stamp))
(defun REPORT-tuple (report) (first report))
(defun REPORT-stamp (report) (second report))
(defun REPORT-param (report) (TUPLE-param (first report)))
```

For example, ((forward far) 1012) indicates that the forward sensor reported far at time 1012. In the following discussion, we never use make-REPORT or make-TUPLE since we do not discuss the parts of the control system that generate data.

Our control algorithm maintains a list of the most recent sensor and control parameter reports. The first routine that we consider, update, takes a list of new reports and a list of old reports and combines them. The old list includes reports from all the sensors and control parameters, but the new list may not. One approach to combining the reports is to consider each of the old reports and check to see if it is updated in the new reports.

The Common Lisp assoc function takes two arguments corresponding to an expression and a list of non-nil lists. The second argument is called an *association list* and allows us to map between symbolic expressions (e.g., ((type truck) (color red) (year 1950))). In its simplest uses, assoc takes a symbol and a list of pairs of symbols and returns the first pair whose first element is eq to the first argument or nil if no such pair exists. For instance, (assoc 'left '((left far) (right near))) would return (left far).

Assoc allows optional arguments specified by keywords. Note that a list of time-stamped reports will contain pairs of the form ((left far) 1).

```
> (assoc '(left far) '(((left far) 1)))
NIL
> (assoc '(left far) '(((left far) 1)) :test #'equal)
((left far) 1)
```

In searching for an updated report, we are looking for a new report on the same parameter with a possibly different value.

```
> (assoc '(left far) '(((left near) 1)) :test #'equal)
NIL
> (assoc '(left far) '(((left near) 1))
        :test #'(lambda (x y) (eq (first x) (first y))))
((left near) 1)
```

Using another optional keyword argument, we can index into the structure of the first element of the pairs in the association list to achieve the same result.

```
> (assoc 'left '(((left far) 1)) :key #'first)
((left far) 1)
```

Instead of testing the first argument of assoc against the first element of each pair in the association list, we test the first argument against the result of applying the function introduced by :key to the first element of each pair in the association list.

We are making progress, but we have a slight problem. In our discussion of assoc, we assume that tuples are implemented as a list of two elements and that reports are implemented as a list of a tuple and an integer. This happens to be true, but an important advantage of introducing a data abstraction is that we should not have to think about how it is implemented. By employing assoc as we did earlier, we violate the data abstraction by taking advantage of a particular implementation. If someone were to change the implementation, for example, they used arrays instead of lists or put the time stamp first instead of last, then we would have to track down all the places where assoc was used and make changes in accord with the new implementation.

We cannot use assoc since we cannot even assume that reports are implemented as lists. What you learned about assoc will not be wasted, however; we use assoc frequently in the coming chapters. Instead of assoc, we use a more general function called find. For our purposes, find takes an arbitrary Lisp object and a list and returns the first element in the list that is eq to the object or nil if no such element exists. Find also takes optional :key and :test arguments. The optional :key function is applied to an element of the list rather than to the first of an element as in assoc. For example, (assoc *item list*) has the same effect as (find *item list* :key #'first).

Using find, we define two functions that perform associations on lists of reports, maintaining the data abstractions. The first function searches for a report with a tuple that has a particular parameter; the second function searches for a report with a particular tuple.

```
(defun param-assoc (param reports)
  (find param reports :key #'REPORT-param))
(defun tuple-assoc (tuple reports)
  (find tuple reports :test #'equal :key #'REPORT-tuple))
```

Now we can specify the algorithm for update as follows. We call update with two lists of time-stamped reports. For each time-stamped report in the list of old reports, check to see if there is a new report with the same parameter. If so, add the new report to the list of reports to be returned by update; otherwise, add the old report to the list of reports to be returned.

This algorithm is implemented in Lisp as follows:

```
(defun update (new old)
  (mapcar #´(lambda (item)
              (or (param-assoc (REPORT-param item) new)
                  item))
          old))
```

The form (or *first second*) is an alternative method of computing (let ((result *first*)) (if (null result) *second* result)).

Consider another possible implementation of update. Suppose in this case that neither the old nor the new reports necessarily include reports on all the sensor and control parameters and that the new reports may even include several reports on the same parameter at different times. In the following implementation, we use the dolist iterative construct and a subroutine fuse that takes a single report and combines it with the old reports. As in the previous algorithm, we call update with two lists of time-stamped reports. In this case, however, we step through the new reports one at a time, updating the list of old reports using the fuse subroutine.

```
(defun update (new old)
  (dolist (item new old) (setq old (fuse item old))))
```

Fuse takes a report and a list of reports and substitutes its first argument for the first report in the list reporting on the same parameter if that report has an earlier time stamp than the first argument or adds the first argument to the end of the list of reports if there is no such report. Fuse uses recursion to take the old list of reports apart with first and rest and put it back together with cons. It either substitutes the new report for an old one with the same parameter or, if no such old report exists, tacks the new report on the end of the old reports.

```
(defun fuse (report old)
  (cond ((null old) (list report))
        ((eq (REPORT-param report) (REPORT-param (first old)))
         (if (> (REPORT-stamp report) (REPORT-stamp (first old)))
             (cons report (rest old)) old))
        (t (cons (first old) (fuse report (rest old))))))
```

The following provides an example showing how update works:

```
> (update ´(((forward near) 2) ((left near) 2) ((left far) 1))
          ´(((forward far) 0) ((left away) 0) ((right near) 1)
            ((rear far) 0) ((speed slow) 1)))
(((LEFT NEAR) 2) ((FORWARD NEAR) 2) ((RIGHT NEAR) 1)
 ((REAR FAR) 0) ((SPEED SLOW) 1))
```

Here is an alternative implementation of fuse using param-assoc and a function remove provided in Common Lisp. Remove takes an expression and a list; the result is a new list that has the same elements as the original except those eq to the expression (e.g., (remove 1 ´(1 2 3 1)) returns (2 3)). Remove takes optional keyword arguments (e.g., (remove ´(1 2) ´(a (1 2) b c) :test #´equal) returns (a b c)).

```
(defun fuse (report old)
  (let ((a (param-assoc (REPORT-param report) old)))
    (cond ((null a) (cons report old))
          ((< (REPORT-stamp report) (REPORT-stamp a)) old)
          (t (cons report (remove a old))))))
```

We could have used (substitute report a old) instead of (cons report (remove a old)). Substitute substitutes its first argument for all occurrences of its second argument appearing as elements of the list corresponding to its third argument. Subst makes substitutions in nested list structures (e.g., (substitute 1 0 ´(0 1 (1 0))) returns (1 1 (1 0)), whereas (subst 1 0 ´(0 1 (1 0))) returns (1 1 (1 1))).

Most of the Common Lisp functions that we describe in this text are more versatile than indicated. For instance, many of the functions mentioned take more keyword arguments than those described. In addition, many of the functions that apply to lists also apply to a more general *sequence* data type that encompasses lists and one-dimensional arrays.

Now that we can update our sensor reports, we need to determine what control actions to take. The control strategy is encoded in a set of rules. We use the following data abstraction for rules:

```
(defun RULE-conditions (rule) (first rule))
(defun RULE-action (rule) (second rule))
```

The conditions correspond to sensor/value pairs, and actions correspond to control-parameter/value pairs. We say that a rule is *applicable* given a set of reports if each of the conditions has associated equal reports. The following functions implement a predicate to determine whether or not a rule is applicable:

```
(defun applicablep (rule reports)
  (aux-applicablep (RULE-conditions rule) reports))
(defun aux-applicablep (tuples reports)
  (or (null tuples)
      (and (tuple-assoc (first tuples) reports)
           (aux-applicablep (rest tuples) reports))))
```

Applicablep takes a rule and a list of time-stamped reports and uses recursion to check if each condition in the rule's list of conditions corresponds to some report in the list of reports. The auxiliary function is used to set up the recursion by introducing the variable tuples that we wish to recurse on. Such auxiliary functions are common in implementing recursive procedures.

We can also implement applicablep using a special mapping function that behaves like a boolean function. The expression (every *test arguments*) returns t if *test* returns non-nil when applied to each cross section of *arguments* (e.g., (every #'oddp '(3 5 9)) and (every #'eq '(a 1) '(a 1)) both return t).

```
(defun applicablep (rule reports)
  (every #'(lambda (tuple) (tuple-assoc tuple reports))
         (RULE-conditions rule)))
```

The following function tests each rule in a set of rules and acts according to the applicable rules:

```
(defun react (rules reports)
  (dolist (rule rules reports)
    (if (applicablep rule reports)
      (setq reports (fuse (act (RULE-action rule)) reports)))))
```

Acting in our simple implementation just consists of adding a time stamp to the action of a rule. The Common Lisp function get-internal-real-time returns an integer representing the current time.

```
(defun act (action) (list action (get-internal-real-time)))
```

Here is a simple example showing the result of reacting.

```
> (react '(((((forward near) (jleft far)) (turn left)))
          '(((forward near) 0) ((turn right) 1) ((jleft far) 1)))
(((TURN LEFT) 2214639) ((FORWARD NEAR) 0) ((JLEFT FAR) 1))
```

Note that if there are two applicable rules with conflicting actions, the function will apply act to each of the actions. In a more realistic implementation, we would provide some means of resolving conflicts involving applicable rules.

We provide an alternative implementation of react that allows us to demonstrate another useful mapping function. Mapcan behaves like mapcar except that it combines its results using nconc (e.g., (mapcan #'rest '((0) (1 a) (2) (3 b) (4 c)) returns (a b c) the same as (apply #'nconc (mapcar #'rest '((0) (1 a) (2) (3 b) (4 c))))).

```
(defun react (rules reports)
  (update (mapcan #'(lambda (rule)
                      (and (applicablep rule reports)
                           (list (act (RULE-action rule)))))
                  rules)
          reports))
```

The function run applies react and update in a cycle using the Lisp iterative construct dotimes. Assume that collect returns the latest sensor reports.

```
(defun run (rules reports)
  (dotimes (index 100 reports)
    (setq reports (react rules (update (collect) reports)))))
```

This function performs 100 cycles with index set to 0, 1, 2, ..., 99. Alternatively, we might implement run using two mutually recursive functions.

```
(defun run (rules reports)
  (aux-update rules (collect) reports 0))
(defun aux-update (rules new old i)
  (if (< i 100) (aux-react rules (update new old) i)))
(defun aux-react (rules reports i)
  (aux-update rules (collect) (react rules reports) (+ i 1)))
```

As illustrated, Common Lisp allows for a lot of variety in implementing algorithms. In the following chapters, we often choose the simplest or most concise implementation.

▼ Summary

This chapter provides an introduction to symbolic programming in Lisp. The chapter covers a subset of Common Lisp, a Lisp dialect that has become a standard in the field. This subset is sufficient for all the programming examples in this book and provides a good basis for further study of Lisp. We start with an example application that involves representing rules as symbolic expressions and manipulating those expressions to perform inference. The chapter ends by showing how to implement a particular rule-based system in Lisp.

The syntax of Lisp is based on expressions, a generalization of lists. A Lisp program is just a sequence of expressions. The semantics of Lisp can be described in terms of two Lisp programs, eval and apply. We began with pure Lisp, involving functions, constants, and boolean operators, but no assignment. Some of the many functions built into Lisp are described along with techniques for defining your own functions, especially recursive functions.

Symbols and variables are the same thing in Lisp. Assignment allows us to change the values associated with variables. Environments are used to keep track of the values of variables. Lisp variables are lexically scoped so that it is easy to determine which parts of a program might possibly change the value of a variable. Environment constructors like let allow the programmer to make use of local variables and to associate local state with functions. Functions with local state can store information about prior invocations.

Lisp allows functions to be passed as arguments to other functions. Many built-in functions have optional keyword arguments that require a function. Function keyword arguments allow the programmer to customize a generic function to suit a specific application. It is also possible to construct unnamed functions called lambda functions that can be built for a particular purpose and then discarded.

Lisp provides a variety of functions for building, accessing, modifying, and searching lists. Lisp lists provide an abstraction of pointers that simplifies many tasks. Symbols can be assigned values that correspond to pointers to list structures in memory. Lists are often the primitive data structure of choice for representing sets, queues, trees, and graphs. We can also use lists to build abstract data types to hide ugly low-level programming details and make code more easily understood.

In this text, we frequently write programs using recursive functions when the underlying algorithm lends itself naturally to a recursive implementation. We also make use of other methods for specifying iteration. Lisp supports several iterative constructs, including mapping functions and both general and specialized forms of iteration.

We describe the basics for handling input and output, debugging, and evaluating functions in files. If you go on to write large programs in Lisp, you will undoubtedly need a more extensive introduction to Lisp. For understanding and experimenting with the programs explored in the following chapters, you should find this introduction sufficient.

● Background

Lisp was invented by John McCarthy and is based roughly on a formal system called the *Lambda calculus*. Lisp is the second oldest (after FORTRAN) computer language still in current use. Lisp was not the first language designed to manipulate lists and symbolic expressions; an earlier list-processing language called IPL was developed by Herbert Simon and Allen Newell for their work in automated problem solving. McCarthy was able to show that a subset of Lisp is able to compute any function that a Turing machine can compute [McCarthy, 1960]. He did so by showing how one could write a *universal function* in Lisp that could interpret any Lisp function; McCarthy's universal function was called eval.

Lisp was designed to facilitate symbolic programming. One important feature that we did not point out but that you may find particularly convenient is that Lisp takes care of allocating and deallocating storage for most data types. You can build up arbitrary list structures, use them temporarily to perform computations, and rely on Lisp to reclaim the associated storage when you are finished using them. The automatic reclamation of storage not referenced (directly or otherwise) by any symbols is called *garbage collection*. Features like garbage collection make Lisp a wonderful language for rapid prototyping and exploratory study.

If you are interested in learning more about Common Lisp, you should consult Steele's description of the language [Steele, 1990]. If you are interested in learning more about how to program in Lisp, you might consider a text specific to Common Lisp (e.g., [Wilensky, 1986]) or one of the many general introductions to Lisp (e.g., [Touretsky, 1984]). For an excellent introduction to programming in Lisp using a dialect of Lisp called *Scheme*, consider the text by Abelson and Sussman [1985].

■ Exercises

2.1 Write your own versions of the Lisp functions member, append, nconc, reverse, and nth. Rename them so that you do not redefine functions that are critical to the proper functioning of your Lisp environment. For append and nconc, it is enough to implement versions for two arguments.

2.2 Create a set of recursive functions for manipulating sets. You should write functions for taking the union, intersection, and complement of sets and testing whether an item is an element of a set. Union and intersection are already defined in Common Lisp, so you should use alternative names for the same reason mentioned in the previous exercise.

2.3 You are given a *dictionary* in the form of a list of "exploded" symbols (e.g., (d e f u n), (s e t q), (s e t f)). Write a recursive function, lookup, that takes a prefix of an exploded symbol (e.g., (s e t)) and a dictionary and returns the list of all items in the dictionary that match this prefix.

2.4 Write a recursive function, distance, to compute the *distance* between two bit vectors of the same length represented by lists of ones and zeros (e.g., (1 0 1 1), (0 1 0 1)) using as a metric the number of bits that are different (e.g., three in the case of (1 0 1 1) and (0 1 0 1)). Write a recursive function, closest, that finds two vectors that are closest in distance in a list of bit vectors. Discuss what would have to be done if the vectors were of different length and composed of uppercase letters instead of ones and zeros. In particular, discuss what distance metric you would use if you were trying to implement a user-friendly spell checker that offers suggestions on what the user might have been trying to spell.

2.5 In this exercise, you are to implement a rule of logical inference. It happens to be a generalization of modus ponens, which you will hear more about in Chapter 3, but you do not need to know the details for this exercise. Suppose that your logician employer has asked you to implement the following specification: Write a recursive function infer that takes a conjunction represented by a list of the form $(Q_1\ Q_2\ \dots\ Q_m)$ and a rule of the form $(Q\ (P_1\ P_2\ \dots\ P_n))$ and returns nil if Q does not appear in the list and otherwise returns a new list in which Q is replaced by $P_1\ P_2\ \dots\ P_n$. Assume that a symbol appears at most once in a conjunction. Here are some examples illustrating the expected behavior of infer.

```
> (infer '(D E A F) '(A (B C)))
(D E B C F)
> (infer '(D E A F) '(A ()))
(D E F)
> (infer '(D) '(A (B C)))
NIL
```

2.6 Rewrite interpolate, nearest-pairs, remember, and estimate using a data abstraction for pairs of the form $(x\ f(x))$.

2.7 Write a recursive function that constructs a labeled binary tree of depth n. Label the root and its subtrees with the integers 0 through 2^n so that no two subtrees have the same label and that, given two subtrees of different depth, the label of the one with the greater depth is larger than the other.

2.8 Write a pair of recursive functions, lookup and enter, that refer to the same local state variable corresponding to an appropriate data structure for the dictionary in Exercise 2.3. Lookup has the same basic input/output behavior as the function of Exercise 2.3 except that it does not require the second argument. Enter takes a single argument corresponding to a new function name and enters it into the dictionary. Use a tree data structure for the dictionary in which function names are stored at the leaves and symbols corresponding to the letters in the function names are stored at internal nodes. Discuss why this tree representation is better than representing the dictionary as a flat list of function names.

2.9 In Chapter 4, we consider an optimization technique that involves simulating evolution. In this technique, Lisp objects are combined and mutated as abstract forms of genetic material. In this exercise, we consider a method for indexing into nested list structures that might be used for selecting subexpressions for mutation or for combining genetic material during reproduction.

Write a recursive Lisp function index that takes two arguments: a nested list structure of a particular restricted form and an integer. Any nonnumeric symbol is of the restricted form, and any list structure of the form $(x\ y)$ is of the restricted form if x and y are of the restricted form. So a, (a b), and (a (b c)) are all of the restricted form, but 1 and (a b c) are not. Note that every restricted form can be represented by a binary tree. Figure 2.14 shows the binary tree for the restricted form (a ((b c) d)) along with the *depth-first numbering* of the nodes in the binary tree. Given a restricted form and an integer, index returns the subtree with the corresponding depth-first numbering. Here are some examples demonstrating index.

```
> (index '(a ((b c) d)) 6)
D
> (index '(a ((b c) d)) 3)
(B C)
> (index '(a ((b c) d)) 0)
(A ((B C) D))
```

That every list has exactly two elements simplifies the recursion considerably. You can assume that the second argument to index corresponds to the depth-first ordering number of a subtree of the first argument.

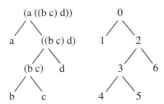

Figure 2.14   A binary tree and its depth-first numbering

2.10 Discuss the problems involved in defining defun in terms of lambda, and mapcar in terms of apply.

2.11 Consider the following variant forms of rules for our rule-based control system:
   a) Suppose that the conditions of rules are specified as boolean combinations of sensor reports (e.g., (and (forward near) (or (jleft near) (jright near)))).
   b) Suppose that parameters have numerical values and we allow inequalities in the conditions of rules (e.g., ((forward < 2) (jleft > 1) (speed > 0))).
   In each case, sketch how you would implement applicablep.

2.12 To access the parameter associated with a time-stamped report, we might evaluate (TUPLE-param (REPORT-tuple report)) or use (REPORT-param report) to directly access the parameter associated with a given report. In some cases, it is convenient to use the same function name to refer to pieces of different data types with the same name.

For example, given a single function for accessing parameters, it would be easy to extract the parameters associated with a mixed list of TUPLEs and REPORTs. In object-oriented languages, objects map *messages* to procedures called *methods*. Two different types of objects can map the same message to different methods. Lisp provides a variety of object-oriented extensions that allow this sort of flexibility. In this exercise, we sketch a simple object-oriented extension to Lisp. The extension is based on the following convention for sending messages to objects, (send *object message*). In the following implementation, an object is just a list of message/method pairs, where methods are implemented as closures. As a simple example, consider how to implement sensor and control parameter reports as objects.

```
(defun make-TUPLE (p v)
  (let ((param p) (value v))
    (list (list 'param #'(lambda () param))
          (list 'value #'(lambda () value)))))
```

Note the use of the let statement to maintain local state. Now we implement time-stamped reports, providing a method for directly accessing the parameter associated with a report.

```
(defun make-REPORT (x y)
  (let ((tuple x) (stamp y))
    (list (list 'tuple #'(lambda () tuple))
          (list 'stamp #'(lambda () stamp))
          (list 'param #'(lambda () (send tuple 'param))))))
```

Send takes an object and a message, looks up the method associated with the message, and uses funcall to invoke the method.

```
(defun send (object message)
  (let ((pair (assoc message object)))
    (if (null pair) (princ "Undefined!")
        (funcall (cadr pair)))))
```

Here we show how we can use the same message to refer to different types of objects.

```
> (progn (setq x (make-TUPLE 'forward 'near)
               y (make-REPORT x 0))
         (eq (send x 'param) (send y 'param)))
T
```

Implement binary trees as objects. You will have to extend this implementation to handle methods that take arguments. One approach is to give send a third argument corresponding to a list of method arguments and then use apply instead of funcall to invoke the method on the list of arguments.

2.13 Writing personalized read-eval-print loops is a popular pastime with Lisp hackers. Here is a simple recursive interpreter that makes use of an alternative version of eval called evil.

```
(defun interpret ()
  (princ "my prompt > ")
  (format t "~%~A" (evil (read)))
  (interpret))
```

Evil makes use of set, which behaves like a version of setq that evaluates its first argument. Set cannot be used to alter the value of a local variable, but it is very useful for implementing interpreters for languages that are embedded in Lisp.

```
(defun evil (expression)
  (cond ((numberp expression) expression)
        ((stringp expression) expression)
        ((symbolp expression) (set expression 0))
        ((eq (first expression) 'setq)
         (set (second expression) (third expression)))
        (t (apply (first expression)
                  (mapcar #'evil (rest expression))))))
```

Evil makes it very difficult to get any useful work done.

```
> (interpret)
my prompt > (setq x 1)
1
my prompt > (setq y 2)
2
my prompt > (+ x y)
0
my prompt > x
0
```

Write a more benevolent interpreter that remembers the last ten list expressions that you have typed and if you type a number between 1 and 10 reevaluates the appropriate expression.

CHAPTER 3

REPRESENTATION AND LOGIC

An engineer for a power plant tells you that if the coolant pump for the plant's generator is functioning properly, then the temperature of the generator housing should be cool to the touch. You have just burnt your hand on the housing. What can you conclude about the coolant pump? How can you represent the knowledge that the engineer conveyed to you, and how can you apply that knowledge to make the desired inference?

An *expert system* uses knowledge encoded in the form of rules to carry out tasks usually performed by expert humans. For instance, there is an expert system called MYCIN that diagnoses bacterial infections and prescribes drug treatments. MYCIN uses rules such as the following:

```
If the patient has a bacterial skin infection and specific
    organisms are not apparent in the patient's blood test,
then there is evidence that the organism causing the
        infection is Staphylococcus.
```

These rules are used to determine the cause of an infection, based on evidence supplied from the patient's history and lab tests. Another expert system called XCON designs configurations of computer components such as disk drives and processors for the customers of Digital Equipment

▲ AI IN PRACTICE

Expert Systems in the Computer Industry

Digital Equipment Corporation had a complicated problem in their shipping department. Each customer order was generally a variety of computer products, that were not guaranteed to be compatible with one another. Sometimes different products or special conversion cards were required. Although there were rules about what computers could be attached to other hardware, because they were difficult to remember, each customer shipment had to be tested for compatibility as an assembly before being shipped.

A computer program was written to solve this problem, an expert system called XCON. XCON was designed to match computers and their peripherals. It checks prerequisites such as cabling and support software based on rules. Other expert systems design local area networks, assess the computing needs of the custorner, and plan the physical placement of the computers.

Because Digital's computer services and products are always changing, the rules for XCON need to change frequently. To facilitate this, rules in XCON are simple. One rule might be "If the Stockman 800 printer and DPK202 computer have been selected, add a printer conversion card, because they are not compatible." Together, these rules form an expert system that has been used successfully for more than a decade.

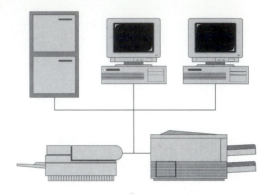

Corporation. Both MYCIN and XCON perform as well as or better than most experts in their corresponding areas of expertise.

Most expert systems rely on some variant of logical inference to justify the strategies they use to arrive at conclusions based on their encoded knowledge. In this chapter, we consider propositional and predicate logic as a basis for representing knowledge. We describe the syntax and semantics of these logics and provide examples of what you can represent using them. We explore some of the computational issues that arise in using logic to encode real-world knowledge and selectively draw conclusions from that knowledge. Finally, we consider strategies for performing practical inference involving knowledge encoded as rules. Our discussion begins with a rather simple but extremely useful logic.

3.1   Propositional Logic

Roughly speaking, a logic is a mathematical tool for constructing and manipulating symbolic expressions. Propositional logic is concerned with symbolic expressions consisting of symbols representing propositions (e.g., "the light is on" or "the door is closed") and symbols representing ways of combining propositions (e.g., the conjunction of two propositions as in "the light is on and the door is closed").

We characterize logics in terms of languages. These languages are like computer languages in that they subscribe to strict syntactic conventions. Logical languages are primarily concerned with describing "what is" rather than "how to," and, for this reason, logical languages are declarative in contrast with computer languages that are imperative or procedural. Think of logical languages as restrictions on a spoken language such as English, and as we investigate specific logical languages, consider how these restricted languages limit what you can express in comparison with the spoken language.

A *formula* is another name for a symbolic expression. A *well-formed formula* or *wff* is a formula that subscribes to a particular criterion for being well formed, and a set of wffs is just a set of formulas, all of which subscribe to the same criterion for being well formed. A *formal language* is defined by a set of wffs. An important aspect of a formal language is that it can be defined without reference to any semantic interpretation. In this section, we consider a particular formal language, the propositional language $\mathcal{P}$. The term *proposition* is used to refer to any wff in $\mathcal{P}$. In this section, we are primarily interested in specifying the syntax that determines the well-formed formulas of $\mathcal{P}$ and semantics that determine the meaning of these formulas.

A *propositional variable* is a symbol used to represent a proposition that is considered to be indivisible. For instance, we might represent "the light is on" using a propositional variable but probably not "the light is on and the door is closed." A *truth-functional connective* is a symbol used to represent a way of combining propositions. Syntactically, formulas in $\mathcal{P}$ correspond to symbolic expressions constructed from a set of propositional variables and a set of truth-functional propositional connectives, including $\land$ (conjunction), $\lor$ (disjunction), $\neg$ (negation), $\supset$ (implication), and $\equiv$ (logical equivalence). These connectives correspond roughly to "and," "or," "not," "implies," and "if and only if" in English.

In other texts, you may see propositional variables called *propositional atoms* to stress that they are syntactically indivisible; we prefer "propositional variables" to stress that semantically they take on *truth values*, either

True or False. A formula that is true no matter what truth values are assigned to its propositional variables is called a *logical truth*. Propositional logic is a theory of those logical truths that can be expressed using propositional variables and truth-functional propositional connectives.

In practice, we often use complex symbolic expressions to represent propositional variables. For example, we might use (status (output device45) high) rather than high45 to represent the proposition that the output of a particular electronic device is high. However, the internal structure of these expressions is intended only to help in reading logical formulas. We use longer expressions rather than shorter ones for the same reason that you use mnemonic variable names in writing good code. The formal meaning of a set of formulas is the same whether the propositional variables are of the form (status (output device45) high) or high45.

Syntax for $\mathcal{P}$

The syntax of a formal language defines the set of well-formed formulas. The syntax of the language $\mathcal{P}$ is described as follows:

- A set of propositional variables
- The connectives $\lor$, $\land$, $\lnot$, $\supset$, and $\equiv$
- A set of wffs inductively defined as
  - The propositional variables
  - $A_1 \lor A_2 \lor \ldots \lor A_n$, where each of the A_i is a wff
  - $A_1 \land A_2 \land \ldots \land A_n$, where each of the A_i is a wff
  - $\lnot A$, where A is a wff
  - $A \supset B$ and $A \equiv B$, where A and B are wffs

We use the terms *conjunction* and *disjunction* to refer to formulas of the form, respectively, $A_1 \land A_2 \land \ldots \land A_n$ and $A_1 \lor A_2 \lor \ldots \lor A_n$, and we use the terms *conjunct* and *disjunct* to refer to their corresponding components, the A_i.

We use parentheses as in standard mathematical notation to indicate the precedence of logical connectives. Using parentheses, we can distinguish ((P1 $\land$ P2) $\supset$ P3), if P1 and P2 then P3, from (P1 $\land$ (P2 $\supset$ P3)), P1 and if P2 then P3.

If P is a propositional variable, then P and $\lnot$P are the *literals* associated with the proposition P. Unnegated variables are called *positive* literals, and negated variables are called *negative* literals. We mentioned that expert systems used knowledge in the form of rules. Unless we indicate otherwise, a *rule* is of the form $A \supset B$, where A and B are either positive literals or conjunctions of positive literals. We can represent the knowledge that the power plant engineer told us using the following rule:

```
coolant-pump-for-generator17-is-normal ⊃
housing-for-generator17-is-cool
```

where the symbols

```
coolant-pump-for-generator17-is-normal
```

and

```
housing-for-generator17-is-cool
```

are propositional variables. Alternatively, we can write the preceding rule using a Lisp-like functional notation.

```
(status (pump generator17) normal) ⊃
( < (temperature (housing generator17)) 50)
```

where in this case

```
(status (pump generator17) normal)
```

and

```
( < (temperature (housing generator17)) 50)
```

are propositional variables. This alternative notation is found in predicate logic, which we discuss later in this chapter. In predicate logic, (pump generator17), (housing generator17), normal, and 50 would denote objects, and status and < would denote relations between objects. In propositional logic, these symbolic (sub)expressions have no meaning. This is because the propositional variables in the formulas of $\mathcal{P}$ have no formally recognized structure. In practice, however, we can use any expression we wish as a propositional variable.

Semantics for $\mathcal{P}$

A semantical theory establishes the meaning of the well-formed formulas for a given representation. Meaning is defined with respect to the different possible ways that we can associate the symbols in a language with the elements of a particular domain of interest. These possible associations are called *interpretations*.

Formally, an interpretation for the language $\mathcal{P}$ is an assignment to each propositional variable either True or False and an assignment to each propositional connective its "usual" truth-functional meaning. Figure 3.1 shows the truth-functional meaning for the standard connectives $\wedge$, $\vee$, $\supset$, and $\neg$, in tabular format called *truth tables*. Since A and B indicate wffs, an assignment to all propositional variables together with the truth tables in Figure 3.1 (page 76) determine an assignment to all formulas in $\mathcal{P}$. For example, if P is assigned False and Q is assigned True, then $\neg P \wedge (P \vee Q)$ is assigned True since both $\neg P$ and $(P \vee Q)$ are assigned True.

Generally in logic, an interpretation I is a *model* for a set of formulas if I assigns True to each formula in the set. A formula is *satisfiable* if it has a model. A formula is *valid* if its negation is not satisfiable. A theory in the

	$A \wedge B$	
	B = True	B = False
A = True	True	False
A = False	False	False

	$A \vee B$	
	B = True	B = False
A = True	True	True
A = False	True	False

	$A \supset B$	
	B = True	B = False
A = True	True	False
A = False	True	True

	$\neg A$
A = True	False
A = False	True

Figure 3.1   Truth functions for standard connectives

propositional logic is nothing more than a set of formulas. A formula A is *valid with respect to a theory T* if A is True in all the models of T. A theory (or formula) is *model theoretically inconsistent* if it has no models. Instead of trying to determine that a formula A is valid, you might try to determine that its negation when added to a theory T results in (model-theoretic) inconsistency. If this is the case and assuming that T and A considered separately are consistent, then A must be valid with respect to T.

A formula in $\mathcal{P}$ that is true no matter what truth values are assigned to its constituent parts is called a *tautology*. The formula $(A \vee \neg A)$ is an example of a tautology.[1] If $A \equiv B$ is a tautology, then A is said to be *logically equivalent* to B. A formula that is false no matter what truth values are assigned to its constituent parts is called a *contradiction*. The formula $(\neg A \wedge A)$ is an example of a contradiction.

Given a theory expressed as a set of formulas, we are often interested in determining whether some additional formula is valid with respect to the theory. One of the most important properties of logic is that it enables us to derive valid statements by performing purely syntactic manipulations. It is believed by some practitioners of AI that much of human knowledge can be captured by statements in a formal logic with reasoning simulated by symbolic manipulation. In the next section, we introduce the machinery for performing such manipulations.

3.2   Formal System for $\mathcal{P}$

We now have a language for representing knowledge in the form of logical formulas. We would like to be able to make use of such knowledge to arrive at valid conclusions. For example, if we know that "the light is off" and "if the light is off then the office is empty," then we might wish to conclude

---

[1]We (informally) defined a logical truth to be a formula that is true no matter what truth values are assigned to its propositional variables. Technically, every logical truth is a tautology, but not every tautology is a logical truth. The expression $\neg A \vee A$, where A is a variable representing any wff, is a tautology but not a logical truth. However, any sentence that results from substituting a wff for A in $\neg A \vee A$ is a logical truth.

that "the office is empty." In this section, we describe formal machinery for arriving at conclusions from knowledge expressed in the language $\mathcal{P}$.

An *axiom* is a wff that constitutes a portion of our knowledge. An axiom might be in the form of a rule as defined in the previous section, or it might be a more complicated formula. An *axiom schema* is a formula that is not well formed but that allows us to specify a large, possibly infinite, set of axioms. In an axiom schema, symbols called *schema variables* are used to indicate places in the schema formula where specified expressions can be filled in. For instance, $A \supset A$ is an axiom schema, and A is a schema variable that can be filled in with any wff. The formula $\mathsf{P} \supset \mathsf{P}$ is an axiom corresponding to an instance of $A \supset A$ with P filled in for A.

The rule about generator coolant pumps is one sort of axiom called a *proper axiom*. Proper axioms are specific to a particular theory describing the world. For example, we might have a set of axioms describing the behavior of equipment in power plants that constitute a theory of power plants. We often refer to a set of proper axioms as a *domain theory* or just *theory*. The axioms in a domain theory are like the physical laws governing the universe.

A *rule of inference* allows us to infer one formula from a set of other formulas. Rules of inference are different from the other sorts of rules discussed in this chapter. A rule of inference is like a procedure that we use to generate new formulas from old. A *formal system* consists of a formal language together with a set of axioms and a set of rules of inference.

Logical Axioms of $\mathcal{P}$

In encoding knowledge about the world, we are interested primarily in writing proper axioms. However, there are also *logical axioms* that are generally considered part of any theory expressed in $\mathcal{P}$. Logical axioms are typically specified as a set of axiom schemas. The following schemas describe the logical axioms of $\mathcal{P}$:

AS1: $A \supset (B \supset A)$
AS2: $A \supset (B \supset C)) \supset ((A \supset B) \supset (A \supset C))$
AS3: $(\neg A \supset \neg B) \supset (B \supset A)$

where A and B are schema variables that can be filled in with any wffs. According to AS1, "if logic is easy then if pigs could fly then logic is easy" is an axiom. AS1 may not appear to be particularly useful but if we want our formal system to be able to derive all the logical truths of $\mathcal{P}$, then we cannot leave AS1 out. Other schemas may appear more likely to be useful. For example, the following formula is an instance of the axiom schema AS3:

$(\neg$ miserable $\supset \neg($wet $\wedge$ cold$)) \supset (($wet $\wedge$ cold$) \supset$ miserable$)$

The axioms AS1-3 are sufficient to derive all the logical truths for the subset of the language $\mathcal{P}$ restricted to include only negation and implication.

To derive logical truths involving the other logical connectives, we have to define the other connectives in terms of negation and implication. The following axiom schemas provide the necessary definitions:

AS4: $(A \equiv B) \supset (A \supset B)$
AS5: $(A \equiv B) \supset (B \supset A)$
AS6: $(A \supset B) \supset ((B \supset A) \supset (A \equiv B))$
AS7: $(A \lor B) \supset (\neg A \supset B)$
AS8: $(A \land B) \supset \neg(A \supset \neg B)$

We can also use axiom schemas to describe sets of proper axioms. For example, the rule about generator17 might apply to several generators and their corresponding coolant pumps. By replacing generator17 with a schema variable,

(status (pump g) normal) $\supset$ ($<$ (temperature (housing g)) 50)

and specifying that g is an element of the set {generator17, generator45, generator9}, we cannot express anything that we could not before, but we are able to specify domain theories more compactly.

Normal Forms

There are often several ways of representing the same logical statement. For instance, P $\supset$ Q, ¬P $\lor$ Q, and ¬(P $\land$ ¬Q) are logically equivalent. It is simpler to write computer programs that manipulate logical formulas if we can establish a convention for representing formulas. Such a convention is called a *canonical* (or *normal*) form, and we use it to standardize the representation of knowledge. A set of formulas can be thought of as a database. A canonical form simplifies automated reasoning much as a standardized format for employee records simplifies searching for information in an employee database.

One very useful canonical form is called the *conjunctive normal form* (CNF). A database of logical formulas is in conjunctive normal form if the database can be represented as a conjunction of disjunctions of literals. Given an arbitrary database of propositional formulas, it is possible to generate an equivalent database in CNF. For example, we can represent a database consisting of P $\supset$ Q, ¬(¬S $\land$ ¬T), and R as (¬P $\lor$ Q) $\land$ (S $\lor$ T) $\land$ R. There is also a disjunctive normal form (DNF) characterized by a disjunction of conjunctions of literals. For every formula in $\mathcal{P}$, there is an equivalent DNF formula.

Here are some additional examples of logically equivalent formulas in which the formulas on the right-hand side of the equivalence are in conjunctive normal form.

((P $\land$ Q) $\supset$ R) $\equiv$ (¬ P $\lor$ ¬ Q $\lor$ R)
(R $\supset$ (P $\lor$ Q)) $\equiv$ (¬ R $\lor$ P $\lor$ Q)
(R $\supset$ (P $\land$ Q)) $\equiv$ ((¬ R $\lor$ P) $\land$ (¬ R $\lor$ Q))

In practice, a database is often represented as the conjunction of a set of rules of the form $(P_1 \wedge \ldots \wedge P_n) \supset Q$, where Q and the P_i are propositional variables. The P_i are called the *antecedents* of the rule, and Q is called the *consequent* of the rule. Given that $(P_1 \wedge \ldots \wedge P_n) \supset Q$ is equivalent to $(\neg P_1 \vee \ldots \vee \neg P_n \vee Q)$, this database representation is a special case of CNF in which each disjunction has exactly one positive literal. In the literature, you may see a disjunction with one positive literal referred to as a *Horn clause* after a logician of the same name. Not every formula can be represented as a conjunction of Horn clauses.

Rules of Inference

In addition to the axioms of a formal system, we need rules of inference to draw conclusions. You unconsciously use rules of inference all the time. For example, you are applying a rule of inference when you conclude that your friend is home from the fact that her car is in the driveway and whenever her car is in the driveway she is home.

A rule of inference consists of two parts: a set of conditions and a conclusion that is warranted given the conditions. For instance, the rule of inference called *modus ponens* can be described as for any wffs A and B, given A and $A \supset B$, we can conclude B. The rule of inference called *conjunction* can be described as given wffs A_1 through A_n, we are warranted in concluding $(A_1 \wedge A_2 \wedge \ldots \wedge A_n)$.

Proofs and Theorems

Given proper axioms P and P $\supset$ Q, we can conclude Q using modus ponens. The previous sentence describes a *proof* of Q from P and P $\supset$ Q. More generally, a *proof* is a sequence of statements in an appropriate language, such as $\mathcal{P}$, where each statement is an axiom or an immediate consequence of some rule of inference and some prior statements in the sequence.

A proof is often written down with one statement on each of several numbered lines. Each statement is followed by a justification indicating that the statement is an axiom or providing the rule of inference employed and the numbers of the preceding lines corresponding to the rule's conditions. In giving justifications in proofs, we abbreviate modus ponens and conjunction as, respectively, MP and CONJ. These two rules are depicted schematically as proofs in Figure 3.2.

Figure 3.3 lists a proof of R given as proper axioms, the set consisting of (P $\wedge$ Q) $\supset$ R, (S $\wedge$ T) $\supset$ Q, S, T, and P plus the two rules of inference,

1.	$A \supset B$			1.	A	
2.	A			2.	B	
3.	B	MP: 1, 2		3.	$A \wedge B$	CONJ: 1, 2

Figure 3.2 Schematic proofs involving modus ponens and conjunction

1.	S	AXIOM
2.	T	AXIOM
3.	S ∧ T	CONJ: 1, 2
4.	(S ∧ T) ⊃ Q	AXIOM
5.	Q	MP: 3, 4
6.	P	AXIOM
7.	P ∧ Q	CONJ: 5, 6
8.	(P ∧ Q) ⊃ R	AXIOM
9.	R	MP: 7, 8

Figure 3.3   A simple proof in propositional logic

modus ponens and conjunction. Each line in a proof is a *theorem* of the formal system.

Modus ponens and conjunction alone do not allow us to make all the conclusions that should follow from a set of proper axioms. For example, if you know that Sonya is either in her office or in the conference room and that both rooms contain a video terminal, then you should be able to conclude that Sonya is in a room that contains a video terminal. Schematically, we wish to conclude Video from Office ∨ Conference, Office ⊃ Video, and Conference ⊃ Video. With a little patience, you could prove this using the logical axioms generated from the axiom schemas AS1-8. However, in some systems for proving theorems, such proofs involving disjunctions are made easy. For example, in some systems, if by assuming Office you can conclude Video and by assuming Conference you can conclude Video, then, given Office ∨ Conference, you can conclude Video.

We could collect a set of rules of inference or add a set of logical axioms to ensure that we derive all the theorems that should follow from a database of logical formulas. However, adding rules of inference and axioms can complicate proving theorems. Fortunately, there is a single rule of inference that does everything that we want.

Resolution Rule of Inference

Consider the rule of inference shown in Figure 3.4. We provide a semantic justification for this rule, known as *resolution*, as follows. By the first line of Figure 3.4, one of $A_1, \ldots, A_i, \neg C, A_{i+1}, \ldots, A_m$ must be true. By the second line, one of $B_1, \ldots, B_j, C, B_{j+1}, \ldots, B_n$ must be true. The *law of the excluded middle* states that every proposition must be either true or false. We know that one of C or $\neg C$ must be true by the law of the excluded

1.	$A_1 \vee \ldots \vee A_i \vee \neg C \vee A_{i+1} \vee \ldots \vee A_m$	
2.	$B_1 \vee \ldots \vee B_j \vee C \vee B_{j+1} \vee \ldots \vee B_n$	
3.	$A_1 \vee \ldots \vee A_m \vee B_1 \vee \ldots \vee B_n$	RR: 1, 2

Figure 3.4   Resolution rule of inference

middle. If C is true, then $\neg C$ is false and one of $A_1, \ldots, A_m$ must be true. If $\neg C$ is true, then C is false and one of $B_1, \ldots, B_n$ must be true. Therefore, since one of C or $\neg C$ must be true, one of $A_1, \ldots, A_m, B_1, \ldots, B_n$ must be true.

Modus ponens is a special case of the resolution rule. To see this, consider the case in which $n = 0$ and $m = 1$. A propositional theorem prover that relies on resolution can be compared to a reduced-instruction-set computer where in the case of the theorem prover, the instruction set consists of rules of inference. Using only a single rule of inference can streamline automated inference by eliminating the need for a theorem prover to consider alternative rules of inference.

Completeness, Soundness, and Decidability

A formal system S is *complete* if all the formulas valid with respect to the axioms of S are also theorems of S.[2] A formal system is *sound* if all its theorems are valid. We would prefer that our formal systems be both sound and complete. In a sound and complete system, the set of valid formulas is identical to the set of theorems.

Since tautologies are valid by definition, the formal system consisting of just resolution is not complete. You cannot prove $(P \lor \neg P)$ using just resolution. There are other notions of completeness, however. A set of rules of inference is *refutation complete* if, given any set of axioms in which each axiom is a disjunction of literals, if the axioms are unsatisfiable then it is possible to derive a contradiction in the form of two formulas P and $\neg P$ for some propositional variable P using only the set of rules of inference. Note that a set of axioms in which each axiom is a disjunction of literals is quite general since any formula or conjunction of formulas can be transformed into conjunctive normal form. The set consisting of just resolution is refutation complete. This observation suggests a procedure for proving theorems. In order to determine if P is a theorem, add $\neg P$ to the set of axioms and try to derive a contradiction using resolution.

A procedure (or method) for answering a given question is *effective* if by following this procedure one obtains a correct answer to the question in a finite number of steps. A formal system is *decidable* if there exists an effective procedure for answering the question for any formula whether or not that formula is a theorem. It so happens that $\mathcal{P}$ together with AS1-8 and resolution is decidable, but this tells only a small part of the story. It

---

[2]In the literature, this is often referred to as *semantic completeness* [Hunter, 1973]. Alternatively, a formal system is *syntactically complete* if and only if for any formula A either A or $\neg A$ is a theorem [Mendelson, 1979]. Syntactic completeness is not particularly useful to us given that we often have theories in which neither P nor $\neg P$ is a theorem as a result of our ignorance.

is not enough just to be able to compute something; we generally wish to compute it efficiently. Unfortunately, a number of computationally difficult problems are associated with $\mathcal{P}$.

Computational Complexity

For a sound and complete formal system, complexity results concerning validity and satisfiability tell us a lot about how difficult it is to check if a given formula is a theorem. Determining if an arbitrary formula in $\mathcal{P}$ is satisfiable is in the class of NP-complete problems. This means that it is highly unlikely that satisfiability can be determined in time polynomial in the length of the formula. The same can be said for formulas in CNF even in the case in which each disjunction has only three literals. However, if each disjunction has no more than two literals, then satisfiability can be determined in polynomial time. Note that a disjunction is satisfied if and only if at least one of its disjuncts can be satisfied. Since each disjunct is simply a conjunction of literals and you can test for the satisfiability of a conjunction of literals in polynomial time, you can test for the satisfiability of a formula in DNF in polynomial time. This last observation tells us that transforming an arbitrary formula into DNF must be hard or result in an exponentially long formula; otherwise, we could determine if an arbitrary formula is satisfiable in polynomial time by transforming it into DNF and determining if the DNF formula is satisfiable.

Given that determining satisfiability is hard, it follows that validity is hard since A is valid if and only if $\neg A$ is not satisfiable. Given that satisfiability is hard and assuming that we are interested in theories that are sound and complete, it is hard to determine whether or not an arbitrary formula is a theorem. These might seem like rather depressing conclusions; however, these results are based on a worst-case analysis. In practice, we can often draw the conclusions we are interested in easily.

Solving Problems with Logic

Propositional logic can be used to represent and solve a variety of problems. For example, in the pharmaceutical industry, logical formulas can be used to represent the constraints governing the atomic structure of large molecules. These formulas can then be used to infer if it is possible to build molecules with particular structures. To illustrate how logic can be used in problem solving, we consider a somewhat simpler problem.

Housing lotteries are often used by university housing administrators to determine which students get first choice of dormitory rooms. In the following example, we try to figure out how four students, Bob, Lisa, Jim, and Mary, are ranked with respect to one another in the housing lottery.

All that we know about the four students is summarized in the following constraints:

1. Lisa is not next to Bob in the ranking.
2. Jim is ranked immediately ahead of a biology major.
3. Bob is ranked immediately ahead of Jim.
4. One of the women is a biology major.
5. Mary or Lisa is ranked first.

If you are good at solving puzzles, you might conclude that Mary is first, Bob is second, Jim is third, and Lisa is last in the ranking for the four students. We can arrive at the same conclusion using logic.

To convert the English statements into logic, we introduce two propositional types, *X*-ahead-of-*Y*, indicating that *X* is immediately ahead of *Y* in the ranking, and *X*-bio-major, indicating that *X* is a biology major. Using these propositional types, we represent that Lisa is not next to Bob in the ranking.

```
(¬ Lisa-ahead-of-Bob  ∧  ¬ Bob-ahead-of-Lisa)
```

Jim is ranked immediately ahead of a biology major.

```
((Jim-ahead-of-Mary ∧ Mary-bio-major) ∨
 (Jim-ahead-of-Bob  ∧ Bob-bio-major)  ∨
 (Jim-ahead-of-Lisa ∧ Lisa-bio-major))
```

One of the women is a biology major.

```
(Mary-bio-major ∨ Lisa-bio-major)
```

Bob is immediately ahead of Jim.

```
Bob-ahead-of-Jim
```

Finally, we represent that either Mary or Lisa is ranked first using a disjunction representing all the possible rankings in which either Mary or Lisa is first.

```
((Mary-ahead-of-Bob  ∧ Bob-ahead-of-Lisa  ∧ Lisa-ahead-of-Jim)  ∨
 (Mary-ahead-of-Bob  ∧ Bob-ahead-of-Jim   ∧ Jim-ahead-of-Lisa)  ∨
 (Mary-ahead-of-Lisa ∧ Lisa-ahead-of-Bob  ∧ Bob-ahead-of-Jim)   ∨
 (Mary-ahead-of-Lisa ∧ Lisa-ahead-of-Jim  ∧ Jim-ahead-of-Bob)   ∨
 (Mary-ahead-of-Jim  ∧ Jim-ahead-of-Lisa  ∧ Lisa-ahead-of-Bob)  ∨
 (Mary-ahead-of-Jim  ∧ Jim-ahead-of-Bob   ∧ Bob-ahead-of-Lisa)  ∨
 (Lisa-ahead-of-Bob  ∧ Bob-ahead-of-Jim   ∧ Jim-ahead-of-Mary)  ∨
 (Lisa-ahead-of-Bob  ∧ Bob-ahead-of-Mary  ∧ Mary-ahead-of-Jim)  ∨
 (Lisa-ahead-of-Mary ∧ Mary-ahead-of-Jim  ∧ Jim-ahead-of-Bob)   ∨
 (Lisa-ahead-of-Mary ∧ Mary-ahead-of-Bob  ∧ Bob-ahead-of-Jim)   ∨
 (Lisa-ahead-of-Jim  ∧ Jim-ahead-of-Bob   ∧ Bob-ahead-of-Mary)  ∨
 (Lisa-ahead-of-Jim  ∧ Jim-ahead-of-Mary  ∧ Mary-ahead-of-Bob))
```

Our method of determining the ranking of the students will be to eliminate disjuncts from the formula until there is only one remaining. In order to eliminate these disjunctions, we need to supplement our representation of the problem.

In addition to the logical translations of the English sentences, we need formulas to represent the common-sense facts that a student can be immediately ahead of at most one other student and that if X is immediately ahead of Y then Y cannot be immediately ahead of X. Here are some example formulas representing such common-sense facts.

```
Bob-ahead-of-Jim  ⊃  ¬ Bob-ahead-of-Lisa
Bob-ahead-of-Jim  ⊃  ¬ Jim-ahead-of-Bob
```

Now, given Bob-ahead-of-Jim, we can prove ¬Bob-ahead-of-Lisa and use this formula to arrive at the following conclusion:

```
¬ (Mary-ahead-of-Bob  ∧  Bob-ahead-of-Lisa  ∧  Lisa-ahead-of-Jim)
```

In this manner, we can eliminate all the disjuncts in which Bob is not ahead of Jim to obtain a disjunction of four possible rankings.

```
((Mary-ahead-of-Bob   ∧  Bob-ahead-of-Jim   ∧  Jim-ahead-of-Lisa)  ∨
 (Mary-ahead-of-Lisa  ∧  Lisa-ahead-of-Bob  ∧  Bob-ahead-of-Jim)   ∨
 (Lisa-ahead-of-Bob   ∧  Bob-ahead-of-Jim   ∧  Jim-ahead-of-Mary)  ∨
 (Lisa-ahead-of-Mary  ∧  Mary-ahead-of-Bob  ∧  Bob-ahead-of-Jim))
```

In a similar manner, we can eliminate disjuncts in which Lisa is next to Bob.

```
((Mary-ahead-of-Bob   ∧  Bob-ahead-of-Jim   ∧  Jim-ahead-of-Lisa)  ∨
 (Lisa-ahead-of-Mary  ∧  Mary-ahead-of-Bob  ∧  Bob-ahead-of-Jim))
```

To arrive at the correct ranking, we have to eliminate the second of the two disjuncts in the formula. This final elimination turns out to be tricky and requires that we modify our representation slightly. We explore the details of this modification in Exercise 3.5. The preceding example should convince you that both representation and proving theorems can be complicated. It is difficult to produce a complete representation (set of formulas) that encodes all the right constraints, and once you have a complete representation, it can be difficult to draw the right conclusions. In the next section, we consider how we might get machines to draw the right conclusions for us.

3.3   Automated Theorem Proving in $\mathcal{P}$

This section describes a simple propositional theorem prover. We assume that the proper axioms of our system are rules of the form $(P_1 \land \ldots \land P_n) \supset Q$, where Q and the P_i are propositional variables. We use the term *fact* to refer to rules without antecedents; a fact is just a propositional variable.

▲ AI IN PRACTICE

Expert Systems in the Credit Card Industry

The American Express Company allows its card holders to make credit card purchases all over the world. Before a card holder can complete a purchase, American Express has to authorize the sales transaction at the point of purchase.

The Authorizer Assistant (AA) is a rule-based expert system that provides the first line of service in credit authorization at a point of sale. AA works as part of a global credit authorization system to guard against unauthorized use of American Express cards. AA tracks each customer's history of transactions looking for unusual activity that might signal fraudulent credit card use. In many routine transactions, human experts are never consulted. If AA detects a possible fraud, it uses an additional set of rules to contact a human expert skilled in handling the particular type of problem encountered.

Another expert system called the Credit Assistant (CA) analyzes customer histories of payments and purchases to detect potential credit risks. AA and CA work together and with other expert systems and human experts at American Express to improve customer service, manage their global business operations, and reduce fraud and credit losses.

Courtesy of American Express

Goal Reduction in $\mathcal{P}$

Goal reduction is a method for proving a conjunction of propositional variables given axioms in the form of rules such as those described earlier. The conjuncts of the conjunction are the *goals*. Suppose we have a goal Q and a rule $(P_1 \wedge \ldots \wedge P_n) \supset Q$. If we can prove $(P_1 \wedge \ldots \wedge P_n)$, then we can prove Q; in this case, proving Q is *reduced* to proving $(P_1 \wedge \ldots \wedge P_n)$.

Here is a nondeterministic algorithm for goal reduction. The algorithm is nondeterministic because it does not stipulate exactly how to make certain choices. To try to prove $(P_1 \wedge \ldots \wedge P_n)$, proceed as follows:

1. If $n = 0$, then stop and signal success.

2. If $n > 0$, then choose some k such that $1 \leq k \leq n$.

3. If P_k is a fact, then (recursively) try to prove $(P_1 \wedge \ldots P_{k-1} \wedge P_{k+1} \wedge P_n)$.

4 If P_k is not a fact, then try to find some rule of the form $(Q_1 \wedge \ldots \wedge Q_m)$ $\supset P_k$ such that $(Q_1 \wedge \ldots \wedge Q_m \wedge P_1 \wedge \ldots P_{k-1} \wedge P_{k+1} \wedge P_n)$ can be (recursively) proved.

5 If P_k is not a fact and an appropriate rule cannot be found in step 4, then stop and signal failure.

With a little effort, we can convert this algorithm into a deterministic algorithm implemented in Lisp.

Rules can be represented in Lisp as lists whose first element is the consequent, followed by the symbol if and any antecedents. For instance, the rule (P $\wedge$ Q) $\supset$ R is represented as (R if P Q). Facts are represented as a list with a single element corresponding to a propositional variable. For instance, P is represented as (P). We codify these conventions in the following data abstraction:

```
(defun consequent (rule) (first rule))
(defun antecedents (rule) (rest (rest rule)))
```

The second definition exploits the fact that the rest of nil is nil so that (antecedents '(P)) is nil.

Figure 3.5 lists the functions for a simple theorem prover based on a deterministic version of the nondeterministic algorithm listed. Instead of relying on a nondeterministic choice, the function theorem tries all the rules in turn. The code in Figure 3.5 implements the following recursive algorithm given a list of conjuncts, a list of rules that have yet to be

```
;; Try to prove a conjunction using a list of rules.
(defun theorem (conjuncts rules)
  (aux-theorem conjuncts rules rules))

;; Keep track of the conjuncts that you have yet to prove,
;; the rules that you have yet to apply to the first conjunct, and
;; the set of all rules for proving the rest of the conjuncts.
(defun aux-theorem (conjuncts untried rules)
  ;; If there are no conjuncts, succeed; no untried rules, fail.
  (cond ((null conjuncts) t)
        ((null untried) nil)
        ;; If the first conjunct is eq to the consequent of the
        ;; first rule and you can prove the antecedents of the first
        ;; rule and the rest of the conjuncts, then you are done.
        ((and (eq (first conjuncts)
                  (consequent (first untried)))
              (aux-theorem (append (antecedents (first untried))
                                   (rest conjuncts))
                           rules rules)) t)
        ;; Otherwise, check out the rest of the rules.
        (t (aux-theorem conjuncts (rest untried) rules))))
```

Figure 3.5 Propositional theorem prover

applied to the first conjunct in the list of conjuncts, and a list of all the rules:

1 If there are no more conjuncts, then return signaling success.

2 If there are no more untried rules, then return signaling failure.

3 If the first conjunct is the same as the consequent of the first untried rule and the conjunction obtained by appending the antecedents of the first untried rule to the rest of the conjuncts is a theorem, then return signaling success.

4 Otherwise, recurse to try the next untried rule.

Here we see `theorem` working for the example shown in Figure 3.3.

```
> (setq rules '((R if P Q) (Q if S T) (P) (Q) (S) (T)))
((R IF P Q) (Q IF S T) (P) (Q) (S) (T))
> (theorem '(R) rules)
T
```

Theorem has some potential problems. Suppose that in addition to `Q` we have an axiom of the form `P ≡ Q` represented as two rules (`P if Q`) and (`Q if P`) and we wish to prove `P`. Here is how `theorem` might respond.

```
> (setq rules '((P if Q) (Q if P) (Q)))
((P IF Q) (Q IF P) (Q))
> (theorem '(P) rules)
STACK OVERFLOW ...
```

Generally, when you get a message like `STACK OVERFLOW`, it means you have a serious problem in your code or in your algorithm. In this case, `theorem` just kept calling itself recursively, first applying the rule (`P if Q`), then (`Q if P`), then (`P if Q`), and so on. Eventually, the recursive calls, each of which requires the construction of a new environment, cause Lisp to run out of memory.

Exercise 3.6 at the end of this chapter involves correcting this problem with `theorem`. With such a correction, we can show that `theorem` can prove any theorem corresponding to a conjunction of positive literals that follows from the axioms in the restricted form described.

Proof by Contradiction

We can justify `theorem` semantically as follows. Suppose that T is a theory corresponding to our list of rules and A is the conjunction that we are trying to prove. Suppose that T and A are both consistent. If T conjoined with $\neg A$ is inconsistent, then $\neg A$ is assigned False in all the models of T; therefore A is assigned True in all the models of T, and A is valid with respect to T. Since a contradiction has no models, if you can derive a contradiction from a theory, then the theory is inconsistent.

Theorem tries to derive a contradiction from the rules and the negation of the conjunction, which is its first argument.

- The negation of a conjunction of positive literals $(A_1 \land \ldots \land A_m)$ is a disjunction of negative literals $(\neg A_1 \lor \ldots \lor \neg A_m)$.
- From $(\neg A_1 \lor \ldots \lor \neg A_m)$ and the rule $(B_1 \land \ldots \land B_n) \supset A_1$ expressed as a disjunction $\neg B_1 \lor \ldots \lor \neg B_n \lor A_1$, we can infer by the resolution rule of inference that $(\neg A_2 \lor \ldots \lor \neg A_m \lor \neg B_1 \lor \ldots \lor \neg B_n)$.
- When theorem is called with a conjunction consisting of a single conjunct A and the rule being applied is the fact A, the negation of the conjunction is $\neg A$, which directly contradicts the fact A.

3.4 Predicate Calculus

In this section, we consider a more expressive formal language called *predicate calculus* ($\mathcal{PC}$). A *predicate* is used to describe properties and relations involving arbitrary objects. $\mathcal{PC}$ allows us to refer to objects, properties of objects, and relations among objects. For example, we can use terms such as block17 or table45 to refer to a toy block and a table. We can represent the property of a particular block being red by red(block17) or the relationship of a block being on a table by on(block17, table45).

A *quantified statement* is a statement that applies to a class of objects. $\mathcal{PC}$ allows us to make quantified statements about arbitrary classes of objects.[3] For instance, the following statement indicates that everything on a particular table is red:

∀ x, on(x,table45) ⊃ red(x)

where the symbol ∀ is a *quantifier*, the symbol x is a *variable*, and the symbol table45 is a *constant*. We read the formula as "for all x, if x is on table45, then x is red." ∀ and ∃ are called, respectively, *universal* and *existential* quantifiers. From the formula and on(block17, table45), we can conclude that block17 must be red because it is on the table.

If we are interested only in a finite set of objects, aside from the convenient syntax for specifying objects and relations, $\mathcal{PC}$ affords us no expressive advantage over propositional logic. However, even for a finite set of objects, $\mathcal{PC}$ offers a compact means of representing knowledge and a powerful calculus for manipulating such knowledge.

---

[3]In this text, we are concerned with *first-order* predicate calculus. In first-order predicate calculus, quantification is only over terms and not over predicates. For example, you can say "all red cars are fast" in $\mathcal{PC}$, but you cannot say "any property that is true of Lynn is also true of Sonya." Second- and higher-order logics allow quantification over predicates.

Syntax for $\mathcal{PC}$

In $\mathcal{PC}$, objects in the domain of interest are specified using expressions called *terms*. Terms are constructed from functions, constants, and variables, and wffs are constructed from terms, predicates, and quantifiers. Each function and predicate takes some number of arguments. We call this number the *arity* of the function or predicate. Technically, a constant is just a function of arity 0, but we treat constants separately from functions. In specifying the syntax of $\mathcal{PC}$, we start with the following entities:

- For each integer $n > 0$, a set of predicates of arity n
- For each integer $n > 0$, a set of functions of arity n
- A set of constant terms
- A set of variable terms

From these entities, we define the set of all terms inductively as

- Constants and variables are terms
- $f(t_1, t_2, \ldots, t_n)$ is a term, where f is a function of arity n and the t_i are terms

We say that $p(t_1, t_2, \ldots, t_n)$ is an *atomic sentence* if p is a predicate of arity n and the t_i are terms. The wffs of $\mathcal{PC}$ are defined inductively as follows:

- The atomic sentences
- $A_1 \vee A_2 \vee \ldots \vee A_n$, where each of the A_i is a wff
- $A_1 \wedge A_2 \wedge \ldots \wedge A_n$, where each of the A_i is a wff
- $\neg A$, where A is a wff
- $A \supset B$ and $A \equiv B$, where A and B are wffs
- $\forall x_1, \ldots, x_n, A$ and $\exists x_1, \ldots, x_n, A$, where A is a wff

The *scope of a quantifier* in a formula is that portion of the formula that the quantifier applies to. The scope of a quantifier is determined parenthetically in a formula just as the scope of a local variable is determined in Lisp. In $((\forall x, p(x)) \wedge (\forall x, q(x)))$, the scope of the first appearance of $\forall x$ is $p(x)$, and the scope of the second appearance is $q(x)$. A variable is considered *free* if it is not in the scope of some quantifier. A *closed* wff is just a wff that contains no free variables. The formula $(\forall x, p(x))$ is closed. A *ground* term or wff is one that contains no variables at all.

There are many choices that have to be made in designing a representation. Predicates are used to represent properties and relations. For instance, we can say that a person is large, heavy, fast, or tall. Large, heavy, fast, and tall are all properties of people. We can have relations involving people such as parent or friend. We choose terms to represent objects based on the name or function of the objects. For instance, the constants Fred and apartment102 can be used to represent Fred and his apartment. We can also represent Fred's apartment functionally using the term apartment(Fred).

Often, in $\mathcal{PC}$, there is more than one way to represent something. We can represent "everyone loves his or her mother" as ∀x,y, mother(y,x) ⊃ loves(x,y) or as ∀x, loves(x,mother(x)), where in the first case mother is used as a predicate, and in the second it is used as a function. Which one is right? They are both right, but one may turn out to be more convenient for certain representation tasks.

Translating English Sentences into Logic

A great deal of human knowledge is encoded in the form of sentences written in natural languages such as English. In building AI systems, it is often necessary to translate such knowledge into a representation suitable for computers to manipulate. To demonstrate how this can be done, we consider a number of English sentences about mushrooms and translate them into predicate calculus, using the predicates mushroom(x), purple(x), and poisonous(x).

- All purple mushrooms are poisonous.

  ∀ x, (mushroom(x) ∧ purple(x)) ⊃ poisonous(x)

- No purple mushroom is poisonous.

  ∀ x, (mushroom(x) ∧ purple(x)) ⊃ ¬ poisonous(x)

- All mushrooms are either purple or poisonous.

  ∀ x, mushroom(x) ⊃ ((purple(x) ∨ poisonous(x)))

- All mushrooms are either purple or poisonous but not both.

  ∀ x, mushroom(x) ⊃
  ((purple(x) ∧ ¬ poisonous(x)) ∨
  (¬ purple(x) ∧ poisonous(x)))

- All purple mushrooms except one are poisonous.

  ∃ x,
  (purple(x) ∧ mushroom(x) ∧ ¬ poisonous(x)) ∧
  (∀ y, (purple(y) ∧ mushroom(y) ∧ ¬ equal (x,y)) ⊃
  poisonous(y))

- There are exactly two purple mushrooms.

  ∃ x, y,
  mushroom(x) ∧ purple(x) ∧
  mushroom(y) ∧ purple(y) ∧ ¬ equal(x,y) ∧
  (∀ z, (mushroom(z) ∧ purple(z)) ⊃ (equal(z,x) ∨ equal(z,y)))

More About Quantification

Quantification allows us to say things about sets of objects. The universal quantifier, ∀, is like a conjunction with possibly an infinite number of conjuncts. If our domain of interest consisted of only Fred and Lynn, we could represent ∀x, loves(x,x) as loves(Fred,Fred) ∧ loves(Lynn,Lynn). This simple trick will not work, however, for ∀x, integer(x) ⊃ (odd(x) ∨ even(x)). The existential quantifier, ∃, is like a disjunction with possibly an infinite number of disjuncts. Assuming the finite domain of Fred and Lynn, ∃x, happy(x) can be represented as happy(Fred) ∨ happy(Lynn). Quantification is always over objects in the domain and not over functions or predicates. Relaxing this restriction produces formulas in what is called second- or higher-order logic.

Formulas involving existential quantifiers can be converted to statements involving universal quantifiers and visa versa using the following equivalences:

$$(\forall\ x,\ A)\ \equiv\ \neg\ (\exists\ x,\ \neg A)$$
$$(\exists\ x,\ A)\ \equiv\ \neg\ (\forall\ x,\ \neg A)$$

To convince yourself that these equivalences are correct, think in terms of quantification over finite sets using disjunction and conjunction. Using these equivalences, we can show that the following five formulas are logically equivalent to one another:

```
∀ x, y, clown(x) ⊃ loves(y,x)
∀ x, clown(x) ⊃ ∀ y, loves(y,x)
∀ x, y, ¬ clown(x) ∨ loves(y,x)
∀ y, ¬ (∃ x, clown(x) ∧ ¬ loves(y,x))
∀ x, clown(x) ⊃ ¬ (∃ y, ¬ loves(y,x))
```

Semantics for 𝒫𝒞

The semantics for a language defines a set of interpretations that associate the symbols in the language with the elements of a particular domain of interest. Given a set of interpretations, we then specify the conditions for an interpretation to satisfy formulas. In the following, we provide a glimpse of how the semantics for predicate calculus deals with predicate and constant symbols and quantifiers and variables. We begin by considering how predicate symbols complicate the picture.

Consider the syntax for a simple language used to reason about the level of fluid in a set of holding tanks. In this language, there is one predicate symbol, overflow, and two constant symbols, tank45 and tank17. In the following, suppose that there are only three well-formed formulas associated with this language:

```
overflow(tank45)
¬ overflow(tank17)
(overflow(tank45) ∧ overflow(tank17))
```

Each interpretation has associated with it a domain corresponding to the set of elements that we are interested in accounting for in our semantics. Suppose that we have in mind a world in which there are three holding tanks, 1, 2, and 3, and so our domain D is the set $\{1, 2, 3\}$. Each interpretation must map each term to some element of the domain. For a particular interpretation, we denote the function mapping terms to domain elements as M_1. In this case, M_1 maps {tank45, tank17} to $\{1, 2, 3\}$. Specifically, M_1 might map tank45 to 1 and tank17 to 2, indicating that in this particular interpretation tank45 corresponds to Tank 1 and tank17 corresponds to Tank 2.

Each predicate symbol denotes a relation on the elements of the domain, and so each interpretation must map each predicate symbol to a relation. For a particular interpretation, we denote the function mapping predicate symbols to relations as M_2. A relation on one variable is just a subset of $\{1, 2, 3\}$, so M_2 maps {overflow} to $2^{\{1,2,3\}}$, where $2^{\{1,2,3\}}$ represents the power set (set of all subsets) of $\{1, 2, 3\}$. Specifically, M_2 might map overflow to $\{1, 3\}$, indicating that in this particular interpretation Tanks 1 and 3 are overflowing. For our simple language, D, M_1, and M_2 together constitute one possible interpretation.

Now we can say what it means for a well-formed formula to satisfy the interpretation (D, M_1, M_2). The interpretation satisfies overflow(tank45) because M_1(tank45) is an element of M_2(overflow). The interpretation satisfies ¬overflow(tank17) since M_1(tank17) is *not* an element of M_2(overflow). Finally, the interpretation does not satisfy overflow(tank45) ∧ overflow(tank17) since $\{M_1(\text{tank17}), M_1(\text{tank45})\}$ is not a subset of M_2(overflow).

More generally, we define what it means for an interpretation to satisfy a formula that has no logical connectives using simple set operations and then inductively define what it means for an interpretation to satisfy a formula that has connectives. The interpretation of a predicate symbol is a relation defined by a set of tuples. For example, if p is a predicate symbol of arity 3, then the interpretation of p is a subset of $D \times D \times D$, corresponding to the set of all triples that stand in a particular relation to one another. If $\langle M_1(\text{t1}), M_1(\text{t2}), M_1(\text{t3}) \rangle$ is an element of the set of triples corresponding to an interpretation of p, then the atomic sentence p(t1,t2,t3) is satisfied by this interpretation of p.

We can formalize these requirements on interpretations as follows. An interpretation I is a triple (D, M_1, M_2) in which M_1 maps terms to D and M_2 maps each predicate symbol of arity n to a set of n-tuples. I is a *model* of a wff φ (written $I \models \varphi$) under the following conditions:

1. $I \models p(t_1, \ldots, t_n)$ iff $\langle M_1(t_1), \ldots, M_1(t_n) \rangle \in M_2(p)$
2. $I \models (\varphi_1 \wedge \varphi_2)$ iff $I \models \varphi_1$ and $I \models \varphi_2$
3. $I \models (\varphi_1 \vee \varphi_2)$ iff $I \models \varphi_1$ or $I \models \varphi_2$
4. $I \models \neg\varphi$ iff $I \not\models \varphi$

The notation $I \not\models \varphi$ indicates that I is *not* a model of φ.

The interpretation of quantified formulas is handled by substituting elements from the domain for the quantified variables. An interpretation is a model for a universally quantified formula if the interpretation is a model for every formula obtained by substituting any domain element for the quantified variable. An interpretation is a model for an existentially quantified formula, if there exists some domain element such that the interpretation is a model for the formula obtained by substituting that domain element for the quantified variable. The notions of satisfiability, validity, and model-theoretic inconsistency carry over from propositional logic.

3.5 Formal System for $\mathcal{PC}$

We need a formal system consisting of axioms and rules of inference in order to construct proofs in $\mathcal{PC}$. In the formal system for $\mathcal{PC}$ discussed in this section, we include the rules of inference for $\mathcal{P}$ and add one additional rule. *Universal instantiation* is a rule of inference that allows us to substitute any term for all occurrences of a universally quantified variable. Figure 3.6 illustrates this rule of inference.

1. $\forall x,\ A$
---
2. A' substituting any term t for all occurrences of x in A UI:$x \rightarrow t$, 1

Figure 3.6 Universal instantiation rule of inference

We represent the statement that Fred is a person by person(Fred) and the statement that Fred is in the lobby by location(Fred,lobby). Suppose that the janitorial robot wants to clean the lobby but cannot do so if the lobby is occupied. Given what we know about the situation can we prove that the lobby is occupied? Figure 3.7 lists the steps in the proof that the lobby is occupied given person(Fred) and location(Fred,lobby). If instead of being given that Fred is in the lobby we are given that everybody is in the lobby, $\forall x$, person(x) $\supset$ location(x,lobby), we could arrive at the same conclusion with a couple of additional steps.

1.   person(fred)   AXIOM
2.   location(fred,lobby)   AXIOM
3. $\forall x,y$, (person(x) $\wedge$ location(x,y))
      $\supset$ occupied(y)   AXIOM
4. $\forall y$, (person(fred) $\wedge$ location(fred,y))
      $\supset$ occupied(y)   UI:$x \rightarrow$fred, 3
5.   (person(fred) $\wedge$ location(fred,lobby))
      $\supset$ occupied(lobby)   UI:$y \rightarrow$lobby, 4
6.   (person(fred) $\wedge$ location(fred,lobby))   CONJ: 1,2
7.   occupied(lobby)   MP: 5,6

Figure 3.7 Simple proof in the predicate calculus

It is often useful to be able to reason about whether or not two terms are equivalent in some sense. For example, we can represent the English sentence "two of the students passed" as $\exists x,y$, passed(x) $\land$ passed(y) $\land$ ¬equal (x,y). To reason about the equal relationship, we would add the following three axioms to capture the reflexive, symmetric, and transitive properties of an equivalence relation:[4]

```
∀ x, equal(x,x)
∀ x,y equal(x,y)  ⊃  equal(y,x)
∀ x,y,z, (equal(x,y)  ∧  equal(y,z))  ⊃  equal(x,z)
```

In a particular domain theory, we might have several equivalence relationships. In reasoning about Lisp, we want to distinguish equality in terms of location in memory from equality in terms of list structure.

Specifying Programs in Prolog

Using the equivalence relation described, we can represent list processing computations of the sort that we encountered in Lisp. For instance, something is a member of a list if it is either equal to the first element of the list or a member of the rest of the list. This declarative specification can be represented by the following axioms:

```
∀ x,list, equal(x,first(list))  ⊃  member(x,list)
∀ x,list, member(x,rest(list))  ⊃  member(x,list)
```

We can use axioms like these to prove theorems about whether an item is a member of a list. In fact, we can specify axioms describing arbitrary operations on lists. The logic programming language *Prolog* allows a programmer to specify programs in the form of such axioms. In the exercises at the end of this chapter, you are given an example of a logic program that can be executed using a goal reduction theorem prover. The procedural specification for such programs is implicit in the way in which Prolog proves theorems. Prolog is particularly interesting in that it illustrates the close connection between logic and computation.

Eliminating Quantifiers

To make it easier for computers to manipulate symbolic expressions, researchers try to design canonical forms for representation. We have already seen examples of canonical forms in the conjunctive and disjunctive normal forms. Quantifiers can complicate the design of canonical forms. Suppose, however, that there is only one type of quantifier, say univer-

---

[4]To completely axiomatize equality, you also need the axiom schema of substitution, $\forall x,y$, equal(x,y) $\supset$ ($\varphi(x) \equiv \varphi(y)$), where φ ranges over all formulas with a free variable.

sal quantifiers, and suppose that we can put any formula in the following form:

$$\forall\ x_1, x_2, \ldots, x_n,\ \varphi(x_1, x_2, \ldots, x_n)$$

where $\varphi(x_1, x_2, \ldots, x_n)$ is an arbitrary formula involving the variables $x_1, x_2, \ldots, x_n$ but no quantifiers. In this case, assuming that we can distinguish variables from other terms, we can eliminate explicit quantifiers entirely and convert $\varphi(x_1, x_2, \ldots, x_n)$ to conjunctive normal form. In the following paragraphs, we demonstrate that it is possible to convert any quantified formula into this form by eliminating explicit existential quantification.

First, note that $\exists x,\ \mathsf{happy(x)}$ is equivalent to $\neg(\forall x,\ \neg\mathsf{happy(x)})$. This equivalence, suitably generalized, allows us to eliminate explicit existential quantification, but it is not enough to get an arbitrary formula into the form mentioned. Another way to eliminate an existential quantifier is to introduce new functions that represent the objects that exist. For example, $\exists x,\ \mathsf{happy(x)}$ would turn into $\mathsf{happy(the\text{-}happy\text{-}one)}$, where $\mathsf{the\text{-}happy\text{-}one}$ is a constant (function of arity 0) that did not exist before. The presence of other quantifiers complicates things somewhat. For example, $\forall x,\ \exists y,\ \mathsf{loves(x,y)}$ would become $\forall x,\ \mathsf{loves(x,\ the\text{-}love\text{-}of(x))}$. The new function $\mathsf{the\text{-}love\text{-}of}$ takes a single argument, the universally quantified variable x, indicating that there is a particular, possibly different love for each possible x.

The functions, $\mathsf{the\text{-}happy\text{-}one}$ and $\mathsf{the\text{-}love\text{-}of}$, are called *Skolem* functions after a logician of that name. Generally, given an expression of the form

$$\forall\ x_1, x_2, \ldots, x_n,\ \exists\ y,\ \varphi(x_1, x_2, \ldots, x_n, y)$$

where $\varphi(x_1, x_2, \ldots, x_n)$ is an arbitrary formula involving the variables $x_1, x_2, \ldots, x_n$, we define the *Skolemization* of the expression to be

$$\forall\ x_1, x_2, \ldots, x_n\ \varphi(x_1, x_2, \ldots, x_n, \mathsf{skm}(x_1, x_2, \ldots, x_n))$$

where skm is a new function that did not exist before. Often Skolem functions are created automatically by theorem-proving systems and given new names like $\mathsf{sk421}$. In the following, we demonstrate how to eliminate existential quantifiers from some example formulas.

Starting with the formula $\forall x,\ \exists y,\ \mathsf{location(y,x)}$, we first Skolemize the existential variables resulting in $\forall x,\ \mathsf{location(sk37(x),x)}$. Next we eliminate the one remaining quantifier to obtain $\mathsf{location(sk37(x),x)}$.

In a more complicated formula, we might have to rename certain variables so that different occurrences of the same variable appearing in different formulas are distinguishable. This process of renaming is called *standardizing the variables apart* and is necessary if the same variable is introduced through two or more quantifiers as in $(\forall x,\ \mathsf{black(x)}) \lor (\forall x,\ \mathsf{white(x)})$. Note that we will also need some method of distinguishing variables from constants.

As a slightly more complicated example, suppose we start with the formula ∀x, human(x) ⊃ (∃y, parent(x,y)). First, we move the quantifiers as far to the left as we can, ∀x, (∃y, human(x) ⊃ parent(x,y)). Next, we Skolemize and convert the implication to a disjunction, ∀x, ¬human(x) ∨ parent(x,sk42(x)). Finally, we eliminate the remaining quantifier and standardize the variables apart ¬human(x64) ∨ parent(x64,sk42(x64)). In Exercise 3.11, you are given a general algorithm for eliminating quantifiers. The only complicated part of this algorithm is in moving the negations inside all the quantifiers so that the formula is in a form that will allow us to apply Skolemization.

Learning and Deductive Inference

In Chapter 5, we study learning with an emphasis on *inductive inference*. In inductive inference, we arrive at general conclusions on the basis of particular examples. For instance, suppose that all the files that you have ever seen with a .lisp extension contain Lisp function definitions. From your observations, you conclude that *every* file with a .lisp extension contains Lisp function definitions.

In this chapter, we are primarily interested in *deductive inference*. In deductive inference, the conclusions follow necessarily from the axioms according to specified rules of inference. In the following paragraphs, we explore how deductive inference can be used to support learning.

Consider a softbot assigned the task of cleaning up the files on a UNIX system. The softbot knows that a super user can delete any file and that it is a super user.

∀ f,u, super(u) ⊃ delete(f,u)
super(bot9)

Using these axioms, the softbot can easily prove that it can delete any particular file. As shown in Figure 3.8, the proof is only five lines long, but in cleaning up the entire file system, the softbot may have to perform the same chain of inference many times. This particular softbot is pretty clever; it notices that the proof would have succeeded for any file and so it proves the following general formula:

∀ f, delete(f,bot9)

The softbot then adds this formula to its set of axioms, and the next time it wants to delete a file, it can prove that it can delete the file in two lines by

1.	super(bot9)	AXIOM
2.	∀f,u, super(u) ⊃ delete(f,u)	AXIOM
3.	∀f, super(bot9) ⊃ delete(f,bot9)	UI:u→bot9, 2
4.	super(bot9) ⊃ delete(tetris,bot9)	UI:f→tetris, 3
5.	delete(tetris,bot9)	MP: 1,4

Figure 3.8 A softbot proves it can delete a file

using the new axiom and one application of universal instantiation. Using this new axiom, the softbot cannot prove anything that it could not before, but it can prove certain things with less effort. The softbot has learned how to accelerate theorem proving, and hence, this type of learning is often called *speedup learning*.

Another name for the type of learning that the softbot performed is *explanation-based generalization*. The proof in Figure 3.8 is an explanation of why the softbot is able to delete a particular file. In explanation-based generalization, the explanation is examined and then generalized by converting some constants to universally quantified variables.

Suppose a softbot is assigned the task of fetching the abstracts for technical papers that are stored on file servers on a network of computers. Here are some of the axioms that the softbot has for reasoning about file servers and abstracts. The first axiom indicates that the abstract for a technical paper is available on the network using the standard network file transfer protocol (FTP) if the abstract is on a file server and you have access to that server.

$\forall$ a,s, (online(a,s) $\land$ access(s)) $\supset$ ftp(a)

An abstract is on the JOSIAH file server if the paper has appeared in a journal published by IEEE.

$\forall$ a,j, (journal(a,j) $\land$ publisher(j,ieee)) $\supset$ online(a,josiah)

If a server provides an anonymous FTP service, then the server is accessible.

$\forall$ s, anonymous(s) $\supset$ access(s)

Finally, Josiah offers anonymous FTP service.

anonymous(josiah)

Suppose that the softbot is asked to retrieve the abstract MCD83. The softbot happens to know that MCD83 appeared in *IEEE Transactions on Pattern Analysis and Machine Intelligence*, a journal published by IEEE Press and affectionately known as PAMI.

journal(mcd83,pami)
publisher(pami,ieee)

Figure 3.9 (page 98) displays a proof that the softbot can FTP the abstract MCD83. In the style of explanation-based generalization, we analyze the proof and see if we can construct a useful generalization. Suppose that we replace MCD83 with a universally quantified variable in the proof. Could we prove $\forall$a, ftp(a)? The answer is no because the proof relies on the abstract being on the JOSIAH server. If every abstract were on the JOSIAH server, then we could prove $\forall$a, ftp(a). In fact, the following formula is a valid generalization:

$\forall$ a, online(a,josiah) $\supset$ ftp(a)

1.	$\forall a,s,$ (online(a,s) $\wedge$ access(s))	
	$\supset$ ftp(a)	AXIOM
2.	$\forall s,$ (online(mcd83,s) $\wedge$ access(s))	
	$\supset$ ftp(mcd83)	UI:a→mcd83, 1
3.	(online(mcd83,josiah) $\wedge$ access(josiah))	
	$\supset$ ftp(mcd83)	UI:s→josiah, 2
4.	$\forall s,$ anonymous(s) $\supset$ access(s)	AXIOM
5.	anonymous(josiah) $\supset$ access(josiah)	UI:s→josiah, 4
6.	anonymous(josiah)	AXIOM
7.	access(josiah)	MP: 5,6
8.	$\forall a,j,$ (journal(a,j) $\wedge$ publisher(j,ieee))	
	$\supset$ online(a,josiah)	AXIOM
9.	$\forall j,$ (journal(mcd83,j) $\wedge$ publisher(j,ieee))	
	$\supset$ online(mcd83,josiah)	UI:a→mcd83, 8
10.	(journal(mcd83,pami) $\wedge$ publisher(pami,ieee))	
	$\supset$ online(mcd83,josiah)	UI:j→pami, 9
11.	journal(mcd83,pami)	AXIOM
12.	publisher(pami,ieee)	AXIOM
13.	(journal(mcd83,pami) $\wedge$ publisher(pami,ieee))	CONJ: 11,12
14.	online(mcd83,josiah)	MP: 10,13
15.	(online(mcd83,josiah) $\wedge$ access(josiah))	CONJ: 7,14
16.	ftp(mcd83)	MP: 3,15

Figure 3.9   A softbot proves it can access a file on the network

We can do a little better. The following generalization is also valid and would result in even shorter proofs:

$$\forall a,j, (journal(a,j) \wedge publisher(j,ieee)) \supset ftp(a)$$

Systems that use explanation-based generalization regularly solve problems by performing some sort of deductive inference. They then analyze the steps and derive a formula that can subsequently be used to speed inference. In Chapter 7, we consider using explanation-based generalization to improve the performance of planning systems.

Decidability

The predicate calculus is not, in general, decidable. That means that there is no effective method for deciding whether a given formula is a theorem. However, there are specific theories that are decidable. For example, any theory with a finite number of terms is decidable. This follows from the fact that with a finite number of terms we can replace universal quantifiers with conjunctions and existential quantifiers with disjunctions and reduce our predicate-calculus theory to a propositional theory. In the next section, we describe a special case of theories with a finite number of constants and predicate symbols for which we can implement an efficient theorem prover.

3.6   Automated Theorem Proving in $\mathcal{PC}$

Consider the following theory:

```
red(block17)
sphere(block17)
red(block41)
cube(block41)
∀x, (red(x) ∧ smooth(x)) ⊃ pleasing(x)
∀x, sphere(x) ⊃ smooth(x)
```

Using the rules of inference for $\mathcal{PC}$, we can prove the formula pleasing(block17) from these axioms. We already know how to represent facts and rules not involving quantifiers from our study of propositional logic. We could represent each universally quantified formula as a conjunction of propositional formulas by substituting block17 and block41 for the quantified variable. Using the resulting propositional theory, we could directly use theorem as defined earlier. In this section, however, instead of converting to a propositional theory, we consider how to implement a particular case of universal instantiation and prove theorems for simple $\mathcal{PC}$ theories.

We will not need to represent quantifiers explicitly since our database is in the canonical form described earlier. We will, however, need to distinguish universally quantified variables from constants. To this end, we introduce an abstract data type for variables in Lisp.

```
(defun make-VAR (var) (list '? var))
(defun is-VAR (x) (and (consp x) (eq (first x) '?)))
```

Any list whose first element is the symbol ? will be interpreted as a universally quantified variable whose scope is the entire expression in which it is found. We represent these axioms as facts and rules in Lisp as follows, being careful to standardize the variables apart to avoid conflicts:

```
((red block17))
((sphere block17))
((red block41))
((cube block41))
((pleasing (? x1)) if (red (? x1)) (smooth (? x1)))
((smooth (? x2)) if (sphere (? x2)))
```

Matching and Universal Instantiation

Universal instantiation allows us to substitute any term for all occurrences of a universally quantified variable in a formula. We say that two formulas *match* if we can find substitutions for the variables appearing in the formula such that the two are syntactically equivalent. We begin by defining a Lisp function that determines if a constant corresponding to a ground formula, such as (pleasing block17), and a pattern corresponding to quantified formula, such as (pleasing (? x)), match. If they do match, the function returns a set of substitutions called *bindings* that map variables to terms. A constant matches another constant if they are equal. An *unbound* variable (one currently without a binding) matches any formula. A bound variable matches a constant if the constant and the value to which the variable is bound are equal.

The following algorithm is used to determine if a pattern and a constant match according to the preceding definition. It is assumed that the initial list of bindings is non-nil so that we can distinguish between a failed match and a successful one involving no variable bindings.

1. If the set of bindings is nil, then return nil indicating failure.

2. If the pattern is an atom, then, if the pattern and the constant are eq, return the list of bindings indicating success; otherwise, return nil indicating failure.

3. If the pattern is a variable, then, if it is already bound, match the constant against the binding for the pattern; otherwise, return a new list of bindings, including the pattern bound to the constant.

4. At this point, we know that the pattern is a non-nil list structure, so if the constant is nil, we return nil.

5. Now, we know that both the pattern and constant are non-nil list structures, and so we match the first element of the pattern and the first element of the constant using the bindings that we obtain from matching the rest of the pattern and the rest of the constant using the bindings that we started with.

Figure 3.10 lists the Lisp code for a recursive function match implementing this algorithm. Recall from Chapter 2 that the Lisp function assoc takes two arguments, an expression and a list of lists, and returns the first list in the list of lists whose first element is eq to the value of the first argument. In our use of assoc in match, we override the default test (eq) with equal by using the optional keyword argument introduced with :test.

Here are some examples showing when match succeeds.

```
> (match '(loves (dog fred) fred)
         '(loves (? x) (? y)))
(((? X) (DOG FRED)) ((? Y) FRED) (MATCH T))
> (match '(loves (dog fred) mary)
         '(loves (dog (? x)) (? y)))
(((? X) FRED) ((? Y) MARY) (MATCH T))
```

Here are some examples showing when match fails.

```
> (match '(loves (dog fred) fred)
         '(loves (? x) (? x)))
NIL
> (match '(loves (dog fred) mary)
         '(loves (dog (? x)) (? x)))
NIL
```

```
;; Determine if a constant and a pattern match.
(defun match (const pat)
  (aux-match const pat '((match t))))

;; Keep track of the bindings established so far.
(defun aux-match (const pat bdgs)
  (cond ((null bdgs) nil)
        ((atom pat) (if (eq pat const) bdgs nil))
        ;; If the pattern is a bound variable, match the
        ;; constant and whatever the variable is bound to.
        ;; If the pattern is a variable and not bound,
        ;; then bind the variable to the constant.
        ((is-VAR pat)
         (let ((bdg (assoc pat bdgs :test #'equal)))
           (cond (bdg (aux-match const (second bdg) bdgs))
                 (t (cons (list pat const) bdgs)))))
        ((or (atom const) (null const)) nil)
        (t (aux-match (first const)
                      (first pat)
                      (aux-match (rest const)
                                 (rest pat) bdgs)))))
```

Figure 3.10   Lisp code for matching constant and pattern expressions

Goal Reduction in $\mathcal{PC}$

Now we can modify theorem to prove (pleasing block17). First, instead of using eq to determine if the consequent of a rule matches a conjunct that we are trying to prove, we use match. Second, after adding the antecedents of a rule to the list of conjuncts we are trying to prove, we make the substitutions indicated by the bindings to all the conjunctions in the list of conjuncts. This is equivalent to applying universal instantiation and modus ponens in succession.

The top graphic in Figure 3.11 (page 102) depicts the structure of the proof as an AND/OR tree. An AND/OR tree is divided into alternating AND and OR layers. The edges through an AND layer connect a conjunction to its conjuncts. The edges through an OR layer connect a conjunct to possible reductions corresponding to rules in the database. A conjunct has a proof in an AND/OR tree if either the conjunct reduces to the empty list or (recursively) the conjunct reduces to a conjunction such that each conjunct has a proof in the AND/OR tree. A *proof tree* for a conjunct in an AND/OR tree is a subtree of the AND/OR tree rooted at that conjunct such that every conjunct has exactly one reduction and the conjunct has a proof in the AND/OR tree. The top AND/OR tree in Figure 3.11 is not very interesting since there is only one possible proof for any conjunct; as such the tree is a proof tree for pleasing(block17). If we add the rule ((pleasing (? x)) if (heavy (? x))) and the fact heavy(block17), then we would have the somewhat more interesting AND/OR tree shown as the

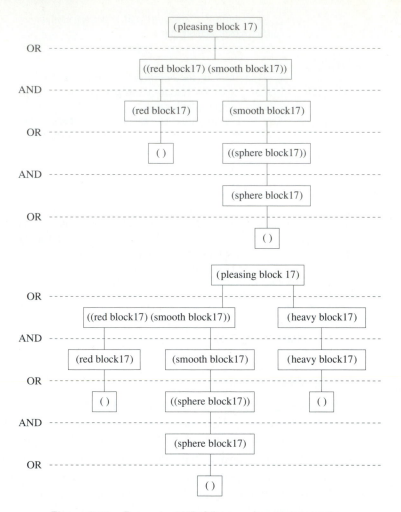

Figure 3.11   Example AND/OR trees for goal reduction

bottom graphic in Figure 3.11, which contains two proof trees for `pleasing`
(`block17`).

The proof for `pleasing(block17)` is a particularly easy one for the reason
that if we make the appropriate substitutions we never add a conjunct that
contains any variables. This means that we always match a constant against
a pattern, which is the only thing that `match` is designed to handle. It is often
useful, however, to try to prove quantified formulas.

We interpret a quantified formula corresponding to a conjunct in an
AND/OR tree as an existential statement. For example, we interpret
(`pleasing (? x)`) in an AND/OR tree as $\exists x$, `pleasing(x)`. Given $\forall x$, `sphere(x)` $\supset$
`smooth(x)`, in order to prove $\exists x$, `smooth(x)` it is enough to prove $\exists x$, `sphere(x)`.
In proving (`pleasing (? x)`), we attempt to find some value v that we can
substitute for x so that we can prove (`pleasing` v). The tricky part in all this
involves matching two formulas, each of which contains variables.

▲ AI IN PRACTICE

Expert Systems in Manufacturing

The General Motors Corporation uses expert systems to help diagnose problems in manufacturing equipment, anticipate failures, and schedule repairs and preventive maintenance. Expert systems allow General Motors to distribute the expertise of its best technicians so that even novice diagnosticians can perform at the level of an expert with many years of experience.

The Boeing Company uses an expert system to advise employees in the proper assembly of complex electrical connectors and cables for airplane manufacturing, maintenance, and repair. The Boeing system is written entirely in Prolog and involves the use of more than 25,000 rules.

The Chrysler Motors Corporation uses an expert system developed at Texas A&M University to aid in the design of automobile cooling systems. The system used by Chrysler generates the design specifications for the cooling system of a vehicle from a description of the subsystems, engine, air conditioning, and transmission that determines the cooling requirements for the vehicle. The expert system allows designers to quickly consider several alternative designs in order to choose the most cost-effective solution for a particular design problem.

Courtesy of Boeing Aircraft, Inc.

Unification

In the following, we consider a more general form of matching called *unification*. The substitutions involved in unification are somewhat more complicated than those employed in the simple form of matching introduced earlier. The two variables x and y are equivalent if we make the substitution ((x fred)(y fred)), but this is too specific a substitution for our purposes. In unifying two patterns, we attempt to find the *most general substitution* that renders the two patterns syntactically equivalent.

The following recursive unification procedure computes the most general substitution for two formulas if there exists such a substitution. The unification procedure makes use of the notion of the *disagreement* between two formulas. If you think of p and q as expressions representing trees, then the *first disagreement* between p and q corresponds to the first differing subexpressions encountered in a side-by-side, depth-first search of the two trees. For example, if p is (loves (mother (? z)) (? z)) and q is (loves (? x) (? y)), then the first disagreement corresponds to (mother (? z)) and (? x). The unification procedure is called with three arguments: two formulas, p and q, and a set of bindings, σ, used to keep track of the substitution.

1 Find the first disagreement between p and q.

2 If there is no disagreement, then signal success and return σ.

3 If there is a disagreement, then see if it can be resolved by making appropriate substitutions for variables.

    a) If neither of the two terms involved in the disagreement is a variable, then fail.

    b) If at least one of the two terms involved in the disagreement is a variable, then call one term corresponding to a variable the variable term and the other term the substitution term and create two new formulas by substituting the substitution term for the variable term in each of the original terms.

    c) Call the resulting formulas p' and q'.

    d) Create a new set of bindings σ' by creating a new binding in which the variable term is bound to the substitution term and adding this binding to σ.

4 Call the unification procedure with p', q', and σ'.

Here is an example showing how the unification procedure works. Let p be (loves (dog (? z)) (dog fred)) and q be (loves (? x) (? x)). The first disagreement between p and q corresponds to (dog (? z)) and (? x). Substituting (dog (? z)) for (? x) in p and q, we obtain p' equal to (loves (dog (? z)) (dog fred)) and q' equal to (loves (dog (? z)) (dog (? z))). The first disagreement between p' and q' corresponds to (? z) and fred. Substituting fred for (? z) in p' and q', we obtain two identical formulas. The unification procedure succeeds with the substitution (((? x) (dog (? z))) ((? z) fred)).

As another example, the unification procedure succeeds on the formulas (loves (mother (? z)) (? z)) and (loves (? x) (? y)), returning the substitution (((? x) (mother (? z))) ((? y) (? z))). Unification fails on the formulas (loves (? z) (? z)) and (loves (mother (? x)) fred).

The unification procedure described has a bug that we should mention. The procedure succeeds on the formulas (loves (mother (? z)) (? z)) and (loves (? x) (? x)) with the substitution (((? x) (mother (? z))) ((? z) (mother (? z)))). The unification procedure does not check to see if the expression that a variable is bound to contains that variable. The unification procedure in Prolog also has this bug. In Prolog, however, this behavior is considered a feature, not a bug, because it allows for some very useful programming techniques and allows unification to run much faster.

```
;; Compute the most general substitution for p and q.
(defun unify (p q)
  (aux-unify p q '((unify t))))

;; Keep track of the bindings established so far.
(defun aux-unify (p q bdgs)
  (let ((d (disagreement p q)))
    ;; If there is no disagreement, then signal success.
    (cond ((null d) bdgs)
          ;; Assume that the first element of the disagreement
          ;; is a variable. If the first element appears in the
          ;; second, then signal failure. If the assumption turns
          ;; out to be false, then the following clause will cope.
          ((occursp (first d) (second d)) nil)
          ((not (is-VAR (first d))) nil)
          ;; Resolve the disagreement by making appropriate
          ;; substitutions and then recurse on the result.
          (t (aux-unify
               (subst (second d) (first d) p :test #'equal)
               (subst (second d) (first d) q :test #'equal)
               (cons d bdgs))))))
```

Figure 3.12   Main routines for computing the most general substitution

Figures 3.12 and 3.13 list the Lisp code for a correct but somewhat inefficient version of unification. Unify returns the most general substitution that renders its two arguments equal if such a substitution exists and returns nil otherwise. In our implementation, we have added an "occurs check" to prevent counterfeit unifications of the sort allowed by Prolog.

```
;; Return subexpressions where p and q first disagree.
(defun disagreement (p q)
  ;; If either p or q is a variable
  ;; and p and q are not equal, then you are done.
  (cond ((is-VAR p) (if (equal p q) nil (list p q)))
        ((is-VAR q) (if (equal p q) nil (list q p)))
        ;; If either p or q is not nil and not a
        ;; list and p and q are not equal, then
        ;; you are done, but p and q will not unify.
        ((or (not (consp p)) (not (consp q)))
         (if (eq p q) nil (list p q)))
        (t (or (disagreement (first p) (first q))
               (disagreement (rest p) (rest q))))))

;; Check to see if x appears anywhere in y.
(defun occursp (x y)
  (cond ((or (null y) (not (consp y))) nil)
        ((is-VAR y) (equal x y))
        (t (or (occursp x (first y)) (occursp x (rest y))))))
```

Figure 3.13   Subroutines required for computing the most general substitution

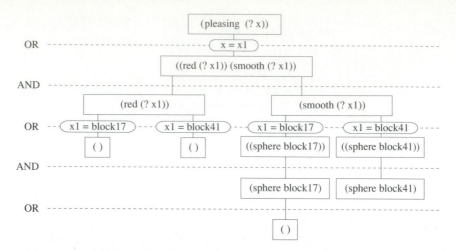

Figure 3.14   Goal reduction with quantified formulas

The version of unification listed in Figures 3.12 and 3.13 works by making repeated substitutions using the Lisp function subst[5] and a function disagreement that computes the corresponding subexpressions in the two formulas at the point that the two formulas first disagree.

Here is a simple example illustrating the operation of unify on two quantified formulas.

```
> (unify '(loves (dog (? x)) (dog fred))
         '(loves (? z) (? z)))
(((? X) FRED) ((? Z) (DOG (? X))) (UNIFY T))
```

Now we can modify theorem once again to prove (pleasing (? x)). For the most part, we proceed as in the case of match but use unify for computing substitutions. One further complication arises in dealing with conjuncts that contain variables. In many cases, it will be necessary to use the same rule more than once in carrying out a proof. To avoid conflicts between variables from different conjuncts arising from separate instantiations of the same rule, we rename all the variables in a rule each time the rule is used.

Figure 3.14 shows the AND/OR graph for (pleasing (? x)). Note that every reduction is now labeled with a substitution. In addition to the requirements mentioned earlier, in a proof tree with substitution, each variable must have at most one binding. Ensuring that each variable has at most one binding is accomplished by maintaining a list of all bindings corresponding to substitutions made in proving earlier conjuncts and passing this list to each recursive call to theorem. Before trying to prove a conjunct, the list of bindings is used to substitute values for the bound variables

---

[5]The expression (subst *new old expr* :test #'equal) returns a copy of *expr* having substituted *new* for every equal occurrence of *old* in *expr*.

in the conjunct. With these additions, theorem implements a simple version of the interpreter for the logic programming language Prolog.

Concept Description Languages

General theorem proving in the predicate calculus is computationally complex. For this reason, researchers try to find subsets of the predicate calculus that are expressive enough to represent a given body of knowledge but that have appealing computational properties. These subsets of the predicate calculus define specialized languages. The rules that we used in goal reduction correspond to just such a specialized language. Using goal reduction rules alone, we cannot represent everything that we can represent in the predicate calculus. However, goal reduction rules do allow us to represent a significant amount of useful knowledge and perform many types of inference involving such knowledge efficiently. In the rest of this section, we introduce another specialized language for which we can support efficient inference.

For our purposes, a *class* is just a set of objects, an *instance* of a class is a member of the corresponding set, and one class is a *subclass* of another class (called the *superclass*) if the set corresponding to the first is a subset of the set corresponding to the second. A *concept description language* is a specialized language that allows us to represent classes of objects, instances of classes, subclass relationships involving classes, and properties of classes and instances.

The simple concept description language that we present here involves three predicates: instance, subclass, and feature. The expression

instance(*object, class*)

represents that *object* is an instance of class. The expression

subclass(*class, superclass*)

represents that *class* is a subclass of *superclass*. Finally,

feature(*class*, *attribute*, *value*)

represents that all objects in *class* can be described as having an *attribute* with *value*.

To represent that Ralph is an instance of the class of robots, we write instance(Ralph,robot). To represent that robots are a subclass of the class of autonomous systems, we write subclass(robot,autonomous-system). To represent that all robots are constructed from mechanical parts, we write feature(robot,construction,mechanical).

There are also some general statements that we can make regarding classes and instances. If an object is an instance of a class, then the object is an instance of all superclasses of that class. The subclass relationship is transitive. If a class has a feature, then all instances of the class have the feature. These statements are represented by the following predicate calculus formulas:

```
∀ x,y,z, subclass(x,y) ∧ instance(z,x) ⊃ instance(z,y)
∀ x,y,z, subclass(x,y) ∧ subclass(y,z) ⊃ subclass(x,z)
∀ x,y,a,v, instance(x,y) ∧ feature(y,a,v) ⊃ feature(x,a,v)
```

Given knowledge encoded in a given concept description language, we are interested in inferring features of instances. For example, we might wish to prove that Ralph is constructed from mechanical parts,

```
feature(Ralph,construction,mechanical)
```

To simplify inference, the knowledge encoded in a concept description language can be converted into a convenient graphical form.

Semantic Networks

A *semantic network* is a directed graph in which the nodes correspond to classes, instances, and the possible values for attributes. The labeled arcs in a semantic network encode instance and subclass relationships, and possible attributes describing classes. Consider the following set of formulas:

```
instance(Fred,human)
instance(Lisa,human)
instance(Ralph,robot)
subclass(robot,autonomous-system)
subclass(human,autonomous-system)
feature(human,construction,biological)
feature(robot,construction,mechanical)
feature(autonomous-system,behavior,adaptive)
```

These formulas are encoded in the semantic network shown in Figure 3.15. Note that there is a node for every instance, class, and attribute value. To compute the value of an attribute for a given instance in a semantic network, follow arcs upward from the instance looking for classes with an arc labeled with the attribute in question. Answering queries regarding the value of attributes can be performed in time linear in the size of the semantic network.

Figure 3.15 represents the simplest sort of semantic network. In more complicated networks, we might have more than one arc leading out of an instance or class node. For example, someone might build a robot that is indistinguishable from a human. This robot might be classified as both a human and a robot, leading to possible ambiguities. In particular, our humanoid robot would have two possible values for the construction attribute.

We might also want to specify an instance that does not have all the features of its class. Such an instance represents an exception to the general rules governing members of its class. For example, we might have a hybrid robot constructed out of mechanical and biological components. In all other respects, the hybrid is like other robots. Exceptions can also apply

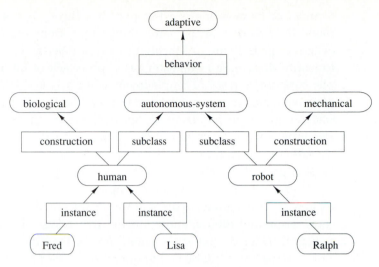

Figure 3.15   Semantic network

to the features of superclasses. For example, we might have a robot that is not capable of adaptive behavior but otherwise has all the features of an autonomous system.

By adding exceptions and other extensions to concept description languages, we increase the expressiveness of those languages. Sometimes this increased expressiveness can also increase the associated computational cost of inference. Trading expressiveness for computational efficiency is an important consideration in designing representations.

3.7 Nonmonotonic Logic

The logics that we have discussed so far are *monotonic* in that, if a formula is a theorem for a particular formal theory, then that formula is still a theorem for any augmented theory obtained by adding axioms to the theory. In a *nonmonotonic logic*, if a formula is a theorem for a formal theory, then that formula need not be a theorem for any augmented theory. Much of common-sense reasoning is nonmonotonic in the sense that adding new information may provide sufficient reasons to retract prior conclusions. For example, you may be willing to believe that you do not have a sister named Alice. However, if you find a birth certificate for a child by the name of Alice with your parents' name on it, you may be willing to retract your prior belief. In this section, we briefly discuss how we can extend traditional monotonic logics to handle nonmonotonic forms of inference.

Closed-World Assumption

A theory is *syntactically complete at the atomic level* if, for every ground atomic formula (one that contains no variables and no connectives), either the formula or its negation is a theorem. If a theory is not syntactically complete, then there may be some things that seem reasonable to conclude even though they are not theorems. A *closed-world assumption* is often used to justify drawing a conclusion based on a lack of information. For example, suppose as head of employment you are asked if Fred is employed in your company. You want to decide if employee(Fred). There is no record of Fred in your employee database, but this does not mean that you can prove ¬employee(Fred). One approach to dealing with this problem is to make a closed-world assumption and *complete* the theory by adding the negation of each ground atomic formula that is not a theorem.

Completing a theory can be complicated when different predicates are related to one another axiomatically. Suppose that we have two predicates, inside and outside, and an axiom that relates them, ∀x, ¬inside(x) ≡ outside(x). If we do not know where Fred is, then there is no reason to add ¬outside(Fred) or ¬inside(Fred) to our theory. The problem is that our choice of predicates is arbitrary. There is no reason to prefer the assumption that Fred is inside over the assumption that Fred is outside. In·general, we would like to have control over what predicates we complete. The following proposal provides just this sort of control.

Suppose that block17 is the only red object that we know of. In fact, we are willing to conclude that any object other than block17 is not red. How can we represent this without explicitly adding ¬red(x) for all x besides block17? One answer is that we can complete the predicate red using the following *completion formula*:

∀ x, red(x) ≡ equal(x,block17)

From the completion formula and the stipulation that two terms are not equal if and only if they are (syntactically) distinct terms, we can easily prove that ¬red(block41). If we later learn that another block is red, say block32, then all we have to do is change the right-hand side of the completion formula.

∀ x, red(x) ≡ (equal(x,block17) ∨ equal(x,block32))

Things are a bit more complicated if the predicate that we wish to complete is implicated in some additional formulas. For instance, suppose that in addition to knowing that block17 is red we know that ∀x, on(x,table32) ⊃ red(x). Now we have the following completion formula:

∀ x, red(x) ≡ (equal(x,block17) ∨ on(x,table32))

A number of special cases of the closed-world assumption appear frequently in the literature on nonmonotonic logics. The first is called the *domain-closure assumption*, and it is the assumption that the only objects in the domain are those that can be named using the constants and functions

$$
\begin{array}{lll}
1. & \alpha & \\
2. & C(\beta) & \\
\hline
3. & \beta & \text{DF: 1, 2}
\end{array}
\qquad
\begin{array}{lll}
1. & \alpha \supset \beta & \\
2. & \beta & \\
3. & C(\alpha) & \\
\hline
4. & \alpha & \text{AB: 1, 2, 3}
\end{array}
$$

Figure 3.16   Two general forms for specifying nonmonotonic rules of inference

specified in the theory. The second is called the *unique-names assumption*, and it is the assumption that if two ground terms cannot be proved equal then they are assumed to be unequal. Such assumptions are often implicit in the operation of working programs.

Abductive and Default Reasoning

We can exert even more control over what sort of nonmonotonic conclusions to allow by adding special-purpose rules of inference. To specify these rules of inference, we introduce a special symbol C, for consistent. Intuitively, for any wff α, $C(\alpha)$ follows if adding α as an axiom does not result in a contradiction. C is called a *pseudo-predicate* since it is not part of the formal language; you cannot prove theorems of the form $C(\alpha)$. Figure 3.16 lists the general form for two types of special-purpose rules of inference in which, for any particular instance of the general form, α and β correspond to particular wffs. Note that the forms shown in Figure 3.16 are *not* schemas such as those shown in Figures 3.2 and 3.4; you cannot substitute any wffs for α and β.

The first type of rule represented in Figure 3.16 is called a *default rule of inference*. The idea is that if we can prove some necessary condition α, and β is consistent with the theory, then we can conclude β.[6] We would not want to allow the substitution of any α and β, but here is an instance of the general type shown in Figure 3.16 that we may wish to add to a theory.

$$
\begin{array}{lll}
1. & \text{engineer}(x) & \\
2. & C(\text{practical}(x)) & \\
\hline
3. & \text{practical}(x) & \text{PR: 1, 2}
\end{array}
$$

The default rule PR says that an engineer is practical if it is consistent to believe so.

Taken by itself, a rule such as PR may seem innocuous. However, it is possible for default rules to come into contention with one another. For

---

[6]The pseudo-predicate C complicates both the syntactic notion of proof and the semantics for logics involving default rules of inference. C introduces a circularity into the traditional concept of proof; the concept of proof uses the notion of an immediate consequence of a rule of inference that may involve C, which is concerned with whether or not one can prove a contradiction.

example, suppose that we add the following rule,

1.	scientist(x)
2.	C(theoretical(x))
3.	theoretical(x) TH: 1, 2

along with the (erroneous) belief that someone cannot be both practical and theoretical, $\forall x$, theoretical(x) ≡ ¬practical(x), and that Lynn is both a scientist, scientist(Lynn), and an engineer, engineer(Lynn). Now we can add only one of theoretical(Lynn) or practical(Lynn) to the theory without making the theory inconsistent. This means that we can apply only one of the two rules PR or TH. In monotonic logic, the order in which you apply rules of inference does not affect what theorems you can derive. In some nonmonotonic logics, however, the order does make a difference.

The second form of nonmonotonic rule of inference shown in Figure 3.16 is called an *abductive rule of inference*. Abduction warrants concluding the antecedent of an implication given the consequent if doing so is consistent. Such a rule is often invoked in diagnostic reasoning. For example, if there is no gas in your car, then it will not start. Using abduction, if your car will not start, you might conclude that it is out of gas, assuming that you have no reason to believe otherwise (perhaps you just filled the tank). The following rule of inference captures this diagnostic strategy:

1.	¬gas(x) ⊃ ¬start(x)
2.	¬start(x)
3.	C(¬gas(x))
4.	¬gas(x) NG: 1, 2, 3

We return to abductive reasoning and reasoning with incomplete and uncertain information in Chapter 8.

Minimal Models

Yet another approach to nonmonotonic logic is based on the notion of *minimal models*. To illustrate, consider the following rule:

$\forall x$, (bird(x) ∧ ¬ abnormal(x)) ⊃ flies(x)

Given bird(Ralph), we can prove flies(Ralph) if we can also prove Ralph is normal. It may be that we cannot prove ¬abnormal(Ralph), but suppose that we are generally willing to conclude that someone is normal unless we can prove otherwise. Using the definition of validity for propositional logic, such a conclusion is not likely to be valid given that there will be interpretations in which abnormal(Ralph) is True and those in which it will be False. In the following, we provide an alternative notion of validity that is concerned only with interpretations that are minimally abnormal (maximally normal).

To define the notion of a minimally abnormal interpretation, we introduce a preference relation over interpretations. We prefer one interpretation I_1 over another I_2 (written $I_1 \gg I_2$) if the following conditions are met:

1. I_1 and I_2 agree on the interpretation of all function and relation symbols other than abnormal.
2. For all x if $I_1 \models \text{abnormal}(x)$, then $I_2 \models \text{abnormal}(x)$.
3. There exists some x, for which $I_2 \models \text{abnormal}(x)$, but $I_1 \not\models \text{abnormal}(x)$.

In other words, one interpretation is preferred to another if they differ only in that the former satisfies a proper subset of the abnormalities of the latter. An interpretation I is minimally abnormal if there is no other interpretation I' such that $I' \gg I$.

If we relax our notion of validity to correspond to satisfiability in all minimally abnormal interpretations, then in the theory consisting of bird(Ralph) and $\forall x, (\text{bird}(x) \land \neg \text{abnormal}(x)) \supset \text{flies}(x)$, the formula $\neg$abnormal(Ralph) will be True in all minimally abnormal interpretations and hence so will be flies(Ralph).

In the approach using minimally abnormal interpretations, we retained the syntax of $\mathcal{PC}$, but we changed the semantics. Unfortunately, our formal systems for $\mathcal{P}$ and $\mathcal{PC}$ are not sufficient to produce a sound and complete theory for this alternative semantical theory. However, the literature on nonmonotonic logic contains a variety of proof techniques that build naturally on the formal systems described earlier in this chapter.

The issues concerning nonmonotonic reasoning in general and nonmonotonic logic in particular form an important subarea of artificial intelligence. A comprehensive treatment of the technical issues is beyond the scope of this text, but we will address particular issues regarding nonmonotonic reasoning in the following chapters.

3.8 Deductive Retrieval Systems

There is more to logical inference than proving theorems. A *deductive retrieval system* refers to any system that stores knowledge in the form of rules and implements procedures for drawing conclusions from that knowledge. Deductive retrieval systems are similar in some respects to theorem proving systems, but are generally tailored for a particular type of problem solving. Most expert systems can be characterized as deductive retrieval systems.

One thing that both deductive retrieval systems and theorem provers have in common is that they represent knowledge symbolically and declaratively. A typical deductive retrieval system consists of a database of facts and rules, and a collection of procedures that operate on that database, answering queries, noticing when certain conclusions are warranted, expanding the facts and rules as new data are added, and cleaning up when data are withdrawn. In this section, we consider some of these component procedures.

The database in most deductive retrieval systems is more than a passive repository for facts and rules. Often when you add or remove an item from a database you initiate a complex set of processes. Some of those processes might reorganize the database for easier data retrieval. In some databases, predicate calculus formulas are stored in a structure called a *discrimination tree* that speeds the search for such formulas. In Chapter 4, we describe discrimination trees in some detail.

Often the information stored in a database is supplemented as well as organized. For example, suppose that the database contains the predicate-calculus formulas (precedes a b) and (precedes b c). Precedes is generally represented as a transitive relation. Given a set of formulas representing precedence between pairs of elements, the *transitive closure* of that set is a set, including the original formulas plus any formulas that are implied by transitivity. Given (precedes a b) and (precedes b c), a deductive retrieval system might add (precedes a c) thereby completing the transitive closure of the two formulas. By storing conclusions in the database, the system can avoid having to derive the same information repeatedly.

Databases do not simply grow monotonically; information can be deleted from the database. This requires that, if we automatically extend the information in the database with conclusions warranted by the data, then we also have to retract those conclusions when the data they depend on are removed. We consider methods for handling data dependencies later in this section.

Forward and Backward Chaining

Inference in deductive retrieval systems is initiated by adding and deleting information and by asking queries. *Forward and backward chaining* are standard methods for performing inference in deductive retrieval systems. A typical forward chaining rule consists of an action part and a conditional part,

$$(A \text{ if } P_1, \dots, P_n)$$

where the P_i correspond to propositions that must be present in the database before performing the action A. The action in a forward chaining rule might correspond to adding something to the database, deleting something from the database, or even running a Lisp program.

You have already been introduced to backward chaining rules. The rules that we introduced in describing goal reduction are a form of backward chaining rule. As a backward chaining rule, the rule

$$(Q \text{ if } P_1, \dots, P_n)$$

is interpreted procedurally as, if you want to prove Q, it suffices to prove $P_1 \wedge \ldots \wedge P_n$. As a forward chaining rule, the same rule is interpreted procedurally as, if you have added P_1 through P_n to the database, then you should add Q as well.

Unification is used to instantiate the variables in forward and backward chaining rules. Deductive retrieval systems are used to perform complex computations disguised as deductions. Some of the most frequently performed computations involve answering questions posed as logical formulas and drawing selected conclusions that follow from the addition of a particular formula to the database. The former is usually handled by some form of backward chaining such as described earlier in this chapter. The latter is often referred to as *pattern-directed inference* and primarily involves forward chaining.

Pattern-directed inference systems (also called *production* or *blackboard* systems) perform computations by forward chaining. A computation is initiated by adding a formula to the database. This formula is matched against the antecedents of forward chaining rules in the database and combined with other formulas in the database that match other antecedents to draw additional conclusions.

As an example, suppose that the database contains the fact (precedes b c) and the rule ((precedes (? x) (? z)) if (precedes (? x) (? y)) (precedes (? y) (? z))) and the user asserts (precedes a b). Here is a step-by-step account of how a pattern-directed inference system might respond to such a query. First of all, the system tries to match (precedes a b) against the antecedents of rules in the database. In particular, the system obtains the following match for the first antecedent of the mentioned rule:

```
> (setq rule '((precedes (? x) (? z)) if
               (precedes (? x) (? y)) (precedes (? y) (? z))))
((PRECEDES (? X) (? Z)) IF (PRECEDES (? X) (? Y))
                          (PRECEDES (? Y) (? Z)))
> (setq bdgs (unify '(precedes a b)
                   (first (antecedents rule))))
(((? Y) B) ((? X) A) (UNIFY T))
```

It uses the resulting substitution to instantiate the rule. Instantiation is performed using a function varsubst, which performs a sequence of substitutions on a quantified formula; varsubst is given as an exercise at the end of this chapter.

```
> (setq rule (varsubst rule bdgs))
((PRECEDES A (? Z)) IF (PRECEDES A B) (PRECEDES B (? Z)))
```

Next the system finds a match for the second antecedent and obtains the consequent of the rule as a conclusion.

```
> (setq bdgs (unify '(precedes b c)
                    (second (antecedents rule)))))
(((? Z) C) (UNIFY T))
> (consequent (varsubst rule bdgs))
(PRECEDES A C)
```

After trying all the other rules in the database with (precedes a b), the system asserts all the conclusions each one in turn just as if the user asserted them. The system continues in this manner until no new assertions are made. The literature on pattern-directed inference systems abounds with sophisticated techniques for expediting this process. The addition of a single assertion typically results in the recursive addition of many other assertions. Removing assertions from the database is a bit more complicated.

Reason Maintenance Systems

Suppose the proposition Q is added to the database on the basis of P and P $\supset$ Q being in the database. It would be useful to have an automatic method of removing Q if P is ever removed.

More generally, we would like to be able to require that a particular formula should be present in the database whenever certain other facts and rules are present (or absent) in the database. For example, when programming a robot, a programmer might specify that as long as all the sensors report no objects within five meters, the robot should maintain its top speed. *Reason maintenance systems* perform computations on noticing when particular facts and rules change. We describe one simple form of reason maintenance next.

A *dependency graph* specifies how items that might be stored in a database depend on one another. A dependency graph is used to keep track of which items are actually stored in the database; to do so effectively, it often has to refer to items that were deleted from or never added to the database. For example, a dependency graph can represent that Q should be in the database whenever P and P $\supset$ Q are in the database. IN is used to indicate that an item is in the database and OUT to indicate that it is not in the database. A dependency graph consists of nodes that are labeled IN or OUT, and connections between nodes that are called *justifications*. A justification connects a set of nodes called the *justifiers* of the justification to a single node called the *justificand* of the justification.

The basic types of justifications are shown in Figure 3.17 with nodes in the dependency graph shown as squares and justifications shown as circles. A *premise* is a node with a justification having no justifiers (see Figure 3.17a). Many justifications involve one or more justifiers (see Figure 3.17b) and nodes often have more than one justification (see Figure 3.17c).

To maintain a dependency graph, we must correctly assign labels to the nodes in the graph as items are added to and deleted from the database. An

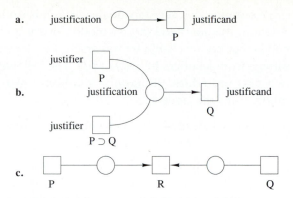

Figure 3.17   Premises and justifications

assignment of labels to nodes is *consistent* if, for each justification, whenever all the justification's justifiers are labeled IN, the justification's justificand is labeled IN. An assignment of labels to nodes is *well-founded* if, for each node labeled IN, there is some justification whose justificand is the node and whose justifiers are all labeled IN. We want to compute a consistent and well-founded assignment of labels to all the nodes in a dependency graph.

Note that it is possible to have circular data dependencies. For example, consider the dependency graph shown in Figure 3.18. Assigning IN to all nodes is a consistent and well-founded assignment for the graph of Figure 3.18. If we were to remove justification J1, the resulting consistent and well-founded assignment of labels would assign IN to D2 and OUT to all other nodes.

The standard operations on dependency graphs include adding a justification to a node and deleting a justification from a node. After each addition or deletion, the graph is updated by computing a consistent and well-founded assignment of labels to all nodes. Updating the dependency graph is done in two passes. In the first pass, the old labels are erased and marked as having been visited. In the second pass, new labels are assigned, and these assignments are propagated along justifications from justifiers to justificands.

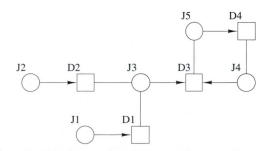

Figure 3.18   Circular data dependencies

Assuming that the dependency graph is updated after each addition or deletion, it is not necessary to modify every node in the graph, only those nodes that are reachable by traversing the dependency graph along justifications from justifiers to justificands. The following algorithm describes the two-pass procedure. Suppose that we have just added or deleted a justification from the node n.

1 Set the labels of all reachable nodes to visited by applying the following recursive subroutine starting from n:
   a) If the node is already labeled visited, then return nil.
   b) If the node is not labeled visited, then label it so, and apply this subroutine recursively to all the justificands of the node.

In the worst case, this subroutine runs in time proportional to the size of the graph.

2 Relabel all the nodes by applying the following recursive subroutine starting from n:
   a) If the node has some justification all of whose justifiers are IN, then set the label of the node to IN; otherwise, set the label of the node to OUT.
   b) If the label of the node was changed in the previous step, then apply this subroutine recursively to all the justificands of the node.

This subroutine computes a consistent and well-founded assignment of labels for all nodes in the dependency graph. In the worst case, it runs in time proportional to the square of the size of the graph.

Nonmonotonic Data Dependencies

There is a nonmonotonic extension to the preceding scheme in which the justifiers in a justification are divided into IN justifiers and OUT justifiers. For a justification to warrant its justificand being IN, all its IN justifiers must be IN, and all its OUT justifiers must be OUT.

For example, suppose you believe that all engineers have practical inclinations unless known to be theoretical. For a particular person p, this rule is encoded in the dependency graph of Figure 3.19a, where the node marked + is an IN justifier and the node marked − is an OUT justifier. Figure 3.19a specifies that practical(p) should be in the database whenever engineer(p) is in the database and theoretical(p) is not in the database.

Nonmonotonic data dependencies have some of the same complications that arise in nonmonotonic logics. Suppose that you also believe that all scientists have theoretical inclinations unless known to be practical and that p is a scientist as well as an engineer. Now we have the same problem that arose in our discussion of default rules in nonmonotonic logic. The dependency graph in Figure 3.19b has two consistent and well-founded assignments to the labels of its nodes.

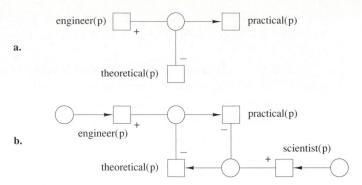

Figure 3.19   Nonmonotonic data dependencies

There are a variety of reason maintenance systems, each of which is suited to a particular range of tasks. Our discussion provides just a glimpse into the techniques and issues. Reason maintenance systems keep track of conclusions derived from facts and rules and automatically retract conclusions that are no longer warranted as a result of changes to the facts and rules. In some cases, a reason maintenance system can improve the performance of a deductive retrieval system by allowing the system to avoid repeatedly deriving the same conclusions. However, the designer of a deductive retrieval system has to be careful to ensure that the time spent in updating the dependency graph does not actually end up degrading performance.

▼ Summary

This chapter is concerned with using logic to represent knowledge about the world. In expert systems, knowledge is represented in the form of rules that are used to carry out tasks usually performed by expert humans. Most expert systems rely on some variant of logical inference to justify their basic operations.

Propositional logic is a theory of those logical truths that can be expressed using propositional variables and truth-functional propositional connectives. Normal forms are used to restrict the syntax of a logic to provide conventions for specifying knowledge in databases. Formal systems provide axioms and rules of inference such as modus ponens to construct proofs. A proof is a sequence of inferential steps sanctioned by the axioms and rules of inference of a formal system. A theorem is the result of a step in a proof.

We provide a semantic theory for propositional logic in terms of interpretations that assign True or False to each formula. A formula is satisfiable if there exists some interpretation that assigns the formula True. Determining if a proposition is satisfiable is computationally difficult. This complexity forces us to consider tradeoffs in designing representations based on logic.

Intuitively, a formal system is complete if you can prove everything that you should be able to prove, sound if you cannot prove anything that you should not be able to prove, and decidable if you can determine whether or not something is a theorem in a finite number of steps. In theory, we would like our formal systems to be sound, complete, and decidable; in practice, we have to make concessions by restricting the syntax for representing knowledge about the world.

Predicate calculus builds on the propositional logic by adding functions, variables, and quantifiers. Predicate calculus allows us to quantify over infinite domains and provides a compact representation for finite domains. We add universal instantiation to the rules of inference for the propositional logic to prove theorems involving quantified formulas. Matching and unification allow us to employ universal instantiation for automatic theorem proving involving quantified formulas.

Explanation-based generalization is a learning technique that relies on deductive inference and is used to improve the performance of automated reasoning systems. Systems that use explanation-based generalization solve problems, analyze the steps taken during problem solving, and then derive expressions to speed future problem solving.

Concept description languages allow us to encode knowledge about objects, classes, and the properties of objects and classes. Graph traversal algorithms operating on semantic networks constitute a special case of automated theorem proving applied to concept description languages. By representing a proper subset of the predicate calculus, concept description languages trade expressiveness for efficiency of inference.

In monotonic logics, adding axioms adds only to the set of theorems. In nonmonotonic logics, adding axioms may force us to retract statements that were previously sanctioned. The closed-world assumption licenses a particular sort of nonmonotonic inference that allows us to draw conclusions on the basis of the absence of information. Special rules of inference can be used to support nonmonotonic inference involving default and diagnostic reasoning.

Deductive retrieval systems are concerned with practical methods for logical inference. Such systems employ strategies for forward and backward chaining to expedite answering questions posed as logical formulas. Deductive retrieval systems often make use of reason maintenance systems to keep track of the justifications for adding and removing information from a database.

In Chapter 2, we mentioned that Lisp is based on a logic (and formal system) called the Lambda calculus. The two primary rules of inference used in the Lambda calculus are known as *beta reduction* and *lambda ab-*

straction. In beta reduction, an expression is reduced to a simpler one. For instance, we obtain 5 from (+ 2 3) by beta reduction. In lambda abstraction, we abstract a general procedure from a particular expression by creating a lambda function in which we replace certain subexpressions by variables. For instance, we obtain (lambda (x) (+ x 3)) from (+ 2 3) by lambda abstraction. Ignoring side effects (the results of setq and defun), the Lisp evaluator can be thought of as applying rules of inference to determine the value of Lisp expressions. In this chapter, we show how it is possible to perform computations by proving theorems, further illustrating the close connection between logic and computation.

● **Background**

For more about expert systems in general, see Jackson [1990]. For more about the MYCIN expert system in particular, see Shortliffe [1976]. MYCIN uses backward chaining as its primary method of inference. Davis [1982] describes automated methods for acquiring and managing a large database of MYCIN rules. XCON is described by McDermott [1982]. Barker and O'Connor [1989] provide an interesting industrial perspective on the effectiveness of XCON. XCON uses forward chaining as its primary method of inference. For more on the use of expert systems at the American Express Company, see Dzierzanowsk et al. [1992]. For more on the application of expert systems in manufacturing, see Schorr and Rappaport [1989].

For a good general introduction to formal logic, read Mendelson [1979]. For more on the metatheory of first-order logic covering consistency, completeness, and decidability, read Hunter [1973]. Manna and Waldinger [1983] provide an excellent introduction to logic for computer scientists. Schagrin et al. [1985] present propositional and predicate logic along with programs for automated theorem proving.

The resolution rule of inference is due to Robinson [1965] and was critical in the development of practical automated theorem-proving systems. For more on automated theorem proving with applications in program analysis and synthesis, see Chang and Lee [1973]. Wos et al. [1984] provide thorough coverage of automated theorem-proving techniques along with applications in circuit validation, real-time control, and expert systems. For an introduction to explanation-based generalization techniques, see Chapters 4 and 5 of the collection edited by Shavlik and Dietterich [1990].

For an introduction to Prolog, see Bratko [1986], Clocksin and Mellish [1987], or Sterling and Shapiro [1986]. Shoham [1994] provides a more advanced treatment of AI programming techniques in Prolog, including reason maintenance systems and pattern-directed inference. Kowalski [1979] offers insights into using logic for automated problem solving.

See Brachman [1985] for an overview of issues concerning semantic networks, concept description languages, and related issues in knowledge representation. Minsky [1975] is generally credited with the idea of building representations that collect and encapsulate all the knowledge pertaining to individual objects and of recognizing the computational advantages of such representations. Schank and Abelson [1977] demonstrated how such representations could be used to explain and simulate high-level cognitive capabilities.

For more about nonmonotonic reasoning, see Genesereth and Nilsson [1987] or Davis [1990] for excellent overviews of the basic techniques. Our treatment of default rules of inference is based on a theory by Reiter [1980]. Our treatment of preferences over interpretations is based on the preferential semantics of Shoham [1986]. You might also want to read some other early foundational papers, particularly McCarthy's theory of circumscription [1980] and McDermott and Doyle's nonmonotonic modal theories [1980].

Charniak et al. [1987] describe how to implement in Lisp a variety of deductive retrieval and reason maintenance systems (also called *truth maintenance systems* in the literature). Forbus and de Kleer [1994] provide more depth on deductive retrieval systems with an especially detailed treatment of reason maintenance systems. Waterman and Hayes-Roth [1978] edited a collection of articles on pattern-directed inference using forward chaining.

■ Exercises

3.1 Use the axiom schemata AS1-3 and the rule of inference modus ponens to prove $P \supset P$.

3.2 Consider the sentence "Heads I win; tails you lose." We can represent this sentence plus associated domain knowledge in the propositional logic using the following proper axioms, where Heads, Tails, WinMe, and LoseYou are propositional variables:

```
Heads  ⊃  WinMe
Tails  ⊃  LoseYou
¬ Heads  ⊃  Tails
LoseYou  ⊃  WinMe
```

   a) Determine if it is possible to prove WinMe using just the rule of inference modus ponens and these four axioms.
   b) Convert each of the four axioms to a disjunction of literals.
   c) For each of the resulting disjunctions, specify if it is a Horn clause.
   d) Determine if it is possible to prove WinMe using just the resolution rule of inference and the four axioms written as disjunctions of literals.

3.3 Design a Lisp representation for propositional formulas. You will have to map nonalphanumeric symbols to alphanumeric ones (e.g., ∨ maps to OR, ≡ maps to IFF). You may find it easier to use prefix rather than infix notation (e.g., (AND A B C) rather than (A AND B AND C)). You may also find it easier to deal with boolean operators that take only two arguments (e.g., ((A AND B) AND C) rather than (A AND B AND C)). To make use of your design, write a recursive function to eliminate implication in a formula by replacing subexpressions of the form $(A \supset B)$ with $(\neg A \lor B)$. Your implementation should expand equivalences so that expressions of the form $A \equiv B$ are replaced by $(A \supset B) \land (B \supset A)$ and the implications subsequently eliminated.

3.4 Using the representation developed for Exercise 3.3, write a recursive function to convert an arbitrary formula in $\mathcal{P}$ into conjunctive normal form. Justify each step in terms of de Morgan's laws,

$$\neg(A_1 \wedge \ldots \wedge A_n) \equiv (\neg A_1 \vee \ldots \vee \neg A_n)$$
$$\neg(A_1 \vee \ldots \vee A_n) \equiv (\neg A_1 \wedge \ldots \wedge \neg A_n)$$

the fact that $\vee$ and $\wedge$ are commutative (e.g., $(A \wedge B) \equiv (B \wedge A)$), distributive (e.g., $((A \wedge B) \vee C) \equiv ((A \vee C) \wedge (B \vee C)))$, and associative (e.g., $((A \wedge B) \wedge C) \equiv (A \wedge (B \wedge C)))$, and the rule that two negations cancel $\neg(\neg A) \equiv A$. The following steps provide an algorithm for carrying out the conversion:

a) Eliminate implication using $(A \supset B) \equiv (\neg A \vee B)$.

b) Move negation in as far as possible using de Morgan's laws.

c) Distribute $\wedge$ and $\vee$ so that you can write the formula as a conjunction of disjunctions.

d) Cancel double negations wherever possible.

3.5 In the housing lottery example, we started to prove a ranking in the lottery for the four students, Bob, Lisa, Jim, and Mary. Our objective in this exercise is to complete the proof and derive the following formula:

```
(Mary-ahead-of-Bob ∧ Bob-ahead-of-Jim ∧ Jim-ahead-of-Lisa)
```

With a little work, you should be able to conclude that Jim is immediately ahead of either Mary or Lisa in the ranking.

```
(Jim-ahead-of-Mary ∨ Jim-ahead-of-Lisa)
```

From this formula and the following disjunction that we derived in the text, you would like to arrive at the desired conclusion.

```
((Mary-ahead-of-Bob   ∧ Bob-ahead-of-Jim   ∧ Jim-ahead-of-Lisa) ∨
 (Lisa-ahead-of-Mary  ∧ Mary-ahead-of-Bob  ∧ Bob-ahead-of-Jim))
```

Unfortunately, the desired conclusion does not follow logically. The problem is that Jim-ahead-of-Lisa does not contradict the second disjunct of the disjunction. To complete the proof, we need an alternative method of representing a complete ranking. The following representation will suit our purposes:

```
(Nobody-ahead-of-Lisa ∧ Lisa-ahead-of-Mary ∧
 Mary-ahead-of-Bob ∧ Bob-ahead-of-Jim ∧ Jim-ahead-of-Nobody)
```

Modify the formulas representing the housing lottery problem, and complete the proof of the ranking.

3.6 In this exercise, we consider an alternative implementation for theorem. Let the status of a proposition be one of {new, working, t, nil}, where t indicates that the proposition is a theorem, nil indicates that it is not, working indicates that we are in the process of trying to prove the proposition, and new that we have yet to encounter the proposition.

In the following, assume that the three operations corresponding to (a) determining the status of a proposition, (b) setting the status of a proposition, and (c) retrieving the list of possible reductions licensed by the various rules associated with a given proposition can be done in constant time independent of the number of proposition symbols or the size of the database of rules. This is not true of the following implementations, but with a little extra effort we could provide such constant-time operations. Set is like setq except that it evaluates its first argument, which must evaluate to a symbol. With a somewhat more complicated data structure for representing propositional variables, we could avoid the use of eval and set.

```
(defun status (p) (eval p))
(defun set-status (p s) (set p s))
(defun reductions (p)
  (rest (assoc p '((P (U V) (Q R)) (Q (S)) (U (P W)
                  (S U)) (S ()) (R ()))))))
```

We assume that all the proposition symbols initially have the status new. In the following, (every #'f l) is non-nil just in case f applied to each element of l is non-nil. Similarly (some #'f l) is non-nil just in case f applied to at least one element of l is non-nil. Recall that t and nil evaluate to themselves.

```
(defun theorem (p)
  (cond ((eq (status p) t) t)
        ((not (eq (status p) 'new)) nil)
        (t (set-status p 'working)
           (if (some #'(lambda (c) (every #'theorem c))
                     (reductions p))
               (set-status p t)
             (set-status p nil)))))
```

Prove that theorem runs in time linear in the size of the database and that, for any proposition P and database T expressed in the preceding format, theorem will return non-nil for P if and only if P is a consequence of T.

3.7 Represent the following English sentences using predicate calculus:
   a) Every cruise ship was accompanied by at least one tug.
   b) At least one tanker was accompanied by more than one tug.
   c) The governor's top aides issued conflicting statements.
   d) All the fishing boats but one returned safely to port.
   e) There are problems that have no solutions.
   f) John is taller than any of the other students.
   g) There are exactly two students with a grade less than B.

3.8 We represent the statement that everything is representable in predicate calculus as $\forall x,$ represents(pc,x). General Problem Solver (GPS) is a system for automated problem solving discussed in Chapter 7 [Ernst, Newell, and Simon, 1969]. We represent the statement that all problems representable in predicate calculus are solvable using GPS as $\forall x,$ (problem(x) $\land$ represents(pc,x)) $\supset$ solves(gps,x). (By the way, neither of these two statements is strictly true.) Now using these two statements and the fact that the Traveling Salesperson Problem (TSP) is a problem (problem(tsp)), prove that GPS solves it.

3.9 Provide arguments to justify the following equivalences:

(∃ x, competent(x)) ≡ (¬∀ x, ¬ competent(x))
((∀ x, black(x)) ∨ (∀ y, white(y))) ≡
(∀ x,y, (black(x) ∨ white(y)))
(∀ x, ((∃ y, loves(x,y)) ⊃ happy(x))) ≡
(∀ x,y, (loves(x,y) ⊃ happy(x)))

3.10 Convert the following sentences into a form in which all the quantifiers are as far to the left as possible (e.g., (∀x, ∃y, φ), where φ contains no quantifiers):

(∀ x, ((∃ y, loves(x,y) ∨ loves(y,x)) ⊃ happy(x)))
(∀ x, happy(x) ⊃ (∃ y, loves(x,y)))
((∀ x, black(x)) ∧ ¬(∃ x, white(x))) ∨ (∀ x, white(x))

3.11 The general algorithm for eliminating quantifiers is as follows.
   a) Eliminate implication to expose negation using $(A \supset B) \equiv (\neg A \vee B)$.
   b) Move negation in as far as possible using de Morgan's laws (see Exercise 3.4 for a listing of de Morgan's laws) and $(\forall x, \varphi) \equiv \neg(\exists x, \neg\varphi)$, where φ is an arbitrary formula in which x may appear free.
   c) Standardize variables apart.
   d) Use Skolemization to eliminate existentials.
   e) Move the quantifiers to the outside.
   f) Eliminate the quantifiers making sure that variables are distinguished from constants.

Implement the algorithm in Lisp using your solution to Exercise 3.3 augmented to handle quantifiers.

3.12 Modify theorem to handle quantified conjuncts. In particular, write a recursive function varsubst to make substitutions in quantified formulas and a function rename that substitutes new variable names for existing names in quantified formulas. To implement rename, use the Lisp function gensym, which creates a brand new symbol each time it is called. (make-VAR (gensym)) creates a new variable.

3.13 In this exercise, we introduce the function cons to reason about membership in lists. Using cons, the list (a b) would be represented as (cons a (cons b ())). The following two rules illustrate how we might implement member for use with the extended version of theorem described in Exercise 3.12:

((member (? x) (cons (? x) (? y))))
((member (? x) (cons (? z) (? y))) if (member (? x) (? y)))

Write similar rules to implement append and reverse.

3.14 *Vivid* reasoning is a strategy for coping with complexity arising from incompleteness [Levesque, 1986]. Incompleteness can arise from disjunction (e.g., given red(car32) ∨ green(car32), car32 could be red or it could be green), existential quantification (e.g., given ∃x, red(x), car32 could be red or something else could be red), and negation (e.g., given ¬red(car32), car32 could be green, blue, or some other color besides red).

   In this exercise, we consider problems that arise from disjunction. For instance, suppose that you want to prove to yourself that your friend will call you and you only know that your friend is either at home or at the office. From the axioms home $\lor$ office, home $\supset$ call, and office $\supset$ call, you can prove call using a disjunctive proof.[7] However, in general, such proofs can lead to combinatorial explosion. Suppose that we throw caution to the wind and arbitrarily select one of the disjuncts and pretend that it is true; this idea forms the basis of a general strategy for dealing with disjunctions. In the example, we might select home, and then prove call.

a) As presented, the strategy outlined here can lead to problems. Indicate why. Consider tautologies and the disjunctive form of implications.

b) Consider the following restricted syntactic form, based on Horn clauses: $(C_1 \land \ldots C_n) \supset (D_1 \lor \ldots D_m)$, where C_i and D_i are positive literals. Using this restricted form, we represent the example by the following three clauses, true $\supset$ (home $\lor$ office), home $\supset$ call, and office $\supset$ call, where true is an axiom. Now specify a decision procedure based on the aforementioned approach to implement tractable (polynomial time) inference for the restricted language presented. Your procedure need not be sound or it may be sound but occasionally return "maybe" instead of "yes" or "no." Consider only the propositional case.

c) Consider situations in which the approach to vivid reasoning is likely to be advantageous and those in which it is likely to lead to problems.

3.15 Write a pair of recursive functions, element and insert, that operate on a database and take care of adding to and retrieving items from the database. The database is implemented as a variable (local to insert and element) bound to a list of expressions. Each function takes a single argument corresponding to an item to be added or checked for membership. Insert adds an item to the end of the database if it is not already present, using equal to determine membership. Element checks if the item is present by going through the list one item at a time checking for membership using equal. If the item is present, then the database is reorganized so that the item is one step closer to the front of the list and the element returns t; otherwise, element returns nil. Over time, the most frequently checked for items will bubble up to the front of the list. If the database is initially (A B C D), then (element 'C) will result in (A C B D). If we repeat (element 'C), then the database will look like (C A B D).

3.16 Modify delete-just so that it uses a different test function than equal to find and remove a justification from a node in a dependency graph. The current implementation relies on two justifications being equal.

3.17 Write a simple production system. In particular, write a recursive function assert that adds a formula to the database and then performs forward chaining.

3.18 Building on the previous exercise, add dependencies to your production system, and implement a function retract that "removes" a formula from the database along with all the additional formulas that depend on it. Rather than physically removing items from the database, your implementation should simply mark items in the database as either IN or OUT and forward chain accordingly.

---

[7]In a disjunctive proof, to prove r from p $\lor$ q, show that r follows given p and r follows given q.

▶ LISP IMPLEMENTATION

Data Dependencies

In this section, we define Lisp procedures for creating and modifying data dependency graphs. We begin with the data structures for representing dependency graphs.

An instance of the abstract data type node consists of a name, a label IN or OUT, a list of its justifications, and a list of the nodes that it justifies. Each justification is represented as a list of justifiers.

```
(defun make-NODE (name) (list name 'OUT () ()))
(defun NODE-label (node) (second node))
(defun NODE-justifications (node) (third node))
(defun NODE-justificands (node) (fourth node))
```

All the elements of a node are settable except name, which is specified when an instance of type node is created.

```
(defun set-NODE-label (node l) (setf (second node) l))
(defun set-NODE-justifications (node j) (setf (third node) j))
(defun set-NODE-justificands (node j) (setf (fourth node) j))
```

Add a justification to an existing dependency node.

```
(defun add-justification (node justification)
  (set-NODE-justifications node
    (cons justification (NODE-justifications node)))
  (mapc #'(lambda (n)
            (set-NODE-justificands n
              (cons node (NODE-justificands node))))
        justification)
  (update-dependency-graph node))
```

Delete a justification from an existing dependency node. We use remove and its optional :test argument to invoke equal to find and remove a justification from a list of justifications and a justificand from a list of justificands. This simple approach has some limitations that you are challenged to overcome in the exercises at the end of this chapter.

```
(defun delete-justification (node justification)
  (set-NODE-justifications node
    (remove justification (NODE-justifications node)
            :test #'equal))
  (mapc #'(lambda (n)
            (set-NODE-justificands n
              (remove node (NODE-justificands node)
                      :test #'equal)))
        justification)
  (update-dependency-graph node))
```

Update a dependency graph in two passes starting from node. The first pass erases the existing labels of all reachable nodes and relabels them as visited. The second pass assigns new labels to all reachable nodes.

```
(defun update-dependency-graph (node)
  (erase-labels node)
  (relabel node))
```

Label as visited all nodes reachable from node by traversing justifications from justifiers to justificands.

```
(defun erase-labels (node)
  (cond ((eq (NODE-label node) 'VISITED) nil)
        (t (set-NODE-label node 'VISITED)
           (mapc #'erase-labels (NODE-justificands node)))))
```

Propagate labels forward along justifications from justifiers to justificands starting from node. If the label at a node does not require changing, then stop propagating labels forward.

```
(defun relabel (node)
  (let ((label (if (consistent node) 'IN 'OUT)))
    (cond ((eq (NODE-label node) label) nil)
          (t (set-NODE-label node label)
             (mapc #'relabel (NODE-justificands node))))))
```

It is consistent to label a node IN if it has some justification all of whose justifiers are labeled IN; otherwise, it should be labeled OUT. As we described in Chapter 2, every and some are similar in form and operation to mapcar. The invocation (every *test args*) returns t if every application of *test* to some cross section of *args* returns non-nil and nil otherwise. The invocation (some *test args*) returns t if at least one invocation of *test* on some cross section of *args* returns non-nil and nil otherwise.

```
(defun consistent (node)
  (some #'justified (NODE-justifications node)))
```

Check to see if all the justifiers of a justification are labeled IN.

```
(defun justified (justification)
  (every #'(lambda (node) (eq (NODE-label node) 'IN))
         justification))
```

With this code, we can build the dependency graph of Figure 3.18 and test the code using the examples given in the text.

```lisp
(let ((D1 (make-NODE 'D1))
      (D2 (make-NODE 'D2))
      (D3 (make-NODE 'D3))
      (D4 (make-NODE 'D4)))
  (add-justification D1 ())
  (add-justification D2 ())
  (add-justification D3 (list D1 D2))
  (add-justification D4 (list D3))
  (add-justification D3 (list D4))
  (defun test ()
    (let (test1-result test2-result)
      ;; The label of D3 should be IN.
      (setq test1-result (eq 'IN (NODE-label D3)))
      ;; Delete the only justification from D1.
      (delete-justification D1 ())
      ;; Now the label of D3 should be OUT.
      (setq test2-result (eq 'OUT (NODE-label D3)))
      ;; The function test should return t.
      (and test1-result test2-result))))
```

CHAPTER 4

SEARCH

Suppose you are preparing for a vacation and need airline tickets, car rentals, and hotel accommodations to suit your complicated itinerary. You may have to consider many combinations of flights, cars, and hotels before finding one that satisfies your requirements. In addition to just being in particular places at particular times, there are generally other considerations. You would like to save money but at the same time you want reliable airlines, comfortable cars, and quality hotels. It would be convenient to have a system that knew your personal preferences and could find you the best possible combination of flights, car rentals, and hotels.

The travel arrangements problem of the previous paragraph is generally considered a *search* problem because we must search through many possibilities for one that satisfies specified requirements. Search problems arise often in artificial intelligence. For example, a robot vehicle would search for a route to a given destination, and an automated air traffic controller would search for a safe landing sequence for a set of incoming planes. Search problems also arise in games of strategy, such as chess or checkers, in which you search for a sequence of moves to vanquish your opponent.

Stated generally, search involves trying to find a particular object from a large number of such objects. In some cases, you do not even have to consider the other objects. For example, no search is needed to find the number

▲ AI in Practice

Scheduling Space Shuttle Maintenance

The Space Shuttle flights are popular television news features because people have an interest in the excitement of working in space. But when the Space Shuttle lands at Kennedy Space Center, the mission is not yet over. Kennedy Space Center has extensive facilities and personnel for inspecting, fixing, and testing each component of the Space Shuttle system. Preparing a Space Shuttle for a new flight is a difficult dynamic scheduling problem. Ordered parts can arrive late, and tools can break unexpectedly. Until the Space Shuttle is thoroughly inspected, no one is even sure what will need to be repaired.

The Kennedy Space Center has created a program called the Ground Processing Scheduling System (GPSS) that schedules Space Shuttle maintenance based on available personnel, time, and resources. Using a technique called constraint-based iterative repair, GPSS begins with a tangled and unusable schedule, but then resolves scheduling conflicts one by one until a workable schedule is found. Determining which parts of the schedule to fix first is a challenging search problem.

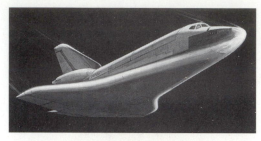

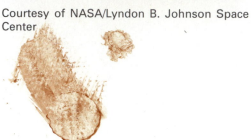

Courtesy of NASA/Lyndon B. Johnson Space Center

---

that is the product of 2 and 3. In other cases, you may need to consider and reject many objects before finding the one you are looking for. It is difficult to find the prime factorizations of large integers quickly because there are so many possibilities to search through. For this reason, private electronic messages are often encrypted using combinations of primes that are known only to the sender and receiver of the message.

What you know about a problem can significantly improve your chances of solving it quickly or determining if a solution exists at all. For example, the *four-color theorem* states that any map of countries can be colored so that no two adjacent countries are colored the same using only four colors [Appel and Haken, 1976]. However, determining whether a map can be similarly colored using only three colors is NP-complete [Karp, 1972]. If you are asked to color a map with four or more colors, then there always exists a solution though it may take some time to find. If you are asked to color a map with three colors, then just determining whether or not a solution exists may be time consuming.

In some problems, you may have no other recourse than to consider all the other objects. For example, you may have to search through all the employees in the company database to find one whose parents have the same initials. In other cases, you can reduce the time required to find a particular object by organizing the objects. For example, if you divide a database of blood donors into sections determined by blood type and further divide these sections into subsections determined by rh factor, then it is easy to find a donor with a particular blood type and rh factor. You just look in the right section and subsection of the database.

In this chapter, we consider search techniques for finding particular objects in a set of such objects by enumerating and testing some subset of those objects. We look at *blind* search techniques in which we are given no guidance in searching among the set of objects and *heuristic* search techniques in which we are given some form of guidance. We consider search techniques that are used to solve *optimization* problems in which the objective is to find the best object or at least a very good one. As a special application of search, we consider search methods for two-person games such as chess or checkers. We also describe *indexing* techniques for organizing sets of objects to reduce the number of objects examined during search.

Search problems are common in AI. Planning and learning especially make use of search techniques. Some researchers view planning as a special case of search and search as a special case of learning; certainly search is important in both planning and learning. This chapter describes general search techniques and provides background and terminology for subsequent chapters. We introduce several examples in this chapter, but you should also think of other problems that you would like a system to solve. As we describe the techniques in this chapter, think about how they might also apply to your problems.

4.1 Basic Search Issues

We begin with some examples of search problems.

- Board games like chess or checkers are often cast as search problems. In playing a game, the system searches for a move that is likely to lead to a winning configuration of pieces.

- Scheduling is often thought of in terms of search. For instance, you might appreciate a system that would figure out what classes you should register for given the classes that you have to take, the classes that you would like to take, a schedule for classes, and your preferences for class times.

- Theorem proving is also a search problem. Given a set of axioms and rules of inference, the objective in this case is to find a proof whose last line is the formula that you wish to prove.

Search Spaces and Operators

A *search space* defines the set of objects that we are interested in searching among. An object in this search space might be a configuration of pieces in a game such as chess, a registration form with zero or more classes filled in for class scheduling, or a proof in the case of proving theorems.

Objects in a search space are related to each another by *operators* that transform one object into another. A legal move in chess is an operator that transforms one configuration of pieces into another. Signing up for an additional course transforms one partially filled out class registration form into another. The application of a rule of inference such as modus ponens is an operator that transforms one proof into another.

In searching a given space, we often have a particular *goal* in mind that describes what we are searching for. For our immediate purposes, a goal is just a subset of the set of all objects in the search space. For instance, in chess the goal is the set of all configurations of pieces in which your opponent's king is in checkmate. In class scheduling, the goal might be the set of all registration forms that allow you to graduate in a total of four years having never taken a class that begins earlier than noon. In theorem proving, the goal might be the set of all proofs whose last line is the formula you are trying to prove.

Most search methods proceed by systematically applying operators and checking after each transformation whether the resulting object is an element of the goal set. In some cases, there is no useful information to guide the search. In these cases, search is said to be *blind* and must rely on exhaustive enumeration of the objects in the search space.

For our purposes, a *metric on a space* allows us to compute some measure of the distance between two objects in the space or some measure of the value of a given object in the space. It is sometimes possible to define a metric on the objects in a search space in order to provide some estimate of how close a given object is to the goal. This metric can direct the search on the assumption that applying operators to an object estimated to be close to the goal will lead to the goal more quickly than applying operators to an object more distant from the goal.

A metric for a search space is usually implemented as a comparison function or as an evaluation function. A comparison function is given two objects and determines which is estimated to be closer to the goal or which has a greater value. An evaluation function is given a single object and returns an estimate of the distance to the goal or an estimate of the object's value.

Search methods that employ metrics to guide search are called *heuristic* in that they are based on techniques that are supposed to perform well in practice but provide no iron-clad guarantees. In chess, board configurations are often ranked on the basis of a metric that accounts for (among other things) the number of pieces belonging to each player and their strategic value. In most cases, a queen is far more valuable strategically than a pawn. A class schedule might be ranked by how many classes are still required to receive a degree.

The basic steps involved in solving a given search problem are as follows:

1. Create a representation for the objects and operators.
2. Define a metric on the search space.
3. Design an efficient method for comparing or evaluating objects consistent with the metric.
4. Design an efficient method for selecting the next object to consider in searching the space.

Appliance Assembly Example

Suppose that you own a factory that assembles custom appliances. The factory consists of several robotic work cells and each work cell is capable of performing different assembly operations. For example, one work cell installs wires and makes electrical connections, and another work cell positions parts and fastens them together with screws. Each appliance requires some number of assembly operations, and these operations often depend on one another. For example, the wiring robot cannot install the power cord on a blender before the motor is fastened to the base. Mobile robots carry partially assembled appliances from one work cell to another.

Given a particular appliance, we might want to arrange the robotic work cells to form an assembly line to perform all the required assembly operations accounting for the dependencies among operations. In this case, the search space corresponds to all permutations of work cells; operators serve to reorder the work cells in a permutation. If there are n work cells, then there are $n!$ permutations. Figure 4.1a depicts one possibility for representing the search space for the mechanical assembly example for the case in which there are three work cells, notated 1, 2, and 3. In Figure 4.1a, each permutation is represented as an ordered set, and the operators serve to swap adjacent work cells starting at the root, $\{1, 2, 3\}$.

Instead of using the space of all permutations of work cells, we might consider the space of all sequences of work cells. In this case, operators would extend a sequence by adding a work cell not already in the sequence. The space of sequences properly contains the space of permutations and hence is larger, but it provides a different perspective on the problem and suggests different, possibly more efficient search procedures. Figure 4.1b shows the search space for the appliance assembly example as a tree whose nodes correspond to sequences. Each operator in Figure 4.1b adds a work cell not already present in the sequence.

It may be that no permutation corresponding to a complete ordering of the work cells will suffice to assemble the appliance. To assemble the

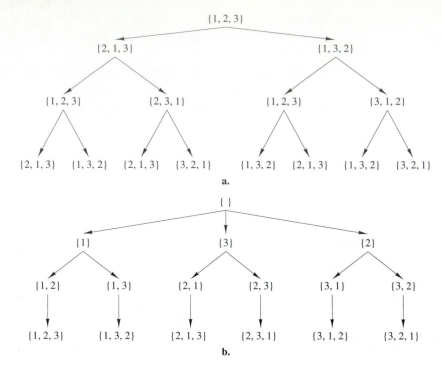

Figure 4.1   Search spaces for the appliance assembly problem

appliance, the partially assembled appliances may have to be transferred back and forth several times between the same work cells. In this case, you might want to find the shortest sequence of transfers that will result in the appliance being properly assembled. It is even possible that performing some operations may require that a previously completed operation be reversed. In this case, the appliance may be so poorly designed that it is impossible to assemble.

Exploiting Structure to Expedite Search

We use the term *useful structure* with respect to a search problem to describe information about the problem that can be used to speed search. Each of the different ways of describing the appliance assembly example that we considered poses a slightly different problem. Each problem has a certain amount of useful structure in terms of information regarding the dependencies between assembly operations. If we are clever in exploiting the available useful structure, we may be able to reduce the amount of search considerably or even do away with it altogether.

If it is possible to assemble the appliance by using each work cell exactly once, then you can solve the problem by examining the dependencies between the assembly operations. The dependencies induce a partial order on work cells; any total order consistent with this partial order satisfies the goal.

If it is possible to assemble the appliance with multiple visits to the same work cell, then finding some solution is easy. However, finding a solution that involves the fewest possible transfers between workstations is more difficult. If some assembly operations result in reversing previous operations, it is even difficult to determine if it is possible to assemble the appliance.

The less structured a problem is, the less information we have to guide our search. In the worst case, we may find ourselves checking a large portion of the objects in the search space. Even for these problems, it is important that we explore the search space in a systematic manner so that we do not check objects that we have visited before. In the next section, we consider methods for systematically searching spaces that either lack useful structure to exploit or require more work than we are willing to do to figure out how to make use of that structure.

4.2 Blind Search

Blind search is best illustrated using a search space with a particular restricted structure. A *tree-structured* search space can be represented as a tree in which each node corresponds to an object in the search space. There is a directed arc from one node to another if there is an operator that transforms the object corresponding to the first node into the object corresponding to the second. If there is an arc from n_1 to n_2, then n_1 is called the *parent* of n_2, and n_2 is called the *child* of n_1. The *out degree* of a node is the number of arcs emanating from the node.

For purposes of analysis, we assume that the out degree of every node is the same and refer to this as the tree's *branching factor* and denote it b. In addition, we assume that an object satisfying the goal is found at a certain depth d. The depth is the length of the path from the root of the tree to the node corresponding to the goal. Figure 4.2 shows a simple tree-structured search space with $b = d = 2$ assuming that the node labeled G is a goal node.

The algorithms in this section are called *blind* because they make no use of information concerning where the goal might be located in the search space. Instead, they exhaustively search the space, checking each object for a possible goal. In the following, we analyze the basic blind search algorithms in terms of time and storage space. The time is the number of nodes visited

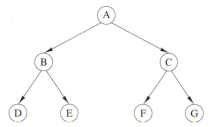

Figure 4.2 Simple tree-structured search space

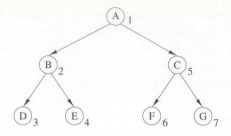

Figure 4.3   Order in which nodes are visited during depth-first search

prior to finding a goal. The storage space is the maximum amount of storage required to keep track of the search. We say that an algorithm for a particular computational task is *asymptotically optimal* in time (space) if the amount of time (space) required by the algorithm is within some additive or multiplicative factor of the minimum amount of time (space) required for the task.

Depth-First Search

The first algorithm we consider is called *depth-first* search because it always prefers to search deeper in the tree rather than wider. The algorithm is described as follows:

1. Set *N* to be a list of initial nodes.
2. If *N* is empty, then exit and signal failure.
3. Set *n* to be the first node in *N*, and remove *n* from *N*.
4. If *n* is a goal node, then exit and signal success.
5. Otherwise, add the children of *n* to the front of *N* and return to step 2.

Figure 4.3 shows the order in which nodes are visited during a depth-first search of the search space shown in Figure 4.2, starting with a list of initial nodes consisting of the node labeled A.

Figure 4.4 shows a Lisp implementation for depth-first search. The function dfs takes a list of nodes that it has not yet explored, a function that

```
;; This depth-first search procedure takes a set of nodes,
;; a function that tests to see if a node is a goal node,
;; and a function that takes a node and returns its children.
(defun dfs (nodes goalp next)
  (cond ((null nodes) nil)
        ;; Return the first node if it is a goal node.
        ((funcall goalp (first nodes)) (first nodes))
        ;; Put the children at the front of the list.
        (t (dfs (append (funcall next (first nodes))
                        (rest nodes))
             goalp
             next))))
```

Figure 4.4   Depth-first search

checks for the goal, and a function that returns the children of a node in the tree-structured search space. The following code implements an abstract data type for trees so that we can test our search methods:

```
(defun make-TREE (label value children)
  (list 'tree label value children))
(defun TREE-label (tree) (second tree))
(defun TREE-value (tree) (third tree))
(defun TREE-children (tree) (fourth tree))
(defun TREE-print (tree) (princ (TREE-label tree)))
```

Using this abstract data type, we can construct a Lisp object corresponding to the tree in Figure 4.2.

```
> (setq tree
      (make-TREE 'a 6
          (list (make-TREE 'b 3
                    (list (make-TREE 'd 5 nil)
                          (make-TREE 'e 4 nil)))
                (make-TREE 'c 1
                    (list (make-TREE 'f 2 nil)
                          (make-TREE 'g 0 nil))))))
(TREE A 6 ((TREE B 3 ((TREE D 5 NIL)
                      (TREE E 4 NIL)))
          (TREE C 1 ((TREE F 2 NIL)
                     (TREE G 0 NIL)))))
```

The following function invocation illustrates the order in which depth-first search visits nodes in the search space. The function checking for the goal prints out the label of the node it is at before checking to see if the label corresponds to the goal node.

```
> (dfs (list tree)
       #'(lambda (x) (TREE-print x) (eq 'g (TREE-label x)))
       #'TREE-children)
ABDECFG
(TREE G 0 NIL)
```

Depth-First Search Is Space Efficient

We analyze the time and storage requirements for depth-first search as follows. In general, timing is a bit tricky since, with an infinite tree, depth-first search may not find a node satisfying the goal and, worse, it may not terminate. If the tree is the same depth as the goal, in the worst case, depth-first search examines every node. In this case, the total time is $1 + b + b^2 + b^3 + \ldots + b^d = (b^{d+1} - 1)/(b - 1)$. The average number of nodes visited by depth-first search is given by

$$\frac{b^{d+1} + db + b - d - 2}{2(b - 1)}$$

which is the average of $d + 1$, the number of nodes visited if the goal is on the far left, and $(b^{d+1} - 1)/(b - 1)$, the number of nodes visited if the goal is on the far right of the search tree.

Calculating space usage is more encouraging. At each node n in the search space, depth-first search has to keep track of the root node and of the children of each node in the path from the root to n excepting n. Since the length of the longest such path is d, in the worst case, depth-first search uses a modest amount of space proportional to $d(b - 1) + 1$. It turns out that depth-first search is asymptotically optimal in its use of space.

Breadth-First Search

The second algorithm we consider is called *breadth-first* search because it explores all the nodes at a given depth before proceeding deeper in the tree. Breadth-first search is superficially similar to depth-first search; the only difference is in the last step. In depth-first search, we place the children of the current node at the beginning of the list of nodes to explore next, and in breadth-first search, we place the children at the end of the list.

1. Set N to be a list of initial nodes.
2. If N is empty, then exit and signal failure.
3. Set n to be the first node in N, and remove n from N.
4. If n is a goal node, then exit and signal success.
5. Otherwise, add the children of n to the end of N and return to step 2.

Figure 4.5 shows the order in which nodes are visited during a breadth-first search of the search space shown in Figure 4.2, starting with a list of initial nodes consisting of the node labeled A.

Figure 4.6 lists the code for a Lisp implementation of breadth-first search. Note that the implementation of breadth-first search is identical to that for depth first with the exception of the order of the arguments to append. The following function invocation illustrates the order in which

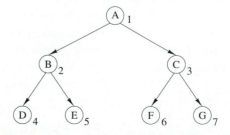

Figure 4.5   Order in which nodes are visited during breadth-first search

```
;; This breadth-first search procedure takes a set of nodes,
;; a function that tests to see if a node is a goal node,
;; and a function that takes a node and returns its children.
(defun bfs (nodes goalp next)
  (cond ((null nodes) nil)
        ;; Return the first node if it is a goal node.
        ((funcall goalp (first nodes)) (first nodes))
        ;; Put the children at the end of the list.
        (t (bfs (append (rest nodes)
                        (funcall next (first nodes)))
              goalp
              next))))
```

Figure 4.6   Breadth-first search

breadth-first search visits nodes in the search space:

```
> (bfs (list tree)
       #'(lambda (x) (TREE-print x) (eq 'g (TREE-label x)))
       #'TREE-children)
ABCDEFG
(TREE G 0 NIL)
```

Breadth-First Search Is Guaranteed

Breadth-first search provides stronger guarantees of finding a goal node if such a node exists but exacts a price in terms of the space required to keep track of where the algorithm is in the search. In the worst case, breadth-first search uses the same amount of time as depth-first search. Breadth-first search has the advantage that it will find a goal node if such a node exists even if the tree has infinite depth. The disadvantage of breadth-first search is that it uses space proportional to b^d. Breadth-first search has to keep track of the entire set of unexplored nodes, which is roughly the set of all nodes at depth d.

The average number of nodes visited by breadth-first search is the sum of all the internal nodes visited, $(b^d - 1)/(b - 1)$, and the average number of nodes visited at depth d, $(b^d + 1)/2$, for a total of

$$\frac{b^d - 1}{b - 1} + \frac{b^d + 1}{2} = \frac{b^{d+1} + b^d + b - 3}{2(b - 1)}$$

It turns out that breadth-first search is computationally more expensive in time than depth-first search by a factor of approximately $(b + 1)/b$, which approaches the limit of 1 as b becomes arbitrarily large.

Iterative-Deepening Search

Neither breadth-first nor depth-first search is asymptotically optimal in both time and space. There does exist an asymptotically optimal algorithm, called *iterative deepening*, that uses a variant of depth-first search as a subroutine.

```
;; This procedure searches depth first to a fixed maximum depth.
;; The procedure takes as arguments a single node, a function
;; that tests to see if a node is a goal node, a function that
;; takes a node and returns its children, an integer specifying
;; the current depth, and an integer specifying the maximum depth.
(defun dfs-fd (node goalp next depth max)
  (cond ((funcall goalp node) node)
        ;; Quit if you are at the maximum depth.
        ((= depth max) nil)
        ;; Increment the depth and extend the search.
        (t (some #'(lambda (n)
                     (dfs-fd n goalp next (+ 1 depth) max))
                 (funcall next node)))))
```

Figure 4.7   Depth-first search to a fixed depth

The following algorithm searches depth first to a fixed depth of max allowing us to exhaustively search a tree to a depth d using only $d(b-1)+1$ of storage:

1. Set N to be a list of initial nodes.
2. If N is empty, then exit and signal failure.
3. Set n to be the first node in N, and remove n from N.
4. If n is a goal node, then exit and signal success.
5. If the depth of n is equal to max, then go to step 2.
6. Otherwise, add the children of n to the front of N and return to step 2.

Figure 4.7 lists the code for a Lisp implementation of the algorithm.

Iterative deepening works by making repeated depth-first searches to a fixed depth, increasing the depth on each search until a goal node is found. This method of using repeated searches causes iterative deepening to revisit the same nodes in the search tree many times. The cost of these repeated visits is negligible from an asymptotic perspective. Figure 4.8 shows the order in which nodes are visited during iterative-deepening search of the search space shown in Figure 4.2 starting with a list of initial nodes consisting of the node labeled A. The following Lisp code implements iterative-

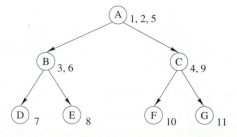

Figure 4.8   Order in which nodes are visited during iterative-deepening search

deepening search:

```
(defun ids (start goalp next depth)
  ;; First search to the current depth.
  (or (dfs-fd start goalp next 0 depth)
      ;; Then look deeper if unnecessary.
      (ids start goalp next (+ 1 depth))))
```

Here we see the order in which iterative deepening visits the nodes in the tree shown in Figure 4.2.

```
> (ids tree
      #'(lambda (x) (TREE-print x) (eq 'g (TREE-label x)))
      #'TREE-children 0)
AABCABDECFG
(TREE G 0 NIL)
```

Iterative-Deepening Search Is Asymptotically Optimal

Iterative deepening is an asymptotically optimal blind search procedure. The space requirements for iterative deepening are the same as for depth-first search, and the time requirements are roughly the same as breadth-first search. In addition, iterative deepening is guaranteed to find a goal node if one exists. The total number of nodes examined in the failed searches is

$$= \sum_{j=0}^{d-1} \frac{(b^{j+1} - 1)}{(b-1)}$$

$$= \frac{1}{(b-1)} \left[b \left(\sum_{j=0}^{d-1} b^j \right) - \sum_{j=0}^{d-1} 1 \right]$$

$$= \frac{b^{d+1} - bd - b + d}{(b-1)^2}$$

We can combine this total with our estimate of the average time required for depth-first search to obtain the average time for iterative deepening. The time required for iterative deepening is dominated by $(b+1)b^{d+1}/2(b-1)^2$, whereas the time required for depth-first search is dominated by $b^{d+1}/2(b-1)$. Therefore, the approximate ratio of time needed by iterative deepening to that required by depth-first search is $(b+1)/(b-1)$.

Although iterative deepening is asymptotically optimal, there are plenty of occasions in which we might prefer either depth-first search or breadth-first search. For instance, depth-first search is preferred for searching a finite tree-structured search space with goal nodes at the leaves of the tree. Breadth-first search is often preferred in cases with a small branching factor, operators that are expensive to apply, and goal nodes expected at a reasonable depth. In this analysis, iterative deepening is determined to be slower than depth-first search. However, in a finite tree-structured search space, if the depth of the tree is much greater than the depth of the goal node, then iterative deepening will often be faster than depth-first search.

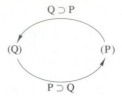

Figure 4.9   Simple graph-structured search space for theorem proving

Searching in Graphs

Many search spaces correspond to graphs instead of trees. For example, the search space shown in Figure 4.1a includes multiple nodes representing the same permutation. This means that the search space of Figure 4.1a is actually a graph and not a tree as shown.

In searching a graph, it is possible to arrive at the same node using different paths corresponding to different sequences of operators. One consequence of there being multiple paths from the starting node to other nodes in the graph is that, if we pretend the search space is a tree, then we may duplicate effort. Recall from Chapter 3 that in trying to prove P from $(P \equiv Q)$ the conjunctions (P) and (Q) kept reappearing without our having made any progress toward the goal of deriving the null clause (). Figure 4.9 shows the graph-structured search space for the simple case in which there are two nodes, (P) and (Q), and two operators, $(P \supset Q)$ and $(Q \supset P)$.

To avoid considering nodes more than once, we keep a list of the nodes already visited. There is some overhead in both time and space associated with checking for previously visited nodes. If we are clever, we can sometimes avoid this overhead by transforming a graph-structured search space into tree-structured space. In Chapter 7, we simplify search by using a tree-structured search space to represent planning problems.

4.3   Heuristic Search

With blind search, we assume that we do not use any information about the structure of the search space to guide our search. Instead, we perform an exhaustive exploration of the possible objects in the search space. Now we turn our attention to search problems for which we take advantage of information about the structure of the search space. We assume a metric on objects in the search space that allows us to estimate the distance from a node to a goal. We use this metric to compare two nodes in determining which nodes to explore next during search. In the appliance assembly example, we might use the number of assembly operations that have yet to be successfully carried out by a particular sequence of robotic work cells as a measure of how close the sequence is to the goal of successfully carrying out all the assembly operations.

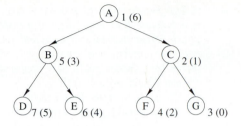

Figure 4.10 Order in which nodes are visited during best-first search. The values used to guide search are shown in parentheses.

A *heuristic* is any rule or method that provides guidance in decision making. A useful heuristic need not always improve decision making, but it should improve decision making more often than not. Choosing to stand in the shortest checkout line at the supermarket does not always get you out of the store quickly, but it is a useful heuristic if you have no other information to go on. In this section, we make use of heuristics to speed search by determining which nodes to explore next.

Best-First Search

The following algorithm is called *best-first* search. It works by sorting the list of nodes to be explored next according to their estimated distance from a goal.

1. Set N to be a sorted list of initial nodes.
2. If N is empty, then exit and signal failure.
3. Set n to be the first node in N, and remove n from N.
4. If n is a goal node, then exit and signal success.
5. Otherwise, add the children of n to N, sort the nodes in N[1] according to their estimated distance from a goal, and return to step 2.

Best-first search attempts to find a goal node quickly by searching nodes that are estimated to be close to a goal. It should be noted that the cost of computing each node's estimated distance to a goal is hidden in the preceding description. In some cases, this cost can be significant, and we would want to avoid computing it more than once.

Figure 4.10 shows the order in which nodes are visited during a best-first search starting with a list of initial nodes consisting of the node labeled A. The values corresponding to the estimated distance to a goal are shown in parentheses. We assume that there are no goal nodes in the tree in order to show how the entire tree is searched.

---

[1]Since the nodes in N are already sorted, it is more efficient to sort the children of n and merge the result with N, but we ignore such optimizations here and elsewhere to simplify the presentation.

```
;; This best-first search procedure takes a set of nodes,
;; a function that tests to see if a node is a goal node,
;; a function that takes a node and returns its children,
;; and a function that compares the value of two nodes.
(defun best (nodes goalp next comparep)
  (cond ((null nodes) nil)
        ;; Return the first node if it is a goal node.
        ((funcall goalp (first nodes)) (first nodes))
        ;; Append the children to the set of old nodes
        ;; and then sort them all according to value.
        (t (best (sort (append (funcall next (first nodes))
                               (rest nodes))
                       comparep)
                 goalp
                 next
                 comparep))))
```

Figure 4.11   Best-first search

Figure 4.11 shows a Lisp function implementing best-first search. The function sort takes two arguments; the first is a list, string, or array, and the second is a comparison function, which takes two arguments and returns non-nil if the first argument is strictly less than the second (in some appropriate sense). Sort may destructively modify its first argument. For this reason, the order of the arguments to append in best is important. Append copies all but its last argument. If we reversed the arguments to append, it would destructively modify the tree that best is searching. The notion of "better" or "best" is supplied by a function that takes two nodes in the search tree and determines which one is better. We augment the abstract data type for trees to include an operation comparing two trees on the basis of their value.

```
(defun TREE-comparator (tree1 tree2)
  (< (TREE-value tree1) (TREE-value tree2)))
```

The following demonstration of best-first search illustrates the order in which best-first search visits the nodes in the tree of Figure 4.2. We provide a function for checking for the goal that always fails in order to show how best-first search examines the entire tree.

```
> (best (list tree)
        #'(lambda (x) (TREE-print x) nil)
        #'TREE-children
        #'TREE-comparator)
ACGFBED
NIL
```

Admissible Evaluation Functions

Best-first search relies on the use of an *evaluation function* to compare objects in the search space. In the preceding example, the function TREE-value implements the evaluation function. The time and space complexity of best-first search depends on how well this function performs. We say that a search algorithm is *heuristically adequate* if it always finds a goal that is nearest to the start node. Note that breadth-first search is heuristically adequate. We would like to do better than breadth-first search if we have good heuristics to guide our search.

Consider the following form for an evaluation function,

$$e(n) = g(n) + h'(n),$$

where n is a node, $g(n)$ is the distance from the root to the node, and $h'(n)$ is an estimate of the distance from the node to the nearest goal. Note that, if $h'(n) = 0$ for all nodes n in the search space, then best-first search reduces to breadth-first search. An evaluation function, h', is *admissible* if $h'(n) \leq h(n)$ for all n, where $h(n)$ is the actual distance to the nearest goal. If h' is admissible, then the resulting variant of best-first search, called A^*, is heuristically adequate.

Suppose a robot is searching for a path from one location to another in a rectangular grid of locations. Figure 4.12 depicts such a grid in which there are arcs between adjacent pairs of locations. Some arcs are obstructed as indicated by the shaded regions thereby preventing passage. The robot can move across any unobstructed arc to an adjacent location. The *Manhattan distance* between two locations is the length of the shortest path between the locations ignoring obstructions. In Figure 4.12, the location of the robot is labeled S, and the destination is labeled G. The Manhattan distance from S to G is four, and the length of the shortest unobstructed path is six. The Manhattan distance provides an admissible heuristic evaluation function for this path planning problem.

An evaluation function imposes structure on the objects of a search space. In some cases, that structure can be illustrated graphically. The

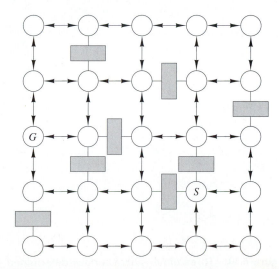

Figure 4.12   Searching for paths in a grid environment

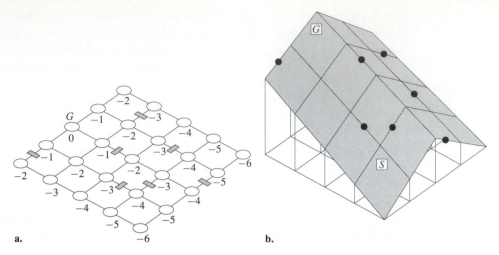

a.   b.

Figure 4.13 Three-dimensional surface determined using the Manhattan distance to the goal as a metric for the grid environment shown in Figure 4.12

diagram shown in Figure 4.13a depicts the grid environment shown in Figure 4.12 as if the grid is laid out on a horizontal plane. Each node in the grid environment is labeled with the additive inverse of the Manhattan distance to the goal for each location in the grid. The surface shown in Figure 4.13a is determined by these distances. Each intersection of lines on the surface corresponds to a node in the search space, and two nodes are connected unless there is a black circle blocking them.

Different metrics and hence evaluation functions result in different surfaces. Figure 4.14 shows what the surface would look like if we used as a metric the shortest distance to the goal accounting for obstructions. Note that the goal node corresponds to the highest point in the surfaces depicted

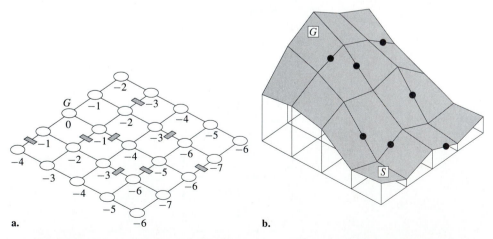

a.   b.

Figure 4.14 Three-dimensional surface determined using the shortest distance to the goal as a metric for the grid environment shown in Figure 4.12

in Figures 4.13 and 4.14, and searching consists of moving about on a surface looking for the highest point. In the next section, we consider how methods for searching for the highest point on a surface can be used to solve problems of great practical interest.

4.4   Optimization and Search

Best-first search uses an evaluation function to guide search for a goal node. Suppose that we forget about goals for a while. Think of the evaluation function as providing a measure of the intrinsic value of objects in the search space and the objective of search to find the highest-value object in the search space. From this perspective, search techniques can be used to address optimization problems that involve finding an object that maximizes or minimizes a particular evaluation function.

Trying to find a schedule for flights to minimize congestion at an airport or find a route that visits a set of cities to minimize the total distance traveled are examples of optimization problems. Typically, these problems are so hard that we cannot find an optimal solution and satisfy ourselves with finding a very good solution. For large scheduling problems like those faced by the airlines, finding a better schedule can mean saving a great deal of money.

A simple approach to solving optimization problems would be to use a best-first search algorithm modified to keep track of the highest-value object seen thus far. Unfortunately, in most optimization problems, the branching factor is very large. This slows best-first search to a crawl because it has to store so many nodes to keep track of what nodes to explore next. To make matters worse, improving an existing route or schedule often requires searching to a considerable depth.

Hill-Climbing Search

In the following, we consider a variant of best-first search called *hill-climbing* search that requires only a constant amount of storage for a search space with bounded out-degree. Hill-climbing search manages this low storage complexity by not keeping track of any previously encountered nodes except the best encountered so far.

1. Set n to be the initial node.
2. If the value of n is greater than the value of any of its children, then exit and return n.
3. Otherwise, set n to be the highest-value child of n and return to step 2.

This algorithm is designed to maximize the evaluation function. If you are interested in minimizing rather than maximizing, then change "greater" to "less" and "highest" to "lowest."

▲ AI IN PRACTICE

Scheduling Astronomical Observations

Powerful telescopes for observing the stars and planets are a valuable and scarce resource for the scientific community. Increasingly, these telescopes are located in space or in remote locations on the earth's surface where the light from human habitation cannot disturb the sensitive instruments. These remote telescopes are aimed and the data collected from observations under computer control. Using networked computers, much of the control can be handled from sites far from the actual locations of the telescopes.

Researchers at the NASA Ames Research Center have developed a real-time scheduling system called CERES that takes requests from astronomers for particular observations and schedules those observations on automatic telescopes. CERES combines scheduling of requested observations with the control of the telescopes and can dynamically respond and reschedule in the event of conditions that make an observation impossible. Astronomers can request astronomical observations on remote equipment and receive the resulting data without ever leaving their home institutions. Such automated management of telescopes reduces the telescope support staff and operations costs while improving the utilization of telescopes and providing scientists with increased flexibility.

Courtesy of NASA Ames Research Center

For simplicity, we assume that every node in the search space has at least one child. Hill-climbing search terminates in a solution that is said to be *locally optimal* because no nodes of higher value are reachable by applying a single operator. We cannot, however, guarantee that the solution returned by hill-climbing search is *globally optimal* in the sense that there are no nodes of higher value anywhere in the search space.

Figure 4.15 depicts a simple optimization problem in which the objective is to find a node reachable from the node labeled S minimizing the Manhattan distance to the node labeled G. Any two nodes connected by an arc that is not blocked by the shaded obstruction are adjacent in the search space. Since G is reachable from S, G is the optimal solution. Hill-climbing search will terminate immediately returning S if it is started in S. A variant of best-first search that keeps track of all previously visited nodes and

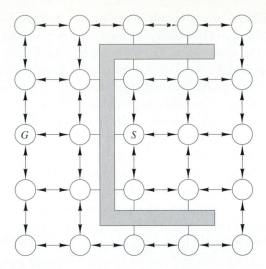

Figure 4.15   Grid environment with a *cul de sac*

never explores the same node twice will find *G* starting from *S*, but such an algorithm is impractical for any real optimization problem.

Local Minima and Maxima

Figure 4.16 depicts the grid environment shown in Figure 4.15 with each node labeled with the additive inverse of the Manhattan distance to the goal; the resulting surface is shown in Figure 4.16b. The node labeled *S* in Figure 4.16b represents a *local minimum* in the search space. A local maximum (minimum) in a search space corresponds to an object all of whose neighboring objects have lower (higher) value. A *global* maximum (minimum) is an object with the lowest (highest) value. Local minima and maxima are

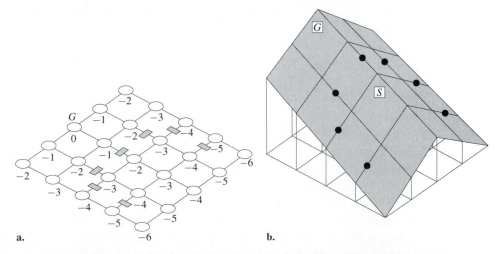

a.   b.

Figure 4.16   Local maximum in the grid environment of Figure 4.15

the bane of optimization techniques and tend to foil even the best heuristic evaluation functions. The problem is to figure out how to maneuver in a search space so as to avoid getting stuck in a local maximum (minimum) that is not also a global maximum (minimum).

The search methods that we have considered so far either search blindly or employ heuristics to guide search. Often in practical applications, good heuristics are difficult to come up with, and blind search methods turn out to be impractical. In the rest of this section, we consider two search methods that attempt to address the problem of local minima and maxima. Both methods are inspired by physical processes and implemented by simulating those processes on a computer.

The algorithms that we consider in this chapter extend search from an already examined object using operators to transform one object into another. Search algorithms like best-first search and hill-climbing search use an evaluation function to choose where to look next in the search space. A potential problem with these algorithms is that the paths traversed during search are constrained by the operators that define the structure (or connectivity) of the search space. There is no way to jump to distant parts of the search space without first exploring some portion of the intervening area. Moreover, there is often no incentive to explore the intervening area since it may contain only objects of lower value. Often the only paths through the search space from one object to another object of higher value require examining objects of lower value.

We could, of course, just add *macro* operators corresponding to sequences of more primitive operators. Such operators would allow us to take larger steps in the search space in an effort to span regions consisting of objects with low value. In Chapter 7, we consider how we might use such macro operators to speed planning. Unfortunately, indiscriminate use of such operators can increase the branching factor of the search space enormously and add to the complexity of the search. To cope with complexity, we need to somehow regulate how frequently and how far we are willing to jump about in the search space. The approaches in this section make use of randomization to help choose when and how far to jump.

The first approach we consider uses an adjustable parameter to decide what steps to take during search. The value of this parameter starts out high and is gradually reduced to zero over the course of the search. If the value of the parameter is high, then with high probability we take large steps. If the value of the parameter is low, then with high probability we take small steps. This strategy has the property that early on in search we are willing to move about the search space boldly, whereas later we are more conservative having surveyed large portions of the space to obtain a global perspective. To illustrate, we consider a method for searching continuous spaces that turns out to be useful in Chapter 5.

Gradient Search

Gradient search is a hill-climbing method from calculus for finding the minima and maxima of continuous, differentiable functions. Suppose that $\Phi(x)$ is the evaluation function and we are searching in the space defined by the real numbers, $\mathbf{R}$. We want to find some $x \in \mathbf{R}$ maximizing $\Phi(x)$. The gradient, in this case defined to be $\frac{d\Phi(x)}{dx}$, indicates the direction in which to change x to maximize the increase in Φ in a small region about x. The simplest gradient search algorithm is to repeatedly execute $x \leftarrow x + \beta \frac{d\Phi(x)}{dx}$, until $-\epsilon \leq \frac{d\Phi(x)}{dx} \leq \epsilon$, where β and ϵ are small positive constants indicating, respectively, the step rate and stopping criterion. By taking many small steps in the direction indicated by the gradient, we are guaranteed to find a *local* maximum corresponding to a value of x such that $\frac{d\Phi(x)}{dx}$ is zero or very nearly so. A local maximum need not also be a global maximum, and gradient search is not guaranteed to find a global maximum. Figure 4.17 illustrates a space with two local maxima and the steps that a gradient search algorithm might take in searching that space starting from the far left of the graph.

Simulated Annealing

To find a global maximum, we might adopt the following strategy. Most of the time we take small steps in the direction indicated by the gradient, but occasionally we take large steps in the direction indicated by the gradient or in some other direction. *Simulated annealing* is an optimization technique that employs a similar strategy. Simulated annealing makes use of a *temperature* parameter that is adjusted during search. If the temperature is high, then large steps are more probable. If the temperature is low, then smaller steps are more probable. Initially, the temperature is high, but over time it is gradually reduced to zero.

Simulated annealing was inspired by a technique used by metallurgists to obtain metals with particular properties. In annealing metals, the materials are heated and cooled, sometimes repeatedly, to achieve a

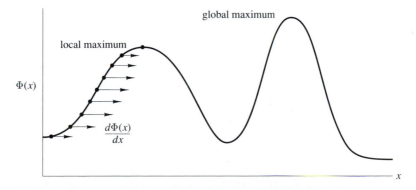

Figure 4.17   Gradient search with multiple local maxima

particular crystalline structure. Annealing can be used to obtain metals that are malleable and less likely to break when subjected to shock. Simulated annealing has been applied successfully to a number of optimization problems in scheduling and vehicle routing. It obtains its power from making random choices according to a changing distribution that initially favors large steps but later favors more conservative steps. The next method we consider also makes random choices on occasion but in addition provides techniques for choosing where to look next in the search space.

Simulated Evolution and Genetic Algorithms

Genetic algorithms search by simulating evolution. Genetic algorithms take their motivation from the mechanics of natural selection and genetics. In natural selection, individuals compete for the opportunity to reproduce. Individuals with new features are introduced into the population when existing individuals exchange genetic material during reproduction and when mutations occur. In the following, we implement a simple genetic algorithm.

The terminology of genetic algorithms is an odd mix of computer science and genetics. An individual has a data structure that describes the genetic structure of the individual. We assume that an individual's genetic structure can be described as a bit string represented as a list of 1's and 0's. In genetics, the strings are called *chromosomes*, the bits are called *alleles,* and the string associated with a given individual is called the individual's *genotype.* Selection is based on the *fitness* of individuals. Fitness in an optimization problem is the value of an individual determined by an evaluation function.

The genetic algorithms presented in the rest of this section operate on populations of individuals called *generations*. Given a population of individuals corresponding to one generation, the algorithm simulates natural selection and reproduction to obtain the next generation. The algorithm involves three basic operations: *reproduction* in which individuals from one generation are selected for the next generation, *crossover* in which genetic material from one individual is exchanged with the genetic material of another individual, and *mutation* in which the genetic material is altered. All three operations make use of randomization.

Figure 4.18 shows the three operations being used to obtain a new generation from an existing population; arrows with smooth lines indicate copying; arrows with squiggly lines indicate mutation. The circled numbers indicate the fitness of the individual located to the left. Note that one not particularly fit individual with genotype (0 1 0 0) was not allowed to reproduce and another, very fit individual with genotype (1 0 1 1) was allowed two offspring.

We want to bias the selection of individuals that are allowed to reproduce on the basis of their fitness. Given a population of individuals, we derive a distribution to govern selection as follows. For each distinct geno-

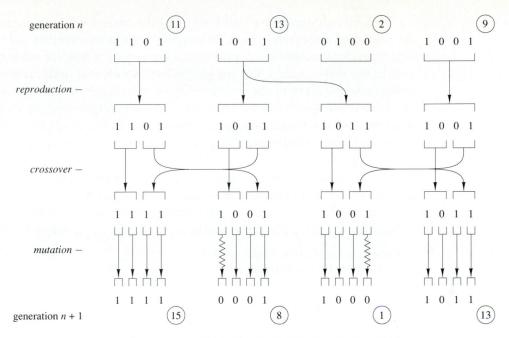

Figure 4.18   Basic operations in simulated evolution

type, the probability of selecting an individual with that genotype is the fitness of the genotype normalized by dividing by the sum of the fitness over the set of all genotypes. The algorithm for creating a new generation of individuals from an existing generation is as follows:

1 Let G be the current generation of individuals.

2 Create a probability distribution based on G. Let T be the set of all genotypes in G and define $\Pr(T)$ as

$$\Pr(t) = \frac{f(t)}{\sum_{t' \in F} f(t')}$$

where $f(t)$ denotes the fitness of an individual of genotype t.

3 Let G' be initially empty.

4 For $i = 1$ to $|G|/2$,

a) Randomly choose two parents p and p' according to $\Pr(T)$ (reproduction).

b) Randomly swap bits in p and p' to obtain two new individuals (crossover).

c) Mutate the new individuals by randomly flipping a small number of bits and add the resulting individuals to the next generation G' (mutation).

5 Return G'.

To search for a solution, you simulate evolution for some number of generations and select the fittest individual in the final generation as your solution.

To investigate genetic algorithms in a little more detail, we implement the preceding algorithm in Lisp. To simplify our implementation, we represent individuals as lists of 1's and 0's and fitness as a function from individuals to the real numbers. For the purpose of search and optimization, the string corresponding to the genotype of an individual is used to describe an object in the search space. For instance, (1 0 0 1) might describe an object in a search space determined by four binary attributes. Two Lisp variables reference the same individual if they are eq. Two individuals have the same genotype if they are equal.

We are interested in finding strings that have a high value with respect to a given evaluation function. In keeping with the natural selection motivation, the evaluation function is called fitness. The distribution for selecting individuals that are allowed to reproduce is described as follows:[2]

```
(defun distribution (population)
  (let* ((genotypes (noduplicates population))
         (sum (apply #'+ (mapcar #'fitness genotypes))))
    (mapcar #'(lambda (x) (cons (/ (fitness x) sum) x))
            genotypes)))
```

Given an existing population, we compute the next generation by selecting pairs of individuals according to this distribution. Each pair is given an opportunity to exchange genetic material by calling the function crossover, which with some probability, destructively modifies the list structures corresponding to the chromosomes of the two individuals.

```
(defun reproduce (population)
  (let ((offspring nil) (d (distribution population)))
    (dotimes (i (/ (length population) 2))
      (let ((x (select d)) (y (select d)))
        (crossover x y)
        (setq offspring (nconc (list x y) offspring))))
    offspring))
```

Select takes a distribution and returns an individual chosen in accord with the given distribution. Select also invokes a procedure that serves to mutate the selected genotype in constructing the new individual.

```
(defun select (distribution)
  (let ((random (random 1.0)) (prob 0) genotype)
    (some #'(lambda (pair)
              (setq prob (+ prob (first pair)))
              (if (> random prob) nil
                  (setq genotype (rest pair))))
          distribution)
    (mutate genotype)))
```

---

[2]Noduplicates takes a list of expressions and returns a list consisting of all those expressions in the original list, eliminating duplicates determined by equal.

Mutation is carried out by creating a new string in which each bit is copied from the old to the new without change with probability 0.97, and a bit is inverted with probability 0.03.

```
(defun mutate (genotype)
  (mapcar #'(lambda (x)
              (if (> (random 1.0) 0.03) x (if (= x 1) 0 1)))
          genotype))
```

Crossover corresponds to two individuals exchanging genetic material. In this implementation, crossover occurs between a selected pair of individuals with probability 0.6. A *crossover site* is an integer specifying an element of a list representing a bit string. Given two strings, with probability 0.6, crossover randomly chooses a crossover site, and exchanges the substrings beginning immediately following the site in each of the strings. For instance, given (0 1 1 0 1) and (1 1 0 1 1), crossover might choose the (0-based) site location of 1 and then destructively modify the two strings to obtain (0 1 0 1 1) and (1 1 1 0 1). The crossover rate of 0.6 and the mutation rate of 0.03 are recommended as initial values for these parameters [Goldberg, 1989], but often it is necessary to experiment to find values that work well for a given application.

```
(defun crossover (x y)
  (if (> (random 1.0) 0.6) (list x y)
      (let* ((site (random (length x)))
             (swap (rest (nthcdr site x))))
        (setf (rest (nthcdr site x)) (rest (nthcdr site y))
              (rest (nthcdr site y)) swap))))
```

To test our algorithm, we interpret a list of n 1's and 0's as a binary number in the range from 0 to $2^n - 1$ with bits ordered from least to most significant. To make the problem interesting, let $n = 30$. We consider two different fitness functions. The first (shown in Figure 4.19b) is defined by $f(x) = (x/2^{30} - 1)^{10}$ and is chosen so that $0 \leq f(x) \leq 1$ and the average fitness is relatively low to make the problem harder. The problem is harder because the evaluation function provides less useful information on average. The second fitness function (shown in Figure 4.19d) is designed to have multiple maxima.[3]

Note that the search space for this problem is quite large (2^{30}), and though *you* may understand what the bits in a given string mean, the genetic algorithm does not. Figure 4.19a plots the value of the fittest individual (solid) and the average fitness (dashed) for 10 generations using the fitness functions shown in Figure 4.19b and starting with an initial population of

---

[3]In case you want to replicate the experiments, the fitness function shown in Figure 4.19d is defined as $f(x) = g(\frac{x}{2^{30}-1})$, where $g(x) = \sum_{i=1}^{4} v_i e^{\frac{1}{2w}(x-c_i)^2}$ and $v_1 = 0.50$, $v_2 = 0.25$, $v_3 = 1.0$, $v_4 = 0.25$, $c_1 = 0.125$, $c_2 = 0.375$, $c_3 = 0.625$, $c_4 = 0.875$, and $w = 0.003$.

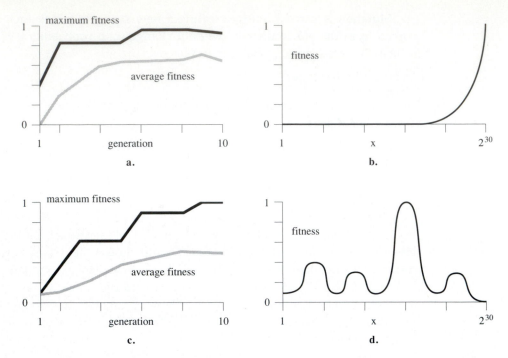

Figure 4.19   Performance of the genetic algorithm for different fitness functions

30 randomly chosen individuals. Figure 4.19c plots the value of the fittest individual (solid) and the average fitness (dashed) for 10 generations using the fitness functions shown in Figure 4.19d. In the case of Figure 4.19c, we start with a population of 30 individuals chosen from the range $[0, 2^{10}]$ to avoid the genetic algorithm starting off with an individual very near to optimal.

Although the experiments described here illustrate the ability of genetic algorithms to deal with combinatorics, they do little to demonstrate any practical advantages of genetic algorithms. In addressing most practical applications, we are immediately challenged by how to represent the objects in the search space as strings. In the following, we consider a classic problem in optimization.

Application to Vehicle Routing

In the *traveling salesperson problem*, a salesperson has to visit a number of cities and wishes to minimize the total distance traveled. Solutions to the traveling salesperson problem are often applied to vehicle-routing problems. For example, a company might want to find the shortest route for its fleet of delivery trucks that visits all the company's customers.

An instance of the traveling salesperson problem consists of a set of n cities and an $n \times n$ (symmetric) matrix indicating the distance between any pair of cities along a direct route. If there is no direct route between two cities, the distance between them is infinite. A *tour* is a permutation of the n cities, indicating the order in which to visit the cities. We want to visit all the cities exactly once and end up back at the first. The objective is to find a short tour.

Notating the n cities $1, 2, \ldots, n$ and considering strings over the alphabet $\{1, 2, \ldots, n\}$, we represent a tour as a string, such as (3 4 9 5 7). So far so good. A problem arises, however, with regard to crossover and mutation. If we cross (1 3 2) and (3 1 2) after the first position, we obtain (1 1 2) and (3 3 2), neither of which corresponds to a tour. If we mutate (1 2 3) by randomly selecting alternative cities, we also run the risk of obtaining strings that are not tours. Since relatively few strings correspond to tours, the mutation and crossover operations more often than not result in strings that are not tours and thus should not be considered during search. An alternative method of mutation is to simply swap the cities at two sites. An alternative crossover operation called *partially matched crossover* is sketched in the following paragraph.

Given two strings representing legal tours, we determine two sites marking the beginning and end of the tour segments to be exchanged. For instance, given the following two tours:

$$T_1 = 134|275|68$$

$$T_2 = 236|751|84$$

where the |'s delimit the exchange area, we exchange the substrings (2 7 5) and (7 5 1) to obtain 134|751|68 and 236|275|84, neither of which represents a tour. We then construct an *exchange map* in which each city not inside the exchange area is mapped to itself, and each city within the exchange area is mapped according to the exchange. For instance, 1 is mapped to 2 given the exchanges, $1 \rightarrow 5 \rightarrow 7 \rightarrow 2$, involving T_1 and T_2. We apply the exchange map to the cities outside the exchange area to obtain two tours.

$$T_1' = 234|751|68$$

$$T_2' = 136|275|84$$

Using the mutation and crossover operations, we can employ a variant of the basic method described earlier to generate a new generation of tours from an existing population of tours. Both simulated annealing and genetic algorithms have been applied with considerable success to instances of the traveling salesperson problem with greater than 200 cities. However, for both methods, success largely depends on devising an appropriate method for representing the problem and coming up with clever methods for maneuvering in the search space. Exercise 4.11 investigates how genetic algorithms can be used to solve problems in propositional logic, and Exercise 4.12 investigates an alternative to genetic algorithms for solving such problems. More than anything else, simulated annealing and genetic algorithms provide particular approaches to search that exercise different intuitions and thereby suggest what are often useful representations for solving hard search problems.

4.5   Adversary Search

In this section, we consider search techniques for two-person games such as chess, checkers, and tic-tac-toe in which the two players alternate moves. These games have the property that both players have perfect information about the location of the pieces on the board in the case of chess or checkers or the marks on the grid in the case of tic-tac-toe. Many card games involve imperfect information in that players typically hide their cards from other players.

In a two-person game of perfect information, each player in turn has to determine a next move. This next-move decision requires thinking about how your opponent will move in response, how you will respond to their response, and so on. Search in this case involves considering various sequences of alternating moves by the two players to assess the consequences of the immediately available options for moving. In chess, for example, moving a pawn may allow your opponent to initiate a sequence of moves that will result in your losing the game no matter how you respond. You would like to anticipate this sequence of moves and thereby avoid moving your pawn.

Minimax Search

A *game tree* is a tree consisting of nodes that represent options for the players to move in a two-person game. The nodes in a game tree alternate between options for the two players. The nodes implicitly represent states of the game, for example, configurations of the playing board in the case of chess or checkers. The state resulting from a move is completely determined by the move and the state immediately prior to the move. Typically, the root of a game tree represents the current state of the game.

Figure 4.20 shows a simple game tree in which the nodes are shown in levels, called *plies*, that correspond to the options of the two players. Terminal nodes indicate moves that result in one of the two players winning the game and are assigned a value of either 1 or −1 depending on which player wins. The objective of one player, called the *maximizer*, is to reach a node with value 1, and the objective of the other player, called the *minimizer*, is to reach a node with value −1. If it is possible for a game to end in a draw, we assign nodes resulting in a draw with a value of 0. Players prefer a win over a draw and a draw over a loss, and we assume that they choose their moves accordingly.

In order to choose a next move, we need to evaluate the consequences of every option, including those corresponding to internal nodes in the game tree. The value of the node labeled p in Figure 4.20 is 1 because the maxi-

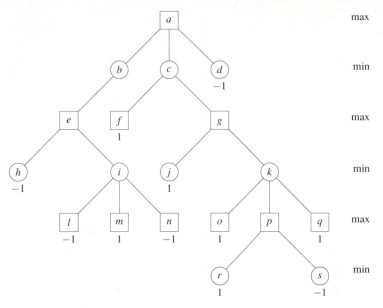

Figure 4.20 A simple game tree. Nodes corresponding to options of the maximizer are shown as squares, and nodes corresponding to options of the minimizer are shown as circles. Terminal nodes are assigned a value of 1 if the maximizer wins and −1 if the minimizer wins.

mizer gets to choose the next move. The value of the node labeled k is also 1 because the minimizer has no better choice. However, the value of the node labeled i is −1 because the minimizer gets to choose the next move. We can assign values to the entire tree in this way starting from the terminal nodes and working our way up to the root of the tree. Figure 4.21 (page 162) shows the values of all the internal nodes of the game tree shown in Figure 4.20.

The strategy for assigning values to nodes in a game tree sketched in the previous paragraph uses an amount of storage exponential in the depth of the tree. In practice, we are interested in computing the value of specific nodes corresponding to possible next moves. The following algorithm, called *minimax* search, reduces the amount of storage required for determining the value of a particular node m by performing a depth-first search of the game tree rooted at m.

1. Set N to be the list consisting of the single element, m.
2. Let n be the first node in N.
3. If $n = m$ and n has been assigned a value, then exit returning this value.
4. If n has been assigned a value, then remove n from N.
5. If n has not been assigned a value and is a terminal node, then assign n the value 1, −1, or 0 depending on whether it is a win for the maximizer, a win for the minimizer, or a draw.
6. If n has not been assigned a value and all its children have been assigned values, then if n is a maximizing node, assign n the maximum of the

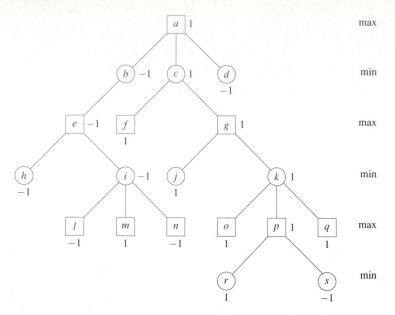

Figure 4.21   A game tree with all the internal nodes assigned values

values of its children; otherwise, assign n the minimum of the values of its children.

7 If n has not been assigned a value and all its children have not been assigned values, then add the children of n to the front of N.

8 Return to step 2.

Note that once we have assigned a value to a node we no longer have to store the values for the children of that node.

This procedure is impractical because the game tree for any interesting games is extremely large. If there are a minimum of b options for each player on each turn and the minimum number of moves required to end in a win or a draw is d, then the procedure will take time proportional to b^d. Instead of analyzing a game all the way to a win or draw, we might search far enough ahead so that we can compute a good estimate of which player is likely to win in various nonterminal nodes. We then use these nonterminal nodes with estimated values as if they were terminal nodes and proceed as before.

To determine which move to make next without searching the entire game tree, we need an evaluation function, $e(n)$, which when applied to a node n returns an estimate of its value. If $e(n) = 1$, then n should lead to a win for the maximizer with certainty. If $e(n) = -1$, then n should lead to a win for the minimizer with certainty. Intermediate values reflect lower levels of certainty. If $e(n) = 0$, then n should have no advantage for either player.

Simple evaluation functions are easy to come by. In the case of chess, we might assign a value to each piece with the more powerful pieces like rooks and queens assigned higher values. Let $w(n)$ be the sum of the values of all the white pieces on the board in the state corresponding to n, and $b(n)$ be the sum of the values of all the black pieces on the board. If the maximizer is controlling the white pieces, then a crude approximation of the value of node can be computed as follows:

$$e(n) = \frac{w(n) - b(n)}{w(n) + b(n)}$$

This evaluation function for chess does not account for positional advantages. Obviously, there is little advantage in having more pieces than your opponent if your king is in jeopardy and losing is inevitable. Calculating positional advantages is generally more costly from a computational standpoint than simply adding up the value of pieces on a board. Given a finite amount of time, there is a tradeoff between time spent searching deeper in the tree and time spent in evaluating individual nodes.

In addition to evaluating nonterminal nodes, the search algorithm has to determine when to stop searching deeper in the tree. There is always the possibility that, if we were to search one ply deeper in the tree, we would discover an advantageous move for one of the two players that was not accounted for by the evaluation function applied to shallower nodes. There is no way of knowing for sure that such a move exists or not without doing the requisite search, but researchers have developed heuristics for determining whether or not to cut off search. One such heuristic is to extend search only on nodes for which the evaluation function is rapidly changing from one ply to the next. A rapidly changing value is often an indicator of a position that indicates a tactical advantage for one of the two players.

α-β Search

Although it is generally difficult to determine exactly how far ahead to search, there are some cases in which, given the nodes that are already evaluated, there is no use in extending the search at other nodes. Consider the partially expanded game tree shown in Figure 4.22 (page 164). Note that, if the maximizer chooses c, it can do no better than -0.2. The maximizer will choose b over c no matter what it learns in expanding d, so it might as well simply prune away the entire subtree rooted at c.

Figure 4.23 illustrates another case in which we can prune the search space. At node g, the minimizer has an option with value -0.3. In this case, there is no need to expand h since the maximizer can always choose b and do better than -0.3. It may be worthwhile expanding d and f, however, since the c option may yet prove to be better than the b option.

The general case for pruning a node is as follows. Suppose that n is a node at which the maximizer gets to move and that n has a sibling with a value v. Suppose further that there is some node m on the path from the root of the tree to n such that the minimizer gets to move and m has a sibling with a value greater than v. In this case, the node n can be pruned

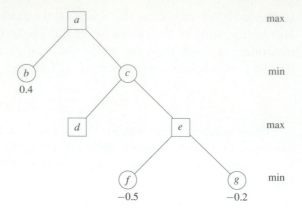

Figure 4.22 The subtree rooted at *c* can be pruned from the search space since the maximizer can always do better by choosing *b*

from the search space. A similar argument works for nodes at which the minimizer gets to move.

To implement this pruning strategy, it is necessary to keep track of the current best estimated value for a node even though the subtree rooted at that node has only partially been explored. When we encounter a new node, if it is a terminal node or we have decided not to expand the tree further, then we apply the evaluation function and assign the resulting value to the node. If the new node is not a terminal node and we intend to expand it later if it is not pruned, then we assign it $-\infty$ if it is a maximizing node and $+\infty$ if it is a minimizing node.

When we assign a value to a node using the evaluation function, we then propagate the value up the tree to the ancestors of the node. This is

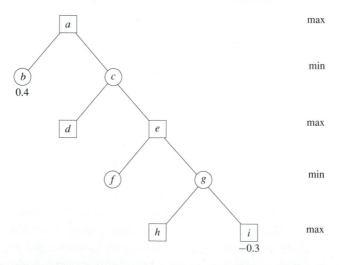

Figure 4.23 The subtree rooted at *h* can be pruned from the search space since the minimizer already has a choice that is better than the best alternative of the maximizer

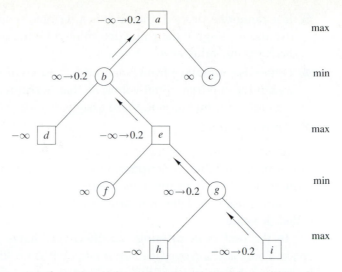

Figure 4.24   Backing up the value at node *i*. Initially, all the maximizing nodes are assigned $-\infty$, and all the minimizing nodes are assigned $+\infty$. When the value of *i* is changed to 0.2, the ancestors of *i* are updated accordingly.

referred to as *backing up* the value at a node. Figure 4.24 shows how the values are backed up in a tree in which all the nodes are initially assigned $\pm\infty$. It is not always necessary to update all the ancestors of a node since some of them need not change. Here is a recursive procedure for backing up the value at a node *n*.

1. Let *v* be the current value of *n*.
2. Let *m* be the parent of *n* and *u* the current value of *m*.
3. If *m* is a maximizing node, then set the value of *m* to be the maximum of *u* and *v*.
4. If *m* is a minimizing node, then set the value of *m* to be the minimum of *u* and *v*.
5. If *m* is the root node or the value of *m* is unchanged, then quit; otherwise, back up the value at *m*.

Here is a complete algorithm for evaluating a node *m* in a game tree that uses the pruning method described earlier.

1. Set *N* to be the list consisting of the single element, *m*.
2. Let *n* be the first node in *N*.
3. If *n* = *m* and *n* has been assigned a value, then exit returning this value.
4. Try to prune *n* as follows. If *n* is a maximizing node, let *v* be the minimum of the values of siblings of *n*, and *u* be the maximum of the values of siblings of ancestors of *n* that are minimizing nodes. If $v \geq u$, then you can remove *n* and its siblings and any successors of *n* and its siblings from *N*. If *m* is a minimizing node, then proceed similarly switching min for max, max for min, and $\leq$ for $\geq$.

5 If n cannot be pruned, then if n is a terminal node or we decide not to expand n, assign n the value determined by the evaluation function and back up the value at n.

6 Otherwise, remove n from N, add the children of n to the front of N, and assign the children initial values so that maximizing nodes are assigned $-\infty$ and minimizing nodes are assigned $+\infty$.

7 Return to step 2.

In the search literature, the preceding procedure is called α-β search because, in the original description of the algorithm, the values used to determine whether to prune a maximizing node were called α values, and the values used to determine whether to prune a minimizing node were called β values.

In the best case, pruning can effectively halve the size of the search space. There is some overhead associated with checking to see if a node can be pruned, but in practice this overhead is more than compensated for by the resulting reduction in the search space. Exactly how much of a reduction is actually realized depends a lot on how the children of a node are ordered in the list of nodes to consider next. It helps to examine the best options first, and chess programs often employ sophisticated techniques in an effort to try to order children best to worst.

4.6   Indexing in Discrimination Trees

Some applications require repeatedly searching through the same set of objects. For example, such repeated searching is often required in answering database queries. The effort required in these searches can often be reduced by appropriately adding structure to the set of objects. In this section, we consider methods for adding such structure. Note that the methods of this section differ from those in earlier sections in an important way. In earlier sections, we were interested in searching a combinatorial space that is only implicitly specified by a set of operators. In this section, we are concerned with repeatedly searching a space that is explicitly stored in memory in its entirety.

A *discrimination tree* or, more generally, a *discrimination network* is a data structure used for storing and retrieving large numbers of symbolic objects. Storing items in a discrimination network is somewhat more expensive in terms of time and space than storing them in a flat list. However, we expect to recoup that initial cost many times over in repeatedly retrieving the same objects from the database. If you are clever, it is possible to store n items in such a way that retrieval can be performed in log n time in the worst case.

The basic idea behind discrimination networks is to recursively partition a set of objects. Each partition divides the set of objects into subsets based on some simple rule. For instance, we might partition the set of employees represented in a database into two sets on the basis of salary: those with a salary $\leq \$50,000$ in one set and those with a salary $> \$50,000$ in the other. The partition could involve more than two sets. For example, we might partition employee salaries into the ranges $0–$10,000, $10,000–$20,000, $20,000–$50,000, $50,000–$70,000, and $> \$70,000$.

Storing and Retrieving Predicate Calculus Formulas

In the following, we consider a simple scheme for storing and retrieving predicate calculus formulas. A *key* is a symbol that corresponds to some part of a Lisp expression representing a formula. We associate with each formula an ordered sequence of keys. Given a formula, we can generate an appropriate set of keys to successively partition the data for either storage or retrieval. The function make-key-list takes an expression and returns a flat list of keys,

```
> (make-key-list '(on block1 (floor room17)))
(*BEGIN* ON BLOCK1 *BEGIN* FLOOR ROOM17 *END* *END*)
```

In the list of keys returned by make-key-list, *BEGIN* and *END* are keys indicating the beginning and end of subexpressions, and the other keys correspond to symbols found in the expression. Keys are used to find (or create) a path in a discrimination tree from the root to a terminal node in which objects are actually stored. Consider the following set of formulas:

```
(on block1 block2)
(on block2 (floor room17))
(instance block1 block)
(instance block2 block)
(on (? x) (? y))
(on (? z) (? z))
```

Figure 4.25 shows a discrimination tree used to store these formulas. In this discrimination tree, all variables are associated with the same key, *VAR*. This means that (on (? x) (? y)) will be stored in the same terminal node as (on (? z) (? z)). Items stored in the same terminal node have to be further differentiated using matching or unification. Indexing using discrimination networks works hand in hand with matching and unification to efficiently access facts and rules.

There are also occasions when it is useful to store formulas indexed by subformulas. For instance, the following rule:

```
((on (? x) (? y)) if
 (on (? x) (? z)) (on (? z) (? y)))
```

might be indexed under (on (? x) (? y)). This method of storage would facilitate retrieving rules with a particular consequent pattern to speed goal reduction.

In the Lisp Implementation section at the end of this chapter, we include a simple implementation of discrimination trees. The function index takes a formula and a discrimination tree, stores the formula in a terminal node of

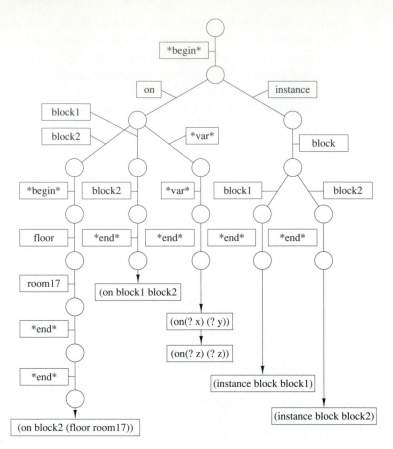

Figure 4.25   Discrimination tree for storing predicate calculus formulas

the tree creating new nodes in the tree if necessary, and returns the terminal. The function extract takes a formula and a discrimination tree and returns the set of all terminals in the tree that contain items that might match the formula. The Lisp Implementation section lists functions that add and fetch formulas from a given discrimination tree. Here we see fetch operating on the discrimination tree shown in Figure 4.25.

```
> (fetch ´(on (? w) (? w)))
((ON (? Z) (? Z)) (ON (? X) (? Z))
 (ON BLOCK1 TABLE2) (ON BLOCK2 (FLOOR ROOM17)))
> (fetch ´(on a b))
((ON (? Z) (? Z)) (ON (? X) (? Z)))
> (fetch ´(on (? x) (floor (? y))))
((ON (? Z) (? Z)) (ON (? X) (? Z))
 (ON BLOCK2 (FLOOR ROOM17)))
```

Decision Trees

Decision trees are closely related to discrimination trees. A decision tree is a representation for a particular sort of procedure. In a decision tree, each

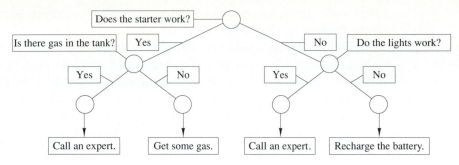

Figure 4.26   Decision tree for deciding what to do when your car fails to start

nonterminal corresponds to a question, and each arc corresponds to an answer. The procedure is executed starting at the root by asking the question posed at a node and traversing the arc corresponding to the answer. If the resulting node is terminal, then generally some data or action is associated with that node. If the resulting node is not terminal, then there is another question to ask.

Figure 4.26 shows a simple decision tree for what to do if your car fails to start when you turn the key. According to the decision tree shown in Figure 4.26, if the starter manages to turn the engine over and you find that there is no gas in the tank, then you should get some gas. Decision trees and discrimination networks are used in a wide variety of techniques for compactly representing decision procedures and for structuring large amounts of data.

▼ Summary

In this chapter, we focus on search: the problem of finding particular objects in a large set of objects. We describe the objects in terms of a search space and a set of operators that allow us to transform one object into another. When searching, we often have a particular goal in mind corresponding to a set of objects in the state space that meet a particular criterion. A tree-structured state space is one in which each object corresponds to a node in a tree whose arcs correspond to operators. Most of the analysis in this chapter assumes that we are dealing with finite, tree-structured state spaces. The algorithms presented here can be applied to arbitrary graph-structured state spaces if they are modified to handle repeated visits to the same object.

Blind search methods such as depth-first, breadth-first, and iterative-deepening search are appropriate when there is no structure in the search space that might guide search. Depth-first search has modest space requirements but may not find a goal node in an infinite tree-structured search space. Breadth-first search will always find a goal node if it does not run out of storage space trying to keep track of which nodes to examine next. Iterative-deepening is optimal in terms of both time and storage space.

However, there are occasions when it is more appropriate to use either breadth-first or depth-first search.

Heuristic search uses knowledge about the structure of the search space to guide search. In particular, heuristic search employs evaluation functions that are applied to a given object to compute an estimate of the distance from that object to the nearest goal. These estimates are used to determine whose children to examine next. Best-first and hill-climbing search are general heuristic search methods. A* search is a variant of best-first search in which the value of the heuristic function at a node is the distance from the root to the node plus an estimate of the distance from the node to the nearest goal.

Search methods can also be used to solve optimization problems. In optimization, evaluation functions provide a measure of the value of the objects in the state space. The objective of optimization is to find objects that are maximal with respect to the evaluation function. A local maximum in a search space is an object such that all the nearby objects have lower value. A global maximum is an object such that no other object in the search space has a higher value. One of the major difficulties in optimization is how to maneuver in a search space to avoid getting stuck in a local maximum that is not also a global maximum. Simulated annealing and simulated evolution employing genetic algorithms use randomization to jump about in the search space looking for a global maximum.

In two-person games such as chess or checkers, both players have perfect information about the state of the game. Game-playing algorithms search a game tree that represents the alternation of moves for the two players in a two-person game. Minimax search looks ahead some number of moves and uses a heuristic evaluation function to try to determine the best next move. α-β search is an extension of minimax search that avoids searching portions of the search space that could not possibly affect the next move decision.

Discrimination trees and networks are used for efficiently storing and retrieving data. In the text, we give the example of storing predicate calculus formulas so that they can be easily retrieved by an automated reasoning system. By storing data in a discrimination network, we can avoid expensive search in retrieval. Discrimination trees are closely related to decision trees that are used for specifying procedures in a graphical format.

Search algorithms are important in a wide variety of applications from factory automation to airline scheduling and robot path planning. Goal-driven techniques that allow any solution satisfying a specified criterion are appropriate in applications like theorem proving and certain types of mechanical assembly in which any solution will suffice. Optimization techniques that seek to maximize some measure of value are appropriate in applications like airline scheduling in which the costs of different solutions vary significantly. Issues of search arise throughout the rest of this text and especially in the chapters on learning and planning.

● Background

This chapter contains a variety of techniques for solving search problems. Some of these techniques are in the standard repertoire of computer science, and others were developed in response to specific problems encountered in AI, research. We mentioned that search problems are common in AI, but in fact search problems are common in most applications of computer science.

Depth-first and breadth-first search are basic graph-searching algorithms in computer science. Korf [1985] is responsible for introducing iterative deepening to researchers in AI, and his analysis provided theoretical evidence of the algorithm's utility. Iterative deepening has probably been reinvented many times, but according to Korf the first appearance in the literature is due to Slate and Atkin [1977], who used the technique in a chess-playing program. The A* algorithm was developed by Hart et al. [1968]. Nilsson [1980] includes an introduction to admissible heuristic evaluation functions. Pearl [1985] provides what is perhaps the most comprehensive treatment of heuristic search issues. Pearl [1982] describes an optimal pruning algorithm for α-β search.

There has been a great deal of work in developing efficient optimization algorithms. Papadimitriou and Steiglitz [1982] provide an introduction for computer scientists. Simulated annealing was developed by Kirkpatrick et al. [1983]. For a good introduction to the use of genetic algorithms for applications in learning and optimization see the text by Goldberg [1989] or Holland et al. [1987].

Discrimination networks are used in many deductive retrieval systems to organize knowledge encoded in the form of predicate calculus formulas. For more information on discrimination network algorithms, see Charniak et al. [1987].

■ Exercises

4.1 Write a heuristic search function `hill-climbing-search` that implements the hill-climbing search algorithm described in the text.

4.2 Write a heuristic search function `beam-search` that operates like breadth-first search in that it proceeds level by level, but different in that it recursively searches at most m children of the nodes expanded at the previous level. At each level, there will be a set of nodes of size less than or equal to m. Determine all the children of those nodes, and rank them using the heuristic evaluation function. Choose the top m of these nodes and recurse. Note that the space requirements for `beam-search` are $O(mb)$, where b is the branching factor of the search space. Note also that, even in the case of a finite tree, `beam-search` may not search the entire space.

4.3 Reimplement the `theorem` function of Chapter 3 using the generic depth-first search routine defined in this chapter. In the search problem addressed by `theorem`, a search state is just a conjunction, the goal is the empty conjunction, and the next-state function takes a conjunction and returns a list of all conjunctions obtained by replacing the first conjunct by the antecedents of a rule such that the consequent of the rule matches the first conjunct. For example, given the conjunction (P Q) and the set of

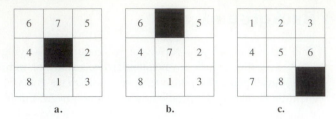

Figure 4.27   Possible configurations for the Eight Puzzle

rules ((P if R) (Q if S) (P if U V)), the next state function would return ((R Q) (U V Q)). Your goal and next-state functions should work with any of the other generic search routines defined in this chapter.

4.4 The *Eight Puzzle* is a game in which there are eight 1×1 tiles arranged on a 3×3 square so that there is one 1×1 uncovered area on the square. The tiles are labeled 1 through 8, and initially they are arranged in some random order. A tile with a face adjacent to the uncovered area can be transferred to the uncovered area in a single move. Figure 4.27 shows three possible configurations for the Eight Puzzle. The second can be obtained from the first with a single move, and the third can be obtained from the second after a sequence of moves. Figure 4.27c corresponds to the goal configuration. Define the state space for the Eight Puzzle, and provide an abstract data type for puzzle configurations. Then write Lisp functions to test for a goal state, and generate all configurations reachable from an initial configuration in a single move. Try depth-first and breadth-first search to solve the Eight Puzzle starting from various initial configurations.

4.5 Consider the Eight Puzzle described in Exercise 4.4, and determine if the heuristic evaluation function that assigns to a board configuration the number of tiles that are not in their final position in the goal configuration is admissible. Implement this evaluation function, and then try best-first search to solve the Eight Puzzle starting from various initial configurations.

4.6 There is an iterative-deepening variant of A* called IDA* that avoids the space problems with A*. IDA* works by using as a cutoff not the depth but rather the estimated distance from the root to the nearest goal provided by the evaluation function, $e(n)$. Implement a version of IDA* in Lisp, and test it using the robot navigation domain and the Manhattan distance as a heuristic evaluation function.

4.7 Modify the implementation of discrimination trees to be more driven by the data. The current implementation stores all objects at the leaves of the tree and generates an index for every key in a formula. In your modified implementation, objects may be stored at internal nodes in the discrimination tree. An index is added to a node just in case the number of objects stored at a node exceeds a fixed threshold provided as a global variable. Initially, all objects will be stored in the root node. When the number of objects stored in a node exceeds the threshold, a new index is created, and some of the objects are transferred to the newly created subtree. Your implementation should choose a new index that partitions the existing objects into two sets whose sizes are as close to one another as is possible.

4.8 Consider the problem of assembling appliances that was introduced in section 4.1. Suppose that the search space consists of the set of all permutations of work cells and each operator transforms a particular permutation by swapping two consecutive work cells. For example, {1, 2, 3} is a permutation for the case of three work cells, there are two operators that apply to {1, 2, 3}, one that swaps cells 1 and 2 and a second that swaps cells 2 and 3, and {1, 2, 3} has two children, {2, 1, 3} and {1, 3, 2}. Let the value of a permutation correspond to the number of assembly operations that can be successfully performed using the sequence of work cells described by the permutation and given the dependencies on assembly operations. Discuss the prospects for searching this space using hill-climbing search.

4.9 Implement a gradient search algorithm using simulated annealing to find the global maximum of a scalar function with multiple maxima. As a target function, select a particularly bumpy nth-order polynomial or a bumpier version of the sum of gaussians used in evaluating the genetic algorithms in this chapter. Devise a strategy for adjusting the temperature parameter from 1.0 to 0.0. If (> (random 1.0) temperature), then set x to be (+ x (* beta (gradient x)), where beta is some small number determined empirically; otherwise, set x to be (+ x (* gamma (gradient x))), where gamma is chosen randomly according to some heuristic strategy of your own choosing. Keep around a small set of the best values of x found so far and rotate among them to extend the search.

4.10 Implement the genetic operators described for the traveling salesperson problem, and apply the resulting genetic algorithm to solving instances of the traveling salesperson problem. To evaluate the performance of your algorithm, implement an alternative heuristic strategy such as Lin and Kernighan's edge-exchange algorithm [1973].

4.11 In this exercise, we consider how to represent satisfiability for formulas in propositional logic as a search problem. The reason that researchers are interested in satisfiability is that many combinatorial problems can be represented as formulas in the propositional logic. For example, in Chapter 3, we mentioned that propositional formulas are used in the pharmaceutical industry to represent the constraints governing the atomic structure of large molecules. The question of whether or not it is possible to build a molecule with a particular structure can be answered in terms of whether or not a particular formula is satisfiable.

The search space for satisfiability is the set of all assignments to propositional variables where each assignment can be represented as a string of 1's and 0's. For example, if there are four propositional variables {v_1, v_2, v_3, v_4}, then 1100 represents the assignment ((v_1True)(v_2True)(v_3False)(v_4False)). Assume that all formulas are represented in conjunctive normal form (that is, as a conjunction of disjunctions of literals). As an evaluation function for such formulas, we use the number of conjuncts satisfied. For example, if the formula is (($v_1 \lor v_2 \lor \neg v_3$) $\land$ ($\neg v_1 \lor v_3 \lor v_4$)), then the assignment 1100 has the value 1 and the assignment 1111 has the value 2. Modify the genetic algorithm code to search for a satisfying assignment.

4.12 Given the method of representing satisfiability described in Exercise 4.11, consider the following simple algorithm for determining if a formula is satisfiable. Let MAX-TRIES and MAX-FLIPS be constants and q be a formula in conjunctive normal form.

a) For $i = 1$ to MAX-TRIES

    i. Set T to be a randomly generated truth assignment.

    ii. For $j = 1$ to MAX-FLIPS

        A. If T satisfies q, return T and signal success.

        B. Otherwise, set v to be the propositional variable such that flipping its truth value in T results in the largest increase in the total number of conjuncts of q that are satisfied by T.

        C. Set T' to be T with the truth value of v flipped.

        D. Set T to T'.

b) Return and signal failure.

Implement the algorithm, and empirically determine reasonable values for the constants MAX-TRIES and MAX-FLIPS.

It turns out that it is actually quite easy to determine satisfiability for many propositional formulas. How hard it is to determine satisfiability for a set of formulas depends on the number of variables N, the number of literals per conjunct K, and the number of conjuncts L. For the case in which $K = 3$, experiments have shown that the hardest formulas appear when L is approximately equal to $4.3N$ [Selman et al., 1992]. The algorithm does quite well on these formulas.

4.13 Determine for each node in Figures 4.22 and 4.23 whether or not the node can be pruned from the search space.

4.14 Implement α-β search in Lisp, and use your algorithm to play a perfect game of tic-tac-toe.

4.15 Define an evaluation function for checkers based on the number of men and kings each side has.

▶ LISP IMPLEMENTATION

Discrimination Trees

Here is the code for a simple implementation of discrimination trees. For completeness, we begin with the abstract data types for variables.

```
(defun make-VAR (var) (list '? var))
(defun is-VAR (x) (and x (listp x) (eq (first x) '?)))
```

Indices are abstracted even though they are relatively simple.

```
(defun make-INDEX (key dt) (list key dt))
(defun INDEX-key (dt) (first dt))
(defun INDEX-dt (dt) (second dt))
```

We also make explicit our use of special symbols for indicating specific types of discrimination keys.

```
(defun is-var-key (key) (eq key '*var*))
(defun is-begin-key (key) (eq key '*begin*))
(defun is-end-key (key) (eq key '*end*))
```

Here is the abstract data type for representing discrimination trees.

```
(defun make-DTREE () (list 'DTREE nil nil))
(defun is-DTREE (x) (and x (listp x) (eq (first x) 'DTREE)))
(defun DTREE-links (dt) (second dt))
(defun DTREE-contents (dt) (third dt))
(defun set-DTREE-links (dt links) (setf (second dt) links))
(defun set-DTREE-contents (dt contents) (setf (third dt) contents))
```

Other basic operations on discrimination trees are recorded here in an effort to keep most of the discrimination tree specific code centralized. To simplify the code, we make use of the Common Lisp iterative construct, do, described in Chapter 2.

```
(defun DTREE-link-existing-index (dt key)
  (let ((link (assoc key (DTREE-links dt))))
    (if link (INDEX-dt link) nil)))


(defun DTREE-rawcontents (dt)
  (append
   (DTREE-contents dt)
   (do ((dts (mapcar #'INDEX-dt (DTREE-links dt)) (rest dts))
        (contents nil (append contents
                              (DTREE-rawcontents (first dts)))))
       ((null dts) contents))))


(defun DTREE-link-index (dt key)
  (let ((link (assoc key (DTREE-links dt))))
    (if link (INDEX-dt link)
      (progn (setq link (make-INDEX key (make-DTREE)))
             (set-DTREE-links dt (cons link (DTREE-links dt)))
             (INDEX-dt link)))))
```

Make-key-list takes a pattern expression and returns a flattened list of discrimination keys.

```
(defun make-key-list (pat)
  (cond ((null pat) (list nil))
        ((is-VAR pat) (list '*var*))
        ((symbolp pat) (list pat))
        (t (cons '*begin*
                 (nconc (mapcan #'make-key-list pat)
                        (list '*end*))))))
```

Given a pattern and a discrimination tree, index returns a terminal discrimination tree corresponding to that pattern.

```
(defun index (pattern dt)
  (aux-index (make-key-list pattern) dt))
(defun aux-index (keys dt)
  (if (null keys) dt
    (aux-index (rest keys)
               (DTREE-link-index dt (first keys)))))
```

Given a pattern and a discrimination tree, extract returns all terminal nodes that might possibly match. Note that extract is not supposed to perform unification. In a complete system, the resulting list would be filtered using a more discriminating form of matching to eliminate false matches. For example, unification would eliminate (on (? x) (? x)) as a match for (on a b).

```
(defun extract (pattern dt)
  (aux-extract (make-key-list pattern) dt))
(defun aux-extract (keys dt)
  (cond ((null keys) (list dt))
        ((is-var-key (first keys))
         (var-extract (rest keys) dt))
        ((is-begin-key (first keys))
         (subexp-extract keys dt))
        ((is-end-key (first keys))
         (key-extract (first keys) (rest keys) dt))
        (t (nconc (key-extract (first keys) (rest keys) dt)
                  (key-extract '*var* (rest keys) dt)))))
```

Key-extract takes a key, a list of keys, and a discrimination tree and returns a list of discrimination trees.

```
(defun key-extract (key keys dt)
  (let ((dt-maybe (DTREE-link-existing-index dt key)))
    (if dt-maybe (aux-extract keys dt-maybe) nil)))
```

Subexp-extract takes a list of keys and a discrimination tree and returns a list of discrimination trees. If the key indicates the beginning of a subexpression, traverse the *begin* and *var* links. In the latter case, eliminate the keys corresponding to the subexpression.

```
(defun subexp-extract (keys dt)
  (nconc
   (key-extract (first keys) (rest keys) dt)
   (key-extract '*var* (strip-off-subexp-keys (rest keys) 1) dt)))
```

Var-extract takes a list of keys and a discrimination network and traverses all atomic indices plus all sets of links corresponding to subexpressions. Var-extract returns a list of discrimination networks.

```
(defun var-extract (keys dt)
  (mapcan #'(lambda (link)
              (cond ((is-begin-key (INDEX-key link))
                     (skip-subexp keys (INDEX-dt link) 1))
                    ((is-end-key (INDEX-key link))
                     (error "VAR-EXTRACT: Ill formed list"))
                    (t (aux-extract keys (INDEX-dt link)))))
          (DTREE-links dt)))
```

Subexp-extract is called with its first argument, keys, bound to the list (*begin* ...), and its second argument, dt, bound to some discrimination tree. To extract discrimination trees from the *var* branch of a discrimination tree, we ignore the keys corresponding to the indicated subexpression. To do so, invoke strip-off-subexp-keys with (rest keys) and 1.

```
(defun strip-off-subexp-keys (keys level)
  (cond ((= level 0) keys)
        ((is-begin-key (first keys))
         (strip-off-subexp-keys (rest keys) (+ level 1)))
        ((is-end-key (first keys))
         (strip-off-subexp-keys (rest keys) (- level 1)))
        (t (strip-off-subexp-keys (rest keys) level))))
```

In discriminating on a variable key, you have to skip over (or suspend discrimination on) all sets of indices corresponding to subexpressions. The level argument to skip-subexp indicates the level of nesting (the number of *begin* keys encountered). Skip-subexp is called while discriminating on a variable key when a *begin* key is encountered, and hence the level argument is initialized to 1.

```
(defun skip-subexp (keys dt level)
  (if (= level 0) (aux-extract keys dt)
    (mapcan
      #'(lambda (link)
          (cond ((is-begin-key (INDEX-key link))
                 (skip-subexp keys (INDEX-dt link) (+ level 1)))
                ((is-end-key (INDEX-key link))
                 (skip-subexp keys (INDEX-dt link) (- level 1)))
                (t (skip-subexp keys (INDEX-dt link) level))))
      (DTREE-links dt))))
```

Here are some routines with a local variable corresponding to a discrimination tree used for storing logical formulas. Again we make use of the Common Lisp iterative construct do. The function add inserts a pattern into the database, and the function fetch retrieves all objects matching the pattern.

```
(let ((dt* (make-DTREE)))
  (defun add (pat)
    (let ((dt (index pat dt*)))
      (if (member pat (DTREE-contents dt)) pat
        (set-DTREE-contents dt (cons pat (DTREE-contents dt))))))
  (defun fetch (pat)
    (do ((dts (extract pat dt*) (rest dts))
         (results nil (append results (DTREE-contents (first dts)))))
        ((null dts) results))))
```

The following constructs the database described in the chapter and shown in Figure 4.25:

```
(mapc #'add '((on block2 (floor room17))
              (on block1 table2)
              (on (? x) (? y))
              (on (? z) (? z))
              (instance block block1)
              (instance block block2)))
```

CHAPTER 5

Learning

Arobot janitor aims its camera at the nameplate next to an office door. The robot is looking for recycling bins so that it can gather recyclable materials for the trash collection tomorrow. The robot's text recognition system indicates that this is the office of an assistant professor. The last three offices belonging to professors that the robot has entered contained recycling bins, but they were located on the fifth floor; this office is on the fourth floor. Pausing before the door, the robot consults the output of its classification system. The classification system indicates that the office does not contain a recycling bin, but there is not enough data for the robot to be confident in this conclusion, so it enters the office and begins searching for a bin. Contradicting the classification system, the robot finds a bin, and so it adjusts the system to account for the fact that a professor's office on the fourth floor can contain a recycling bin.

The robot classifies offices as either containing recycling bins or not. The adjustments that the robot makes to its classification system constitute a particular sort of *learning*. Learning involves changes to the content and organization of a system's knowledge enabling it to improve its performance on a particular task or set of tasks [Simon, 1981]. Learning occurs when the system acquires new knowledge from its environment or when it organizes its current knowledge to make better use of it.

In Chapter 3, we considered a learning method called explanation-based generalization that uses deductive inference to improve the performance of an automated reasoning system. In this chapter, we are concerned primarily with learning methods that use *inductive inference*. Inductive inference arrives at general conclusions by examining particular examples. For instance, if all the offices belonging to professors that the janitor robot enters contain recycling bins, then the robot can conclude with some confidence that all offices belonging to professors, whether or not the robot has entered them, contain recycling bins.

We consider a variety of inductive learning methods in this chapter. Some of these methods make use of techniques in statistical decision making, and others borrow ideas from biological systems to perform inductive inferences. We begin by classifying inductive learning problems. Next we present the basic theory involving inductive inference techniques. The rest of the chapter consists of descriptions of specific learning methods, including implementations and experiments. You are encouraged to replicate the results of the experiments described in this chapter and to design your own experiments. Learning provides an excellent example of how theory and practice work together to advance science.

5.1   Classifying Inductive Learning Problems

Learning based on inductive inference can be divided into *supervised* and *unsupervised learning*. In learning involving inductive inference, the learning program tries to infer an association between specific inputs and outputs. The "supervision" in supervised learning happens when the learning program is given both the input and the correct output. In other cases, there is no supervisor to provide the program with the correct output. In unsupervised learning, the learning program must rely on other sources of feedback to determine whether or not it is learning correctly. In learning to navigate in corridors, bumping into the walls provides a robot with feedback, indicating that its navigation procedure needs some adjustment.

Supervised Learning

In supervised learning, the learning program is given a sequence of input/output pairs of the form $\langle x_i, y_i \rangle$, where x_i is a possible input, and y_i is the output associated with x_i. The input/output pairs are called *examples* and are assumed to come from some unknown function. The learning program is expected to learn a function f that accounts for the examples seen so far, $f(x_i) = y_i$ for all i, and that makes a good guess for the outputs of inputs that it has not seen. The inputs can be descriptions of objects and the outputs classes that the objects belong to. Alternatively, the inputs can be descriptions of situations and the outputs actions or predictions. For example, the inputs might be descriptions of offices, including the floor that

▲ AI IN PRACTICE

Learning to Navigate

Humans are good at adapting to change, but programs are less so. Most programs are written for a specific task and fail to work when the unexpected happens. We would like our programs to make a best guess at handling new situations and learn from experience. For example, a robot delivery van must make steering decisions based on where it finds the road in video pictures. It should be able to drive down a variety of roads, not just the one it was initially tested on. A learning program can solve this problem by finding similarities between roads it knows how to drive and those it does not.

Carnegie Mellon University has developed an autonomous vehicle called ALVINN (Autonomous Land Vehicle In a Neural Network), which learns to drive. First, a human drives the vehicle to demonstrate how to navigate under normal conditions. Then, ALVINN is given a simulated driving experience, showing what the road would look like if ALVINN were veering off to one side and should take emergency action. From this training, ALVINN learns how to drive anywhere on a certain type of road. After training on a variety of road types, ALVINN can handle any of them. Taking 10 video pictures a second, ALVINN has driven as fast as 55 mph and for as long as 90 miles without human intervention. The figures show ALVINN and two low-resolution binary images corresponding to what ALVINN sees in driving on two roads.

Courtesy of the Robotics Institute/Carnegie Mellon University

---

the office is located on and whether or not it is occupied by a professor, and the outputs might be yes or no, indicating whether or not the office contains a recycling bin.

As an example of a supervised learning task, suppose that we want a robot to learn to drive a vehicle from examples of a human driving. The inputs are the images produced by a camera mounted on the vehicle and corresponding to what the driver sees of the road. The outputs are the actions taken by the human driver to steer the vehicle or adjust its speed. Figure 5.1a illustrates the examples presented to a learning program for

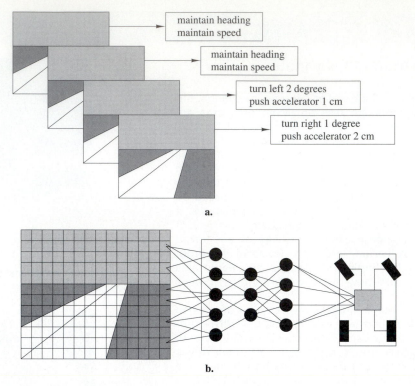

Figure 5.1 A learning program can learn to navigate a vehicle by observing an expert driver. The top figure depicts a sequence of input/output pairs consisting of images taken by a camera mounted on the vehicle and the associated steering and acceleration adjustments made by the expert driver. The bottom figure depicts the result of learning shown as a network implementing a function mapping images to control actions.

this task. Using these examples, we would run the learning program to obtain a function mapping images to actions. This function should generalize to cover situations not encountered in the examples. The learned function would then be implemented as a program to control the vehicle as shown in Figure 5.1b.

Classification and Concept Learning

If the function is discrete valued, then the outputs are called *classes* and the learning task is called *classification*. A system designed to monitor highway traffic might learn to classify vehicles into four classes: passenger cars, small trucks and vans, medium-sized trucks and buses, and large trucks. If there are only two possible outputs, then the learned function is called a *concept*. Each input either satisfies the concept or not. Learning in this case is called *concept learning*. For instance, a robot might learn the concept of a movable object. Every object either is or is not movable. Using such a concept, the robot might recognize a movable object without actually trying to move it.

Unsupervised Learning

In unsupervised learning, the learning program is not presented with a conveniently packaged sequence of inputs and outputs. A form of unsupervised learning called *reinforcement learning* uses a feedback signal that gives the learning program an indication of whether or not what it has learned is correct. Learning to play chess is an example of reinforcement learning in which the feedback signal is a function of pieces lost and taken and games won and lost. In many applications, including learning to play chess, the system learns to associate situations with actions to perform in those situations. Feedback is in the form of rewards that result as a consequence of performing a long sequence of actions in particular situations. The objective in this type of reinforcement learning is to maximize the expectation of reward.

In other forms of unsupervised learning, the objectives are highly problem dependent. *Clustering* is a form of unsupervised learning employed in pattern recognition tasks. A clustering algorithm partitions the inputs into a fixed number of subsets or *clusters* so that inputs in the same cluster are close to one another with respect to some metric on the space of possible inputs. In *map learning*, the objective is to learn a representation of space that facilitates navigation. In *discovery* learning, the objective is to uncover new relations in the data. A robot might discover for itself the concept "door" for describing objects that can be used to gain access to locations that are otherwise inaccessible.

Online and Batch Learning Methods

In some applications, the learning program might be given a large set of examples and allowed to process them all at once. Learning systems that process large sets of examples all at once are called *batch* methods. In other applications, the learning program might be expected to process examples one at a time and not store an entire sequence of examples. Learning systems that process examples one at a time are called *online* methods. In this chapter, we investigate both batch and online methods. Before we look at specific methods, we consider some theoretical issues that provide insight into the nature of inductive inference.

5.2 Theory of Inductive Inference

In this section, we investigate some of the basic theoretical results concerning inductive inference. We focus on concept learning, but much of what we have to say applies to other forms of learning. We assume a set X from which all of our examples are drawn. Formally, a concept is a subset $C \subset X$ corresponding to all examples belonging to the concept. In concept learning, the learning program is presented with a set of *training* examples, drawn

from X, labeled *positive* or *negative* depending on whether the example belongs to the concept. The objective is to learn a rule for correctly labeling
any example drawn from X.

The learning program is given examples of the form $\langle x, y \rangle$, where $x \in X$,
and if $x \in C$, then $y = 1$, otherwise $y = 0$. The objective is to learn a function
f such that $f(x) = 1$ if $x \in C$ and $f(x) = 0$ if $x \notin C$. The function f can be
expressed in a variety of ways as a set of rules, a procedure, or a network
of computing elements modeling neurons.

The Role of Inductive Bias

As described so far, the learning problem is not well enough defined for
us to precisely formulate a solution. We need to specify the set of functions from which we select f and provide some criterion for choosing one
function over another. Given a set of training examples, we can easily generate a function that accounts for the examples. A table that maps the input for each example to its respective output accounts for the examples
already seen, but provides no guidance in the case of yet unseen examples. Given no constraint on f, we have no reason to believe that there is
any better representation than the table that accounts for all the training
examples.

In the following, we assume that f is drawn from a space of possible
hypotheses; we notate this *hypothesis space* by H. To make concept learning
well defined, we need to introduce constraints on H. Such a constraint is
called an *inductive bias* (or just *bias*). A bias provides a learning program
with some basis for choosing among the possible representations for f. A
completely unbiased learning program has no justification for choosing any
function that predicts beyond the training examples. Guided by a particular
bias, a learning program can justify choosing a function that generalizes
beyond the observed training examples.

If an elementary school student is asked to solve a math problem, then it
is likely that a method for solving the problem can be found in the student's
mathematics textbook. The textbook provides a bias that restricts the search
for solutions. The student need not look in textbooks on advanced calculus
to find a solution. An inductive bias performs a similar service in learning
by providing guidance in selecting functions that generalize beyond the
observed examples.

Restricted Hypothesis Space Biases

The first type of bias that we consider guides the selection of a hypothesis by
restricting the set of possible hypotheses, H. Such a bias is called a *restricted
hypothesis space bias*. If a table including exactly the training examples is not
in H, then the learning program cannot choose such a table. Restricting
H can make learning easy in cases where a less restricted hypothesis space

would result in computational difficulty. It is also possible that restricting H can exclude the "right" hypothesis, and so restrictions must be considered with care.

Consider the space of all boolean functions defined on n variables, $\{x_1, x_2, \ldots, x_n\}$. In the robot janitor example, we might have a boolean variable x_1 for whether or not an office belongs to a professor and another one x_2 for whether or not the office is located on the fifth floor. A training example would assign True or False to each variable. A hypothesis f is said to be *consistent with a set of training examples* $\{\langle x_i, y_i \rangle | 1 \le i \le k\}$ if $f(x_i) = y_i$ for $1 \le i \le k$. Finding an arbitrary boolean function that is consistent with a set of training examples is easy. In this case, any function that maps every positive example to True and every negative example to False is consistent with the training examples.

Now consider some restricted spaces of boolean functions. We can represent any boolean function as a boolean formula. For instance, the boolean function represented by $(x_1 \lor (\neg x_2 \land x_3))$ returns True if and only if either x_1 is assigned True or x_2 is assigned False and x_3 is assigned True. One restriction on the space of boolean functions is the space defined by all conjunctions of positive literals. For instance, $\{x_1, x_2, (x_1 \land x_2)\}$ is the set of all conjunctions of positive literals involving up to two variables. If we restrict the hypothesis space to conjunctions of positive literals, then we can find a consistent hypothesis in time polynomial in the number of variables. The same can be said if we restrict our attention to the space of all formulas in k-DNF or k-CNF. A formula in k-DNF corresponds to a boolean formula in disjunctive normal form with an arbitrary number of disjunctions but with at most k conjuncts in each conjunction. k-CNF is defined by switching conjunctions and disjunctions in the definition of k-DNF.

Some restrictions on H are not enough to have a significant impact on the computational complexity. A boolean formula is k-term-DNF if it is in disjunctive normal form with at most k disjuncts. Interestingly, finding a consistent hypothesis in the case of a hypothesis space restricted to k-term-DNF, which forms a subset of the boolean functions in k-CNF, is NP-hard.

Similar results have been obtained for the neural-network models that we consider later in this chapter. Neural networks are often classified in terms of the number of layers of neural-like computing elements that they have. Finding a consistent three-layer network of neural-like computing elements is NP-hard, whereas finding a two-layer network can be done in time polynomial in the size of the network.

Preference Biases

The second type of bias that we consider is called a *preference bias* and provides the learning program with an ordering or metric that serves as the basis for a preference relation on H. Often we prefer short or simple explanations in accord with Occam's razor. Occam's razor is a heuristic frequently applied in science and philosophy and credited to the 14th century English philosopher William of Occam. Occam's razor counsels preferring the simplest of theories that account for the observed data and avoiding the proliferation of unnecessary concepts and terminology in explaining unknown phenomena.

For preference biases, the computational picture is more complicated. There do not appear to be polynomial algorithms for finding the most preferred hypothesis given typical notions of preference. For example, there are no known polynomial-time algorithms for finding the smallest conjunction or three-layer network consistent with a set of training examples. Although it may be difficult to find the simplest hypothesis, it may be easy to find a hypothesis that is within some factor of the simplest, where the factor is polynomial in the number of boolean variables or the size of the network. Such polynomial approximations to the simplest hypotheses can be computed in polynomial time in the case of conjunctions of positive literals, but not in the case of hypotheses restricted to finite state machines.

The problem of finding a hypothesis consistent with the training examples given a restricted hypothesis bias, and the problem of finding a simple hypothesis given a preference bias, are problems of implementing biases. We still need some notion of what it means to learn something correctly. In particular, assuming we have some control over the number of training examples, we do not know when to stop considering additional examples and commit to a particular hypothesis. Valiant [1984] provided a theoretical answer to the problem of when to stop considering additional examples.

Valiant's approach provides a bound, called the *sample complexity*, on the number of training examples required for a particular bias so that a hypothesis consistent with the examples seen so far is usually correct. The basic idea is that, if the hypothesis space is small, then any hypothesis consistent with the training examples is likely to be correct. This assumes that the set of training examples is somehow representative of the set of all examples.

Probably Approximately Correct Learning

Suppose that the training examples are selected from X according to some probability distribution $\Pr(X)$. We define the error associated with a given hypothesis f and concept C as

$$\text{Error}(f) = \sum_{x \in D} \Pr(x)$$

where D is the set of all examples on which f disagrees with C,

$$D = \{x | (f(x) = 0 \land x \in C) \lor (f(x) = 1 \land x \notin C)\}$$

We are interested in finding hypotheses with small error. We say that a hypothesis f is *approximately correct* with accuracy ϵ if and only if $\text{Error}(f) \leq$

ϵ. We accept the inevitable, that learning programs will make errors, and then we try to bound those errors.

We can further relax our requirements for learning by allowing some probability of deviating outside the error bounds. We say that a learning program is *probably approximately correct (PAC)* with probability δ and accuracy ϵ, if given any set of training examples drawn according to the distribution Pr, the program outputs a hypothesis f such that $\Pr(\text{Error}(f) > \epsilon) < \delta$. As is only fair, the distribution governing the selection of training examples must be the same distribution used in the measurement of performance. You would be upset if you took a class and the final exam had nothing to do with the textbook or the exercises assigned for homework.

In some cases, we can obtain a program that is PAC by using an algorithm that simply finds a hypothesis that is consistent with the training examples. Suppose that the hypothesis space is finite. If the hypothesis space is small, then it does not take many training examples to eliminate all those hypotheses that are not PAC. More precisely, a program that returns any hypothesis consistent with the training examples is PAC whenever the number of training examples is greater than $\ln(\delta/|H|)/\ln(1-\epsilon)$, where $|H|$ is the number of hypotheses in H. To see that this is so, consider the following argument.

If f is not approximately correct, then $\text{Error}(f)$ is greater than ϵ, so the probability of f being correct on a single example is less than $1 - \epsilon$, and the probability of f being correct on all m examples is less than $(1 - \epsilon)^m$. There are $|H|$ hypotheses in the restricted hypothesis space, and hence, the probability that there is some hypothesis in H that correctly classifies all m examples and is not approximately correct is bounded by $|H|(1-\epsilon)^m$. Solving for m in $|H|(1-\epsilon)^m < \delta$, we obtain $\ln(\delta/|H|)/\ln(1-\epsilon)$. Note that this result is independent of the particular distribution governing the selection of training examples and measurement of error. For this reason, PAC learning results are often referred to as *distribution-free learning* results.

In terms of efficiency, we are interested in how fast ϵ and δ decrease as the number of examples grows or, alternatively, how fast $1/\epsilon$ and $1/\delta$ increase as the number of examples grow. As a function of increasing $1/\delta$ and $1/\epsilon$, $\ln(\delta/|H|)/\ln(1 - \epsilon)$ is relatively slow growing. For 10^2 hypotheses, about 70 examples are required to reduce the error below 0.1 with probability 0.9; for 10^3 hypotheses, about 90 examples suffice; for 10^4 hypotheses, about 110 examples suffice. Multiply the number of examples by 10 to obtain rough bounds for an accuracy of 0.01 with probability 0.99, or by 10^2 to obtain rough bounds for an accuracy of 0.001 with probability 0.999.

PAC Learnable Concept Classes

We want programs that are not only accurate with high probability but that are relatively fast and provide high-probability accuracy after only a small number of examples. We also want programs that run in time polynomial in the relevant parameters of the problem, including the size of input descriptions and the number of examples. Putting all these requirements together, we can define what it means for a class of concepts to be PAC learnable by a given hypothesis space.

Let C be a class of concepts such that for each $C \in \mathcal{C}$, $C \subset X$. To account for reading and storing the training examples, we assume that the time required to process a given element of X is bounded by some small constant. $\mathcal{C}$ is said to be *PAC learnable by a hypothesis space H* if there exists a polynomial-time algorithm A and polynomial function p such that for all $C \in \mathcal{C}$, all distributions $\Pr(X)$, and any $\epsilon > 0$ and $0 \leq \delta < 1$, if A is given at least $p(1/\epsilon, 1/\delta)$ training examples drawn according to $\Pr$, then with probability $1 - \delta$, A returns a hypothesis f such that $\text{Error}(f) \leq \epsilon$. The class of k-DNF and k-CNF concepts are PAC learnable for the case in which the class of concepts to be learned and the hypothesis space are the same.

These PAC learning results are worst case, and hence, they are generally pessimistic. In practice, many concepts are much easier to learn than the PAC learning results indicate. This does not contradict the PAC results; it suggests, however, that many practical problems have structure that is not taken into account in the existing PAC results, and could be used to expedite learning. Now that we have described how inductive bias plays a role in learning, we explore some practical methods for implementing useful biases.

Finding Consistent Hypotheses

Learning theory tells us that, in some cases, finding a hypothesis consistent with the training examples is sufficient for effective learning. However, finding such a hypothesis can be time consuming. Computational complexity poses a challenge for researchers building learning systems that implement a particular bias.

The next two sections describe methods for implementing two inductive biases. The first method, called the *version-space method*, exploits the structure of a restricted hypothesis space to maintain bounds on the set of *all* concepts consistent with a set of training examples. This method proceeds by processing one training example at a time and is asymptotically optimal for the restricted hypothesis space consisting of conjunctions of positive literals.

The second method, called the *decision-tree method*, uses a very general hypothesis space and employs a preference bias and a heuristic to guide the search for a compact, consistent hypothesis that generalizes to yet unseen examples. The second method is an example of a batch method.

5.3 Version Spaces

A concept C_1, considered as a set of examples, is a *specialization* of a concept C_2 if $C_1 \subset C_2$. If C_1 is a specialization of C_2, then C_2 is a *generalization* of C_1. For instance, the concept "an office on the fifth floor" is more general than the concept "an office on the fifth floor belonging to an assistant professor." Specialization and generalization are transitive relationships on concepts. We say that C_1 is an *immediate specialization* of C_2 if there is no other concept that is both a specialization of C_2 and a generalization of C_1.

A *version space* defines a graph whose nodes are concepts and whose arcs specify that one concept is an immediate specialization of another. The method presented in this section uses a version space to maintain a compact representation of the set of all concepts consistent with the examples seen so far. This representation provides bounds, general and specific, on the set of consistent hypotheses using the ordering induced by the specialization relationship. The version-space method is optimal for conjunctions of positive literals in the sense that no method does less work in implementing the bias that restricts attention to conjunctions of positive literals. In principle, the method works for other hypothesis spaces, but the computational overhead can be prohibitive.

To make the following discussion more concrete, we return to the example of the janitorial robot that roams the top three floors of a university building collecting trash and looking for recyclable materials. The robot is trying to learn which offices have recycling bins. For a given office, it might know the following information: the status of its occupants, faculty, staff, or student; the floor that the office is located on, three, four, or five; the department that its occupants are associated with, electrical engineering or computer science; and the size of the office, large, medium, or small. This information defines the structure of the space of possible training examples.

Attributes, Features, and Dimensions

An *attribute* is a variable used to describe the objects in the space of possible training examples X. For a given $x \in X$, each attribute is assigned exactly one of its possible values. An attribute together with *all* its possible values is called a *dimension* of X. An attribute together with *one* of its values is called a *feature*. In the robot example, there are four dimensions described and notated (status, {faculty, staff, student}), (floor, {three, four, five}), (dept, {ee, cs}), and (size, {large, medium, small}).

We describe concepts as boolean combinations of features. In the examples in this text, there is no overlap between the sets of possible values for the different attributes, and so we often abbreviate features using the values of the attributes. Next, we list some examples of concepts in different restricted hypothesis spaces. A conjunction of positive literals can represent the concept corresponding to the offices on the fifth floor belonging to computer science faculty.

`faculty` $\land$ `cs` $\land$ `fifth`

The concept corresponding to large or student offices is a purely disjunctive concept.

large ∨ student

Finally, an example of a concept expressed in a conjunctive normal form in which each conjunction has at most two boolean variables corresponds to offices containing students from any department or faculty members in computer science.

student ∨ (faculty ∧ cs)

Specializing and Generalizing Concepts

Consider the version space corresponding to conjunctions of positive literals for the space of examples generated by the following three dimensions: (status, {faculty, staff}), (floor, {four, five}), and (dept, {ee, cs}). The most general concept is represented as True or as the degenerate conjunction with no conjuncts, ∧. Immediately more specific than ∧ are any concepts corresponding to a single literal. The concepts ee and faculty are immediately more specific than ∧. Immediate specializations of single literals are conjunctions of two literals. Immediate specializations of conjunctions of two literals are conjunctions of three literals. In our restricted representation language, conjunctions of three literals correspond to examples.

Figure 5.2 depicts the version space for our robot example assuming the restriction to conjunctions of positive literals and the three-dimensional space of examples. In the rest of this section, we present an online algorithm that modifies a *general* and a *specific boundary* after each training example. Initially, the general boundary consists of just ∧, and the specific boundary consists of the set of all conjunctions of three literals. Some of the two- and three-conjunct concepts are not shown in Figure 5.2 to keep the drawing from becoming too cluttered.

The boundaries are modified after each training example is presented. If the training example is positive, then generalize each concept in the

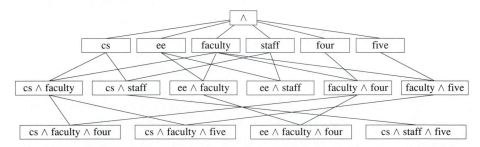

Figure 5.2   Simple version space for the robot example. Boxes denote concepts and are labeled with conjunctions of positive literals. An arc between two boxes indicates that the concept on the bottom is an immediate specialization of the concept on the top.

specific boundary until it is consistent with the example. In the case of conjunctions of positive literals, generalization consists of dropping conjuncts. For example, if there is a concept "purple and smooth" in the specific boundary and "purple and rough" is a positive training example, then we might generalize "purple and smooth" to "purple." In a more expressive hypothesis space, we might also generalize by introducing a disjunction or by turning concepts involving constants into quantified formulas.

If the training example is negative, then specialize each concept in the general boundary until it is *not* consistent with the example. Specialization in our restricted hypothesis space consists of adding conjuncts. In a more expressive hypothesis space, we might specialize by dropping disjuncts or instantiating universally quantified formulas.

If the specific and general boundaries are maintained according to these rules, then a concept is guaranteed to include all positive examples and exclude all negative examples if it falls within the general and specific boundaries. More precisely, a concept C is guaranteed to include all positive examples and exclude all negative examples if there exist C' and C'' defined as follows:

1. C' is in the general boundary.
2. C is equal to or more specific than C'.
3. C'' is in the specific boundary.
4. C is equal to or more general than C''.
5. C' is equal to or more general than C''.

Maintaining Version-Space Boundaries

If we want the boundaries to converge to a single concept, we have to do a little more work to eliminate concepts from the boundaries. The complete algorithm for maintaining the boundaries is listed here. This algorithm guarantees convergence to a single concept if there is just one concept consistent with all the training examples.

I If the example is positive, then perform the following steps:
   a) Eliminate all concepts in the general boundary that are not consistent with the example.
   b) Minimally generalize all concepts in the specific boundary until they are consistent with the example, and eliminate those that fail to satisfy the following requirements:
      i. Each concept is a specialization of some concept in the general boundary.
      ii. Each concept is not a generalization of some other concept in the specific boundary.

2 If the example is negative, then perform the following steps:

a) Eliminate all concepts in the specific boundary that are consistent with the example.

b) Minimally specialize all concepts in the general boundary until they are not consistent with the example, and eliminate those that fail to satisfy the following requirements:

i. Each concept is a generalization of some concept in the specific boundary.

ii. Each concept is not a specialization of some other concept in the general boundary.

Figure 5.3 shows a succession of version spaces labeled with boundaries and the positive and negative examples that gave rise to them. For simplicity, examples are represented by their corresponding three-conjunct conjunction, with a + or − to indicate, respectively, positive and negative examples. In the top drawing, there is a single positive example, and boundaries correspond to the example and the most general concept, ∧. In the second drawing, cs ∧ staff ∧ five is presented as a negative training example, and the general boundary consisting of just ∧ is specialized to faculty and staff. In the third drawing, cs ∧ faculty ∧ five is presented as a positive example, and both boundaries are changed. Finally, in the bottom drawing, the boundaries converge to a single concept as the last, negative example is added.

Data Structures for Learning

In this chapter, we provide Lisp implementations for several learning algorithms. In learning, as in most other areas of AI, theoretical investigations are no substitute for empirical investigations. Often it is only by running experiments that we gain useful insight into the limitations of learning algorithms. To implement learning algorithms in Lisp, we introduce the following abstract data types. A FEATURE is an attribute together with a value.

```
(defun make-FEATURE (attribute value) (list attribute value))
(defun FEATURE-attribute (feature) (first feature))
(defun FEATURE-value (feature) (second feature))
```

A DIMENSION is an attribute together with a set of possible values.

```
(defun make-DIMENSION (attribute values) (list attribute values))
(defun DIMENSION-attribute (dimension) (first dimension))
(defun DIMENSION-values (dimension) (second dimension))
```

An EXAMPLE is an identifying symbol together with a set of features that describe the example and an expression representing a class. In the examples in the text, there will be only two classes represented by the symbols yes and no.

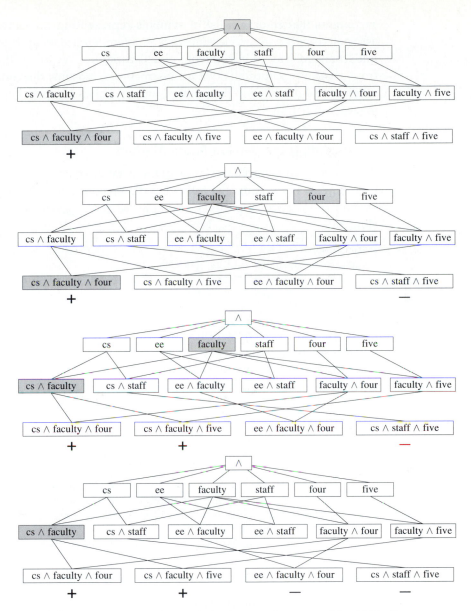

Figure 5.3 Convergence of boundaries in a version space. Plus (+) indicates a positive training example, and minus (−) indicates a negative example. Shaded boxes show the boundaries of the version space given the indicated training examples.

```
(defun make-EXAMPLE (id features class) (list id features class))
(defun EXAMPLE-id (example) (first example))
(defun EXAMPLE-features (example) (second example))
(defun EXAMPLE-class (example) (third example))
```

Dimensions is a function of no arguments that returns the list of dimensions associated with a given problem. Classes is another function of no arguments that returns a list of symbols representing the different classes associated with a given classification problem. Dimensions and classes are an underhanded way of introducing global variables. We allow this deviation from good programming style for instructional reasons; the code is simpler when we do not have to pass dimensions and classes around as parameters to every function.

Implementing the Version-Space Method

We provide a Lisp implementation of the version-space method at the end of this chapter. We assume the following dimensions and classes exist, where yes and no refer to, respectively, whether or not a given office has a recycling bin.

```
(defun dimensions ()
  (list (make-DIMENSION 'status '(faculty staff))
        (make-DIMENSION 'floor '(four five))
        (make-DIMENSION 'dept '(cs ee))))
(defun classes () '(yes no))
```

A training example is represented as a list of features. For our restricted hypothesis space, a concept is also represented as a list of features. The Lisp representation of the initial boundaries and the four training examples from Figure 5.3 is given in Figure 5.4. We set the specific boundary to include all concepts corresponding to the features of training examples. The general boundary is just the degenerate conjunction represented as the empty list.

Figure 5.5 shows the output of the Lisp implementation of the version-space method listed in the Lisp Implementation section with the training

```
;; Examples are represented by an identifier corresponding to
;; a room number, a list of features, and either yes or no
;; indicating whether or not the room contains a recycling bin.
(setq examples
      (list (make-EXAMPLE '412 '((status faculty) (floor four)
                                 (dept cs)) 'yes)
            (make-EXAMPLE '509 '((status staff) (floor five)
                                 (dept cs)) 'no)
            (make-EXAMPLE '517 '((status faculty) (floor five)
                                 (dept cs)) 'yes)
            (make-EXAMPLE '507 '((status faculty) (floor five)
                                 (dept ee)) 'no)))

;; The initial general boundary is the empty list representing a
;; conjunction with no conjuncts. The initial specific boundary
;; consists of lists of example features representing concepts.
(setq boundaries
      (list (list '())
            (mapcar #'EXAMPLE-features examples)))
```

Figure 5.4   Lisp encoding of training examples and initial boundaries

```
> (version examples boundaries)
Example: (412 ((STATUS FACULTY) (FLOOR FOUR) (DEPT CS)) YES)
General: (())
Specific: (((STATUS FACULTY) (FLOOR FOUR) (DEPT CS)))
Example: (509 ((STATUS STAFF) (FLOOR FIVE) (DEPT CS)) NO)
General: (((FLOOR FOUR)) (AND (STATUS FACULTY)))
Specific: (((STATUS FACULTY) (FLOOR FOUR) (DEPT CS)))
Example: (517 ((STATUS FACULTY) (FLOOR FIVE) (DEPT CS)) YES)
General: (((STATUS FACULTY)))
Specific: (((STATUS FACULTY) (DEPT CS)))
Example: (507 ((STATUS FACULTY) (FLOOR FIVE) (DEPT EE)) NO)
General: (((DEPT CS) (STATUS FACULTY)))
Specific: (((STATUS FACULTY) (DEPT CS)))
```

Figure 5.5   Refining the version-space boundaries

examples and initial boundaries shown in Figure 5.4. Note that following the final training example, the general and specific boundaries have converged to a single concept.

Optimal Method for Conjunctions of Positive Literals

The version-space method is asymptotically optimal for the restricted hypothesis space of conjunctions of positive literals. The method will work with other hypothesis spaces, but in some cases the number of possible concepts makes the method impractical. In the hypothesis space of all possible boolean formulas, individual concepts can become quite large, and the boundaries in the version space for certain concepts can become impractical to represent explicitly. In such cases, we may have to abandon the desirable goal of representing all hypotheses consistent with the training examples and be satisfied with finding a hypothesis consistent with the training examples that is relatively small and easy to represent. In the following section, we consider the merits of a heuristic method for doing exactly that.

5.4   Decision Trees

One of the simplest forms of learning, rote learning, consists of just remembering everything you have experienced. For concept learning, this would require remembering every example along with whether it was positive or negative. Of course, rote learning does not help with new examples; some means of generalizing beyond old examples is needed to correctly classify new examples. Suppose, however, that instead of remembering every feature of every example, you remember examples only in terms of those features that serve to distinguish positive from negative. For instance, in the version space of Figure 5.2, the offices belonging to computer science faculty are positive, and the rest are negative; the other features are not important for classification.

#	status	floor	department	size	recycling bin?
TABLE 5.1 Training examples for the robot janitor problem					
307	faculty	three	ee	large	no
309	staff	three	ee	small	no
408	faculty	four	cs	medium	yes
415	student	four	ee	large	yes
509	staff	five	cs	medium	no
517	faculty	five	cs	large	yes
316	student	three	ee	small	yes
420	staff	four	cs	medium	no

In Chapter 4, we considered the use of decision trees (also called discrimination trees) for storing information and retrieving it efficiently. In this chapter, we use decision trees to build a special-purpose memory to be used for classification. Recall that each nonterminal node of a decision tree is associated with a question that can be applied to the items stored in the tree. The answers are associated with the branches leading to the children of the node and help determine where in the tree items are to be stored. A path from the root of a decision tree to some other node corresponds to a sequence of questions and answers. The items stored in a terminal node are all those items that fit the questions and answers on the path from the root to the node. In this chapter, the questions correspond to attributes, and the answers to attribute values. The questions and answers on a path from the root to a node determine a conjunction of features defining a subset of the set of all possible examples.

For classification purposes, a terminal node can store any number of items as long as they all belong to the same class. Table 5.1 shows some training examples for a variant of the robot janitor problem; the last column indicates whether or not there is a recycling bin in the office. Figure 5.6 shows a decision tree for the examples in Table 5.1. The shaded items represent offices with recycling bins. Note that 509 and 420 are stored in the same terminal node.

Implementing a Preference for Small Decision Trees

The problem with the decision tree in Figure 5.6 is that it is not very useful for generalizing to new examples. For instance, it tells us nothing about medium-sized offices housing electrical engineering students. The decision tree in Figure 5.7 also discriminates among the examples according to class, but it is much smaller. From this tree, we might conclude that medium-sized offices housing electrical engineering students have recycling bins; indeed, this decision tree indicates that all student offices have recycling bins, a reasonable hypothesis given the data. Both decision trees represent

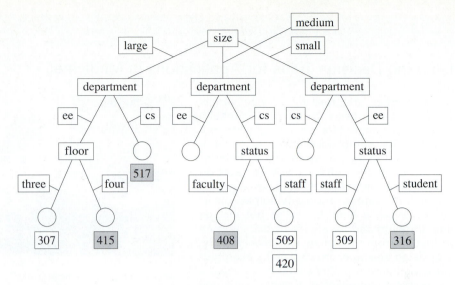

Figure 5.6   Decision tree for the robot janitor problem. Nonterminal nodes are labeled with attributes. Arcs are labeled with attribute values. Terminal nodes are shown as circles, and the training examples corresponding to offices that are stored at a terminal node are shown as boxes labeled with office numbers and listed below the node. Shaded boxes identify offices with recycling bins.

hypotheses about the target classification function; Occam's razor counsels us to choose the smaller of the two. In the following, we show how to implement this preference bias.

Preference biases give rise to optimization problems that tend to be hard. Choosing the smallest decision tree consistent with the training examples is computationally difficult. In lieu of an efficient exact solution, we seek a heuristic that will provide an approximate solution. The method for generating decision trees described in the following does not guarantee finding the smallest decision tree; however, the method has been demonstrated to perform quite well in practice.

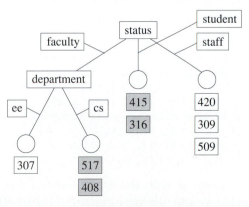

Figure 5.7   Compact decision tree for the robot janitor problem

▲ AI IN PRACTICE

Learning Decision Trees for Applications in Medicine

Decision trees are used for a wide variety of classification tasks in the field of health care. If a patient enters the emergency room of a hospital complaining of chest pains, it is important to quickly determine whether or not the patient is suffering from a heart attack and if so immediately begin appropriate treatment. Features for classifying patients as either having a heart attack or not include age, duration and frequency of pain, and information from the patient's medical history. A decision tree is constructed using examples corresponding to patients who have entered the hospital complaining of chest pains and subsequently been determined to have either suffered a heart attack or not.

The resulting decision tree serves as a procedure for emergency room personnel to follow in diagnosing incoming patients suspected of having heart attacks. Decision tree methods have been shown to outperform physicians in diagnosing heart attacks. Decision trees also have been shown to perform well in guiding physicians in the care and treatment of patients following heart attacks. In particular, decision trees have been used to judge the benefits of various treatments and diagnostic tests that are expensive or present some risk or possible discomfort to the patient.

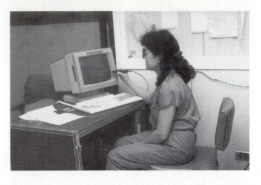

Alain McGlaughlin/Benjamin/Cummings Publ.

To implement decision trees, we need an abstract data type for nodes. A decision-tree node consists of an attribute, a list of examples, and a list of child nodes.

```
(defun make-NODE (examples) (list nil examples nil))
(defun NODE-attribute (node) (first node))
(defun NODE-examples (node) (second node))
(defun NODE-children (node) (third node))
(defun set-NODE-attribute (node attribute)
  (setf (first node) attribute))
(defun set-NODE-children (node children)
  (setf (third node) children))
```

In keeping with the examples in Table 5.1, the space of possible examples has four dimensions, and the particular classification task involves two classes.

```
(defun dimensions ()
  (list (make-DIMENSION 'status '(faculty staff student))
        (make-DIMENSION 'floor '(three four five))
        (make-DIMENSION 'dept '(cs ee))
        (make-DIMENSION 'size '(large medium small))))
(defun classes () '(yes no))
```

The decision tree method works by building a decision tree from the root down. The root is associated with the set of all training examples. All other nodes are associated with some subset of the examples determined by the path from the root to the node. A node is terminal if all the examples associated with that node fall in a single class; in this case, no further discrimination is necessary for classification purposes.

In the Lisp Implementation section, we describe a function `buildtree` that builds a decision tree. `Buildtree` is a recursive function that is invoked initially with a single instance of the `NODE` data type containing all the training examples but with no attribute or children specified. The algorithm that `buildtree` implements is described as follows:

1. If all the examples in the node fall in the same class, then quit.
2. If all the examples in the node do not fall in the same class, then perform the following steps:
   a) Choose some attribute and set it to be the attribute of the node.
   b) Partition the examples into subsets according to the values for the chosen attribute.
   c) Create new nodes for each nonempty subset of examples in the partition.
   d) Set the list of new nodes to be the children of the node.
   e) Apply `buildtree` recursively to each of the new nodes.

The only difficult step in the algorithm is choosing an attribute. If we choose an attribute that results in a partition in which all the examples are in the same subset, then we have added to the size of the decision tree without improving its ability to classify the training examples. In the following, we describe a disciplined approach to choosing attributes that leads to small decision trees in practice.

Disorder and Information Theory

Let S be the set of all training examples. Think of the decision tree as storing all the elements of S in its leaves. In classifying a new example, we want to be able to find the leaf containing the example by asking as few questions as possible; to this end, we would like a decision tree as small as possible. Since finding the smallest tree is computationally difficult, we build the tree from the root down (heuristically) choosing the question (attribute) that minimizes a particular measure of the *disorder* in the subtree rooted at a given node.

Information theory links the notions of disorder and information. The more disorderly a set, the more information is required to correctly guess an element of that set. For instance, someone might select a number from a set of numbers and ask to guess the selected number. Given an arbitrary finite set, the best strategy for guessing an element of that set is to repeatedly divide the set in half, ask which half the element is in, and then apply the strategy recursively to the half corresponding to the answer. The number of questions required to guess an element of S using this strategy is $\log_2 |S|$. Think of this quantity as the information value of being told x instead of having to spend time guessing it.

Let U be a subset of S. The information value of being told x after finding out whether or not $x \in U$ is

$$\log_2 |S| - \left[\Pr(x \in U) \log_2 |U| + \Pr(x \notin U) \log_2 |S - U| \right]$$

where $\Pr(x \in U)$ is just the ratio $|U|/|S|$ and $\Pr(x \notin U)$ is $1 - \Pr(x \in U) = |S - U|/|S|$. The sets U and $S - U$ partition S. Rewriting the equation for a partition $\{P, N\}$, where $P \cup N = S$, we obtain the information value of being told x after finding out whether $x \in P$ or $x \in N$.

$$I(\{P, N\}) = \log_2(|S|) - \frac{|P|}{|S|} \log_2 |P| - \frac{|N|}{|S|} \log_2 |N|$$

The attribute associated with a decision-tree node serves to partition the examples associated with that node according to the possible values for that attribute. All the subsets of the attribute partition are themselves partitioned by the possible classes.

To understand the difference between class partitions and attribute partitions, let $S = \{307, 309, 316, 408, 415, 420, 509, 517\}$ be the set of examples in Table 5.1 identified by number. $\{\{316, 517, 415, 408\}, \{420, 509, 309, 307\}\}$ is the class partition of S. $\{\{517, 408, 307\}, \{420, 509, 309\}, \{316, 415\}\}$ is the attribute partition of S according to the status attribute. $\{\{408, 517\}, \{307\}\}$, $\{\{\}, \{309, 509, 420\}\}$, and $\{\{415, 316\}, \{\}\}$ are the class partitions of the three subsets of the attribute partition of S according to status.

We are interested in choosing an attribute for a node that minimizes the disorder in the corresponding attribute partition for the examples associated with that node. This method of choosing attributes is not guaranteed to find a decision tree of minimum size (see Exercise 5.8), but it works well enough in practice. Let $\{S_i | 1 \le i \le n\}$ be a partition of S resulting from a particular attribute. Consider the case of concept learning involving only two classes, and let $P(S_i)$ be the set of positive examples in S_i and $N(S_i)$ be the set of negative examples. The information value or disorder associated with the attribute partition is the probability weighted sum over all S_i of the information value of the class partition $\{P(S_i), N(S_i)\}$,

$$V(\{S_i | 1 \le i \le n\}) = \sum_{i=1}^{n} \frac{|S_i|}{|S|} I(\{P(S_i), N(S_i)\})$$

TABLE 5.2 **Disorder and resulting class partitions for various attributes**

attribute	disorder	resulting class partitions
status	0.34	{{408,517},{307}} {{},{309,509,420}} {{415,316},{}}
floor	0.94	{{316},{307,309}} {{408,415},{420}} {{517},{509}}
department	1.00	{{408,517},{509,420}} {{415,316},{307,309}}
size	0.94	{{415,517},{307}} {{408},{509,420}} {{316},{309}}

Table 5.2 lists the disorder and the resulting class partitions associated with four attributes for a node containing the examples of Table 5.1. Table 5.2 indicates that this node should be assigned the status attribute.

Generalizing to an arbitrary class partition $\{X_i | 1 \leq i \leq n\}$, the value of knowing the subset of the partition containing the sought-after element is

$$I(\{X_i | 1 \leq i \leq n\}) = \log_2 |X| - \sum_{i=1}^{n} \frac{|X_i|}{|X|} \log_2 |X_i|$$

where $X = X_1 \cup X_2 \cup \cdots \cup X_n$.

We use this measure of disorder to help in selecting an attribute to partition the examples associated with a node. This measure has been shown to perform well in practice. However, other measures appear to perform equally well. An effective measure should reach a maximum when the examples are divided equally among all classes, and a minimum when all the examples belong to a single class.

Figure 5.8 shows the Lisp representation of the training examples shown in Table 5.1. Figure 5.9 illustrates the operation of buildtree on the set of

```
(setq examples
    (list
      (make-EXAMPLE '307 '((status faculty) (floor three)
                           (dept ee) (size large)) 'no)
      (make-EXAMPLE '309 '((status staff) (floor three)
                           (dept ee) (size small)) 'no)
      (make-EXAMPLE '408 '((status faculty) (floor four)
                           (dept cs) (size medium)) 'yes)
      (make-EXAMPLE '415 '((status student) (floor four)
                           (dept ee) (size large)) 'yes)
      (make-EXAMPLE '509 '((status staff) (floor five)
                           (dept cs) (size medium)) 'no)
      (make-EXAMPLE '517 '((status faculty) (floor five)
                           (dept cs) (size large)) 'yes)
      (make-EXAMPLE '316 '((status student) (floor three)
                           (dept ee) (size small)) 'yes)
      (make-EXAMPLE '420 '((status staff) (floor four)
                           (dept cs) (size medium)) 'no)))
```

Figure 5.8 Lisp encoding of a set of training examples

```
> (buildtree (make-NODE examples))
Class distribution: (4 4)     Attribute chosen: STATUS
Class distribution: (2 1)     Attribute chosen: FLOOR
Class distribution: (0 1)     Terminal node.
Class distribution: (1 0)     Terminal node.
Class distribution: (1 0)     Terminal node.
Class distribution: (0 3)     Terminal node.
Class distribution: (2 0)     Terminal node.
```

Figure 5.9   Illustration of buildtree constructing a decision tree. Each line following the function invocation lists the number of examples in the different subsets of the class partition for the set of examples of the node that buildtree is being applied to and either the attribute chosen for that node or an indication that the node is terminal.

training examples from Table 5.1. Note that buildtree generates a different decision tree from that shown in Figure 5.7, but it is of exactly the same size.

Decision Trees in Practice

There is great deal more to building decision trees for real-world applications. Techniques are available for dealing with attributes with continuous values, large sets of discrete values, and cases in which training examples are missing values for attributes. Noise is another issue that arises frequently in practice (see Exercise 5.6). Suppose that, in the case of our robot janitor, occasionally the robot mistakes a computer science office for an electrical engineering office. Various statistical tests can be used to exclude from consideration spurious examples, but to use these tests, more training examples are often required. As another example, suppose that the light being on or off in the office is considered a dimension of the learning problem. In the case of classifying offices with recycling bins, we would probably want to ignore this dimension altogether, but if it were relevant to the problem, its time-variant property would make it difficult to deal with. The basic decision-tree method is one of the most widely used and successful learning methods, and a large literature exists to assist the practitioner in its application (see for example, Quinlan [1986] or Breiman et al. [1984]).

5.5   Network Learning Methods

In this and the following three sections, we consider learning methods based on *network parallel computing models*. A network parallel computing model is composed of units that compute simple functions. These components are connected to compute more complex functions. Computation is performed by propagating values from inputs to outputs with individual units performing their local computations in parallel either synchronously or asynchronously depending on the particular model.

Figure 5.10 illustrates three of the most common components employed in network computing models. A *summation unit* takes *n* inputs and com-

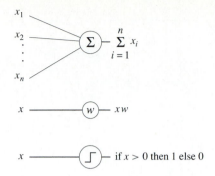

Figure 5.10   Basic components for network computing models. The top component is a summation unit that takes *n* inputs and computes their sum. The middle component is a multiplication unit that multiples its single input by a constant *w*. The bottom component is a thresholding unit that outputs 1 if its single input is greater than 0 and outputs 0 otherwise.

putes their sum, $f(x_1, x_2, ..., x_n) = \sum_{i=1}^{n} x_i$. A *multiplication unit* multiplies its single input by a constant w, $f(x) = wx$. Finally, a *thresholding unit* outputs 1 if its single input is greater than 0 and 0 otherwise:

$$f(x) = \begin{cases} 1 \text{ if } x > 0 \\ 0 \text{ otherwise} \end{cases}$$

These three units are combined in what is called a *linear threshold unit* shown in Figure 5.11.

Model for Computation in Biological Systems

Neurons are assumed to be the basis for computation in biological systems. The linear threshold unit has been used as a model for neurons. This model is commonly referred to as the McCulloch-Pitts neuron. Real neurons have complications not modeled by the McCulloch-Pitts neuron. For instance, real neurons appear to perform nonlinear, rather than linear, summations and provide graded rather than binary responses. Whatever its merits as a biological model, the linear threshold unit and related component units are

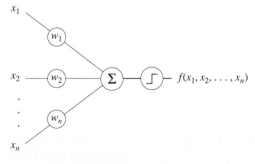

Figure 5.11   A linear threshold unit outputs 1 if the weighted sum of its *n* inputs is greater than 0 and outputs 0 otherwise

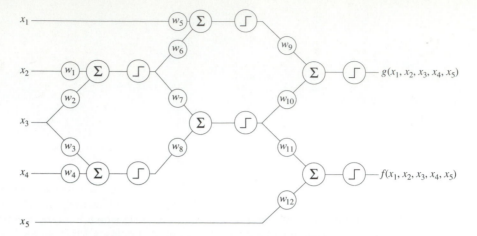

Figure 5.12   A network of neural-like computing elements

very interesting for the possible role they might play in parallel computation and learning. In the following, we largely ignore the biological modeling issues associated with network computing models.

A single linear threshold unit is of limited utility as a computing device. However, networks of linear threshold units such as the one shown in Figure 5.12 can be used to compute arbitrary boolean functions. Such networks are often called *artificial neural networks*. Network models can also be used to compute continuous functions.

Two functions typically used as computing elements for networks representing continuous functions are shown in Figure 5.13. They are the *gaussian* function, $f(x_1, x_2, ..., x_n) = e^{-\frac{1}{2\sigma}\sum_{i=1}^{n}(x_i - c_i)^2}$, where σ and the c_i are constants, and the *sigmoid* (or *logistic*) function, $f(x) = 1/(1 + e^{-x})$. Examples of gaussian and sigmoid functions are shown in Figure 5.14.

The response of a gaussian unit is determined by the distance from the input to the gaussian's *center* $\langle c_1, c_2, ..., c_n \rangle$ in the *n*-dimensional input

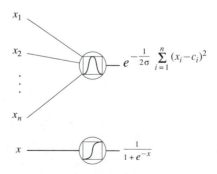

Figure 5.13   Additional components for network computing models. The component on the top is a multivariate (multiple input) gaussian function with *n* inputs. The component on the bottom is a continuous version of a thresholding unit called a sigmoid (or logistic) function.

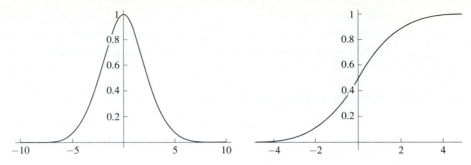

Figure 5.14 Graphs of two computing elements representing continuous functions. The graph on the left shows the univariate (single input) gaussian function with center 0 and width 5. The graph on the right shows the sigmoid (or logistic) function.

space. The magnitude of the response for an input whose distance is more than twice the *width* σ from the center is negligible. This sort of localized response is typical of certain neural structures found in biological systems and for that reason is popular among neural-modeling researchers. It also has mathematical properties that make it convenient for analysis. Later, we show how gaussian functions can be used to approximate other functions.

The sigmoid function provides a continuous, differentiable alternative to the thresholding unit. Networks such as the one shown in Figure 5.12 with the thresholding units replaced by sigmoid functions represent continuous, differentiable functions and as such are easier to handle mathematically. A linear threshold unit in which the thresholding unit is replaced by a sigmoid function is called *sigmoidal unit*.

Adjustable Weights and Restricted Hypothesis Spaces

As described so far, network models are just computing devices. Such networks can be used for learning by allowing a learning program to modify some of the parameters describing the network components. These modifiable parameters are called *adjustable weights* (or just *weights*). The adjustable weights define a *parameter space* whose dimensionality is determined by the number of adjustable weights. For instance, in the units that perform multiplication by a constant, the constant is treated as an adjustable weight. Similarly, we might wish to adjust the width and center of a gaussian unit. An adjustable threshold can be implemented in a linear threshold unit by using a standard zero-threshold unit and adding an additional multiplication unit with an adjustable weight set to a nonzero, fixed input.

A network model together with a set of adjustable weights defines a restricted hypothesis space corresponding to a family of functions. For instance, a summation unit whose n inputs are multiplied by n adjustable weights defines an n-dimensional parameter space and the following family of functions $\{f(x_1, \ldots, x_n) = \sum_{i=1}^{n} x_i w_i | w_i \in \mathbf{R}\}$. We now have a method of representing inductive biases using network models. In the next three sections, we consider methods for implementing such biases.

5.6 Gradient Guided Search

In this section, we consider the problem of finding a consistent hypothesis from a restricted hypothesis space specified as a network model with adjustable weights. We measure performance with respect to a hypothesis f using the mean of the squared error,

$$P = -\frac{1}{|T|} \sum_{\langle x, y \rangle \in T} (f(x) - y)^2$$

where T is the set of training examples. P is called the *performance function*.

We wish to find the best hypothesis, the one that maximizes the performance function. In general, finding such a hypothesis involves searching in the hypothesis space. Suppose that the hypothesis space is defined in terms of a network composed of units corresponding to continuous, differentiable functions with adjustable weights. To simplify the notation, assume that the hypothesis space consists of scalar functions. We can represent a hypothesis f from this space as a function $f(x) = F(\mathbf{w}, x)$, where $\mathbf{w}$ is a vector of adjustable weights. Note that F is also continuous and differentiable and that the performance function P is now a function of $\mathbf{w}$.

In some very simple cases, we can find the best hypothesis by setting the gradient of the performance function to 0 and solving the resulting system of equations for the weights. Alternatively, we can use the gradient to guide search; the gradient tells us the direction in which to adjust the weights so that the squared error decreases most quickly. If we make many small adjustments to the weights in the direction indicated by the gradient, then eventually we will reach some setting for the weights so that performance does not improve no matter what direction the weights are adjusted; this is called a local maximum of the performance function. If we are lucky, the local maximum is also a global maximum, and we have found the hypothesis minimizing the mean of the squared error.

Consider the following restricted hypothesis space:

$$\left\{ f(x) = \sum_{i=1}^{m} w_i \phi_i(x) | w_i \in \mathbf{R} \wedge \forall x \in \mathbf{R}, \phi_i(x) \in \mathbf{R} \right\}$$

where the ϕ_i are differentiable, real-valued functions. The gradient of the performance function, ∇P, is the vector of the partial derivatives with respect to the different weights,

$$\nabla P = \left[\frac{\partial P}{\partial w_1}, \frac{\partial P}{\partial w_2}, \ldots, \frac{\partial P}{\partial w_m} \right]$$

where

$$\frac{\partial P}{\partial w_i} = -\frac{2}{|T|} \sum_{\langle x,y \rangle \in T} (f(x) - y)\phi_i(x)$$

obtained by taking the derivative of P with respect to w_i keeping all the w_j for $j \neq i$ constant.

Gradient methods usually employ a *learning rate* that determines how much the weights are adjusted in the direction indicated by the gradient. The rule for adjusting the ith weight according to the gradient method is

$$w_i \leftarrow w_i + \beta \frac{\partial P}{\partial w_i}$$

where β is the learning rate, and $\leftarrow$ indicates that the expression on the left-hand side of the arrow is assigned the value of the expression on the right-hand side of the arrow.

This rule for adjusting weights uses the entire set of training examples. The following rule, due to Widrow and Hoff [1960], represents an online approximation to the preceding rule that uses only one training example at a time $\langle x, y \rangle$:

$$w_i \leftarrow w_i + \beta(f(x) - y)\phi_i(x)$$

Searching in Linear Function Spaces

The restricted hypothesis space described earlier is called a *linear function space* since each function in the space can be specified as a linear combination of the $\{\phi_i\}$. The $\{\phi_i\}$ are called the *basis functions* for the space of functions. The basis functions are often referred to as the *features of the input space* and need not be linear themselves. In the case of a linear function space, the performance function is quadratic in the weights. Quadratic functions are a special case of *convex* functions that are characterized by having a single (global) maximum. If the hypothesis space is a linear function space and the function being learned is in the hypothesis space, then by making a sufficient number of small adjustments in the direction indicated by the gradient, we can find a hypothesis such that the mean of the squared error is arbitrarily small.

As an example, suppose that the restricted hypothesis space is $\{f(x) = w_0 + w_1x + w_2x^2 + w_3x^3 | w_i \in \mathbf{R}\}$ and suppose we are trying to learn the cubic polynomial shown as the solid curve in Figure 5.15 (page 208). The set of training examples consists of 40 input/output pairs, with the inputs randomly selected from the set $\{x| -1 \leq x \leq 1\}$. Figure 5.16a (page 209) shows the performance of the rule for adjusting weights that uses all the examples to compute the gradient and $\beta = 0.1$. The hypothesis after 100 adjustments is shown as the dashed curve in Figure 5.15. Figure 5.16b shows the performance of the rule for adjusting weights that uses a single

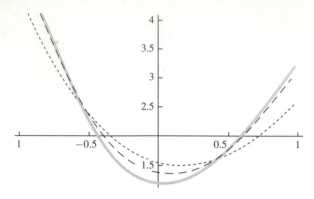

Figure 5.15   Cubic polynomials for the gradient method example. The solid curve is the function we are trying to learn. The dashed curve is the function learned after 100 adjustments using all 40 examples to compute the gradient. The dotted curve is the function learned after 100 adjustments using one randomly chosen example per adjustment to estimate the gradient.

example chosen randomly from the set of examples for each adjustment and $\beta = 0.1$.[1] The hypothesis after 100 adjustments is shown as the dotted curve in Figure 5.15. The adjustment rule using a single randomly chosen example does quite well given how little information it has to go on in making an adjustment.

Experimental Validation

Much of our confidence in learning programs comes from empirical studies. In the following paragraphs, we briefly consider how to evaluate learning programs empirically. In Figure 5.16, we used the set of training examples to evaluate the performance of the two gradient methods. In practice, using the training examples for evaluation purposes is to be avoided if at all possible.

Suppose that we want to evaluate a particular learning program. First, we need a source of examples. Ideally, we are given an example generator

---

[1]Some complications arise in using a single example to estimate the gradient. If the features of a given input are significantly different in magnitude (e.g., x versus x^3), then it is often necessary to normalize them in some fashion to avoid disproportionate changes in the weights. For the example of learning a cubic polynomial, we used the following rule for adjusting the weights:

$$w_i \leftarrow w_i + \beta(f(x) - y)\left[\frac{\phi_i(x)}{\sum_{i=1}^{m} \text{abs}(\phi_i(x))}\right]$$

where

$$\text{abs}(x) = \begin{cases} x & \text{if } x > 0 \\ -x & \text{otherwise} \end{cases}$$

This problem is avoided by averaging over all the examples, as is done when computing the exact gradient.

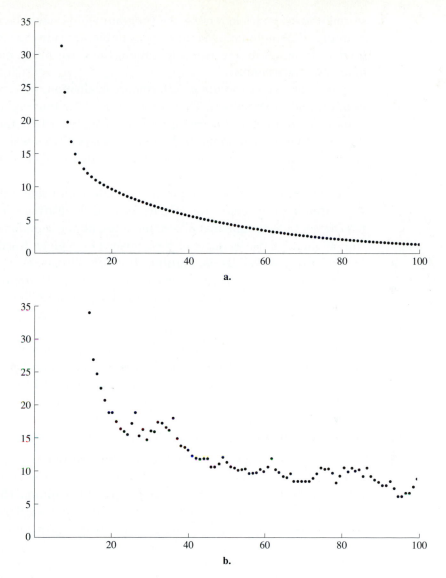

Figure 5.16 Graphs illustrating the performance of two gradient methods. Each graph shows the mean of the squared error over a set of 40 examples as a function of the number of adjustments. In (a) each adjustment uses all 40 examples; in (b) each adjustment uses one randomly chosen example.

that we can use to generate as many examples as we want. However, in many cases, the best we can hope for is to be given a single set of examples of fixed size.

We could give the whole set of examples to a learning program, have it construct a hypothesis, and then evaluate its performance by computing the sum of the errors on the examples. This approach gives the program an advantage that it would not have in a more realistic situation. By simply storing the examples in a table, the program would never be wrong on the examples but might not generalize to examples outside the set of examples used in training. In any real application, there are many more examples than training examples.

To obtain a more accurate performance evaluation, we can partition the examples into two subsets. One subset is used for training, and the other is used for testing. The learning program chooses a hypothesis based on the subset used for training. If the hypothesis performs well on the subset used for testing, then we gain confidence in that program for similar sets of examples.

If the set of training examples T is small, then using only a subset of T for training can reduce the effectiveness of the learning program. *Cross validation* is a technique that allows us to use all the training examples and still obtain a reliable estimate of performance for a given learning program. To perform cross validation, partition T into V subsets, $T_1, T_2, \ldots, T_V$, of as nearly equal size as possible. For each $v = 1, 2, \ldots, V$, apply the learning program using $T - T_v$ as the set of training examples, and let P_v be the performance of the resulting hypothesis as measured using T_v, the subset of examples that were not used in training. The *v-fold cross-validation estimate* for the hypothesis generated by the learning program using all of T is defined by $\frac{1}{V} \sum_{i=1}^{V} P_v$. Cross validation is recommended for evaluating the performance of learning programs in cases in which relatively few examples are available for training.

Nonlinear Function Spaces and Artificial Neural Networks

For hypothesis spaces corresponding to nonlinear function spaces, it is still possible to use gradient guided search; however, for such spaces, gradient methods do not guarantee finding a global maximum. The strategy for searching in nonlinear function spaces involves occasionally making large adjustments in the adjustable weights to escape from local maxima that are not global maxima. Making large adjustments in the direction indicated by the gradient is not guaranteed to result in a hypothesis with smaller squared error. By way of example, we consider a class of hypothesis spaces that are typical of the sort of artificial neural networks found in the learning literature.

The artificial neural networks that we consider are composed of sigmoidal units and are arranged in a sequence of layers. Each layer is associated with a set of inputs to or outputs from sigmoidal units. The inputs to a sigmoidal unit whose output is associated with one layer must come from layers that appear earlier in the sequence. Every network includes an *input layer* corresponding to the set of inputs for the network and an *output layer* corresponding to the set of outputs for the network. All the layers except the input layer are associated with the outputs from sigmoidal units. Layers other than the input and output layers are called *hidden layers*.

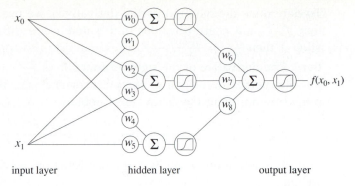

Figure 5.17   A three-layer artificial neural network. The input layer consists of the set of inputs. The hidden and output layers consist of sigmoidal units and their associated outputs.

The artificial neural network shown in Figure 5.17 is a three-layer network: an input layer consisting of two inputs, a hidden layer consisting of the outputs from three sigmoidal units, and an output layer consisting of the output of one sigmoidal unit.[2] It can be shown that a three-layer network with a sufficient number of units in the hidden layer suffices for representing any function. Unfortunately, this result does not help in determining how many units to add to a network for learning a particular function, and adding unnecessary units can slow learning. In the following discussion, we assume that we are given a network and wish to use it to learn a particular function.

Deriving the Gradient for Multilayer Networks

We use a gradient method to adjust the weights of the artificial neural network. We begin by deriving the gradient for an artificial neural network with multiple layers. To demonstrate the mathematics, we take the simplest possible case of a three-layer network, consisting of one input and a single-input sigmoidal unit at each of the hidden and output layers. The corresponding function is $\sigma(w\sigma(w'x))$, where $\sigma(u) = \frac{1}{(1+e^{-u})}$. We define performance in terms of the mean of the squared error, but we consider only a single training example $\langle x, y \rangle$,

$$P = -(F(w, w') - y)^2$$

where $F(w, w') = \sigma(w\sigma(w'x))$. The gradient for the case of a single training example is the vector of the partial derivatives of P with respect to w and w',

$$\nabla P = \left[\frac{\partial P}{\partial w}, \frac{\partial P}{\partial w'} \right]$$

---

[2]Be careful when reading the literature on artificial neural networks; some researchers do not count the inputs as a layer, and the network shown in Figure 5.17 would be considered a two-layer network.

To determine the required partial derivatives, we use the *chain rule*: Given that f, g, and u are functions and g and u are differentiable, if $f(x) = g[u(x)]$, then $\frac{df(x)}{dx} = \frac{dg(u(x))}{du(x)} \frac{du(x)}{dx}$. The chain rule also applies to partial derivatives. The derivative of the sigmoid function is $\frac{d\sigma(x)}{dx} = \sigma(x)[1 - \sigma(x)]$.

The partial derivative of the performance with respect to w is determined by applying the chain rule to obtain

$$\frac{\partial P}{\partial w} = \frac{dP}{dF(w, w')} \frac{\partial F(w, w')}{\partial w}$$

From the definition of the performance function, solving for the first term, we get

$$\frac{dP}{dF(w, w')} = -2(F(w, w') - y)$$

Solving for the second term requires another application of the chain rule.

$$\frac{\partial F(w, w')}{\partial w} = \frac{dF(w, w')}{dw\sigma(w'x)} \frac{\partial w\sigma(w'x)}{\partial w}$$

$$= F(w, w')[1 - F(w, w')]\sigma(w'x)$$

The partial derivative of the performance with respect to w' is determined in a similar fashion.

$$\frac{\partial P}{\partial w'} = \frac{dP}{dF(w, w')} \frac{\partial F(w, w')}{\partial w'}$$

The first term is the same as the one we encountered in the previous derivation. The second term can be determined by applying the chain rule multiple times.

$$\frac{\partial F(w, w')}{\partial w'} = \frac{dF(w, w')}{dw\sigma(w'x)} \frac{\partial w\sigma(w'x)}{\partial w'}$$

$$= F(w, w')[1 - F(w, w')]\frac{\partial w\sigma(w'x)}{\partial \sigma(w'x)} \frac{d\sigma(w'x)}{dw'}$$

$$= F(w, w')[1 - F(w, w')]w\frac{d\sigma(w'x)}{dw'x} \frac{dw'x}{dw'}$$

$$= F(w, w')[1 - F(w, w')]w\sigma(w'x)[1 - \sigma(w'x)]x$$

$$= \sigma(w\sigma(w'x))[1 - \sigma(w\sigma(w'x))]w\sigma(w'x)[1 - \sigma(w'x)]x$$

Error Backpropagation Procedure

The preceding analysis allows us to compute the gradient for a simple multilayer network. We can generalize on this analysis to obtain a procedure called *error backpropagation* for adjusting the weights of an artificial neural network in accord with the gradient method. As a convention, the rightmost or output layer is designated as the first layer. We also want to refer to intermediate outputs. An output at the ith layer is the output of a sigmoidal

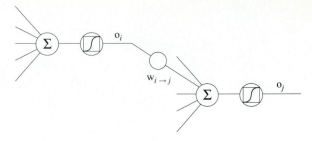

Figure 5.18 Illustration of the conventions used in the text for referring to the components of a network associated with a particular weight $w_{i \to j}$

unit at that layer or (abusing the terminology somewhat) an input if i is the input layer. Let $w_{i \to j}$ be a weight from the ith layer to the jth layer. Note that j need not be $i + 1$. In referring to $w_{i \to j}$, o_i is the output at the ith layer, which is multiplied by $w_{i \to j}$, and o_j is the output at the jth layer, which the product of o_i and $w_{i \to j}$ feeds into. Figure 5.18 illustrates these conventions. We assume that each weight is input to exactly one sigmoidal unit so that, given a particular output o_i and weight $w_{i \to j}$, the output o_j is uniquely defined.

Let **w** be the vector of adjustable weights in a given network and T be the set of training examples. The performance function is defined by

$$ P = -\frac{1}{|T|} \sum_{\langle x, y \rangle \in T} (F(\mathbf{w}, x) - y)^2 $$

where $F(\mathbf{w}, x)$ is the output of the network for a given input x and setting of the weights **w**. The gradient of the performance function is the sum of the gradients for each of the training examples. Let $P_{\langle x, y \rangle} = (F(\mathbf{w}, x) - y)^2$ so that $P = -\frac{1}{|T|} \sum_{\langle x, y \rangle \in T} P_{\langle x, y \rangle}$. Extending the analysis described earlier, we arrive at the following method for computing $\frac{\partial P_{\langle x, y \rangle}}{\partial w_{i \to j}}$ in an arbitrary network of sigmoidal units:

$$ \frac{\partial P_{\langle x, y \rangle}}{\partial w_{i \to j}} = o_i o_j (1 - o_j) \delta_j $$

where $\delta_1 = -(F(\mathbf{w}, x) - y)$ and $\delta_j = w_{j \to k} o_k (1 - o_k) \delta_k$ for $j > 1$. Each iteration of the gradient method adjusts the weights in the network as follows:

$$ w_{i \to j} \leftarrow w_{i \to j} + \beta \sum_{\langle x, y \rangle \in T} \frac{\partial P_{\langle x, y \rangle}}{\partial w_{i \to j}} $$

where β is the learning rate.

As we mentioned earlier, a three-layer network with enough units in the hidden layer can, at least in theory, be used to represent any function. In practice, however, designing an appropriate network and strategy for adjusting the weights can be quite tricky. Learning involves searching in the large, multidimensional space defined by the adjustable weights, and the gradient provides guidance only on how to find local maxima.

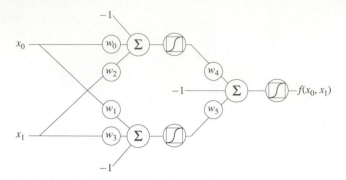

Figure 5.19   A three-layer, two-hidden-unit, fixed-threshold network

If we use a fixed learning rate, then we would like one that is large enough to escape from suboptimal local maxima but small enough to remain in a global maximum once it finds one. In general, it is impossible to find a fixed learning rate that satisfies these requirements. Instead of using a fixed learning rate, some learning systems adjust the learning rate over time using simulated annealing (see Chapter 4). In the following, we describe a Lisp implementation for artificial neural networks and examine some of the complications that arise in using error backpropagation and the gradient method to learn two-input boolean functions.

Implementing Artificial Neural Networks in Lisp

The first network we consider, shown in Figure 5.19, is a three-layer network with two hidden units. Since we want to learn boolean functions, we cannot use sigmoidal units approximating zero thresholds. Following standard practice, we remedy this problem by using fixed, nonzero thresholds implemented by subtracting one from the input of each sigmoidal unit.

```
(defun sigmoid (x) (/ 1 (+ 1 (exp (- 1 x)))))
```

Figure 5.20 lists the definition of the function net, which implements the network shown in Figure 5.19. Net takes two arguments, a list of the inputs to a two-input boolean function and a list of six weights. We represent

```
;; Compute the output of the network shown in Figure 5.19 for
;; a specified input and setting of the six adjustable weights.
(defun net (input weights)
  (sigmoid (+ (* (nth 4 weights)
                 (sigmoid (+ (* (nth 0 weights) (nth 0 input))
                             (* (nth 2 weights) (nth 1 input)))))
              (* (nth 5 weights)
                 (sigmoid (+ (* (nth 1 weights) (nth 0 input))
                             (* (nth 3 weights) (nth 1 input))))))))
```

Figure 5.20   Implementation of the two-hidden-unit, fixed-threshold network

the target boolean functions as lists consisting of pairs of inputs and their corresponding outputs. A pair of the form ((1 0) 1) indicates that the output of the function is 1 whenever it is input 1 and 0. Here are the representations for the boolean or, and, and xor (exclusive or) functions.

```
(setq or  '(((0 0) 0) ((1 0) 1) ((0 1) 1) ((1 1) 1))
      and '(((0 0) 0) ((1 0) 0) ((0 1) 0) ((1 1) 1))
      xor '(((0 0) 0) ((1 0) 1) ((0 1) 1) ((1 1) 0)))
```

We use error backpropagation and the gradient method for adjusting the weights to learn a given boolean function. Figure 5.21 lists the code for computing the gradient of the mean-squared-error performance function at the point in the parameter space specified by a set of weights. Gradient takes a set of training examples and a set of weights and returns the gradient at the point specified by the weights. The expression (mapcar #'+ v w), where v and w are lists of numbers representing vectors, implements vector addition. The contribution of the gradient for a particular training example is computed by the function delta in accord with the general error backpropagation procedure presented earlier.

```
;; Sum the contributions to the gradient for each example
;; at a point in parameter space specified by the weights.
(defun gradient (examples weights)
  (reduce #'(lambda (v w) (mapcar #'+ v w))
          (mapcar #'(lambda (pair)
                      (delta (first pair) (second pair) weights))
                  examples)))

;; Compute the contribution to the gradient for a single
;; training example for the network shown in Figure 5.19.
(defun delta (input output weights)
  (let ((error (- output (net input weights)))
        (out (net input weights))
        (hout1 (sigmoid (+ (* (nth 0 weights) (nth 0 input))
                           (* (nth 2 weights) (nth 1 input)))))
        (hout2 (sigmoid (+ (* (nth 1 weights) (nth 0 input))
                           (* (nth 3 weights) (nth 1 input))))))
    (list (* (nth 0 input) hout1 (- 1 hout1)
             (nth 4 weights) out (- 1 out) error)
          (* (nth 0 input) hout2 (- 1 hout2)
             (nth 5 weights) out (- 1 out) error)
          (* (nth 1 input) hout1 (- 1 hout1)
             (nth 4 weights) out (- 1 out) error)
          (* (nth 1 input) hout2 (- 1 hout2)
             (nth 5 weights) out (- 1 out) error)
          (* hout1 out (- 1 out) error)
          (* hout2 out (- 1 out) error))))
```

Figure 5.21   Computing the gradient for the two-hidden-unit, fixed-threshold network

Train takes a two-input boolean function and a set of weights for the network shown in Figure 5.19. If the weights successfully implement the target function, then train exits, printing the weights. Otherwise, train determines the gradient of the performance function, computes a new set of weights by adding the gradient to the old weights, and then calls itself recursively on the new set of weights. Train assumes a learning rate β of one. To use a different learning rate, multiply each element of the list of numbers returned from gradient by the desired learning rate. Note that, in the following implementation, the set of training examples includes the entire input space. For a larger input space, this is not likely to be true.

```
(defun train (target weights)
  (if (successp target weights) (princ weights)
    (train target (mapcar #'+ weights (gradient target weights)))))
```

For a given input, the sigmoid function corresponding to the output of the network provides a value between 0 and 1. A given set of weights is considered to have successfully implemented a target function if the difference between the actual and desired outputs is less than 0.4. All that is absolutely necessary is that the difference is strictly less than 0.5 so that the rounded output is equal to the desired output. The function abs is built into Common Lisp and returns the absolute value of its single argument.

```
(defun successp (target weights)
  (every #'(lambda (x)
             (< (abs (- (second x)
                         (net (first x) weights))) 0.4))
         target))
```

The choice of initial weights is important in learning in multilayer networks. Generally, it is a bad idea to have all the weights initially the same. We use a vector of real-valued random weights in the range from 0 to 2.

```
(defun init ()
  (mapcar #'random '(2.0 2.0 2.0 2.0 2.0 2.0)))
```

The procedure described here can learn only and, or, and xor for some sets of initial weights. For other sets of initial weights, train runs indefinitely without finding a solution. This is because train becomes stuck in a local maximum that is not a global maximum. It is possible to get train unstuck by increasing the learning rate, but this does not guarantee success. Here is an example of the weights determined in learning the xor function.

```
> (train xor (init))
(5.67 1.80 6.84 1.27 4.49 -4.39)
```

In a moment, we introduce another network for learning two-input boolean functions and compare the performance of the two networks. First, however, we consider some of the factors that influence performance.

▲ AI IN PRACTICE

Applications of Artificial Neural Networks

Artificial neural networks have been used to recognize and generate speech, navigate vehicles, recognize hand writing, predict price fluctuations in the stock market, and play games. NETtalk is an artificial neural network program that takes as input sequences of characters from written text and produces as output a sequence of phonemic codes that can be used to generate speech. The network consists of 7×29 inputs encoding a moving window of 7 characters, 80 hidden units, and 26 output units for representing the phonemic codes. NETtalk was trained on 1,024 words from a side-by-side source pairing English words with their corresponding phonemic codes. The program performed quite well demonstrating 95% accuracy on the training examples and 78% accuracy on additional words taken from the side-by-side source but not in the set of training examples.

Another artificial neural network program called Neurogammon has learned to play the game of backgammon. On each move, Neurogammon has a choice of approximately 20 possible moves depending on the roll of a pair of dice. Neurogammon is trained to associate a score between -100 (terrible move) and 100 (excellent move) with each triple, consisting of a position, an outcome for the two dice, and a possible move. The program is trained on 3,000 examples hand scored by an expert player. Neurogammon won the gold medal at the 1989 computer olympiad in London beating five commercial programs and challenging even expert human players.

Representational and Computational Issues

Learning boolean functions with multilayer networks is not particularly fast. Train learned successfully only after several hundred adjustments to the weights. Recall, however, that implementing the bias corresponding to three-layer networks is known to be difficult. Finding weights for a three-layer network so that it is consistent with a set of training examples is NP-hard. In some cases, the process can be expedited by using a larger learning rate, but too large a rate can introduce instabilities leading to undesirable behavior.

With a little work, we can generate weights for the network in Figure 5.19 that implement an xor function. For instance, suppose that the weights for the top hidden unit are 2 and -2, those for the bottom hidden unit are -2 and 2, and the weights for the output unit are 2 and 2. With these weights and a threshold of 1, the top hidden unit approximates a function that outputs a 1 only when x_0 is 1 and x_1 is 0. The bottom unit approximates a function that outputs a 1 only when x_1 is 1 and x_0 is 0. The output unit approximates an or function. Together, these three functions implement xor.

There are other weight settings that implement different solutions to the xor problem. For instance, the procedure just defined finds a solution in which those for the top hidden unit are 5.7 and 6.8, those for the bottom hidden unit are 1.8 and 1.3, and those for the output unit are 4.5 and -4.4. In this case, the top hidden unit approximates a function that is always 1 unless both inputs are 0, the bottom unit approximates a function that is always 0 unless both inputs are 1, and the output unit approximates a function that is 1 only if the top hidden unit outputs a 1 and the bottom hidden unit outputs a 0. Collectively, these functions implement $((x_0 \vee x_1) \wedge \neg(x_0 \wedge x_1))$, which is the boolean xor function.

In solving a problem, an *internal representation* is a representation that is not explicitly mentioned in describing either the inputs or the outputs associated with the problem. In chess, the input is described as a configuration of pieces arranged on a chess board, and the output as a legal move. An internal representation for playing chess might describe groups of pieces as units that can be used in strategic operations. The hidden units in an artificial neural network constitute an internal representation. By setting the weights for the hidden units, we are partially determining a representation for the target function. The only parameters left unknown are the weights combining the hidden units. If we are given a correct set of weights for the hidden units, then determining the weights for the output unit is easy using the gradient method. If the weights for the hidden units are fixed, we are searching in a linear function space with the hidden units serving as the basis functions and a convex performance function.

Learning in multilayer networks involves searching in a very large space of possible internal representations. This is why error backpropagation and the gradient method take so long to find a solution. In fact, the space of internal representations is even larger considering that we as designers can choose the number and arrangement of the hidden units. Next, we consider a different network for learning two-input boolean functions.

Networks with Adjustable Thresholds

The next network we consider is a three-layer network with a single hidden unit. This network, shown in Figure 5.22, is said to be *fully connected* because every unit at a given layer feeds into every unit at each layer closer to the output layer. The network of Figure 5.22 has adjustable rather than fixed

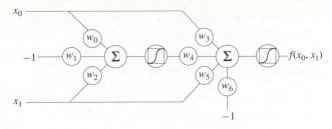

Figure 5.22   A three-layer, one-hidden-unit, adjustable-threshold network

thresholds. The network with its seven weights is implemented in Lisp as shown in Figure 5.23.

The only other function we need to change is the delta function, which computes the contribution to the gradient for a particular training example and set of weights. The definition of the delta function for the network of Figure 5.22 is shown in Figure 5.24.

```lisp
;; Compute the output of the network shown in Figure 5.22 for
;; a specified input and setting of the seven adjustable weights.
(defun net (input weights)
  (sigmoid (+ (* (nth 3 weights) (nth 0 input))
              (* (nth 4 weights)
                 (sigmoid (+ (* (nth 0 weights) (nth 0 input))
                             (* (nth 1 weights) -1)
                             (* (nth 2 weights) (nth 1 input)))))
              (* (nth 5 weights) (nth 1 input))
              (* (nth 6 weights) -1))))
```

Figure 5.23   Implementation of the one-hidden-unit, adjustable-threshold network

```lisp
;; Compute the contribution to the gradient for a single
;; training example for the network shown in Figure 5.22.
(defun delta (input output weights)
  (let ((error (- output (net input weights)))
        (out (net input weights)) (rate 10)
        (hout (sigmoid (+ (* (nth 0 weights) (nth 0 input))
                          (* (nth 1 weights) -1)
                          (* (nth 2 weights) (nth 1 input))))))
    (list (* (nth 0 input) hout (- 1 hout)
             (nth 4 weights) out (- 1 out) error)
          (* -1 hout (- 1 hout)
             (nth 4 weights) out (- 1 out) error)
          (* (nth 1 input) hout (- 1 hout)
             (nth 4 weights) out (- 1 out) error)
          (* (nth 0 input) out (- 1 out) error)
          (* hout out (- 1 out) error)
          (* (nth 1 input) out (- 1 out) error)
          (* -1 out (- 1 out) error))))
```

Figure 5.24   Computing the gradient for the one-hidden-unit, adjustable-threshold network

Here is an example of the weights determined in learning the xor function using the network of Figure 5.22.

```
> (train xor (init))
(-5.75 -1.71 -4.95 -4.02 -6.53 -3.02 -4.64)
```

The network of Figure 5.22 is a two-input boolean function followed by a three-input boolean function. The solution that the procedure finds has the hidden layer approximating a boolean function that produces a 1 only if both inputs are 0. The output layer approximates a boolean function that produces a 1 only when exactly one of the two inputs is 1 and the output of the hidden layer is 0 or when both inputs and the output of the hidden layer are 0.

Comparing the Performance of Different Networks

The network of Figure 5.22 has one more weight than the network shown in Figure 5.19, so you might think that it would take longer to learn, searching in a larger space of possible weights. In practice, this does not seem to be the case. Table 5.3 provides some data for different networks, learning rates, and boolean functions. The network of Figure 5.19 with two hidden units is denoted 2HU, and the network of Figure 5.22 with a single hidden unit is denoted 1HU. We tried two learning rates: 1.0 and 2.0. For each combination of network, learning rate, and target function, we ran the training procedure with 10 different initial sets of weights. Each time we allowed a maximum of 1,000 weight adjustments. The statistics in Table 5.3 are of the form $k(h/10)$, where k is the average number of adjustments over those times that the procedure successfully learned the target in less than 1,000 adjustments, and h is the number of times out of 10 that the procedure was successful. Note that 1HU performs better than 2HU in all cases but that both encounter some difficulty learning the xor function.

		Target Function		
Network	Rate	Or	And	Xor
2HU	1.0	297 (3/10)	301 (3/10)	394 (3/10)
2HU	2.0	345 (5/10)	152 (6/10)	199 (6/10)
1HU	1.0	5 (10/10)	12 (10/10)	264 (9/10)
1HU	2.0	5 (10/10)	6 (10/10)	145 (10/10)

TABLE 5.3   Average number of adjustments for different rates and networks

The story is somewhat more complicated than Table 5.3 indicates, but we leave it up to you to experiment with different learning rates, networks, initial weights, combinations of fixed and adjustable thresholds, and maximum number of adjustments before counting a run as unsuccessful. Currently, designing learning algorithms based on multilayer networks is more of an art than a science. However, in the following two sections, we provide a little more insight into what can be learned by network models and how we might guide the design process.

5.7 Perceptrons

In this section, we take a brief look at a special network model called the *perceptron*. Perceptrons use a restricted hypothesis space of boolean functions

$$\left\{ f(\mathbf{x}) = \sum_{i=1}^{m} w_i \phi_i(\mathbf{x}) > \theta \,\middle|\, w_i \in \mathbf{R} \wedge \forall \mathbf{x} \in \{0,1\}^n, \phi_i(\mathbf{x}) \in \{0,1\} \right\}$$

where $\mathbf{x} = \langle x_1, \ldots, x_n \rangle$, the basis functions $\{\phi_i\}$ are arbitrary boolean functions, and θ is a fixed threshold. Figure 5.25 shows a perceptron as a network computing model. Aside from the thresholded output, this function space is composed of functions that are linear combinations of the basis functions, and you might suspect that learning is easy for such a bias. This suspicion turns out to be well founded for an important class of concepts, called *linearly separable*, that we define later in this section. Of course, we cannot use the gradient method since both the basis functions and the thresholding produce a discontinuous and nondifferentiable function. There is, however, a very simple weight-adjustment rule that is guaranteed to work for linearly separable concepts.

Figure 5.26 depicts a simple perceptron for learning two-input boolean functions; it is called a *straight-through* logic-threshold unit since the inputs feed straight through to the weights. In a straight-through logic-threshold unit, the basis functions are trivial: $\{\phi_i(\langle x_1, \ldots, x_n \rangle) = x_i\}$. The weight adjustment rule works on the following intuition. If the perceptron produces the desired output for a particular input, then clearly we should leave the

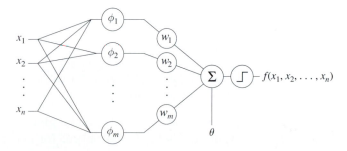

Figure 5.25 Perceptron depicted as a network computing model. The basis functions $\phi_1, \phi_2, \ldots, \phi_m$ represent arbitrary boolean functions, and θ is a fixed threshold.

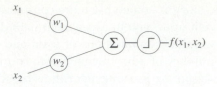

Figure 5.26   A perceptron for learning two-input boolean functions

weights as they are. Suppose, however, that the perceptron produces a 0 when it should produce a 1. In an effort to correct this error in the future, we increase the weights for those basis functions (inputs in the case of a straight-through, logic-threshold unit) that output 1. Similarly, if the perceptron produces a 1 when it should produce a 0, we decrease the weights for those basis functions that output 1. We never adjust the weights for basis functions that output 0 since these weights cannot affect the outcome for the particular input.

Perceptron Learning Rule

We can codify our intuitions in the following weight-adjustment strategy called the *perceptron learning rule*.

1. If the perceptron produces the wrong result, then

    a) If the perceptron produces a 1 when it should produce a 0, then decrement each weight by the output of its corresponding basis function.

    b) If the perceptron produces a 0 when it should produce a 1, then increment each weight by the output of its corresponding basis function.

2. Otherwise make no changes to the weights.

We implement this in Lisp as follows. First, we provide an implementation for straight-through, logic-threshold units with a fixed threshold of 1 for any length of input and weight vectors.

```
(defun ltu (input weights)
  (if (< 1 (apply #'+ (mapcar #'* input weights))) 1 0))
```

Here is an implementation of the perceptron learning rule.

```
(defun adjust (input output weights)
  (cond ((= (ltu input weights) output) weights)
        ((= (ltu input weights) 0) (mapcar #'+ weights input))
        (t (mapcar #'- weights input))))
```

A perceptron has successfully learned a given target function when the perceptron output equals the target output for every input.

```
(defun successp (target weights)
  (every #'(lambda (x) (= (ltu (first x) weights) (second x))) target))
```

For our experiments, training consists of choosing random input/output pairs from the target and adjusting the weights according to the perceptron learning rule until the target is successfully learned.

```
(defun train (target weights)
  (if (successp target weights) nil
    (let ((pair (nth (random (length target)) target)))
      (train target (adjust (first pair) (second pair) weights)))))
```

We ran the training program with a target of the or function 20 times. It took an average of 8 trials, as few as 3 trials, and as many as 18 trials to learn this function. Here is some example output from a version of train modified to provide running commentary and summary statistics.

```
> (test or '(0 0))
Training example: ((1 1) 1)   Adjusted weights: (1 1)
Training example: ((0 1) 1)   Adjusted weights: (1 2)
Training example: ((0 1) 1)   Adjusted weights: (1 2)
Training example: ((1 0) 1)   Adjusted weights: (2 2)
Number of adjustments: 4
```

For this run, the learning algorithm was not even presented with all the possible inputs, and still it managed to learn the function. The initial setting of the weights plays a role in how quickly a perceptron learns. However, this procedure is guaranteed to find a correct set of weights no matter what the initial weights are. Perceptrons appear to work far more quickly than the multilayer networks studied in the previous section. Unfortunately, the perceptron of Figure 5.26 cannot learn any two-input boolean function.

Linearly Separable Functions

The set of inputs, $x_1, \ldots, x_n$, define an n-dimensional space. A boolean function defining a concept is said to be *linearly separable* if there exists a hyperplane dividing the space into inputs for which the function produces a 1 and inputs for which the function produces a 0. The perceptron learning rule for straight-through, logic-threshold units works only for concepts that are linearly separable.[3] Figure 5.27 provides examples of two-input boolean functions that are linearly separable and examples of functions that are not linearly separable. A hyperplane in a two-dimensional input space is just a line. Note that the xor function that gave our multilayer networks so much trouble is not linearly separable.

Perceptrons are fast, but limited. Note, however, that we can transform any concept into a linearly separable concept by making the concept be one

---

[3]In order to learn any linearly separable boolean function using the perceptron learning rule, we have to add an adjustable threshold as we did earlier by providing an additional adjustable weight wired to a nonzero, fixed input.

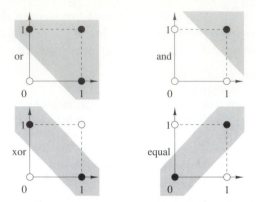

Figure 5.27   Boolean functions and linear separability. The or and and functions are linearly separable. For these two functions, the hyperplane separating the inputs that produce a 1 from those that produce a 0 is shown as the border between the shaded and unshaded regions of the input space. The xor and equal functions are not linearly separable. For these two functions, no hyperplane separates the inputs that produce a 1 from those that produce a 0.

of the basis functions. This gets back to the problem of determining a good internal representation that we mentioned in the previous section; learning is easy if you start with the right representation. In the next section, we provide some insight into the problem of finding good internal representations for network learning models.

5.8   Radial Basis Functions

Linear function spaces are appealing for two important reasons. First, gradient search techniques are guaranteed to find a global maximum in such spaces. Second, given the right set of basis functions, it is possible to learn any function. Of course, the second reason is trivial since we can always add the target function as one of the basis functions. It turns out, however, that a variety of problems can be solved by using a class of basis functions called *radial* basis functions. In this section, we focus on learning by approximating functions. The objective in learning by approximating functions is to find a hypothesis with small mean squared error.

Earlier, we considered learning functions using polynomials as basis functions. In the case of polynomial basis functions, such as those in the set $\{1, x, x^2, x^3\}$, each basis function has some nonnegligible influence on the output of the network throughout the input space. If $w_0 = w_1 = w_2 = w_3$, then the basis function x^2 significantly influences the output of $w_0 + w_1 x + w_2 x^2 + w_3 x^3$ except when x is close to 0. In this section, we consider basis functions whose influence is more localized.

A *radial basis function* is one whose output is symmetric about some fixed point or *center* in the input space and whose magnitude is negligible outside some bound determined by its *width*. Figure 5.28 shows some

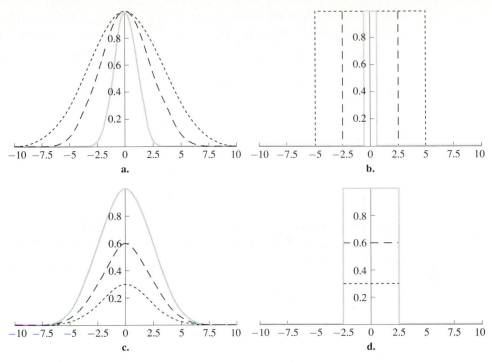

Figure 5.28 Continuous and discontinuous radial basis functions. (a) and (b) show, respectively, gaussian and step radial basis functions of widths 1 (solid), 5 (dashed), and 10 (dotted). (c) and (d) show, respectively, gaussian and step radial basis functions of width 5 multiplied by 1.0 (solid), 0.6 (dashed), and 0.3 (dotted) to provide some idea of how such functions behave when attenuated.

simple radial basis functions centered on 0 with varying widths. In approximating functions, the centers of the radial basis functions are hardly ever centered on the same point; instead, they are spread out in the input space.

Approximating Functions by Combining Gaussians

If the target function is a linear combination of gaussian functions, then learning using a linear function space whose basis functions are gaussians makes perfect sense. However, what if the hypothesis space is different from the concept space? For instance, what if we are trying to learn cubic polynomials? Will gaussian basis functions help here as well? The answer is yes. With enough gaussian functions having the right centers and widths, we can approximate any function to any degree of precision. This is exactly the claim that we made for multilayer networks. In the case of radial basis functions, however, the truth of the claim is a little easier to grasp intuitively.

Think of the step functions in Figure 5.28 as piecewise-constant approximations to the gaussians, and consider a basis of step functions. Each step function is nonzero on some region of the input space determined by its center and width. Suppose that we use four piecewise-constant functions with centers −0.75, −0.25, 0.25, and 0.75 and width 0.5.

$$h_1(x) = \begin{cases} 1 \text{ if } -1 \leq x < -0.5 \\ 0 \text{ otherwise} \end{cases}$$

$$h_2(x) = \begin{cases} 1 \text{ if } -0.5 \leq x < 0 \\ 0 \text{ otherwise} \end{cases}$$

$$h_3(x) = \begin{cases} 1 \text{ if } 0 \leq x < 0.5 \\ 0 \text{ otherwise} \end{cases}$$

$$h_4(x) = \begin{cases} 1 \text{ if } 0.5 \leq x \leq 1 \\ 0 \text{ otherwise} \end{cases}$$

The corresponding restricted hypothesis space is defined by $\{w_1 h_1 + w_2 h_2 + w_3 h_3 + w_4 h_4 | w_i \in \mathbf{R}\}$. Assigning a value to each of the four weights, we obtain the piecewise-constant approximation of the cubic polynomial shown in Figure 5.29. The resulting approximation serves as a table in which there is an entry for each of the nonzero regions defined by the basis functions. This entry is the weight associated with a given step function, and it is set to the average of the outputs of the target function over the nonzero region. Using small enough regions, we can approximate any function to any degree of accuracy.

The region of the input space determined by the width and center of a radial basis function is called its *receptive field*. When using gaussian basis functions, the receptive fields often overlap to some extent; in this case, several basis functions may contribute significantly to the output corresponding to a particular input. The resulting function with its overlapping receptive fields provides a smooth approximation to the target function. We can control the smoothness by modifying the widths of the basis functions. When we use a small number of training examples, the resulting function

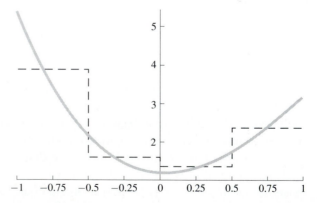

Figure 5.29 Approximating a polynomial with piecewise-constant functions. The solid line indicates the cubic polynomial we are trying to learn. The dashed line indicates a piecewise-constant approximation to the polynomial.

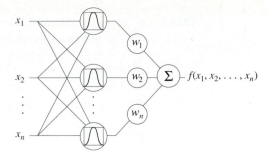

Figure 5.30   A network for approximating functions

computes the value for a new input by using the smoothed function to interpolate between the values for two old inputs.

Figure 5.30 provides the general structure for a network representing a linear combination of gaussian basis functions. We distinguish the w_i from the other adjustable parameters of the network, the centers and widths of the radial basis functions, by referring to them as the *coefficients*, of the network. The parameter space associated with a network is defined by the coefficients of the network and the centers and widths of the radial basis functions. To learn using such a network, we could use gradient methods to search the parameter space for a global maximum of the performance function. However, this would probably not result in much of an improvement over the same method applied to multilayer networks.

Two-Step Strategy for Adjusting Weights

Instead of adjusting all the weights simultaneously, we can decompose the learning problem into two steps. First, we generate a rough representation of the target function by assigning radial basis functions to regions of the input space. This step fixes the widths and centers of the radial basis functions. We might assign many narrow-width basis functions to portions of the input space that are important or in which the target function varies considerably. In learning to estimate the position of objects for the purpose of obstacle avoidance, a robot does not need a precise estimate for objects at a considerable distance. The learning program would allocate most of the radial basis functions to regions of the input space corresponding to portions of physical space near the robot. In the second step, we refine the representation by determining how each receptive field contributes to the output of the learned function. This step determines the coefficients of the network.

Each step might require some experimentation. In fact, we might jump back and forth between these two steps, performing experiments in an effort to learn more about the structure of the target function. Consider how we might apply these steps to a particular problem.

TABLE 5.4   Error for different centers and widths
of the basis functions

Centers				Widths	Error
−0.75	−0.375	0.0	0.50	1.0	48.10
−0.75	−0.375	0.0	0.50	0.5	9.45
−0.75	−0.25	0.25	0.75	1.0	38.19
−0.75	−0.25	0.25	0.75	0.5	5.22
−1.00	−0.500	0.0	1.00	1.0	16.51
−1.00	−0.500	0.0	1.00	0.5	2.64

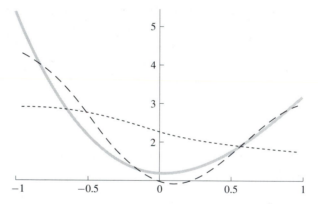

Figure 5.31   Approximating a cubic polynomial with gaussian basis functions. The solid curve is the target function. The dashed curve is the approximation using a width of 0.5 and centers of −1.0, −0.5, 0.0, and 1.0. The dotted curve is the approximation using a width of 1.0 and centers of −0.75, −0.25, 0.25, and 0.75.

Suppose that we use a set of radial basis functions, $\{\eta_{c_1,\sigma_1}, \eta_{c_2,\sigma_2}, \eta_{c_3,\sigma_3}, \eta_{c_4,\sigma_4}\}$, where $\eta_{c,\sigma}(x) = e^{-\frac{1}{2\sigma}(x-c)^2}$, to approximate the cubic polynomial that we considered in Figure 5.29. We fix the centers and widths for different values and, using 40 input/output pairs with inputs drawn randomly from the range $[-1, 1]$, we applied the gradient method for 500 steps using all 40 examples each time to compute the gradient.[4] Table 5.4 shows some of the selected values for the widths and centers along with the mean squared error of the resulting approximation computed over the same 40 examples. Figure 5.31 shows the target function and two representative approximations.

---

[4]More steps did not have any appreciable additional impact on performance.

Changes in the widths and centers significantly affect the performance of the resulting approximation. Barring divine inspiration, how can we find appropriate settings for the widths and centers? There is no easy answer to this question, but we consider one strategy that often works in practice. Suppose that we are given a small set of training examples drawn from throughout the input space. We hope that each example is somehow typical of examples that are nearby in the input space, but we cannot guarantee this. We are going to use these training examples to set the centers and widths of the gaussian basis functions.

Suppose that we choose four training examples of the form $\langle x_i, y_i \rangle$. Let $x_1 = -0.8$, $x_2 = -0.2$, $x_3 = 0.3$, $x_4 = 0.9$, and $y_i = g(x_i)$, where the target function g is defined by $g(x) = 1.20 - 0.20x + 3.10x^2 - 0.90x^3$. Let the x_i be the centers of the gaussian functions and 0.5 be the width since the x_i are about 0.5 apart. The resulting function f is defined by

$$f(x) = w_1 e^{-\frac{1}{2\sigma}(x-x_1)^2} + w_2 e^{-\frac{1}{2\sigma}(x-x_2)^2} + w_3 e^{-\frac{1}{2\sigma}(x-x_3)^2} + w_4 e^{-\frac{1}{2\sigma}(x-x_4)^2}$$

where $\sigma = 0.5$. We can solve for the w_i using the following system of simultaneous equations so that $f(x_i) = y_i$ for $1 \le i \le 4$:

$$y_1 = w_1 e^{-\frac{1}{2\sigma}(x_1-x_1)^2} + w_2 e^{-\frac{1}{2\sigma}(x_1-x_2)^2} + w_3 e^{-\frac{1}{2\sigma}(x_1-x_3)^2} + w_4 e^{-\frac{1}{2\sigma}(x_1-x_4)^2}$$

$$y_2 = w_1 e^{-\frac{1}{2\sigma}(x_2-x_1)^2} + w_2 e^{-\frac{1}{2\sigma}(x_2-x_2)^2} + w_3 e^{-\frac{1}{2\sigma}(x_2-x_3)^2} + w_4 e^{-\frac{1}{2\sigma}(x_2-x_4)^2}$$

$$y_3 = w_1 e^{-\frac{1}{2\sigma}(x_3-x_1)^2} + w_2 e^{-\frac{1}{2\sigma}(x_3-x_2)^2} + w_3 e^{-\frac{1}{2\sigma}(x_3-x_3)^2} + w_4 e^{-\frac{1}{2\sigma}(x_3-x_4)^2}$$

$$y_4 = w_1 e^{-\frac{1}{2\sigma}(x_4-x_1)^2} + w_2 e^{-\frac{1}{2\sigma}(x_4-x_2)^2} + w_3 e^{-\frac{1}{2\sigma}(x_4-x_3)^2} + w_4 e^{-\frac{1}{2\sigma}(x_4-x_4)^2}$$

The resulting approximation is shown in Figure 5.32. We can refine this initial approximation by using the gradient method and additional examples to fine-tune the w_i but already we have a pretty good approximation to the

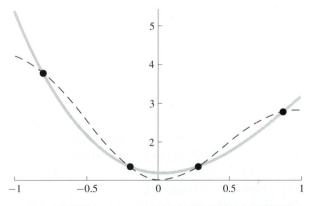

Figure 5.32 Approximation for a cubic polynomial. The solid curve is the target function. The dashed curve is the approximation using a width of 0.5 and centers of -0.8, -0.2, 0.3, and 0.9. The approximation is exact at the centers indicated the four black dots.

target function after seeing only four examples. There is no magic here. The two-step method does not solve the problem of coming up with a good representation for the target function. However, thinking of radial basis functions in terms of receptive fields often does help in choosing basis functions.

Functions with Multidimensional Input Spaces

There is one other issue that is important in all network models but that is manifested clearly in the case of radial basis functions. This problem is concerned with functions involving several dimensions that are scaled differently. In solving a physics word problem, it is important to know what the units are; it makes a difference whether we are using feet rather than meters to measure distance or Fahrenheit rather than Celsius to measure temperature.

In using gaussians to approximate functions with multidimensional input spaces, we make use of the multivariate gaussian

$$f(x_1, x_2, \ldots, x_n) = e^{-\frac{1}{2\sigma} \sum_{i=1}^{n} (x_i - c_i)^2}$$

where the sum $\sum_{i=1}^{n} (x_i - c_i)^2$ is a measure of distance also written $\| \mathbf{x} - \mathbf{c} \|$ in vector notation, where $\mathbf{x} = \langle x_1, \ldots, x_n \rangle$ and $\mathbf{c} = \langle c_1, \ldots, c_n \rangle$. $\mathbf{c}$ is the center of the gaussian in the n-dimensional input space. This particular distance measure is called the Euclidean distance metric. (You might also hear it referred to as the L_2 metric.)

If the scale of the individual inputs is very different, then the Euclidean metric may provide an inaccurate measure of distance. For example, if we have a two-dimensional space and x_1 measured in millimeters and x_2 in kilometers, then $\langle 0, 0 \rangle$ will be close to $\langle 1, 0 \rangle$ but far from $\langle 0, 1 \rangle$. To correct for this scaling effect, we can employ a weighted distance metric so that

$$f(\mathbf{x}) = e^{-\frac{1}{2\sigma} \| \mathbf{x} - \mathbf{c} \|_{\mathbf{w}}}$$

where

$$\| \mathbf{x} - \mathbf{c} \|_{\mathbf{w}} = \sum_{i=1}^{n} w_i (x_i - c_i)^2$$

for $\mathbf{w} = \langle w_1, \ldots, w_n \rangle$. This solves the scale problem at the cost of adding n additional adjustable parameters to the learning problem and making the underlying search problem that much more difficult.

Without some prior knowledge in the form of a strong bias, many learning problems are practically impossible. We can specify a large number of learning problems in terms of network models, but finding satisfactory values for the adjustable weights can require a great deal of time. As a general rule of thumb: The more parameters a learning method has, the more difficult it is to apply in practice.

5.9 Learning in Dynamic Environments

In this chapter, we focus primarily on inductive inference and supervised learning. In the exercises, we say a bit about how genetic algorithms can be used to support learning, and in other chapters, we describe explanation-based generalization for speedup learning. These topics by no means exhaust machine learning. In this section, we provide a brief introduction to some related problems in unsupervised learning concerned with how a system might learn to function in a *dynamic environment*. A dynamic environment is defined by a set of states and a set of physical laws that govern how the state of the environment changes over time.

Reinforcement Learning

We are interested in how a system embedded in a dynamic environment and provided with feedback in the form of rewards might learn to react to its environment so as to maximize its long-term cumulative rewards. A small child learns to maximize the attention he or she receives by figuring out how to behave on the basis of parental feedback. This feedback reinforces some behaviors and discourages others, and so this type of learning is called *reinforcement learning*.

We model a system embedded in a dynamic environment with a set of *states*, a set of *actions*, and a *state-transition function*. The state-transition function models the physical laws governing the dynamic environment and determines the next state given an initial state and an action performed by the system. The methods we consider are very general and apply to a wide variety of applications from game playing to optimizing computer networks, but to exercise your physical intuitions we consider the situation faced by a delivery robot in an office environment.

For our delivery robot, states are offices, and actions correspond to the robot traversing a corridor from one office to another. Figure 5.33 depicts a particularly simple office environment as a graph, called a *state-transition diagram* with states as nodes and state transitions as arcs labeled with actions. There are four states corresponding to four offices labeled 0, 1, 2, and 3. The offices are connected in a ring, and the robot can perform three actions; it can move in a clockwise direction (+), in a counterclockwise direction (−), or it can stay where it is (@).

We generally assume that there is a clock governing the passage of time and that at each tick of the clock the robot has to perform some action. What state the robot ends up in after the next tick is completely determined by what state the robot is in and what action it performs. An environment in which there is a unique next state resulting from any initial state and action is *deterministic*. The office environment in Figure 5.33 is deterministic. For the time being, we assume that the robot always knows what state it is in, but later we consider relaxing this assumption.

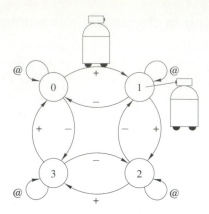

Figure 5.33 State-transition diagram for a deterministic environment. Nodes represent states labeled 0, 1, 2, and 3. Arcs represent actions labeled +, −, and @. The robot can observe the label of the state it is in and perform any action corresponding to an arc leading out of its current state.

Each time the robot performs an action, it receives a *reward* (possibly 0) that depends on the state that the robot ends up in. For the environment shown in Figure 5.33, suppose that the robot receives a reward of 10 whenever it ends up in state 3 and a reward of 0 for ending up in any of the other three states. In many applications, the reward also depends on the action and the state the robot starts out in, but here we consider a simpler case.

Now the robot can assign a value to performing a sequence of actions starting from a given state. For instance, starting in state 0, performing the + action for four ticks results in a total reward of 10; performing the + action for eight ticks results in a total reward of 20.

The actions performed by the robot are determined by a simple program called a *policy* that maps states to actions. The policy tells the robot which action to take in a given state. A policy together with the state-transition function for a deterministic environment uniquely determines an infinite sequence of states starting in any initial state. Now we can talk about the value of a state with respect to a particular policy assuming that we follow the policy forever.

The value of state 0 with respect to the policy that maps each state to @ is 0 because the robot will never perform @ and end up in state 3, the only state with a nonzero reward. The value of state 0 with respect to the policy that maps each state to + is infinite because the robot will perform + and end up in state 3 infinitely often. Unfortunately, value of state 0 with respect to the policy that maps state 3 to @ and the other states to + is also infinite even though this policy seems clearly better than the policy that maps each state to +. Let policy 0 be the policy that maps each state to + and policy 1 be the policy that maps state 3 to @ and the other states to +. We might distinguish these policies in two ways.

First, instead of taking the sum of the rewards, we might compute the average reward per tick. In the limit, the average reward per tick for state 0 with respect to policy 0 is 10/4, and the average reward per tick for state 0 with respect to policy 1 is 10. Alternatively, we might assume that the robot associates a higher value with more immediate rewards and therefore discounts future rewards. The *discount rate* is a number between 0 and 1 used to discount future rewards. Let γ denote the discount rate. The *discounted cumulative reward* for a particular state with respect to a given policy is the sum for n from 0 to infinity of γ^n times the reward associated with the state reached after the nth tick of the clock. For a discount rate of 0.5, the discounted cumulative reward for state 0 with respect to policy 0 is 1.33. The discounted cumulative reward for state 0 with respect to policy 1 is 2.5. In the following, we use discounted cumulative reward to compare the performance of policies.

How did we calculate the discounted cumulative rewards? We used an iterative method based on dynamic programming. In dynamic programming, a problem is broken down recursively into smaller problems. These problems are then solved, proceeding from the smallest to the largest. Solutions to smaller problems are used to solve larger problems. To calculate discounted cumulative rewards for a given policy, we first compute the discounted cumulative reward assuming that we follow the policy for just one tick. Given the results of the calculations for n ticks, we calculate the discounted cumulative rewards for $n + 1$ ticks.

Suppose that the rewards are independent of actions, and let $R(j)$ be the reward for ending up in state j. Let π denote a fixed policy and $\pi(j)$ denote the action dictated by π in state j. Let $f(j, \alpha)$ be the next state given that the robot starts in state j and performs the action α. Let $V_\pi^i(j)$ be the estimated value of state j with respect to the policy π after the ith iteration of our dynamic programming algorithm. The dynamic programming algorithm for computing the value of each state with respect to a fixed policy π is described as follows:

1. For each j, set $V_\pi^0(j)$ to 0.
2. Set i to 0.
3. For each j, set $V_\pi^{i+1}(j)$ to $R(j) + \gamma V_\pi^i(f(j, \pi(j)))$.
4. Set i to $i + 1$.
5. If i is equal to the maximum number of iterations, then return V_π^i; otherwise, return to step 3.

The *value function* for the policy π, denoted V_π, is defined in the limit by V_π^i as $i \to \infty$. In practice, the dynamic programming algorithm provides a good estimate of V_π after a small number of iterations.

Figure 5.34 lists the reward function, the state-transition functions associated with policies 0 and 1, and the Lisp implementation of the dynamic

```
;; Reward function for the environment shown in Figure 5.33.
(defun reward (state)
  (second (assoc state '((0 0.0) (1 0.0) (2 0.0) (3 10.0)))))

;; Deterministic state-transition function for the fixed
;; policy that maps each state to the action +
(defun deterministic-transition-0 (state)
  (second (assoc state '((0 1) (1 2) (2 3) (3 0)))))

;; Deterministic state-transition function for the fixed
;; policy that maps state 3 to @ and every other state to +
(defun deterministic-transition-1 (state)
  (second (assoc state '((0 1) (1 2) (2 3) (3 3)))))

;; Dynamic programming algorithm for computing the value of each
;; state in Figure 5.33 for a given state-transition function
(defun dynamic (next discount iterations)
  (let ((values (list 0 0 0 0)))
    (dotimes (i iterations values)
      (dotimes (state 4)
        (setf (nth state values)
              (+ (reward state)
                 (* discount (nth (funcall next state) values))))))))
```

Figure 5.34   Functions for computing the discounted cumulative reward

programming algorithm. We compute the values for each state for both of the policies assuming a discount rate of 0.5 as follows:

```
> (dynamic #'deterministic-transition-0 0.5 100)
(1.33 2.66 5.33 10.66)
> (dynamic #'deterministic-transition-1 0.5 100)
(2.5 5.0 10.0 20.0)
```

Our dynamic programming algorithm provides one possible solution to an important problem in machine learning. The problem is called the *temporal credit assignment problem*, and it is concerned with assigning credit or blame to the actions in a sequence of actions where feedback is available only at the end of the sequence. When you lose a game of chess or checkers, the blame for your loss cannot necessarily be attributed to the last move you made or even the next-to-last move. You may have made some mistakes and corrected for them. The mistakes were part of the sequence of actions but did not contribute to your losing the game. Figuring out which moves are responsible for your loss is what the temporal credit assignment problem is all about. Dynamic programming solves the temporal credit assignment problem by propagating rewards backwards to earlier states and hence to actions earlier in the sequence of actions determined by a policy. Given a method for estimating the value of states with respect to a fixed policy, it is possible to find an optimal policy.

Computing an Optimal Policy

Now we have an algorithm that can compute the value of a state for a given policy. A number of methods use this algorithm as a subroutine to find a policy that maximizes the discounted cumulative reward. We describe one such method called *policy iteration* [Howard, 1960].

A policy π is said to be the *optimal policy* if there is no other policy π' and state j such that $V_{\pi'}(j) > V_\pi(j)$ and for all $k \neq j$ $V_{\pi'}(k) \geq V_\pi(k)$. The following algorithm is guaranteed to terminate in a finite number of steps with an optimal policy:

1. Let π_0 be an arbitrary policy.
2. Set i to 0.
3. Compute $V_{\pi_i}(j)$ for each j.
4. Compute a new policy π_{i+1} so that $\pi_{i+1}(j)$ is the action α maximizing $R(j) + \gamma V_{\pi_i}(f(j, \alpha))$.
5. If $\pi_{i+1} = \pi_i$, then return π_i; otherwise, set i to $i + 1$, and go to step 3.

We have shown how computing the value of states with respect to a policy can help in computing optimal policies. In the following paragraphs, we consider some additional issues in learning value functions.

Online Methods for Learning Value Functions

The dynamic programming algorithm described earlier assumes we know the reward function and state-transition function for a given environment. In many applications, this information is not known to the robot. However, the robot can learn about these functions by interacting with its environment. In the following, we provide online methods for learning a value function that do not require knowing either the state-transition function or the reward function.

Figure 5.35 lists the code for a generic environment simulator. The function simulate takes a state-transition function associated with a fixed

```
;; Simulate a robot following a particular policy and updating
;; the value of the current state for that policy on each tick.
(defun simulate (transition update discount iterations)
  (do ((n 1 (+ n 1)) (values (list 0 0 0 0)) (state 0 next)
       (next (funcall transition 0) (funcall transition next)))
      ((= n iterations) values)
    (funcall update state next values discount)))

;; Update the value of a state given a particular next state
;; and assuming a deterministic state-transition function.
(defun deterministic-update (state next values discount)
  (setf (nth state values)
        (+ (reward state) (* discount (nth next values)))))
```

Figure 5.35   Functions for simulating policies and updating the value of states

policy, a function for updating a value function implemented as a vector of values (one for each state), a discount rate, and an integer indicating how many ticks to simulate. The function deterministic-update takes as arguments the information available in a given state, namely, the current state, the next state, the current estimated value function, and the discount rate, and uses this information to update the estimated value function. Deterministic-update works by updating the estimated value function one state each iteration rather than all states each iteration as in the dynamic programming algorithm, but it still converges to the same value function, at least for states that are visited infinitely often in an infinite number of transitions.

```
> (simulate #´deterministic-transition-0
             #´deterministic-update 0.5 100)
(1.33 2.66 5.33 10.66)
> (simulate #´deterministic-transition-1
             #´deterministic-update 0.5 100)
(0.0 0.0 0.0 20.0)
```

Note that using policy 1, the system never returns to states 0, 1, or 2 after visiting state 3.

So far we have assumed that the environment is deterministic. In a *stochastic* environment, the next state for a given initial state and action is determined by a probability distribution on the set of states. Figure 5.36 shows the transition probabilities for a stochastic variant of the office environment of Figure 5.33. According to Figure 5.36, if the robot performs action + in state 0, then 70% of the time the robot will end up in state 1, and 30% of the time the robot will remain in state 0. Figure 5.37 lists the stochastic state-transition functions for the two policies considered earlier. In the code in Figure 5.37, each state is associated with a distribution represented

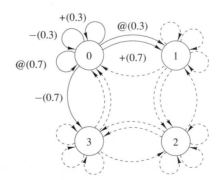

Figure 5.36   State-transition diagram for a stochastic environment. The transition probabilities are shown only for state 0. The transition probabilities for other states are identical.

```
;; Stochastic state-transition function for the fixed
;; policy that maps each state to the action +
(defun stochastic-transition-0 (state)
  (let ((distribution (rest (assoc state '((0 0.7 1 0)
                                           (1 0.7 2 1)
                                           (2 0.7 3 2)
                                           (3 0.7 0 3))))))
    (if (< (random 1.0) (first distribution))
        (second distribution)
        (third distribution))))
```

```
;; Stochastic state-transition function for the fixed policy
;; that maps state 3 to @ and every other state to +
(defun stochastic-transition-1 (state)
  (let ((distribution (rest (assoc state '((0 0.7 1 0)
                                           (1 0.7 2 1)
                                           (2 0.7 3 2)
                                           (3 0.7 3 0))))))
    (if (< (random 1.0) (first distribution))
        (second distribution)
        (third distribution))))
```

Figure 5.37   Stochastic state-transition functions for two fixed policies

in the form (*state probability-of-most-likely-next-state most-likely-next-state next-most-likely-next-state*), where we assume that any given state has at most two possible next states. For instance, (2 0.7 3 2) indicates that 70% of the time when the robot is in state 2 it ends up in state 3, and the remainder of the time it ends up back in state 2.

The deterministic update strategy of Figure 5.34 does not work in a stochastic environment. We define the *expected value of a state* with respect to a fixed policy to be the discounted cumulative reward averaged over sequences of state transitions determined by the distributions governing the stochastic environment. We are interested in determining the expected value of a state. The value functions computed using the deterministic update strategy tend to change erratically, and in some cases, do not allow us to distinguish between the two policies considered earlier.

```
> (simulate #'stochastic-transition-0
            #'deterministic-update 0.5 100)
(1.33 2.66 5.33 10.66)
> (simulate #'stochastic-transition-1
            #'deterministic-update 0.5 100)
(1.33 2.66 5.33 10.66)
```

The expected value of a state in a stochastic environment is the sum of the reward in the state and the probability-weighted sum of the expected values of the possible next states. For the policy that maps each state to +, the value of state 0 is the sum of the reward in state 0 and 0.7 times the value of state 1 plus 0.3 times the value of state 0. It is straightforward to modify the dynamic programming algorithm to compute a probability-weighted sum of the values of the possible next states. To estimate the expected value using an online update algorithm, we use the fact that the states visited by the robot while following its policy are determined by the distributions governing the stochastic environment. After each transition, the robot makes a small adjustment in the estimated value for the state prior to the transition. Over many transitions, these small adjustments result in an estimate of the sum of the reward for the state and the probability-weighted sum of the values of the possible next states. An online algorithm with an adjustment rate of β between 0 and 1 and a discount rate of γ is given as follows:

1. For each i, initialize $V_\pi(i)$ to be 0.
2. Set j to be the initial state.
3. Set r to be the reward received in j.
4. Perform $\pi(j)$, and set k to be the resulting state.
5. Set $V_\pi(j)$ to be $V_\pi(j) + \beta[(r + \gamma V_\pi(k) - V_\pi(j)]$.
6. Set j to be k, and go to step 3.

This algorithm does not converge to the actual expected values. Instead, after some number of transitions, the algorithm achieves a steady state in which the estimated values are confined to an interval about the expected values. The size of this interval depends on the adjustment rate. An adjustment rate close to 1 results in a larger interval but fewer transitions to achieve steady state. A smaller adjustment rate results in a smaller interval but requires more transitions to achieve steady state. In Exercise 5.16, you are encouraged to experiment with various adjustment rates. Figure 5.38 lists an implementation of the algorithm.

```
> (simulate #'stochastic-transition-0 #'stochastic-update 0.5 1000)
(0.16 0.81 3.35 10.88)
> (simulate #'stochastic-transition-1 #'stochastic-update 0.5 1000)
(0.14 0.83 3.99 14.33)
```

```
;; Update the value of a state given a particular next state
;; and assuming a stochastic state-transition function.
(defun stochastic-update (state next values discount)
  (let ((rate 0.01))
    (setf (nth state values)
          (+ (nth state values)
             (* rate (- (+ (reward state)
                           (* discount (nth next values)))
                        (nth state values)))))))
```

Figure 5.38   Function for updating the value of states in a stochastic environment

Learning by Exploration

We are interested in how systems interact with and learn about their environment. In the techniques discussed, the robot learns about its environment by exploring that environment following a given policy. We assumed that the robot did not know what rewards it would receive in a state or what state it would end up in by performing a given action. Our online algorithms did not bother to learn either the reward or the state-transition functions. It seems plausible, however, that learning these functions could speed learning policies.

Next, we focus on learning the state-transition function for an environment. If we associate states with physical locations and actions with strategies for moving between physical locations, then learning a state-transition function is analogous to learning a map of the environment. For the environment in Figure 5.33, it is simple to learn the state-transition function assuming that the robot can observe what state it is in.

Uncertainty makes learning state-transition functions more complicated. In the following, we consider uncertainty in action and uncertainty in observation. In the stochastic environment shown in Figure 5.36, there is uncertainty in action, but observation of states is certain. When it performs an action, the robot cannot predict with certainty what state it will end up in. Learning the probabilistic state-transition function for Figure 5.36 is still relatively easy using statistical techniques.

Uncertainty in observation can arise even in a deterministic environment. In many cases, it is not possible to determine exactly what state you are in. If you are somehow teleported to a McDonald's restaurant, you may realize that you are in a McDonald's restaurant without knowing which one; all McDonald's restaurants look more-or-less alike. It is as though all the states are assigned labels and some states have the same label.

Stochastic environments can introduce another source of uncertainty in observation. Suppose that your vision system is governed by a stochastic process. Most of the time when you are in a McDonald's restaurant it looks like a McDonald's restaurant, but some of the time it looks like a Burger King restaurant. In this case, it is as though there is a probability distribution that governs what label you see when you are in a given state.

Rather than consider stochastic environments, we might assume that the environment is deterministic but that perception is governed by a stochastic process. For instance, we might perceive that we are in a Burger King restaurant when in fact we are in a McDonald's restaurant, or the robot might perceive itself moving in a counterclockwise direction when in fact it is moving in a clockwise direction. Figure 5.39 depicts the situation faced by a robot when some states have the same labels. The robot can make errors in perceiving the labels and in determining which transitions it actually performs.

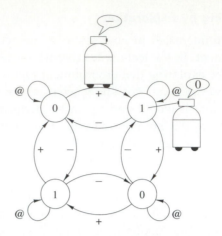

Figure 5.39   Perceptual errors in a deterministic environment

It turns out that learning an arbitrary state-transition diagram of the sort depicted in Figure 5.39 is difficult, even if we assume that perception is error free. In some cases, it is not even possible. For instance, it is impossible to distinguish the environment shown in Figure 5.39 from an environment consisting of only two states, one labeled by 1 and the other labeled by 0. But even if we ignore the complications introduced by indistinguishable environments, learning environments is hard in the general case. The basic problem of inferring an environment that is consistent with the actions and states observed by the robot and whose size is bounded by some polynomial factor of the size of the actual environment is intractable given widely believed assumptions.

In the literature on learning, environments of the sort shown in Figures 5.33 and 5.39 are represented as finite-state automata. Much of the recent work on learning finite-state automata is concerned with discovering classes of automata that are PAC learnable. For instance, in many realistic environments, a robot can distinguish any two states by considering the sequence of labels observed in carrying out the actions in a specified sequence. Environments for which you can find such a sequence are PAC learnable. Developing algorithms for learning finite-state automata is just one of many areas of active research in machine learning.

▼ Summary

Learning involves changes to the content and organization of a system's knowledge, enabling it to improve its performance on a set of tasks. In this chapter, we consider a particular form of learning called inductive inference, which arrives at general conclusions by examining particular examples. We focus primarily on supervised learning, in which the learning system is given a set of training examples in the form of input/output pairs from a target function. The learning system constructs a hypothesis, another function, that accounts for the training examples and generalizes to unseen input/output pairs.

If the space of possible hypotheses is not restricted, then there is no justification for the system choosing a function that generalizes beyond the training examples. By restricting the space of hypothesis or preferring certain hypotheses to others, we introduce an inductive bias that serves as a justification for generalizing beyond the training examples. For instance, in learning boolean functions, we might restrict hypotheses to conjunctions of positive literals or prefer smaller boolean functions to larger ones.

Errors are inevitable in learning. Probably approximately correct (PAC) learning is a computational model of learning that establishes a tolerance for errors (the approximate part) and an allowance that occasionally the tolerance is not met (the probable part). A class of functions is PAC learnable with respect to a space of hypotheses if there exists a polynomial-time algorithm that, given any tolerance requirements and instance of the class of functions, returns a hypothesis that, with high probability, satisfies the tolerance requirements with a polynomial number of training examples. In many cases, given a large enough number of training examples, it is sufficient for PAC learning to find a hypothesis that is consistent with the training examples.

Implementing an inductive bias consists of finding a hypothesis that subscribes to the bias and is consistent with the training examples. Some biases are easier to implement than others. For a hypothesis space consisting of conjunctions of positive literals, the problem of finding a consistent hypothesis can be solved in polynomial time. For a hypothesis space consisting of formulas in disjunctive normal form with at most k disjuncts, the problem of finding a consistent hypothesis is NP-hard.

The version-space method is an online method that proceeds by bounding the set of all hypotheses consistent with the examples observed so far. The version-space method is optimal for the space of hypotheses consisting of conjunctions of positive literals. The decision-tree method is a batch method that takes a set of training examples and uses a heuristic to search for a small decision tree that classifies the examples. The heuristic is based on a measure of disorder from information theory. Decision trees are used in a wide variety of applications from recognizing defective products in quality control systems to predicting good investments in the stock market.

Networks of simple computational units can be used to implement a wide range of computing devices. Such networks can be used to describe hypothesis spaces by adding a set of adjustable weights that define a family of functions. Gradient methods are used to adjust the weights to find hypotheses that minimize the error with respect to a set of training examples. For networks describing linear function spaces, gradient methods are guaranteed to converge to a hypothesis minimizing the errors. For networks describing nonlinear function spaces, no such guarantee can be made, but gradient methods can still be applied and often yield good performance in practice. For one class of relatively simple networks called perceptrons, there exists a rule for adjusting the weights that is guaranteed to converge to a hypothesis minimizing the errors for the class of linearly separable functions.

In general, designing networks and applying strategies to adjust their weights for learning particular functions is quite complicated and requires a certain amount of trial and error. Networks that compute a sum of gaussians provide a model of learning as memory with particular portions of memory assigned the task of approximating the output of the target function on particular regions of the input space. This network model allows the designer to approach learning in two steps: first, assign memory to portions of the input space and, second, approximate the function over regions of the input space assigned to each portion of memory.

Reinforcement learning is a form of unsupervised learning in which the system is given feedback in the form or rewards indicating whether or not a hypothesis is correct. The temporal credit assignment problem is concerned with assigning credit or blame to the actions in a sequence of actions in which feedback is available only at the end of the sequence. Dynamic programming provides an approach to solving the temporal credit assignment problem for reinforcement learning problems. Some reinforcement learning methods perform without a model of the environment in which they are learning. Another form of unsupervised learning involves inferring a model of the environment in the process of exploring that environment. By inferring a model of the environment, it is possible to expedite reinforcement learning.

Learning is not a panacea for all the difficult problems faced by AI. On the contrary, efficient learning seems to require you narrow the search for a hypothesis by giving the learning system an appropriate inductive bias. In learning, as in search, representation plays a key computational role. Choosing a representation for hypotheses introduces an inductive bias that ultimately determines what a system can learn and how quickly.

● Background

For a general overview of machine learning, read the survey by Dietterich [1990]. Michalski et al. [1983] and Shavlik and Dietterich [1990] have edited collections of papers that provide a good initial introduction to the large literature on machine learning.

Mitchell [1977] makes a case for the necessity of an inductive bias in learning. The probably approximately correct model of learning was introduced by Valiant

[1984], spurring theoretical work in machine learning. Our PAC learning analyses borrow from those of Blumer et al. [1987].

Version spaces were developed by Mitchell [1982] as part of a strategy for searching for good generalizations. Decision trees have a long history in learning and statistical analysis. The treatment of decision trees in this chapter borrows primarily from Quinlan [1986], but see Breiman et al. [1984] for an alternative perspective. The medical applications featured in this chapter are described in Breiman et al. [1984]. There is also a close connection between learning based on decision trees and certain methods for performing data compression [Lin and Vitter, 1992].

Much of the work on network models of computation derives from the model of the nervous system developed by McCulloch and Pitts [1943]. In particular, the linear threshold unit is a specialization of their general model. Perceptrons as an important special case of linear threshold units are generally credited to Rosenblatt [1961]. See the texts by Nilsson [1965] or Minsky and Papert [1969] for a more detailed discussion of perceptrons and their limitations, including a proof that the perceptron learning rule converges.

An efficient method for computing the gradient in multilayer networks was introduced by Werbos [1974]. The method discussed in this chapter is called backpropagation and is due to Rumelhart et al. [1986]. Network models that use radial basis functions for approximating functions are described in Poggio and Girosi [1989]. Hertz et al. [1991] provide an introduction to the theoretical foundations of artificial neural networks.

Pomerleau [1991] describes ALVINN and the application of artificial neural networks to vehicle navigation. Sejnowski and Rosenberg [1987] describe NETtalk, an artificial neural network program for pronouncing English text. Learning programs for playing backgammon are described in Tesauro and Sejnowski [1987] and Tesauro [1992].

Barto et al. [1990] provide a survey of reinforcement learning techniques. Sutton [1988] describes a general set of techniques for solving the temporal credit assignment problem. Tesauro [1992] describes how reinforcement learning techniques have been applied to learning to play tournament-level backgammon. The idea of representing environments as finite automata goes back to Moore [1956]. For a sampling of theoretical results in learning automata, see Angluin [1987], Rivest and Schapire [1987], and Basye et al. [1995]. The exercise on classifier systems employing genetic algorithms is based on the work of Holland [1975].

■ Exercises

5.1 An isothetic rectangle is a rectangle with two sides parallel to one axis of a two-dimensional space and the other two sides parallel to the other axis of the space. More generally, an isothetic hyperrectangle in an m-dimensional space is an m-dimensional solid whose projection onto any two-dimensional subspace is an isothetic rectangle. Isothetic hyperrectangles are PAC learnable for the case in which the class of concepts to be learned and the hypothesis space are the same.

In this exercise, you are to write a Lisp procedure that, given a set of positive and negative examples corresponding to points in an m-dimensional space, returns two

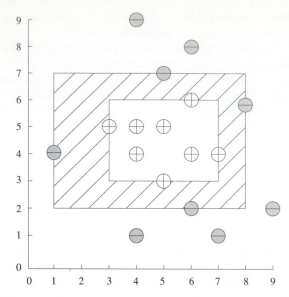

Figure 5.40 Isothetic rectangles representing consistent hypotheses

hyperrectangles representing consistent hypotheses. For simplicity, assume k positive examples and k negative examples. The jth positive example is described as $p_j = \langle p_{j,1}, p_{j,2}, \ldots, p_{j,m} \rangle$. The jth negative example is described as $n_j = \langle n_{j,1}, n_{j,2}, \ldots, n_{j,m} \rangle$. We wish to compute two hyperrectangles, p and q, represented as m pairs of lower and upper bounds,

$$p = \langle \langle pl_1, ph_1 \rangle, \langle pl_2, ph_2 \rangle, \ldots, \langle pl_m, ph_m \rangle \rangle$$

$$n = \langle \langle nl_1, nh_1 \rangle, \langle nl_2, nh_2 \rangle, \ldots, \langle nl_m, nh_m \rangle \rangle$$

where the ith component of p is defined by $ph_i = \max\{p_{j,i} | 1 \le j \le k\}$ and $pl_i = \min\{p_{j,i} | 1 \le j \le k\}$[5], and given p, the ith component of n is defined by $nh_i = \min\{n_{j,i} \ge ph_i | 1 \le j \le k\}$ and $nl_i = \max\{n_{j,i} \le pl_i | 1 \le j \le k\}$. Figure 5.40 illustrates the bounding rectangles for a two-dimensional case; positive examples are indicated by $\oplus$, and negative examples by $\ominus$.

It is easy to show that any hyperrectangle consistent with the examples must contain the first of the two hyperrectangles. Prove by counterexample that it is *not* the case that any hyperrectangle consistent with the examples is contained in the second of the two hyperrectangles.

5.2 Consider the following two hypothesis spaces, and in each case, derive a formula for determining the size of the space for arbitrary n and m and the number of examples that are required to reduce the error below 0.1 with probability 0.9 for the case in which $n = 10$ and $m = 5$.

---

[5]It is possible that the indicated sets are empty. In your implementation, you can assume upper and lower bounds on the values in each dimension. For instance, restrict examples to $[0, 1]^n$.

a) Conjunctions of positive literals in which there are n attributes and exactly m attribute values for each attribute.

b) Isothetic hyperrectangles in which each example corresponds to a point in $\{0, 1, 2, \ldots, m\}^n$ ($\langle 3, 7, 4 \rangle \in \{0, 1, 2, \ldots, 9\}^3$).

5.3 For a finite hypothesis space H, any hypothesis consistent with the training examples is PAC whenever the number of training examples is greater than $\ln(\delta/|H|)/\ln(1-\epsilon)$. Plot this function for different fixed values of δ and ϵ. Using Lisp lists and functions, create a sample space X ($\{i | 0 \le i \le 99\}$) and a space of possible concepts (any collection of subsets of X will do). Let $\Pr(X)$ be the uniform distribution on X ((random 100)). Assume the space of concepts and the hypothesis space are the same. Write a program to empirically determine the number of examples that are required to obtain various PAC guarantees (less than 0.1 error 90% of the time). Plot the results, and compare with plots for the theoretical bounds.

5.4 The Lisp implementation of refine provided in this chapter for refining version-space boundaries is not guaranteed to converge to a unique concept. In this exercise, you are to modify refine in accord with the complete algorithm given in the text. Here are the basic modifications to refine.

```
(defun refine (example general specific)
  (if (eq (EXAMPLE-class example) 'yes)
      (simplify-specific (prune-general example general)
                         (generalize-specific example specific))
      (simplify-general (specialize-general example general)
                        (prune-specific example specific))))
```

Pruning is straightforward. Here is a function for pruning the general boundary when presented with a positive example.

```
(defun prune-general (example general)
  (findall general
           #'(lambda (concept)
               (consistent (EXAMPLE-features example) concept))))
```

You are to write the functions for pruning the specific boundary and simplifying the boundaries. You will have to ensure that your simplification routines return a list of the two boundaries.

5.5 Learning is complicated when training examples are misclassified. One model for how this might happen is that correctly classified examples are generated by the teacher but then transmitted to the learning system along a noisy channel so that occasionally some features are corrupted or the class changed. In transmitting examples along a noisy channel, (dept cs) might be changed to (dept ee) or the class changed from yes to no.

Write functions for generating training examples for concepts expressed as boolean combinations of features. Your generator should provide control over the frequency of positive and negative examples, and allow for the introduction of noise by corrupting features according to a specified distribution. For example, for a particular attribute, 90% of the time a feature with that attribute is transmitted without error, and 10% of the time a feature with that attribute is corrupted during transmission by substituting a feature with the same attribute but a different value.

Rewrite buildtree and the abstract data type for nodes to keep track of (a) the attribute that each node is split on, (b) the list of attributes on the path from the root to the node, (c) the feature determining that subset of the examples of the node's parent that are stored at the node, and (d) the class name corresponding to the majority class for those examples stored in terminal nodes. Modify buildtree so that it does not split a node when all the examples are in the same class or by using an attribute that has already been used in arriving at that node.

Write a function performance that takes a decision tree and a set of examples and returns the percentage of correctly classified examples. Write functions size and depth that, when applied to a decision tree, return, respectively, the number of nodes in the tree and the length of the longest path from the root to a terminal node. Use these functions to test buildtree on a variety of concepts with differing noise models.

5.6 In this exercise, you are to experiment with two methods for dealing with noise, making use of the functions developed in the previous exercise. The first method is the simpler but less effective of the two. In this method, we introduce a *threshold* parameter and prevent splitting a node when the most discriminating attribute for that node ((splitter node)) is found not to be discriminating enough ((> (evaluate node dim) threshold)). The threshold parameter should be set to a value between 0.0 and 1.0.

Thresholding is not particularly effective for dealing with noise. The problem is that a threshold large enough to prevent splitting on irrelevant attributes is usually large enough to prevent splitting on relevant attributes as well. The second method considered in this exercise uses a statistical test to determine if an attribute is relevant or not.

Let α be an attribute with v values, and suppose that we are considering whether or not to split a node corresponding to the set of examples C using the attribute α. Restricting our attention to concept learning, suppose that there are p positive examples and n negative examples in C. Suppose further that α splits C into the subsets $C_1, C_2, \ldots, C_v$ such that there are p_i positive examples and n_i negative examples in C_i. If α is irrelevant in classifying C, then the expected number $\hat{p}_i$ of positive examples in C_i should be

$$\hat{p}_i = p \left(\frac{p_i + n_i}{p + n} \right)$$

and similarly for the expected number $\hat{n}_i$ of negative examples. We can use a standard statistical test to determine the probability that α is irrelevant. The distribution of the statistic

$$\gamma = \sum_{i=1}^{v} \frac{(p_i - \hat{p}_i)^2}{\hat{p}_i} + \frac{(n_i - \hat{n}_i)^2}{\hat{n}_i}$$

is approximately χ^2 (read "chi-square") with $v - 1$ degrees of freedom. We accept the hypothesis that α is irrelevant for the case of $v = 2$ as long as $\gamma \leq 3.8415$ in accord with the following table indicating the probability that a χ^2 random variable exceeds various bounds:

	$\Pr(\chi^2 > x) = \rho$			
	$\rho = 0.050$	$\rho = 0.025$	$\rho = 0.010$	$\rho = 0.005$
$v - 1 = 1$	3.8415	5.0238	6.6349	7.8794
$v - 1 = 2$	5.9915	7.3777	9.2103	10.5966
$v - 1 = 3$	7.8147	9.3484	11.3449	12.8381
$v - 1 = 4$	9.4877	11.1433	13.2767	14.8602

Implement both methods, and compare their performance using the functions developed in Exercise 5.6.

5.7 Decision-tree methods can also be used to learn concepts involving attributes with continuous values, such as temperature or wind speed. One strategy for splitting a node using a continuous attribute is to choose an attribute value that partitions the set of examples at the node into two, approximately equal sets. Rewrite `buildtree`, the abstract data type functions, and any additional supporting functions to handle attributes with continuous values. To test your implementation, consult a physics or chemistry text to obtain training examples that given a particular temperature and barometric pressure indicate whether or not water will boil.

5.8 Exclusive-or functions are particularly difficult for methods such as `buildtree` that use limited lookahead. Here is an example of exclusive-or for the robot-janitor domain.

```
(((status faculty) ∧ ¬(dept cs)) ∨
(¬(status faculty) ∧ (dept cs)))
```

Note that ¬(status faculty) ≡ ((status student) ∨ (status staff)) and ¬(dept cs) ≡ (dept ee). Demonstrate by example that it is not always possible to choose the smallest decision tree using a limited lookahead search such as the one implemented by `buildtree`.

5.9 Repeat the experiments used to generate the graphs in Figure 5.16, but this time use cross validation to measure performance of different learning programs. Given a training set of 40 examples, use a 10-fold cross-validation estimate to compare the performance of 10 different learning programs corresponding to the 2 different gradient methods with learning rates $\beta = 0.05, 0.1, 0.2, 0.4, 0.8$. In each case, use 100 adjustments for training.

5.10 Modify the network of Figure 5.19 to incorporate adjustable thresholds as in the network of Figure 5.22. The resulting network is shown in Figure 5.41 (page 248). Compile statistics similar to those of Table 5.3 to compare the performance of the new network with that of the networks in Figures 5.19 and 5.22.

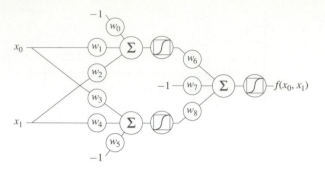

Figure 5.41   A three-layer, two-hidden-unit, adjustable-threshold network

5.11 Run experiments with the perceptron learning rule to determine the effect of variations in the initial weights on the number of adjustments required to learn various boolean functions.

5.12 Describe the grid world and the problem of evaluating different navigation strategies, for example, using the Manhattan (L_1) metric to choose which direction to head in.

5.13 Discuss the possible advantages of using simulated annealing to adjust the weights in an artificial neural network.

5.14 Genetic algorithms of the sort considered in Chapter 4 can be used as part of an effective learning strategy. In this exercise, we consider how to learn boolean functions of n inputs by searching in a space of simple rule-based systems. A *classifier system* is a set of rules called *classifiers* that are represented as strings. Each classifier consists of a *condition* and an *action*. For our purposes, a condition is a string from the set $\{0, 1, *\}^n$, and an action is either 1 or 0. The target function is represented as a list of input/output pairs of the sort used in this chapter. An input matches a condition if the individual components match, where * matches anything. The input (0 1 1 0) matches the condition (0 1 * *) but not (* 0 1 0).

In most genetic algorithms for learning classifier systems, rules are evaluated in a simulated competition that determines the fitness of each rule; in this exercise, we take a simpler approach. Let $C(r)$ be the set of inputs matching r's condition, $R(x, r)$ be the set of rules with conditions matching x and action the same as r, and $d(r, f, x) = 1$ if r agrees with the target function f on the input x and -1 otherwise. We define the fitness of a rule r as

$$\sum_{x \in C(r)} \frac{d(r, f, x)}{|R(x, r)|}$$

This definition rewards a rule for getting the output right on a given input, penalizes for getting it wrong, and adjusts the reward or penalty according to the number of other rules that respond in the same way.

In addition to redefining fitness, you will have to modify mutate to handle the extended string alphabet. You might also consider modifying reproduce so that some proportion of the population is carried over to the next generation. Note that in this application of genetic algorithms the entire population of rules corresponding to a classifier system is the result of learning. You can evaluate a given classifier in terms of the number of inputs for which at least one rule has a matching condition and gets the right output and no rule has a matching condition and gets the wrong output.

5.15 Implement an online version of the policy iteration algorithm for computing an optimal policy. Use the online method for computing the value of states with respect to a fixed policy, and then devise a strategy to switch between learning the values of states with respect to the current policy and figuring out how to improve the current policy. When learning the value of states with respect to the current policy, you should follow the policy exclusively. When figuring out how to improve the current policy, you will have to experiment with actions other than those dictated by the current policy.

5.16 Modify the dynamic programming algorithm for computing value functions to work with stochastic transitions. In particular, make use of the state-transition probabilities to compute the probability-weighted sum of the values of the possible next states. Use the values computed by your dynamic programming algorithm to test the online method described in the text with different learning rates. Run the online algorithm 20 times for each of several different learning rates $(0.1, 0.2, \ldots, 0.9)$. For each run, compute the error for the run as the sum of the squares of the error over the values for all states using the values computed by your dynamic programming algorithm as the correct values. Compile a table listing the average of the error over all runs using a given learning rate.

▶ LISP IMPLEMENTATION
Learning Algorithms in Lisp

This section provides the Lisp code for implementing learning algorithms based on version spaces and decision trees. Before listing the code for these algorithms, we describe two utilities that will be used for both algorithms.

The function findall takes a list and a function and returns all items in the list such that the function returns non-nil when applied to the item.

```
(defun findall (list test)
  (do ((items list (rest items)) (results nil))
      ((null items) results)
      (if (funcall test (first items))
          (setq results (adjoin (first items) results
                                :test #'equal)))))
```

We will want to refer on occasion to the set of all features allowed by the dimensions of the problem. Features uses dimensions to generate the list of all features for a given problem.

```
(defun features ()
  (mapcan #'(lambda (dim)
              (mapcar #'(lambda (value)
                          (list (DIMENSION-attribute dim)
                                value))
                      (DIMENSION-values dim)))
          (dimensions)))
```

Refining Boundaries in Version Spaces

In the following, we provide code for modifying the boundaries in a version space given a new training example. The code provided is not guaranteed to converge to a unique concept. In Exercise 5.4, you are shown how to modify the code to implement the complete algorithm given in the text.

Refine takes a single training example and two lists of concepts representing the general and specific boundaries. A conjunctive concept is represented as a list of features. Refine determines whether the training example is positive, yes, or not, no, and then proceeds to, respectively, generalize the concepts in the specific boundary or specialize the concepts in the general boundary.

```
(defun refine (example general specific)
  (if (eq (EXAMPLE-class example) 'yes)
      (list general (generalize-specific example specific))
    (list (specialize-general example general) specific)))
```

Generalizing the specific boundary consists of generalizing each concept in the boundary until it is consistent with the (positive) example.

```
(defun generalize-specific (example boundary)
  (mapcan #'(lambda (concept)
              (aux-generalize-specific example concept))
          boundary))
(defun aux-generalize-specific (example concept)
  (if (consistent (EXAMPLE-features example) concept)
      (list concept)
    (generalize-specific example (generalize concept))))
```

Specializing the general boundary consists of specializing each concept in the boundary until it is not consistent with the (negative) example.

```
(defun specialize-general (example boundary)
  (mapcan #'(lambda (concept)
              (aux-specialize-general example concept))
          boundary))
(defun aux-specialize-general (example concept)
  (if (not (consistent (EXAMPLE-features example) concept))
      (list concept)
    (specialize-general example (specialize concept))))
```

A concept is consistent with an example if for each feature (conjunct) in the concept, either the attribute of the feature is not mentioned in the list of features describing the example, or if it is mentioned, the corresponding feature has the same attribute value. For instance, if an example corresponds to an office on the third floor, then any concept consistent with that example must either not mention a floor or indicate the third floor.

```
(defun consistent (features concept)
  (every #'(lambda (f)
             (or (not (assq (FEATURE-attribute f) features))
                 (member f features :test #'equal)))
         concept))
```

For the restricted hypothesis space consisting of conjunctions of positive literals, generalization corresponds to removing features from a concept represented as a list of features.

```
(defun generalize (concept)
  (mapcar #'(lambda (feature)
              (remove feature concept :test #'equal))
          concept))
```

Specialization corresponds to adding features that are consistent with the concept. Both specialize and generalize return concepts that are, respectively, minimally more specific and minimally more general than the concept provided as an argument to the function.

```
(defun specialize (concept)
  (mapcar #'(lambda (feature) (cons feature concept))
          (findall (features)
                   #'(lambda (feature)
                       (and (consistent (list feature) concept)
                            (not (member feature concept
                                         :test #'equal)))))))
```

Versions takes a set of training examples and a pair of initial boundaries and refines the boundaries by processing each training example in turn.

```
(defun versions (examples boundaries)
  (mapc #'(lambda (example)
            (setq boundaries (refine example
                                     (first boundaries)
                                     (second boundaries)))
            (format t "Example: ~A~%General: ~A~%Specific: ~A~%"
                    example (first boundaries) (second boundaries)))
          examples))
```

Building Decision Trees

Given a set of examples, classify partitions the examples into classes.

```
(defun classify (examples)
  (mapcar #'(lambda (class)
              (findall examples #'(lambda (s)
                                    (eq class (EXAMPLE-class s)))))
          (classes)))
```

Partition takes a set of examples and partitions by the attribute of a dimension according to the values for that attribute.

```
(defun partition (examples dimension)
  (let ((attribute (DIMENSION-attribute dimension)))
    (mapcar #'(lambda (value)
                (findall examples
                         #'(lambda (example)
                             (member (list attribute value)
                                     (EXAMPLE-features example)
                                     :test #'equal))))
            (DIMENSION-values dimension))))
```

Buildtree implements the basic recursive function for constructing decision trees.

```
(defun buildtree (node)
  (format t "Class distribution: ~A~%"
          (mapcar #'length (classify (NODE-examples node))))
  (if (< 1 (length (findall (classify (NODE-examples node))
                            #'(lambda (s) (not (null s))))))
      (let ((dim (splitter node)))
        (format t "Dimension chosen: ~A~%" dim)
        (set-NODE-attribute node (DIMENSION-attribute node))
        (set-NODE-children node
                           (mapcar #'make-NODE
                                   (partition (NODE-examples node) dim)))
        (mapc #'buildtree (NODE-children node)))
      (format t "Terminal node.~%")))
```

Splitter finds the attribute that minimizes a particular evaluation function implemented by evaluate.

```
(defun splitter (node)
  (do* ((dims (rest (dimensions)) (rest dims))
        (value (evaluate node (first (dimensions))))
        (splitter (first (dimensions))) (min value))
       ((null dims) splitter)
    (setq value (evaluate node (first dims)))
    (if (< value min)
        (setq splitter (first dims) min value))))
```

The function evaluate computes the weighted sum of the disorder over all class partitions for a given attribute partition.

```
(defun evaluate (node dimension)
  (let ((total (length (NODE-examples node))))
    (apply #'+
           (mapcar #'(lambda (subset)
                       (* (/ (length subset) total)
                          (disorder (classify subset))))
                   (partition (NODE-examples node) dimension)))))
```

Disorder computes the information value (disorder) associated with a particular class partition according to the formula listed in the section on decision trees.

```
(defun disorder (partition)
  (let* ((sizes (mapcar #'length partition))
         (total (apply #'+ sizes)))
    (if (= total 0) 0
      (- (log total 2)
         (apply #'+ (mapcar #'(lambda (s)
                                (if (= s 0) 0
                                  (* (/ s total) (log s 2))))
                            sizes))))))
```

CHAPTER 6

ADVANCED
REPRESENTATION

In this chapter, we explore some of the issues involved in reasoning about time, space, and belief. The notions of time passing and change are central to our understanding of the dynamic world in which we live. Much of our common-sense knowledge about the world can be represented in terms of cause-and-effect relations that govern our interactions with the environment. We are embedded in space as well as time and our knowledge of the shape and position of objects is essential for our survival and for our appreciation of the world around us. Finally, we are social beings, and in order to communicate and coordinate our behavior with those around us, we have to reason about what other people believe and how those beliefs change over time.

We start by considering representations of time using first-order predicate logic. Certain problems in representation lead us to investigate the use of nonmonotonic logic for reasoning about time. We discuss methods of automating temporal reasoning and describe an algorithm for predicting the consequences of a set of events. We then consider logics for reasoning about knowledge and belief. We also consider methods for reasoning about space for applications in robotics. Our discussion begins with the issues of time and change.

6.1 Temporal Reasoning

A *theory of change* describes how various aspects of the world change over time and how events bring about such changes. *Temporal reasoning* involves using a theory of change to predict the future or explain the past or present. Figure 6.1 depicts a fantasy-game world that we will use to illustrate issues in temporal reasoning.

In the fantasy-game world of Figure 6.1, the dragon is in his hoard guarding his treasure, the wizard is in his chamber frozen in a block of ice, and the knight is in the castle dungeon contemplating a mission to steal the treasure from the dragon's hoard. In this world of dungeons and dragons, there are statements that are true at some times and false at others. For example, in Figure 6.1 the knight is in the dungeon, but we can easily imagine situations in which this is not the case. Events bring about changes in the status of statements. For example, if the knight moves into the wizard's chamber, then the knight will no longer be in the dungeon.

A theory of change can be described in terms of a set of rules that govern the physics of the world. For example, one rule describes how the knight might release the wizard from the block of ice, "If the wizard is frozen and the knight thaws the wizard with a torch, then the wizard will no longer be frozen." Another rule describes how the wizard can be bribed to unlock the dragon's hoard, "If the wizard is not frozen and the door to the dragon's hoard is locked and the knight bribes the wizard with a jewel, then the door to the dragon's hoard will be unlocked." These rules are often called *causal rules* because they define cause-and-effect relationships.

Given a set of such causal rules, a set of initially true statements, "The wizard is frozen" and "The dragon's hoard is locked," and a sequence of events, "The knight thaws the wizard" followed by "The knight bribes the wizard," we can predict the consequences of the events. Figure 6.2 shows

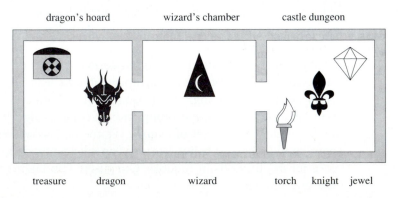

dragon's hoard   wizard's chamber   castle dungeon

treasure   dragon   wizard   torch   knight   jewel

Figure 6.1   The knight is on a mission to steal the treasure from the dragon's hoard. The jewel and the torch will help him succeed.

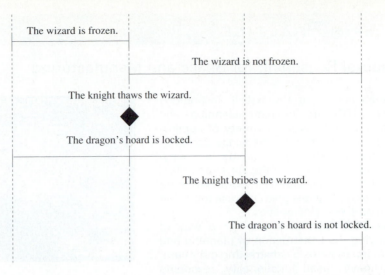

Figure 6.2   The knight uses a torch to thaw the frozen wizard and then bribes the wizard with a jewel to unlock the dragon's hoard

a set of statements and intervals during which they are true. The intervals are depicted as horizontal lines, events as black diamonds, and particular instants in time are drawn as vertical lines. The depiction in Figure 6.2 is called a *time map* because it allows us to examine changes over time much as we would examine a map of physical space.

It may also be useful to reason about durations and the length of intervals of time. For example, in the world of dungeons and dragons, if the wizard is not bribed within five minutes of being thawed by the knight, then the wizard will freeze the knight into a block of ice. Change and the passage of time are fundamental in our understanding of the world around us. In the following three sections, we consider how we might formalize such reasoning and write programs to make automatic predictions. We begin with a discussion of a calculus for reasoning about time and change that is cast entirely within the first-order predicate calculus.

6.2   The Situation Calculus

In the following, we describe the *situation calculus,* which is a first-order predicate calculus theory developed by John McCarthy for reasoning about change over time. We begin by introducing a number of technical terms that will figure prominently in our discussion. An *event* is something that can happen. The knight thawing the frozen wizard is an event. A *fluent* is a description that applies to some intervals of time and does not apply to others. For example, the description "the knight is in the dungeon" applies only to intervals in which the knight is in the dungeon. A *situation* is an interval of time during which nothing changes. Our theories of time and change are expressed in terms of events, fluents, and situations. We restrict

▲ AI IN PRACTICE

Temporal Reasoning for Space and Manufacturing

Researchers at the Honeywell Technology Center (HTC) are building planning and scheduling systems for a variety of applications in manufacturing and space domains. The basis for all these systems is Honeywell's implementation of the Time Map Manager (TMM), a specialized temporal reasoning system originally designed by researchers at Brown and Yale Universities.

The TMM was conceived as a way of simplifying the construction of planning and scheduling systems by abstracting out a common, heavily used functionality: reasoning about the ordering and extent of events and the resulting changes in the state of the world. The TMM supports cause-and-effect reasoning and provides for the efficient incremental modification of existing plans and schedules. The system has been applied to problems involving more than 10,000 activities.

HTC researchers have developed planning and scheduling systems based on the TMM for scheduling a circuit board manufacturing plant, planning operations for science modules on the NASA space shuttle (see accompanying figure), processing and analyzing satellite data, and processor and communication scheduling for flight management systems. Customers for these systems include three divisions of Honeywell and several NASA centers.

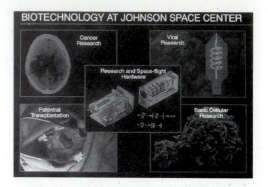

Courtesy of NASA/Lyndon B. Johnson Space Center

our attention to describing how things change over time in response to a single process or the actions of a single agent.

In describing any theory expressed in the predicate calculus, we have to indicate the relevant predicates, constants, and functions. Events, fluents, and situations are represented by terms. For instance, we might represent the location of an object with a fluent location(*thing, place*), where location is a function mapping an object *thing* and a location *place* to the fluent of the object being in that place. While we are using fluents to reason about propositions—statements that are either true or false—it is important to keep in mind that fluents are terms and not propositions in the logic. Think about what obstacles there are to reasoning about fluents as propositions; we return to this subject in the next section.

We also introduce a function result that takes an initial situation and an event and returns the situation resulting when the event occurs in the initial situation. For instance, there is a situation during which the light is off in a room; if in this situation, a robot toggles the light switch, then in the resulting situation, the light will be on in the room. Each situation determines a set of fluents that are true throughout the interval associated with the situation.

In the version of the situation calculus presented here, there is only one predicate, holds. The formula holds(s, f) indicates that the fluent f is true in the situation s. Consider how we might represent knowledge about dungeons and dragons using the situation calculus. The following formulas represent that the wizard is frozen and the dragon's hoard is locked in the situation denoted by 0.

```
holds(0, frozen)
holds(0, locked)
```

Using the result function, we can represent the consequences of events occurring in particular situations. The following causal rule indicates that, if the knight thaws the wizard in a situation in which the wizard is frozen, then in the resulting situation, the wizard is no longer frozen.

```
∀ s,
 holds(s, frozen) ⊃ holds(result(s, thaw), not(frozen))
```

In the situation calculus, not is a function that takes a fluent and returns another fluent.

The next rule indicates that if the wizard is not frozen and the dragon's hoard is locked and the knight bribes the wizard, then dragon's hoard will be unlocked.

```
∀ s,
 (holds(s, not(frozen)) ∧ holds(s, locked)) ⊃
 holds(result(s, bribe), not(locked))
```

Given the preceding axioms, we can prove that the wizard is not frozen in the situation that results from the knight thawing the wizard in the situation denoted by 0.

```
holds(result(0, thaw), not(frozen))
```

Note that we represented the wizard being frozen as frozen and the wizard not being frozen as not(frozen). Keep in mind that frozen and not(frozen) are terms and not well-formed formulas. We could not substitute ¬frozen for not(frozen) since the former is syntactically ill formed in the predicate calculus. It is important to note that the semantics for the predicate calculus does not constrain the fluents not(frozen) and frozen. If we want it to be the case that only one of these two fluents is true in any given situation, we have to add appropriate axioms to enforce such conditions.

Constraining Fluents in Situations

Fluents are often constrained by one another in situations. For example, it may be that Ralph and Fred are inseparable; they are always located in the same place. We can express this constraint using the following axiom:

```
∀ s,p,
 holds(s, location(Fred, p)) ≡
 holds(s, location(Ralph, p))
```

We can also express the constraint that, whenever Fred and Lynn are in the same place, then Sam will also be there.

```
∀ s,p,
 (holds(s, location(Fred, p)) ∧
  holds(s, location(Lynn, p))) ⊃
 holds(s, location(Sam, p))
```

We mentioned before that fluents are not modeled as propositions in the situation calculus. However, by adding appropriate axioms, we can make fluents behave more or less like propositions. Specifically, we can add axioms that simulate truth functional operators. For example, we might model negation using the function not and disjunction using the function or.

```
∀ s,f,
 holds(s, not(f)) ≡ ¬holds(s, f)
∀ s,f,g,
 holds(s, or(f, g)) ≡ (holds(s, f) ∨ holds(s, f))
```

Using the axioms for simulating negation and disjunction, we can rewrite the axiom involving Fred, Lynn, and Sam as follows:

```
∀ s,p,
 holds(s, or(or(not(location(Fred, p)),
               not(location(Lynn, p))),
            location(Sam, p)))
```

Frame Problem

Given the axioms for reasoning about dungeons and dragons introduced earlier, we were able to prove the following formula:

```
holds(result(0, thaw), not(frozen))
```

Given these same axioms, however, we are not able to prove that the dragon's hoard is still locked following the wizard's thawing.

```
holds(result(0 ,thaw), locked)
```

The causal rules provided specify what changes follow as the result of the knight thawing the wizard, but we have no way of inferring what things do not change. We have not specified what fluents persist from one situation to the next. For the particular case of the dragon's hoard, we could add the following axiom:

```
∀ s,
holds(s, locked) ⊃ holds(result(s, thaw), locked)
```

Using this special axiom and the other axioms introduced earlier, we can now prove that if the knight first thaws and then bribes the wizard, then in the resulting situation, the hoard will be unlocked.

```
holds(result(result(0, thaw), bribe), not(locked))
```

The complete proof is shown in Figure 6.3.

The special axiom indicating that thawing the wizard does not affect the locked hoard allowed our proof to go through. In general, however, we would need to add axioms to handle every possible combination of event and fluent whether or not the event changes the fluent. The problem of representing exactly what things do not change as a consequence of an event is called the *frame problem*, and axioms such as the one given are called

1.	holds(0, frozen)	AXIOM
2.	holds(0, locked)	AXIOM
3.	∀s, holds(s, frozen) ⊃ holds(result(s, thaw), not(frozen))	AXIOM
4.	holds(0, frozen) ⊃ holds(result(0, thaw), not(frozen))	UI: s→0, 3
5.	holds(result(0, thaw), not(frozen))	MP: 1, 3
6.	∀s, holds(s, locked) ⊃ holds(result(s,thaw),locked)	AXIOM
7.	holds(0 ,locked) ⊃ holds(result(0, thaw), locked)	UI: s→0, 6
8.	holds(result(0, thaw), locked)	MP: 2, 7
9.	holds(result(0, thaw), not(frozen)) ∧ holds(result(0, thaw), locked)	CONJ: 5, 8
10.	∀s, (holds(s, not(frozen)) ∧ holds(s, locked)) ⊃ holds(result(s, bribe), not(locked))	AXIOM
11.	(holds(result(0, thaw), not(frozen)) ∧ holds(result(0, thaw), locked)) ⊃ holds(result(result(0, thaw), bribe), not(locked))	UI: s→ result(0, thaw), 10
12.	holds(result(result(0, thaw), bribe), not(locked))	MP: 9, 11

Figure 6.3   Simple proof in the situation calculus

frame axioms. In a motion picture film, action is captured in a sequence of images called frames. Generally, very little changes from one frame to the next; in particular, often the entire background remains unchanged. The frame problem is concerned with the intuition that it should be possible to compactly represent the evolution of a set of fluents over time by simply representing those things that do change.

It might seem that axioms of the following sort can be used to solve frame problem:

```
∀ s, f,
 ¬(f = frozen) ⊃
 (holds(s,f) ≡ holds(result(s, thaw), f))
```

It would seem that, using this sort of rule, we need one additional rule per event. In addition, however, we need many axioms of the form ¬(f = g), where f and g are fluents. By departing from the predicate logic just a bit, we can dispense with the need for such negated equality statements. The unique-names assumption, taken from our discussion of nonmonotonic logic in Chapter 3, enables us to infer that two terms are not equal if they are syntactically distinct. The literature is full of solutions to the frame problem, many of which rely on some form of nonmonotonic logic. As we will see later, in practice, the frame problem can often be solved by straightforward bookkeeping techniques.

Qualification Problem

There is a problem with the approach to reasoning about change described earlier. The problem stems from the fact that it reduces cause-and-effect reasoning to logical implication. Modeling causation in terms of implication requires us to provide sufficient conditions for a given event to have a particular consequence. In practice, it is quite difficult to provide such conditions; there are invariably circumstances that force us to qualify such rules. Generally, if you toggle the switch to a light that is not on, then it will come on.

```
∀ s,
 holds(s, not(on(light))) ⊃
 holds(result(s, toggle), on(light))
```

However, toggling a switch will have no effect on the light if the light is damaged or the wires or equipment supplying power to the light are interrupted. This problem of correctly stating the conditions under which a given event will have a particular consequence is called the *qualification problem*. The qualification problem can also be solved by an appropriate application of nonmonotonic reasoning. In the following version of the axiom, we make use of the abnormal predicate introduced in Chapter 3.

∀ s,
(holds(s, not(on(light))) ∧ ¬abnormal(s, light)) ⊃
holds(result(s, toggle), on(light))

This qualified formula indicates that as long as there is nothing abnormal about the light, then toggling it in a situation in which it is not on will result in it coming on.

Now we can introduce a qualification as follows. If the power being supplied to a location is interrupted, then the light will not come on when the light switch is toggled.

∀ s, holds(s, not(on(power))) ⊃ abnormal(s, light)

Now we can try to use the notion of satisfiability in all minimally abnormal interpretations, introduced in Chapter 3, to obtain the desired conclusion that the light will be on unless we can prove that the power is off. Unfortunately, the preference criterion that prefers minimally abnormal interpretations is not quite satisfactory. Let us suppose that if there is nothing special about the power supplied to a location, then, if there is an earthquake, the power will be out.

∀ s,
¬abnormal(s, power) ⊃
holds(result(s, quake), not(on(power)))

The power supplied to a location might be considered abnormal if, for example, there is a diesel generator that provides emergency power.

Suppose that the power is on and the light is not on in the situation denoted by 0. Let 1 denote the situation result(0, quake) and 2 denote the situation result(1, toggle). We add a special frame axiom to represent that if a light is not on before a quake then it is still not on after the quake.

∀ s,
holds(s, not(on(light))) ⊃
holds(result(s, quake), not(on(light)))

You might expect that holds(2, not(on(light))) is true in all minimally abnormal interpretations. Unfortunately, there are minimally abnormal interpretations in which this formula is true and ones in which it is not. Figure 6.4 (page 264) illustrates two such interpretations. We can correct this problem by employing a slightly more complicated preference relation over interpretations: one that prefers interpretations in which the fewest abnormalities occur and those that do occur do so as late as possible.

To make this more precise, we introduce a chronological ordering on situations. Given two situations s and s', we say that s immediately precedes s' if there exists an event e such that result$(s, e) = s'$. We say that $s \prec s'$ if either s immediately precedes s' or there exists s'' such that s'' immediately precedes s' and $s \prec s''$. We say that $s \preceq s'$ if either $s \prec s'$ or $s = s'$. We now define a new preference order, $\gg_t$, such that $I_1 \gg_t I_2$ if there exists a

Interpretation 1	Interpretation 2
holds(0, on(power))	holds(0, on(power))
holds(0, not(on(light)))	holds(0, not(on(light)))
¬abnormal(0, light)	¬abnormal(0, light)
¬abnormal(0, power)	abnormal(0, power)
holds(1, not(on(power)))	holds(1, on(power))
holds(1, not(on(light)))	holds(1, not(on(light)))
abnormal(1, light)	¬abnormal(1, light)
¬abnormal(1, power)	¬abnormal(1, power)
holds(2, not(on(power)))	holds(2, on(power))
holds(2, not(on(light)))	holds(2, on(light))

Figure 6.4   Two minimally abnormal interpretations for the earthquake example

situation s satisfying the following conditions:

1. I_1 and I_2 agree on the interpretation of all function and relation symbols other than abnormal.
2. For all x and $s' \prec s$, if $I_2 \models$ abnormal(s', x), $I_1 \models$ abnormal(s', x).
3. For all x and $s' \preceq s$, if $I_1 \models$ abnormal(s', x), $I_2 \models$ abnormal(s', x).
4. There exists some x, for which $I_2 \models$ abnormal(s, x), but $I_1 \not\models$ abnormal(s, x).

Using $\gg_t$, we prefer interpretations in which abnormalities can be explained by prior conditions rather than simply occur spontaneously. Given $\gg_t$, the interpretation shown on the left in Figure 6.4 is preferable to the interpretation shown on the right. It should be noted that the preference criterion works for prediction, but it behaves counterintuitively for explanation. For example, if you were to walk in a room and find the light on, then using the preference criterion you would conclude that the light was turned on just before you entered the room.

The variant of the situation calculus described here has a number of expressive limitations. First, it is complicated to reason about two or more events occurring simultaneously. For instance, it is difficult to model two people cooperating to lift a large or heavy object. Second, this variant of the situation calculus deals only with discrete time, making it difficult to reason about continuous change. For example, we cannot reason about bathtubs overflowing or water coming to a boil. These expressive limitations can be eliminated by extending the situation calculus. However, in the following section, we consider an alternative representation for time and change in which these expressive limitations do not arise in the first place.

6.3   First-Order Interval Temporal Logic

In the situation calculus, we modeled fluents using terms, but we were able to do so without leaving the predicate calculus. Alternatively, it is possible to model fluents as atomic sentences within the predicate calculus by simply adding another argument to every predicate. For instance, to model the changes in the location of an object over time, we would employ a three-place predicate location(*object*, *place*, *time*). The formula location(Ralph, room509, 12:15) represents that Ralph is in Room 509 at 12:15. If time is iso-morphic to the integers, then we can represent the consequences of toggling the switch to a light that is not on as follows:

$\forall$ t,
(¬on(light, t) $\wedge$ toggle(t)) $\supset$ on(light, t+1)

What is wrong with this approach to modeling time and change? With respect to the emphasis of this chapter, it accords no special status to time and hence does not immediately provide a basis for organizing and structuring knowledge. Of course, the simple syntactic convention of using the last argument as a temporal index could provide a basis for structuring statements according to the times at which they are true. We prefer, however, to emphasize the role of time both syntactically and semantically. In the following, we present a logic that does exactly that. We refer to this logic as the *first-order interval temporal logic* or simply the *interval logic*.

In modeling physical processes, we need to reason about the truth of propositions over intervals of time. The propositions correspond to properties of the world that are subject to change. For instance, we might want to say something about whether or not a light is turned on at a particular time; to do so, we introduce a unary relation, on, and a constant, light, denoting the light that we have in mind. Since the light is on at some times and off at others, the proposition, on(light), must be interpreted differently with respect to different times. The temporal logic that we employ here is essentially a calculus for reasoning about the association between time intervals and propositions.

Syntax for the Interval Logic

We choose to treat time points as primitive and reason about intervals in terms of points. We introduce a binary relation, $\preceq$, on time points indicating temporal precedence. The symbol $\prec$ denotes the strict version of temporal precedence, that is, t1 $\prec$ t2 iff t1 $\preceq$ t2 but not t2 $\preceq$ t1. If t1 and t2 are time points such that t1 $\preceq$ t2, then (t1, t2) is an interval. The formula, (p, (t1, t2)), where p is a propositional symbol, allows us to associate propositions with intervals in which they hold. Following common practice in artificial intelligence, we substitute holds(t1, t2, p) for (p, (t1, t2)). Note, however, that holds is not predicate in the interval logic. The intervals employed here are more general than those associated with situations in the situation calculus. Unlike in the situation calculus, a lot can go on in an interval in the interval logic. We are also free to choose the structure for time in the interval logic; the set of time points might correspond to the integers, the rationals, or the reals if we so choose. To simplify the following discussion, we assume that time is isomorphic to the integers.

We present the syntax for the propositional version of the interval logic. The full first-order version with function and predicate symbols is a straight-forward extension. We introduce a set of time point symbols, T, a set of propositional symbols, P, and a set of temporal variables, TV. The set of well-formed formulas (wffs) is defined inductively.

1. If t1 and t2 are in $T \cup TV$ and p is in P, then t1 $\prec$ t2, t1 $\preceq$ t2, and holds(t1, t2, p) are wffs.

2. If φ_1 and φ_2 are wffs, then so are $\varphi_1 \wedge \varphi_2$ and $\neg\varphi_1$.

3. If φ is a wff and t is in TV, then $\forall$t, φ is a wff.

We assume the standard definitions of $\vee$, $\supset$, $\equiv$, and $\exists$. For convenience, we allow the following abbreviations specified as syntactic transformation rules:

holds(t,φ) $\Rightarrow$ holds(t,t,φ)
holds(t1,t2,$\varphi_1 \wedge \varphi_2$) $\Rightarrow$ holds(t1,t2,φ_1) $\wedge$ holds(t1,t2,φ_2)
holds(t1,t2,$\neg\varphi$) $\Rightarrow$ $\neg$holds(t1,t2,φ)

Note that the formulas on the left-hand side are syntactically ill formed. Think of a transformation rule *lhs* $\Rightarrow$ *rhs* as indicating that whenever we write *lhs* what we really mean is *rhs*.

The last of the three transformation rules provides a definition for a proposition not being true in an interval. This definition is generally referred to as *weak negation*. An alternative definition referred to as *strong negation* is provided by the following transformation:

holds(t1,t2,$\neg\varphi$) $\Rightarrow$ $\forall$ t, (t1 $\preceq$ t $\preceq$ t2) $\supset$ $\neg$holds(t,φ)

We can define disjunction in terms of negation and conjunction.

holds(t1,t2,(p $\vee$ q)) $\Rightarrow$ holds(t1,t2,$\neg$($\neg$p $\wedge$ $\neg$q))

As the designer of a representation, you have many choices to make. The choice between strong and weak negation provides a good example of how choices can have far-reaching consequences. If a security guard asks you if you were not in the building during the weekend, then the guard probably has strong negation in mind. If you answer positively, then he will likely interpret your answer as meaning that at no time during the weekend were you in the building.

Of course, strong and weak negation have certain representational con-sequences in common. For instance, both forms of negation allow us to "cancel" negations. Here are the sequence of transformations that show

how this property follows from weak negation,

```
holds(t1,t2,¬¬p) ⇒
¬holds(t1,t2,¬p) ⇒
¬¬holds(t1,t2,p) ⇒
holds(t1,t2,p)
```

Here are the sequence of transformations that show how to "cancel" negations using the stronger form of negation.

```
holds(t1,t2,¬¬p) ⇒
∀ t, ((t1 ≼ t) ∧ (t ≼ t2)) ⊃ ¬holds(t,¬p) ⇒
∀ t, ((t1 ≼ t) ∧ (t ≼ t2)) ⊃
¬(∀ t´, ((t1 ≼ t´) ∧ (t´ ≼ t2)) ⊃ ¬holds(t´,p)) ⇒
∀ t, ((t1 ≼ t) ∧ (t ≼ t2)) ⊃ ¬¬holds(t,p) ⇒
∀ t, ((t1 ≼ t) ∧ (t ≼ t2)) ⊃ holds(t,p)
```

There are also properties that only one form of negation possesses. For instance, using the weak form of negation, you can prove (holds(t1,t2,p) ∨ holds(t1,t2,q)) from the formula holds(t1,t2,(p ∨ q)).

```
holds(t1,t2, p ∨ q) ⇒
holds(t1,t2,¬(¬p ∧ ¬q)) ⇒
¬(holds(t1,t2,¬p) ∧ holds(t1,t2,¬q)) ⇒
¬(¬holds(t1,t2,p) ∧ ¬holds(t1,t2,q)) ⇒
holds(t1,t2,p) ∨ holds(t1,t2,q)
```

However, a similar proof is not possible for strong negation.

Representing Change in the Interval Logic

In the interval logic, fluents and events are both modeled as propositions. In the interval logic, we do not distinguish syntactically fluentlike propositions such as "the light is on" from eventlike propositions such as "he toggled the switch." In some cases, however, it is useful to make such distinctions axiomatically. An eventlike proposition is one that, if it is true in an interval, it is not true in any proper subinterval. A fluentlike proposition is one that, if it is true of an interval, it is true of every subinterval. If φ is a fluentlike proposition, we might add an axiom of the form

```
∀ t1, t2, t3,
 (holds(t1, t2, φ) ∧ (t1 ≼ t3) ∧ (t3 ≼ t2)) ⊃ holds(t3, φ)
```

By introducing appropriate relation and function symbols, we can develop notations for representing a variety of phenomena using the preceding syntax. For example,

```
holds(t1, t2, location(knight,chamber(wizard)))
```

is meant to represent the fact that the knight is located in the wizard's chamber from t1 to t2.

The following axiom in the interval logic represents the rule that we introduced earlier in the situation calculus that, whenever we toggle the switch for a light that is off, the light will come on:

```
∀ r, p, t,
 (holds(t, ¬on(light)) ∧ holds(t, toggle)) ⊃
 holds(t+1, on(light))
```

We can also represent cause-and-effect relations that require reasoning about duration and delay. Since the structure of time is generally isomorphic to the integers or the reals, we assume that the addition and subtraction of temporal terms is well defined and extend the syntax accordingly. For example, in the world of dungeons and dragons, if the wizard is not bribed with the jewel within five minutes of being thawed by the knight, then the wizard will freeze the knight into a block of ice.

```
∀ t1, t2,
 (((t2 - t1) > 5) ∧
  holds(t1, t2, not(frozen(wizard))) ∧
  holds(t1, t2, not(possess(wizard, jewel)))) ⊃
 holds(t2, frozen(knight))
```

Semantics for the Interval Logic

The two things that logicians are most concerned about in a logic are its semantics and its associated formal system. Since we will not undertake to prove theorems, we omit the formal system for the interval logic. We are, however, concerned that our notations have precise meaning. In developing an algorithm for deriving statements from a set of other statements, we want to ensure that our conclusions are valid; for this we require a semantic theory for our temporal logic.

Intuitively, the formula holds(t1,t2,on(light)) should be true if the light is on at every time point between t1 and t2. In the interval logic presented here, we think of each proposition as denoting a set of time intervals. For example, on(light) denotes the set of intervals in which the light is on. In this case, holds(t1,t2,on(light)) should be true if the interval (t1, t2) is an element of the set of intervals assigned to on(light). The full semantics for first-order interval temporal logic simply expands on this basic idea.

To address the frame and qualification problems, we can invoke various forms of nonmonotonic logic as we did in the case of the situation calculus. The method of handling the qualification problem is similar to that employed for the situation calculus.

```
∀ t,
 (holds(t, ¬on(light)) ∧ holds(t, toggle) ∧
  ¬abnormal(t, light)) ⊃
 holds(t+1, on(light))
```

Semantically, our definition of validity prefers interpretations in which the fewest abnormalities occur and those that do occur do so as late as possible.

To address the frame problem, we cannot quantify over fluents as we did in the situation calculus. Instead, we augment our temporal logic so that propositions, once they become true, tend to persist in the absence of any information to the contrary. This tendency is often referred to as the *default rule of persistence* or the *common-sense law of inertia*. The justification for this default rule is not based on any natural law. In fact, it does not appear to be appropriate for reasoning about propositions in general. However, it is appropriate for reasoning about propositions describing many of the processes that humans cope with on a day-to-day basis. This statement is based on an assessment of our perceptual and cognitive capabilities; we simply cannot cope with processes whose important properties are not discernible by our senses or that change so rapidly or seemingly randomly that we cannot keep track of them.

We begin by introducing a special case of abnormality. Since propositions tend to persist, times at which they change should be rare or abnormal. We refer to the abnormality in which a proposition φ changes its truth value at time t as a *clipping* and notate it as clips(t, φ). The following axiom schema allows us to infer clippings in appropriate circumstances:

$\forall$ t, (holds(t, φ) $\land$ holds(t+1, $\neg\varphi$)) $\supset$ clips(t, φ)

The common-sense law of inertia is captured in the following formula:

$\forall$ t, (holds(t, φ) $\land$ $\neg$clips(t, φ)) $\supset$ holds(t+1, φ)

Since statements of the form $\neg$clips(t, φ) generally do not follow from the axioms, there will be models, for any t and φ, in which $\neg$clips(t, φ) is true, as well as models in which it is false. Semantically, we are interested only in models in which the abnormalities and clippings are minimized in the chronological sense mentioned earlier.

We have investigated two logics for reasoning about time and change. Using the situation calculus, we could prove theorems about the consequences of events using the techniques described in Chapter 3. Generally, however, we can reason more efficiently if we take advantage of the structure afforded by time, specifically, that events propagate consequences forward in time. In the next section, we consider how to reason about time and change efficiently using a restricted version of the interval logic.

6.4   Managing Temporal Knowledge

In this section, we are concerned with managing a database encoding knowledge about the truth of propositions over intervals of time. To speak about the structure of time itself, we refer to points and intervals of time. We distinguish between a general type of proposition, "the robot recharged its batteries," and a specific instance of a general type, "the robot recharged its batteries at noon." The latter are referred to as *time tokens* or simply *tokens*. As in the previous two sections, we distinguish between propositions corresponding to events and those corresponding to fluents.

A token associates a general type of event or fluent with a specific interval of time over which the event occurs or the fluent holds. The beginning and ending of an interval are time points. In the following discussion, a time point is either an integer or the symbol ∞. An interval is constrained by changing its beginning and ending.

Our algorithms for reasoning about time will be concerned with manipulating time tokens stored in a database referred to as a *time map*. Given some set of initial tokens, we will want to generate additional tokens corresponding to the consequences of the events represented in the initial tokens. We notate general types of events and fluents using atomic propositions and their negations. For example, the fluent "the light in room 101 is on" might be represented as on(light(room101)), and its negation as ¬on(light(room101)). Similarly, the event type "Ralph toggles the switch for the light in room 101" might appear as toggle(Ralph, light(room101)). To simplify matters, we assume that all events are point events in that their beginning and ending time points are the same.

For tokens corresponding to fluents, we would like to predict how long the corresponding propositions persist once they become true. For example, suppose that we know the light is turned on in room101 at time t1 but we also know that at some time later t2 the light is turned off. In accord with the common-sense law of inertia, we wish to infer that the light is on throughout the interval from t1 until t2, assuming no evidence to the contrary. In general, we require that the interval corresponding to a token persist until the first subsequent interval corresponding to a token of a contradictory type. For any proposition type p, p and ¬p are said to be contradictory. We refer to the process of enforcing this requirement by constraining the ending of token intervals as *persistence clipping*. An interval whose beginning is an integer and whose ending is ∞ is said to *persist indefinitely*.

A temporal query of the form holds(t1, t2, p) should succeed if there is a token in the database of type p constrained to begin before or coincident with t1, and not constrained to end before t2. Complex temporal queries involving conjunctions and disjunctions can be defined in terms of simpler queries but we do not consider such extensions.

Persistence clipping is one kind of routine inference important in reasoning about time and change. There is a second kind of routine inference, called *projection*, that we would like to be able to handle. Projection is concerned with inferring the consequences of events based on a model specified in terms of the cause-and-effect relationships that exist between various event types. A *causal rule* describes such a cause-and-effect relationship. We use the following format to notate causal rules:

crule(*antecedents, trigger, consequents*)

to indicate that, if an event of type *trigger* occurs, and the *antecedents* hold at the time of the triggering event, then the *consequents* will hold following the event. The triggering event is specified as an event type, the antecedents are specified as a set of fluent types, the consequents are specified in terms of types of events or fluents and delays indicating how long after the triggering event the consequent effects manifest themselves.

The basic algorithm for handling both projection and persistence clipping is described next. The algorithm takes as input a set of initial tokens—roughly corresponding to the boundary conditions in a physics problem—and a set of causal rules.

1. Set database to be the set of initial tokens.
2. Set closed to be the empty list.
3. Set current to be the earliest token corresponding to an event that is in database but not in closed. If there is no such token, then quit.
4. Find all causal rules whose trigger event type unifies with the type of current.
5. For each causal rule found in step 4 whose antecedents are true at the time of current, add to database tokens corresponding to the types specified in the consequents, and constrain them according to the specified delays.
6. For each new token added in step 5 whose type corresponds to a fluent, find all tokens of a contradictory type that begin before the newly added token, and constrain them to end before the beginning of the new token.
7. Add current to closed, and go to step 3.

This algorithm ensures that the resulting database contains all and only those tokens warranted by the set of initial tokens and the projection rules. Since it is possible to specify causal rules that describe processes of indefinite duration, we cannot guarantee that the algorithm will terminate. Nevertheless, the algorithm will predict n steps into the future in time polynomial in n and the sizes of the set of conditions and the set of causal rules.

Answering temporal queries is handled by searching through the set of tokens.

Consider a simple example. Suppose that at time 0 fluents of type P and Q are true and that an event of type E occurs at time 10. Initially, the database contains three tokens: a token of type E corresponding to an event that begins and ends at time 10 and two tokens, one of type P and another of type Q, corresponding to propositions that begin at time 0 and persist indefinitely. Suppose that we are given the following three causal rules:

```
crule({P},E,{fact(R,0)})
crule({Q},E,{event(F,5)})
crule({R,Q},F,{fact(¬P,0)})
```

where we use fact and event to distinguish consequences corresponding to propositions from those corresponding to events. The first rule indicates that, if an event of type E occurs at time t and P is true at t, then R will become true at t and persist indefinitely unless constrained to end earlier. The second rule indicates that, if an event of type E occurs at time t and Q is true at t, then an event of type F will occur at $t + 5$. The third rule indicates that, if an event of type F occurs at time t and R and Q are true at t, then ¬P will become true at t and persist indefinitely unless constrained to end earlier.

Projection and persistence clipping proceed as follows. The earliest token corresponding to an event is the token of type E at time 10. There are two rules associated with events of type E, and in both cases, their antecedents are true at time 10. These two rules result in adding two new tokens to the database: a token of type R that begins at time 10 and persists indefinitely and a token of type F that begins and ends at time 15.

The next token in the database corresponding to an event is the token of type F at time 15. There is only one rule associated with events of type F, and its antecedents are true at time 15. This rule results in adding one token to the database: a token of type ¬P that begins at time 15 and persists indefinitely. In adding the token of type ¬P to the database, the earlier-occurring token of type P is constrained to end at time 15. Since there are no additional tokens corresponding to events, we are done. In the resulting database, the query holds(5, P) succeeds, whereas the query holds(20, P) does not. Figure 6.5 provides a graphical depiction of the contents of the database following projection and persistence clipping.

Projection and persistence clipping can be used to validate robot plans. A plan can be represented as a sequence of actions. For example, the following sequence of actions represents a plan to pick up a package, package47, in one room, room101, and deliver it to another room, room109.

```
goto(Ralph, room101)
pickup(Ralph, package47)
goto(Ralph, room109)
putdown(Ralph, package47)
```

A plan successfully achieves location(package47, room109) if this formula is true following the last action in the plan. We return to the issues involved in planning and plan validation in Chapter 7.

The Lisp Implementation section provides an example of this projection and persistence clipping algorithm. This implementation can be extended easily to handle qualifications on causal rules and more complicated sorts of contradictory types. The exercises at the end of this chapter consider such

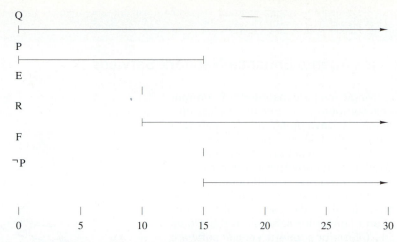

Figure 6.5 Time map illustrating projection and persistence clipping. Each token is identified by its type shown on the left and a horizontal line representing its interval. The beginning of an interval is shown as a short vertical line. The ending of an interval is also shown as a short vertical line unless the interval persists indefinitely, in which case an arrow is shown extending to the right.

extensions. Extensions that deal with uncertainty in the time of occurrence of events are more complicated. In general, reasoning about partially ordered events is computationally difficult. We should note, however, that we have already accepted certain expressive limitations in the format for expressing causal rules. For example, we do not allow disjunctive effects. You cannot represent that, after the horse race, the gambler will be either $100 poorer or $10,000 richer. In reasoning about time, as elsewhere in knowledge representation, we need to make tradeoffs to build practical systems.

6.5 Knowledge and Belief

In this section, we use the term *agent* to refer to any person, program, or device capable of reasoning and decision making. It is often useful for an agent to be aware of what it knows or believes or what some other agent believes or even what some other agent believes about what other agents believe. If a robot currently does not know some piece of information and knows that it does not know this information, then it can formulate a plan to obtain the information. If two robots are working together, and one knows the location of a tool that the other one needs, then the robot that knows where the tool is should tell the other one.

One of the most interesting applications for systems that can reason about the beliefs of other agents is in the area of softbots that act as automated personal assistants. You might have heard them called *personal digital assistants* or *PDAs*. PDAs are being designed to search networks of computers for requested information. In many cases, PDAs will have to ask questions of other PDAs to obtain the information they are seeking.

▲ AI IN PRACTICE

Software Agents Enhance Network Services

General Magic Inc., a consortium of communications, computer, and consumer-electronic companies, is developing a new software technology called Telescript to assist consumers in taking advantage of the many services available on computer networks worldwide. With Telescript, consumers can use home computers or hand-held personal digital assistants to make use of online information and consumer services in the global network. Telescript supports special software agents that assist in shopping, planning travel arrangements, retrieving information, and filtering and responding to electronic messages.

Consumers would purchase specialized software agents that would make use of the Telescript technology to perform particular chores. These software agents would take requests from the consumer and then travel through the computer networks, possibly enlisting the aid of other agents, and perhaps even spawning new agents to assist in carrying out the request. Software agents would behave much like benign versions of the software viruses that occasionally plague computer networks.

As an example of a software agent, a business traveler might employ a personal software agent to book airline flights. The agent would know the traveler's preferred travel times and have the authority to represent the traveler and even make purchases in his or her behalf. The agent would search the networks for the best price and alert the traveler if it found a special deal that might warrant a change in itinerary. On the day of the flight, another agent might periodically communicate with an agent at the airline to monitor the status of the flight and alert the traveler of any delays.

Computer and communications experts are providing the infrastructure for local and global electronic marketplaces where software agents representing consumers and suppliers will interact. Software agents and networked computers herald a brave new world of automated electronic commerce.

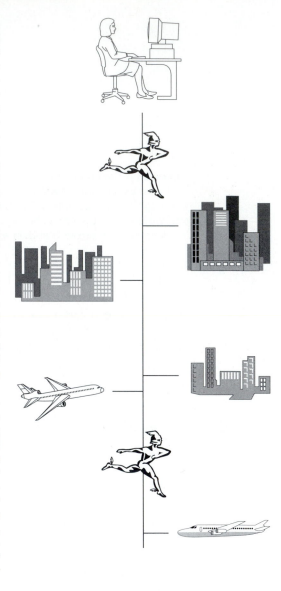

There is considerable controversy in philosophy regarding the relationship between knowledge and belief. One proposal is that knowledge is justified true belief. In this proposal, an agent is said to know φ if φ is true, the agent believes φ, and the agent is justified in believing φ. The controversy arises in trying to specify exactly what it means for an agent to be justified in believing something. In this section, we sidestep the philosophical controversy by focusing on belief and providing axioms for a theory of belief. Ultimately, we want to integrate machinery for reasoning about belief with machinery for reasoning about time, so we can represent how the beliefs of agents change over time. The interested reader should consult the references at the end of this chapter for ideas about how to manage this integration.

A *modal logic* is an extension of predicate calculus with one or more operators, called *modal operators*, that take well-formed formulas as arguments. In this section, we use the notation of a particular modal logic [Davis, 1990] to illustrate a number of points regarding reasoning about belief. We describe the syntax and semantics for the logic informally. The set of wffs include all the wffs of predicate calculus plus any formula believe(α, φ), where α is any term denoting an agent, φ is any wff, and believe is a modal operator for representing the beliefs of agents. Nested belief statements such as believe(a, believe(b, φ)) are syntactically well formed and common-place in theories of belief.

The following axioms are presented as possible axioms for inclusion in a theory of belief. It is up to the designer of a representation for belief to choose from these axioms in formulating a theory for a particular application. Some of the axioms attribute powerful computational capabilities to agents. The first axiom stipulates that belief is closed under modus ponens. In the following, unless stated otherwise, ϑ and φ correspond to arbitrary closed sentences in the logic.

$\forall$ a, (believe(a, ϑ) $\wedge$ believe(a, $\vartheta \supset \varphi$)) $\supset$ believe(a, φ)

Although this axiom seems innocuous enough when one considers a single application of modus ponens, the same axiom suggests that an agent is capable of inferences that require an arbitrary number of applications of modus ponens. Since we expect agents to have limited computational capabilities, this axiom seems too strong. It is difficult to write axioms that allow one application of modus ponens without allowing any number of such applications.

We assume that an agent believes all the logical axioms and all the axioms of belief. In the following axiom schema, φ is any logical axiom or axiom of belief, including any instance of itself. Again, this axiom suggests an agent with very powerful inferential capabilities.

$\forall$ a, believe(a, φ)

It may be useful to assume that an agent is consistent in its beliefs. Though we occasionally hold contradictory beliefs, most of us would insist that we are consistent about those of our beliefs that are important for day-to-day living.

∀ a, ¬(believe(a, φ) ∧ believe(a, ¬φ))

Most of us are willing to assume that if we believe that we believe something, then indeed we believe it. Similarly, if we believe that we do not believe something, then indeed we do not believe it. The following axiom schemas cover this assumption:

∀ a, believe(a, believe(a, φ)) ⊃ believe(a, φ)
∀ a, believe(a, ¬believe(a, φ)) ⊃ ¬believe(a, φ)

An agent generally believes that if it believes some proposition, then that proposition is true. Without such a belief, an agent might not be willing to act on its beliefs. There are degrees of belief, but we ignore this complication in the following axiom schema:

∀ a, believe(a, (believe(a, φ) ⊃ φ))

We assume that an agent can introspect about its beliefs. In particular, if an agent believes some proposition, then the agent believes that it believes the proposition. Furthermore, if an agent does not believe some proposition, then the agent believes that it does not believe the proposition. The following two schemas, referred to, respectively, as positive and negative introspection, cover the assumptions regarding introspection:

∀ a, believe(a, φ) ⊃ believe(a, believe(a, ¬φ))
∀ a, ¬believe(a, φ) ⊃ believe(a, ¬believe(a, φ))

We need operators for belief, time, and for reasoning about communication. In planning, agents have to reason about offering, requesting, sending, and receiving information. In general, such issues are far too complicated for this introductory text. However, to give you some idea of the capabilities that more complicated modal logics offer, the following axiom schema provides useful advice for an agent interested in determining information in a situation in which the agent believes that some other agent possesses the desired information:

∀ s, a, b,
 holds(s, ¬believe(a, φ) ∧ ¬believe(a, ¬φ) ∧
         believe(a, (believe(b, φ) ∨ believe(b, ¬φ)))) ⊃
 holds(s, believe(a, holds(result(s, ask(a, b, believe(b, φ))),
                     believe(a, φ) ∨ believe(a, ¬φ))))

In this schema, we are assuming that, if a asks b whether b believes φ, then b will answer truthfully according to its beliefs. We are also assuming that b is reliable in the sense that if b believes φ, then a should be willing to believe φ as well. If b believes φ, should a believe it also? It depends on φ. We may believe that b can reliably tell the time of day. We may be unwilling to accept b's beliefs regarding who should be the next president.

In the preceding axiom schema, we have muddled various logics for time and belief. Combining modal operators to reason about everyday communication and interaction between agents is a fascinating area of research but beyond the scope of this text.

Possible-Worlds Semantics

We have syntax for representing beliefs. We need semantics so that we can specify what it means for a program to draw valid conclusions about its beliefs and those of other agents. The most popular semantics for the sort of modal logic described earlier is called *possible-worlds semantics*, or *Kripke semantics* after the philosopher of the same name. A possible world is an assignment of true or false to each closed wff, like the interpretations that we considered in Chapter 3.

Roughly speaking, a possible world w is *accessible* from another world w' if everything that is believed in w is true in w'. An *accessibility relation* determines for any two possible worlds if one world is belief accessible to the other. We obtain different theories depending on whether the accessibility relation is transitive, symmetric, or reflexive. If there are several agents, then there is a different accessibility relation for each agent. For a given agent α and world w, we are generally interested in all those worlds that are α-*accessible* to w. The α-accessible worlds are those worlds that are possible given what α believes.

A *Kripke structure* is a set of possible worlds together with an accessibility relation. Suppose that φ is a closed wff that contains no modal operators. A Kripke structure S and a particular world w are said to be a model for φ with respect to a given agent α (written $S, w \models_\alpha \varphi$), if w models φ in the propositional semantics described in Chapter 3. Formulas involving modal operators are treated differently.

In possible-worlds semantics, we quantify over possible worlds. A modal operator can be thought of as a particular sort of quantifier. For instance, a Kripke structure S and a particular world w are said to be a model for believe(α, φ) (written $S, w \models_\alpha$ believe(α, φ)) if $S, w' \models_\alpha \varphi$ for all w' α-accessible from w. A wff is satisfiable if it has a model. A wff is valid if its negation has no model.

Figure 6.6 (page 278) illustrates the structure of possible worlds for a single agent's beliefs. The nesting of belief operators results in nested quantification over possible worlds. Note that if ¬believe(α,φ) is true in a world then there exists α-accessible worlds in which φ is false, and possibly α-accessible worlds in which it is true, if in addition ¬believe($\alpha,\neg\varphi$) is true.

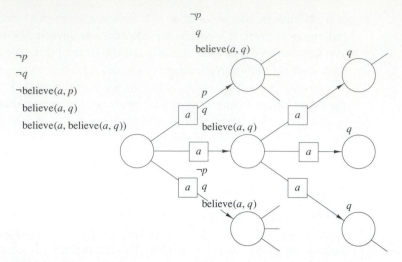

Figure 6.6 Possible worlds for the beliefs of a single agent. Every possible world assigns true or false to every formula, but only selected assignments are shown in the diagram.

If the accessibility relation for α is reflexive, then if α believes φ in a world w, then φ must be true in w. In general, however, not everything that we believe is true, and what one agent may believe is true another may believe is false. A theory of belief would not be very interesting if it did not allow for differences in belief. Figure 6.7 depicts the structure of possible worlds for a case in which two agents have conflicting beliefs.

The issues we have considered in this section just scratch the surface of reasoning about knowledge and belief. Applications in distributed computing and personal digital assistants are driving the research. In this

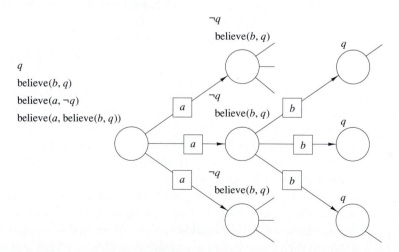

Figure 6.7 Possible worlds for agents with conflicting beliefs

world of networks and information highways, computers communicate with one another routinely, and their conversations are becoming increasingly sophisticated.

6.6   Spatial Reasoning

In some respects, spatial and temporal reasoning are similar. In each case, there is a metric space with various objects (points, intervals) related to one another by quantitative and qualitative constraints. There are also significant differences that make reasoning about space more challenging from a computational and representational perspective. Physical space has three dimensions rather than just one, and there are many more options for moving through space than through time.

It seems as if representing space in a computer should be easy. However, actually constructing a representation for a particular application can be quite difficult. Of course, some applications are easier than others. If you wish to represent the space occupied by a simple geometric object such as a cube or cylinder, then there are a host of techniques available. There is a large software industry devoted to providing computer-aided design (CAD) tools that are used to assist in the design and manufacture of products.

For the most part, CAD techniques rely on representing objects as composites of simple geometric primitives. For example, objects are typically represented by combining cylinders, rectangular parallelopipeds, and other simple shapes. CAD techniques are poor at representing trees, grass, and animals. In this section, we consider a number of spatial representation techniques. We do not provide a solution to the difficult problems of representing clouds and waterfalls, but we outline some techniques useful to a robot planning how to move about in its environment.

Representing Spatial Knowledge

Spatial inference often requires quantitative reasoning involving geometric relations to represent the physical surfaces of real objects. To recognize an object, it may be necessary to determine the distance or angle between two lines. Spatial inference also requires qualitative reasoning involving topological relations such as touching, overlapping, and containing. We could employ formal logic as the basis for our representations; however, it will be easier for our immediate purposes to focus on geometric and graph-based representations.

The top two panels in Figure 6.8 (page 280) show representations of the space occupied by two different objects. In each case, the representation is compact because it is constructed from a small number of geometric primitives. The representation on the left corresponds to the specification of a machined part, whereas the representation on the right corresponds to a crude characterization of a human being. All representations approximate

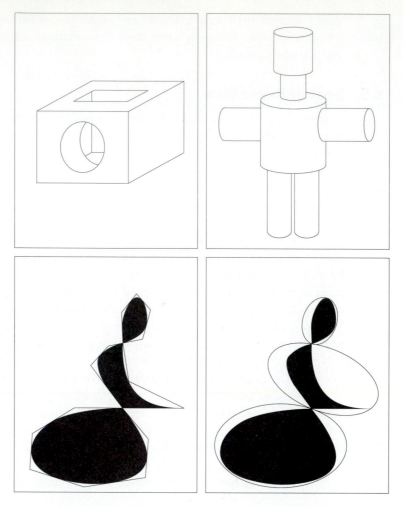

Figure 6.8   Three-dimensional shape representations for a machined part (top left) and a human being (top right). Two-dimensional shape representations composed of polygons (bottom left) and ellipses (bottom right).

what they represent. The suitability of the representation depends on what it is to be used for. The representation of a human being as a composite of cylinders may be perfectly reasonable for some purposes even though it is obviously inadequate for others. Using a rough shape representation, a surveillance robot might be able to identify possible intruders but not be able to distinguish between people.

The bottom panels in Figure 6.8 show two different representations of a two-dimensional shape. The geometric primitives used in these representations correspond to polygons and ellipses. The representation on the left approximates the shape using three polygons. The number of polygons and the number of edges per polygon will depend on the degree of precision required. The representation on the right approximates the shape using three ellipses. Each ellipse is specified in terms of its position, orientation, and the length of its minor and major axes.

The process (as well as the result) of decomposing an object into distinct components each of which is represented by one or more primitives is called *segmentation*. Segmentation is important in vision for finding objects in a cluttered scene. The representations in the bottom two panels of Figure 6.8 each employ the same segmentation. The representation using polygons approximates the boundaries of the shape more closely than the representation using ellipses. However, the ellipses provide a more compact representation since they require fewer parameters to specify.

To make the discussion of spatial representations more concrete, we now consider a particular task, path planning for mobile robots, and a general approach to representing the spatial properties of robots and their environments for purposes of navigation and obstacle avoidance.

Planning Paths in Configuration Space

In planning paths for robots, we are given as input a geometric model describing a robot, the objects surrounding it, their initial relative positions and orientations, and some target configuration describing a final position and orientation of the robot. The output is a path from the initial configuration to the target configuration that avoids the obstacles. A mobile robot plans paths to navigate from one room to another in an office building. A fixed robot plans paths for a manipulator attached to a robotic arm to grasp and move objects in its workspace.

To represent the state of the robot with respect to its surrounding physical environment, we introduce the idea of a space of possible configurations [Lozano-Pérez, 1983]. We represent the robot, $\mathcal{R}$, and the objects corresponding to obstacles in its environment, $\mathcal{B}_1, \mathcal{B}_2, \ldots, \mathcal{B}_m$, as closed subsets of the environment space, $\mathcal{E} = \mathbf{R}^n$, where $n = 2$ or 3. Both the robot and the obstacles in the environment are assumed to be rigid, nondeformable objects. A *Cartesian frame of reference* is a coordinate system used to describe the points that comprise an object. Let $\mathcal{F}_{\mathcal{R}}$ and $\mathcal{F}_{\mathcal{E}}$ be Cartesian frames of reference used to specify the points in $\mathcal{R}$ and $\mathcal{E}$, respectively. We assume that $\mathcal{F}_{\mathcal{E}}$ is fixed and $\mathcal{F}_{\mathcal{R}}$ is allowed to move with respect to $\mathcal{F}_{\mathcal{E}}$. Figure 6.9 (page 282) shows three objects and a robot specified with respect to two Cartesian frames of reference.

A *configuration*, q, of an object is a specification of the position and orientation of $\mathcal{F}_{\mathcal{R}}$ with respect to $\mathcal{F}_{\mathcal{E}}$. The *configuration space*, $\mathcal{C}$, is the set of all configurations of $\mathcal{R}$. We define the *free space*, $\mathcal{C}_{free}$, to be

$$\mathcal{C}_{free} = \{q \mid q \in \mathcal{C} \wedge \mathcal{R}(q) \cap (\mathcal{B}_1 \cup \mathcal{B}_2 \cup \cdots \cup \mathcal{B}_m) = \emptyset\}$$

where $\mathcal{R}(q)$ is that subset of $\mathcal{E}$ occupied by $\mathcal{R}$ in configuration q. A *free path* (or just a *path*) of $\mathcal{R}$ from some initial configuration, q, to the target

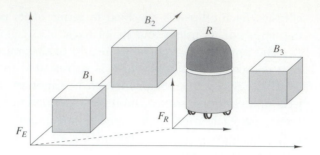

Figure 6.9   Two Cartesian frames of reference, F_E and F_R, showing three objects, B_1, B_2, and B_3, specified with respect to F_E, and a robot, R, specified with respect to F_R

configuration, q^*, is a continuous map

$$\pi : [0, 1] \rightarrow \mathcal{C}_{free}$$

subject to the constraints that $\pi(0) = q$ and $\pi(1) = q^*$.

Suppose that we can represent the robot and the obstacles in its environment using two-dimensional shapes. Suppose further that either the robot is represented by a circle or that the robot cannot rotate but only translate in the plane; in either case, the resulting configuration space is only two dimensional. If the robot was some noncircular shape and we were to allow the robot to rotate about some point, the resulting configuration space would be three dimensional, with the third dimension ranging over the possible rotations of the robot about the point. Generally, the configuration space has one dimension for every degree of freedom of the robot.

The top two panels in Figure 6.10 show two different robots in an environment consisting of two obstacles. To construct the resulting configuration spaces, we identify a point on each robot and then define the free space by finding all possible coordinates for that point such that the robot does now overlap with any obstacle. The middle two panels in Figure 6.10 illustrate a simple scheme for determining the boundaries for the obstacles in configuration space by sweeping the robot shape about the surfaces of the obstacles. The bottom two panels in Figure 6.10 show the resulting configuration spaces in which the free space is shaded.

Path Planning as Graph Search

There are a variety of techniques for finding a free path given a configuration space. Let us suppose that the boundaries of the obstacles in the configuration space can be represented as polygons. We can reduce finding a free path to searching for a path in a graph as follows. The *visibility graph* for a configuration space consisting of polygonal obstacles is constructed from the set of vertices corresponding to the vertices of the polygons plus the initial and target configurations. There is an edge between two vertices

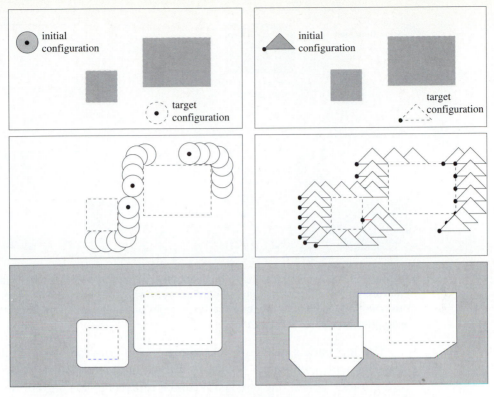

Figure 6.10   Two-dimensional configuration spaces. The top two panels show an environment with two obstacles. The top left panel shows a circular robot, and the top right panel shows a triangular-shaped robot. The center panels show how to construct the configuration spaces for the two different situations, and the lower panels show the resulting configuration spaces.

in the visibility graph if it is possible to draw a line segment between the two vertices that does not intersect any obstacle. Figure 6.11 (page 284) shows how a visibility graph is constructed from a configuration space and a path found from the initial to the target configuration. We can use any of the methods developed in Chapter 4 for searching for a path in a visibility graph.

If the configuration space obstacles are not polygonally shaped, it is necessary to generate some sort of polygonal approximation such as that shown in the lower left panel of Figure 6.8. An alternative to generating such a polygonal approximation and its corresponding visibility graph is to generate an approximate shape by breaking the object into discrete cells to construct a *discretized configuration space*. We obtain a discretized configuration space by superimposing a grid of cells on the continuous configuration space. A cell is marked occupied if it intersects an obstacle, and free otherwise.

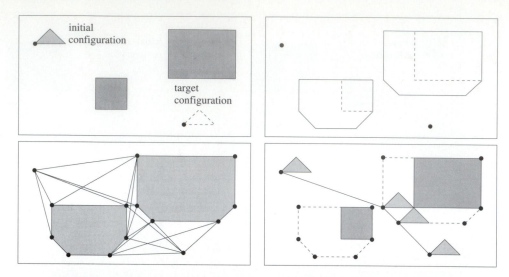

Figure 6.11 Searching for a path in a visibility graph. The top two panels show an environment and its corresponding configuration space. The lower left panel shows the resulting visibility graph, and the lower right panel shows a free path found by searching in the visibility graph.

The top panels in Figure 6.12 show a configuration space containing obstacles with continuous boundary curves and the resulting discretized configuration space. The free space can be represented as a graph in which the vertices correspond to unoccupied cells and there is an edge between any vertices whose corresponding cells are adjacent. As shown in the lower

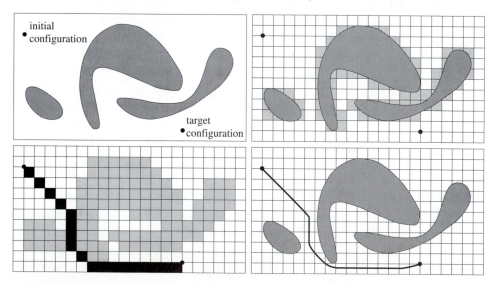

Figure 6.12 Discretized configuration space. A continuous configuration space (upper left) is approximated by a grid of discrete cells (upper right). A free path consists of a connected sequence of cells (lower left) corresponding to a path (lower right) in the graph in which each cell is a vertex connected to all eight of its adjacent cells.

panels in Figure 6.12, we can search this graph to obtain a path from the initial configuration to the target configuration. Note that in the discretized configuration space, the two larger obstacles are touching, but they were not in the continuous space. The effect of such inaccuracies can be ameliorated by using a finer-grained grid at the expense of a larger search space and more expensive path finding.

Locally Distinctive Places

In the approaches described, we assume that it is possible to somehow obtain reasonably accurate descriptions of the shapes of obstacles. Such descriptions are not always required for navigation purposes. For instance, there exist mobile robots that are capable of navigating along the corridor of office buildings, recognizing when they have entered into a junction where two or more corridors meet, and generally moving about without the use of a complex geometric representation of objects and their surfaces. For such robots, the world is composed of corridors to traverse and junctions to enter and leave from.

The top left panel in Figure 6.13 shows a portion of a simple office building composed entirely of corridors and junctions. As long as it is in one of the shaded areas shown in the top right panel in Figure 6.13, the robot knows that it is in a junction and that the junction is shaped like a T, L, or some other legal meeting of corridors. The junctions are often referred to as *locally distinctive places* because the robot can distinguish the space near a junction from the space elsewhere in its environment. The bottom

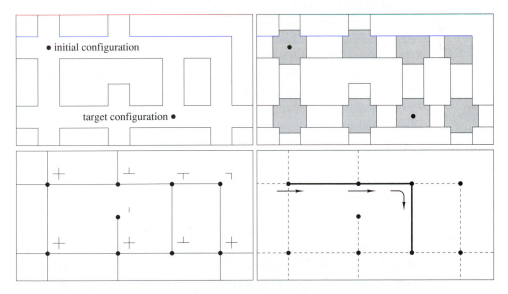

Figure 6.13   Graph of locally distinctive places. An office layout (top left) is broken up into regions (top right) that are used to construct a graph (lower left) that can be searched to find a path (lower right) from the initial to the target configuration.

left panel in Figure 6.13 shows a graph with the locally distinctive places as vertices labeled with type of the corresponding junction and edges between vertices corresponding to junctions joined by a corridor. The bottom right panel shows a path from the initial configuration to the target location.

To be useful, the graph of locally distinctive places relies on having sensing and navigation routines for identifying locally distinctive places, traversing corridors, and finding how to exit from a junction into a particular corridor. This representation has the advantage that it is simple, compact, easy to search, and tuned to the robot's sensing and navigation capabilities. In order to design a practical spatial representation, it is important to have a clear idea of what the representation is to be used for.

▼ Summary

It is often useful in organizing knowledge to accord special status to those aspects of our understanding of the world that play an important representational role. Many aspects of our daily existence can be described in terms of the passage of time, the structure of the space, and what people believe. In this chapter, we sampled some techniques for reasoning about time, space, and belief.

A situation is an interval of time in which things do not change. A situation is described in terms of a set of fluents that can change from one situation to another. Events serve to change one situation into another. In the situation calculus, situations, events, and fluents are represented as terms in first-order predicate logic. The situation calculus allows us to represent cause-and-effect relationships involving events and fluents and to reason about the consequences of sequences of events.

The frame problem is concerned with representing what things do not change as a result of an event occurring in a situation. The qualification problem is concerned with stating the conditions under which a given event will have a particular consequence. Common-sense reasoning about time and change requires solutions to the frame and qualification problems. Techniques from nonmonotonic logic have provided a variety of solutions to these problems.

In first-order interval temporal logic, events and fluents are represented as propositions. In this logic, we can reason about points and intervals of time, discrete and continuous time, delays between when an event occurs and when its consequences occur, and the possibility of several events occurring at the same time. In general, reasoning about time is computationally difficult. However, for a restricted interval temporal logic involving simplified causal rules, temporal reasoning can be performed in polynomial time.

Modal logics can be used to reason about what an agent believes or knows. Many choices are involved in axiomatizing belief. In some theories, an agent believes all the logical axioms and any logical consequence of those axioms and the agent's other beliefs. We can also require that an agent is consistent in its beliefs. A logic of belief enables a system to reason about how to acquire information and about when to volunteer information to others.

The semantics for modal logics are specified in terms of possible worlds and an accessibility relationship on such worlds. Each possible world corresponds to an interpretation in the semantics for the predicate calculus. If an agent believes φ in one possible world, then φ is true in all possible worlds accessible from that world. Possible-worlds semantics enables the logician to think about the theories of belief in graphical terms.

In reasoning about physical objects, it is important to choose spatial primitives that allow us to represent the important spatial properties of the objects while allowing us to efficiently encode spatial information and draw appropriate conclusions. In most applications, spatial representations only approximate the spatial structure of physical objects. In robot navigation planning, the feasible positions of the robot and its surroundings are described as a space of configurations. Planning consists of finding a path from one configuration to another that avoids portions of configuration space occupied by obstacles. In configuration space, the surfaces of objects can be approximated by polygonal shapes or by a grid of discrete cells that are either occupied by obstacles or not. In some cases, physical space can be represented as a graph of locations in which the arcs between locations represent procedures that the robot can employ to move from one location to another.

Time, belief, and space present significant challenges for automated reasoning systems. Fortunately, time, belief, and space have structure that can be exploited to expedite reasoning. This structure is apparent in the forward flow of time, the continuity of space, and the relationships involving an agent's beliefs. Automated reasoning systems will have to take advantage of this structure to provide acceptable levels of performance.

● Background

McCarthy [1963] introduced the notion of situations for reasoning about change. McCarthy and Hayes [1969] present the situation calculus along with a description of the frame problem. McDermott [1982] describes a temporal logic for reasoning about continuous change. Allen [1984] developed a temporal logic in which intervals rather than points were primitive. Dean and Boddy [1988a] describe computational problems involved in reasoning about events whose relative ordering is not known.

Many articles have been published describing solutions to the frame and qualification problems [Hanks and McDermott, 1987; Kautz, 1986; Lifschitz, 1987; Dean and Kanazawa, 1988; Morgenstern and Stein, 1988; Lin and Shoham, 1991; Sandewall, 1989]. The methods for dealing with the frame and qualification problems described in this text were adapted from the work of Shoham [1988]. The implementation of projection and persistence clipping is based on techniques described in Dean and McDermott [1987].

Davis [1990] reviews methods for reasoning about knowledge and belief. Moore [1980] describes an approach for reasoning about belief and time. For more about modal logics of belief, read Halpern and Moses [1985], Levesque [1986], or Fagin et al. [1994]. Kripke [1971] developed the possible-worlds semantics for modal logics.

Brooks [1981] describes a spatial representation based on cylinders and conic sections. McDermott and Davis [1982] describe a symbolic approach to spatial reasoning that uses discrimination trees to store spatial knowledge. Kuipers [1978] describes an approach to representing large-scale space based on a graph of locally distinctive places. Davis [1986] provides representations and algorithms for acquiring spatial knowledge. Lozano-Pérez [1983] introduced the idea of configuration space to computer scientists and demonstrated its applicability to robotics. Latombe [1990] provides a comprehensive treatment of configuration-space methods for path planning.

■ Exercises

6.1 Consider the following digital circuit.

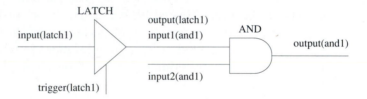

We model the behavior of the circuit using the situation calculus. The output of a LATCH is whatever its input is when the LATCH is triggered.

```
∀ s, b,
 holds(s, status(input(latch1), b))  ⊃
 holds(result(s, pulse(trigger(latch1))),
      status(output(latch1), b))
```

The output of an AND gate is determined by the appropriate boolean function.

```
∀ s, b1, b2, b3,
 (holds(s, status(input1(and1), b1))  ∧
  holds(s, status(input2(and1), b2))  ∧
  b3 = boolean_and(b1, b2))  ⊃
 holds(s, status(output(and1), b3))
```

The output of latch1 and first input of and1 are the same.

```
output(latch1) = input1(and1)
```

Here are some initial conditions.

```
holds(s1, status(input1(latch1), 0))
holds(s1, status(output(latch1), 1))
holds(s1, status(input1(and1), 1))
holds(s1, status(input2(and1), 1))
```

What additional axioms are needed in order to prove the following statement?

```
holds(result(s1, pulse(trigger(latch1))),
      status(output(and1), 0))
```

6.2 Suppose there is an event called chance that has the result of either p or q. We represent this in the situation calculus using the following formula:

∀ s, holds(result(s, chance), or(p, q))

Describe how this formula complicates the simple approach to solving the frame problem described in the text. In particular, consider what will happen if not(p) and not(q) are true of a situation.

6.3 If you toggle the switch to a light and the light is off, then the light will come on, at least assuming that the electric power is behaving normally. If you toggle the switch to a light in a situation during which the power is interrupted, then the light will not come on. If the power is subsequently restored, then the light will come on if the switch is still in the appropriate position. Provide axioms in the situation calculus to model the consequences of any sequence of switch togglings and interruptions and restorations of power.

6.4 Consider the following boolean circuit:

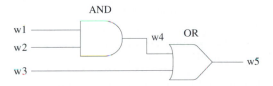

a) Write a causal theory in the form of a set of axioms in the interval logic to reason about how signals might propagate in this boolean circuit. Your theory should capture the constraint that it takes eight units of time for a signal to propagate through an AND gate and five units of time to propagate through an OR gate. You can assume that wires propagate signals instantly. A wire is either high or low at any given time.

b) Translate your theory into a set of Lisp CRULEs. Assume that initially w1 and w2 are high, w3 is low, w4 and w5 are determined by the AND and OR gates, and that the system is quiescent in the sense that all the signals have had a chance to propagate throughout the circuit. Use project to predict what will happen to w5 if at time 10 w1 goes low and at time 40 it goes high.

6.5 Write a set of causal rules in the interval temporal logic that capture the following physical laws for the world of dungeons and dragons:

a) To move from A to B, the knight must be alive, not frozen, in A, and A must be adjacent to B. If all these conditions are satisfied, then the knight will enter B two time units later. Entering a place immediately changes the knight's location to that place.

b) If the dragon is not enchanted, whenever the knight enters the dragon's hoard, the dragon will try to toast the knight one time unit later. Should the knight still be in the hoard when the dragon tries to make toast of him, the knight will die immediately.

c) The wizard will immediately become unfrozen should the knight decide to thaw him. The knight can thaw the wizard only if the knight is in the wizard's chamber, possesses the torch, and the wizard is frozen. Once thawed, the wizard will try to freeze the knight six time units later, unless the wizard possesses the jewel by then. The knight will be immediately frozen only if he is in the wizard's chamber when the wizard tries to freeze him.

d) Picking up something immediately results in possessing it. The knight can only pick up the torch or jewel if he is in the dungeon and the treasure if he is in the dragon's hoard.

e) The knight can only give away the jewel if he possesses it and the receiver is in the same room as he. Giving something away immediately results in the receiver becoming the new possessor. If the wizard is given the jewel when he is not frozen, the wizard will enchant the dragon (hence the dragon will become enchanted) two time units later. The wizard cannot receive things while he is frozen.

6.6 Change the Lisp function contra so that (location r x) contradicts (location r y) just in case (not (equal x y)). Implement causal rules that determine the location of the robot as a result of actions of the form (move r x y), where x and y are locations.

6.7 Suppose that we represent space hierarchically so that someone can be in a building while in an office in that building. How does this complicate the task of computing the effects of an action? Think of the complications introduced by moving objects from one location to another. For example, how would you keep track of the location of the robot and the car in the sequence: The robot got in the car, the car was in the garage, the car was driven to the beach.

6.8 Extend the routines for managing temporal databases to handle qualifications. Give each rule a name (R47), and then, before applying a rule, check to see if there are any qualifications in effect that would override applying the rule in the present circumstances. Your solution should be able to handle qualifications on qualifications as long as there are no circularities.

6.9 Suppose that Fred believes that his neighbor's house is on fire. Suppose further that Fred believes that if his neighbor's house is on fire then the right thing to do is to call the fire department. Using the axioms described in this chapter, prove that Fred believes that the right thing to do is to call the fire department.

6.10 Suppose that Ralph wants to use Lynn's computer account to read a paper that they are working on jointly. In order to use Lynn's account, Ralph needs to know Lynn's password. Suppose that Lynn and Ralph are good friends so Lynn will tell Ralph her password if he asks her. Write axioms using the situation calculus so that you can prove that Ralph can read the paper.

You will have to write axioms that specify, among other things, that if Lynn tells Ralph her password, then he will know it. In order to write these axioms, you will need knows, asks, and other functions for describing knowledge and communication.

6.11 Write a program that, given a set of convex polygons representing obstacles in the plane, the length of a side of a triangular robot with three equal sides, and two points representing the initial and target configurations for the robot, plans a free path from the starting configuration to the target configuration using the visibility graph method. Assume that the robot can move only via translation in the plane (no rotations). As abstract data types, you might implement a point as a pair of numbers, a line segment as a pair of points, and a polygon as a connected sequence of line segments. You will have to write (or otherwise obtain) routines for determining if two line segments intersect and performing a variety of other simple geometric calculations.

6.12 Suppose that you have to navigate blindfolded using touch alone. Describe some familiar area, for instance, your apartment or a portion of your workplace, in terms of a graph of locally distinctive places. You will have to develop a set of features that are recognizable using touch. For example, you may be able to easily recognize door jambs. You will also have to develop a set of navigation procedures for getting from one place to another. For example, you may have a procedure for traversing a hall by trailing your hand along one wall feeling for a door jamb or other discontinuity.

▶ LISP IMPLEMENTATION

Temporal Reasoning

In this section, we provide an implementation for the projection and persistence clipping algorithm described in the text. We begin with the abstract data type for causal rules. A CRULE consists of a list of antecedent conditions, an expression indicating the type of the triggering event, and a list of consequent effects.

```
(defun make-CRULE (antecedents trigger effects)
  (list 'CRULE antecedents trigger effects))
(defun CRULE-antecedents (rule) (second rule))
(defun CRULE-trigger (rule) (third rule))
(defun CRULE-effects (rule) (fourth rule))
```

The effects specified in a causal rule correspond to potential events or propositions (facts) that become true and persist for some time. The abstract data type for effects encodes whether the effect is a potential event or fact, the type of the event or fact, and a delay indicating how much time elapses from when the triggering event occurs to when the fact or event becomes true. An effect is *instantiated* in the process of projection when a causal rule is found to apply to a particular event. The only thing we do with effects is create new ones or instantiate existing ones.

```
(defun make-EFFECT (event-or-fact type delay)
  (list event-or-fact type delay))
(defun EFFECT-instantiate (effect time)
  (cond ((eq (first effect) 'EVENT)
         (make-EVENT (second effect) (+ time (third effect))))
        ((eq (first effect) 'FACT)
         (make-FACT (second effect) (+ time (third effect))))))
```

Having differentiated between facts and events, we have to introduce abstract data types for each. All events are point events, so we need only an event type and time of occurrence.

```
(defun make-EVENT (type time) (list 'EVENT type time))
(defun is-EVENT (x) (and x (listp x) (eq (first x) 'EVENT)))
(defun EVENT-type (event) (second event))
(defun EVENT-time (event) (third event))
```

Facts are similar to events except that they persist over intervals of time. All facts are initially assumed to persist indefinitely. To represent indefinite persistence, we introduce a special symbol infty meant to indicate that there is no upper bound on the duration of the corresponding interval. Since we may have to revise this bound in the light of additional information, we make the ends of facts settable.

```
(defun make-FACT (type begin) (list 'FACT type begin 'infty))
(defun is-FACT (x) (and x (listp x) (eq (first x) 'FACT)))
(defun FACT-type (fact) (second fact))
(defun FACT-begin (fact) (third fact))
(defun FACT-end (fact) (fourth fact))
(defun set-FACT-end (fact time) (setf (fourth fact) time))
```

Here is the Lisp representation of the causal rule indicating that whenever a robot toggles the switch for a light that is off, the light will come on.

```
(make-CRULE '((location Ralph room101)
              (not (on (light room101))))
            '(toggle Ralph (switch (light room101)))
            (list (make-EFFECT 'FACT '(on (light room101)) 0)))
```

Now we can list the rest of the code for projection and persistence clipping. We proceed in a top-down manner starting with the function project that takes a list of initial facts true at time 0, a list of events known to occur at various times, and a list of causal rules. Project does not return anything of interest; it modifies certain internal state variables to construct a time map in the form of a list of tokens representing propositions that are true over intervals of time.

```
(defun project (conditions events rules)
  (initialize-database conditions events)
  (aux-project rules))
```

We separate the database into facts and events. At this point, all we need to know about facts and events is that we can add new ones and that we can reset the lists of facts and events to the empty list. Initialization consists of adding the information corresponding to the initial conditions and events to the corresponding portions of the database.

```
(defun initialize-database (conditions events)
  (reset-facts)
  (mapc #'(lambda (type)
            (add-fact (make-FACT type 0)))
        conditions)
```

```
(reset-events)
(mapc #'(lambda (spec)
          (add-event (make-EVENT (first spec) (second spec))))
      events))
```

The events are stored in a sorted queue in the order of their occurrence, earliest to latest. In aux-project, the earliest occurring event is removed from the list of events, and all the causal rules with the corresponding triggering event type are checked to see if their antecedents are true at the time of the event.

```
(defun aux-project (rules)
  (let ((event (pop-event)))
    (if (null event) nil
      (progn (mapc #'(lambda (rule) (apply-rule event rule))
                   (fetch-rules event rules))
             (aux-project rules)))))
```

Fetch-rules takes an event and a set of causal rules and returns all rules with triggering event type that corresponds to the type of the event given as the first argument.

```
(defun fetch-rules (event rules)
  (cond ((null rules) nil)
        ((equal (EVENT-type event) (CRULE-trigger (first rules)))
         (cons (first rules) (fetch-rules event (rest rules))))
        (t (fetch-rules event (rest rules)))))
```

Apply-rule takes an event and a causal rule and, if the antecedents of the rule are satisfied at the time of the event, then it adds to the database the appropriate events and facts corresponding to the effects supplied in consequents of the rule.

```
(defun apply-rule (event rule)
  (let ((time (EVENT-time event)))
    (if (check-antecedents (CRULE-antecedents rule) time)
        (mapc #'(lambda (token)
                    (if (is-FACT token)
                      (add-fact token)
                      (add-event token)))
              (mapcar #'(lambda (effect)
                          (EFFECT-instantiate effect time))
                      (CRULE-effects rule))))))
```

To determine if the antecedents of a rule are satisfied at a particular time, check-antecedents invokes the function holds, which determines whether or not a proposition is true at a time by looking at the facts in the database. Projection proceeds by sweeping forward in time so that, when a causal rule is considered with respect to a particular triggering event, the database is complete until the time of that event.

```
(defun check-antecedents (antecedents time)
  (cond ((null antecedents) t)
        ((not (holds time (first antecedents))) nil)
        (t (check-antecedents (rest antecedents) time))))
```

Now we describe the database and the operations on the database. We introduce local state variables for the functions that operate on facts and events. We can reset the list of facts to the empty list, add a new fact or determine if there is a fact of a particular type in the database whose interval spans a given time point. In adding a new fact, we clip the persistence of any existing fact of a contradictory type. We use the Common Lisp find function to search through the list of facts to find one with a given type that begins at or before a given time and persists beyond that time. Find returns the first element of its second argument such that the test function applied to this element and the first argument returns non-nil.

```lisp
(let ((facts nil))
  (defun reset-facts () (setq facts nil))
  (defun holds (time type)
    (find type facts
          :test #'(lambda (type fact) (is-true type fact time))))
  (defun add-fact (fact)
    (if (holds (FACT-begin fact) (FACT-type fact)) nil
      (let (contra (time (FACT-begin fact)))
        (setq contra (find (contradicts (FACT-type fact)) facts
                           :test #'(lambda (type fact)
                                     (is-true type fact time))))
      (if contra (set-FACT-end contra (FACT-begin fact)))
      (setq facts (cons fact facts)))))))
```

The following method of determining a contradictory type will suffice for our examples:

```lisp
(defun contradicts (type)
  (if (and type (listp type) (eq (first type) 'NOT))
      (second type) (list 'NOT type)))
```

A proposition (type) is true at a time given a fact (token) if the type of the fact is the same as the proposition and the fact begins before or coincident with the time and ends prior to the time.

```lisp
(defun is-true (type fact time)
  (and (equal type (FACT-type fact))
       (or (t< (FACT-begin fact) time)
           (= (FACT-begin fact) time))
       (t< time (FACT-end fact))))
```

Temporal precedence is complicated somewhat by the symbol, infty, used to represent the indefinite upper bound on the duration of fact tokens.

```lisp
(defun t< (time1 time2)
  (or (eq time2 'infty)
      (and (integerp time1)
           (integerp time2)
           (< time1 time2))))
```

In this implementation, we keep track only of events to use in predicting additional facts and events. We maintain the list of events in a queue ordered by time. Since events can cause only future events and facts, we pop the events off the queue one at a time in performing our sweep forward in time for projection.

```
(let ((events nil))
  (defun reset-events () (setq events nil))
  (defun add-event (event)
    (setq events
          (sort (cons event events)
                #'(lambda (f g) (t< (EVENT-time f)
                                    (EVENT-time g))))))
  (defun pop-event ()
    (let ((item (first events)))
      (setq events (rest events))
      item)))
```

Here is a simple test illustrating how project performs for the example shown in Figure 6.5.

```
(let ((rules
       (list (make-CRULE '(P) 'E (list (make-EFFECT 'FACT 'R 0)))
             (make-CRULE '(R Q) 'F (list (make-EFFECT 'FACT '(NOT P) 0)))
             (make-CRULE '(Q) 'E (list (make-EFFECT 'EVENT 'F 5))))))
  (defun test ()
    (project '(P Q) '((E 10)) rules)
    (and (holds 5 'P)
         (not (holds 20 'P)))))
```

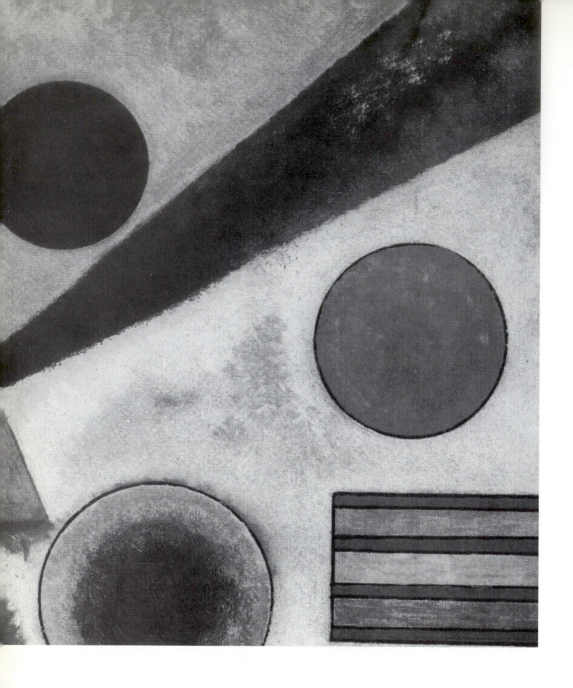

CHAPTER 7

PLANNING

A robot forklift truck is unloading engine blocks from a flatbed trailer when it is told that the main production line in the factory is being held up for lack of parts (Figure 7.1). The robot finishes unloading the engine block that it is currently carrying and at the same time inquires about what parts

Figure 7.1 A robot forklift communicating with an automated factory plans to deliver a load of gaskets that is holding up production in the factory

are needed to continue production. Having discovered that an assembly unit on the production line has run out of a certain kind of gasket, the robot travels to the right location in the warehouse, picks up the required gaskets, delivers them to the assembly unit in the factory, and then resumes unloading the engine blocks.

In the scenario, the robot forklift truck has a general goal to maintain production in the factory. In response to information that production is halted, the robot formulates a plan for getting production started again. The plan consists of the following steps: Unload the engine block currently being carried, gather information about the needed parts and their location in the warehouse, travel to the right location in the warehouse, pick up the parts, travel to the right location in the factory, place the parts so that they can be used by the assembly unit.

The need to plan sequences of actions to achieve goals arises in many applications. The following examples should give you some idea of the diversity of planning applications.

- **Scheduling scientific experiments**—Expensive pieces of NASA equipment like the space shuttle and the Hubble space telescope are in great demand by scientists. Planning systems have been developed to schedule experiments that require using such equipment.
- **Managing scarce resources in brewing beer**—Fermentation vats constitute a scarce resource in the brewing industry. Planning systems are used to allocate available fermentation vats to produce small batches of beer and ale in custom breweries.
- **Sequencing in the shipping industry**—In seaports, huge cranes are used for loading and unloading containerized freight from ships. Planning systems are used to determine the order in which to process ships and to assign cranes to get the job done.

As will become apparent, planning has a lot in common with search, and most problems of practical interest have combinatorial aspects that raise issues of computational complexity.

7.1 State-Space Search

What Is Planning?

Intuitively, a *plan* is a strategy for acting. Planning involves choosing a plan by considering alternative plans and reasoning about their consequences. Consider a simple case. Suppose that a particular robot can perform exactly one of several alternative actions and no actions thereafter. Suppose further that the robot can predict the consequences of its actions and that each action results in a different future. In this simple case, choosing an action corresponds to choosing a future.

▲ AI IN PRACTICE

Planning for Spacecraft Assembly

A consortium, including Computer Resources International, Matra Marconi Space, and researchers at AIAI, University of Edinburgh, has developed a system for planning and scheduling the activities involved in the assembly and testing of spacecraft for the European Space Agency (ESA). The system, called OPTIMUM-AIV, supports the entire life cycle of spacecraft assembly and testing, not only scheduling activities but also monitoring the execution of plans. State-of-the-art knowledge-based techniques have been applied to automate planning and scheduling. Operators representing preconditions and effects for spacecraft assembly activities are used to coordinate activities and verify plans. Failures of tests can be fixed using recovery plans.

As with other software used in the real world, the OPTIMUM-AIV planning system has to integrate its activities with other systems and human experts. OPTIMUM-AIV allows engineers to participate in the planning process and supports replanning to deal with problems encountered during plan execution. The system also works in concert with the ARTEMIS project management system already in use for spacecraft assembly, integration, and test support at the European Space Agency.

Courtesy of ESA

You can imagine different criteria that the robot might use to choose between the alternative actions and, hence, futures. For instance, there might be some proposition (say, your being independently wealthy) that, if true of a possible future, makes that future more desirable than futures in which the proposition is false. Such a proposition is called a *goal*. An agent that chooses an action because it results in a future in which particular goals are true is *satisficing*. As another strategy for choosing actions, suppose that the agent can assign a value to each possible future where higher values are better in some sense. An agent that chooses an action whose future has the maximum value is *optimizing*.

We have already encountered algorithms for satisficing and optimizing in Chapter 4. Planning is a special case of search in which we are concerned with finding plans that result in desirable futures.

Planning as Search

In the first formulation of planning as search explored in this chapter, the search space is the set of all possible states of the world. The objective is to find a state in which the goal is satisfied. Operators correspond to actions that transform one state into another. Any sequence of operators that transforms the initial state into a state satisfying the goal corresponds to a successful plan. For obvious reasons, this approach to planning as searching in the space of states is called *state-space search*.

As an alternative formulation of planning as search, we might use a search space consisting of all possible plans. In this case, operators transform one plan into another, by adding or reordering *plan steps* that correspond to actions. The advantage of this alternative formulation is that we can think of plans as something other than simple sequences of actions. For instance, representing plans as partially ordered sets of actions allows us to avoid commitment to the order in which actions are carried out when order does not matter.

Planning so as to coordinate with other agents and processes complicates the problem quite a bit. Even if the agent is restricted to taking exactly one action, it still has to consider all the myriad ways that other agents and processes might alter the consequences of its action. If the agent is contemplating a series of actions, then it must consider how to counter the effects of other agents and processes.

In the case in which there are no other agents or processes but there is some uncertainty regarding the consequences of an agent's actions, a fixed sequence of actions may not be the best plan. Assuming that the agent can observe the immediate consequences of its actions, the agent might construct what is called a *conditional plan* specifying for each step in the plan the correct action to take given the observations following the previous step. For instance, a plan for getting milk late at night might be to drive to the market in town and, if the market is open (something we can observe once at the market), then purchase the milk at the market; otherwise, drive to the convenience store and purchase the milk there.

In some cases, the future is uncertain and no amount of observation will enable us to resolve the uncertainty before having to take action. For example, it might be important for a successful vacation that the weather be warm and sunny; unfortunately, long-range weather prediction is not accurate, and for any number of reasons you might have to plan your vacation well in advance. In such cases, it is useful to be able to reason about the probability of uncertain consequences. For instance, you might find out that at your desired vacation spot there is a 70% chance that it will be warm and sunny on any given day in August but only a 30% chance that it will be warm and sunny in December. By making use of these probabilities and accounting for the value associated with a successful vacation at the two different times of year, you can choose a course of action that maximizes the value you can expect given the probabilities. We do not discuss probabilistic modeling issues in this chapter. We will have something to say about planning under uncertainty in Chapter 8.

We focus on planning rather than acting in this chapter though the two are typically interleaved in practice. In many cases, we can successfully interact with the world to achieve our goals without careful planning or being able to accurately predict the future. In the literature on planning and acting, directly responding to events as they happen is often referred to as *situated activity*.

If your goal is to get a high score in a fast-paced video game, then carefully planning out each move in advance is likely to interfere with your performance. To play a high-scoring game, you have to be quick to observe events as they occur and adapt to situations as they evolve over time. The rule-based reactive system described in Chapter 2 is a simple example of a system designed for situated activity. We consider some of the perceptual issues involved with situated activity in Chapter 9.

In this chapter, we investigate several approaches to planning. We begin by describing planning in terms of state-space search. We then build on the basic representation for actions used in state-space search to develop a more general representation for plans and consider how to search in the space of such plans. We present a planning approach that speeds planning by representing the planning problem at several different levels of abstraction and proceeding from the most abstract level to the least abstract level through a series of refinements. Another approach speeds planning by remembering past solutions and then adapting them to present circumstances. This adaptive approach to planning corresponds to a form of learning. We also consider an approach to planning with incomplete information. Finally, we discuss some of the issues involved in planning with more expressive representations for actions.

Representing and Solving Search Problems

In this section, we introduce a general approach for representing and solving search problems cast in terms of planning. This approach to search appears as the first section of a chapter on planning to emphasize the strong connection between planning and search.

In the following section, we refer to a node in the search space as a *state*, and we use the terms *search space* and *state space* interchangeably. In the simple propositional version of planning described in this chapter, the set of all states is determined by a set of *propositional state variables* $\mathcal{P} = \{P_1, \ldots, P_n\}$. For example, the propositional state variables might consist of "the light is on" and "the door is closed." A particular state corresponds to a truth assignment $\sigma : \mathcal{P} \to \{\text{True}, \text{False}\}$. For example, there is the state in which "the light is on" is assigned True and "the door is closed" is assigned False.

A goal is a partial assignment $\gamma : Q \rightarrow \{\text{True}, \text{False}\}$, where $Q \subseteq P$. For instance, we might require that the state variable "the door is closed" be assigned True but not care about the truth value assigned to "the light is on." Given a goal γ, the objective of state-space search is to transform some initial state σ into a state σ' such that σ' implies γ.

State transformations result from applying a sequence of operators chosen from a set of such operators. Each operator can be expressed as a rule that determines the circumstances under which an operator can be applied to a state and provides a description of the resulting state. For instance, we might have an operator for closing the door that can be applied only if the light is on and the door is open and will result in the door being closed. In terms of truth assignments, this operator might be expressed as if "the light is on" is assigned True, and "the door is closed" is assigned False, then the result of applying the door closing operator is that "the door is closed" is assigned True, and the other truth assignments remain the same as they were before the operator was applied.

It is often convenient to represent states, goals, and operators in set-theoretic terms. A *condition* corresponds to a state variable or its negation. In set-theoretic terms, a state is the set of conditions assigned True. For any state variable P and state S, either $P \in S$ or $\neg P \in S$ but not both. A state S *satisfies* a goal G if $G \subseteq S$.

It will never be the case that we allow both P and $\neg P$ in a state S, but it will be convenient to relax the requirement that for every state variable P, either $P \in S$ or $\neg P \in S$. For instance, if a state contains a condition indicating that an object is colored red, we might not want to include conditions indicating that it is not blue, not green, and so on. This method of implicitly assigning truth values to state variables corresponds to an instance of the closed-world assumption that was discussed in Chapter 3 in the section on nonmonotonic reasoning.

In set-theoretic terms, an operator is a triple (P, A, D) consisting of three sets of conditions: a set of *Preconditions* that must be true in any state in which the operator is applied, a set of *Additions* that must be true in any state that results from the operator being applied, and a set of *Deletions* that must be false in any state that results from the operator being applied.

State Progression

Applying an operator in the forward direction (transforming a state into another state) is called *state progression*. An operator, $\alpha = (P, A, D)$, can be applied in the forward direction to a state, S, if P is a subset of S; the resulting state is

$$f_\alpha(S) = A \cup (S - D)$$

where $\cup$ indicates set union, and $-$ indicates set difference.

The function f_α is said to compute the *strongest provable postconditions* since the progressed state retains as much as possible from the original state taking into account what must be true in a state resulting from the application of the operator. We assume that anything true in the original state that is not mentioned explicitly in the operator's delete list is true in the progressed state.

Goal Regression

Applying an operator in the backward direction (transforming a goal into another goal) is called *goal regression*. An operator, $\alpha = (P, A, D)$, can be applied in the backward direction to a goal, G, if the intersection of D and G is empty; the resulting goal is

$$b_\alpha(G) = P \cup (G - A)$$

The function b_α is said to compute the *weakest provable preconditions* since the regressed goal retains as little as possible from the original goal while still ensuring that the original goal will be satisfied following the application of the operator if the regressed goal is satisfied prior to the operator being applied. For instance, given the goal "the door is closed" and the door closing operator described earlier, the regressed goal obtained using the door closing operator consists of "the light is on" and "the door is open."

Using state progression, we can search forward from the initial state looking for a progressed state satisfying the goal. Using goal regression, we can search backward from the goal looking for a regressed goal that is satisfied by the initial state. There are also search strategies that simultaneously search forward and backward.

Means/Ends Analysis

The set difference, $G - S$, between a goal G and a state S provides a weak but often useful measure of the distance from a state to a goal. A *difference* is something true in the goal and false in the state. *Means/ends analysis* is a heuristic strategy that prefers to apply operators in a state so as to reduce the number of differences between the state and the goal.

For instance, if we are in a state in which the door is open and the light is on and our goal is to have the door closed, then we will prefer operators that close the door to those that turn the light off. There will be times when we have to choose operators contrary to the advice of means/ends analysis. Suppose that we have three operators: one that closes the door if the light is on and the door open, a second that turns the light on if it is off, and a third that turns the light off if it is on. If we are in a state in which the door is open and the light is off and our goal is to have the door closed and the light off, then we will have to turn on the light,

```
;; Given a set of operators and an initial state, return the
;; set of all resulting states obtained by applying operators
;; whose preconditions are satisfied in the initial state.
(defun apply-operators (operators state)
  (if (null operators) nil
    (let ((operator (first operators)))
      (if (subsetp (preconditions operator) state :test #'equal)
          (cons (union (additions operator)
                       (set-difference state
                                       (deletions operator)
                                       :test #'equal)
                       :test #'equal)
                (apply-operators (rest operators) state))
        (apply-operators (rest operators) state)))))
```

Figure 7.2   Generating the next states for state-space search

close the door, and turn off the light to achieve the goal. The first step of turning on the light increases rather than reduces the number of differences.

We can implement a simple version of state-space search relying on state progression rather easily. We begin with a data abstraction for operators.

```
(defun make-OPERATOR (preconditions additions deletions)
  (list preconditions additions  deletions))
(defun preconditions (operator) (first operator))
(defun additions (operator) (second operator))
(defun deletions (operator) (third operator))
```

Figure 7.2 provides a function that, given a set of operators and a state, applies all those operators whose preconditions are true in the state and returns the list of resulting states. The implementation of apply-operators makes use of the Common Lisp routines for manipulating sets represented as lists. Subsetp, union, and set-difference perform the obvious set-theoretic operations on sets. Each of these functions takes an optional keyword argument corresponding to a function used to test for equality among elements of sets; since it will be convenient to use arbitrary expressions to represent conditions, we use equal to test for equality. Using apply-operators, we can implement state-space search using the generic search routines defined in Chapter 4.

Figure 7.3 lists two versions of state-space search. The first version, sss, uses the generic breadth-first search routine in which the goal function is implemented using the Common Lisp subsetp routine, and the function for generating the children of a node is implemented using apply-operators. The second version, mea, employs means/ends analysis by applying best-first search with a distance measure based on the number of differences between a state and the goal. The breadth-first version will always find a solution if one exists, assuming that you do not run out of computer memory.

```
;; State-space search using a breadth-first strategy
(defun sss (states goal operators)
  (bfs states
       #'(lambda (state) (subsetp goal state :test #'equal))
       #'(lambda (state) (apply-operators operators state))))

;; State-space search using a best-first strategy
(defun mea (states goal operators)
  (best states
        #'(lambda (state) (subsetp goal state :test #'equal))
        #'(lambda (state) (apply-operators operators state))
        #'(lambda (state1 state2) (< (distance state1 goal)
                                     (distance state2 goal)))))

;; A distance measure for state-space search
(defun distance (state goal)
  (length (set-difference goal state :test #'equal)))
```

Figure 7.3   Two implementations for state-space search

Machine Assembly Example

Here is a simple example illustrating the preceding versions of state-space search. Suppose that we have a robot trying to figure out how to assemble a machine consisting of three components. Initially, none of the components are assembled, and the robot's goal is to assemble all three.

Four operators reflect certain interactions involving the order in which the components are assembled. One operator assembles the first component if it is not already assembled. Another operator assembles the third component only if the first two are already assembled. The assembly of the second component is governed by two operators, one of which applies if the first component is assembled, and the other applies if it is not. Assembling the second component in a state in which the first is already assembled results in the first component being disassembled. Figure 7.4 (page 306) shows the Lisp representation for the initial state, goal, and operators.

Both versions of state-space search find a solution easily for this small problem. The version using means/ends analysis takes about half the time to find a solution. The reason for the difference in running times is apparent when we examine underlying search space.

Figure 7.5 (page 307) depicts the state space for the machine assembly example. The four operators are notated a, b, c, and d. At the top of Figure 7.5, each operator is depicted schematically as a partitioned box, indicating preconditions on the left, additions on the upper right, and deletions on the lower right. At the bottom of Figure 7.5, the search space is shown with the integers 1 through 3 used to denote the three components. An integer with a bar over it indicates that the corresponding component is not assembled, and an integer without a bar indicates that the component is

```
;; Initial state
'((not (assembled 1)) (not (assembled 2)) (not (assembled 3)))

;; Goal specification
'((assembled 1) (assembled 2) (assembled 3))

;; List of operators
(list (make-OPERATOR '((not (assembled 1)))      ;; Preconditions
                     '((assembled 1))            ;; Additions
                     '((not (assembled 1))))     ;; Deletions
      (make-OPERATOR '((not (assembled 1)))
                     '((assembled 2))
                     '((not (assembled 2))))
      (make-OPERATOR '((assembled 1))
                     '((assembled 2) (not (assembled 1)))
                     '((not (assembled 2)) (assembled 1)))
      (make-OPERATOR '((assembled 1) (assembled 2))
                     '((assembled 3))
                     '((not (assembled 3)))))
```

Figure 7.4   Initial state, operators, and goal for the machine assembly example

assembled. States are represented as sets. For instance, $\{\bar{1}, 2, \bar{3}\}$ corresponds to the state in which component two is assembled and components one and three are not assembled.

The dashed arcs in Figure 7.5 correspond to transformations that reduce the number of differences. In this case, means/ends analysis enables the search to head almost directly to a solution. As mentioned earlier in this section, means/ends analysis does not always provide useful guidance since there are times when it is necessary to increase the number of differences in order to find a solution.

Operator Schemas

Specifying operators can become tedious in cases in which a given type of operator applies to many different objects. Suppose, for instance, that you have a movement operator that allows you to move forward one step whenever the space immediately in front of you is clear. Rather than write down a separate operator for each possible location, we can use an *operator schema* to compactly represent the set of all such movement operators.

Operator schemas in state-space search serve much the same purpose as axiom schemas for proving theorems in propositional logic. We use the matching and variable substitution techniques from Chapter 3 to implement operator schemas in Lisp. In particular, the form (? x) is used to represent a *schema variable* that ranges over all the objects in a specified domain. In the exercises at the end of this chapter, you are asked to modify apply-operators to work with operator schemas using the functions match and varsubst from Chapter 3.

a	
(NOT (ASSEMBLED 1))	+ (ASSEMBLED 1)
	− (NOT (ASSEMBLED 1))

c	
(ASSEMBLED 1)	+ (NOT (ASSEMBLED 1)) (ASSEMBLED 2)
	− (ASSEMBLED 1) (NOT (ASSEMBLED 2))

b	
(NOT (ASSEMBLED 1))	+ (ASSEMBLED 2)
	− (NOT (ASSEMBLED 2))

d	
(ASSEMBLED 1) (ASSEMBLED 2)	+ (ASSEMBLED 3)
	− (NOT (ASSEMBLED 3))

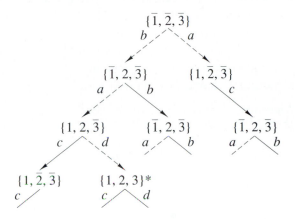

Figure 7.5 State-space search for the machine assembly example. The four opera-tors, *a*, *b*, *c*, and *d*, are shown on the top as partitioned boxes with preconditions on the left and additions (+) and deletions (−) shown on the right. The search space is shown on the bottom with each state represented as a set and arcs labeled by operators. For example, $\{1, \bar{2}, \bar{3}\} \xrightarrow{c} \{\bar{1}, 2, \bar{3}\}$ indicates that the operator *c* transforms the state in which only the first component is assembled into the state in which only the second component is assembled. Dashed arcs represent transformations that reduce differences. The goal state is marked with an asterisk.

Block-Stacking Problems

To illustrate the use of operator schemas, we introduce a class of problems called *block-stacking problems*. The particular block-stacking problems that we consider in this text involve a set of blocks and a table. Each block is either on the table or on some other block. Each block is either clear or there is exactly one block on top of it. The conditions that change as a result of applying an operator are of the form (on (? x) (? y)) or (clear (? x)). In addition, there is a set of *static conditions* of the form (not (equal (? x) (? y))) that allow us to distinguish blocks from the table and from one another.

There are no conditions of the form (not (on (? x) (? y))) explicitly men-tioned in states. If (on x y) is contained in a state, then, for all $z \neq y$, (not (on x z)) is implicitly contained in that state. Similarly, if (on x y) is contained in a state and y is a block and not the table, then, for all $z \neq x$, (not (on z y)) is implicitly contained in that state. Here is an example of an operator to move a block currently on another block to the table.

```
;; Move block (? x) from block (? y) to the table.
(make-OPERATOR ;; Preconditions
               '((on (? x) (? y)) (clear (? x))
                 (not (equal (? y) table)))
               ;; Additions
               '((on (? x) table) (clear (? y)))
               ;; Deletions
               '((on (? x) (? y))))
```

This operator schema indicates that you can apply an instance of the schema in a state with (? x) and (? y) bound to particular blocks if (? x) is clear and on (? y). If the preconditions are satisfied in a state, then in the resulting state (? y) is clear and (? x) is on the table and not on (? y). The following expression corresponds to an instance of the given operator schema with (? x) bound to a and (? y) bound to b:

```
;; Move block a from block b to the table.
(make-OPERATOR ;; Preconditions
               '((on a b) (clear a)
                 (not (equal b table)))
               ;; Additions
               '((on a table) (clear b))
               ;; Deletions
               '((on a b)))
```

In the operator schema, note that (not (equal (? y) table)) is necessary to ensure that the operator is not applied when (? x) is already on the table. Note also that for each block a every state must contain (not (equal a table)), and for each a and b every state must contain (not (equal a b)). In the next section, we consider a somewhat more elegant method of handling static conditions without expanding the state.

7.2   Least Commitment Planning

The state-space search method described in the previous section constructs sequences of operators working forward from the initial state or backward from the target goal. A plan is just a sequence of operators. The general problem of finding a sequence of operators that satisfies a goal is computationally complex[1] and hence we are resigned to searching for solutions.

Often enough, the method of the previous section places one operator after another for no particular reason; in many cases, the two operators might be applied in either order or even in parallel. In solving a block-

---

[1]The problem of finding a sequence of operators of the sort defined in Chapter 4 that transforms a given state into one satisfying a given goal is in the class of PSPACE-complete problems. A problem is in the class PSPACE if its space requirements are bounded by some polynomial. The class NP (nondeterministic polynomial time) is contained in the class PSPACE. PSPACE completeness is to the class PSPACE what NP-completeness is to the class NP.

stacking problem in which block a must be placed on b and c on d, the method of the previous section always orders the two operators whether or not there is any reason to order them.

Suppose that you have to go to the grocery store and to a baseball game. Think of these two activities as steps in a plan. Initially, you think you might carry out these steps in either order, so you don't consider them as ordered in time. Later, you remember that the baseball game might last for several hours, and so you think about picking up some food to take to the game. You realize that going to the grocery store first will allow you to satisfy a precondition for the baseball game, namely, having some food to eat at the game. In this case, delaying commitment as to the order of the steps in the plan reduces the number of alternative plans that have to be considered in the process of planning.

The method described in this section never orders any two operators unless it has some justification for doing so. The heuristic strategy underlying this method involves making minimal commitments to the order of operators, and for this reason, the method is called *least commitment planning*.

Search in the Space of Partially Ordered Plans

In least commitment planning, a plan is defined by a set of sequences of operators compactly represented as a partially ordered set of operators and referred to as a *partially ordered plan*. Figure 7.6 shows a partially ordered plan with operators numbered 1 through 5. An arc between two operators indicates that the operator from which the arc emanates must precede the operator that the arc points to. The graph in Figure 7.6 represents the set of operator sequences $\{\{1, 2, 3, 4, 5\}, \{1, 3, 2, 4, 5\}, \{1, 3, 4, 2, 5\}\}$. Note that any partially ordered set of operators can be represented as a set of sequences of operators but not vice versa. Instead of searching in the space of possible states, least commitment planning searches in the space of possible partially ordered plans. Using this alternative method of search, a planner is often able to consider fewer plans in solving a given planning problem.

In the following, we describe an implementation of least commitment planning. We begin with the case in which operators that transform one

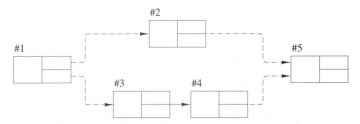

Figure 7.6 A partially ordered plan consisting of five steps. The dashed arcs represent constraints on the ordering of steps.

state into another contain no variables, and then explain how to extend the implementation to the case of operators with variables. We use the same data abstraction for operators as in the previous section. We will need additional data abstractions to represent plans.

In the following, a plan consists of a set of *steps* corresponding to operators, *constraints* on the order in which these steps are to be carried out, and information regarding how the steps depend on one another. The dependency information is of three different types. First, there are records called *requirements* indicating propositions that are required in order that certain operators have their desired effect. Next, there are records called *links* describing how the consequences of one operator are used to satisfy the requirements of another. Finally, there are records called *conflicts* describing potential undesirable interactions between operators. As an example of a conflict, one operator might delete a proposition that another operator adds, where the deleted proposition is required for the plan to succeed.

```
(defun make-PLAN (steps constraints conflicts links requirements)
  (list steps constraints conflicts links requirements))
(defun PLAN-steps (plan) (first plan))
(defun PLAN-constraints (plan) (second plan))
(defun PLAN-conflicts (plan) (third plan))
(defun PLAN-links (plan) (fourth plan))
(defun PLAN-requirements (plan) (fifth plan))
```

We represent constraints in terms of their begin and end steps, and assign each step a unique integer to distinguish different steps employing the same operator.

```
(let ((n 0)) (defun make-STEP (operator)
               (list (setq n (+ n 1)) operator)))
(defun STEP-id (step) (first step))
(defun STEP-operator (step) (second step))
(defun make-CONSTRAINT (begin end) (list begin end))
(defun begin (constraint) (first constraint))
(defun end (constraint) (second constraint))
```

As in the previous section, we describe a state as a set of conditions. A requirement corresponds to a step and a condition that must be true immediately prior to that step. The condition of the requirement corresponds to a precondition of the operator indicated in the step.

```
(defun make-REQUIREMENT (step condition) (list step condition))
(defun REQUIREMENT-step (req) (first req))
(defun REQUIREMENT-condition (req) (second req))
```

A link involves two steps and a condition. One step, called the *producer*, has the condition in the list of additions for its associated operator. The producer makes the condition true. The other step, called the *consumer*, has the condition in the list of preconditions for its associated operator. The consumer requires that the condition be true. Links are created to satisfy requirements.

```
(defun make-LINK (producer condition consumer)
  (list producer condition consumer))
(defun LINK-producer (link) (first link))
(defun LINK-condition (link) (second link))
(defun LINK-consumer (link) (third link))
```

A conflict involves a link and a step. The step, called the *clobberer*, has the condition of the link in the list of deletions for its associated operator. A conflict arises when a step is added to a plan and that step might be carried out after the producer of a link and before the consumer, preventing the link from satisfying the requirement that the link was introduced to satisfy. When a conflict occurs, the clobberer is said to *threaten* link.

```
(defun make-CONFLICT (link clobberer) (list link clobberer))
(defun CONFLICT-link (conflict) (first conflict))
(defun CONFLICT-clobberer (conflict) (second conflict))
```

An instance of a planning problem is given as an initial state and a target goal where states and goals are represented as lists of conditions. We can represent such an instance as a plan consisting of two steps. The first step is a pseudo operator with a set of additions corresponding to the initial state and no preconditions or deletions. The second step is another pseudo operator with a set of preconditions corresponding to the target goal and no additions or deletions. The plan has one constraint indicating that the first step must precede the second step, and one requirement for each condition in the list of conditions corresponding to the target goal.

An example of some partially ordered plans will help us get some of this terminology straight. Recall the machine assembly example from the previous section. Figure 7.7 (page 312) shows two plans for assembling the three components for the machine assembly example. The plan on the top of Figure 7.7 has only two steps corresponding to the two pseudo operators for representing the initial conditions and the goal. In this plan, there is one constraint ordering the two steps and three requirements corresponding to assembling each of the three components.

The plan on the bottom of Figure 7.7 has five steps corresponding to the two pseudo operators and three additional steps for assembling the three components. Adding the three assembly operators results in the addition of four new requirements, but all seven requirements are satisfied by links in the bottom plan. There is one conflict in the bottom plan where one step requires that the first component not be assembled and another step results in the first component being assembled.

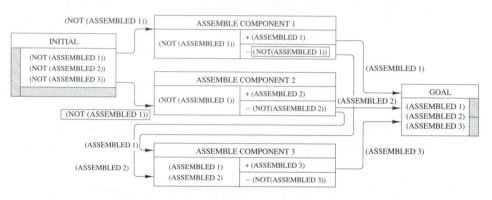

Figure 7.7 Two partially ordered plans for the machine assembly example. Each operator corresponding to a step in the plan is shown as a partitioned box, including (top) a description of the operator, (left) the set of preconditions, (upper right) the set of additions, and (lower right) the set of deletions. Each link is indicated by a solid arc from the producer step to the consumer step labeled with the associated condition. Each link implies a constraint between the producer and the consumer. A dashed arc implies a constraint but no link. There is one conflict in the bottom plan identified by a box drawn around the condition giving rise to the conflict where it appears in the link that is threatened and in the deletions of the step doing the threatening.

Sound, Complete, and Systematic Search

In the following paragraphs, we describe a method for systematically searching the space of partially ordered plans. We say that a search procedure is *systematic* if the procedure never examines the same node in the search space twice. We say that a search procedure is *sound* if whenever it returns a plan then any total order of the steps in the plan consistent with the partial order specified is guaranteed to transform the initial state into a state satisfying the goal. Finally, we say that a search procedure is *complete* if it always finds a solution when one exists. If there is no solution, then we will not be able to guarantee termination.

We have a representation for partially ordered plans, but in order to completely describe the search space for partially ordered plans, we need to specify some means of generating new plans from existing ones. The operators that we have for transforming one state into another will not serve for transforming one partially ordered plan into another. We refer to the process of transforming one partially ordered plan into another as *plan refinement*. We refine a plan either by adding constraints to eliminate conflicts or by linking new or existing steps to existing ones to eliminate requirements.

- The only way that you can eliminate a conflict is by constraining the clobberer to come before the producer or after the consumer of the threatened link.
- The only way that you can eliminate a requirement with condition r for step q is to add a link l with producer p, consumer q, and condition r, where p is a new or existing step that adds r.

In generating new plans from existing ones through the process of plan refinement, we want the new plans to have the following properties:

- A new plan must have all the steps, constraints, and links of the plan it was generated from.
- If, in a given plan, there is a link l with producer p, consumer q, and condition r, then there must be corresponding steps p and q so that p adds r and q has r as a precondition.
- If, in a given plan, there is a link l with producer p, consumer q, and condition r and a step c that, given the current set of constraints, could come between p and q and deletes r, then there is conflict with link l and clobberer c.

The following algorithm takes a plan and a set of operators and generates a set of plans to explore next:

1. If there are any conflicts, then choose a conflict and resolve it by adding constraints. In this case, there could be zero, one, or two new plans generated; zero if the conflict cannot be avoided.
2. If there are no conflicts, then choose a requirement and satisfy the requirement in all possible ways using both existing steps and new steps constructed using the supplied set of operators.

In the Lisp Implementation section, we provide an example of the preceding algorithm. The corresponding Lisp function is called refinements and takes two arguments, a plan, and a list of operators.

Block-Stacking Example

To illustrate the approach to searching in the space of plans, we consider a simple block-stacking problem. Figure 7.8 (page 314) depicts the initial state and a state that satisfies the goal for a particular block-stacking problem. Figure 7.9 (page 314) shows how to construct the initial plan and a set of operators to solve the block-stacking problem shown in Figure 7.8. We use best-first search as the basis for planning, and so we need to specify a function goalp to test for satisfying the goal, a function comparep for comparing two states of the search space, and a function next for generating new plans from old.

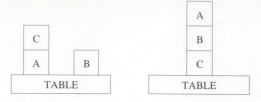

Figure 7.8   Initial and goal state for a simple block-stacking problem

```
;; The start step uses a pseudo operator to encode the initial conditions.
(setq start
      (make-STEP
       (make-OPERATOR nil
                      '((on c a) (on a table) (on b table)
                        (clear c) (clear b))
                      nil)))
;; The finish step uses a pseudo operator to encode the goal conditions.
(setq finish
      (make-STEP (make-OPERATOR '((on a b) (on b c)) nil nil)))

;; The initial requirements correspond to the goal conditions.
(setq requirements (list (make-REQUIREMENT finish '(on a b))
                         (make-REQUIREMENT finish '(on b c))))

;; The initial plan steps consist of the start and finish steps.
(setq plan (make-PLAN (list start finish)
                      (list (make-CONSTRAINT start finish))
                      nil nil requirements))

;; We show only the operators needed for the example.
(setq operators
      (list ;; Put block c on the table.
            (make-OPERATOR '((on c a) (clear c))       ;; Preconditions
                           '((on c table) (clear a)) ;; Additions
                           '((on c a)))              ;; Deletions
            ;; Put block a on block b.
            (make-OPERATOR '((on a table) (clear a) (clear b))
                           '((on a b))
                           '((on a table) (clear b)))
            ;; Put block b on block c.
            (make-OPERATOR '((on b table) (clear b) (clear c))
                           '((on b c))
                           '((on b table) (clear c)))))
```

Figure 7.9   Specification for the block-stacking example

1. A plan achieves the target goal when there are no outstanding conflicts
   or requirements.

```
(defun goalp (plan)
  (and (null (PLAN-conflicts plan))
       (null (PLAN-requirements plan))
```

2. There are any number of ways of comparing two plans; in the following, one plan is better than another if it has fewer requirements:

```
(defun comparep (p q)
  (< (length (PLAN-requirements p))
     (length (PLAN-requirements q))))
```

3. For a specified set of operators, we define the next search-state generator as follows:

```
(defun next (plan)
  (refinements plan operators))
```

The following illustrates a solution returned by the search procedure on the block-stacking problem of Figure 7.8. We have added a print routine to the goal function to display the resulting plan.

```
> (best (list plan) #'goalp #'next #'comparep)
Steps: (5 (((ON B TABLE) (CLEAR B) (CLEAR C))
           ((ON B C))
           ((ON B TABLE) (CLEAR C))))
        (4 (((ON C A) (CLEAR C))
           ((ON C TABLE) (CLEAR A))
           ((ON C A))))
        (3 (((ON A TABLE) (CLEAR A) (CLEAR B))
           ((ON A B))
           ((ON A TABLE) (CLEAR B))))
        (2 (((ON A B) (ON B C))
           NIL
           NIL))
        (1 (NIL
           ((ON C A) (CLEAR C) (CLEAR B)
            (ON A TABLE) (ON B TABLE))
           NIL))
Order: ((1) (4) (5) (3) (2))
```

The partial-order information is interpreted as follows. Each element of the list corresponds to one of the steps in the plan identified by its unique integer. These elements are ranked according to the partial order specified in the plan. If the plan does not specify a total order, then the ranking is just one of possibly several total orders consistent with the partial order. If a step is unordered with respect to other steps, then those steps are listed in the rest of the element corresponding to that step. In the plan listed, the steps are totally ordered.

Figure 7.10 (page 316) shows a block-stacking problem that admits to a solution with partially ordered steps. Unordered steps in a partially ordered plan imply that the steps can be executed in either order. The following solution found by our implementation indicates that the steps of putting c

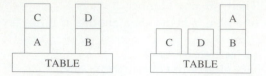

Figure 7.10 In transforming the state on the left into the state on the right, the steps of putting c and d on the table can be executed in either order

and d on the table can be executed in either order:

```
Steps: (5 (((ON D B) (CLEAR D))
          ((ON D TABLE) (CLEAR B))
          ((ON D B))))
       (4 (((ON C A) (CLEAR C))
          ((ON C TABLE) (CLEAR A))
          ((ON C A))))
       (3 (((ON A TABLE) (CLEAR A) (CLEAR B))
          ((ON A B))
          ((ON A TABLE) (CLEAR B))))
       (2 (((ON A B))
          NIL
          NIL))
       (1 (NIL
          ((ON C A) (ON D B) (ON A TABLE)
           (ON B TABLE) (CLEAR C) (CLEAR D))
          NIL))
Order: ((1) (5 4) (4 5) (3) (2))
```

Recognizing and Resolving Conflicts

Figures 7.11 and 7.12 illustrate how links are created and conflicts recognized and resolved during planning. These two figures depict four partially ordered plans created in the process of solving the problem shown in Figure 7.8. The top plan in Figure 7.11 represents the initial plan. In the bottom plan in Figure 7.11, the requirement (on a b) has been eliminated by adding a step to put a on b. This generates three additional requirements, two of which are taken care of by links to the step corresponding to the initial conditions.

In the top plan in Figure 7.12 (page 318), another new step is added to eliminate the requirement (on b c). In this case, all three of the requirements resulting from the new step are satisfied in the initial conditions. There is a conflict, however, since the operator that puts b on c has (clear b) as a precondition, and the operator that puts a on b deletes (clear b). This conflict can be resolved in only one way by putting b on c before putting a on b.

In the bottom plan shown in Figure 7.12, the last remaining requirement is taken care of by adding a step to put c on the table. This step, which requires (clear c), conflicts with the step of putting b on c, which

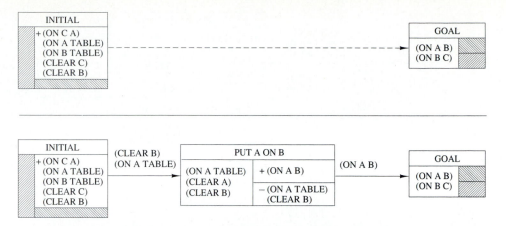

Figure 7.11   Two partially ordered plans illustrating the links created in the process of solving a simple block-stacking problem. Each operator corresponding to a step in a partially ordered plan is shown as a partitioned box, including (top) a description of the operator, (left) the set of preconditions, (upper right) the set of additions, and (lower right) the set of deletions. Each link is indicated by a solid arc from the producer step to the consumer step labeled with the associated condition. If a producer/consumer pair is involved in more than one link, then a single arc is shown labeled with all the associated conditions.

deletes (clear c). The conflict is resolved by putting c on table before putting b on c.

It would be nice if we could guarantee that we were always making progress toward the goal. Unfortunately, this is difficult to realize in general. Figure 7.13 (page 318) shows a block-stacking problem in which a partially constructed tower has to be torn down before it can be completely constructed. The preceding implementation will generate a plan in which the step corresponding to the goal is linked to the step corresponding to the initial conditions to satisfy the requirement (on a b). This plan cannot be extended to a solution. Although it is easy to see that this particular plan will not work, there are other hopeless cases that are quite difficult to recognize.

Variables in Partially Ordered Plans

Extending the implementation to handle operator schemas involving variables is relatively straightforward and introduces another way of resolving conflicts. To extend the implementation to handle operator schemas, we employ the unification (unify) and variable substitution (varsubst) routines from Chapter 3 instead of equal to find and instantiate appropriate operators and to create links and find conflicts. There are some subtleties in using operator schemas for least commitment planning.

Operator schemas for least commitment planning generally include another component in addition to the sets of preconditions, additions, and deletions. This additional component consists of constraints on how the

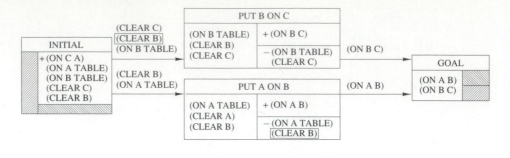

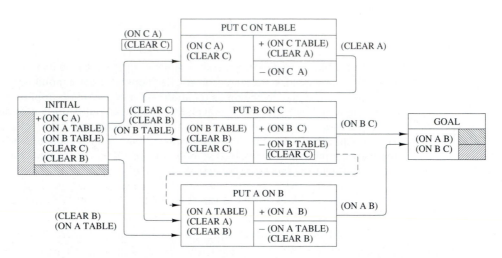

Figure 7.12 Two partially ordered plans illustrating the conflicts generated in the process of solving a simple block-stacking problem. Conflicts are identified by drawing a box around the condition giving rise to the conflict where it appears in the link that is threatened and in the deletions of the step doing the threatening. The bottom plan shows a dashed arc indicating a constraint added to resolve the conflict found in the middle plan.

variables are to be bound. These constraints serve two purposes. First, they allow us to specify static conditions on the application of operators without enumerating a large number of static conditions in states as we had to in the previous section. Second, they provide us with another means of resolving conflicts in partially ordered plans.

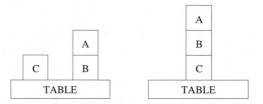

Figure 7.13 In order to transform the state on the left into the state on the right, it is necessary to undo what appears to be a partial solution

```
;; Move block (? x) from block (? z) to the table.
(make-OPERATOR ;; Preconditions
               '((on (? x) (? z)) (clear (? x)))
               ;; Additions
               '((on (? x) table) (clear (? z)))
               ;; Deletions
               '((on (? x) (? z)))
               ;; Constraints
               '((not (equal (? x) (? z)))
                 (not (equal (? x) table))
                 (not (equal (? z) table))))

;; Move block (? x) from block (? z) to block (? y).
(make-OPERATOR ;; Preconditions
               '((on (? x) (? z)) (clear (? x)) (clear (? y)))
               ;; Additions
               '((on (? x) (? y)) (clear (? z)))
               ;; Deletions
               '((on (? x) (? z)) (clear (? y)))
               ;; Constraints
               '((not (equal (? x) (? y)))
                 (not (equal (? x) (? z)))
                 (not (equal (? y) (? z)))
                 (not (equal (? x) table))
                 (not (equal (? y) table))
                 (not (equal (? z) table))))
```

Figure 7.14   Operator schemas for stacking blocks

Figure 7.14 shows the operator schemas for solving block-stacking problems. Two basic schemas are shown: one for moving a block from a block to the table and one for moving a block from a block to another block. We assume that the table can support any number of blocks and that at least one block is always on the table. Given this last assumption, the table is never clear. The list of constraints corresponding to the last component in an operator schema ensures that the operators are not inappropriately used. For instance, the constraints dictate that you cannot put a block on top of itself, clear the table, or put the table on top of a block. Note that we need one additional operator schema to cover the case of moving a block from the table to another block.

A constraint of the form (not (equal *x y*)) is satisfied if the variables *x* and *y* do *not* unify. One method that we might use to find an operator to satisfy a requirement with condition (on a b) is as follows. We attempt to unify (on a b) with all the additions of all the operators. (In practice, we would employ a more efficient indexing scheme.) The attempt succeeds with the first addition of the second operator. Substituting for variables from the bindings returned by unification, we obtain the following partially instantiated operator in which all the constraints are satisfied:

```
(;; Preconditions
 ((on a (? z)) (clear a) (clear b))
 ;; Additions
 ((on a b) (clear (? z)))
 ;; Deletions
 ((on a (? z)) (clear b))
 ;; Constraints
 ((not (equal a b)) (not (equal a (? z)))
  (not (equal b (? z))) (not (equal a table))
  (not (equal b table))))
```

In an actual implementation, we would rename all the variables. This partially instantiated operator would be added as a step to the plan. Note that it is because we have plan steps with partially instantiated operators that we need unify rather than the simpler match in dealing with variables in partially ordered plans.

This operator deletes the condition (on a (? z)). Suppose that at some point there is a link with condition (on a d). The two conditions (on a (? z)) and (on a d) unify with one another, and all the constraints are still satisfied. This means that there is a potential conflict that can be resolved by adding ordering constraints so that the clobberer is executed either before the producer or after the consumer. We can also resolve the conflict by adding the constraint (not (equal (? z) d)). The list of constraints associated with the operator of a given step will increase in size in cases where such constraints are used to resolve conflicts.

To use one step to satisfy a requirement associated with another step, we unify the conditions of the corresponding operators—one step will serve as a producer, the other as a consumer—and check to see that the constraints are satisfied. If they are satisfied, then the appropriate substitutions are made to both operators, and we proceed as in the ground case.

Planners that operate by adding constraints are often referred to as *constraint-posting planners* in the literature. The combination of posting constraints and delaying commitment serves as the basis for many automated planners. For most applications, efficiency requires that we employ additional techniques for guiding search. In the following section, we consider one such technique.

7.3   Planning in a Hierarchy of Abstraction Spaces

Suppose that we are trying to plan the construction of a large office building. Planning involves coordinating the actions of a large number of contractors responsible for various aspects of the building. For example, the primary contractor has to coordinate the activities of subcontractors responsible for digging foundations, erecting masonry walls, woodworking, plumbing, wiring, and plastering. To make the planning problem more tractable, we *abstract* the problem by considering a smaller search space that ignores some of the detail in the full problem. In fact, we consider a hierarchy of search spaces ranging from the most abstract to the most concrete.

For instance, we might begin by focusing entirely on the contractors responsible for putting in the foundations and erecting the basic floors and walls. Having found a solution in this abstract space, we might then proceed to refine the solution taking into account additional aspects of the problem. For instance, given a plan for the basic structure, we might refine the plan to account for the plumbers and electricians. This corresponds to continuing the search in a more concrete, less abstract search space. Finally, having accounted for the basic structure, plumbing, and wiring, we might integrate the plasterers and other contractors responsible for the finish work. In the ideal case, work done at one level of abstraction is not disturbed in making refinements at less abstract levels.

Analysis of Planning with Levels of Abstraction

Suppose that we search a given space so that we always examine plans of length l before examining plans of length $l + 1$. For a problem whose smallest solution is length l and whose branching factor is b, finding such a solution has a worst-case complexity of $O(b^l)$.

Now suppose that we introduce n levels of abstraction so that the length of a solution at level i is $1/k$ times the length of the solution at level $i - 1$, where $k > 0$ is some constant. Different levels of abstraction allow us to focus on a subset of the set of all conditions in planning at a given level of abstraction. Conditions outside the subset of conditions being considered are ignored during planning. Only at the least abstract, most concrete level of abstraction are all the conditions accounted for. In the ideal case, a solution at level i gives rise to l/k^{n-i} subproblems of equal solution size at level $i + 1$, where a subproblem corresponds to a condition appearing in the solution and ignored at the previous level. Suppose that $n = \log_k l$ and that the solutions to different subproblems at a given level of abstraction do not interfere with one another so that they can be solved independently. Given these rather strong assumptions, it can be shown that the complexity of planning in a hierarchical abstraction space is

$$O\left(\frac{l-1}{k-1}b^k\right)$$

or just $O(l)$ for fixed b and k [Knoblock, 1991].

In general, it is not possible to satisfy the assumptions introduced here. There are classes of problems, however, that do satisfy these assumptions and for which we can achieve asymptotically the aforementioned exponential speedup. In the following, we consider such a class of problems called *towers-of-Hanoi* problems.

Towers-of-Hanoi Problems

Instances of the towers-of-Hanoi problem involve a set of pegs and a set of disks of varying size. Each disk has a hole in the center so that it can be positioned over any one of the pegs. Each disk must be on some peg and several disks can be on the same peg at a time as long as no disk is on a disk of smaller size. A disk can be moved from one peg to another if it is clear of all disks and all the disks on the destination peg are larger than the disk we are trying to move. In general, instances can have any number of pegs and disks and any initial and target arrangements of disks. In the following, however, when we talk about an instance of the towers-of-Hanoi problem, we mean a problem instance with n disks and n pegs, all the disks initially on one peg, and the goal of stacking all the disks on some other peg. Figure 7.15 shows the initial and target state for the case of $n = 3$.

The representation used in Figure 7.15 is similar to that used for block-stacking problems. We treat disks like blocks and pegs like tables. The possible configurations for disks are constrained by the size of the disks and how they are stacked. Think of the pegs as disks that are immovable and larger than any movable disks. Every movable disk has to be on some other disk and each disk can have at most one disk (directly) on it.

Figure 7.16 lists a search-space representation for the towers-of-Hanoi problem. In this case, there is a single operator for moving a disk from one peg to another. For the n disk problem, the length of the shortest solution is $2^n - 1$. Blind search in the corresponding search space can be computationally daunting even in cases involving small numbers of disks.

We reduce the amount of search by employing a hierarchy of abstraction spaces. An abstraction space is just a search space defined by a set of operators and a set of conditions determining a state space. We are given a set of operators and a set of conditions that determine the least abstract, or *ground*, space. From these operators and conditions, we construct a hierarchy of spaces as follows. We partition the set of conditions to define an ordered set of abstraction levels where each level corresponds to a subset of the set of conditions. Each level defines an abstraction space in which we

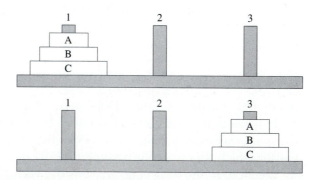

Figure 7.15   Initial and goal state for an instance of the towers-of-Hanoi problem

```
;; Initially all the disks are stacked on the first peg.
(setq initial '((on a b) (on b c) (on c 1) (clear a)
                (smaller a b) (smaller b c) (smaller a c)
                (smaller a 1) (smaller a 2) (smaller a 3)
                (smaller b 1) (smaller b 2) (smaller b 3)
                (smaller c 1) (smaller c 2) (smaller c 3)))

;; The goal is to have the disks stacked on the third peg.
(setq goal '((on a b) (on b c) (on c 3)))

;; One operator schema suffices for this version of the problem.
(setq operators
      (list (make-OPERATOR ;; Preconditions
                   '((on (? x) (? y)) (clear (? x))
                     (clear (? z)) (smaller (? x) (? z)))
                   ;; Additions
                   '((clear (? y)) (on (? x) (? z)))
                   ;; Deletions
                   '((on (? x) (? y)) (clear (? z)))
                   ;; Constraints
                   '((not (equal (? z) (? y)))
                     (not (equal (? z) (? x)))
                     (not (equal (? y) (? x)))))))
```

Figure 7.16 Nonhierarchical representation for the towers-of-Hanoi problem

attend to only the conditions in that or higher levels. For all lower levels, we just pretend as if the conditions do not exist.

Planning proceeds as follows. Given initial conditions and a goal, find a solution using only the conditions listed at the highest level of abstraction. Once you have a solution at this level, refine the plan at the next, more concrete level of abstraction. Continue refining the plan level by level until you have a plan at the most concrete level.

Figure 7.17 (page 324) lists an alternative search-space representation for the towers-of-Hanoi problem. In this representation, we depart from the previous approach by representing that more than one disk can reside on a given peg. The constraint that prevents us from setting a larger disk on a smaller one is handled by introducing a hierarchy of abstractions. We provide the operators for the case of $n = 3$; for arbitrary n, there are n operator schemas, one for each disk. In Figure 7.17, there are three operators, which we notate as (move_c (? p) (? q)), (move_b (? p) (? q)), and (move_a (? p) (? q)), where (? p) and (? q) range over pegs. There are three condition types represented in the operators: (on_c (? p)), (on_b (? p)), and (on_a (? p)). We assign the conditions to levels of abstraction as follows. The condition (on_c (? p)) is assigned level 2, (on_b (? p)) is assigned level 1, and (on_a (? p)) is assigned level 0.

This hierarchical decomposition of the towers-of-Hanoi problem satisfies the assumptions that we listed for the ideal situation. The length of the shortest solution in the ground space is $l = 2^n - 1$, the number of abstraction

```
;; There is a condition type for each of the three disks.
(setq initial '((on_a 1) (on_b 1) (on_c 1)
                (not (on_a 2)) (not (on_b 2)) (not (on_c 2))
                (not (on_a 3)) (not (on_b 3)) (not (on_c 3))))

(setq goal '((on_a 3) (on_b 3) (on_c 3)))

;; There is an operator for moving each of the three disks.
(setq operators
      (list (make-OPERATOR ;; Preconditions
                 '((on_c (? p))
                   (not (on_a (? p))) (not (on_a (? q)))
                   (not (on_b (? p))) (not (on_b (? q))))
                 ;; Additions
                 '((on_c (? q)) (not (on_c (? p))))
                 ;; Deletions
                 '((on_c (? p)) (not (on_c (? q))))
                 ;; Constraints
                 '((not (equal (? p) (? q)))))
            (make-OPERATOR ;; Preconditions
                 '((on_b (? p))
                   (not (on_a (? p))) (not (on_a (? q))))
                 ;; Additions
                 '((on_b (? q)) (not (on_b (? p))))
                 ;; Deletions
                 '((on_b (? p)) (not (on_b (? q))))
                 ;; Constraints
                 '((not (equal (? p) (? q)))))
            (make-OPERATOR ;; Preconditions
                 '((on_a (? p)))
                 ;; Additions
                 '((on_a (? q)) (not (on_a (? p))))
                 ;; Deletions
                 '((on_a (? p)) (not (on_a (? q))))
                 ;; Constraints
                 '((not (equal (? p) (? q)))))))
```

Figure 7.17   Hierarchical representation for the towers-of-Hanoi problem

levels is $O(\log_2 l)$, the ratio of the shortest solution length between the levels is two, and the subproblems at a given level are independent.

Figure 7.18 shows a solution to the instance of the towers-of-Hanoi problem shown in Figure 7.15. Note that the plan generated at each level of abstraction is a refinement of the plan generated at the previous level.

In practice, it is difficult to realize the same sort of performance gains as we did in the towers-of-Hanoi problem, but often some increased efficiency can be realized with an appropriate abstraction hierarchy. In some cases, it is possible to automatically generate an abstraction hierarchy by examining the dependencies between operators determined by their preconditions and postconditions. Generating such abstraction hierarchies corresponds to

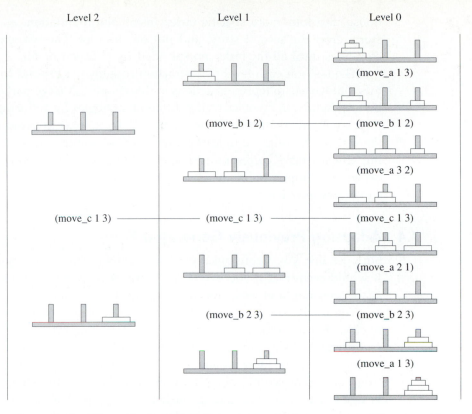

Level 2	Level 1	Level 0
		(move_a 1 3)
	(move_b 1 2) ————	———— (move_b 1 2)
		(move_a 3 2)
(move_c 1 3) ————	———— (move_c 1 3) ————	———— (move_c 1 3)
		(move_a 2 1)
	(move_b 2 3) ————	———— (move_b 2 3)
		(move_a 1 3)

Figure 7.18 Hierarchical solution for an instance of the towers-of-Hanoi problem. The sequence of steps runs from the top to the bottom.

finding inherent structure in combinatorial problems and is a powerful approach to reducing search.

Task Reduction Planning

Abstraction plays a role in many different approaches to planning. One of the most important practical approaches to planning is organized around the concept of a *task*, which is an abstract operation that the planner commits to carrying out. Tasks are abstract in that they dictate the general nature of what an operation is to accomplish without necessarily specifying precise details. For example, a building contractor may have the task to construct a two-story colonial house. Before such a task can be accomplished, the contractor must supply sufficient detail so that the construction can be carried out by carpenters, electricians, plumbers, and other skilled workers.

One way of increasing detail is to replace an abstract task with a more specific task or collection of more specific tasks. This process of refining the level of abstraction is called *task reduction*. By *reducing* an abstract task, the planner commits to carrying out the more specific tasks. For example, the contractor might reduce the task of building a two-story colonial house into four more specific tasks: install the foundation, erect the first story, erect the second story, and put on the roof. The reduction process continues until all the tasks are specified in sufficient detail.

The tasks at each level of abstraction roughly correspond to the operators that we use to represent actions in this chapter. A large part of planning by task reduction involves trying different strategies for reducing tasks and then trying to coordinate the tasks at each level so as to avoid conflicts of the sort we investigated in least commitment planning. Strategies for reducing abstract tasks correspond to standard methods for breaking problems down into simpler problems. A related idea involves adapting old plans to solve new problems.

7.4   Adapting Previously Generated Plans

Suppose that you figure out a plan for traveling from one city to another. It would seem that if you ever have to travel between the same two cities again, you might at least consider reusing the old plan.

You might even consider generalizing your plan to work for other pairs of cities. For instance, suppose that you are traveling from Cambridge, Massachusetts, to Palo Alto, California. You might take a bus from Cambridge to Logan Airport, fly from Logan to San Francisco Airport, and take a bus from San Francisco to Palo Alto. From this plan for traveling from Cambridge to Palo Alto, you might construct a general plan that involves using ground transportation to get to the nearest airport, flying to the airport nearest your destination, and then using ground transportation to get to your final destination.

Many planning systems make use of a *library* of existing plans. In some cases, these plans correspond to previously constructed plans. In other cases, the plans are provided by someone expert in a given application domain. When such planning systems are confronted by a new problem, they find an existing plan in the library and adapt it to solve the new problem. In some cases, such planners may make use of several library plans to solve various subproblems that arise in solving a given problem. In the following, we consider one particular approach to adapting previously generated plans.

Indexing, Retrieving, and Adapting Plans

We consider three basic issues in the rest of this section.

1. Given a plan that solves one problem, how might you index it so that it can subsequently be retrieved to solve similar problems?
2. Given a problem to solve, how might you retrieve an old plan from a library of plans to adapt to solve the present problem?
3. Given an old plan, how might you adapt it to solve a new problem?

```
Steps: (5 (((ON B TABLE) (CLEAR B) (CLEAR C))
          ((ON B C))
          ((ON B TABLE) (CLEAR C))))
       (4 (((ON C A) (CLEAR C))
          ((ON C TABLE) (CLEAR A))
          ((ON C A))))
       (3 (((ON A TABLE) (CLEAR A) (CLEAR B))
          ((ON A B))
          ((ON A TABLE) (CLEAR B))))
       (2 (((ON A B) (ON B C))
          NIL
          NIL))
       (1 (NIL
          ((ON C A) (ON A TABLE) (ON B TABLE)
          (CLEAR C) (CLEAR B))
          NIL))
Order: ((1) (4) (5) (3) (2))
```

Figure 7.19 Solution to a block-stacking problem

We begin by considering what to do with the solution to one problem so that we might be in a position to apply it to another problem in the future.

Figure 7.19 shows a solution to the block-stacking problem shown in Figure 7.8. Note that this solution will work for any three blocks that are in the same initial configuration and are required to be in the same goal configuration. Given this observation, we want to construct a plan schema that will work for any problem involving three blocks with the corresponding initial and goal configurations. To assist in subsequent indexing, we also make clear the general form of the initial state and goal that the plan is designed to solve.

Figure 7.20 shows the plan schema generalized from the solution to the problem in Figure 7.8 along with the initial conditions and goal used to index it in a library of plans. The process of generalizing plans is a form of explanation-based generalization that we investigated in Chapter 3. We

```
   Goal: ((ON (? x) (? y)) (ON (? y) (? z)))
Initial: ((ON (? z) (? x)) (ON (? x) TABLE)
         (ON (? y) TABLE) (CLEAR (? z)) (CLEAR (? y)))
  Steps: (1 (((ON (? z) (? x)) (CLEAR (? z)))
            ((ON (? z) TABLE) (CLEAR (? x)))
            ((ON (? z) (? x)))))
         (2 (((ON (? y) TABLE) (CLEAR (? y)) (CLEAR (? z)))
            ((ON (? y) (? z)))
            ((ON (? y) TABLE) (CLEAR (? z)))))
         (3 (((ON (? x) TABLE) (CLEAR (? x)) (CLEAR (? y)))
            ((ON (? x) (? y)))
            ((ON (? x) TABLE) (CLEAR (? y)))))
  Order: ((1) (2) (3))
```

Figure 7.20 Library plan for stacking three blocks

▲ AI IN PRACTICE

Domain-Dependent Planning Technology

Researchers at the SRI AI Center have developed a knowledge-based planning system called SIPE-2 that has been applied to problems in manufacturing, the military, construction tasks, and planning the actions of a mobile robot. In a factory setting, SIPE-2 generates plans with more than a thousand actions for handling multiple production lines turning out dozens of orders and hundreds of products.

SIPE-2 provides a general-purpose formalism for describing actions and employs a variety of heuristics to deal with the combinatorics of complicated domains. A causal theory deduces context-dependent effects of actions. SIPE-2 can modify plans in response to unexpected events during plan execution. SIPE-2 is designed to work in cooperation with human planners and features a sophisticated graphical interface for displaying and manipulating plans, and controlling the planning process.

A version of SIPE-2 is incorporated into the SRI Cypress system being developed for joint military operations planning under the guidance of the United States Air Force and the Advanced Research Projects Agency. Input to the Cypress system includes threat assessments, terrain analysis, transportation capabilities, and operational constraints. Cypress generates and then monitors the execution of deployment plans for coordinating the movement of troops, equipment, and supplies to meet military objectives.

© Hank Morgan/Photo Researchers, Inc.

---

also assume that dependency information in the form of links is also part of the plan though it is not shown in Figure 7.20.

There are some important issues that we ignored in the preceding discussion that we mention here so as not to mislead the reader into thinking that constructing a useful library of plans is easy. For instance, there may be conditions in the initial state or steps in the plan that do not affect the success of the plan; clearly, we would like to identify these and eliminate them from the library plan. Another issue that we do not consider concerns the size of the library; the more plans that are stored in the library, the more plans have to be considered in planning and the greater the difficulty in retrieving potentially applicable library plans. In the following, we assume that we have a reasonably sized and formulated library of plans.

Next we consider how we might retrieve plans from a library of plans and then *fit* them so as to construct plans to use for purposes of refinement. Fitting corresponds to taking a library plan and modifying it so that it has the initial conditions and goal corresponding to the problem we are trying to solve. Refinement involves a slightly modified version of the algorithm that we introduced in the section on least commitment planning. Adaptation involves both fitting and refinement.

Suppose we are given a new problem to solve corresponding to a set of initial conditions and a goal. Adaptation proceeds as follows. For each library plan, try to match the goal of the library plan against the new goal. For instance, the library plan may have the goal to achieve P and Q, and the new goal requires only Q. We also allow for partial matches. For instance, the library plan achieves only P, and the new goal requires P *and* Q. The method that we describe in the following will produce a correct plan (assuming one exists) no matter what library plan we choose, but it will perform less search if we start with a library plan that closely matches the new goal and initial conditions. If there are several matches, choose among the plans on the basis of how well the initial conditions of the library plans match the new initial conditions. Specifically, consider how many new requirements would have to be added to the plan during fitting.

Given a library plan whose goal matches the new goal, fit the plan to the new problem as follows:

1. Instantiate the library plan using the variable substitution obtained in matching.

2. Replace the goal of the library plan with the new goal.

3. Add requirements for each condition appearing in the new goal but not appearing in the library plan.

4. Replace the initial conditions of the library plan with the new initial conditions.

5. Eliminate each link in the plan with a condition satisfied by the old initial conditions but not satisfied by the new initial conditions. For each such link removed, add a requirement with the condition and consumer of the link.

6. Eliminate each link in the plan that satisfies a condition that was present in the old goal but not present in the new goal.

Figure 7.21 (page 330) illustrates the process of fitting. The plan at the top of Figure 7.21 depicts a library plan. The plan in the middle of Figure 7.21 shows a new goal and initial conditions. Note that the goals for the

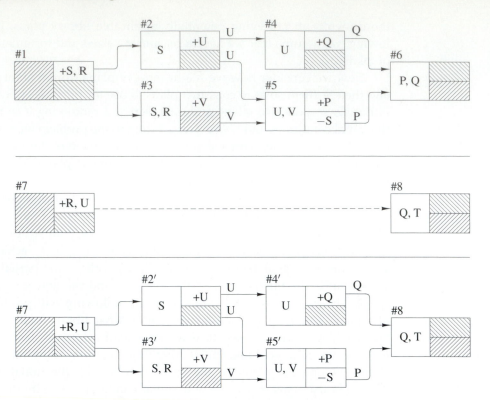

Figure 7.21 Fitting an existing plan to a new goal and initial conditions. The plan at the top represents a library plan. The plan in the middle represents the initial plan for a new goal and initial conditions. The plan at the bottom is the result of fitting the library plan to the new goal and initial conditions. Note that in the fitted plan, links have been removed and replaced with simple ordering constraints.

plans at the top and middle of Figure 7.21 only partially match. The plan at the bottom of Figure 7.21 shows the result of fitting the library plan to the new goal and initial conditions. The fitted plan has two requirements: achieve T for the step labeled #8 and achieve S for the step labeled #2′. You might ask yourself why it is important to remove the link from #5′ to #8 with condition P. Note also that #2′ does not appear to be necessary given that U is in the initial conditions; of course, the same could be said for the steps labeled #3′ and #5′. You might consider how such steps could be eliminated to produce a better fitted plan.

At this point, we should have one or more plans that we can refine in an attempt to obtain a solution to the new problem. Our previous method of generating refinements will not work for plan adaptation. The reason is that it may not be possible to reach a solution starting from the plans obtained from library plans by fitting. In order to reach a solution, we may have to retract steps, links, or ordering constraints in the refitted library plans.

What this means in terms of search is that we may have to move up as well as down in the search tree. The options for refining a particular refitted

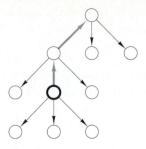

Figure 7.22   Extending and revising plans during refinement

plan are illustrated in Figure 7.22, where the refitted plan is indicated by **O**, and the edges, indicated by ⟶ , correspond to refinements that retract steps and constraints in the refitted plan. In order to search the space systematically, we have to be careful not to traverse any edge twice. This was never a problem in the case of the algorithm for least commitment planning since we assumed that the search space was a tree and the algorithm only moved down in the tree.

To achieve systematicity, we mark each plan corresponding to a search state as either ↑ or ↓. During planning, we maintain a queue of such plans to explore next. In refining a plan, if it is marked ↓, we apply refinements, mark each of the resulting plans with ↓, and place them all on the queue. To refine a plan π marked ↑, we retract exactly one prior refinement to π to obtain a single new plan π' which is marked ↑ and added to the queue. We then apply refinements to π' to obtain a set of plans, one of which will be π. Each of these refinements except π is marked ↓ and added to the queue. This strategy assures that we visit each state (plan) in the search space at most once.

Analysis of Adaptive Planning

Note that the approach of refitting existing plans does not guarantee that we will do any less work during planning. We could even do more work if we start with a really poor plan. To get some idea of when adapting previously generated plans is a good idea, consider the following simple analysis adapted from Hanks and Weld [1992].

First, note that in adapting plans, we have exactly one additional option over those available in the approach to least commitment planning introduced earlier; we can go up as well as down in the tree corresponding to the search space. Suppose that the branching factor for the least commitment search is b, and the shortest-length plan for a given problem is n. Our breadth-first search implementation of least commitment planning will require b^n time.

Now suppose that we initialize our adaptive planner with a refitted plan that can be used to generate a plan that achieves the goal using k adaptations corresponding to retractions and refinements. In this case, adaptation requires less time whenever

$$(b+1)^k < b^n$$

This inequality is satisfied whenever $k/n < \log_{b+1} b$. In most practical planning problems, b is at least 3. Given that $\log_4 3 = 0.79$, we conclude that adaptation is preferable if the retrieval and refitting routines always return a plan that requires at most 80% as many adaptations as the basic least commitment strategy requires refinements. Empirical studies indicate that adaptation strategies often do quite well in practice.

7.5   Planning with Incomplete Information

For the sort of planning described in the previous sections, it is not necessary to know the complete state of the world at any given time. In order to apply an operator, however, it is necessary to know those conditions listed in the preconditions of the operator.

In general, a planner cannot rely on knowing all the conditions relevant to a particular planning problem. In most situations, there are conditions that the planner knows nothing about, and there are conditions that the planner knew about at one time or another but is unsure of their present status. In this section, we consider the case in which for each condition either the planner knows—in the sense of justified true belief—that the condition is True, knows that it is False, or knows neither. This last corresponds to the excluded middle of classical two-valued logic and is denoted Unknown.

Since a state now assigns each condition one of True, False, or Unknown, we can no longer represent a state simply as a list of the true conditions. A state is now represented as a complete assignment. For example, the state in which the planner knows that a is on b and b is not on a but does not know whether or not b is on c is represented as (((on a b) True) ((on b a) False) ((on b c) Unknown)). In specifying operators, we combine additions and deletions into a single set of *postconditions*. Both preconditions and postconditions are specified as assignments to conditions.

The Copier-Repair Problem

Now that we can represent ignorance, what use can we make of this increased expressive power? Consider the following problem. A copier in an office building is not working ((working copier) False), and the robot is given the goal of fixing it ((working copier) True). Suppose that the only reasons for the copier not working are that (1) its paper storage tray is empty, (2) its replaceable cartridge is in need of replacement, or (3) it experienced some momentary hardware or software problem and needs to be reset (Figure 7.23). We refer to this as the *copier-repair problem*.

The standard practice for fixing the copier is to fill the paper tray if it is empty, replace the cartridge if necessary, and then reset the machine. To

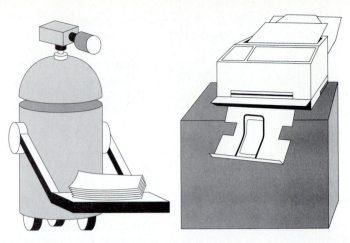

Figure 7.23   A robot has to find out what is wrong with the copier in order to fix it by either loading the paper storage tray, replacing the printing cartridge, or resetting the machine

fill the paper tray, the tray must be empty, the robot must be at the copier, and the robot must have some paper. To replace the cartridge, the cartridge must be spent, the robot must be at the copier, and the robot must have a replacement cartridge. To reset the machine, the paper tray must not be empty, and the cartridge must not be spent. The corresponding three operators are shown in Figure 7.24 (page 334).

Suppose, however, that the robot does not know and cannot find out the status of the cartridge and paper tray without examining the copier, that is, ((empty_paper copier) Unknown) and ((spent_cartridge copier) Unknown). Finally, suppose that the robot is currently in a lab some distance from the room in which the copier is kept.

One plan for fixing the copier is to travel to the room in which the copier is located, diagnose the problem, and then take whatever steps are required to fix the problem. In order to come up with such a plan, the robot needs to represent operators for determining the status, True or False, of conditions that are currently Unknown.

Figure 7.25 (page 334) lists operators for determining if the replacement cartridge is in need of replacement and determining if the paper tray is empty. In each case, there is a precondition that some condition is Unknown, and a postcondition corresponding to a disjunction indicating that after the operator is applied the condition will be known to be True or known to be False.

That the robot not know whether or not the copier is out of paper as a precondition for observing whether or not the copier is out of paper may seem a bit strange. Certainly such a precondition of ignorance is very different from the precondition requiring the robot to be at the copier in order to observe whether or not the copier is out of paper. In a more expressive

```
;; Fill the paper tray if it is empty.
(make-OPERATOR ;; Preconditions
                '(((empty_paper copier) True)
                  ((at robot copier) True)
                  ((has robot paper) True))
                ;; Postconditions
                '(((empty_paper copier) False)
                  ((has robot paper) False)))


;; Replace the cartridge if necessary.
(make-OPERATOR ;; Preconditions
                '(((spent_cartridge copier) True)
                  ((at robot copier) True)
                  ((has robot cartridge) True))
                ;; Postconditions
                '(((spent_cartridge copier) False)
                  ((has robot cartridge) False)))


;; Reset the machine.
(make-OPERATOR ;; Preconditions
                '(((working copier) False)
                  ((at robot copier) True)
                  ((spent_cartridge copier) False)
                  ((empty_paper copier) False))
                ;; Postconditions
                '(((working copier) True)))
```

Figure 7.24   Operators for the copier-repair problem

operator language, we would distinguish actions that result in uncertainty, such as spinning a roulette wheel, from actions that result in resolving uncertainty, such as observing the roulette wheel when it has stopped spinning [Etzioni et al., 1992]. In the following discussion, however, we will not make such a distinction.

```
;; Determine if the cartridge is spent.
(make-OPERATOR ;; Preconditions
                '(((spent_cartridge copier) Unknown)
                  ((at robot copier) True))
                ;; Postconditions
                '((or (spent_cartridge copier) True)
                     (spent_cartridge copier) False))


;; Determine if the copier is out of paper.
(make-OPERATOR ;; Preconditions
                '(((empty_paper copier) Unknown)
                  ((at robot copier) True))
                ;; Postconditions
                '((or (empty_paper copier) True)
                     (empty_paper copier) False))
```

Figure 7.25   Operators for acquiring information

The disjunctions in the postconditions are not something that we are able to handle using the state-space search methods introduced earlier.[2] However, we can deal with disjunctions in postconditions by using a standard strategy for proving theorems. If you can prove r given p and prove r given q, then you can prove r given p ∨ q. This strategy is often referred to as *reasoning by cases*. In planning to repair the copier, we do something very similar.

First, we plan to determine what is wrong with the copier. We refer to this as the *unconditional* part of the plan. This plan would entail the robot traveling to the copy room and examining both the paper tray and the replacement cartridge. Following these examinations, one of four cases will be determined: There is paper and the cartridge is in need of replacement; there is no paper and the cartridge is fine; both the paper and the cartridge need attention; and neither the paper nor the cartridge is at fault, and there must have been a momentary hardware or software problem. Only at execution time will the robot know which one of these four cases corresponds to the actual state of affairs.

Generating Conditional Plans

In addition to the unconditional part of the plan, we construct four contingency plans, one for each of the four possible cases. At execution time, we execute the unconditional part of the plan to determine which of the four cases actually obtains and then execute the contingency plan corresponding to the actual case. The entire plan is called a *conditional plan*. In a conditional plan, whether or not the robot executes certain steps depends on conditions whose status, True or False, is determined during the execution of the plan.

Incompleteness introduces additional choices in planning. For instance, a requirement can be satisfied by either taking steps to make it True or by observing that it is True. Often it is useful to explicitly indicate that an operator precondition can be achieved only by observation. One way of finding an office with a green door is to find any office and paint its door green, but presumably we would prefer our office robots reject such a solution.

Using the preceding operators, it is not possible to fix a problem copier caused by an empty paper tray or spent replacement cartridge unless you know that the tray is empty or the cartridge spent. In practice, however, it is common to replace a part in trying to repair a machine without knowing that the part is defective; this is often because determining whether or not a part is defective is more expensive than just purchasing a replacement and installing it whether or not the part is defective.

---

[2]Note that the disjunction in the list of additions is not a tautology given that a condition can be assigned True, False, or Unknown.

In this approach, we can save some planning effort by simply planning to gather the necessary information, carrying out that plan, and then, having determined the necessary information, planning for the specific situation determined as a result of information gathering. However, though this might save some computation, it might also result in an expensive plan to execute.

Suppose that the stock of paper and replacement cartridges is located in the lab where the robot is initially located. A clever robot might take along a new cartridge and a carton of paper in order to be prepared no matter what turns out to be wrong with the copier. In many cases, it is worthwhile trying to come up with a plan in which the robot performs actions in anticipation of different possible observations.

Of course, it is one thing to anticipate a problem and quite another to prepare for it. It may be that the robot cannot carry both a replacement cartridge and a carton of paper. In this case, the robot has to choose between the two, perhaps on the basis of statistics concerning which of the two possible causes for copier malfunction is more likely to occur. Planning with incomplete information involves combining plans to deal with different possible futures.

In the following, we describe an algorithm for planning with incomplete information. To simplify the discussion, we assume that each operator has at most one postcondition corresponding to a disjunction and that this disjunction is always of the form (or (*condition* True) (*condition* False)). We refer to a disjunct of such a disjunction for an operator appearing in a plan as an *observation*.

Contexts Represent Possible Sets of Observations

To keep track of the different possible cases corresponding to unknown conditions, we introduce the notion of a *context*. A context assigns True or False to a set of conditions; each context corresponds to a set of observations.[3] Two contexts are said to be *compatible* if they agree on assignments for all conditions that they both assign values to. For instance, the context ((condition1 True) (condition2 True)) is compatible with () and ((condition1 True) (condition3 False)) but incompatible with ((condition2 False)).

In the previous section, we started the search algorithm with a plan consisting of two steps: one with a pseudo operator whose postcondi-

---

[3]For some applications, it may be useful to represent operators that result in certain conditions becoming Unknown. For example, if the robot leaves a room, it may no longer be sure of the occupants of that room. This complicates the notion of context since conditions can alternate between being known and being unknown any number of times. In this section, we assume that once the truth value for a condition becomes True or False, it never again becomes Unknown. We can extend our approach to deal with conditions alternating between Unknown and either True or False by distinguishing different instances of observations regarding the same condition.

tions correspond to the initial conditions and one with a pseudo operator whose preconditions correspond to the goal conditions. In planning with incomplete information, we begin as in the case of complete information; however, we label the steps with contexts to keep track of the observations that those steps depend on. Although we wish to construct a plan that succeeds no matter what we observe at execution time, there is no reason to execute steps that depend on conditions that were not observed.

The *derived context* for a step includes an observation if and only if the step is the consumer in a link in which either the condition of the link is the observation or the context of the producer of the link includes the observation. The context for a step that is not a goal is just the derived context. In planning with incomplete information, we typically create several goal steps corresponding to different, incompatible contexts. The *initial context* for a goal step is assigned at the time the step is created. The context for a goal step is the union of its derived context and its initial context. Only goal steps have initial contexts.

Planning proceeds as follows. Create an initial plan as in the case with complete information. Assign the goal step the empty context as its initial context. Proceed as in the case with complete information with two important differences. First, you can link one step to another only if the two steps have compatible contexts; after linking, the context of the consumer should logically entail the context of the producer. Second, a step conflicts with a link only if the context of the consumer of the link is compatible with the context of the step.

The criterion for a correct plan with incomplete information is as follows. First, the plan has no requirements or conflicts as in the case of complete information. Second, the contexts for the goal steps must correspond to a tautology for a two-valued logic with just True and False. This second requirement ensures that for any possible set of actual observations, there is some goal step whose context is compatible with that set of observations. If a point is reached during planning where there are no requirements or conflicts and the contexts for the goal steps do not form a tautology, then create a new goal step with a context that is incompatible with each of the contexts for existing goal steps and continue planning.

To illustrate the planning algorithm, we consider a simple version of the copier-repair problem. We begin by defining the set of conditions: working, the copier is working; atlab, the robot is in the lab; atcopier, the robot is in the copier room; empty, the copier paper tray is empty; spent, the copier replacement cartridge is in need of replacement; cart, the robot has a replacement cartridge; paper, the robot has paper for the copier. We represent the three possible assignments True, False, and Unknown for the condition c as, respectively, c, ¬c, and ?c. Table 7.1 lists the preconditions

TABLE 7.1   Operators for copier-repair problem

operator	preconditions	postconditions
goal	working	
initial		atlab ¬paper ¬cart ¬atcopier ¬working
getcart	atlab	cart
getpaper	atlab	paper
gocopier	atlab	atcopier
checkcart	atcopier ?spent	(or spent ¬spent)
checkpaper	atcopier ?empty	(or empty ¬empty)
changecart	atcopier cart spent	¬spent
addpaper	atcopier empty paper	¬empty
reset	atcopier ¬spent ¬empty	working

and postconditions for the set of operators used to solve the copier-repair problem.

We initialize the goal step with the empty context. Figure 7.26 shows a plan for solving the copier-repair problem for the context in which the cartridge is not in need of replacement and the paper tray is not empty. Each step is displayed with boxed text indicating the corresponding operator, and preconditions and postconditions are displayed as unboxed text. Every step is labeled with its context. The goal step is labeled with its initial context followed by its derived context. Disjunctions of observations are indicated graphically by ⨉.

Figure 7.27 shows two additional plans. The top plan works whether the cartridge needs replacing or not as long as the paper tray is not empty. The bottom plan works unless the cartridge needs replacing and the paper tray

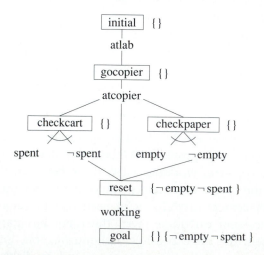

Figure 7.26   Solution to the copier-repair problem for one possible context

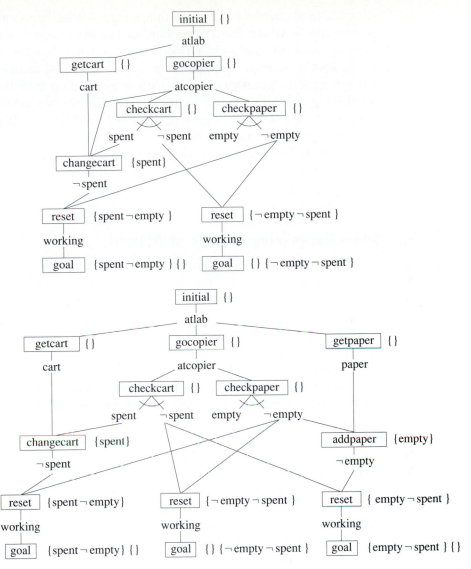

Figure 7.27 Solutions to the copier-repair problem for additional contexts. To avoid cluttering the figure, the fact that reset requires the precondition atcopier is not made explicit.

is empty. By adding another goal step with an initial context of {spent empty}, the planner will generate a plan that works no matter what observations are made at execution time.

For the copier-repair problem, we had to consider all possible contexts to construct a plan that would work no matter what conditions are observed at execution time. In general, there will be 2^n contexts assuming $2n$ observations and the model described. Planning is already hard in the case of complete information; incomplete information just exacerbates the computational problems. To make things even worse, there may very well be contexts for which there is no solution. For instance, suppose that reset depends on additional preconditions that the robot has no control over. In the best of worlds, we might hope for a sound and complete planner, but asking for a guarantee of termination in addition may be asking too much. For practical planning, we need good, domain-dependent heuristics; we need to know when to give up in trying to solve a difficult problem and how to recover from failure.

All the techniques that we have considered so far rely on a very simple model of action. In the next section, we consider some of the consequences of moving to a more sophisticated representation for actions and change over time.

7.6 More Expressive Models of Action

The planning methods in the previous sections represent actions using operators that transform one state into another. Each operator is specified in terms of preconditions and postconditions. If the preconditions are not satisfied in a state, then the operator does not apply in that state. The planning methods presented ensure that the preconditions of an operator are satisfied in the state just prior to the operator and the postconditions are true in the state immediately following the operator.

The different representations for operators that we have considered so far have certain expressive limitations that we consider overcoming in this section. In particular, we consider conditional effects in which the state immediately following an operator depends on the state immediately before the operator and universally quantified effects that range over sets of objects. In the previous sections, we used propositional logic to represent states of the world and operator preconditions and postconditions. In the following, we introduce universal quantifiers as a representational convenience. We assume a finite domain, and therefore, we can transform universally quantified statements into conjunctions and remain entirely within the propositional logic.

In many cases, increased expressiveness results in increased computational overhead. We already considered one extension for operators that resulted in additional computational overhead. The use of disjunctive postconditions to represent uncertainty in the effects of operators can increase the size search space exponentially in the number of disjunctive postconditions. In this section, we focus on extensions that result in relatively modest increases in computational overhead.

To encode operators in this section, we revise our notation for operator schemas one more time. For the rest of this section, an operator consists of two formulas: one formula describing the preconditions of the operator and another formula describing the postconditions. Using this notation, we represent an operator to move one block (? x) from another block (? y) to the table as follows:

```
(make-OPERATOR ;; Preconditions
              '(and (on (? x) (? y))
                    (clear (? x))
                    (not (equal (? y) table)))
              ;; Postconditions
              '(and (on (? x) table)
                    (clear (? y))
                    (not (on (? x) (? y)))))
```

Both additions and deletions appear in the postcondition formula of the operator with the deletions negated to indicate that they are not true in the state immediately following an instance of the operator.

Conditional Effects

Recall that in our discussion of the machine assembly example in the section on state-space search we needed to use two operators to model the action of assembling the second component. If the first component is already assembled at the time that the second component is assembled, then the first component has to be disassembled in the process of assembling the second. One operator handles the case in which the first component is assembled before attempting the assembly of the second component. The second operator handles the case in which the first component is not assembled before attempting the assembly of the second component.

We say that the resulting status of the first component, assembled or not, is a *conditional effect* of the action of assembling the second component. To reason about conditional effects, we employ the notation (when *antecedent consequent*) to represent that whenever the *antecedent* condition is true of the state immediately preceding the operator, the *consequent* condition will be true of the state immediately following the operator.

Figure 7.28 (page 342) shows the revised operators for the machine assembly example. The following example illustrates how conditional effects are handled in least commitment planning.

Suppose that in the initial state all three of the components are unassembled, and the goal is to have all three of the components assembled. Planning begins with three requirements, one for each of the three components to be assembled. To satisfy these requirements, we add all three operators, generating two additional requirements, namely, that components one and two be assembled before component three. Ordering constraints are added to satisfy these two new requirements, and now the plan consists of assembling components one and two in either order followed by assembling component three.

We know that component two must be assembled before component one. Here is how a least commitment planner would use the conditional effect to arrive at the same conclusion. The planner notes that the condition

```
;; Assemble the first component.
(make-OPERATOR ;; Preconditions
               '(not (assembled 1))
               ;; Postconditions
               '(assembled 1))

;; Assemble the second component.
(make-OPERATOR ;; Preconditions
               '(not (assembled 2))
               ;; Postconditions
               '(and (assembled 2)
                     (when (assembled 1)
                           (not (assembled 1)))))

;; Assemble the third component.
(make-OPERATOR ;; Preconditions
               '(and (assembled 1)
                     (assembled 2) (not (assembled 3)))
               ;; Postconditions
               '(assembled 3))
```

Figure 7.28   Revised set of operators for the machine assembly example

(assembled 1) of the link between the step of assembling component one and the goal step contradicts the consequent (not (assembled 1)) of the conditional effect in the operator for assembling the second component. To ensure that the consequent of the conditional effect is not realized, the planner adds a requirement that the negation of the antecedent of the conditional effect be true immediately before the step of assembling the second component.

This new requirement introduces a conflict that can be resolved in only one way, by assembling the second component before the first component. The strategy for handling conditional effects that we sketched can easily be added to the algorithm for least commitment planning with only a small increase in computation.

Disjunctive Preconditions

In the section on planning with incomplete information, we used postconditions containing disjunctions to represent uncertainty. We can also add disjunctions to preconditions, but in this case, the additional computational overhead is more reasonable.

In one sense, disjunctions in preconditions are unnecessary since an operator with a disjunctive precondition can be expanded into two or more operators, one for each of the disjuncts in the disjunction. However, representing the disjunctions explicitly is often more natural, and in some cases, clarifies the scope of the operator. Disjunctions in preconditions are often used to ensure that an operator is applied in the appropriate context.

Often the disjuncts in disjunctive preconditions make use of static conditions. We already have encountered static conditions of the form (not (equal

```
(make-OPERATOR ;; Preconditions
               '(and (on (? x) (? y))
                     (block (? x))
                     (clear (? x))
                     (or (and (block (? z))
                              (clear (? z)))
                         (equal (? z) table))
                     (not (equal (? x) (? y)))
                     (not (equal (? x) (? z)))
                     (not (equal (? y) (? z))))
               ;; Postconditions
               '(and (on (? x) (? z))
                     (not (on (? x) (? y)))
                     (when (not (equal (? y) table))
                           (clear (? y)))
                     (when (not (equal (? z) table))
                           (not (clear (? z)))))))
```

Figure 7.29   General operator schema for stacking blocks

x *y*)). Static conditions are also often used to specify the *types* of objects. For example, the static condition (block a) indicates that the object a is of type block.

We assume that the set of objects and their type designations are static in the sense that actions cannot result in the creation or destruction of objects or changes in their types. In particular, you cannot write an operator with a postcondition (not (block b)).

Figure 7.29 shows a single operator schema that uses disjunctive preconditions and conditional effects to represent the action of moving a block. This single operator correctly handles the cases of moving a block from a block to another block, from a block to the table, and from the table to a block.

In order to handle disjunctive preconditions in least commitment planning, we need to add machinery that adds requirements for each disjunct and then removes the other disjuncts when one is satisfied. Disjunctive preconditions increase the size of the search space but are often convenient when used in moderation.

Universally Quantified Effects

It is sometimes useful to describe preconditions and postconditions that involve a whole class of objects. Such preconditions and postconditions can be represented using universally quantified formulas.

For example, instead of using a special clear predicate, we can represent (clear (? y)) using the following quantified formula, where explicit typing information is used to restrict the scope of the quantifier:

```
(forall (block (? x))
        (not (on (? x) (? y))))
```

Representing such universally quantified statements does not require any additional machinery. We can take advantage of the fact that typing information is static and the domain is finite to convert the universally quantified formulas into conjunctions. For example, if there are just three blocks, a, b, and c, then the preceding quantified formula can be represented by the following conjunction:

```
(and (not (on a (? y))) (not (on b (? y))) (not (on c (? y))))
```

In practice, universally quantified preconditions are expanded directly into the equivalent conjunction, and universally quantified postconditions are expanded on demand in response to appropriate requirements and potential conflicts.

Wandering Briefcase Example

To illustrate the utility of conditional effects and quantified postconditions, suppose that your briefcase is at home and currently contains your paycheck, and your goal is to have your briefcase at the office and your paycheck at home. Figure 7.30 lists two operators: one operator moves the briefcase and its contents from one location to another, and the second operator removes an object from the briefcase.

Initially, we have (at b home), (in c b), and (at c home), where b is the briefcase and c is the paycheck. Our goal is to have (at b office) and (at c home). Since (at c home) is already true in the initial state, we link the initial step

```
;; Move a briefcase (? b) from (? x) to (? y).
(make-OPERATOR ;; Preconditions
             '(and (briefcase (? b))
                   (location (? x))
                   (location (? y))
                   (at (? b) (? x))
                   (not (equal (? x) (? y))))
             ;; Postconditions
             '(and (at (? b) (? y))
                   (not (at (? b) (? x)))
                   (forall (object (? z))
                           (when (in (? z) (? b))
                                 (and (at (? z) (? y))
                                      (not (at (? z) (? x)))))))))

;; Remove an object (? x) from a briefcase (? b).
(make-OPERATOR ;; Preconditions
             '(and (object (? x))
                   (briefcase (? b))
                   (in (? x) (? b)))
             ;; Postconditions
             '(not (in (? x) (? b)))))
```

Figure 7.30 Operators for reasoning about briefcases

to the goal step with the condition (at c home). To achieve (at b office), we instantiate an operator to move b from home to office. The planner notices that one of the consequences of the following conditional effect, an instance of the quantified postcondition, contradicts the link with condition (at c home):

(when (in c b) (and (at c office) (not (at c home))))

If the paycheck remains in the briefcase, then it will end up at the office and not at home as required. In order that the conditional effect not be realized, we set up a requirement that the negation of the antecedent of the conditional effect be true immediately prior to the operator moving the briefcase to the office. To satisfy this requirement, we add another operator to remove the paycheck from the briefcase before moving it to the office, thereby forming a complete plan to achieve the goal.

As an aside, in this chapter, we have concerned ourselves exclusively with goals of achievement. In real planning systems, goals of *maintenance* are just as important. As an example of a goal of maintenance, you might have the goal to put a spare house key in your briefcase and then keep it there so that you will have it in emergencies. Goals of maintenance are relatively straightforward to implement in least commitment planning.

Processes Outside the Planner's Control

The techniques described here are quite useful in practice but still limited in expressiveness. For example, extending the techniques to handle arbitrarily nested containers is nontrivial. Containment is usually represented as a transitive, irreflexive, and antisymmetric relation. What happens to the contents of a briefcase if we put the briefcase inside a suitcase and then move the suitcase?

Reasoning about plans is even more complicated when we try to account for events outside the planner's control. Even in the simplest domains, the planner has no control over the passage of time. The problem is further complicated when we consider other agents and processes outside the planner's control. We can often represent the consequences of other agents' actions if we know what those actions are. The question is whether or not we can afford to account for those consequences in planning given the computational overhead.

Chapter 6 provides some additional ideas on reasoning about cause-and-effect relationships that can be applied to reasoning about the consequences of actions. Temporal reasoning and planning have always been closely associated in the literature. In both of these subfields, a critical issue involves building representations that balance expressiveness and computational complexity.

▼ Summary

Planning involves reasoning about the consequences of acting so as to choose actions that bring about desirable consequences. In this chapter, we consider planning as a special case of search. As in the case of other search problems, the way in which we represent the search space can have a significant impact on performance.

State-space search casts planning as search in the space of possible states of the world. A planning problem is specified as an initial state and a target goal representing a set of states. Operators transform one state into another. A solution to a planning problem corresponds to a sequence of operators that transforms the initial state into a goal state.

As an alternative to searching in the space of possible states of the world, we can search in the space of possible plans. Least commitment planning makes use of a search space consisting of plans represented as a partially ordered set of operators. Each partially ordered set of operators can represent one or more sequences of operators. We provide a search procedure for least commitment planning that is sound (if the procedure claims something is a solution, then it is a solution), complete (if there is a solution to the problem posed, then the procedure will find a solution), and systematic (the procedure will never examine the same node in the search space twice).

Planning is computationally complex. Abstraction provides one approach to reducing complexity. An abstraction space is a search space that ignores certain details in order to expedite search. By defining a hierarchy of increasingly more abstract abstraction spaces, it is possible to speed planning dramatically.

Another approach to speed planning involves storing previously generated plans in a library of such plans. When faced with a new problem, the planner looks in the library for a plan used to solve a similar problem and then adapts the library plan to the new problem. This technique of adapting previously generated plans attempts to amortize the cost of storing and retrieving plans over many adaptations.

In most applications, the planner does not have complete information about the state of the world. Planning for such applications involves figuring out what to do in the absence of information. Sometimes we can plan to gather the necessary information. Other times we must proceed in ignorance making use of whatever information there is available. Coping with incomplete information adds yet another dimension of computationally complexity to planning.

For most of this chapter, we employ the simple representation for actions developed in the section on state-space search. This representation is not sufficiently expressive to handle even relatively simple consequences of everyday actions and processes. It turns out to be relatively easy to extend our representation to handle conditional effects and quantification over finite sets of objects. Further extensions to handle disjunctions and metric time raise difficult representational problems. Reasoning about continuous quantities and processes outside the control of the planner poses even more daunting problems. These difficulties stem not so much from the problem of formally describing such consequences but from the problem of providing an efficient representation accounting for computation. Developing effective methods for reasoning about real-world processes is an important area for research in automated planning.

Background

The material on state-space search draws on the work of Ernst, Newell, and Simon [1969] in developing General Problem Solver (GPS), a program intended to model human performance in solving search problems. GPS was tremendously influential, and many of the ideas in GPS have been incorporated into modern planning and search systems. The particular approach to state-space search that we consider in detail is based on the representations used by the Stanford Research Institute Planning System (STRIPS) [Fikes and Nilsson, 1971]. The STRIPS representation for actions serves as the representational basis for many planning systems.

The section on least commitment planning derives from the work of Sacerdoti [1977] and Tate [1977] employing partially ordered plans, Sussman's work [1975] on identifying and resolving conflicts, and Stefik's work [1981] on constraint-posting planners. Chapman [1987] provided a more rigorous reconstruction of the earlier work on planning with partially ordered plans, and McAllester and Rosenblitt [1991] refined these ideas even further to develop the approach described in this chapter.

The original work on planning in a hierarchy of abstraction spaces is credited to Sacerdoti [1974]. Our treatment here follows that of Knoblock [1991] and is related to the analysis of Korf [1987] on planning as search.

The work on adapting plans corresponds to particular sort of learning, and related research appears in the literature cast in terms of plan reuse, speedup learning, adaptive planning, plan debugging, and case-based planning [Fikes et al., 1972; Schank and Abelson, 1977; Minton, 1988; Alterman, 1986; Simmons and Davis, 1987; Hammond, 1989; Kambhampati and Hendler, 1992]. The particular treatment presented in this chapter is due to Hanks and Weld [1992].

There has been a great deal of work on planners that produce conditional plans aimed at providing more flexibility at execution time [Warren, 1974; Dean, 1985; Schoppers, 1987; Collins and Pryor, 1992; Peot and Smith, 1992; Etzioni et al., 1992]. To provide even greater flexibility, researchers have developed systems that plan and execute at the same time [McDermott, 1978; Georgeff and Lansky, 1987; Firby, 1987; Krebsbach et al., 1992]. If the world changes quickly or unpredictably, it may be reasonable not to do any planning at all but simply to react to the environment and not bother with complicated and likely useless calculations for prediction and planning [Agre and Chapman, 1987; Brooks, 1986; Rosenschein and Kaelbling, 1986].

Extensions to handle more expressive representations for action are covered in Green [1969], Pednault [1988], Dean et al. [1988], Penberthy and Weld [1992]. Our discussion of more expressive representations for action borrows from Weld [1994]. For an interesting discussion of how the ideas in this chapter might be applied in practice, see Wilkins [1988]. For more on planning and scheduling systems for applications in space, see Aarup et al. [1987].

■ Exercises

7.1 Modify the implementations of sss and mea to print out the list of operators applied to achieve a given state. This can be done by augmenting the representation for states to include the list of operators applied to achieve the state starting from the initial state. You should define an appropriate data abstraction for states to accomplish this extension.

7.2 Generate a variant of the machine assembly example for which mea will not find a solution even though one exists.

7.3 Implement a state-space search strategy that uses both state progression and goal regression. One approach is to develop a new search space in which the nodes correspond to state/goal pairs. Operators in this search space correspond to the traditional state-space search operators used for either state progression or goal regression.

7.4 Modify apply-operators to work with operator schemas. Use the functions match and varsubst from Chapter 3 to implement your modified apply-operators.

7.5 Consider the following operator schema for block stacking:

```
(make-OPERATOR ;; Preconditions
              `((on (? x) (? z)) (clear (? x))
                (clear (? y)) (not (equal (? x) (? y)))
                (not (equal (? y) (? z))))
              ;; Additions
              `((on (? x) (? y)) (clear (? z)))
              ;; Deletions
              `((on (? x) (? z)) (clear (? y))))
```

Assume that (clear table) is true in the initial state no matter how many blocks are on the table and that (clear table) is never deleted from a state. Determine what, if any, additional operator schemas are required for solving block-stacking problems.

7.6 Write a complete set of operators for the Eight Puzzle, which was described in the exercises for Chapter 4. You will need conditions to represent the location of the uncovered area, (blank (? x) (? y)), and the locations of the eight tiles, (tile (? n) (? x) (? y)). If you are clever, you can specify the complete set of operators as four operator schemas, one for each direction in which it is possible to move a tile relative to the uncovered area. In writing these operator schemas, you will need to refer to the tile above, below, right, or left of the uncovered area. This would be trivial if you could apply functions during matching (for example, (tile 1 (+ 1 2) 3) would match (tile 1 3 3)). As an alternative to using arithmetic functions, consider representing addition as a relation of the form (+ (? x) (? y) (? z)), where (? z) is the sum of (? x) and (? y). Note that, given a static condition of the form (+ 1 2 3), you can determine the sum of 1 and 3 by matching (+ 1 2 (? z)) and the number one less than 3 by matching (+ 1 (? y) 3).

7.7 Consider problems that involve planning paths from one location to another given a graph with vertices corresponding to locations and edges corresponding to roads or corridors connecting locations. Construct an operator schema to move from one location to another given that the two locations are connected. Discuss what, if any, advantages might result from using a least commitment planning strategy for solving such problems.

7.8 Construct operators to represent actions corresponding to a robot grasping and ungrasping objects that result in the robot holding an object or not. Assume that the robot can hold exactly one object and that that object must be light and not heavy. Your operators should represent the fact that, if the robot moves from one location to another while grasping an object, then the object will move with the robot; in particular, if the robot ungrasps the object, then the object will be located wherever the robot is located when the ungrasp occurs.

7.9 Devise a method for reasoning about resources using operator schemas. Your method should allow you to reason about *pools* of objects that can be allocated and then later returned to the pool. For instance, in a factory domain, there might be a pool of work cells. For a particular factory order, you might allocate three cells for the interval of time required to complete the order. A robot with two or more multipurpose manipulators might reason about these manipulators as a resource.

    The resources considered in this exercise correspond to discrete, reusable resources. Consider the complications involved in reasoning about continuous (for example, fuel), nonreusable (for example, parts), and sharable (for example, vehicles) resources.

7.10 The goals considered in this chapter are all goals of achievement: Take steps to ensure that a proposition is true at some time or in some situation. In this exercise, we consider goals of *maintenance* and *prevention*. Maintenance goals involve propositions that must remain true over a given interval of time. Prevention goals involve propositions that must never become true over a given interval of time. Discuss how maintenance and prevention goals can be handled by the least commitment planning method described in this chapter.

7.11 Write a program that, given a plan consisting of a partially ordered set of steps and a set of initial conditions, chooses a total order consistent with the partially ordered steps and then simulates the execution of the resulting plan. For each step in the plan, your program should print the corresponding operator and the resulting state.

7.12 Rewrite the code for the least commitment planner to handle operator schemas with variables and constraints on variable bindings. You will have to modify the abstract data types to keep track of constraints on variable bindings. You will also have to rewrite refinements and several of the functions that it depends on to implement the method described for detecting potential conflicts and then resolving them by adding constraints on variable bindings. You might find it convenient to write a version of unify that takes three arguments corresponding to two patterns and a list of constraints that have to be satisfied. This version should succeed just in case the two patterns can be unified and also satisfy the constraints.

7.13 This exercise builds on the copier-repair problem described in our discussion of planning with incomplete information. Suppose there is another operator that enables the robot to use a computer in the lab to determine whether or not the paper tray is empty. Construct a plan to get the copier working that makes use of this operator. Indicate exactly what steps are executed for the different possible observations that the robot might make in the course of executing this plan.

7.14 A robot working on the police bomb squad is faced with the following problem. There are two packages in the room, and exactly one of them contains a bomb. The robot has a bomb-defusing device that will prevent the bomb from exploding if the correct package is placed in the device and the device is activated. Represent the problem, and then discuss whether or not the method for dealing with incomplete information described in this chapter will solve the problem. What if, instead of a bomb-defusing device, the robot is equipped with a blast-containment device that will fit exactly one of the two packages?

7.15 Many tasks in the real world require repeating some action until some condition is met. For instance, you hit a nail until it is flush with the surface that you are nailing, or you continue hailing taxi cabs until one stops and picks you up. Discuss the problems involved in reasoning about such tasks using the methods described in this chapter for dealing with incomplete information.

7.16 Consider a variation on the block-stacking domain in which the blocks are arranged on a table in n^2 locations corresponding to the cells of an $n \times n$ grid. At most, one block can be located in a given location. As an additional complication, suppose that blocks can be stacked no more than h high. Define the operators for moving blocks between locations, between blocks, and between locations and blocks. Define a two-level abstraction hierarchy using your operators, and discuss the potential for improving search using this hierarchy.

7.17 Consider the problem of planning for simultaneous actions. Suppose that there are two operators push-left and push-right that can be used in concert to lift a heavy object but that either operator used in isolation results in the object being moved outside the reach of the robot. Consider how such operators might be represented in the situation calculus and the interval temporal logic. Modify the projection routines from Chapter 6 to handle such operators.

7.18 Extend the algorithm for least commitment planning to handle operators with conditional effects. You will have to detect when the consequent of a conditional effect contradicts the condition of a link. Once such a contradiction is detected, you can resolve it just as you would a conflict, or you can ensure that the conditional effect is never realized by adding a new requirement that the negation of the antecedent of the conditional effect be true just prior to the step with the offending conditional effect.

7.19 Given a plan consisting of a sequence of actions, a set of initial conditions, and a causal theory, the projection routines of Chapter 6 can be used to verify whether or not the plan achieves the target goal. Discuss how these projection routines might be used as part of a strategy for solving planning problems that require reasoning about other processes and complex models of action.

▶ LISP IMPLEMENTATION

Refining Partially Ordered Plans

The Lisp implementation for refinements is provided as follows. Recall that, unless the plan satisfies the goal, it has either conflicts or requirements.

```
(defun refinements (plan operators)
  (if (PLAN-conflicts plan)
      (resolve-conflict (first (PLAN-conflicts plan)) plan)
    (append (resolve-req-new-step (first (PLAN-requirements plan))
                                  operators plan)
            (resolve-req-existing-step (first (PLAN-requirements plan))
                                       plan))))
```

Conflicts are resolved by constraining the clobberer to occur before the producer of the associated link or after the consumer of the link.

```
(defun resolve-conflict (conflict plan)
  (let ((link (CONFLICT-link conflict))
        (step (CONFLICT-clobberer conflict)))
    (append (constrain step (LINK-producer link) plan)
            (constrain (LINK-consumer link) step plan))))
```

A new plan is created with one step to occur before another if the two steps are not already constrained to occur in the opposite order.

```
(defun constrain (step1 step2 plan)
  (if (precedes step2 step1 (PLAN-constraints plan)) nil
    (list (make-PLAN (PLAN-steps plan)
                     (adjoin (make-CONSTRAINT step1 step2)
                             (PLAN-constraints plan)
                             :test #'equal)
                     (rest (PLAN-conflicts plan))
                     (PLAN-links plan)
                     (PLAN-requirements plan)))))
```

Precedes determines if one step precedes another given a set of constraints.

```
(defun precedes (step1 step2 constraints)
  (or (equal step1 step2)
      (some #'(lambda (c)
                (and (equal step1 (begin c))
                     (precedes (end c) step2 constraints)))
            constraints)))
```

To eliminate a requirement by adding a new step, create a new plan for each applicable operator.

```
(defun resolve-req-new-step (req operators plan)
  (mapcan #'(lambda (p) (applicablep p req plan)) operators))
```

An operator is applicable just in case the condition of the requirement is added by the operator. If applicable, create a new plan from the old one by adding a new step, constraining the new step to precede the step of the resolved requirement, eliminating this requirement, adding a link resolving the requirement with the new step as producer, adding a new set of requirements corresponding to the preconditions of the operator, and updating the set of conflicts. Conflicts can arise when the deletions of the new step threaten existing links or when existing steps threaten the new link.

```
(defun applicablep (operator req plan)
  (if (not (member (REQUIREMENT-condition req)
                   (additions operator) :test #'equal)) nil
    (let* ((step (make-STEP operator))
           (constraint (make-CONSTRAINT step (REQUIREMENT-step req)))
           (link (make-LINK step (REQUIREMENT-condition req)
                            (REQUIREMENT-step req))))
      (list (make-PLAN (cons step (PLAN-steps plan))
                       (adjoin constraint (PLAN-constraints plan)
                               :test #'equal)
                       (append (LINK-conflicts link plan)
                               (STEP-conflicts step plan)
                               (PLAN-conflicts plan))
                       (cons link (PLAN-links plan))
                       (append (generate-requirements operator step)
                               (rest (PLAN-requirements plan))))))))
```

When a link is added, find all steps that might conflict with it. This function extends the data abstraction for objects of type LINK.

```
(defun LINK-conflicts (link plan)
  (mapcan #'(lambda (step) (conflictp link step)) (PLAN-steps plan)))
```

When a step is added, find all links that might conflict with it. This function extends the data abstraction for objects of type STEP.

```
(defun STEP-conflicts (step plan)
  (mapcan #'(lambda (link) (conflictp link step)) (PLAN-links plan)))
```

A link and a step conflict whenever the operator of the step deletes the condition of the link, unless the step is the consumer of the link.

```
(defun conflictp (link step)
  (if (and (not (equal step (LINK-consumer link)))
           (member (LINK-condition link)
                   (deletions (STEP-operator step))
                   :test #'equal))
    (list (make-CONFLICT link step)) nil))
```

The operator of a step has associated with it one requirement for each of its preconditions.

```
(defun generate-requirements (operator step)
  (mapcar #'(lambda (p) (make-REQUIREMENT step p))
          (preconditions operator)))
```

To eliminate a requirement using an existing step, create a new plan for each existing step that can be linked to satisfy the requirement.

```
(defun resolve-req-existing-step (req plan)
  (mapcan #'(lambda (s) (linkablep s req plan)) (PLAN-steps plan)))
```

An existing step can be linked to satisfy a requirement just in case its associated operator adds the condition of the requirement and the existing step is not constrained to follow the step of the requirement. If this criterion is met, create a new plan from the old one by constraining the existing step to the step of the resolved requirement, eliminating this requirement, adding a link resolving the requirement with the existing step as producer, and updating the set of conflicts.

```
(defun linkablep (step req plan)
  (if (or (not (member (REQUIREMENT-condition req)
                       (additions (STEP-operator step)) :test #'equal))
          (precedes (REQUIREMENT-step req) step
                    (PLAN-constraints plan)))  nil
    (let ((link (make-LINK step
                           (REQUIREMENT-condition req)
                           (REQUIREMENT-step req)))
          (constraint (list step (REQUIREMENT-step req))))
      (list (make-PLAN (PLAN-steps plan)
                       (adjoin constraint (PLAN-constraints plan)
                               :test #'equal)
                       (append (LINK-conflicts link plan)
                               (PLAN-conflicts plan))
                       (cons link (PLAN-links plan))
                       (rest (PLAN-requirements plan)))))))
```

This implementation with a slight modification is systematic. The modification extends the criterion for conflict so that a step and a link are said to conflict if the condition of the link is added *or* deleted by the operator of the step. In practice, this modification is typically not implemented, and practitioners report no deleterious consequences.

This implementation is also sound and complete. There are also various modifications that guarantee termination, but they all require considerable computational overhead since they involve checking for cycles in which a sequence of steps arrives at the same state multiple times.

CHAPTER 8

Uncertainty

Fred is debugging a program written in Lisp. He just typed an expression to the Lisp interpreter, and now it will not respond to any further typing. The visual prompt that usually indicates the interpreter is waiting for further input is not displayed. As far as Fred knows, there are only two situations that could cause the Lisp interpreter to stop running: either there are problems with the computer hardware or there is a bug in Fred's code that has caused the Lisp interpreter to get stuck in one of its strange, uncooperative states.

Fred's first thought is that the computer hardware is malfunctioning. Fortunately, if there is a hardware problem, then there is other evidence available to help Fred determine this. For instance, Fred is also running a text editor to edit his Lisp code; if the hardware is functioning properly, then the text editor should still be running. Moreover, if the editor is running, then the editor's cursor should be flashing. Fred checks the screen and, sure enough, the cursor is flashing. At this point, Fred reluctantly concludes that the computer is not experiencing hardware problems and that the reason the Lisp interpreter is misbehaving is that there are bugs in his Lisp code.

Consider the knowledge required for Fred to arrive at this conclusion. The most important knowledge required involves cause-and-effect relationships. If the hardware is functioning correctly, then the editor should be

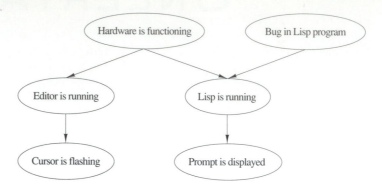

Figure 8.1   Causal relationships for the buggy Lisp code example

running, and if the editor is running, then the cursor should be flashing. If the hardware is functioning correctly and there are no bugs in the Lisp code, then the Lisp interpreter should be running, and if the Lisp interpreter is running, then the prompt should be displayed. These cause-and-effect relationships are depicted in Figure 8.1, where events are shown as ellipses, and arcs are drawn from causes to effects.

Of course, characterizing cause-and-effect relationships in terms of implications is somewhat misleading. There are times that Lisp stops running when the hardware is functioning perfectly and the code is known to be bug free. Similarly, the prompt can occasionally fail to appear immediately following a typed expression when the Lisp interpreter is running fine if perhaps a little slowly. What we really want to say is something like "most of the time, when the hardware is functioning correctly and the code is bug free, the Lisp interpreter is running." We may even be able to be a little more precise, as in "seventy-five percent of the time, when the hardware is functioning correctly and the code is bug free, the Lisp interpreter is running."

Even if we could model cause-and-effect relationships in terms of implication, we still could not arrive at the definite conclusion that the code has bugs in it. From "if the editor is running, then the cursor is flashing" and "the cursor is flashing," Fred cannot conclude necessarily that "the editor is running." In this chapter, we explore a calculus that differs from the propositional and predicate logics that we considered in Chapter 3 in that it allows us to express degrees of belief regarding the truth of a proposition or the occurrence of an event. This added flexibility allows us to draw useful conclusions in a variety of situations in which the propositional and predicate logics would not provide useful guidance.

The calculus that we consider in this chapter is based on probability theory. Probability theory allows us to make qualitative claims like "the cursor flashing depends on the editor running" and quantitative claims like "ninety percent of the time when the editor is running the cursor is flashing." We start by considering the various sources of uncertainty that motivate the consideration of probability theory. We provide a very basic introduction to probability theory, and then we consider a method of representing uncertain knowledge in networks. The treatment of representation issues includes a discussion of computational methods for inference. Finally, we consider how the methods for reasoning under uncertainty discussed in this chapter can be used to support decision making.

8.1 Motivation for Reasoning Under Uncertainty

There are many propositions whose truth values you do not know and cannot easily determine prior to your having to make a decision that depends on them. You may not know, for example, whether or not a class that you are enrolled in will meet on a particular snowy winter morning, but you still have to decide whether or not to get up and trek down to school. Uncertainty with regard to the truth of propositions and the occurrence of events is unavoidable in many real-world applications.

Sources of Uncertainty

Uncertainty can arise from a number of different sources. It may be that there are processes such as those involving the decay of radioactive substances whose behavior cannot be explained by any deterministic model. In such cases, the best that we can do is describe the process in terms of the frequencies with which events occur or propositions turn out to be true.

Alternatively, we may be dealing with processes that we don't understand very well. For instance, modern medicine does not yet understand the exact mechanism whereby the common cold is transmitted from one person to another. To reason about the possibility of our catching a cold when exposed to someone who already has one, we may resort to the frequency with which persons similarly exposed end up catching a cold.

Even in the case of processes that are deterministic and for which we do have detailed models, we may choose to represent their behavior as uncertain to avoid the computational overhead involved in using the detailed, deterministic model. For instance, given a particular Lisp program and the initial state of a particular computer, we can determine if the program will crash on the machine. However, making this determination could be quite time consuming. Instead, it may be enough to obtain some measure of the frequency with which a typical Lisp program will crash on a typical machine.

Representing Uncertain Knowledge

Representation involving uncertain knowledge is at least as hard as representation involving certain knowledge. It is still necessary to identify the relevant events and propositions and to determine how they relate to one another. It is also often necessary from a computational standpoint to ignore propositions and events that are not relevant to whatever particular task we have in mind.

For instance, if you are building a system to diagnose and repair automobile transmissions, you may wish to ignore the car's electrical and fuel systems. Determining that one set of propositions can be considered independently of another given a particular body of evidence is an important consideration in representing uncertain knowledge. A similar issue arises in representing knowledge in the propositional or predicate logic. In general, if we are concerned with determining the answer to a particular question, we would like to limit our attention to that subset of knowledge that is relevant and ignore the rest.

There is an issue that arises in methods for representing uncertain knowledge that does not arise in representing knowledge in propositional and predicate logic. Having determined that a given relationship between propositions or events exists, it remains to quantify that relationship. For instance, to quantify the relationship between catching a cold and being exposed to someone with a cold, we can ask a large number of people who have been exposed to someone with a cold whether or not they caught a cold immediately after and use this information to compute the frequency with which exposure to a cold results in catching a cold.

There are cases where quantifying a relationship can be quite difficult. For instance, you may notice that the amount of sleep you have the night before an exam affects the grade you receive on the exam. By the time you get enough data to accurately quantify such a relationship, you may be nearly finished with school. Instead, you may have a very rough estimate based on intuition or hearsay. Carefully justifying this estimate can be difficult, but you may feel that using the rough estimate is better than ignoring sleep altogether in deciding on a strategy for passing an exam.

Applications Involving Uncertainty

A wide range of applications for expert systems deal with uncertain knowledge. There are systems that identify problems in complicated pieces of equipment like the large gas turbines used for power generation. There are systems that are used to diagnose diseases from patient symptoms and records. Diagnostic systems are in daily use to assist doctors in identifying cancers, neuromuscular disorders, sleeping problems, and bacterial infections. Systems are also in use to assist companies in determining where to mine for minerals or drill for oil or natural gas.

In addition to systems that are in use today, systems are being developed for applications in robotics, airline scheduling, decision making for managing disaster planning, and understanding printed and spoken language. The primary obstacles to applying the methods of this chapter are acquiring the necessary qualitative and quantitative relationships and devising efficient methods for computing useful answers from uncertain knowledge.

8.2 Probability Theory

Suppose that you have observed the light on in Sonya's office a large number of times, and 90% of those times Sonya has actually turned out to be in her office. Now you observe the light on in Sonya's office. You might say there is a 0.9 chance that Sonya is in her office. A *probability* is a number in the range from 0 to 1 expressing the chance that a proposition is true or that some event occurred. If a proposition has probability 1, then it is certainly true. If a proposition has probability 0, then it is certainly false.

Frequency Interpretation of Probability

There are different interpretations of statements involving probabilities. In the *frequentist* interpretation, a probability is a property of a set of similar events. Suppose that we have a set S of objects. An event corresponds to selecting an object from S. Assume that we are equally likely to select any object in S. Now suppose that we partition S into two subsets P and N so that $P \cup N = S$ and $P \cap N = \emptyset$. The probability that we select an object belonging to P is $|P|/|S|$, corresponding to the *frequency* with which we expect to select objects belonging to P. The probability of selecting an object that does not belong to P is $|S - P|/|S| = |N|/|S|$.

Suppose that you visited Sonya's lighted office 100 times over the last month and in 90 of those visits Sonya was in her office. If you select a visit with an equal likelihood of selecting any one of the 100 visits, then the probability of selecting a visit such that Sonya was in her office would be 90/100. In a strict frequentist interpretation, the information regarding the 100 visits in the past tells you nothing about whether Sonya will be in her office tomorrow if we visit her office and find the light on. If there is an obviously repeatable sequence of events such as flipping a coin, a somewhat more complicated interpretation can be used to justify generalizing to future events. However, there are many situations in which no obvious interpretation in terms of frequencies applies.

Subjective Interpretation of Probability

There is also an interpretation of probability statements that involves what are called *subjective probabilities*. A subjective probability is a probability expressing a person's degree of belief in a proposition or the occurrence of an event. Suppose that you have spent all weekend studying for an exam and you feel pretty confident that you can pass the exam. You might say that the degree of your belief in the proposition that you will pass the exam is 0.9. This subjective probability can be used in combination with other probabilities to determine whether additional studying could significantly improve your chances of passing the exam. The mathematics involved in manipulating probabilities is the same whether we assign a frequentist or subjective interpretation. By allowing the use of subjective probabilities, we considerably extend the scope of applicability of the methods described in this chapter.

Probabilities that can be easily given a frequency interpretation are generally uncontroversial. However, subjective probabilities are sometimes considered suspect by practitioners who would prefer that probabilities be considered as existing apart from any given observer. The primary distinction between those willing to use subjective probabilities and those that restrict themselves to probabilities that can be given a frequency interpretation is that the former are willing to assign probabilities to events that are not elements of any obvious repeatable sequence of events. For instance, an advocate of subjective probabilities might assign a probability to the event that dinosaurs will again roam the earth as a result of advances in genetic engineering. Despite the misgivings of some practitioners, subjective probabilities can be given a quite reasonable and coherent interpretation.

Degrees of Belief

Suppose that you claim to be 90% certain that you will pass your math exam on Monday. One interpretation of this statement is that you would be prepared to offer a bet in which you pay out nine units if you fail the exam and you receive one unit if you pass the exam. In gambling terms, this corresponds to offering 9 to 1 odds on passing against not passing. Your degree of belief corresponds to the highest odds you are willing to offer. If your degree of belief is 0.9, then you would be eager to bet at 8 to 1 odds but unwilling to bet at 10 to 1 odds. Experts in the field of decision analysis have sophisticated tools for eliciting degrees of belief from subjects based on consistent betting behavior. These experts ask probing questions of subjects to assign numbers corresponding to degrees of belief that obey the mathematical rules for probabilities.

Generally, we are interested in a person's degree of belief in a proposition given a particular body of evidence and background knowledge. Detractors of subjective probabilities often complain that different people assign different subjective probabilities to the same propositions. Advocates of subjective probabilities counter that such variation is due to the fact that different people have different background knowledge and evidence, and hence it is natural that they have differing degrees of beliefs. In this text, we freely mix frequencies and degrees of belief in our discussion of probabilities; the mathematics and the computational techniques developed in this chapter apply to both interpretations of probabilities.

Random Variables and Distributions

We need a mathematical framework for representing uncertainty about propositions and events. To this end, we introduce a probabilistic analog of propositional variables to represent propositions that take on values true or false, events that take on values occurred or not occurred, and generally, variables that take on values from some set of possible values. As far as we are concerned, a *random variable* is a variable that can take on values from a set of mutually exclusive and exhaustive values referred to as the *sample space* of the random variable. For instance, a random variable representing a proposition would take on values from {True, False}. These values are mutually exclusive given that a proposition cannot be both True and False and exhaustive given that a proposition must be either True or False. A random variable representing the color of a car can take on values from {red, blue, green, other}, where other corresponds to any color other than red, blue, or green. The value other ensures that the set of values is exhaustive. To ensure that the values are mutually exclusive, we require that cars be classified as at most one of red, blue, green, or other.

In the following sections, we notate random variables using uppercase letters, for example, X or Y, and the values of random variables using lowercase letters, for example, x or y. The sample space of a variable X is notated by Ω_X. All sample spaces considered in this text are finite. If X and Y are random variables, then $Z = (X, Y)$ is a random variable representing the conjunction of X and Y, and the sample space for Z is the product of the sample spaces for X and Y, $\Omega_Z = \Omega_X \times \Omega_Y$. If $\Omega_X = \Omega_Y = \{\text{True}, \text{False}\}$, then the sample space for (X, Y) is the set of all boolean pairs: $\{\langle \text{True}, \text{True}\rangle, \langle \text{True}, \text{False}\rangle, \langle \text{False}, \text{True}\rangle, \langle \text{False}, \text{False}\rangle\}$. Generally, we are concerned with a set of random variables. For the set of random variables $\{X_1, \ldots, X_n\}$, the *joint sample space* is defined as the product of the sample spaces for the X_i,

$$\Omega_{X_1} \times \Omega_{X_2} \cdots \Omega_{X_n} = \prod_{i=1}^{n} \Omega_{X_i}$$

A random variable represents one aspect of a possible situation. The notation $X = x$ indicates that the variable X takes on the value x in a given situation. We can also talk about situations in which several variables take on specific values. For instance, the notation $(X = x, Y = y)$ indicates that the variables X and Y take on the values x and y, respectively, in a given situation; the comma separating $X = x$ and $Y = y$ represents conjunction.

The function, Pr, is a *probability distribution* over a finite sample space Ω_X for a random variable X if

$$0 \leq \Pr(X = x) \leq 1, \forall x \in \Omega_X$$

and

$$1 = \sum_{x \in \Omega_X} \Pr(X = x)$$

Since we are concerned only with finite sample spaces, all the distributions in this text are said to be *discrete*. Unless stated otherwise, we will assume that all random variables are boolean valued ($\Omega_X = \{\text{True}, \text{False}\}$). It should be mentioned, however, that all the methods in the text can be applied to arbitrary discrete distributions and that some of the methods can be extended to handle distributions over continuous sample spaces such as the real numbers.

The distribution over the joint sample space for a set of random variables is called the *joint distribution*. If $\{A, B, C\}$ is a set of random variables such that $\Omega_A = \Omega_B = \Omega_C = \{\text{True}, \text{False}\}$, we notate the joint distribution over $\{A, B, C\}$ as $\Pr(A, B, C)$. The statement $\Pr(A = \text{False}, B = \text{False}, C = \text{True})$ represents the probability that A and B are false and C is true. For a distribution involving a single variable A, we can specify the distribution as a one-dimensional table.

	Pr(A)
$A = $ True	0.3
$A = $ False	0.7

For a joint distribution involving two variables A and B, we can use a two-dimensional table.

	Pr(A,B)	
	$B = $ True	$B = $ False
$A = $ True	0.1	0.2
$A = $ False	0.3	0.4

Note that, according to our definition of a probability distribution, the numbers in each of these tables must sum to 1.

The joint distribution tells us everything we want to know about a set of random variables. Specifying a joint distribution in the general case requires space exponential in the number of random variables. We are concerned with representing a joint distribution compactly and with efficiently using such a representation to compute specific probabilities of interest.

Conditional Probability

Often we are interested in the probability of a proposition or event given some additional information or evidence. To represent this sort of knowl-

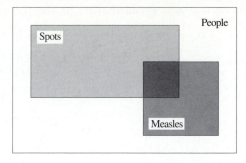

Figure 8.2 Venn diagram representing relationships involving three sets, *People*, *Measles*, and *Spots*. The largest rectangle represents the set, *People*, of all people. The smallest rectangle represents the set, *Measles*, of all people with measles. The remaining rectangle represents the set, *Spots*, of all people who have red spots on their skin. The intersection of the two smaller rectangles represents the set, *Measles* ∩ *Spots*, of all people with measles who also have red spots on their skin.

edge, we introduce *conditional probabilities* defined as follows:[1]

$$\Pr(A|B) = \frac{\Pr(A, B)}{\Pr(B)}$$

Read the expression $\Pr(A|B)$ as "the probability of A given B." The function $\Pr(A|B)$ is called a *conditional probability distribution*.

Almost all probability statements involve either implicit or explicit conditions. For example, a doctor might assign a probability to a patient having the measles. Implicitly, the doctor assumes that the patient is a person and not, say, a household pet. By making conditions explicit, we obtain an intuitive characterization of probabilities. Let M be a random variable representing the proposition that a patient has the measles and P a random variable representing the proposition that the patient is a person. Let *Measles* represent the set of all patients with measles and *People* represent the set of all people. If we assume that it is equally likely that any given person will walk into the doctor's office and furthermore that only people get the measles, then the probability that the next patient entering the doctor's office has the measles is defined as follows:

$$\Pr(M = \text{True}|P = \text{True}) = \frac{|Measles \cap People|}{|People|} = \frac{|Measles|}{|People|}$$

As another example, let S be a random variable representing the proposition that a person has red spots on his or her skin, and *Spots* represent the set of all patients with red spots on their skin. Figure 8.2 illustrates the relationships involving the three sets, *People*, *Measles*, and *Spots*. $\Pr(S = \text{True}|M = \text{True})$ represents the probability that a patient has red spots

---

[1]As far as we are concerned in this text, $\Pr(A|B)$ is not defined if $\Pr(B)$ is 0.

on his or her skin given that he or she has the measles.

$$
\begin{aligned}
\Pr(S = \text{True}|M = \text{True}) &= \Pr(S = \text{True}|M = \text{True}, P = \text{True}) \\
&= \frac{\Pr(S = \text{True}, M = \text{True}|P = \text{True})}{\Pr(M = \text{True}|P = \text{True})} \\
&= \frac{|Spots \cap Measles|}{|People|} \times \frac{|People|}{|Measles|} \\
&= \frac{|Spots \cap Measles|}{|Measles|}
\end{aligned}
$$

Since only people get the measles, we can suppress the condition that the patient is a person.

Calculus for Combining Probabilities

We need a calculus for combining probabilities that allows us to infer new knowledge from old. In particular, we need some means of taking evidence into account to update our beliefs. In the basic cycle of inference, we start with some initial or *prior* beliefs. We are given evidence in the form of new information. We then use the evidence and the prior beliefs to compute the updated or *posterior* beliefs. In the example given in the introduction to this chapter, Fred initially believes that his problems with the Lisp interpreter are due to malfunctioning hardware, but once he has evidence that the hardware is functioning properly, he shifts the blame to his Lisp code. In the following paragraphs, we introduce a number of rules for manipulating expressions involving probabilities to perform inference. These rules are expressed in the form of equalities that justify our substituting one expression for another.

Given a joint distribution $\Pr(A, B, C)$ over the set of random variables $\{A, B, C\}$, we can compute a distribution for any conjunction of random variables. For instance, suppose we wish to compute $\Pr(A, B)$, we can do so using the joint distribution as follows:

$$
\Pr(A, B) = \sum_{c \in \Omega_C} \Pr(A, B, C = c)
$$

which is shorthand for

$$
\Pr(A = a, B = b) = \sum_{c \in \Omega_C} \Pr(A = a, B = b, C = c)
$$

where a and b are elements of Ω_A and Ω_B, respectively. This operation is referred to as *marginalizing the joint distribution to* $\{A, B\}$, and $\Pr(A, B)$ is the *marginal distribution with respect to* $\{A, B\}$. To marginalize multiple variables, we employ nested sums where the order of nesting is immaterial.

$$
\Pr(C) = \sum_{a \in \Omega_A} \sum_{b \in \Omega_B} \Pr(A = a, B = b, C)
$$

Note that the distributions for $\Pr(A)$ and $\Pr(A, B)$ constrain one another since we can compute $\Pr(A)$ from $\Pr(A, B)$ by marginalizing the joint distribution $\Pr(A, B)$ to $\{A\}$.

Here is an important rule used in probabilistic reasoning called the *addition rule*.

$$\Pr(A) = \sum_{b \in \Omega_B} \Pr(A|B = b)\Pr(B = b)$$

Note that the addition rule follows immediately from marginalization and the definition of conditional probability. As an example application of the addition rule, suppose that you know the probability that Sonya is in her office given that her light is on and the probability that Sonya is in her office given that her light is off. If in addition, you know the probability that the light is on and the probability that the light is off, then you can compute the probability that Sonya is in her office in the absence of any observation whether her light is on or off.

Another important rule for manipulating expressions involving probabilities is called the *chain rule*.

$$\Pr(X_1, X_2, \ldots, X_n) =$$

$$\Pr(X_1|X_2, \ldots, X_n)\Pr(X_2|X_3, \ldots, X_n)\cdots\Pr(X_{n-1}|X_n)\Pr(X_n)$$

The chain rule enables us to factor a joint distribution into a product of conditional probabilities just as you can factor an integer into a product of smaller integers or a polynomial into a product of polynomials of smaller degree. Using the chain rule, there are as many factorizations as there are ways of ordering the set of random variables. The ability to factor the joint distribution turns out to be important in developing a compact representation for a joint distribution.

To give you some examples that involve manipulating probabilities, here is a proof of the chain rule for the special case of the joint distribution $\Pr(A, B, C)$. The steps in the following derivation follow from the definition of conditional probability:

$$\Pr(A, B, C) = \Pr(A|B, C)\Pr(B, C)$$

$$= \Pr(A|B, C)\Pr(B|C)\Pr(C)$$

Perhaps the best known rule for manipulating conditional probabilities is called *Bayes' rule*.

$$\Pr(A|B) = \frac{\Pr(B|A)\Pr(A)}{\Pr(B)}$$

Note that in order to compute $\Pr(A|B)$ using Bayes' rule, it is enough to know $\Pr(B|A)$ and $\Pr(A)$ since we can compute $\Pr(B)$ from $\Pr(B|A)$ and $\Pr(A)$ using the addition rule. Bayes' rule follows directly from the definition of conditional probability.

$$\Pr(A|B) = \frac{\Pr(A, B)}{\Pr(B)}$$

$$= \frac{\Pr(B|A)\,\Pr(A)}{\Pr(B)}$$

Bayes' rule often allows us to make inferences using whatever probabilities we happen to have on hand. Suppose we know the probability that a patient has red spots given that the patient has the measles, but we wish to know the probability that a patient has the measles given that the patient has red spots. In diagnostic terms, we wish to determine the probability that a patient has a particular disease (measles) given that the patient has a particular symptom (red spots). Given the probability of having measles, the probability of having red spots, and the probability of having red spots given measles, we can compute the probability of having measles given red spots using Bayes' rule.

Conditional Independence

In general, specifying a distribution for n variables may require an n-dimensional table. For the set $\{X_1, \ldots, X_n\}$, where $\Omega_{X_i} = \{\text{True}, \text{False}\}$ for all $1 \leq i \leq n$, specifying $\Pr(X_1, \ldots, X_n)$ may require as many as 2^n numbers.

In many cases, however, we can get by with considerably fewer numbers and consequently less space by exploiting the fact that some variables do not depend on others, allowing us to decompose the specification of a joint distribution into manageable pieces. In this subsection, we say precisely what it means for one set of variables to depend on another and demonstrate how we can use dependency information to develop a compact representation for a joint distribution.

The random variable A is *conditionally independent of B given C* if

$$\Pr(A|B, C) = \Pr(A|C)$$

If A is not conditionally independent of B given C, then A is *conditionally dependent on B given C*. Note that, if A is conditionally independent of B given C, then we can compute the joint distribution over $\{A, B\}$ given C rather easily.

$$\Pr(A, B|C) = \Pr(A|C)\,\Pr(B|C)$$

This is proved as follows. Suppose that $\Pr(A|B, C) = \Pr(A|C)$, then

$$\Pr(A, B|C) = \Pr(A|B, C)\,\Pr(B|C)$$

$$= \Pr(A|C)\,\Pr(B|C)$$

The first step is justified by the definition of conditional probability and the second step by conditional independence. Note also that conditional independence is a symmetric relationship. In the exercises at the end of this chapter, you are asked to prove this.

Now we are ready to see how the chain rule and conditional independence allow us to represent joint distributions compactly. Consider the set of variables $\{A, B, C, D\}$, where $\Omega_A = \Omega_B = \Omega_C = \Omega_D = \{\text{True}, \text{False}\}$. Using the chain rule, we can factor the joint distribution as follows:

$$\Pr(A, B, C, D) = \Pr(A|B, C, D)\Pr(B|C, D)\Pr(C|D)\Pr(D)$$

Suppose that we have the following equations describing conditional independence relationships, $\Pr(A|B, C, D) = \Pr(A|B)$ and $\Pr(B|C, D) = \Pr(B|C)$. Substituting in the preceding formula, we obtain

$$\Pr(A, B, C, D) = \Pr(A|B)\Pr(B|C)\Pr(C|D)\Pr(D)$$

Note that given the distribution in the factored form, we can compute any probability specified by the joint distribution. The complete four-dimensional table for $\Pr(A, B, C, D)$ would require 16 numbers. For the factored distribution, each of the functions involving two variables requires a two-dimensional table consisting of four numbers, and the function involving one variable requires a one-dimensional table consisting of two numbers for a total of 14 numbers. This is a small savings, but consider a generalization of this example with the set of variables $\{X_1, \ldots, X_n\}$ and conditional independence relationships, $\Pr(X_i|X_{i+1}, \ldots, X_n) = \Pr(X_i|X_{i+1})$.[2] In this case, the complete n-dimensional table would require 2^n numbers, but we can manage with $n - 1$ two-dimensional tables and a one-dimensional table for a total of $2 + 4(n - 1)$ numbers. Although in general we won't be able to realize such space savings, we can often manage significant reductions in space by exploiting conditional independence between random variables.

Maintaining Consistency

There is another problem that arises in specifying a joint distribution that we have ignored until now. The problem is that, if we are not careful in specifying the numbers, we can introduce inconsistencies. For example, suppose we are given $\Pr(A = a|B = b) = 0.7$, $\Pr(B = b|A = a) = 0.3$, and $\Pr(B = b) = 0.5$, then by Bayes' rule we have

$$\Pr(A = a) = \frac{\Pr(B = b)\Pr(A = a|B = b)}{Pr(B = a|A = a)} = \frac{0.5 \times 0.7}{0.3} = \frac{0.35}{0.3} > 1.0$$

failing our criteria for Pr being a probability distribution. These probabilities are said to be *inconsistent*.

Fortunately, if we factor the joint distribution into a product of distributions and specify only the distributions in this product, then avoiding

---

[2]Actually, we can get by with half as many numbers for the case of boolean-valued random variables by exploiting the fact that $\Pr(X = \text{False}) = 1 - \Pr(X = \text{True})$.

inconsistencies turns out to be relatively easy. Suppose we factor $\Pr(A, B)$ into $\Pr(B)\Pr(A|B)$. In specifying a one-dimensional distribution,

	Pr(*B*)
B = True	0.4
B = False	0.6

or a two-dimensional conditional probability distribution,

	Pr(*A*|*B*)	
	B = True	*B* = False
A = True	0.8	0.3
A = False	0.2	0.7

it is enough to maintain consistency that the columns of numbers sum to 1. We would not, given the factorization, specify the probabilities for $\Pr(A)$ since these probabilities are already completely determined by $\Pr(B)$ and $\Pr(A|B)$.

You now have the basic mathematical background necessary to discuss issues in representing uncertain knowledge. In the next section, we consider a graphical representation for specifying a joint distribution and algorithms for making useful inferences that account for evidence.

8.3   Probabilistic Networks

In the example at the beginning of this chapter concerning Fred and his problems with Lisp, we were able to characterize how the relevant variables of the problem (problems in the hardware or bugs in Fred's Lisp code) are related to one another. We summarized these relationships in the graph shown in Figure 8.1. This intuitive representation can be formalized to capture both qualitative and quantitative relationships. The formal model will allow us to reason forward from causes to effects and backward from effects to causes. The former is called *predictive reasoning*, and the latter *diagnostic reasoning*.

In reasoning about the behavior of the stock market, for instance, you might know something about conditions that cause fluctuations in stock prices. For example, if a drug company discovers a cure for a crippling disease but the drug has dangerous side effects, you might want to predict how the market will respond so that you can decide whether to buy stock in the company. In reasoning about a patient admitted to a hospital with chest pains, a diagnostic system tries to determine the disease that caused the chest pains so that a physician can treat the disease.

Often it is useful for a system to perform both predictive and diagnostic reasoning. For instance, suppose that a medical diagnosis system determines that the most likely cause of a patient's chest pain is indigestion. The doctor might wish to consider the consequences of accepting this diagnosis and administering treatment accordingly. In particular, if there is some significant chance that the patient is having heart problems, it may be better to proceed as if the patient has heart problems even though it is more likely that the patient is just having problems digesting his or her dinner.

In the next section, we consider a general framework for representing relationships involving random variables. This framework allows us to define algorithms that operate on these representations to perform both predictive and diagnostic reasoning.

Graphical Models

A *probabilistic network* is a directed acyclic graph, $G = (V, E)$, whose vertices, V, are random variables and whose edges, E, indicate dependencies between random variables. We call the random variables in a probabilistic network *chance nodes* or just *nodes*. There is at most one edge connecting any two nodes in a probabilistic network.

An edge from X to Y in $G = (V, E)$, where $X \in V$ and $Y \in V$, is often taken to mean that X causally influences Y. Given such an interpretation for an edge from X to Y, evidence regarding X is said to provide *causal support* for Y, and evidence regarding Y is said to provide *diagnostic support* for X.

In Figure 8.3, we redisplay Figure 8.1 as a probabilistic network in which there are six, boolean-valued random variables. The variables are labeled as follows: H, the computer has Hardware problems; B, there are Bugs in Fred's Lisp code; E, the Editor is running; L, the Lisp interpreter is running; F, the cursor is Flashing; and P, the Prompt is displayed.

For a network $G = (V, E)$, if there is an edge from X to Y in E, where $X \in V$ and $Y \in V$, then X is said to be a *parent* of Y, and Y is said to be a *child* of X. Let Parents(X) denote the parents of $X \in V$ in $G = (V, E)$. For example, Parents(L) = $\{H, B\}$ in Figure 8.3. The *successors* of a node

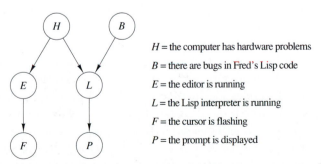

H = the computer has hardware problems

B = there are bugs in Fred's Lisp code

E = the editor is running

L = the Lisp interpreter is running

F = the cursor is flashing

P = the prompt is displayed

Figure 8.3   Probabilistic network for the buggy Lisp code example

▲ AI IN PRACTICE

Diagnosing Problems in Gas Turbines

Knowledge Industries has developed an expert system for the Electric Power Research Institute that diagnoses efficiency problems in large gas turbines used for power generation. Their approach combines expert probabilistic assessments with statistical data and thermodynamic analysis. The system employs a probabilistic network to update the likelihoods of alternative problems given a set of measurements. For a set of measurements, the system suggests the most cost-effective tests to perform to determine the cause of a performance problem.

Uncertainty is ubiquitous in reasoning about complex systems. Inspecting the internal parts of large gas turbines can involve costly downtime for critical power generation systems. In the absence of information regarding the functioning of internal parts, diagnostic systems must reason with uncertainty about the associations between observables and alternative problems that can cause those observations.

The probabilistic network was constructed by consulting with expert diagnosticians. Conversations with these experts revealed the importance of cause-and-effect relationships involving efficiency problems and their observable manifestations. Using the model represented in the probabilistic network, the expert system can suggest tests to distinguish between a faulty pressure gauge, requiring an inexpensive replacement, and a damaged fuel injector, requiring a costly repair.

Courtesy of General Electric

---

consist of the node's children, its childrens' children, its childrens' childrens' children, and so on. The successors of H in Figure 8.3 are E, L, F, and P.

By convention, the independence relationships in a probabilistic network can be succinctly characterized as follows: Each node is conditionally independent of all its nonsuccessors given its parents. For example, in Figure 8.3, P is conditionally independent of E, F, B, and H given L, so we have $\Pr(P|E, F, L, B, H) = \Pr(P|L)$. We can use this characterization in compactly representing the joint distribution for all the variables in a probabilistic network.

A *topological sort* of the variables represented in a network is an ordered list of the variables in which each variable comes after all its children in the network. The ordered list P, F, L, E, B, H is a topological sort of the variables shown in the network of Figure 8.3. Let $X_1, X_2, \ldots, X_n$ be a topological sort of the variables in G. Using the preceding characterization for independence in probabilistic networks, we note the following independence relationships:

$$\Pr(X_i | X_{i+1}, X_{i+2}, \ldots, X_n) = \Pr(X_i | \text{Parents}(X_i))$$

Using the independence relationships and the chain rule, we can specify the joint distribution as

$$\Pr(X_1, X_2, \ldots, X_n) = \prod_{1 \leq i \leq n} \Pr(X_i | \text{Parents}(X_i))$$

In particular, for the network in Figure 8.3, we have

$\Pr(P, F, L, E, B, H)$

$$= \Pr(P | F, L, E, B, H) \Pr(F | L, E, B, H)$$

$$\Pr(L | E, B, H) \Pr(E | B, H) \Pr(B | H) \Pr(H)$$

$$= \Pr(P | L) \Pr(F | E) \Pr(L | H, B) \Pr(E | H) \Pr(B) \Pr(H)$$

Path-Based Characterization of Independence

We can gain additional insight into probabilistic networks by recharacterizing independence relationships in terms of paths through the underlying graph. Consider the network shown in Figure 8.3. Is H independent of B given L? The answer is no. If Lisp has stopped running ($L = $ False), then knowing that the hardware is functioning correctly ($H = $ False) raises the probability that there are bugs in Fred's code ($B = $ True).

As another example, consider a simple chain such as that depicted in the following network:

Suppose that S corresponds to Smoking, D corresponds to lung Damage, and C corresponds to Coughing. Is smoking independent of coughing given lung damage? In the network, the answer is yes. Coughing is influenced by lung damage and by nothing else in the network, so knowing that someone smokes adds nothing to our knowledge of their coughing given that we know whether or not their lung are damaged.

Dependency in a probabilistic network can be determined by paths connecting nodes in the network. An *undirected path* in a probabilistic network is just a path in which we ignore the direction of the arrows. More precisely, an undirected path from n to n' in $G = (V, E)$ is a sequence $n_0, v_1, n_1, \ldots, v_k, n_k$ in which $n = n_0$, $n' = n_k$, for $i \neq j$ $n_i \neq n_j$, and for

$1 \leq i \leq k$ $n_i \in V$, $v_i \in E$, and v_i is either an edge from n_{i-1} to n_i or an edge from n_i to n_{i-1}. We classify the nodes in an undirected path other than the first or last as either *converging*, *diverging*, or *linear* as determined by their adjacent edges in the path.

We say that there is a *dependency-connecting path*, p, from X to Y in $G = (V, E)$ given a set $S \subset V$ if p is an undirected path and for each node n in p either

1. n is linear or diverging and not in S, or

2. n is converging and either n or one of its successors is in S.

Using the notion of dependency-connecting path, we can say precisely what it means for one variable to be dependent on another given a set of additional variables. We say that X *is dependent on Y given a set of variables S* if and only if there exists some dependency-connecting path from X to Y in G.

This definition of dependence completely characterizes the dependence (and independence) relationships in probabilistic networks. In the following network, A and B are dependent no matter how many nodes are in the linear chain as long as none of the X_i are in S, the set of given variables:

This is because information about A will influence our belief in B unless it is subsumed by information about one or more of the X_i. Note that it doesn't matter if the X_i are diverging. In the next example, there is a path between A and B with a converging node.

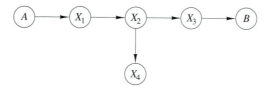

Note that knowledge about X_4 or X_2 allows X_1 to influence X_3 just as in the example where knowledge of Lisp running allows knowledge of hardware problems to influence knowledge of bugs in the Lisp code.

Quantifying Probabilistic Networks

Now we have to supply the numbers for the conditional probability of each node given its parents. For a node representing a boolean-valued random variable with m parents, this involves $2^{(m+1)}$ numbers. To maintain consistency of the joint distribution, we have to be careful that the conditional probabilities for a given assignment to the variables on which we are conditioning sum to 1. For example, if we are trying supply numbers for $\Pr(A|B, C)$ then

$$\forall b \in \Omega_B, c \in \Omega_C, \sum_{a \in \Omega_A} \Pr(A = a|B = b, C = c) = 1$$

We refer to supplying these numbers as *quantifying the network*.

If every node has exactly two parents, then the total amount of storage required for the joint distribution factored as shown is $8n$ rather than 2^n, representing a considerable saving in storage. Acquiring the actual numbers is done by either consulting an expert or by performing a set of experiments to obtain estimates of the desired probabilities.

Suppose that you want an estimate of the probability that Sonya's light is on given that Sonya is in her office. You could stop in Sonya's office each night for several weeks at some set of specified times. On each visit, you would mark down whether or not Sonya is in and whether or not her light is on. Once you have enough data, you would compile a conditional probability table using as probability estimates frequencies extracted from the data. Determining how much data is enough is a question for statisticians and beyond the scope of our discussion. In the Table 8.1, # Light on is the number of times you visited Sonya's office and the light was on. More generally, # φ is the number of times you visited Sonya's office and the proposition φ was true.

In some situations, the network designer must make do with whatever data is available or decide that there is not enough data to obtain a useful estimate for the probabilities. An alternative is to try to find an expert to supply the numbers. We will not discuss this approach except to mention that there is a discipline called *decision analysis* that is concerned with how humans make decisions and how they might make better decisions. Decision analysts have developed sophisticated tools for eliciting useful probability estimates from experts.

Inference in Probabilistic Networks

Now that we can represent uncertain knowledge using probabilistic networks, we need methods for inferring conclusions from what we know and

TABLE 8.1 Estimated probabilities		
	Pr(Sonya in/out | Light on/off)	
	Light on	Light off
Sonya in	$\dfrac{\text{\# Light on and Sonya in}}{\text{\# Light on}}$	$\dfrac{\text{\# Light off and Sonya in}}{\text{\# Light off}}$
Sonya out	$\dfrac{\text{\# Light on and Sonya out}}{\text{\# Light on}}$	$\dfrac{\text{\# Light off and Sonya out}}{\text{\# Light off}}$

whatever evidence we have acquired. The sort of inference we are interested in involves computing the probabilities of the nodes in a network given some evidence. In probabilistic networks, evidence is represented by assigning values to random variables from their respective sample spaces.

Given evidence $\mathcal{E}$ and some variable of interest X, we are interested in computing $\Pr(X|\mathcal{E})$. This conditional probability distribution is called the *posterior distribution*. In performing diagnosis, a doctor might wish to compute the probability of various diseases given evidence in the form of symptoms and lab tests. $\Pr(X|\mathcal{E})$ summarizes our beliefs regarding X. Methods for computing posterior distributions are to probabilistic networks what methods for applying resolution are to rule-based systems. We could compute the posterior distribution directly from the joint distribution in its factored form using marginalization, but it may take considerable time given that we will have to sum over the entire product space.

The general problem of exactly computing the posterior distribution is in the class of NP-hard problems. In certain special cases, however, the posterior distribution can be computed in polynomial time. There are also algorithms that compute an approximation to the posterior distribution that work well in practice. In the following sections, we describe polynomial-time exact algorithms for two special cases of probabilistic networks and an approximate algorithm for the general case.

Exact Inference in Tree-Structured Networks

In this section, we consider a method for computing the posterior distributions for variables in networks in which each node has at most one parent. Such networks are trees and hence are called *tree-structured networks*. We are interested in computing $\Pr(X|\mathcal{E})$ for all X in a tree-structured network. For a tree-structured network $G = (V, E)$, the method described in this section computes the posterior distribution $\Pr(X|\mathcal{E})$ for all variables $X \in V$ in time proportional to $\sum_{X \in V} |\Omega_X|$ or $2|V|$ in the case of boolean-valued random variables.

Consider the tree-structured probabilistic network shown in Figure 8.4. Suppose we wish to compute $\Pr(X|Z, Y_1, \dots, Y_n)$. Applying Bayes' rule, we have

$$\Pr(X|Z, Y_1, \dots, Y_n) = \frac{\Pr(Y_1, \dots, Y_n|X, Z)\Pr(X|Z)}{\sum_{x \in \Omega_X} \Pr(Y_1, \dots, Y_n|X = x, Z)\Pr(X = x|Z)}$$

Note that in Figure 8.4, the Y_i are conditionally independent of Z and each other given X. Therefore, we can simplify $\Pr(X|Z, Y_1, \dots, Y_n)$ to

$$\frac{\Pr(X|Z)\Pr(Y_1|X) \cdots \Pr(Y_n|X)}{\sum_{x \in \Omega_X} \Pr(X = x|Z)\Pr(Y_1|X = x) \cdots \Pr(Y_n|X = x)}$$

Note that this expression requires only the conditional probabilities associated with the nodes $X, Y_1, \dots, Y_n$.

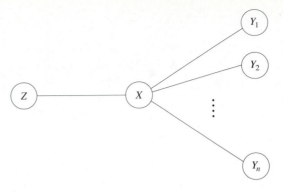

Figure 8.4 Simple tree-structured probabilistic network

Variables at the *boundary of a network* are variables with either no parents or no children. For the problems we consider, evidence corresponds to the instantiation of variables at the boundary of the network. We compute the impact of evidence on variables not on the boundary by propagating the evidential information through intervening variables. In Figure 8.4, the boundary comprises variables in the set $\{Z, Y_1, \ldots, Y_n\}$. Some or all of the variables in the boundary may be instantiated as evidence. As new evidence is added, the posterior distributions require updating. In Figure 8.4, we may compute $\Pr(X|\mathcal{E})$ for the evidence $\mathcal{E} = \{Y_1 = y_1, \ldots, Y_n = y_n\}$, where $y_i \in \Omega_{Y_i}$. If later we discover that $Z = z$ for some $z \in \Omega_Z$, then we will want to update $\Pr(X|\mathcal{E})$ for the evidence $\mathcal{E} = \{Z = z, Y_1 = y_1, \ldots, Y_n = y_n\}$.

Let $\mathcal{E}$ denote all the evidence obtained thus far. Removing a variable X from a tree-structured network separates the network into $n + 1$ subtrees associated with the single parent of X and its n children. We partition $\mathcal{E}$ into $n + 1$ components corresponding to these $n + 1$ subtrees. Let $\mathcal{E}^+$ be the evidence associated with the parent of X, and $\mathcal{E}_i^-$ be the evidence associated with the ith child of X. Figure 8.5 illustrates this partition graphically. Suppose that X can obtain $\Pr(Z|\mathcal{E}^+)$ from Z, and $\Pr(\mathcal{E}_i^-|X)$ from Y_i. Given this information, we can compute $\Pr(X|\mathcal{E})$ in a manner similar to that used in computing $\Pr(X|Z, Y_1, \ldots, Y_n)$,

$$\Pr(X|\mathcal{E}) = \Pr(X|\mathcal{E}^+, \mathcal{E}_1^-, \ldots, \mathcal{E}_n^-)$$

$$= \frac{\Pr(X|\mathcal{E}^+)\Pr(\mathcal{E}_1^-|X) \cdots \Pr(\mathcal{E}_n^-|X)}{\sum_{x \in \Omega_X} \Pr(X = x|\mathcal{E}^+)\Pr(\mathcal{E}_1^-|X = x) \cdots \Pr(\mathcal{E}_n^-|X = x)}$$

where $\Pr(X|\mathcal{E}^+)$ is derived from $\Pr(X|Z)$ and $\Pr(Z|\mathcal{E}^+)$,

$$\Pr(X|\mathcal{E}^+) = \sum_{z \in \Omega_Z} \Pr(X|Z = z)\Pr(Z = z|\mathcal{E}^+)$$

and $\Pr(\mathcal{E}_i^-|X)$ is obtained from the ith child of X. $\Pr(Z|\mathcal{E}^+)$ represents the causal support for X contributed by its single parent Z, and $\Pr(\mathcal{E}_i^-|X)$ represents the diagnostic support for X contributed by its ith child.

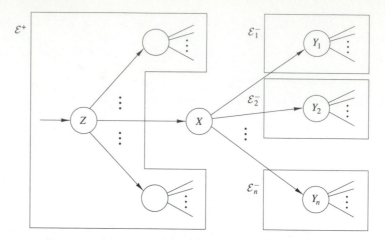

Figure 8.5 Partitioning evidence in a tree-structured network

Evidence propagates through the network by propagating causal support from parents to children and diagnostic support from children to parents, where causal and diagnostic support correspond to distributions. Each of the distributions, $\Pr(Z|\mathcal{E}^+)$ and $\Pr(\mathcal{E}_i^-|X)$, representing support involves only a single variable, Z or X, and so can be represented as a vector (list) of probabilities.

In propagating evidence by propagating causal and diagnostic support, the computations performed with respect to a given node are *local* in the sense that they depend only on support from the node's children and single parent. Each node keeps track of the most recent support received from its single parent and each of its n children. In the case of the network shown in Figure 8.5, the node X receives the support $\Pr(Z|\mathcal{E}^+)$ from its single parent and support $\Pr(\mathcal{E}_i^-|X)$ for $1 \le i \le n$ from its children.

The node corresponding to X recomputes the support for its single parent and children only in the event that it receives support from a parent or child differing from the last support received from that same parent or child. In tree-structured networks, propagation stops at nodes corresponding to evidence. The diagnostic support that X sends to its parent is

$$\Pr(\mathcal{E}_1^-, \ldots, \mathcal{E}_n^-|Z) = \sum_{x \in \Omega_X} \left(\Pr(X = x|Z) \prod_{i=1}^n \Pr(\mathcal{E}_i^-|X = x) \right)$$

and the causal support that X sends to its kth child is

$$\Pr(X|\mathcal{E}^+, \mathcal{E}_1^-, \ldots, \mathcal{E}_{k-1}^-, \mathcal{E}_{k+1}^-, \ldots, \mathcal{E}_n^-)$$

which can be computed by simply eliminating the $\Pr(\mathcal{E}_k^-|X)$ factor in the expression for $\Pr(X|\mathcal{E})$. Figure 8.6 depicts the causal and diagnostic support involving the node X required in computing the posterior distribution $\Pr(X|\mathcal{E})$.

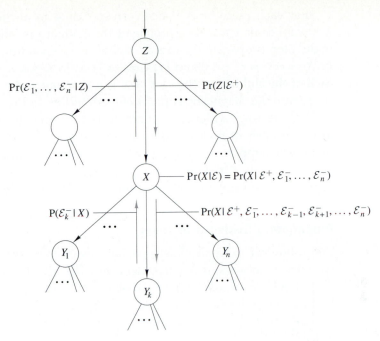

Figure 8.6 Causal and diagnostic support involving the node X required in computing the posterior distribution $\Pr(X|\mathcal{E})$. The node X exchanges support with all its children even though only the exchanges involving Y_k are shown.

We now describe an algorithm for computing $\Pr(X|\mathcal{E})$ for all nodes in a network. The algorithm depends on two recursive subroutines: one for propagating diagnostic support up from child to parent and one for propagating causal support down from parent to child.

The first subroutine propagates diagnostic support up from a child c to its parent p. If the diagnostic support from c is unchanged or p is an instantiated root node, then the subroutine terminates; otherwise, it updates the diagnostic support from c in p, propagates diagnostic support up to the parent of p, and propagates causal support down to the children of p except c.

The second subroutine propagates causal support down from a parent p to a child c. If the causal support from p is unchanged or c is an instantiated terminal node, then the subroutine terminates; otherwise, it updates the causal support from p in c and propagates causal support down to each child of c.

Before we can propagate evidence in a network, we have to initialize the causal and diagnostic support for all nodes. In the absence of any evidence, the diagnostic support for X from its ith child is $\Pr(\mathcal{E}_i^-|X = x) = \Pr(\{\}|X = x) = 1.0$ for all $x \in \Omega_X$. The initial causal support is determined by setting $\Pr(X|\mathcal{E}^+) = \Pr(X|\{\}) = \Pr(X)$ for the root node, computing the causal support for each of the children of the root node, and then propagating this causal support down from the root to the children.

For each piece of evidence corresponding to an instantiated variable $X = x$ for some $x \in \Omega_X$, we propagate the evidence as follows. If X is the root node, then propagate the causal support corresponding to $\Pr(X = x|\mathcal{E}^+) = \Pr(X = x|X = x) = 1.0$ and $\Pr(X \neq x|\mathcal{E}^+) = \Pr(X \neq x|X = x) = 0.0$ down to each of the children of the root. If X is a terminal node with parent Z, then propagate the diagnostic support corresponding to $\Pr(X = x|Z)$ up to Z.

Propagating evidence is guaranteed to terminate in time polynomial in the number of nodes in the network. If we take computing causal and diagnostic support at a node as unit cost, then the complexity of updating $\Pr(X|\mathcal{E})$ for all $X \in V$ in response to new evidence is $O(|V|)$. There is a complete Lisp implementation of the algorithm at the end of this chapter.

Propagating Evidence in Trees

The following example illustrates how evidence is propagated in a tree-structured network using the algorithm described earlier. We introduce three boolean-valued random variables: O, Sonya is in her Office; L, the Light is on in Sonya's office; and C, Sonya is logged on to her Computer. Suppose that we have the following distribution on Sonya being in her office:

	$\Pr(O)$
$O = $ True	0.4
$O = $ False	0.6

We also have a conditional probability distribution for the light in Sonya's office being on given information about Sonya being in her office. Note that Sonya is often in her office with the light off (she likes to work at her computer with the light off), and her light is seldom on if she is not in the office.

	$\Pr(L|O)$	
	$O = $ True	$O = $ False
$L = $ True	0.6	0.1
$L = $ False	0.4	0.9

Finally, we have a conditional probability distribution for Sonya being logged on to her computer given information about Sonya being in her office. Note that Sonya occasionally logs on to her computer from somewhere outside her office by using the telephone and a modem.

	Pr($C|O$)	
	O = True	O = False
C = True	0.8	0.3
C = False	0.2	0.7

The resulting tree-structured network is shown in Figure 8.7.

Now, suppose that Fred is working with Sonya on a research paper. Fred noticed a while ago that the light in Sonya's office was on, so he assumes that it is still on, L = True. Sonya has the latest draft of the paper, and Fred would like to look at it but he doesn't know which directory on Sonya's computer contains the paper. If Sonya is logged on to her computer, Fred can send her an electronic message asking for the directory containing the paper. Fred wishes to determine the conditional probability that Sonya is logged on to her computer given that the light in her office is on, Pr(C = True|L = True).

For this simple three-variable network, we can easily compute any probability involving $\{O, L, C\}$ using the joint distribution

$$\Pr(O, C, L) = \Pr(C|O)\,\Pr(L|O)\,\Pr(O)$$

For example, we can determine Pr(C = True) by marginalizing the joint distribution to $\{C\}$. The particular probability we are interested in is

$$\Pr(C = \text{True}|L = \text{True}) = \frac{\Pr(C = \text{True}, L = \text{True})}{\Pr(L = \text{True})}$$

which we can compute by marginalizing the joint distribution. Summing the numerator over Ω_O and the denominator over $\Omega_O \times \Omega_C$, we obtain the result Pr(C = True|L = True) = 0.7. Now we consider how to obtain this same value by propagating causal and diagnostic support.

Prior to obtaining any evidence, the diagnostic support for O from C and L is initialized to be Pr($\{\}|O = o) = 1.0$ for all $o \in \Omega_O$, where $\{\}$ represents that there is no evidence in the subtrees rooted at C and L. Causal support is initialized by propagating the prior causal support Pr(O) to C and L. On this initialization, Pr(C = True) = 0.5 since

$$\sum_{o \in \Omega_O} \Pr(C = \text{True}|O = o)\,\Pr(O = o) = (0.8 \times 0.4) + (0.3 \times 0.6) = 0.5$$

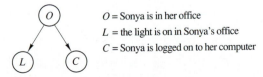

O = Sonya is in her office
L = the light is on in Sonya's office
C = Sonya is logged on to her computer

Figure 8.7 Example for illustrating how evidence is propagated in trees

After obtaining the evidence $L = \text{True}$, L sends the diagnostic support $\Pr(L = \text{True}|O)$ to O. In response, O updates the causal support for C as follows:

$$\Pr(O|L = \text{True}) = \frac{\Pr(O)\Pr(L = \text{True}|O)}{\sum_{o \in \Omega_O} \Pr(O = o)\Pr(L = \text{True}|O = o)}$$

No further propagation is required, and so we can determine the posterior distribution $\Pr(C|\mathcal{E}) = \Pr(C|L = \text{True})$ using the current causal and diagnostic support at C.

$$\Pr(C|L = \text{True}) = \Pr(C|O = \text{True})\Pr(O = \text{True}|L = \text{True}) +$$

$$\Pr(C|O = \text{False})\Pr(O = \text{False}|L = \text{True})$$

From this, we compute $\Pr(C = \text{True}|L = \text{True}) = 0.7$, the same value obtained directly from the joint distribution.

Exact Inference in Singly Connected Networks

The method just described can be extended to handle networks in which nodes have more than one parent, but there is exactly one undirected path between any two nodes. Such networks are called *singly connected* networks. The method of propagating causal and diagnostic support can be used to perform exact inference in singly connected networks.

The basic equations are similar to those for tree-structured networks with the exception that in singly connected networks we may have to handle evidence from more than one parent. Figure 8.8 shows how the evidence is partitioned in a singly connected network for a node X with m parents, $Z_1, \ldots, Z_m$, and n children, $Y_1, \ldots, Y_n$. In this case, the causal support for X originating in the subtrees associated with X's parents is described by

$$\Pr(X|\mathcal{E}^+) = \Pr(X|\mathcal{E}_1^+, \ldots, \mathcal{E}_m^+)$$

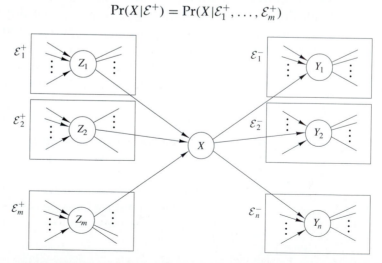

Figure 8.8　Partitioning evidence in a singly connected network

where

$$\Pr(X|\mathcal{E}_1^+, \ldots, \mathcal{E}_m^+) =$$

$$\sum_{z_1 \in \Omega_{Z_1}} \cdots \sum_{z_m \in \Omega_{Z_m}} \left(\Pr(X|Z_1 = z_1, \ldots, Z_m = z_m) \prod_{i=1}^{m} \Pr(Z_i = z_i|\mathcal{E}_i^+) \right)$$

Using $\Pr(X|\mathcal{E}^+)$ we can compute $\Pr(X|\mathcal{E})$ as before.

The diagnostic support that X sends to its jth parent is

$$\Pr(\mathcal{E}_1^-, \ldots, \mathcal{E}_n^-|Z_j) = \sum_{x \in \Omega_X} \left(\Pr(X = x|Z_j) \prod_{i=1}^{n} \Pr(\mathcal{E}_i^-|X = x) \right)$$

where $\Pr(X|Z_j)$ is obtained by marginalization as follows:

$$\Pr(X|Z_j) = \sum_{z_1 \in \Omega_{Z_1}} \cdots \sum_{z_{j-1} \in \Omega_{Z_{j-1}}} \sum_{z_{j+1} \in \Omega_{Z_{j+1}}} \cdots \sum_{z_m \in \Omega_{Z_m}}$$

$$\Pr(X|Z_1 = z_1, \ldots, Z_{j-1} = z_{j-1}, Z_j, Z_{j+1} = z_{j+1}, \ldots, Z_m = z_m)$$

The causal support that X sends to its children is similar to that sent in the case of tree-structured networks.

$$\Pr(X|\mathcal{E}_1^+, \ldots, \mathcal{E}_m^+, \mathcal{E}_1^-, \ldots, \mathcal{E}_{k-1}^-, \mathcal{E}_{k+1}^-, \ldots, \mathcal{E}_n^-)$$

In the case of tree-structured networks, we said that propagation stops at nodes corresponding to evidence. In the case of singly connected networks, propagation stops at root nodes corresponding to evidence, but the parents of a terminal node corresponding to evidence are conditionally dependent on one another by our path-based characterization of independence. By this same characterization, however, the parents of a terminal node that is not instantiated as evidence are independent of one another. From these dependency arguments, we see that propagation in a singly connected network stops at an uninstantiated terminal node and continues at an instantiated terminal node.

In order to propagate evidence in a singly connected network, we need only modify the subroutine that propagates causal support down from a parent p to a child c. If the causal support from p is unchanged or c is an uninstantiated terminal node, then the subroutine terminates; otherwise, it updates the causal support from p in c, propagates diagnostic support up to each parent of c except p, and propagates causal support down to each child of c. Using the path-based characterization of independence, you can devise a more general technique for determining whether or not to continue propagation in singly connected network.

For a singly connected network $G = (V, E)$, the method sketched computes the posterior distribution $\Pr(X|\mathcal{E})$ for all variables $X \in V$ in time proportional to

$$\sum_{X \in V} \left(\prod_{Y \in \text{Parents}(X)} |\Omega_Y| \right)$$

Note that this is exponential in the maximum number of parents for any given node but polynomial in the number of nodes, which is no worse than the storage required for the distributions used to quantify the network.

Approximate Inference Using Stochastic Simulation

As mentioned earlier, the general problem of computing the posterior distribution given some evidence is NP-hard. Complexity arises in what are called *multiply connected networks*, networks in which there are two or more undirected paths between some nodes.

The complexity results from keeping track of the impact of evidence. It is impossible to keep track of the impact of evidence in multiply connected networks using the sort of local computations employed in propagating causal and diagnostic support. For instance, in the multiply connected, four-node network shown on the left in Figure 8.9, evidence concerning A is propagated forward to B and C. When D wishes to combine the evidence from B and C, it cannot assume that the information stored at B and C is independent. In order for D to combine the information stored at B and C correctly, it must know exactly how B and C both depend on A, information that requires a more global view.

Evidence propagated in multiply connected networks tends to cycle. As an analogy, suppose you start a rumor that Fred is having a party. You are just guessing that Fred is having a party based on a fragment of a phone conversation that you overheard. You tell Sonya that Fred is having a party, Sonya tells someone else, and after a while Ralph comes up to you and tells you that Fred is having a party. Should you be more convinced that Fred is having a party based on Ralph's testimony? He may just be propagating your original rumor back to you. There is a way to avoid evidence cycling in multiply connected networks, but it has a computational cost.

In the network shown on the left in Figure 8.9, note that since $\Pr(B|C, A) = \Pr(B|A)$, we have $\Pr(B, C|A) = \Pr(B|A)\Pr(C|A)$. Using this result, we can create a new variable (B, C) with sample space $\Omega_B \times \Omega_C$ and convert the multiply connected network shown on the left in Figure 8.9 into the singly connected network shown on the right in Figure 8.9. In fact, we can convert any multiply connected network into a singly connected

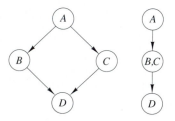

Figure 8.9   A simple multiply connected network (left) and its singly connected counterpart (right)

network using a strategy similar to the aforementioned. One problem with the technique for converting multiply connected networks into singly connected networks by combining variables is that the size of the sample spaces for the combined variables grows exponentially in the number of variables combined in a single node. It turns out that the problem of exactly calculating the posterior distributions in multiply connected networks is NP-hard; all known algorithms take time exponential in the size of the network for some networks.

In many cases, however, we do not require an exact calculation; an approximation will often suffice. In the following paragraphs, we consider approximation methods that work by generating assignments to random variables according to the distributions associated with the variables. These assignments are treated as though they come from data collected in the real world, and frequency estimates are computed to estimate the real probabilities. Algorithms that generate assignments in this way are called *stochastic simulation algorithms* or *Monte Carlo methods* and are important for practical applications of probabilistic networks.

Consider a very simple network G consisting of two nodes A and B corresponding to boolean-valued random variables with an edge from A to B. Suppose that we are given $Pr(B|A)$ and $Pr(A)$ and we want to approximate $Pr(B = \text{True})$ using stochastic simulation. We assume we have some means of generating random real numbers in the range from 0.0 to 1.0. We begin by setting $\#(B = \text{True})$ equal to 0; the $\#$ function will be used to keep track of the number of times the variable B is assigned True during simulation.

We then simulate G for m iterations, where each iteration proceeds as follows. First, generate two random numbers p and q. If p is less than $Pr(A = \text{True})$, then A is assigned True in this iteration, and if q is less than $Pr(B = \text{True}|A = \text{True})$, set $\#(B = \text{True})$ to $1 + \#(B = \text{True})$. If p is greater than or equal to $Pr(A = \text{True})$, then A is assigned False in this iteration, and if q is less than $Pr(B = \text{True}|A = \text{False})$, set $\#(B = \text{True})$ to $1 + \#(B = \text{True})$. After m iterations, the estimate of $Pr(B = \text{True})$ denoted $\hat{Pr}(B = \text{True})$ is $\frac{\#(B=\text{True})}{m}$. As $m \to \infty$, $\hat{Pr}(B = \text{True})$ is guaranteed to converge to $Pr(B = \text{True})$ with high probability.

If there are nodes assigned values by the evidence, then the corresponding variables are assigned the values indicated by the evidence in every iteration. For the case in which all nodes assigned values by the evidence have no parents, we can construct an algorithm that works for any network $G = (V, E)$. Let $\mathcal{E}$ represent all the evidence. If X is assigned a value by the evidence, then let $\mathcal{E}(X)$ be that value. The simulation algorithm for the case in which all nodes assigned values by the evidence have no parents is as follows:

1 For each $X \in V$, for each $x \in \Omega_X$, set $\#(X = x)$ to 0.

2 Perform the following simulation subroutine m times:

a) Set N to be a list of all the nodes in V.

b) For all X in N, if X is assigned a value by the evidence, then set X to be $\mathcal{E}(X)$; otherwise, set the value of X to be $\bot$. This step marks nodes so that no attempt is made to set the value of a node before setting the value of its parents.

c) If N is empty, then exit the subroutine.

d) Set X to be the first element in N.

e) If X is already assigned a value, then remove X from N and go to step 2c.

f) If X has one or more parents with value $\bot$, then remove X from N and go to step 2c. If X is removed at this step, then it must be the case that one or more of X's parents are still on the list N.

g) Let p be the probability that $X = \text{True}$ given the values assigned to the parents of X.

h) Let q be a random number between 0.0 and 1.0.

i) If $q < p$, then set X to be True and set $\#(X = \text{True})$ to be $1 + \#(X = \text{True})$; otherwise, set X to be False and set $\#(X = \text{False})$ to be $1 + \#(X = \text{False})$.

j) Remove X from N, add the children of X to N, and go to step 2c.

3 For each $X \in V$ that is not assigned a value by the evidence, for each $x \in \Omega_X$, set $\hat{\Pr}(X = x | \mathcal{E})$ to be $\frac{\#(X=x)}{m}$.

Each time the simulation subroutine is run it generates an assignment to all the variables in the network called a *sample*. Assuming that no variables assigned values by the evidence have parents, every sample generated by the simulation subroutine agrees with the values assigned by the evidence.

If the evidence contains variables with parents, then computing an approximation is more complicated. One way of dealing with such evidence is to use the simulation subroutine to generate a lot of samples ignoring the evidence and then just throw away all those samples that do not agree with the evidence. This simple approach is guaranteed to converge to the actual probabilities in the limit, but it will take a long time to converge in the case of rare evidence since most of the samples will be thrown away.

Likelihood-Weighting Algorithm

In the algorithm described, each sample is given the same weight, namely 1, and we use the ratio of the number of samples in which $X = x$ to the total number of samples as our approximation of $\Pr(X = x | \mathcal{E})$. In the following algorithm, if a sample does not agree with the evidence, instead of throwing it away we give the sample the following weight:

$$\prod_{X \in \mathcal{E}} \Pr(X = \mathcal{E}(X) | \text{Parents}(X) = \text{Sample}(\text{Parents}(X)))$$

where $\text{Sample}(\text{Parents}(X))$ indicates the values assigned by the sample to the parents of X. Though it may not be apparent that this is the right thing to do in general, consider the case in which all the evidence involves nodes in the network that have no children. In this case, the weight assigned to a given sample is the probability of the evidence given the sample.

An algorithm based on this weighting scheme called the *likelihood-weighting algorithm* is described next. Instead of keeping track of the number of times each variable is assigned a given variable ($\#(X = x)$), we keep track of a running score ($\text{Score}(X = x)$). Let $G = (V, E)$ be a probabilistic network, $\mathcal{E}$ an assignment to some subset of the variables in V, and $\text{Sample}(X)$ represent the value assigned to X by the current sample generated by the algorithm.

1 For each $X \in V$, for each $x \in \Omega_X$, set $\text{Score}(X = x)$ to 0.

2 Perform the following simulation subroutine m times:

  a) Set N to be a list of all the nodes in V.

  b) For all X in N, if X is assigned a value by the evidence, and X has no parents in G, then set X to be $\mathcal{E}(X)$; otherwise, set the value of X to be $\perp$.

  c) If N is empty, then perform the following steps:

   i. Let w be $\prod_{X \in \mathcal{E}} \Pr(X = \mathcal{E}(X)|\text{Parents}(X) = \text{Sample}(\text{Parents}(X)))$.

   ii. For each $X \in V$, set $\text{Score}(X = \text{Sample}(X))$ to be $w + \text{Score}(X = \text{Sample}(X))$.

   iii. Exit the subroutine.

  d) Set X to be the first element in N.

  e) If X is already assigned a value, then remove X from N, and go to step 2c.

  f) If X has one or more parents with value $\perp$, then remove X from N, and go to step 2c.

  g) Let p be the probability that $X = \text{True}$ given the values assigned to the parents of X.

  h) Let q be a random number between 0.0 and 1.0.

  i) If $q < p$, then set X to be True; otherwise, set X to be False.

  j) Remove X from N, add the children of X to N, and go to step 2c.

3 For each $X \in V$ that is not assigned a value by the evidence, for each $x \in \Omega_X$, set $\hat{\Pr}(X = x|\mathcal{E})$ to be $\text{Score}(X = x)/\sum_{x' \in \Omega_X} \text{Score}(X = x')$.

In computing $\hat{\Pr}(C = \text{True}|L = \text{True})$ for the network shown in Figure 8.7, after 100 samples, the absolute error corresponding to the absolute value of $0.7 - \hat{\Pr}(C = \text{True}|L = \text{True})$ is less than 0.1 and after 1,000 samples the absolute error is less than 0.01. There is a Lisp implementation of the likelihood-weighting algorithm at the end of this chapter. In the exercises, you are encouraged to experiment with this algorithm for a variety of networks.

In practice, likelihood weighting performs quite well even on multiply connected networks and networks with probabilities close to 1 or 0. Probabilities close to 1 or 0 often pose convergence problems for other stochastic simulation methods. Of course, given that computing the posterior distribution for an arbitrary network is NP-hard (even computing an approximation of the posterior distribution has been shown to be NP-hard), it is possible that there are networks arising in practice for which likelihood weighting will perform poorly. Quantifying the tradeoffs involved in using exact versus approximate methods is an area of active research.

Probabilistic Reasoning in Medicine

In a simplified view of medical diagnosis, the patient has a disease that is not known and a set of symptoms caused by the disease that are known. The task of diagnosis is to determine the most likely disease given evidence in the form of observed symptoms. To simplify the model describing how diseases cause symptoms, we assume that the patient has exactly one disease at a time and that symptoms are independent given a disease.

Figure 8.10 shows the structure of probabilistic network that captures this simplified model. In Figure 8.10, H represents the hypothesis concerning the patient's disease, and the F_i represent findings such as symptoms or lab results. The sample space for H is the set of all possible diseases. Note that, according to the structure of the network in Figure 8.10, $\Pr(F_i|F_j, H) = \Pr(F_i|H)$ for $i \neq j$. The most likely hypothesis given evidence $\mathcal{E}$ in the form of a set of findings is that $h \in \Omega_H$ maximizing $\Pr(H = h|\mathcal{E})$.

In practice, of course, neither the assumption of one disease at a time nor the assumption that symptoms are conditionally independent given diseases is justified. Even so, researchers were able to build systems based on this simple model that demonstrated impressive performance. For example, using a similar model, de Dombal and his colleagues built a system that averaged 90% correct diagnoses of acute abdominal pain for problems such as appendicitis. Expert physicians averaged 65% to 80% correct diagnoses on the same task.

The same basic network shown in Figure 8.10 can also be used for tasks involving the interpretation of sensor data for applications in robotics. For instance, the sample space for the hypothesis node might range over possible objects that a robot might observe (for example, chair, desk, file cabinet), and the findings might correspond to features of objects (for example, large

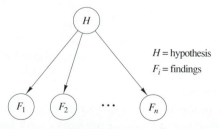

Figure 8.10   Simple tree-structured network for diagnostic reasoning

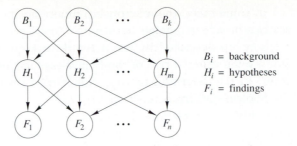

Figure 8.11   Multiply connected network for diagnostic reasoning

flat horizontal surface, rectangular shape). Quantifying the network can be handled by running a series of experiments with the robot.

The simple network of Figure 8.10 has limitations due in part to the fact that patients often have more than one problem and symptoms are rarely independent of one another given a disease. As methods for computing posterior distributions improve, researchers are willing to consider more complicated models. One of the most ambitious models so far is called the Quick Medical Reference (QMR) and is designed to serve as knowledge base and diagnostic aid for internal medicine.

The basic structure for the probabilistic network version of QMR is shown in Figure 8.11. In this network, the B_i represent background information such as the age or sex of the patient, the H_i represent diagnostic hypotheses such as the patient has an ulcer or a kidney infection, and the F_i represent findings such as symptoms or lab results. The QMR network encodes knowledge of almost 600 diseases and 4,000 findings. The network is multiply connected with approximately 40,000 edges linking nodes.

QMR serves to push the state of the art in representing uncertain knowledge. Due to the size and connectivity of the network, existing exact algorithms are rendered impractical. Researchers have met with some success in applying stochastic sampling methods to the network, but other practical limitations are involved in quantifying the network. For example, often a finding will be influenced by a number of hypotheses, as shown in Figure 8.12. If there are n hypotheses represented by n boolean-valued random variables, then there will be $0(2^{n+1})$ numbers required to quantify the relationship; generally, there will be many more as in the case of QMR where most random variables are not boolean valued.

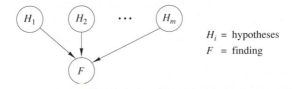

Figure 8.12   Network representing a noisy-OR dependency relationship

In some cases, the relationship involving the finding and the hypotheses can be approximated by a much simpler relationship. For instance, a relationship described by the network in Figure 8.12 might be characterized by the rule, "if one of the hypotheses is true, then the finding will be true." In the deterministic case, this sort of relationship is represented by the boolean-OR truth function: $(H_1 \vee H_2 \vee \cdots \vee H_n) \equiv F$. In the stochastic case, this sort of relationship can be represented by a *noisy-OR* relationship, in which each of the (boolean-valued) hypotheses is considered a separate possible cause for the finding. Each hypothesis is associated with a parameter representing the probability of the finding given that the hypothesis is true and all the alternative hypotheses are false. The resulting probabilistic relationship involves only n parameters

$$\{p_i = \Pr(F \mid H_i, \bar{H}_{j \neq i}) \mid 1 \leq i \leq n\}$$

where

$$\bar{H}_{j \neq i} \equiv (H_1 = \text{False}, H_2 = \text{False}, \ldots, H_{i-1} = \text{False}, H_{i+1} = \text{False}, \ldots, H_n = \text{False})$$

and is represented by the following conditional probability distribution:

$$\Pr(F \mid H_1, H_2, \ldots, H_n) = 1 - \prod_{i=1}^{n}(1 - p_i)$$

Noisy-OR relationships are used as a practical expedient to support inference involving complex probabilistic models. Given the computational complexity of reasoning in general networks, representational techniques like noisy-OR modeling and computational techniques like stochastic simulation are necessary in building practical systems that use uncertain knowledge.

8.4   Decision Theory

We motivated our investigation of uncertain reasoning by saying that we need to deal with uncertainty in decision making. So far we have talked about only prediction and diagnosis. Once you have computed the probability that there will be school today given that it is snowing, or the probability that you have a stomach virus given that you have a temperature of 98°, you still have to decide whether or not to attend classes or whether or not to call a doctor.

In Chapter 7, we discussed how to construct plans of action to achieve goals. Planning is one form of decision making. Planning in particular and decision making in general are complicated by uncertainty. How can you plan to go to the store if you do not know whether or not the car will start? How can you evaluate a plan that involves driving to the store given 0.2 probability that the car will not start? *Decision theory* is a discipline concerned with mathematical theories of decision making. In the following paragraphs, we sketch answers to these questions based on ideas from decision theory adapted for use in automated decision-making systems.

▲ AI IN PRACTICE

Troubleshooting Problems in Computer Networks

Researchers at Microsoft Corporation are investigating the use of probabilistic networks for diagnosing problems in computer hardware and software. For example, in a typical office environment, several personal computers are connected to a network so that they can share centralized services for storing files and printing documents. When a user sitting at a personal computer enters a command to print a document, the print command initiates a complex sequence of operations involving several machines and a variety of software. Probabilistic networks can be used to identify the hardware and software components responsible for a document failing to print and to suggest steps to take to correct the problem.

Microsoft researchers have developed a diagnostic tool employing a probabilistic network that determines likely problems encountered in printing in networked computer systems. The diagnostic tool considers evidence obtained from calls to the operating system (referred to as "sniffing") as well as inputs provided by the user. This evidence is used to update the probabilities of various problems, such as a loose cable or incompatible printing software. The diagnostic tool engages in a simple dialog with the user, asking questions to determine what is wrong and making recommendations regarding various fixes and repairs.

It can be very frustrating when something goes wrong in a networked computer system since many operations involve hardware and software components from several different suppliers. Diagnostic tools can increase customer satisfaction by allowing problems to be resolved quickly by the user, without the irritation of finding a local expert or trying to find the right supplier to call for customer support.

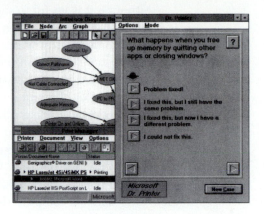

Preferences and Utilities

The consequences of decision making are represented by a set of *outcomes* Ω that represent all aspects of the world that the decision maker cares about. For example, in planning to go to the store, it may be that the only thing you care about is how long it takes. In this case, the set of outcomes can be represented by the set of positive real numbers. As decision makers, we generally have preferences over outcomes. For example, a 5-minute trip to the store is better than a 10-minute trip.

Although it is useful to say that we prefer one outcome over another, it is often more useful to assign to each outcome a number, called the *utility* of the outcome, that provides a measure of the value of a given outcome. A *utility function U* maps outcomes ($\omega \in \Omega$) to the real numbers.

Suppose that we are considering driving the car to the store. If the car starts, it will take 10 minutes to drive to the store. If the car does not start, it will take 5 minutes to determine that the car will not start and an additional 15 minutes to use the bus to get to the store for a total of 20 minutes. In this example, utility is inversely related to the time required to get to the store. How can we evaluate the plan that involves trying to drive to the store given that there is a 0.2 probability that the car will not start? The answer is that we compute the *expected utility* $E_\pi[U]$ associated with plan π defined as follows:

$$E_\pi[U] = \sum_{\omega \in \Omega} \Pr(\omega) U(\omega)$$

In the case of the driving plan, the expected utility (the additive inverse of the expected time to get to the store) is -12.

$$-20 \times 0.2 + -10 \times 0.8 = -12$$

Decision theory posits that a rational decision maker possessed of all the available facts and unlimited time for decision making will always choose the plan that maximizes expected value. In the preceding example, a rational decision maker would choose the driving plan ($E_\pi[U] = -12$) over the plan of immediately trying the bus ($E_{\pi'}[U] = -15$).

Decision Tree Methods

Now we sketch a general method for representing decision problems and computing a plan that maximizes expected utility. We represent a decision problem as a decision tree in which there are *decision nodes* and *chance nodes*. A decision node represents a choice of actions for the decision maker. A chance node represents uncertainty in the consequences of acting. A terminal leaf in a decision tree is a degenerate chance node corresponding to a particular outcome. In the following example, we demonstrate how to represent a decision problem in terms of a decision tree.

Gort is a delivery robot that works in the computer science department, which occupies the fourth and fifth floors of an office building. Gort is currently in Fred's office on the fifth floor and has been instructed to find Sonya and deliver a package. As far as Gort knows, Sonya is either in her office on the fifth floor or in the conference room on the fourth floor. The layout for the computer science department is shown in Figure 8.13.

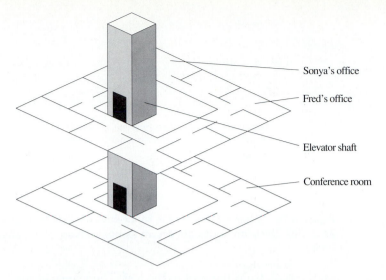

Figure 8.13   Office layout for the robot delivery example

Gort is considering two possible plans for finding Sonya: Go to Sonya's office, and if she is not there, then go to the conference room; or go to the conference room, and if Sonya is not there, go to her office. To go from Fred's office to Sonya's office requires negotiating one corridor and takes Gort 5 minutes. To go from Fred's office to the conference room requires using the elevator and takes Gort 10 minutes. To go from Sonya's office to the conference room or from the conference room to Sonya's office also requires using the elevator and takes Gort 10 minutes.

There are four possible outcomes: two for each of the two plans. These four possible outcomes are listed with the total time indicated in square brackets.

1. Gort checks the conference room first.

    a) Sonya is in her office. [20]
    b) Sonya is in the conference room. [10]

2. Gort checks Sonya's office first.

    a) Sonya is in her office. [5]
    b) Sonya is in the conference room. [15]

Utility is inversely proportional to the total time time spent in transit. Suppose that Sonya is either in her office or in the conference room and that as far as Gort is concerned there is a 0.5 chance of her being in either.

Figure 8.14 shows the decision tree for the robot delivery example. Decision nodes are indicated by squares and chance nodes by circles. Branches leading out of decision nodes are labeled by an action, and branches leading out of chance nodes are labeled by a proposition and the probability that it is true. The outcomes at leaves are determined actions and propositions

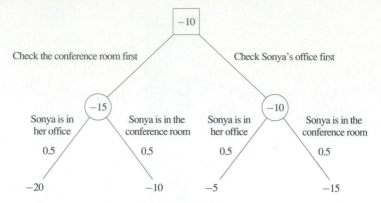

Figure 8.14   Decision tree for the robot delivery example. Chance nodes are drawn as circles. Decision nodes are drawn as boxes. Nodes are labeled by their expected utility.

on the path from the root to the leaf. The leaves of the tree are labeled with the utility of the corresponding outcome.

A decision tree represents all the information necessary to compute a plan that maximizes expected utility. In Figure 8.14, chance and decision nodes are labeled with their expected utility. At a branch node, the decision maker should choose the action maximizing expected utility. In Figure 8.14, decision branches with a short perpendicular line through them indicate actions that do not maximize expected utility. The decision tree in Figure 8.14 suggests that Gort should visit Sonya's office first. Note that, if the probability that Sonya is in her office is less than 0.25, Gort should visit the conference room first.

The following procedure describes how to assign each node in a decision tree an expected value:

1. Set N to be a list of all the terminal nodes.
2. If N is empty, then quit.
3. Set n to be some node in N, and remove n from N.
4. If n is a terminal node, then assign n the utility of the corresponding outcome.
5. If n has children that are not assigned expected values, then go to step 2.
6. If n is a chance node, then assign n to be the sum of expected values assigned to its children weighted by the probabilities on the branches linking n to its children.
7. If n is a decision node, then assign n the maximum of the expected values assigned to its children.
8. Add the single parent of n to N, and go to step 2.

Decision trees can be used to reason about more complicated types of decision making. In Chapter 4, we discussed conditional plans in which actions are determined by the results of observations. Gort's plans for delivering the package to Sonya are actually conditional plans in that Gort plans to go to one place to check for Sonya and then go to another place if Sonya is not there. In the next example, we consider how Gort can decide whether to perform an action whose purpose is to gather information.

Computing the Value of Information

Suppose that there is a computer network connection in Fred's office that Gort can plug into and determine whether or not Sonya is logged on to her computer. If Sonya is logged on to her computer, then she is in her office; otherwise, she is in the conference room. Suppose that this operation will take 2 minutes and will result in Gort knowing with certainty if Sonya is in her office or in the conference room. Prior to plugging into the network, Gort believes the probability that Sonya is logged on is 0.5. Should Gort use the network connection to check on Sonya?

If Gort knows Sonya's location, it will take him 5 minutes to deliver the package if she is in her office and 10 minutes if she is in the conference room. How much is the information regarding Sonya's location worth to Gort? The 0.5 probability that Sonya is logged on means that there is 0.5 probability that Sonya is in her office and a 0.5 probability that she is in the conference room. The *value of the information* is the difference between the expected value of proceeding with the information, $(-5 \times 0.5) + (-10 \times 0.5) = -7.5$, and proceeding without the information, -10 according to the decision tree in Figure 8.14, which is 2.5, the expected time saved by obtaining the information. The cost of acquiring the information is the 2 minutes of time required to use the network connection. Since the expected time saved is greater than the time spent in acquiring the information, Gort should use the network connection to check on Sonya.

Figure 8.15 (page 394) shows the decision tree for the extended robot delivery example. The left branch of the tree is not shown and is summarized by its expected utility. The left branch is identical to the decision tree in Figure 8.14. For all outcomes in the right branch of the tree, Gort takes 2 additional minutes to use the network connection to check on Sonya. The bottom layer of the tree is repetitious, and two of the nodes have been summarized by their expected utility. According to the decision tree of Figure 8.15, Gort should take the extra 2 minutes to use the network connection.

Decision trees for nontrivial applications can become quite large. If there are n actions, then the size of the tree could be as large as 2^n. Researchers have developed more compact means of representing decision problems. There are techniques that eliminate redundancy in decision trees. There is also a generalization of probabilistic networks that provides a compact representation for prediction, diagnosis, and decision making. Of course, it is not enough to represent problems compactly; we also want to generate decisions quickly. Not surprisingly, generating conditional plans with uncertain knowledge is computationally complex, leading researchers to consider a

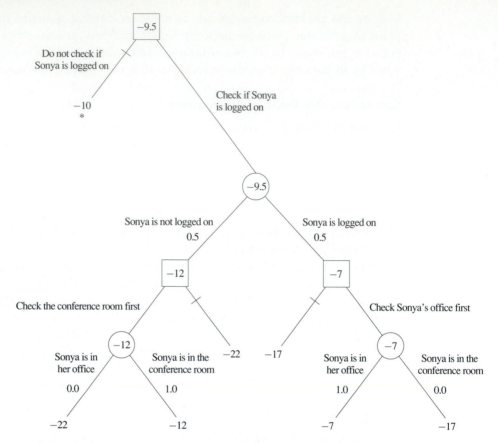

Figure 8.15 Decision tree for the extended robot delivery example in which the robot has to decide if it is worthwhile to gather additional information. Some portions of the complete tree are not shown to simplify the drawing. The node labeled with an asterisk (∗) corresponds to the root of the tree in Figure 8.14.

wide range of representational and computational techniques to expedite decision making.

Automated Decision Making in Medicine

A patient comes to see a physician complaining of chest pains. The patient is worried about the possibility of a heart attack. The patient has a history that indicates a high probability of coronary artery disease. The physician can perform a surgical operation called *coronary artery bypass surgery* that can greatly reduce the chances of a heart attack if the patient is suffering from coronary artery disease. The physician can also perform a test called an *angiogram* to determine the extent of coronary artery disease. However, this test is expensive and has some risk. Should the physician perform the bypass surgery immediately or perform the angiogram test and decide whether to operate on the basis of the test results? In some cases, it may even be better not to perform the test or the operation.

In this problem, utility is determined by the length and quality of the patient's life and the cost of medical treatment. We could represent this problem using a decision tree or an augmented probabilistic network, and build a system that takes as input information about a particular patient and provides as output a plan for treatment that maximizes expected utility. In fact, the technology and expertise now exist for building a wide variety of such decision-making aids, and several are currently under development.

However, building the system is a small part of the overall process of solving a problem in the real world, especially in the case of decision problems in medicine. Such systems must be subjected to careful testing in the field. The underlying probabilistic models must be scrutinized by experts, and the actual recommendations must be compared with the recommendations of experts. Even if the system performs the same or better than the leading experts, there are questions of liability.

As you might expect, relying on machines for such sensitive decisions is fraught with medical, social, and legal complications. If the patient dies and the decision regarding treatment is questioned, who is legally responsible? Is it the person who designed the system, the hospital that purchased the system, or the surgeon who operated on the recommendation of the system? In the coming years, we are likely to see an increased number of automated decision-making aids in hospitals and physicians' offices. Initially, they may be used as a check on recommendations made by a qualified physician. As the reliability of these systems improves, however, reliance on their recommendations will increase. You can expect some interesting court battles in the future regarding negligence in cases involving automated decision-making aids.

▼ Summary

Uncertainty arises in reasoning about complex processes that we do not understand very well. We care about uncertainty because it affects our ability to make good decisions. Uncertainty can be represented by disjunctions in logic or random variables in probability theory. In this chapter, we use probability theory to represent uncertainty.

A random variable can be used to represent a proposition being true or false, an event occurring or not, or generally, a variable taking on some value from a set of values. A probability is a number between 0 and 1 expressing the chance that a random variable takes on a particular value in a given situation. Probability theory allows us to make qualitative statements about how propositions and events relate to one another, and quantitative statements regarding such relations in terms of probabilities. In particular, probability theory allows us to specify that two variables are independent of one another (or not) given a set of other variables.

The joint distribution of a set of variables tells us everything that we could wish to know about the set of variables. Specifying a joint distribution in general can require a great deal of space to store all the probabilities. By exploiting independence involving sets of variables, we can often specify a joint distribution in a compact factored form. We can represent a joint distribution in its compact factored form as a network of nodes, corresponding to random variables, connected by arcs, indicating dependency between variables.

A basic operation on a probabilistic network is to compute the posterior distribution of one variable given some evidence in the form of assignments of values to other variables. In singly connected networks, computing the posterior distribution of one or all of the variables given some evidence is easy. In general networks, however, this operation is computationally complex. To avoid complexity in networks that are not singly connected, stochastic simulation algorithms compute approximations of the posterior distributions that converge to the actual distributions in the limit and often generate useful approximations in practice.

In decision theory, outcomes are associated with the consequences of actions. Utility functions map outcomes to numbers indicating their value for decision-making purposes. Decision theory posits that a rational decision maker given the necessary time and information will always choose to act so as to maximize expected utility. Decision trees are used to describe decision problems involving uncertainty. Given a decision tree representing a particular decision problem, it is possible to compute a plan that maximizes expected utility in accord with the axioms of decision theory.

Probability and decision theory have been applied to a wide variety of problems ranging from diagnosis and prediction involving equipment failures to diagnosis involving human diseases. In medicine, probabilistic networks have been used to diagnose sleep disorders, diseases of the lymph node, and neuromuscular disorders. Automated decision-making aids are likely to play an increasingly important role in hospitals and clinics as the technology improves and patients and physicians come to accept the idea of machines making decisions that directly affect human lives.

● Background

For a comprehensive introduction to the theory of probabilistic networks, see the text by Pearl [1988]. Neapolitan [1990] provides an overview of the theory and practice of using probability theory in expert systems. Our discussion of subjective probabilities borrows from Lindley [1980], which in turn borrows from Savage [1972]. For a treatment of issues in decision theory, see Howard and Matheson [1984] or Raiffa [1968]. Howard and Matheson [1984] describe a generalization of probabilistic networks called *influence diagrams* for decision making. For an introduction to decision analysis from the perspective of building expert systems, see Henrion et al. [1991].

For a discussion of how decision analysis is used to assess the costs and benefits of government policy, see Morgan [1993]. For instance, if we allow the utility companies to burn coal with a high sulphur content, we may benefit from lower electricity costs, but we may also pay higher costs for health care as a consequence of increased respiratory problems.

For descriptions of practical procedures for the exact computation of posterior distributions, see Pearl [1988], Lauritzen and Spiegelhalter [1988], and Jensen et al. [1990]. Cooper [1987] provides a proof that the exact computation of posterior distributions in arbitrary probabilistic networks is NP-hard, and Dagum and Luby [1993] show that even computing an approximation of the posterior distribution is NP-hard. There are a variety of methods for the approximate computation of posterior distributions [Pearl, 1988; Henrion, 1988]. The particular approximate computation method described in the Lisp Implementation section of this chapter is due to Peot and Shachter [1991].

A large number of applications involve manipulating uncertain knowledge. MYCIN [Shortliffe, 1976] was already mentioned in the context of expert systems in Chapter 3. Prospector [Duda et al., 1981] is a system for evaluating the prospects for finding mineral deposits in an area. De Dombal et al. [1974] describe the performance of a system for diagnosing abdominal pain. Szolovits [1982] provides a good overview of AI in medicine prior to 1982. PATHFINDER is a system used to diagnose diseases of the lymph node [Heckerman et al., 1992]. INTELLIPATH is a commercially available system based on the ideas in PATHFINDER that provides a practical decision aid for surgical pathologists. MUNIN [Andreassen et al., 1987] is a system designed to diagnose neuromuscular disorders. MUNIN uses a probabilistic network consisting of approximately 1,000 nodes; the network is multiply connected, and exact computation of the posterior distribution takes under 5 seconds.

Probabilistic techniques are also being used for applications in robotics and natural language processing. Charniak and Goldman [1991] describe how probabilistic networks can be used to recognize plans in understanding written text. Charniak [1993] provides an overview of how probabilistic methods can be used in natural language processing. Dean and Wellman [1991] describe how probabilistic networks can be used for automated planning in robotics.

■ Exercises

8.1 Using the definitions for probability distribution and conditional probability, answer the following questions:
   a) Given $\Pr(A = a)$, what can you say about $\Pr(A \neq a)$?
   b) Given $\Pr(A|B)$ and $\Pr(B)$, what can you say about $\Pr(A, B)$?
   c) Given that $\Pr(A = a|B = b) = 0$, what can you say about
   $\Pr(B = b|A = a)$?

8.2 Prove that the conditional independence relationship is symmetric. Specifically, use the definition of conditional probability to prove that $\Pr(A|B, C) = \Pr(A|C)$ implies $\Pr(B|A, C) = \Pr(B|C)$.

8.3 Consider a familiar probabilistic relationship that you can easily acquire data regarding. For example, you might consider the probability that the professor teaching a particular class is present in the classroom at the exact time when the class is scheduled to begin, or you might consider the probability that the cafeteria will serve a

particular dessert. First, estimate the corresponding distribution based on your expertise. Second, gather as much data as you can, and estimate the distribution using
the frequencies obtained from the data. In some cases, you may be able to get data
without observing it directly. For example, the cafeteria may keep past menus, or
the cafeteria manager may actually have a deterministic policy for serving desserts.
Finally, compare your subjective distribution and the distribution based on the data.
You might also consider getting together two or more people to quantify the same
relationship independently and afterward compare results.

8.4 In this chapter, we talk primarily about the probability of a random variable being
assigned a value in a particular situation. We also talk about conjunctions of such
assignments, but we do not explicitly mention disjunctions. Let $((X = x) \lor (Y = y))$
describe any situation in which either $X = x$ or $Y = y$. Use de Morgan's law,
$\neg(\neg p \land \neg q) \equiv (p \lor q)$, and the fact $\Pr(X = x) = 1 - \Pr(X \neq x)$, to prove the following equivalence:

$$\Pr(((X = x) \lor (Y = y))) = \Pr(X = x) + \Pr(Y = y) - \Pr(X = x, Y = y)$$

8.5 Construct a probabilistic network for a predictive or diagnostic task that you perform
regularly and consider yourself expert in. For example, suppose that you regularly
buy lunch at a specific sandwich shop. Some days the shop is crowded, and you have
to wait in line for a long time, and other days you are served immediately. Build a
network to predict whether there will be a long, medium, or short wait. Determine
the factors that influence the wait. For instance, weather, time of day, holidays, and
day of the week may all be factors. To quantify your network, generate numbers for
the probabilities based on your subjective estimates. See if the network makes predictions in accord with your expert judgement; if not, reconsider the subjective probabilities and the structure of the network looking for flaws in your predictive model.

8.6 Write a Lisp program to compute the posterior distribution for any variable in a
network given any evidence using marginalization and the joint distribution in the
factored form given in the text. Use the data structures provided in the Lisp Implementation section for representing probabilistic networks.

8.7 Consider the following probabilistic network shown in Figure 8.16, and answer the
following questions about conditional independence:
   a) Is A conditionally independent of B given $\{X_4, X_6\}$?
   b) Is A conditionally independent of B given $\{X_1, X_2, X_4\}$?
   c) Is A conditionally independent of B given $\{X_2, X_6\}$?

8.8 How many numbers are required to quantify the network shown in Figure 8.3 assuming that all the variables are boolean valued? How many numbers would be
required to specify the complete joint distribution if we could not make any independence assumptions regarding the variables?

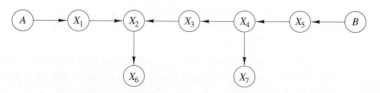

Figure 8.16   Probabilistic network for Exercise 8.7.

8.9 Modify the algorithm for exact inference in tree-structured networks listed in the Lisp Implementation to handle arbitrary singly connected networks. The evidence propagation routines are already correct for singly connected networks. All you need to do is modify the routines for computing causal and diagnostic support.

8.10 Building on your solution to Exercise 8.6, construct a set of three small networks, including a multiply connected network of the form shown in Figure 8.9. Compare the performance of the likelihood-weighting algorithm described in the Lisp Implementation with the exact computations performed using marginalization and the factored joint distribution.

▶ LISP IMPLEMENTATION

Inference in Probabilistic Networks

In this section, we provide two implementations for computing the posterior distributions of random variables in probabilistic networks given evidence in the form of instantiated variables. First, we implement an algorithm for exact computation of posterior distributions by propagating causal and diagnostic support. Second, we implement the likelihood-weighting algorithm for estimating posterior distributions using stochastic simulation. We begin with the data structures for representing probabilistic networks that will be used in both implementations.

In the following implementations, we assume that all random variables are boolean valued and that only boundary nodes are instantiated as evidence. The value of a random variable is represented as either 0 (False) or 1 (True). An instance of the abstract data type NODE consists of a name for the associated random variable, a list of parents, a list of children, causal and diagnostic support represented as association lists mapping contributing nodes to support vectors, a number representing the probability that the associated random variable is True given the evidence, a distribution providing the conditional probability of the random variable given its parents, a value used to keep track of the value assigned to evidence and for generating samples in stochastic simulation, and a pair of scores used in stochastic simulation to keep track of the accumulated scores for the values 0 and 1.

```
(defun make-NODE (name)
  (list name nil nil nil nil nil nil nil nil))
(defun NODE-name (n) (first n))
(defun NODE-parents (n) (second n))
(defun NODE-children (n) (third n))
(defun NODE-distribution (n) (fourth n))
(defun NODE-causal (n m) (second (assoc m (fifth n))))
(defun NODE-diagnostic (n m) (second (assoc m (sixth n))))
(defun NODE-probability (n) (seventh n))
(defun NODE-value (n) (eighth n))
(defun NODE-scores (n) (ninth n))
```

All the elements of a node are settable except its name, which is specified when an instance of type NODE is created. At the time that the parents and children are set, association lists are created that map nodes contributing support to causal and diagnostic support vectors represented by lists of numbers. Causal and diagnostic support vectors are accessed and set by specifying the node receiving the support and the node contributing the support.

```
(defun set-NODE-parents (n p)
  (setf (fifth n) (mapcar #'(lambda (m) (list m nil)) p))
  (setf (second n) p))
(defun set-NODE-children (n c)
  (setf (sixth n) (mapcar #'(lambda (m) (list m nil)) c))
  (setf (third n) c))
(defun set-NODE-distribution (n d) (setf (fourth n) d))
(defun set-NODE-causal (n m s)
  (setf (second (assoc m (fifth n))) s))
(defun set-NODE-diagnostic (n m s)
  (setf (second (assoc m (sixth n))) s))
(defun set-NODE-probability (n b) (setf (seventh n) b))
(defun set-NODE-value (n v) (setf (eighth n) v))
(defun set-NODE-scores (n s) (setf (ninth n) s))
```

A conditional distribution is represented as a nested list structure.[3] There is one level of nesting for each random variable. Note that the order of the nodes listed in parents must be consistent with the order in which the probabilities are listed in distribution. Since we represent truth values by 0 and 1, in the Lisp implementations of the examples in the text, the listing of probabilities is reversed from how it appears in the text. The following is a conditional distribution for a variable with two parents:

```
(setq distribution '(((0.2 0.8)
                      (0.3 0.7))
                     ((0.1 0.9)
                      (0.8 0.2))))
```

In the exact inference algorithm for tree-structured networks, we use the function nth to access probability distributions. This access method is relatively straightforward in tree-structured networks since each node has at most one parent, and each conditional distribution consists of a pair of pairs of numbers. For example, the following expression is used to refer to the probability $\Pr(L = \text{True}|O = \text{False})$ for the network shown in Figure 8.7 and the conditional probability distribution given in the text:

```
(nth 1 (nth 0 '((0.9 0.1)
                (0.4 0.6))))
```

Exact Inference in Tree-Structured Networks

Now we begin the details of our implementation of exact inference by propagating evidence in tree-structured networks. The following propagation code applies to any singly connected network. However, the code for computing causal and diagnostic support applies only to tree-structured networks. In Exercise 8.9, you are asked to modify this implementation to handle any singly connected network.

---

[3]We could have represented distributions using Common Lisp arrays. If you are interested in knowing more about Common Lisp, you might consult Steele [1990] and reimplement distributions using arrays.

The function up propagates diagnostic support up from a sender node to its parent recipient node. If the diagnostic support from the sender is unchanged or the recipient is an instantiated root node, then quit; otherwise, update the diagnostic support from the sender, propagate diagnostic support up to the parents, and propagate causal support down to each child except the sender.

```
(defun up (recipient sender support)
  ;; Don't propagate support if it has not changed
  ;; or the recipient is an instantiated root node.
  (if (or (equal support (NODE-diagnostic recipient sender))
          (and (null (NODE-parents recipient))
               (NODE-value recipient))) nil
    (progn
      (set-NODE-diagnostic recipient sender support)
      ;; Propagate support up to each parent.
      (mapc #'(lambda (n)
                (up n recipient (diagnostic n recipient)))
            (NODE-parents recipient))
      ;; Propagate support down to each child except the sender.
      (mapc #'(lambda (n)
                (down n recipient (causal n recipient)))
            (remove sender (NODE-children recipient))))))
```

The function down propagates causal support down from a sender node to its child recipient node. If the causal support from the sender is unchanged, then quit; otherwise, update the causal support from the sender. If the recipient is an uninstantiated terminal node, then quit; otherwise, propagate diagnostic support up to each parent except the sender, and propagate causal support down to each child. You might consider adding further optimizations to terminate unnecessary propagation, using the path-based characterization of independence given in the text as a justification.

```
(defun down (recipient sender support)
  (if (not (equal support (NODE-causal recipient sender)))
    (progn
      (set-NODE-causal recipient sender support)
      ;; Don't propagate through an uninstantiated terminal node.
      (if (or (NODE-children recipient) (NODE-value recipient))
        (progn
          ;; Propagate support up to each parent except the sender.
          (mapc #'(lambda (n)
                    (up n recipient (diagnostic n recipient)))
                (remove sender (NODE-parents recipient)))
          ;; Propagate support down to each child.
          (mapc #'(lambda (n)
                    (down n recipient (causal n recipient)))
                (NODE-children recipient)))))))
```

Compute the diagnostic support contributed by node n for recipient r. We do not have to know the recipient for the tree-structured case since the recipient is always the node's single parent. In the following function definition, the formal parameter for the recipient is not used. It is included, however, to facilitate Exercise 8.9, which involves modifying this implementation to handle arbitrary tree-structured networks.

```
(defun diagnostic (r n)
  ;; Handle the special case of terminal nodes.
  (if (null (NODE-children n))
    (if (null (NODE-value n)) '(1.0 1.0)
      (mapcar #'(lambda (v) (nth (NODE-value n)
                                 (nth v (NODE-distribution n))))
              '(0 1)))
    (mapcar #'(lambda (v)
                (sum #'(lambda (u)
                         (* (nth u (nth v (NODE-distribution n)))
                            (prod #'(lambda (m)
                                      (nth u (NODE-diagnostic n m)))
                                  (NODE-children n))))
                     '(0 1)))
            '(0 1))))
```

Compute the causal support contributed by node n for the recipient r. Here we deviate slightly from the treatment in the text; for a variable X with single parent Z, instead of returning $\Pr(Z|\mathcal{E}^+)$, the causal support for X given its single parent, we return $\Pr(X|\mathcal{E}^+)$ having factored out Z using $\Pr(X|Z)$ as described in the text. In the following implementation, when we refer to the causal support for X, we mean $\Pr(X|\mathcal{E}^+)$. As an exercise, you might consider reimplementing the data structures for probability distributions to make the following code reflect the mathematics more obviously. Such a reimplementation will make it much easier to complete Exercise 8.9.

```
(defun causal (r n)
  ;; Handle the special case of instantiated root nodes.
  (if (and (null (NODE-parents n)) (NODE-value n))
    (nth (NODE-value n) (NODE-distribution r))
    (let ((terms
            (mapcar #'(lambda (v)
                        (* (nth v (causal-support n))
                           (prod #'(lambda (m)
                                     (nth v (NODE-diagnostic n m)))
                                 (remove r (NODE-children n)))))
                    '(0 1))) normalizer distribution)
      (setq normalizer (apply #'+ terms))
      (setq distribution
        (mapcar #'(lambda (term) (/ term normalizer)) terms))
      (mapcar #'(lambda (v)
                  (sum #'(lambda (u)
                           (* (nth v (nth u (NODE-distribution r)))
                              (nth u distribution)))
                       '(0 1)))
              '(0 1)))))
```

Fetch the causal support for a node. In the case of singly connected networks, note that each node has at most one parent. The causal support for a root node corresponds to the prior distribution.

```
(defun causal-support (node)
  (if (NODE-parents node)
```

```
    (NODE-causal node (first (NODE-parents node)))
    ;; Handle the special case of root nodes.
    (NODE-distribution node)))
```

The description so far has focused on the details of propagating evidence and computing causal and diagnostic support. Now the description turns top down with a top-level function that computes the posterior distributions for all the nodes in tree-structured network given evidence in the form of a list of pairs assigning values to nodes.

```
(defun exact (nodes evidence)
  (initialize-priors nodes)
  (mapc #'propagate evidence)
  (mapc #'posterior nodes)
  (mapc #'display nodes))
```

Initialize the support for each node in the network by assigning diagnostic support to each node and then propagating the priors from the root nodes down. In the case of tree-structured networks, there will be exactly one root node.

```
(defun initialize-priors (nodes)
  ;; Initialize the diagnostic support for each node.
  (mapc #'(lambda (n)
            (mapc #'(lambda (m)
                      (set-NODE-diagnostic n m '(1.0 1.0)))
                  (NODE-children n)))
        nodes)
  ;; Eliminate any old evidence in the network.
  (mapc #'(lambda (n) (set-NODE-value n nil)) nodes)
  ;; Propagate priors down from the root nodes.
  (mapc #'(lambda (root)
            (mapc #'(lambda (n) (down n root (causal n root)))
                  (NODE-children root)))
        (mapcan #'(lambda (n) (if (NODE-parents n) nil (list n)))
                nodes)))
```

Propagate evidence down from root nodes and up from terminal nodes. Only boundary nodes are allowed to be assigned values as evidence.

```
(defun propagate (evidence)
  (let ((n (first evidence)) (v (second evidence)))
    (set-NODE-value n v)
    (cond ((null (NODE-parents n))
           ;; Propagate support down to each child.
           (mapc #'(lambda (m)
                     (down m n (causal m n)))
                 (NODE-children n)))
          ((null (NODE-children n))
           ;; Propagate support up to each parent.
           (mapc #'(lambda (m)
                     (up m n (diagnostic m n)))
                 (NODE-parents n)))
          (t (princ "Illegal evidence node!")))))
```

Compute the probability that the associated random variable is False given the evidence. The probability that the variable is True is just 1 minus the probability it is False. The function posterior is called when evidence propagation is complete.

```
(defun posterior (n)
  (if (NODE-value n)
    (if (eq (NODE-value n) 1)
      (set-NODE-probability n 0.0) (set-NODE-probability n 1.0))
    (let ((terms
            (mapcar #'(lambda (v)
                        (* (nth v (causal-support n))
                          (prod #'(lambda (m)
                                    (nth v (NODE-diagnostic n m)))
                            (NODE-children n))))
                  '(0 1))))
      (set-NODE-probability n (/ (first terms) (apply #'+ terms))))))
```

Display the name of the node and the posterior distribution of the corresponding variable given the evidence.

```
(defun display (node)
  (format t "Node ~A has distribution (~4,2F, ~4,2F).~%"
          (NODE-name node)
          (NODE-probability node)
          (- 1 (NODE-probability node))))
```

Here are some simple utility routines for taking sums and products.

```
(defun sum (function terms)
  (apply #'+ (mapcar function terms)))
(defun prod (function terms)
  (apply #'* (mapcar function terms)))
```

Approximate Inference Using Stochastic Simulation

Now we provide the functions implementing the likelihood-weighting algorithm. Since the likelihood-weighting algorithm applies to arbitrary networks and in particular to networks with nodes that have more than one parent, we will find it useful to define functions for handling conditional probability distributions with more than one conditioning variable.

Index takes the distribution of a node and a list of values. For our purposes, the length of the list of values should be equal to 1 plus the length of the parents of the node. Index returns the probability given by the distribution for the case in which the values in the list are assigned to the variables. The last value in the list is assigned to the variable corresponding to the node, and the earlier values in the list are in the order determined by the parents of the node.

```
(defun index (distribution values)
  (if (null values) distribution
    (index (nth (first values) distribution)
           (rest values))))
```

Compute the probability that the variable corresponding to a node takes on a particular value given the values of its parents. Note the way that mapcar is used to build a list of the values of the parents, and then the specified value is added to the end of this list using nconc.

```lisp
(defun probability (node value)
  (index (NODE-distribution node)
         (nconc (mapcar #'NODE-value (NODE-parents node))
                (list value))))
```

Estimate the posterior probabilities using likelihood weighting. Evidence is provided as a list of pairs assigning values to nodes.

```lisp
(defun approximate (nodes evidence iterations)
  (initialize-scores nodes)
  (dotimes (i iterations)
    (initialize-values nodes evidence)
    (simulate nodes)
    (update-scores nodes evidence))
  (set-evidence nodes evidence)
  (mapc #'estimate nodes)
  (mapc #'display nodes))
```

The scores for each node are initialized to a pair of 0's.

```lisp
(defun initialize-scores (nodes)
  (mapc #'(lambda (n) (set-NODE-scores n (list 0 0))) nodes))
```

The value of each node is initialized to nil unless the node is assigned a value by the evidence and the node has no parents. Evidence nodes with parents are assigned values by stochastic simulation, but the resulting assignments are weighted.

```lisp
(defun initialize-values (nodes evidence)
  (mapc #'(lambda (n)
            (let ((pair (assoc n evidence)))
              (if (and pair (null (NODE-parents n)))
                  (set-NODE-value n (second pair))
                  (set-NODE-value n nil))))
        nodes))
```

Clean up the values of nodes after stochastic simulation. Only evidence nodes should have values after the clean up.

```lisp
(defun set-evidence (nodes evidence)
  (mapc #'(lambda (n)
            ;; Exploits the fact that second of nil is nil.
            (set-NODE-value n (second (assoc n evidence))))
        nodes))
```

Update the scores of each node using likelihood weighting.

```lisp
(defun update-scores (nodes evidence)
  (let ((w (sample-weight evidence)))
    (mapc #'(lambda (n)
              (let ((s (NODE-scores n)))
                (if (= 0 (NODE-value n))
                    (setf (first s) (+ w (first s)))
                    (setf (second s) (+ w (second s))))))
          nodes)))
```

Compute the likelihood weighting assigned to the evidence given the sample.

```
(defun sample-weight (evidence)
  (apply #'* (mapcar #'(lambda (assignment)
                         (apply #'probability assignment))
                    evidence)))
```

Simulate by propagating values forward through the network.

```
(defun simulate (nodes)
  (cond ((null nodes) nil)
        ;; Ignore a node if it already has a value or
        ;; if it has one or more parents without values.
        ((or (NODE-value (first nodes))
             (some #'(lambda (n) (null (NODE-value n)))
                   (NODE-parents (first nodes))))
         (simulate (rest nodes)))
        (t (let ((number (random 1.0)) (n (first nodes)))
             (if (< number (probability n 0))
               (set-NODE-value n 0) (set-NODE-value n 1))
             (simulate (append (rest nodes)
                               (NODE-children n)))))))
```

Estimate the posterior probability for the case in which the node is assigned False. The probability for the case in which the node is assigned True is just 1 minus the probability it is False.

```
(defun estimate (n)
  (if (NODE-value n)
    ;; No sense in estimating evidence nodes.
    (if (eq (NODE-value n) 1)
      (set-NODE-probability n 0.0) (set-NODE-probability n 1.0))
    (set-NODE-probability n (/ (first (NODE-scores n))
                              (+ (first (NODE-scores n))
                                 (second (NODE-scores n)))))))
```

Lisp code for a network consisting of a subset of the nodes shown in Figure 8.3.

```
(let ((H (make-NODE 'H))
      (B (make-NODE 'B))
      (L (make-NODE 'L)) nodes evidence)
  (set-NODE-children H (list L))
  (set-NODE-children B (list L))
  (set-NODE-parents L (list H B))
  (set-NODE-distribution H '(0.7 0.3))
  (set-NODE-distribution B '(0.2 0.8))
  (set-NODE-distribution L '(((0.2 0.8)
                              (0.3 0.7))
                             ((0.1 0.9)
                              (0.8 0.2))))
  (setq nodes (list H L B)
        evidence (list (list H 0)))
  (defun buggy-approximate (n) (approximate nodes evidence n)))
```

Lisp code for the network shown in Figure 8.7.

```lisp
(let ((O (make-NODE 'O))
      (C (make-NODE 'C))
      (L (make-NODE 'L)) nodes evidence)
  (set-NODE-children O (list C L))
  (set-NODE-parents C (list O))
  (set-NODE-parents L (list O))
  (set-NODE-distribution O '(0.6 0.4))
  (set-NODE-distribution C '((0.7 0.3)
                             (0.2 0.8)))
  (set-NODE-distribution L '((0.9 0.1)
                             (0.4 0.6)))
  (setq nodes (list O C L)
        evidence (list (list L 1)))
  (defun sonya-exact () (exact nodes evidence))
  (defun sonya-approximate (n) (approximate nodes evidence n)))
```

CHAPTER 9

IMAGE UNDERSTANDING

The intelligent robots and softbots of the future will be designed with artificial intelligence principles. Such systems will reason about the world and take appropriate actions by manipulating knowledge stored in internal representations. For a robot to be truly autonomous, it must sense the world directly. No humans can intervene to make suggestions. Biological systems have evolved remarkable senses, some of which can be reproduced with technology; vision, hearing, tactile sense, and sonar are animal senses that AI research has dealt with. The field of vision, also known as *computational perception*, a diverse and interdisciplinary body of knowledge and techniques, has as its goal to understand the principles behind the processes that interpret perceptual signals provided by various sensors.

This chapter concentrates on visual sensors and images. Before describing a set of principles necessary for the design of systems with vision, we take a short detour to explain in general terms parts of the human visual system that we understand. In order to present a complete theory for vision, we need to describe the interface of vision with planning, learning, and reasoning. This is an impossible task in the limits of this textbook. For this reason, we consider vision as the set of processes that recover descriptions of the world from images. Having such descriptions would allow us to design various specific systems, ranging from autonomous vehicles to workstations for radiologists. If images are to be used to extract information about the world, we must understand how they are made. Thus, we begin with the geometric and photometric aspects of image formation, and later we concentrate on developing constraints that relate information about the world with image cues. Finally, we discuss some applications. In particular, we describe computer-guided vehicles and systems that recognize classes of objects.

9.1 Sensors and Images

Sensors are special machines, devices that measure particular aspects of space-time in their environment. They belong to two general categories: *passive* and *active* sensors. Active sensors disturb the environment and measure the extent of the disturbance. Bats use active acoustic sensors to avoid obstacles and catch prey; they disturb the environment by emitting high-pitched sounds. Passive sensors measure the environment without interfering. Visual sensors, biological eyes, or electromechanical cameras passively record image sequences. These sensors record the amount of light in terms of the number of photons with a wavelength within a specified range that enter the sensor.

Digital Images

Most cameras record light visible to humans and map a view to a grid of cells on a Cartesian plane, which is called the *image plane*. Figure 9.1a shows an image, and Figure 9.1b shows the representation of a part of it inside a digital computer. Such a representation is called a *digital image* and is an array of integers representing how bright the image is. This quantity is called *image irradiance*. The creation of digital images involves the problems of *sampling* and *quantization*. Sampling involves selecting a discrete set of locations on the plane of the image for measuring light. Quantization involves assigning to each selected location a discrete integer label that is representative of the range within which the irradiance lies. Figure 9.2 (page 412) illustrates the sampling and quantization of a cone.

Each quantized sample in a digital image is called a *pixel* (picture element). This term is also used for denoting distance on the image plane. The integer value of a pixel at an image location is called *image intensity* or *gray level*. Although a digital image is just an array of numbers, it is more conveniently displayed as an array of gray areas. Each cell in the array represents an individual pixel with respect to both location and brightness.

Noise in Image Processing

Before the images can be understood by computer, they have to be *sensed*. The optical image needs to be converted into an electrical image. This process, along with the processes of sampling and quantization, alters the original image in various ways, or as we say, they introduce *noise*. Noise can

a.

183	196	199	200	214	215	118	226	98	104
208	194	200	226	157	88	76	157	0	43
209	214	199	182	91	71	59	173	217	177
214	214	175	150	88	71	59	138	217	214
193	215	208	199	113	60	55	52	244	199
138	105	137	152	215	109	71	44	70	168
137	120	105	102	104	157	244	137	75	68
140	123	120	123	105	105	120	137	244	199
138	118	139	109	108	138	138	138	138	168
109	114	121	121	138	119	119	138	138	152

b.

Figure 9.1 In a digital image, the image intensities (or brightnesses) are discretely sampled, and the sampled values are quantized to a discrete set of values, usually represented by integers. The elements of the resulting array of numbers are called pixels, and their values are called gray levels. In the figure, the array of numbers represents the array of intensities in the boxed portion of Sarah Bernhardt's eye. (Reproduced from Aloimonos and Rosenfeld [1991] ©1991 AAAS. Photo courtesy of Bettmann Archive.)

make subsequent processing very hard. See Figures 9.3a and 9.3b (page 412) for an example of an image corrupted by noise.

Different sensors provide different types of images. Color Plate 1a shows an image taken by a depth sensor, and Color Plate 2 shows images taken by an infrared sensor. The algorithms and representations needed for the interpretation of an image depend primarily on the type of image and on the sensor used. In this chapter, we concentrate on the computational aspects underlying the process of vision, our most powerful sense.

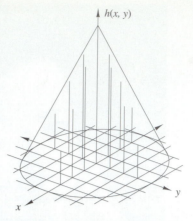

Figure 9.2   The process of sampling discretizes the domain of a function by assigning to each discrete point the value of the function there. In the figure, the *xy* plane over which a cone $h(x, y)$ is defined is discretized by allowing only integer coordinates. Quantization discretizes the range of a function, mapping the value of the function at any point onto a member of a discrete set. In the figure, the magnitude of $h(x, y)$ is discretized by rounding the value down to an integer value. (Reproduced from *A Guided Tour of Computer Vision* by written permission from Addison-Wesley Publishing Company.)

a.   b.

Figure 9.3   (a) A noiseless image of an office space showing portions of the walls, floor, and ceiling, along with part of a chair and a few branches of a large indoor plant. (b) The same image corrupted by noise.

9.2   Computer Vision

Computer vision is the field of AI that describes the automatic understanding of the structure and properties of a possibly changing three-dimensional world from its two-dimensional images. The images are usually sampled in space and time, and the magnitudes of these samples quantized. Thus, they can be easily processed by a digital computer. The images are taken by a

Figure 9.4   An active vision system, usually called head-eye system, constructed by Transitions Research Corporation. The system is similar to a human head with eyes. The cameras are attached to motors, and they can rotate as the human eyes do. Both eyes are resting on a platform (neck) that can rotate around the vertical and horizontal axes. The motors of the system are controlled by a computer that has access to the camera images in real time. This means that the delay between the time that the images are sensed and processed so that an action can be taken is negligible. (Courtesy of Transitions Research Corporation.)

single or multiple cameras that are either static or changing. Mobility, verging of the eyes, focusing, and accommodation of the lens of the camera are some of the ways in which a vision system could be changing. When vision systems are capable of controlling the parameters of their visual apparatus, they are called *active vision* systems[1] (see Figure 9.4 for an example).

Understanding Images

What does it mean to "understand" a three-dimensional (3D) scene from its images? Understanding has puzzled philosophers for thousands of years. Understanding a 3D scene from images has puzzled scientists for decades. There is a wide diversity of biological vision systems; not all organisms see things in a way humans do. Every organism has its own perceptual world, constrained by its sensory capabilities, memory, and computational capacity. There exist insects with eight simple eyes, arthropods with movable eyes, reptiles with infrared sensors, mammals possessing more than one fovea in each eye. Each biological vision system derives from images information about the objective reality. This information is not complete but

---

[1]Not to be confused with active sensing, where the sensor emits a wave.

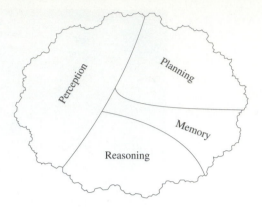

Figure 9.5 A modular view of an intelligent system. The system's intelligence consists of various cognitive modalities: perception, reasoning, memory, and planning. Perception can be seen as a mechanical act whose goal is to create a description of the scene that is used by the rest of the modules in order to successfully perform various actions, make appropriate decisions, and so on.

partial. It is, however, sufficient for allowing a system to accomplish goals and perform tasks needed for survival.

A theoretical approach to studying vision regards it as the process of recovering the three-dimensional world from its images. Figure 9.5 describes this process in detail. Figure 9.5 shows an intelligent system possessing vision in a modular manner, where the modules correspond to different cognitive modalities. The vision module builds a central database of information about the structure of the world and its properties. This database serves planning, reasoning, and memory and allows the system to navigate and recognize objects in its environment (see the AI in Practice box entitled "Object Recognition Systems" in the Color Plate section).

Vision Versus Thought

We separate here seeing and thinking (Nalwa 1993). Kanizsa [1979] argues that visual perception is not an integral part of what we call intelligence. For example, although we can conceive the fragments in Figure 9.6a to form a cube, we do not see one right away. However, the introduction of three opaque stripes in Figure 9.6b changes our perception. The cube becomes perceptually apparent. Researchers have argued that "seeing" is just a mechanical act in that it does not originate anything. It simply infers the state of the world to the extent allowed by the sensed data. Whether this is true in biological systems is of no importance here. This chapter is devoted to the *theoretical* questions related to vision. We explore the question *what could be* inferred about the 3D world from its images. See Nalwa [1993] for a good discussion on this topic.

Why doesn't computer vision just emulate the human visual system? The subject of research in neurophysiology, psychology, and psychophysics

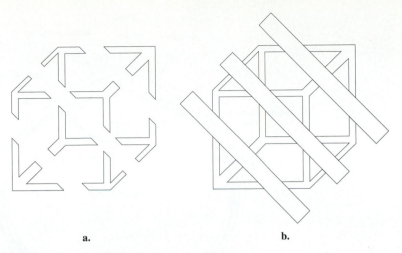

a.   b.

Figure 9.6 An illusion. (Reproduced from *Organization in Vision* by written permission from Greenwood Publishing Group, Inc.)

is about vision in humans and animals. Little is known about human vision beyond the eye. Moreover, a robot may need visual capabilities different from the ones of humans in order to best execute its intentions or goals. Nevertheless, the study of human vision is exciting in its own right and provides insight into our efforts in image understanding.

9.3 Human Vision

Neither objects nor properties of objects such as shape and color exist inside our brains as such. When we see, computations are performed inside our heads that generate hypotheses about objects and their properties. The human eye is an optical instrument. Figure 9.7 (page 416) shows a cross-section of the human eye viewed from above.

Transferring Information from the Eye to the Brain

Sidestepping the details of how the image is formed, we concentrate on the retina. The *retina* is a complex membrane with many photoreceptors that produce electrical nervous signals when they are stimulated by light. These signals are transmitted to the brain via the optic nerve where appropriate processing produces the experience of vision. Two kinds of photoreceptors exist in the retina; they are named *rods* and *cones* after their shapes.

These receptors are sensitive to only a small part of the electromagnetic spectrum. The rods exhibit similar variation in spectral sensitivity as a function of wavelength. The cones, however, appear in three kinds: those that are most sensitive to the red, green, and blue parts of the visible spectrum. The cones give us color vision, and the rods provide night vision capabilities because of their ability to detect light at much lower intensity

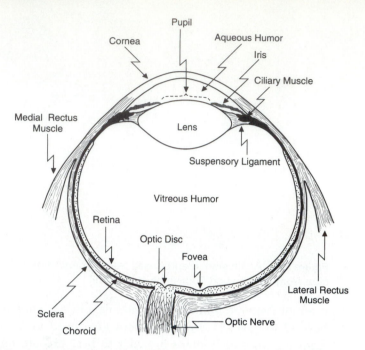

Figure 9.7   A simplified pictorial description of a horizontal cross-section of a human eye, seen from above. Light goes through the cornea, the aqueous humor, the lens, and the vitreous humor to finally form an image on the retina. The fovea is a small part of the retina with a very high concentration of photoreceptors. The optic nerve leaves the retina from the optic disc. The ciliary muscle controls the curvature of the lens, and the iris is a membrane that controls the pupil, the aperture in the iris from which light enters the eye. For a detailed analysis of the physiology of the eye, see Rodieck [1973]. (Reproduced from *A Guided Tour of Computer Vision* by written permission from Addison-Wesley Publishing Company.)

levels than cones [Cornsweet, 1970]. Figure 9.8 gives a simplified schematic description of the major visual pathways from the eyes to the brain. Light striking each retina is encoded into nerve impulses and transmitted to the brain via the optic nerve.

The left part of the visual field, which is formed on the right half of each retina, is transmitted to the right half of the brain, and the right to the left. There, computations on the data make us "see." The cross-over of nerve fibers occurs at the optic chiasma, from where the fibers proceed to the lateral geniculate nuclei via the optic tracts. From here, the signals are transmitted to the striate cortex of the brain. At the center of each retina is an area called the *fovea* where the concentration of photoreceptors is very high, one order of magnitude more than the concentration of the photoreceptors in the periphery. The fovea has only cones, whereas much of the rest of the retina has a much higher concentration of rods than cones. As a result, our day vision is sharp and colored, and our night vision blurred and colorless.

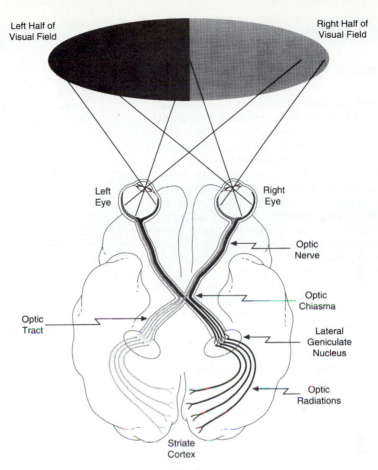

Figure 9.8 A simplified schematic description of the major visual pathways from the eyes to the brain. The cross-over of the optic nerve fibers takes place at the optic chiasma. From there, the nerve fibers proceed to the lateral geniculate nuclei (LGN) via the optic tracts. From the LGN, nerve impulses are transmitted to the striate cortex of the brain via the optic radiations. In comparison to what we know about the human eye, little is known about the function of the parts of the brain dedicated to vision. See Hubel [1988] for a detailed analysis. (Reproduced from *A Guided Tour of Computer Vision* by written permission from Addison-Wesley Publishing Company.)

Compressing Visual Information

An important point to note about human visual machinery is that though the total number of cones is about 6 million and the rods 120 million, the total number of nerve fibers leaving the eye for transferring the image to the brain is of the order of 1 million. Thus, it seems that at least one function of the retinal nerve cells between the photoreceptors and the optic nerve fibers is to compress the information contained in the light falling on the retina. Understanding human vision amounts to discovering the algorithms and representations used by the brain for analyzing the images transferred to the

▲ AI IN PRACTICE

Document Understanding Systems

Advanced document understanding systems have the ability to comprehend a document by capturing and analyzing symbolic and semantic aspects of it. An important problem is the one of page decomposition. One recently addressed component of the page decomposition process involves identifying device, style, and attribute parameters of document components. The goal of page decomposition is to divide the page into homogeneous regions and label them accordingly. There clearly exists a classification hierarchy that extends from high-level text/graphics/halftone discrimination, in the case of text, to a distinction between machine and hand generation to identification of font, style, size, and similar attributes.

Although systems typically rely on spatial proximity for all but the highest level classification, a finer level of discrimination is desired. This type of information is essential not only to preserve stylistic information in the electronic document, but also to allow the system to use specialized recognition algorithms and infer information about the functional aspects of the page.

The figure shows how the identification of bold and italic regions can be used to separate functionally different components in a simple page that are similar with respect to proximity.

Temporal Clues in Handwriting

David S. Doermann
Azriel Rosenfeld
Computer Vision Laboratory
University of Maryland
College Park, MD 20742-3411

Abstract

Handwritten character recognition is typically classified as on-line or off-line depending on the nature of the input data. On-line data consists of a temporal sequence of instrument positions while off-line data is in the form of a 2D image of the writing sample.

On-line recognition techniques have been relatively successful but have the disadvantage of requiring the data to be gathered during the writing process. Although the temporal information from on-line data is not directly available from static images of handwriting, the experience of forensic document examiners assures us that such information can be successfully recovered. This paper presents work on the extraction of temporal information from static images of handwriting and its implications for character recognition.

1 Introduction

The automated interpretation of handwritten text has long been desired as an alternative to traditional data input. Although there have been promising advances in on-line recognition, off-line recognition remains an open problem.

the on-line data onto the writing surface, but as we will see, there is a great deal of additional information contained in the image itself. For off-line recognition, we are faced with a almost infinite shape space in addition to complex image processing tasks.

In this paper we will outline the potential value of using on-line techniques for off-line recognition by converting the off-line representation to one which contains, at least qualitatively, a temporal component.

2 Handwritten Documents

Although there has been a great deal of success in processing machine produced documents, the complexity of the problems associated with hand-produced documents suggests that traditional shape recognition techniques are not sufficient for off-line handwritten data. Alternative approaches such as the use of temporal information should be explored.

The advantage of on-line information is that we are processing a pair of one-dimensional signals. Small perturbations in position may cause significant changes in the processing of a 2D image, but have a relatively small effect on the 1D signals. For this reason, we find that intra-writer variation tends to be

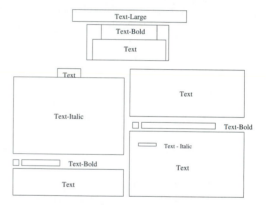

Courtesy of David Doermann, University of Maryland

cortex in order to acquire information necessary for accomplishing a variety of tasks. Our understanding of these processes is very far from complete. For this reason and because we do not study vision here in the context of a larger system that performs a task, we consider vision as a *recovery problem*.

9.4   Vision as a Recovery Problem

Two classes of problems are commonly held to be touchstones for practical vision systems: successful navigation in a complex environment using visual information and recognition of classes of common objects (such as people or trees) in a complex scene. Most research in computer vision addresses one of these goals. If both problems were solved, automatic systems would have many of the capabilities of the human visual system. Unfortunately, constructing such systems presents great difficulties. These difficulties were realized after the failure of early attempts in the 1960s and early 1970s to build entire vision systems that exhibited some vertical integration and used knowledge at all levels, including domain-specific information. "In order to complete the construction of such systems, it is almost inevitable that corners be cut and many overly simplified assumptions be made" (Brady [1982]). This results in a system capable of carrying out a limited number of tasks but not enhancing our general understanding of vision. At about that time, the recovery school of thought started to develop through the work of Marr [1982] and his colleagues.

Recovery means to derive, from one or more images of a scene, an accurate three-dimensional description of the objects in the scene and quantitatively recover their properties, or at least those properties relevant to a given task. If we can recover the properties of an object, we can use them to recognize the object. Thus, recovery in computer vision emphasizes the study of visual abilities, independently of a task.

Even if we consider that the solution to vision problems lies in the recovery of the scene, it is not obvious how to proceed. Luckily, there is a standard way to design large, complex information systems, as research in computational fields has shown [Feldman, 1985]. We divide the system into functional components or subsystems. We analyze these subsystems, choose the representations of information that they use, and the language of communication among them. The subsystems are then tested individually, in pairs, and all together.

We can use this approach in building a visual system, using functionally independent subsystems that recover specific properties of the world from images. We call these subsystems modules. Visual recovery research is devoted to the study of such modules and their integration. There is considerable evidence for the existence of such modules in the human visual system. One source of such evidence is the study of patients with visual disabilities that result from brain lesions [Farah, 1990].

Perceptual processes (processes underlying visual abilities) must be understood at three levels [Marr, 1982].

1. The level of *computational theory*. We must develop, through rigorous mathematical treatment, the relationship between the quantity to be computed and the input in the form of images.
2. The level of *algorithms* and *data structures*. After the computational theory has been completed, we must design algorithms and data structures that, when applied to the input, will output the desired quantity.
3. The level of *implementation*. After the two previous levels have been developed, we must implement the algorithm in hardware or software.

If these three levels are fully understood, we can say that we understand the perceptual process.

What to Recover

What should we attempt to recover from images in order to be able to accomplish visual tasks? The answer defines the nature of the theory of computer vision, that is, image understanding techniques not directed toward specific applications.

It is clear, that one quantity we should be able to recover from images is the shape of objects. A large amount of visual recovery research is devoted to determining the shapes of imaged objects from image cues, such as shading, texture, contour, multiple views, and motion (Color Plate 3). If we can recover the geometry of the environment, we can perform navigational tasks such as avoiding obstacles or finding routes. In addition, if we can find an appropriate representation, we can use shape information for object recognition.

Shape is not the only thing we may want to recover; for example, if we can recover the three-dimensional velocity of a moving object, we can catch it, avoid it, track it. We may want to determine the velocity with which every image point moves, in the case of images obtained by a moving sensor. We may also want to recover the colors of objects; to recover the spatial position and orientation of a known object; to determine the discontinuities of the image intensity, the image contours across which the intensity changes abruptly (Figure 9.9a); to determine a segmentation of the image that corresponds to some well-defined segmentation of the scene (Figure 9.9c); or we may want to recover or restore the ideal image from the actual image, which is corrupted by noise.

Geometric Aspects of Image Formation

Before we discuss visual recovery problems we need to understand the process of image formation. Two issues are involved: the geometric aspect of image formation, where the image of a point will appear; and the photometric aspect, how bright the image of a point will be.

The simplest imaging device is a *pinhole camera* like the one in Figure 9.10 (page 422). It possesses an infinitesimally small aperture, or pinhole, through which light enters the camera and forms an image.

From a geometrical point of view, the image is formed by light rays traveling in straight lines from the object through the aperture to the image plane. This geometry is known as *perspective projection*, and it is illustrated in Figure 9.11 (page 422).

Perspective Projection

Consider, for simplicity, the pinhole to be behind the image plane, as shown in Figure 9.12 (page 423); the geometry remains unchanged. We define the optical axis to be the perpendicular from the pinhole to the image plane. We introduce a Cartesian coordinate system with the origin at the pinhole

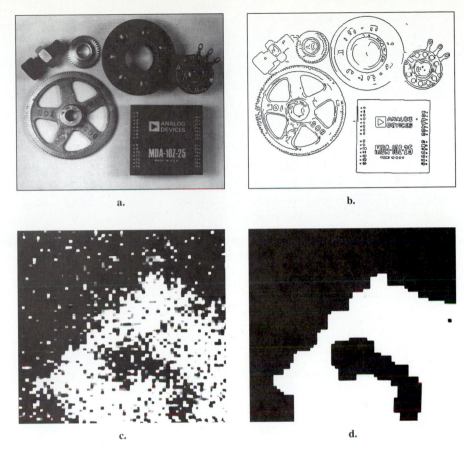

Figure 9.9 The process of recovering edges in images is an example of visual recovery. (b) shows recovered edges for the image in (a). Recovering a segmentation of an image is another example of a difficult recovery task. (d) shows a segmentation for the scene in (c). (Part (a) from "A Computational Approach to Edge Detection," J. Canny, IEEE AAMI, Vol. 8, No. 6, November 1986, pp. 679–698. Parts (c) and (d) from "Stochastic Relaxation, Gibbs Distributions, and Bayesian Restoration of Images," S. Geman and D. Geman, IEEE PAMI, Vol. 6, No. 6, November 1984, pp. 721–741.)

and the Z axis aligned with the optical axis and pointing toward the image. Let A be any point in front of the camera. We assume that nothing lies on the ray from point A to the point O. We would like to compute the position of the image A' of A in the image plane. The *focal length* is the distance of the image plane from the point O. Let $V = (X, Y, Z)$ be the vector connecting O to A and $V' = (x, y, f)$ be the vector connecting O to A', with f the focal length. Then (x, y) are the coordinates of A' on the image plane in the naturally induced coordinate system with origin the point of the intersection for the image plane with the optical axis, and axes x and y parallel to the axes of the camera coordinate system OX and OY. It is easy to see that

$$x = \frac{fX}{Z}, \quad y = \frac{fY}{Z} \tag{9.1}$$

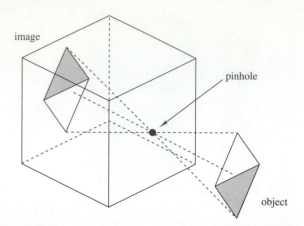

Figure 9.10   A pinhole camera. Rays of light enter the camera through a small opening called a pinhole to form an inverted image on the rear inside surface of the camera.

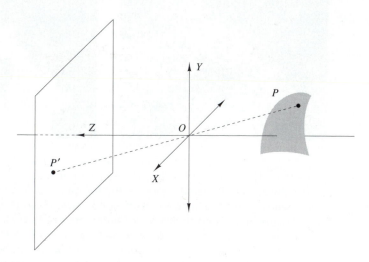

Figure 9.11   Perspective projection with the image plane in the back [Horn, 1986]. The pinhole is at the origin O of the coordinate system defined by the axes X, Y, and Z. Light travels in a straight line from a point P on an object through the infinitesimally small aperture at O to fall on the image plane at the point P'.

These equations relate the world coordinates of a point to the image plane coordinates of its image. Very often, to further simplify the equations, we assume $f = 1$ without loss of generality.

   This is the most widely used model of perspective projection. However, the image formed on the planar film or retina depends on more than just the position of the center of projection; it also depends on the orientation and the position of the planar imaging surface. Such dependencies can be removed by projecting the image onto a sphere centered at the center of projection, as in Figure 9.13. This projection is called *spherical perspective*

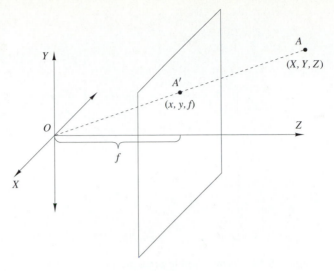

Figure 9.12   Perspective projection with the image plane in front

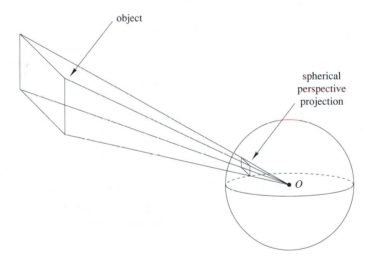

Figure 9.13   In spherical perspective projection, each point on the object is projected along a straight line through the origin *O* onto the surface of a sphere centered
at *O*.

projection and takes place in the vision system of some insects possessing
compound eyes that are almost spherical.

Orthographic Projection

Although perspective projection most accurately models the image formation process, it can result in equations that are difficult to work with. A
simpler model, which can be used in some cases and is easier to work with,
is the one of *orthographic projection*. If, in the perspective projection model,
we have a scene plane that lies parallel to the image plane at $Z = Z_0$,

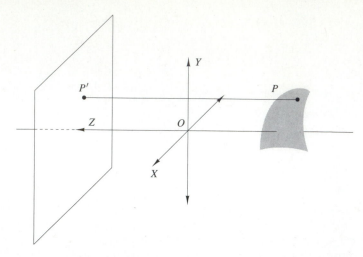

Figure 9.14   Orthographic projection [Horn, 1986]. Each point on the object is projected onto the image plane along a straight line perpendicular to the image plane.

then we define the magnification, μ, as the ratio of the distance between two points measured in the image to the distance between the corresponding points in the scene plane. So, for a small interval (dX, dY, O) on the scene plane and the corresponding small interval (dx, dy) in the image, we have

$$\mu = \frac{\sqrt{(dx)^2 + (dy)^2}}{\sqrt{(dX)^2 + (dY)^2}} = \frac{f}{Z_0}$$

Thus a small object in the scene at average distance Z_0 will produce an image that is magnified by μ. Evidently the magnification is approximately constant when the depth range of the scene is small relative to the average distance of the scene points from the camera. In this case (9.1) becomes

$$x = \mu X, \quad y = \mu Y \tag{9.2}$$

with $\mu = f/Z_0$ and Z_0 the average value of the depth Z. For convenience, if we set $\mu = 1$, (9.2) further simplifies to

$$x = X, \quad y = Y \tag{9.3}$$

Equation (9.3) defines the orthographic projection model, where the rays are parallel to the optical axis (see Figure 9.14). The difference between orthography and perspective is small when the distance to the scene is much larger than the variation in distance among objects in the scene. A rough rule of thumb is that perspective effects are significant when a wide angle lens is used, whereas images taken by telephoto lenses tend to approximate orthographic projection [Horn, 1986].

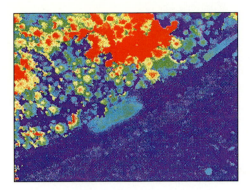 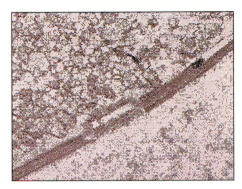

Color Plate 1 Aerial images. (a) Taken by a depth sensor. Red corresponds to the closest points of the scene, and blue corresponds to the farthest ones. All colors of the spectrum in between correspond to intermediate depths. (b) Optical image of the same scene. The road, the truck, and the foliage can be distinguished in the upper left part of the picture. (Courtesy of Vojislav Lalich-Petrich.)

▲ AI IN PRACTICE

Aerial Photo Interpretation

Several photo-interpretation problems are addressed today in an automatic or semiautomatic fashion. This is becoming necessary because of the tremendous amount of images that are collected from airplanes and satellites. These are of vegetation, cities and urban areas, oceans, road networks, and other areas of some important interest. It is becoming impossible for specialists to analyze this data by examining each individual photograph. Thus, computer programs are developed for detecting changes or diseases in vegetation, stress in the trees of large forests, appearance or movement of military equipment and many other activities of civil, medical, ecological, economic or military interest. These programs operate on optical, range or infrared images and they are specialized to address particular problems. In Color Plate 1a we see a

range aerial image of an area containing vegetation (a forest on the upper left side), and a road containing a truck. The contents are more visible on the optical image, which is displayed in Color Plate 1b. Algorithms using some of the techniques described in Chapter 9 perform detection, segmentation, and recognition of some of the contents of the image. Results of this processing are displayed below.

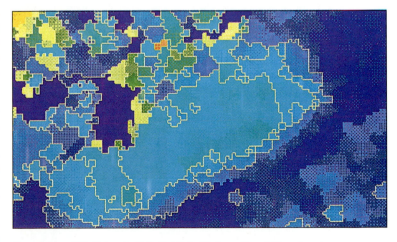

Courtesy of Vojislav Lalich-Petrich, University of Maryland

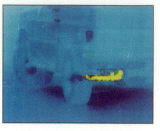
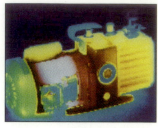

a.   b.   c.

Color Plate 2 Images taken by an infrared sensor. Red denotes more heat; blue denotes more cold. (a) Engine warm-up. (b) Vacuum pump. (c) Night vision, security. (Courtesy of Cincinnati Electronics Corporation.)

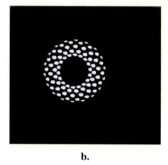

a.   b.

Color Plate 3 Cues such as shading and texture provide information about the shape of the imaged surface. A human can easily perceive the shapes in (a) and (b). The processes of shape from shading and shape from texture are examples of visual recovery.

Color Plate 4 Shaded surface

Color Plate 5 Textured surface (gravel)   **Color Plate 6** Textured surface (ivy)

Color Plate 7 Ivy-covered wall

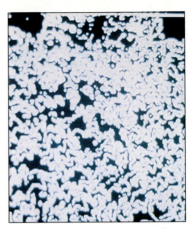

Color Plate 8 Edge image of the wall

Color Plate 9 Image of a patterned sphere

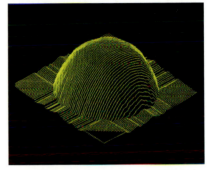

Color Plate 10 Reconstructed sphere (from Color Plate 9)

Color Plates 11, 12, 13 These images show a scene as seen by a UGV and results from a physics-based analysis of that scene. Color Plate 11: Outdoor image seen by a UGV. Color Plate 12: Results of physics-based algorithm indicating regions of the same material as Color Plate 11. Black indicates areas of uncertainty. Color Plate 13: A map indicating shadows: Dark gray denotes umbra, medium gray indicates penumbra, and white indicates directly lit. Note that a wood post in the center of the image has been mistaken for a shadow. The shadows of the fence in the foreground have been partially detected, despite the texture and albedo variations of the ground. (All three images courtesy of Gareth D. Funka-Lee. Plate 11 also courtesy of Martin Marietta Corporation.)

Object Recognition Systems

Today, there is a lot of interest in image understanding systems that remember and can recognize a large number of specific objects. This has led to the development of a subfield known as *image database*. Of extreme importance are images of faces, with applications ranging from security systems to teleconferencing, as well as several *virtual reality* problems. Virtual reality is a field that consists of a blending of vision and graphics; real images are manipulated using methods of graphics and this way an alternate reality is displayed. For example, in the problem of videoconferencing, due to limits in the speed of transmission, new poses and facial expressions are synthesized from existing images. Videoconferencing is then accomplished as follows: For the case of a talking head, instead of transmitting all images, only a small number of initial images are transmitted, and every other image is coded in the form of a vector expressing the difference of pose and facial expression. Then, at the receiver's site, the difference vector is used to synthesize the new image, which appears to be as fully transmitted. In the figure, the face of a person is shown along with intermediate stages of computations of the vector denoting the facial expression (smile).

Other applications are concerned with the controlled change of pictures of existing scenes. For example, an architect could be interested in visualizing how a design fits in some particular environment. Programs exist that, using a few pictures of an environment, can create many other views for the purposes of a realistic walk-through or fly-through.

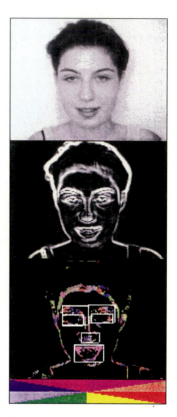

Courtesy of Yaser Yacoob, University of Maryland

Paraperspective Projection

Orthographic projection is a very rough approximation of the projection of light on the fovea, but it is impractical for many machine vision applications. Perspective projection, however, involves more complicated equations and makes the analysis of some problems difficult. *Paraperspective projection* is a good approximation of perspective since it lies between orthography and perspective. Let a coordinate system $OXYZ$ be fixed with respect to the camera, with the Z axis pointing along the optical axis and origin at O. Assuming the focal length $f = 1$, we consider the image plane perpendicular to the Z axis at the point $(0, 0, 1)$. Consider a small planar surface patch S as shown in Figure 9.15 and the projection plane $Z = d$. Paraperspective projection involves two steps:

1. S is projected onto $Z = d$. This projection is performed using the rays that are parallel to the line from O to the center of mass (centroid) of C.

2. The projection of S on $Z = d$ is projected perspectively onto the image plane. Since $Z = d$ is parallel to the image plane, this projection results in magnification by a factor $1/d$.

Paraperspective decomposes the projection of the scene onto the image plane into two parts. Step (1) incorporates the foreshortening distortion

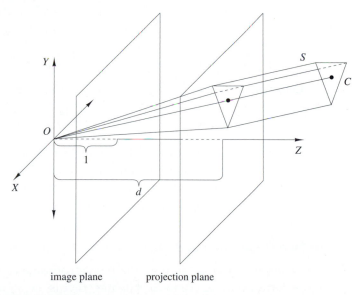

Figure 9.15 Paraperspective projection. The point C is the centroid of the planar surface patch S. The points on S are projected onto the projection plane along a set of straight lines parallel to the line from the origin O to the centroid C. These projected points are then projected onto the image plane as in perspective projection. Paraperspective projection is a good approximation for perspective projection whenever the dimensions of the viewed object are small when compared to the distance from the object to the origin.

and part of the position effect, and step (2) incorporates both the distance and additional position effects. Paraperspective projection is a good approximation for perspective projection whenever the dimensions of the viewed object are small compared to the distance from the object to the origin.

Shape Representation

A visual system analyzes images and produces descriptions of what is imaged. A description might include information about the shapes of the objects in the scene. But the shape of an object does not have a unique description; descriptions can have many levels of detail and be from many points of view. We don't want just any description of what is imaged, but one that allows us to take appropriate action. A reasonable first approximation to describing the shape of an object is to represent the local orientation of its surface. We will consider only this level of description here. Surface orientation is usually represented by the orientation of the surface normal vector. In the following two subsections, we show how the shape of a visible surface can be reconstructed from local orientation information.

Surface Orientation and Shape Under Perspective

The normal vector $\bar{n}$ to the surface $Z = Z(X, Y)$ at the point (X, Y, Z) is

$$\bar{n} = \left(\frac{\partial Z}{\partial X}, \frac{\partial Z}{\partial Y}, -1 \right) \Big/ \left[\left(\frac{\partial Z}{\partial X} \right)^2 + \left(\frac{\partial Z}{\partial Y} \right)^2 + 1 \right]^{1/2}$$

One can show that if $\partial Z/\partial X$, $\partial Z/\partial Y$ are known, the quantity

$$\frac{Z(x + dx, y + dy)}{Z(x, y)}$$

can be computed. This means that if the surface normal is known as a function of position (x, y) in the image, then the depth function $Z(x, y)$ can be computed up to a constant factor. The constant is undetermined; the surface can be small and near the camera or large and far away.

Surface Orientation and Shape Under Orthography

Under orthographic projection, the image coordinates of a point are equal to the corresponding scene coordinates, that is, $(x, y) = (X, Y)$. So

$$\left(\frac{\partial Z}{\partial X}, \frac{\partial Z}{\partial Y} \right) = \left(\frac{\partial Z}{\partial x}, \frac{\partial Z}{\partial y} \right)$$

Since

$$Z(x + dx, \ y + dy) - Z(x, y) = \frac{\partial Z}{\partial x} dx + \frac{\partial Z}{\partial y} dy + (\text{higher order terms})$$

we see that $Z(x, y)$ can be computed up to a constant additive term. Thus, if we know the surface orientation under orthography, we know the surface shape, but we do not know its distance.

Stereographic Projection

Let $p = \partial Z/\partial X$, $q = \partial Z/\partial Y$ at the point of the surface $Z = Z(X, Y)$. We have seen that the surface normal vector is

$$\frac{(p, q, -1)}{(p^2 + q^2 + 1)^{1/2}}$$

The coordinates

$$(a, b, c) = \left(\frac{p}{k}, \frac{q}{k}, \frac{-1}{k} \right) \text{ with } k = (p^2 + q^2 + 1)^{1/2}$$

define the position of a point on the *Gaussian sphere*. This position can also be defined in terms of latitude and longitude angles. Another commonly used representation is in terms of slant and tilt, (σ, τ), where slant is the tangent of the latitude angle and tilt is the longitude angle. We have

$$\sigma = \cos^{-1} \left(\frac{1}{\sqrt{1 + p^2 + q^2}} \right)$$

$$\tau = \tan^{-1} \left(\frac{q}{p} \right)$$

The parameterization of the local surface normal uses the partial derivatives $p = \frac{\partial z}{\partial x}$, $q = \frac{\partial z}{\partial y}$, and gives rise to the concept of *gradient space*. The coordinates p, q define the shape. The parameterization has the disadvantage that the partial derivatives can become infinite at occluding boundaries. An occluding boundary is a place where the surface turns away from the viewer. A similar problem arises with the slant-tilt representation. In this case, we can use a different parameterization (f, g) of surface orientation, which is called *stereographic*. f and g are related to p and q by

$$f = \frac{2p}{1 + \sqrt{1 + p^2 + q^2}}, \; g = \frac{2q}{1 + \sqrt{1 + p^2 + q^2}}$$

Using the Gaussian sphere formalism, we can show that gradient space corresponds to projecting the Gaussian sphere from its center onto a plane tangent to the sphere at its north pole, whereas stereographic space corresponds to projecting from the south pole (see Figures 9.16 and 9.17, page 428).

Geometric Properties of the Perspective Projection

Suppose a line l in the scene is defined by $(x, y, z) + \lambda(\Delta X, \Delta Y, \Delta Z)$ for all values of λ, where (x, y, z) is any point on the line, and $(\Delta X, \Delta Y, \Delta Z)$ is a direction vector of the line (any vector contained in the line). For any λ,

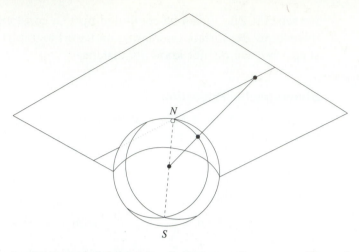

Figure 9.16 Projection of Gaussian sphere on gradient space. (Reproduced from *Robot Vision* by written permission from MIT Press.)

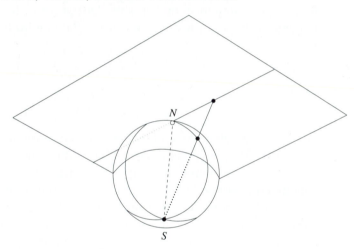

Figure 9.17 Stereographic projection. (Reproduced from *Robot Vision* by written permission from MIT Press.)

the corresponding point on the line is $P_\lambda = (X + \lambda\Delta X, Y + \lambda\Delta Y, Z + \lambda\Delta Z)$, and its image (assuming perspective projection and focal length equal to 1) is the point

$$P_\lambda = \left(\frac{X + \lambda\Delta X}{Z + \lambda\Delta Z}, \frac{Y + \lambda\Delta Y}{Z + \lambda\Delta Z} \right)$$

As λ grows larger, the image point P_λ converges to some point V in the image:

$$V = \lim_{\lambda \to \infty} P_\lambda = \left(\frac{\Delta X}{\Delta Z}, \frac{\Delta Y}{\Delta Z} \right)$$

provided $\Delta Z \neq 0$, that is, the line is not parallel to the image plane. Point V is called the *vanishing point* of line l and is that point in the image beyond

Figure 9.18   Parallel straight lines converge at a single point (called the vanishing point) under perspective projection

which the projection of the line cannot extend. Parallel lines have the same vanishing point. Figure 9.18 illustrates a vanishing point. Figure 9.19 shows that the vanishing point of any given straight line is located at that point in the image where a parallel line through the center of projection intersects the image plane.

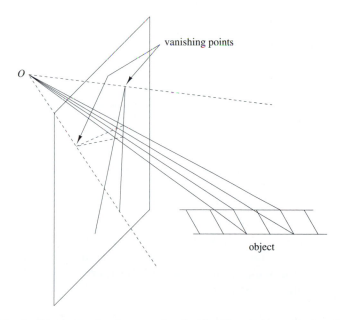

Figure 9.19   In this example, the perceived object is a schematic description of a sidewalk broken into rectangular segments at regular intervals. In the image plane, the parallel edges of the sidewalk converge at one vanishing point, and the parallel edges of the lines (the expansion joints or "cracks" in the sidewalk) dividing the rectangular segments converge in a second vanishing point.

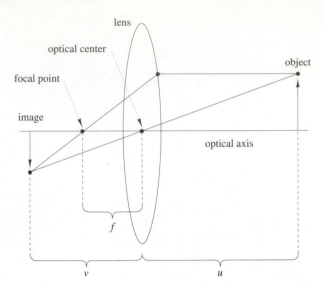

Figure 9.20   Imaging with lenses. The optical center of the lens plays the role of the pinhole in a pinhole camera. A lens gathers light over a much wider aperture than is possible using a pinhole camera while retaining the relatively simple geometry of the pinhole camera.

Imaging with Lenses

So far, we have considered a pinhole camera as a pure geometric entity. However, in real situations, we are imaging with a lens (Figure 9.20).

In a lens, the gathered light comes from an object point toward the lens's aperture and is brought into focus at a single distinct image point. Usually a lens brings into focus only those object points that lie in a plane parallel to the image. Assuming, however, a thin lens whose optical axis is perpendicular to the image, we have the following useful relation:

$$\frac{1}{u} + \frac{1}{v} = \frac{1}{f}$$

where u is the distance of an object point from the plane of the lens, v is the distance of the image point from the lens, and f is the focal length of the lens. The optical center of the lens plays the role of a pinhole in a pinhole camera. The field of view describes the cone of viewing directions of the lens. Wide angle lenses have small focal lengths and, thus, large fields of view. The depth of field refers to the range of depths over which the scene is approximately in focus, and the aperture of the lens is the opening through which light crosses the lens.

Photometric Aspects of Image Formation

An image point's brightness depends on the relationship between the amount of light radiating from a surface point (called *scene radiance*) and the amount of light falling onto the image of the surface point (called *image irradiance*).[2] This analysis has been extensively carried out. For the case of a lens with focal length f and circular aperture of diameter d, it can be shown that

$$\text{Irrad} = \text{Rad}\left(\frac{\pi}{4}\right)\left(\frac{d}{f}\right)^2 \cos^4 \alpha$$

where Rad is the radiance of the surface, Irrad is the irradiance of the image, and α is the angle between the optical axis of the lens and the direction from the lens toward the object area. This fundamental relation demonstrates that the image irradiance is proportional to the scene radiance; indeed, the factor $\frac{\pi}{4}\left(\frac{d}{f}\right)^2$ is constant all over the image. The term $\cos^4 \alpha$, although it varies with the position of the image, could be considered constant when the field of view is not large. Thus it turns out that, in general, bright points in the scene will give rise to bright image points, and dark scene points will create dark images.

9.5   Recovery of Image Descriptions

To make image analysis practical, we must reduce the huge size of most image data. *Edge detection* and *segmentation* are important data reduction steps in most recovery algorithms (see the AI in Practice box entitled "Aerial Photo Interpretation" appearing in the Color Plate section). An *edge* in an image is an image contour across which the brightness of the image changes abruptly. Edges are classified by the way the brightness function[3] is distributed around the edge: *step edges*, *roof edges*, and *line edges*. A *step edge* refers to a contour in the image across which the value of the intensity function changes abruptly. A *roof edge* is a contour across which the orientation of the intensity function changes abruptly. A *line edge* is a pair of adjacent parallel step edges. Our focus here will be on step edges.

Edge Detection

Edges in an image are important because they encode information about the structure of the scene. In Figure 9.21 (page 432), we can distinguish several physical events in a scene that lead to intensity edges in an image of the scene. Among these events are discontinuities in the surface normal, in illumination, in depth, and in surface reflectance or in some combination of these.

---

[2]Informally, both the scene radiance and the image irradiance are called brightness although they represent different quantities.

[3]Recall that what is available to a computer for the purposes of image understanding is a digital image. This image, however, has meaning in the optical image that it represents. The optical image is characterized by the image irradiance function defined over the image plane, and thus we can refer to the continuously defined intensity surface underlying a digital image. Nalwa [1993] explains this in detail.

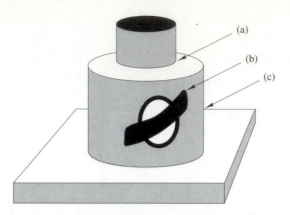

Figure 9.21 (a) Discontinuity in shape. (b) Discontinuity in reflectance. (c) Discontinuity in depth.

Edge detection is a two-step process: First, short linear edge segments are detected, and then these edges are aggregated into extended segments. Algorithms for detecting edges (edge detectors) are usually differentiation based or model based. Differentiation approaches estimate the derivatives of the image intensity function, the idea being that large image derivatives reflect abrupt intensity changes. Model-based approaches try to determine whether the intensities in a small area conform to some model for the edges that we have assumed.

Differentiation Approaches

The gradient of a function $g(x, y)$ is the vector $\nabla g(x, y) = \left(\frac{\partial g}{\partial x}, \frac{\partial g}{\partial y} \right)$. At a step edge, the underlying intensity function has a large gradient pointing across the edge. This is the key idea behind most differentiation approaches to edge detection.

In most techniques, an image point is selected as representing an edge if the image intensity gradient at that point is above a certain threshold. The difference operators described in this section are discrete approximations of the gradient. There are many ways to estimate gradients. Most of the known approaches estimate the directional derivatives of the image intensity at any two orthogonal directions in a single point. If g_1 and g_2 are these orthogonal directional derivatives, then the magnitude of the gradient is $\sqrt{g_1^2 + g_2^2}$, and its direction with regard to g_1's direction is $\tan^{-1}(g_2/g_1)$.

If we consider a 2×2 window in the image and fit a planar surface to the values of the image intensity, then a good approximation to the gradient in the region defined by the window is the gradient of the fitted plane. A discrete approximation to the gradient based on this idea can be computed using *Roberts operators*, as shown in Figure 9.22.

We describe operators in terms of either 2×2 or 3×3 arrays of numbers called *masks* that are used to compute approximations to the directional

g_1 g_2 g_1 g_2

0	1		1	0
−1	0		0	−1

−1	1		1	1
−1	1		−1	−1

a.   **b.**

Figure 9.22 Roberts operators: (a) The indicated masks are used to compute g_1 and g_2 at a 2 × 2 window, along the lines diagonal to the coordinate axes of the image. (b) The indicated masks are used to compute g_1 and g_2 at a 2 × 2 window along the x and y coordinate axes of the image.

g_1

−1	0	1
−1	0	1
−1	0	1

g_2

1	1	1
0	0	0
−1	−1	−1

Figure 9.23 Prewitt operator: These masks provide estimates of the directional derivatives along the coordinate axes of the image at the center of a 3 × 3 window

derivatives at a point. For example, if g_1 is described by a mask of the form $\begin{smallmatrix} 0 & 1 \\ -1 & 0 \end{smallmatrix}$ then the directional derivative g_1 at the point (x, y) in the image is

$$(0 \times I(x, y)) + (1 \times I(x + 1, y)) + (-1 \times I(x, y + 1)) + (0 \times I(x + 1, y + 1))$$

where $I(i, j)$ is the image intensity at the pixel (i, j).

If, on the other hand, we fit a quadratic surface in a 3 × 3 window (instead of a planar surface in a 2 × 2 window) and differentiate the fitted surface to obtain the gradient, we arrive at the discrete masks shown in Figure 9.23 and known as the *Prewitt operator*.

The operators described accentuate image intensity variations, thus detecting edges. Moreover, they also accentuate image noise, and thus detect spurious edges. To account for this, the opposite effect of image smoothing should be employed. Smoothing masks have only positive weights. The masks of the *Sobel operator* are designed following this principle; they are basically equivalent to Roberts operators applied after the image has been smoothed. It can be shown that the Sobel operator is the result of the (discrete) *convolution* of an averaging mask with the horizontal and vertical directional derivative masks (Figure 9.24).

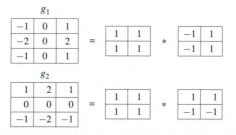

Figure 9.24 Sobel operator: Its application amounts to smoothing followed by differencing

The convolution, denoted by $*$, is the operation of computing the weighted integral (or sum in the case of discrete functions) of one function with another function that has first been reflected about the origin and suitably displaced. If one of the functions is symmetric about the origin, as in the case of the Gaussian, then reflection is unnecessary. The two functions, say f and g, are said to be *convolved*, and the resulting convolution is denoted $f * g$. In the case of two continuous functions f and g of a single variable, $f(x) * g(x) = (f * g)(x) = \int f(x - t)g(t)dt$. Figure 9.25 provides examples illustrating the result of convolving images with functions such as the Gaussian and the Laplacian of the Gaussian.

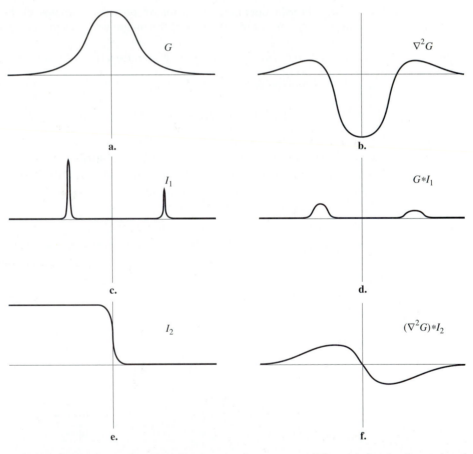

Figure 9.25 Examples illustrating continuous convolution: (a) A one-dimensional Gaussian function G. (b) The Laplacian of the Gaussian $\nabla^2 G$. (c) A function I_1 representing two noise spikes in an otherwise zero intensity one-dimensional slice of an image. (d) I_1 smoothed by convolving it with G thereby reducing the effect of the noise. (e) A function I_2 representing an abrupt change in intensity in a one-dimensional slice of an image. (f) I_2 convolved with the Laplacian of the Gaussian $\nabla^2 G$ where the zero crossing marks the abrupt change in intensity.

In digital image processing, the discrete Gaussian is used to assign to each pixel the weighted average of the intensity of that pixel and the intensities of its neighboring pixels. In the one-dimensional case, the discrete Gaussian $G(i)$ assigns to each integer a positive real number such that $\sum_{-\infty}^{\infty} G(i) = 1.0$. For practical purposes, the weights for integers much greater than 3 or much less than -3 are 0. Here is a simple example of a discrete Gaussian.

$$G(i) = \begin{cases} 0.2 \text{ if } i = -1 \\ 0.6 \text{ if } i = 0 \\ 0.2 \text{ if } i = 1 \\ 0.0 \text{ otherwise} \end{cases}$$

Suppose we have a one-dimensional image slice corresponding to the following vector of image intensities $\langle 10, 10, 10, 10, 25, 10, 10, 10, 10, 10 \rangle$, such that the intensity $I(j)$ at the jth pixel is the jth element of the vector, for example, $I(5) = 25$ and $I(6) = 10$. Convolving the image slice with the discrete Gaussian amounts to computing the following sum for each pixel except those at the boundaries of the image:

$$I'(j) = \sum_{-\infty}^{\infty} I(i)G(j - i)$$

to obtain the smoothed image slice $I'(j)$ (see Figure 9.26) corresponding to the vector $\langle 10, 10, 13, 19, 13, 10, 10, 10 \rangle$.

In the case of a two-dimensional image, smoothing involves a two-dimensional Gaussian function $G(x, y) = \frac{1}{2\pi\sigma^2} e^{-\frac{x^2+y^2}{2\sigma^2}}$ for an appropriately chosen standard deviation σ. A popular edge detector based on Gaussian smoothing is due to Marr and Hildreth [1980]. The Marr–Hildreth operator convolves the image with the Laplacian of a Gaussian function and then takes the zero-crossings of the result to identify edges. In particular, if $\nabla^2 = \frac{\partial^2}{\partial x^2} + \frac{\partial^2}{\partial y^2}$ is the Laplacian operator, G is a Gaussian, and $I(x, y)$ the image

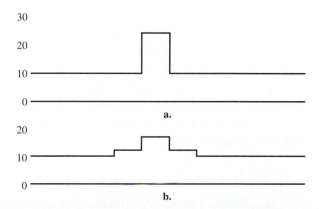

Figure 9.26   (a) The intensities for a one-dimensional image slice. (b) The result of convolving the image slice with a discrete Gaussian.

a.

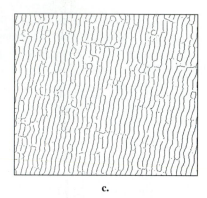

b.   c.

Figure 9.27   (a) Original image. (b) Extracted edges at a fine scale. (c) Extracted edges at a coarse scale. (From "A Computional Approach to Edge Detection," J. Canny, IEEE AAMI, Vol. 8, No. 6, November 1986, pp. 679–698.)

intensity function, their scheme computes.

$$\nabla^2(G * I) = (\nabla^2 G) * I$$

This operator computes the second-order partial derivatives along two orthogonal axes that can be oriented in any fashion since the operator $\nabla^2 G$ is rotationally symmetric. Along a straight step edge, we can orient one axis along the edge and the other axis perpendicular to the edge. Both partial derivatives are zero in both directions, but the derivative across the edge becomes nonzero as we move away from the edge. Thus, the operator $\nabla^2 G$ produces zero-crossings along the edge. Figure 9.27 contains results from the application of the Canny edge detector, which uses several one-dimensional edge-segment detectors at each point in the Gaussian-convolved image as a substitute for the Laplacian.

Model-Based Approaches

The edge detectors described in the previous section are popular because they resemble biological systems. Some low-level retinal computations resemble smoothing and differencing operations. An alternative way to detect

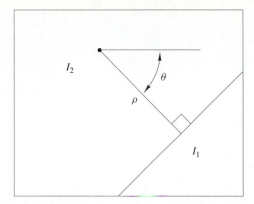

Figure 9.28 A model for a step edge. The parameters I_1, I_2, ρ, and θ represent the four degrees of freedom. An edge is declared present in the image if the model fits the data successfully.

edges is to develop a parametric model for the edges and compute how well it matches the image data.

The most widely known operator in this category is the Hueckel operator [Hueckel, 1973]. The model used by Hueckel is the following: An ideal step edge is a short linear segment of an image intensity edge, and it has four degrees of freedom—orientation, position, and the intensities (assumed constant) on the two sides of the edge (see Figure 9.28). Edge detection then amounts to matching. We seek the least-squares error fit of the parametric model to the image window under consideration.

Edge Grouping and Hough Transform

The edge detectors we described previously produce short linear disjointed segments with position and orientation. To be useful, these segments must be aggregated into extended edges. Curves must be fitted to the edge data. An interesting and useful tool for performing such fittings is the *Hough transform*. Suppose we are given a set of features, such as points or short line segments, and we wish to find the curve to which these features belong. Suppose, also, that we know the parametric form of this curve. Then the parameters of the curve are found in two steps. In the first step, every feature is mapped, using the Hough transform, onto a set of possible parameter values for which the curve passes through the given feature. In the second step, we find the intersection of all the sets of parameter values that have been mapped in the first step. This intersection gives the values of the parameters of the curve we were looking for.

Suppose we are given a set of points lying on a straight line and we wish to find the equation of the line on which they lie. The lines may be noisy, having gaps and wiggles. Consider point $p' = (x', y')$ in Figure 9.29a and the equation for a line $y = \alpha x + \beta$. What are the lines that could pass through p'? It is simply all the lines with α and β satisfying $y' = \alpha x' + \beta$. If

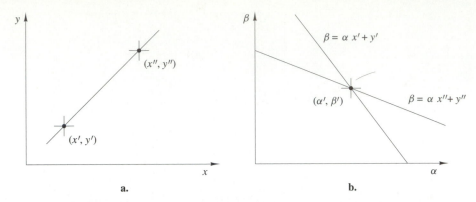

Figure 9.29 (a) A line in image space. (b) A line in parameter space.

we regard (x', y') as fixed, then the last equation is the equation of a line in α-β space, or parameter space. If we repeat this reasoning, a second point $p'' = (x'', y'')$ will have an associated line in parameter space; furthermore, these lines will intersect at the point (α', β') that corresponds to the line $P_1 P_2$ connecting these points. All points on the line $P_1 P_2$ will yield lines in the parameter space that intersect at the point (α', β') (see Figure 9.29b).

If the constraint sets in parameter space have no common intersection, then no curve of the specified parametric form satisfies the given data.

Image Segmentation

Image segmentation means dividing the image into regions or segments, each of which is in some sense homogeneous, but the union of adjacent segments is not homogeneous in the same sense [Nalwa 1993]. Homogeneity here is characterized by some property, for example, smoothly varying intensity, similar statistics, or color. Edge detection is a common precedent to segmentation, since it segments the image into regions of smoothly varying intensity. Segmentation is performed by *pixel classification*, *splitting or merging*, and *optimization methods*. Pixel classification methods are the simplest. In pixel classification, each pixel is classified by its gray value. The gray scale is partitioned into intervals, and every pixel within a gray-level interval is assigned to a single class. Selecting thresholds is difficult. A possible approach to choosing thresholds is to take advantage of the multimodal nature of typical gray-level histograms. Large coherent regions usually generate maxima, whereas edges typically generate minima. Figure 9.30 shows an image, its gray-level histogram, and its segmentation based on thresholds selected in the histogram.

There are several problems with this approach. Pixels assigned to a single class do not necessarily form coherent regions since the spatial locations of the pixels are ignored during the segmentation process. In addition, threshold selection is not performed in a rigorous way: There may be a very large number of maxima and minima. Finally, two areas in the image with

a.

b.

c.

Figure 9.30 Image segmentation based on histogramming. (a) Original image. (b) Gray-level histogram of the image in (a). It plots the number of image pixels that take each gray level. In the figure, we show a candidate set of thresholds that indicate gray-level intervals within each of which pixels may be categorized as belonging to the same class. (c) Segmentation of the original image based on the thresholds in (b). (Vishrjit A. Nalwa, *A Guided Tour of Computer Vision* (pp. 17, 23, 55, 114), ©1993 by AT&T Bell Laboratories. Reprinted by permission of Addison-Wesley Publishing Company.)

the same gray level but separated by an edge are going to be classified in the same segment. Optimization techniques for image segmentation fall in the general paradigm of *relaxation processes*. According to this paradigm, a list of candidate interpretations such as segment labels is assigned to each entity (pixel or segment) independently and given a confidence level. Then the confidence level of each segment is reinforced or inhibited on the basis of

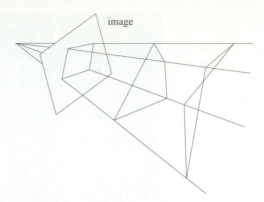

image

Figure 9.31   An infinite number of 3D drawings can give rise to the same image

the compatibility of the label with neighboring ones. This step is repeated until the process converges.

Of course, the compatibility between neighboring labels is measured on the basis of some model that is chosen a priori. The relaxation process can be deterministic or probabilistic, according to how the compatibility among segments is updated.

It is becoming clear through current research that edge detection and segmentation are inherently limited if no other knowledge is utilized such as context and expectations. There are simply too many ways to segment an image when the only information utilized is low level and no use of high-level semantic cues is made.

9.6   Shape from Contour

After we have estimated the brightness edges in an image, we have a line drawing. An important question in visual recovery is to deduce the three-dimensional structure of a scene from its line drawing. Although humans are very good in recovering shape from a single image of a line drawing,[4] an inherent ambiguity exists in this problem. This is because, under perspective projection, the line drawing of any scene event, for example, a depth discontinuity, can restrict the location of the event only to a narrow cone of rays (Figure 9.31).

Most research on *shape from contour* has focused on the images of opaque polyhedra, trying to quantify and qualify the scenes. The goal of shape-from-contour modules is to extract as much information as possible from an image of polyhedral surfaces, like the one in Figure 9.33.

---

[4]Humans possibly employ various assumptions in interpreting line drawings. Nevertheless, they are often subject to experiencing multiple interpretations of a drawing (see, for example, Figure 9.32).

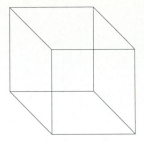

Figure 9.32   The Necker cube. In this drawing, the viewer perceives a box with transparent faces. There are two consistent interpretations of the drawing depending on which of the two box faces drawn as squares is believed to be closest to the viewer. If you stare at the drawing, you may find yourself jumping back and forth between the two interpretations.

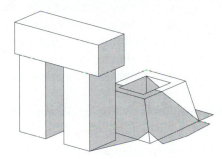

Figure 9.33   A line drawing of a scene consisting of polyhedra. Shaded surfaces are shadows. The goal of the shape-from-contour module is to derive information about the orientation of the various different faces.

Qualitative Analysis Using Edge Labels

Line drawing analysis can be qualitative or quantitative. Qualitatively, with our inability to create an exact three-dimensional interpretation of the scene, we resort to giving the various edges labels. Quantitatively, we attempt to estimate the orientation of the planar faces present. The following taxonomy has been proposed for labeling edges in a line drawing: + (for a nonoccluding convex line), − (for a concave line), and ↑ (for an occluding line). These labels, illustrated in Figure 9.34 (page 442) for a cube resting on the floor, have the following interpretations: + and − denote, respectively, convex and concave edges along which both faces forming the edge are visible, and ↑ signifies an occluding edge.

The occluding matter is to the right of the line looking in the direction of the arrow, and the occluded surface is to the left. Having this labeling taxonomy, an important observation is that every line must have a single label along its entire length; otherwise, the planes forming the edge would need to have nonconstant orientation. Using this observation, we can systematically derive a complete *junction catalog*. This is a catalog of all the

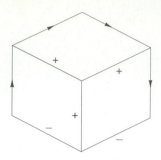

Figure 9.34 A block resting on its bottom surface

possible configurations in which edges meet at a common point in a line drawing (with trihedral vertices) (Figure 9.35).

Thus, given a line drawing, if it cannot be labeled using the junction labels of Figure 9.35, then it cannot exist because it is not possible physically (see Figure 9.36). If, however, it can be labeled, then the labeling immediately provides a qualitative interpretation. The Lisp implementation at the end of this chapter describes an algorithm for labeling line drawings of polyhedral scenes using the junction catalog shown in Figure 9.35.

Quantitative Analysis Using Skewed Symmetries

Among the quantitative approaches, the one of *skewed symmetry* receives much attention for planar contours. Many planar objects are symmetrical about an axis. This axis and another, which is perpendicular to the first

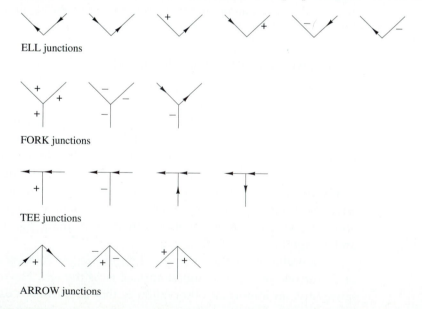

Figure 9.35 The junction catalog for line drawing of trihedral vertex polyhedra. Although 64 (= 4^3) distinct ways of labeling exist, only the ones in the figure are valid.

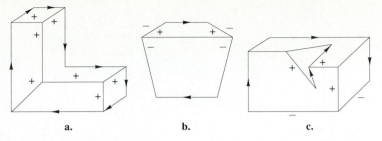

a.   b.   c.

Figure 9.36 Nonsense labelings and nonpolyhedra. (b) After Mackworth [1977]. (c) After Huffman [1971].

one and in the same plane of the object, form a natural coordinate system for the object. If the plane of the object is perpendicular to the line of sight (optical axis), then the coordinate axes appear to be at right angles. Otherwise, the axes appear skewed (see Figure 9.37 for some examples). A skewed symmetry in the image may or may not reflect a real symmetry. If, however, the skewed symmetry results from a tilted real symmetry, then an interesting constraint on the object orientation in gradient space can be developed.

An imaged unit vector with orientation α on the image and lying on a plane with orientation (p, q), must have 3D coordinates given by

$$(\cos\alpha,\ \sin\alpha,\ p\cos\alpha + q\sin\alpha)$$

If the two axes of skewed symmetry make angles α and β with the x axis of the image, then the two vectors $\vec{A}$ and $\vec{B}$ in 3D space must have coordinates

$$\vec{A} = (\cos\alpha,\ \sin\alpha,\ p\cos\alpha + q\sin\alpha)$$
$$\vec{B} = (\cos\beta,\ \sin\beta,\ p\cos\beta + q\sin\beta)$$

Since, however, these vectors in 3D reflect a real symmetry, they must be perpendicular, or $\vec{A}, \vec{B} = 0$, that is,

$$\cos(\alpha - \beta) + (p\cos\alpha + q\sin\alpha)(p\cos\beta + q\sin\beta) = 0$$

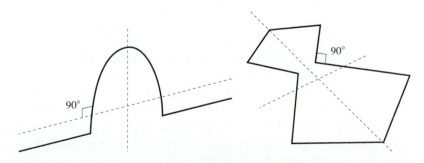

Figure 9.37 Skewed symmetries

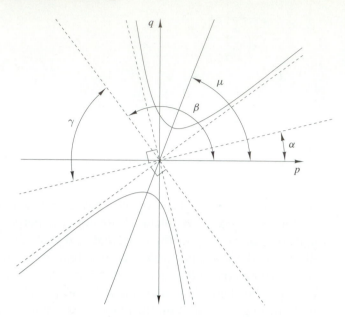

Figure 9.38   Skewed symmetry constraint in gradient space

By appropriate rotation of the axes by an angle $\mu = \frac{\alpha+\beta}{2}$, that is, a change of the p-q coordinate system to

$$p' = p\cos\mu + q\sin\mu$$
$$q' = -p\sin\mu + q\cos\mu$$

the preceding equation becomes

$$p'^2\cos^2\frac{\gamma}{2} - q'^2\sin^2\frac{\gamma}{2} = -\cos\gamma$$

where $\gamma = \alpha - \beta$. Thus, the gradient of the object must lie on a hyperbola with the axis tilted by μ from the x axis and with asymptotes perpendicular to the directions of α and β (see Figure 9.38).

9.7   Shape from Shading

The recovery of surface orientation from gray-level variations (called *shape from shading*) has been extensively studied. Color Plate 4 shows an image that contains shading. Humans can easily perceive, at least qualitatively, the shape of the imaged surface. In this section, we describe methods of recovering surface orientation from shading, together with other assumptions that we describe later.

The amount of light reflected by a surface element, the surface radiance, depends on its microstructure, on its optical properties, and on the angular distribution and state of polarization of the incident illumination. For some surfaces, the fraction of incident illumination (irradiance) reflected in a particular direction depends only on the surface orientation. The reflectance of such a surface can be represented by a function $f(i, g, e)$ of

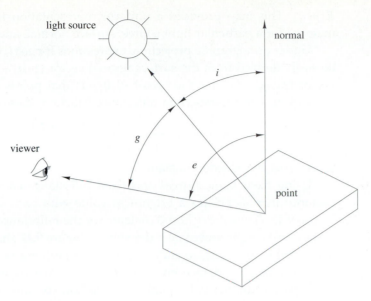

Figure 9.39   Geometry of reflection illustrating the incident (i), phase (g), and emergent (e) angles for a particular viewer, point, and light source

the angles i = incident, g = phase, and e = emergent, as they are defined in Figure 9.39. For example, in perfect specular (mirrorlike) reflection, the incident angle equals the emergent angle, and the incident, emergent, and normal vectors lie in the same plane; the phase angle is given by $g = i + e$. Thus the reflectance function is

$$f(i, e, g) = \begin{vmatrix} 1 \text{ if } i = e \text{ and } i + e = g \\ 0 \text{ otherwise} \end{vmatrix}$$

The most widely used model of surface reflectance is defined by the function $f(i, e, g) = \rho \cos i$, where ρ is constant for a given surface, called the *albedo constant*. This function defines the reflectance of a perfectly diffuse *Lambertian* surface that appears equally bright from all viewing directions. The cosine of the incident angle compensates for the foreshortening of the surface as seen from the light source.

In orthographic projection, the viewing direction and hence the phase angle g are constant for all surface elements. So, for a fixed light source and viewer geometry and a given surface material, the ratio of radiance to irradiance depends only on the surface normal vector. Furthermore, suppose that each surface element receives the same irradiance. Then the surface radiance, and hence the image intensity $I(x, y)$, depends only on the surface normal vector.

Reflectance Maps

When expressed in terms of the surface normal coordinates $p = \frac{\partial z}{\partial x}$, $q = \frac{\partial z}{\partial y}$, the reflectance function is called the *reflectance map* and is denoted by

$R(p, q)$. This map provides a uniform representation for a given surface material for a particular light source, surface normal, and viewer geometry.

Under orthographic projection, expressions for $\cos i$, $\cos e$, and $\cos g$ can be easily derived from the surface normal vector $(p, q, -1)$, the light source vector $(p_s, q_s, -1)$, and the vector $(0, 0, -1)$ that points in the direction of the viewer. For a Lambertian reflectance function, these expressions give

$$R(p, q) = \frac{\rho(1 + p\, p_s + q\, q_s)}{\sqrt{(1 + p^2 + q^2)}\sqrt{(1 + p_s^2 + q_s^2)}}$$

where ρ is the albedo constant.

Using fixed light sources and fixed reflectance characteristics, the reflectance map associates a brightness value with each surface orientation. Figure 9.40 shows *isobrightness contours* for the reflectance map for the same surface and a light source near the viewer. Figure 9.41 shows the reflectance map for the same surface and a light source farther away from the viewer.

The image irradiance equation $I(x, y) = R(p, q)$ is a nonlinear first-order partial differential equation. A method for solving this equation is the *characteristic strip expansion*. This method computes the solution surface $z = g(x, y)$ by finding a family of space curves whose local tangents all lie in the tangent plane of the solution surface. Such a curve can be specified by a one-parameter family of points $(x(s), y(s), z(s))$, where s is the distance along the curve.

Differentiation with respect to s gives

$$p\frac{dx}{ds} + q\frac{dy}{ds} - \frac{dz}{ds} = 0$$

or

$$(p, q, -1) \cdot \left(\frac{dx}{ds}, \frac{dy}{ds}, \frac{dz}{ds}\right) = 0$$

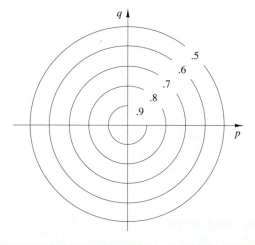

Figure 9.40   Isobrightness contours for a Lambertian surface when the light source is near the observer

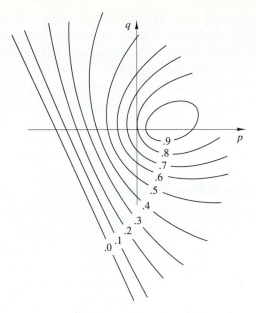

Figure 9.41 Isobrightness contours for a Lambertian surface when the light source is removed from the observer. (Reproduced from *Robot Vision* by written permission from MIT Press.)

The vector $\left(\frac{dx}{ds}, \frac{dy}{ds}, \frac{dz}{ds}\right)$ lies in the tangent plane of the solution surface. Trivially, the vector $(R_p, R_q, pR_p + qR_q)$ also lies in that plane. From this observation, we conclude that

$$\frac{dx}{ds} = R_p \tag{9.4}$$

$$\frac{dy}{ds} = R_q \tag{9.5}$$

$$\frac{dz}{ds} = pR_p + qR_q \tag{9.6}$$

where the subscripts denote partial differentiation.

Differentiating the image irradiance equation with respect to x gives $I_x = R_p\, p_x + R_q\, q_x$, and since $Rp_y = g_{xy} = g_{yx} = q_x$ we have $I_x = R_p\, p_x + R_q\, p_y$, and consequently

$$I_x = \frac{dp}{ds} \tag{9.7}$$

Similarly,

$$I_y = \frac{dq}{ds} \tag{9.8}$$

Thus, if we know that the image point (x_k, y_k) corresponds to a surface patch with orientation (p_i, q_i), we can extend this solution to other points. If we take a step ds along the characteristic strip from (x_i, y_i) to (x_{i+1}, y_{i+1}), and correspondingly from (p_i, q_i) to (p_{i+1}, q_{i+1}), then the five differential equations (9.4)–(9.8) show that the step in the image is in direction (R_p, R_q). This is along the normal to the isobrightness contour in the reflectance map. In the same way, the step in the reflectance map is in the direction normal to the isobrightness contour computed in the image. Thus, if we know the reflectance map, we can compute the surface orientations at a sequence of points along a characteristic strip starting from a point where the surface orientation is known. In order to use this method, we need an initial point with known surface orientation. The algorithm also depends on the assumption that the surface is locally convex at the initial point.

Solving Ill-Posed Problems

A problem is called *ill-posed* when its solution does not exist or it is not unique or does not depend continuously on the data. The problem of shape from shading is ill-posed, so we will need additional constraints. We will now describe how a smoothness constraint, along with boundary conditions, provides a unique solution. Bounding or occluding contours provide boundary conditions for the shape-from-X problems (where X is shading, contour, motion, or stereo). If I_{ij} is the intensity at point (i, j), and (f, g) are the stereographic coordinates of the surface orientation, we look for a surface (f_{ij}, g_{ij}), $(i, j) \in$ image that minimizes

$$e = \sum_i \sum_j (s_{ij} + \lambda r_{ij})$$

where

$$s_{ij} = \frac{1}{4}\left[(f_{i+1,j} - f_{ij})^2 + (f_{ij+1} - f_{ij})^2 + (g_{i+1,j} - g_{ij})^2 + (g_{ij+1} - g_{ij})^2\right]$$

and

$$r_{ij} = (I_{ij} - R(f_{ij}, g_{ij}))$$

The first term in the sum represents departure from smoothness, whereas the second represents departure from the constraint defined by the image irradiance equation. Thus the surface that minimizes e best satisfies the image irradiance equation and is also as smooth as possible. The parameter λ defines the relative importance of the smoothness and the irradiance constraint. We minimize e by differentiating with respect to f_{ij}, g_{ij} and setting the resulting derivatives equal to 0. This gives the following recurrence relations as the basis of an iterative algorithm:

$$f_{ij}^{(n+1)} = \overline{f_{ij}^{(n)}} + \lambda\left(I_{ij} - R(f_{ij}^{(n)}, g_{ij}^{(n)})\right)\frac{\partial R}{\partial f}$$

$$g_{ij}^{(n+1)} = \overline{g_{ij}^{(n)}} + \lambda\left(I_{ij} - R(f_{ij}^{(n)}, g_{ij}^{(n)})\right)\frac{\partial R}{\partial g}$$

where the superscripts in parentheses denote iterates, and the bars denote local averages. Since the surface orientation at the occluding boundaries is known, this recurrence propagates information inward and in a relaxation style computes the orientation everywhere.

Photometric Stereo

Another technique for computing shape from shading using multiple light sources is called *photometric stereo* [Woodham, 1980]. Let the intensity at point (x, y) in the image obtained when only the first light source is used be $I_1(x, y)$. Then the surface orientation at (x, y) is restricted to the isobrightness contour in the reflectance map corresponding to the brightness value computed from $I_1(x, y)$. Similarly, when the second light source is used, the surface orientation is restricted to the isobrightness contour defined by $I_2(x, y)$. Thus when we use both light sources, one at a time, the surface orientation is usually determined by the intersection of two isobrightness contours. Figure 9.42 describes the process. A third source provides complete disambiguation.

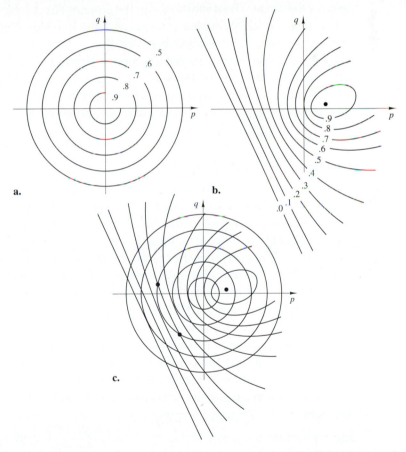

Figure 9.42   An illustration of photometric stereo using two light sources. (a) Isobrightness contours using only the first light source. (b) Isobrightness contours using only the second light source. (c) The isobrightness contours from both light sources superimposed. The surface orientation at a point can often be determined by finding the intersection of the two isobrightness contours corresponding to the intensities at the point for the light sources. (Reproduced from *ACM Computing Surveys* by written permission from the ACM.)

9.8   Shape from Texture

Texture provides an important source of information about the orientations of surfaces. Color Plates 5 and 6 show the perspective images of some natural surfaces. It seems that a human can easily perceive the shapes of the surfaces. To recover shape from texture, the distorting effects of the surface orientation and the imaging geometry must be distinguished from the properties of the texture on which the distortion acts. This requires that assumptions be made about the texture. The problem of recovering the orientation of a planar surface from texture has been extensively studied. These studies were based on different assumptions about the texture and the imaging geometry.

The process of image formation introduces distortions into the appearance of the scene. The distortions are the *distance* effect (objects appear larger when they are closer to the camera) and the *foreshortening* effect (the distortion depends on the angle between the surface normal and the line of sight). The orthographic projection model captures only the foreshortening effect and ignores the distance effect. Therefore, methods for shape from texture that use orthographic projection are valid only in a limited domain. The perspective projection model captures both effects.

Density of Textural Elements

The first to approach the shape-from-texture problem was Gibson [1979]. Trying to develop a theory of how humans perceive surface orientation from texture, he suggested that textures consist of small elements, which we shall call *texels*. Of course, these texels may be arranged very irregularly. We assume, however, that the texels are uniformly distributed on the scene plane in the sense that each unit area on that plane contains approximately the same number of texels. In the image, however, the texel density may not be uniform; it may vary (linearly) with position. The gradient (magnitude and direction of maximum rate of change) of texture density in the image then determines the surface orientation; the magnitude depends on the surface slant and the direction of the tilt.

The mathematics of backprojected texture density are as follows. Let image regions R_1 and R_2 have areas S_1 and S_2 and contain k_1 and k_2 texels, respectively. Under paraperspective projection, the areas of the corresponding regions on the scene plane are $T_1 = \frac{S_1 c^2 \sqrt{1+p^2+q^2}}{(1-A_1 p - B_1 q)^2}$ and $T_2 = \frac{S_2 c^2 \sqrt{1+p^2+q^2}}{(1-A_2 p - B_2 q)^2}$, respectively, where (A_1, B_1), (A_2, B_2) are the centroids of R_1, R_2, and the scene plane has equation $Z = pX + qY + c$. By the uniform density assumption, we have $k_1/T_1 = k_2/T_2$, and this can be transformed to give

$$\left[\left(\frac{k_2}{k_1} \frac{S_1}{S_2} \right)^{\frac{1}{3}} A_2 - A_1 \right] p + \left[\left(\frac{k_2}{k_1} \frac{S_1}{S_2} \right)^{\frac{1}{3}} B_2 - B_1 \right] q = \left(\frac{k_2}{k_1} \frac{S_1}{S_2} \right)^{\frac{1}{3}} - 1$$

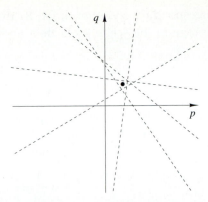

Figure 9.43   Lines in gradient space computed using several pairs of image regions. Each pair of image regions determines a line. Ideally, we can solve for p and q using two pairs of image regions; however, to deal with sampling errors, we use many pairs of image regions and compute the point whose sum of distances from all the lines is minimum.

This equation represents a line in p-q space; thus comparing the counts of texels in two image regions constrains (p, q) to lie on a line in gradient space. Ideally, using two pairs of image regions, we can solve for p and q. But because of the errors introduced by the sampling process (image digitization and density fluctuations of the texels in the regions), this will give unreliable results. To obtain a robust result, we consider many pairs of image regions. Each pair gives us a line in the gradient space, and the desired solution is the point whose sum of distances from all the lines is minimum (see Figure 9.43).

This method requires that the texels be identified so that they can be counted. A more realistic approach uses the total length of edges in an image region; assuming that these are texel edges, their total length should be proportional to the number of texels. Using this method, one can recover the orientations of planar surfaces in real-world scenes. For example, Color Plate 7 shows the image of an ivy-covered wall with orientation (slant = 20°, tilt = 0°). Color Plate 8 shows the extracted edges; this edge image was input to an algorithm that, using the modified uniform density assumption, recovered (slant = 24.5°, tilt = 5.6°).

Research on shape from texture for nonplanar surfaces has been restricted to idealized domains involving surfaces covered with uniformly spaced, identical texels, such as the ones in Color Plate 9.

Textural Reflectance Maps

There exists a technique that applies the methods used in shape from shading to the problem of shape from texture. Assume that all the texels are approximately planar and have the same area and that we use paraperspective projection. Let S_I be the area of an image texels, S_W the area of the corresponding scene texel, (A, B) the centroid of the image texel, and d the range to the scene texel; then (assuming focal length $= 1$), it can be shown that

$$S_I = \frac{S_W}{d^2} \frac{1 - Ap - Bq}{\sqrt{1 + p^2 + q^2}}$$

where (p, q) is the gradient of the plane containing the scene texel. If we call S_I the "textural intensity," and S_W/d^2 the "textural albedo," the preceding equation is very similar to the image irradiance equation

$$I = \omega \frac{1 - Ap - Bq}{\sqrt{(1 + p^2 + q^2)}}$$

where I is the intensity, (p, q) is the gradient of the surface point whose image has intensity I, ω is the albedo at the point, and $(A, B, -1)$ is the direction of the light source. We call

$$R(p, q) = \frac{S_W}{d^2} \frac{1 - Ap - Bq}{\sqrt{(1 + p^2 + q^2)}}$$

the "textural reflectance." If we fix S_W/d^2 and the position (A, B) of the texel on the image, this equation can be graphed conveniently as a series of contours of constant textural intensity. Figure 9.44 illustrates a simple *textural reflectance map*. Using $R(p, q)$, we can recover shape in a region Ω in the same way as we recovered shape from shading and occluding boundaries in Section 9.7, that is, by minimizing an expression of the form

$$\iint\limits_{\Omega} \left\{ (S_I - R)^2 + \frac{\lambda}{d^2}(p_x^2 + p_y^2 + q_x^2 + q_y^2) \right\} dx \, dy$$

with λ a constant weighing the relative importance of the constant versus smoothness. Results obtained using this method are shown in Color Plate 10.

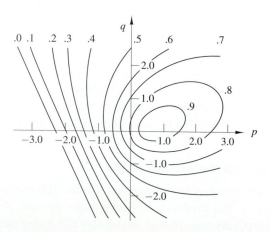

Figure 9.44 Textural reflectance map

9.9   Stereo

The use of stereo in computer vision indicates the recovery of the structure of a three-dimensional scene from two images of the scene, each acquired from a different viewpoint. The basic idea behind the process of stereo is based on triangulation (Figure 9.45). Consider a single image of a scene. The location in three dimensions of any visible object point is restricted to lie on the straight line connecting the center of projection and the image of the point. Thus, given two images from two different viewpoints, the location of any object point that is visible in both images is constrained to lie at the intersection of two straight lines. This process of locating a point in the scene by finding the intersection of two straight lines is called triangulation. In order, however, for triangulation to be feasible, we must "match" the image location of the object point in one image with its location in the other image. Establishing matches between features in a pair of images is known as the *correspondence problem*. When the correspondence between multiple points in two images is ambiguous, triangulation may lead to different interpretations of the scene that can be consistent (see Figure 9.46, page 454).

Addressing the Correspondence Problem

The correspondence problem is among the most difficult problems in computer vision. Many proposals for its solution have been presented and cast away. Some points in one image will have no corresponding points in the other image because the cameras have different fields of view and there may be occlusion.

It would seem that in order to establish correspondence, we would need to search the entire image for every point in the other image. Luckily, such a two-dimensional search is not necessary because a simple and powerful constraint exists that reduces the search requirements, namely, the *epipolar constraint*. Consider Figure 9.47 (page 454). A plane that passes through the

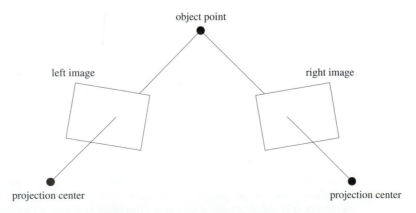

Figure 9.45   Stereo through triangulation

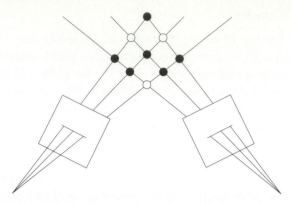

Figure 9.46 Ambiguity in correspondence of image points leads to different consistent scene interpretations

two centers of projection is called an *epipolar plane*. An epipolar plane is a plane containing the baseline. The straight lines that are intersections of the epipolar plane with the two image planes are called corresponding *epipolar lines*. It is clear from Figure 9.47 that the corresponding point of a point on one epipolar line is restricted to the corresponding epipolar line in the other image.

Usually, for reasons of computational convenience, the two image planes are chosen to be coplanar and parallel to their baseline. When the stereo images are coplanar and parallel to their baseline, they are said to be rectified. Finally, a frequently encountered term is disparity, which refers to the vector defined by the difference of two corresponding image points. Consider Figure 9.48, where the image planes of the left and right cameras in the stereo setup are coplanar.

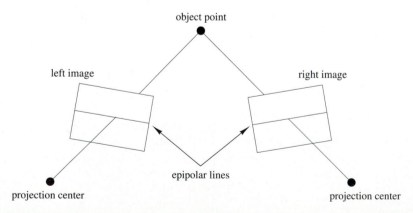

Figure 9.47 Epipolar geometry. Each of the two image planes in the diagram has a different center of projection. A plane that passes through the two centers of projection is called an epipolar plane. The lines at which an epipolar plane intersects one or the other of the two image planes are called epipolar lines.

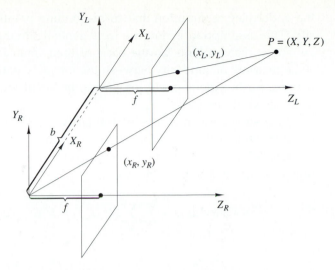

Figure 9.48 A stereo setup with coplanar left and right camera planes. *f* is the focal length of each camera, and *b* is the baseline.

If $P = (X, Y, Z)$ is a point in 3D with regard to the coordinate system of the left camera, then if (x_L, y_L) and (x_R, y_R) are the images of P in the left and right images, respectively, we have

$$x_L = \frac{fX}{Z}, \quad y_L = \frac{fY}{Z}$$

$$x_R = \frac{fX - b}{Z}, \quad y_R = \frac{fY}{Z}$$

Thus,

$$x_L - x_R = \frac{fb}{Z}, \quad \text{and } y_L = y_R$$

These equations signify that there is only horizontal disparity $x_L - x_R \overset{\triangle}{=} d$, and the equation $d = \frac{fb}{Z}$ or $Z = \frac{fb}{d}$ signifies the triangulation process.

The issues involved in establishing correspondence between two images are (a) what entities (features, points) to match in the two images, (b) how to perform the matching, and (c) how to evaluate the successfulness of a match. Correspondence search is constrained along corresponding epipolar lines. There are two general classes of techniques for addressing the stereo correspondence problem: the methods based on matching image intensities and the ones based on matching edges.

Intensity-Based Matching

To establish correspondences along corresponding epipolar lines, we can match points on the basis of their image intensities. This approach makes the underlying assumption that corresponding points have the same intensity. This assumption is not true for a general situation.[5] For this reason, if we are to match points on the basis of their intensity, we must minimize some measure of similarity between the intensity patterns of various image regions. Such regions could, of course, be small windows, epipolar lines, or even whole images.

Two successful measures of similarity are the sum of squared differences (SSD) and the cross-correlation (CC). If $I^L(x, y)$ and $I^R(x, y)$ are the discrete left and right images, respectively, then the SSD and CC over a region W are defined as follows:

$$SSD(\Delta x, \Delta y) = \sum_{i,j \in W} \left(I^L(i, j) - I^R(i - \Delta x, j - \Delta y) \right)^2$$

$$CC(\Delta x, \Delta y) = \sum_{i,j \in W} I^L(i, j) I^R(i - \Delta x, j - \Delta y)$$

To match one image to another, we choose a small window centered at an image point on some epipolar line and find the best matching image window along the corresponding epipolar line. The center of the window can then be chosen as the corresponding point. An important issue in this kind of matching is related to the size of the window used. If the window is too small, then it may not be able to capture enough image structure, and it may be noise sensitive, thus resulting in false matches. If it is too large, it may violate the underlying assumption that intensities around corresponding points are similar. Figure 9.49 shows results from a stereo system performing intensity-based matching.

Edge-Based Matching

With this technique, we detect edges and match the edges' intersections with corresponding epipolar lines. Of course, this technique is ineffective for regions not containing edges or for edges that are along epipolar lines. Edge-based methods take advantage of the *edge continuity constraint*. If the intersection of an edge with an epipolar line in one image matches some intersection of an edge with the corresponding epipolar line, then all other intersections of these two edges with corresponding epipolar lines must also match. Edge-based methods will provide depth at only those image points that are locally distinguishable along epipolar lines. Hence, several techniques have been invented to estimate depths at intermediate points by assuming a surface in view with certain properties.

---

[5]It is true only for perfectly Lambertian surfaces.

a.

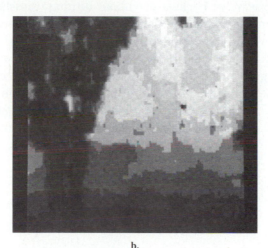

b.

Figure 9.49 (a) Stereo pair of an outdoor scene. (b) Computed disparity image. High intensity indicates a low disparity between image positions of corresponding pixels. Low intensity indicates high disparity. (From "Stochastic Stereo Matching Over Scale," S. Barnard, *International Journal of Computer Vision*, Vol. 3, pp. 17–32, 1989. Courtesy of Kluwer Academic Publishers.)

9.10 Analysis of Visual Motion

The previous sections were restricted to visual perception by a stationary observer. A moving observer can examine much more of the world. When a camera moves in some environment and collects a sequence of images, then the image data is enriched with an additional dimension, namely, the dimension of the moving viewpoint. With more information, performing recovery is easier. Recovery of shape using time-varying imagery is a generalization of stereo recovery since the underlying principles are the same.

Every scene point lies on all its projection rays, and thus multiple rays from a scene point determine the spatial position of the point. The major difference between stereo vision and mobile vision is that in stereo the positioning of the two cameras is known. In motion, the relative positioning of the cameras as they collect successive image frames often is not known. Thus, the use of time-varying imagery requires the relative motion between the camera and the scene to first be determined.

Motion Fields

An important concept in time-varying image analysis is that of the *motion field*, introduced by Gibson. Figure 9.50 shows the motion field on the eye of a pilot looking straight ahead in level flight on an overcast day. The motion field is an assignment of vectors to image points. Each vector represents the image motion of the corresponding scene point. When the observer is moving forward or backward without turning (translating only), all the image motion vectors radiate outward from (if the observer approaches the scene in view) or toward (if the observer moves away from the scene) a single image point called the *focus of expansion* or *focus of contraction*, respectively. As Figure 9.51 indicates, the focus of expansion is defined as the point of intersection of the direction of translation of a translating observer with the image surface. Thus, when the direction of translation is parallel to the image plane, the motion field vectors are parallel, and the focus of expansion lies at infinity (see Figure 9.52).

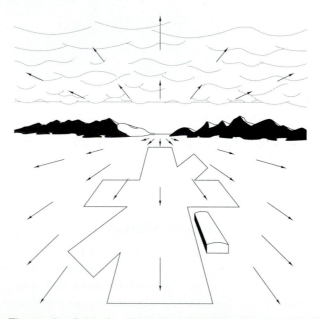

Figure 9.50   The motion field of a pilot looking straight ahead in level flight. (Reproduced from *The Perception of the Visual World* by written permission from Houghton Mifflin Publishing Company.)

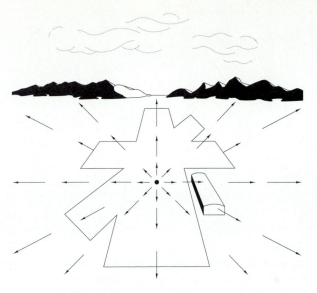

Figure 9.51   The focus of expansion. (Reproduced from *The Perception of the Visual World* by written permission from Houghton Mifflin Publishing Company.)

Alternatively, if the observer rotates only around an axis passing through its origin (and not necessarily along the line of sight), then the motion field is tangential to a set of conic sections. In such a case, every point in 3D moves along a circle in a plane perpendicular to the axis of rotation. The perspective image of this circular path is the intersection of the image plane with the cone defined by the circle and the rotation axis (see Figure 9.53a).

Figure 9.52   The motion field of a pilot looking to the right in level flight. (Reproduced from *The Perception of the Visual World* by written permission from Houghton Mifflin Publishing Company.)

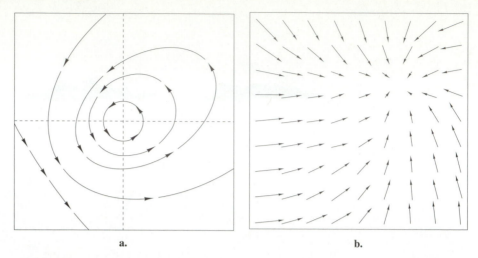

Figure 9.53   (a) Rotational motion field; the center of rotation (at the intersection of the two dashed lines) is the point where the axis of rotation intersects the imaging surface. (b) Motion field for a general rigid motion sampled at points on a 9 × 9 grid.

Depending on the relation between the aperture angle of the cone for a given point and the angle that the image plane forms with the rotation axis, different second-order curves are obtained for the intersection. When, however, the observer is moving in an unrestricted rigid manner (with translation and rotation), then the focus of expansion (or contraction) and the rotation center are not necessarily obvious in the motion field (Figure 9.53b).

As already emphasized, a moving observer, before it proceeds to recover the scene, must recover its own motion using as input the motion field. More formally, the problem of *structure from motion* is defined as follows: For an observer moving rigidly with translation $T = (U, V, W)$ and rotation $\Omega = (\alpha, \beta, \gamma)$ in an environment, recover the motion of the observer and the structure of the scene using as input the series of images collected by the observer (see Figure 9.54).

Clearly, the estimation of motion and structure should happen using as input the motion field, which is not available and must be estimated. Thus, the problem of "structure from motion" consists primarily of two components: the estimation of the motion field and its interpretation.

Here, we do not treat the cases where the scene in view consists of multiple moving objects or objects moving nonrigidly. Further, we are not concerned with problems of visual motion such as pursuit, tracking, and homing or docking. We are concerned only with recovery of motion and structure by a moving observer in a static scene.

Motion Field Estimation

The relative motion of the observer with respect to the scene gives rise to a motion of brightness patterns in the image plane. The instantaneous

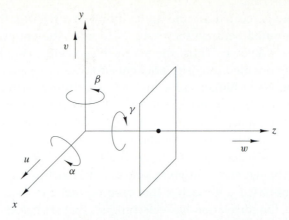

Figure 9.54 A rigidly moving observer

changes of the brightness pattern in the image plane are analyzed to derive the *optical flow field*, a two-dimensional vector field describing the image displacements. Optical flow, the velocity on the image, is our approximation to the motion field.

The optical flow value of each pixel is computed locally; that is, only information of a small spatio-temporal neighborhood is used in order to estimate it. In general, it is not possible to compute an image point's true velocity by observing only a small neighborhood. Imagine that you are watching a feature (line, bar, piece of contour) through an aperture that is small compared to the feature at two instances of time (see Figure 9.55). Watching through this small aperture, it is impossible to determine where each point of the feature moved to exactly. The only information directly available from local measurements is the component of the velocity that is perpendicular to the feature, the so-called *normal flow*. We cannot, however, determine the component of the optical flow parallel to the feature. This ambiguity, which is referred to as the *aperture problem*, exists independently of the technique employed for local estimation of flow. In cases where the

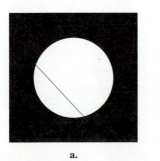
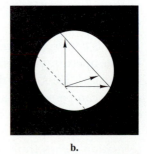

a.   b.

Figure 9.55 (a) Line feature watched through a small aperture at time *t*. (b) At time $t+\delta t$, the feature has moved to a new position. It is not possible to determine where each point exactly moved to. From local measurements only the flow component perpendicular to the line feature can be computed.

aperture is located around an endpoint of a feature, the true velocity may be computed because the exact location of the endpoint at two instances of time is known. Thus, the aperture problem exists in regions that have strongly oriented intensity gradients (for example, edges) and may not exist at locations of higher-order intensity variations, such as corners.

Therefore, any optical flow procedure has to involve two computational mechanisms. In the first step, assuming the conservation of some form of information about the image, locally available velocity information is computed. According to the kind of information that is assumed not to change, three different kinds of approaches can be distinguished: the gradient-based approaches that assume that the image intensity does not change, the correlation-based techniques that are based on the assumption of conservation of local intensity distribution, and the spatio-temporal energy-based approaches that are analogous to the gradient-based approaches in the spatio-temporal frequency space. In a second step, in order to compute the other component of the optical flow vectors, additional assumptions have to be made. Either some kind of smoothness is assumed or the shape of the scene is geometrically modeled to obtain constraints for the optical flow values. Here we describe the gradient-based approaches.

The gradient-based approach introduced by Horn and Schunck [1981] is based on the assumption that for a given scene point the intensity I at the corresponding image point remains constant over time. If a scene point P projects onto the image point (x, y) at time t and onto the image point $(x + \delta x, y + \delta y)$ at time $(t + \delta t)$, one can write

$$I(x, y, t) = I(x + \delta x, y + \delta y, t + \delta t) \tag{9.9}$$

If we develop the right-hand side of equation (9.9) by a first-order Taylor's series expansion and denote by $u(x, y)$, $v(x, y)$ the velocity of image points $\left(\frac{dx}{dt}, \frac{dy}{dt}\right)$ (the components of the optical flow vector), we obtain the following equation that relates the optical flow to the partial derivatives I_x, I_y, I_t of I:

$$I_x u + I_y v + I_t = 0 \tag{9.10}$$

This constraint is called the *optical flow constraint equation*, and it simplifies the aperture problem. The linear equation defines a line in velocity space (u-v space). Thus, only the vector component in the direction of the gradient (I_x, I_y) can be computed. If we employ the motion constraint equation everywhere in the image, the normal flow may be computed (see Figure 9.56).

We need more information in order to estimate optical flow. Such information comes from additional assumptions that we can make about the scene in view. One constraint that has received considerable attention is smoothness, that is, requiring that the flow field is smooth in a way similar to the one presented in Section 9.4 for shape recovery. If we measure departure from smoothness as a quantity like $S = u_x^2 + u_y^2 + v_x^2 + v_y^2$, then flow

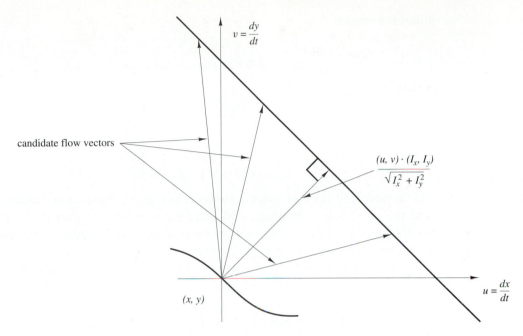

Figure 9.56 Constraints on optical flow. The equation $I_x u + I_y v + I_t = 0$ specifies that only the component of (u, v) along the gradient (I_x, I_y) can be estimated and that we have no information about the component of the flow tangential to the contour through the image point (x, y).

estimation could proceed by minimizing a function of the form

$$\iint_I L^2 dx\, dy + \lambda \iint_I S\, dx\, dy$$

where $L = I_x u + I_y v + I_t$ signifies the geometric constraint. As before, λ weights the relative importance of the constraint versus the assumption of smoothness.

Motion Field Interpretation

After the estimation of the optical flow field, we have an approximation to the motion field that we can relate to 3D motion and shape. When the observer of Figure 9.54 moves with rigid motion (T, Ω), we can consider that the observer is stationary and the scene moves with the opposite motion.

Thus, a point (X, Y, Z) in the observer's coordinate system is moving with velocity $V = -T - \Omega \times (X, Y, Z)$, or

$$\dot{X} = -V - \beta Z + \gamma Y$$
$$\dot{Y} = -V - \gamma X + \alpha Z$$
$$\dot{Z} = -W - \alpha Y + \beta X$$

Considering then the image projection equations $x = \frac{X}{Z}, y = \frac{Y}{Z}$ (where the focal length is assumed to be one unit), and differentiating with respect to time, we obtain

$$\dot{x} = u = u_{\text{trans}} + u_{\text{rot}}$$
$$\dot{y} = v = v_{\text{trans}} + v_{\text{rot}}$$

where

$$u_{\text{trans}} = \frac{-U + xW}{Z}, \quad v_{\text{trans}} = \frac{-V + yW}{Z}$$

$$u_{\text{rot}} = \alpha xy - \beta(1 + x^2) + \gamma y$$
$$v_{\text{rot}} = \alpha(1 + y^2) - \beta xy - \gamma x$$

The motion field at every point consists of two parts, one due to translation and the other due to rotation, with only the translational part depending on the structure (Z) of the scene in view. From the preceding equations, it can be easily derived that the motion field is invariant under scaling of the depth (Z) and the translational vector (U, V, W). Consequently, we can derive the direction of translation $\left(\frac{U}{W}, \frac{V}{W}\right)$ and the depth Z only up to an unknown scale factor (shape).

From the previous equations, we have

$$\frac{u - u_{\text{rot}}}{v - v_{\text{rot}}} = \frac{-\frac{U}{W} + x}{-\frac{V}{W} + y}$$

This is a nonlinear equation in the unknowns $\frac{U}{W}$, $\frac{V}{W}$, α, β, γ and holds at every image point where a measurement of optical flow is available. Solution of a system of such equations provides the 3D motion parameters. The nonlinearity involved in this problem has generated a great deal of research addressing structure from motion.

One set of techniques is based on modeling the shape of the scene in view. Assuming that the surface in view is smooth and that the optical flow field varies smoothly, a series of algorithms appeared that estimate the 3D motion from only local information. The surface patch in the scene around the optical axis is approximated by either a plane or a quadratic. Then, by using information about optical flow and its derivatives, it is possible to obtain 3D motion and shape. However, any method that uses optical flow only locally will be unstable because completely different observer motions produce locally similar motion fields. For example, in an area near the y axis of the image plane, 3D rotation around the X axis produces a flow field similar to the one produced by translation along the Y axis.

In recent years, techniques have appeared that characterize the motion field globally by making use of properties relevant to 3D motion that are defined on the whole visual field. For example, consider a spherical eye in motion, such as the eyes of several insects.[6] The motion field in this

---

[6]Insects can very successfully solve 3D motion estimation problems.

Figure 9.57   Spherical motion field for a sensor translating without rotation

case has very nice global properties. The motion vectors due to translation are along geodesics, all emanating from one point and flowing into another point with the two points separated by 180 degrees (see Figure 9.57 [Nelson and Aloimonos, 1988]). If rotation is present, this structure is not there. The two characteristic points move toward each other. A successful technique for estimating 3D motion is to search for the rotation (α, β, γ), which when subtracted from the whole motion field, leaves the pattern of Figure 9.57 (purely translational). Finally, the flow field on the whole image can be decomposed by considering flow vectors in particular directions [Fermüller, 1993].

9.11   Active Vision

So far we have been concerned with the principles behind scene recovery from image cues for a passive observer. The observer had no control over the image acquisition process. It turned out that recovering the structure of the scene in this case is an extremely difficult, underconstrained problem. However, the vision of most biological organisms is not passive but exploratory and active. Organisms do not just see, they look. Their eyes converge or diverge, they adjust to the level of illumination, and their heads move to obtain a better view of the scene. In the past few years, researchers started examining the computational advantages of active observers over passive ones.

An observer is called *active* when it is trying to control how it sees. The observer controls the parameters of its eye and manipulates the constraints underlying the observed phenomena to improve perception. For example, a monocular observer that moves and can rotate its eyes and track environmental objects is an example of an active observer.

The activities of active observers include touch and motion and others that remain unexplored. In the case where the observer is moving, tracking environmental points or converging the cameras, results have been reported.

TABLE 9.1 Comparing the performance of active and passive observers		
Problem	Passive Observer	Active Observer
Shape from shading	Ill-posed problem. Needs to be regularized. Even then, unique solution is not guaranteed because of nonlinearity.	Well-posed problem. Unique solution, linear equation, stability.
Shape from contour	Ill-posed problem. Has not been regularized up to now in the Tichonov sense. Solvable under restrictive assumptions.	Well-posed problem. Unique solution for both monocular and binocular observer.
Shape from texture	Ill-posed problem. Needs some assumption about the texture.	Well-posed problem. No assumption required.
Structure from motion	Well-posed but unstable. Nonlinear constraints.	Well-posed and stable. Quadratic constraints, simple solution methods, stability.

They state that several shape-from-X problems (where X is shading, contour, motion, or stereo) become well conditioned, and unique solutions are possible. This is not surprising because there is an additional information source, which is controlled by the observer. The basis for the approach lies in the ability to work in a rich stimulus domain with a partially known parameterization.

This knowledge is due to the fact that the viewing transformation is known. As the viewing parameters are continuously varied, the observed visual stimuli undergo local transformations that are measurable and provide powerful constraints for the computation of the unknown scene parameters. It should be pointed out that in the active vision paradigm, one does not work with a small set of discrete observations but with trajectories in the stimulus space termed flow lines. These trajectories are smooth since the viewing transformations we use are themselves smooth and therefore can be computed accurately enough for our purposes. Thus we do not need to rely on the smoothness of properties of the observed scene, such as illumination and depth. Table 9.1 compares the performance of a passive and an active observer in the solution of several basic problems.

9.12   Applications

As we already emphasized, a broad spectrum of computer vision applications exists, ranging from autonomously navigating systems to specialized workstations for the photointerpreter or the radiologist. Here we concentrate on two applications, one related to autonomous navigation and the other to recognition of classes of man-made objects.

Autonomous Vehicle Navigation

Navigation refers to the ability of a system to move about the world with some degree of autonomy. A system that navigates interacts adaptively with the environment. In particular, the movement of the system is governed by sensory feedback that allows it to adapt to variations in the environment rather than being limited to a small set of fixed motions, as is the case with most industrial robots of today.

The U.S. government has sponsored research on autonomous navigation for quite some time. During the 1980s this research gave rise to the Autonomous Land Vehicle (ALV), which was capable of successfully following roads (see Figure 9.58).

The evolution of the ALV is the so-called Unmanned Ground Vehicle (UGV). A UGV is supposed also to move on rough terrain, outside the road network, and perform tasks related to reconnaissance, surveillance, and target acquisition (RSTA). Recall from Section 9.10 that if the vehicle is capable of recovering the shape and 3D motion of the scene from the sequence of images it acquires as it is moving, then it will be able to perform any RSTA task. This amounts, however, to solving the general problem of structure from motion, which is too difficult. Luckily, the vehicle can solve a

Figure 9.58   The Autonomous Land Vehicle, a project sponsored at Martin Marietta Corp. by the Defense Advanced Research Projects Agency (DARPA). The vehicle carried TV cameras and computers, and drove itself along a road network using information about road geometry derived from the TV images. (Courtesy of Martin Marietta Corporation. Approved for Public Release, Distribution Unlimited.)

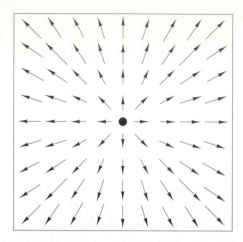

Figure 9.59 A typical flow pattern due to a pure translation. In this case, the observer is approaching the scene, so the arrows radiate outward from a single point called the focus of expansion. If the observer is moving away from the scene, the arrows radiate inward toward a single point called the focus of contraction.

collection of problems whose complexity is much lower than the one of the general structure-from-motion problem. Such problems include finding egomotion, finding independently moving objects,[7] and reasoning about parts of the scene through the understanding of the material by which parts of the scene are made. For example, using a combination of visual and inertial sensors, the vehicle can understand in real time its own motion. This amounts to knowledge of its translation (focus of expansion) and rotation values.

Recall from Section 9.10 that the flow due to the rotation of the sensor does not depend on the depth of the scene. It depends on only the value (α, β, γ) of the rotation. Thus, it can be computed at every point in the image and subtracted from the actual optical flow, leaving only the part of the flow due to translation. This process is known as *derotation*. Assuming that the focus of expansion lies on the image, meaning that the vehicle is looking toward the direction in which it is moving, the flow should be as in Figure 9.59 if no other object is moving in the environment.

If the scene contains independently moving objects, the pattern of Figure 9.59 is destroyed, and moving objects are detected. In addition, if the sensors of the vehicle are *active*, like human eyes, by fixating at different parts of the scene the detection of moving objects becomes easier. Figure 9.60 shows a scene containing moving objects (cars) as seen by a moving UGV. Figure 9.61 (page 470) shows parts of the scene moving independently and discovered by selecting the pixels whose motion does not agree with the

---

[7]This is quite a difficult problem if the vehicle is moving since the whole image is in motion.

Figure 9.60   A sequence of closely sampled images taken by a UGV. (Courtesy of Rajeev Sharma, University of Maryland.)

pattern of Figure 9.59. Finally, after an exploratory activity consisting of successive fixations, information about independent motion is enriched and displayed in Figure 9.62 (page 470).

Another important task that a UGV needs to perform is to find properties of the scene. This is achieved using a set of techniques identified by the name *physics-based* approaches in computer vision. Using properties of the light reflected from the surfaces in the environment, such as color, hue, polarization, and illumination as well as appropriate models of the image formation, a UGV can detect parts of the scene made by the same material, dialectric and metallic objects, and shadows. Color Plate 11 shows an outdoor image seen by a UGV. Color Plates 12 and 13 display results from a physics-based analysis of the scene.

Object Recognition

Another application we discuss here is related to the recognition of a class of man-made objects. Biederman [1985] has observed that a large class of objects consists of a small set of primitive parts that he called *geons*. Several systems based on geons have been constructed that recognize restricted classes of objects. Figure 9.63 (page 471) shows a set of volumetric primitives used in Dickinson et al. [1992]. These primitives can be mathematically defined

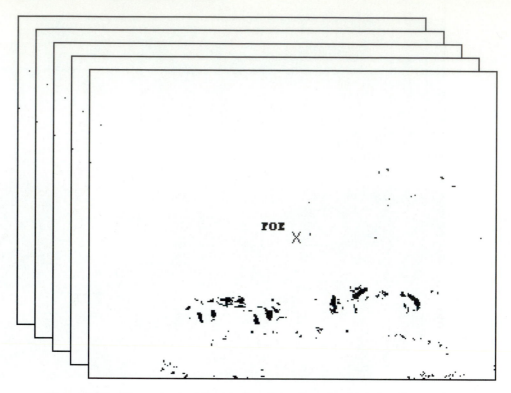

Figure 9.61   The output of the motion detection algorithm by discovering pixels whose flow does not conform to the pattern of Figure 9.59. (Courtesy of Rajeev Sharma, University of Maryland.)

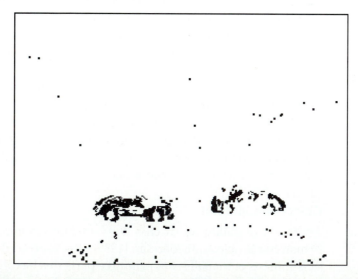

Figure 9.62   The output of the motion detection algorithm after a set of successive fixations by the active sensors of a UGV. (Courtesy of Rajeev Sharma, University of Maryland.)

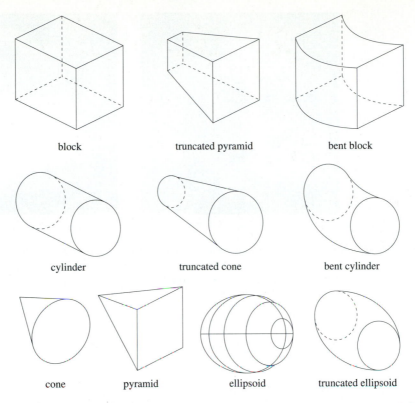

Figure 9.63 Ten primitives for classifying geometric shapes. (Reproduced from Dickinson et al. [1992] © 1992 IEEE.)

using elaborate models of *generalized cylinders*, *generalized cones*, and *superquadrics*.

Recognition then proceeds as follows: Given an image (or several images) of an object, its shape is recovered using the variety of techniques described in this chapter. Having reconstructed the shape, specialized algorithms attempt to fit the geons of Figure 9.63. The successful fitting of geons and the discovery of the relationship of the different geons lead to the recognition of the imaged object. Figures 9.64a and 9.64b (page 472) show the images of two man-made objects, and Figures 9.65a and 9.65b (page 472) demonstrate the fitted parts, along with the identified geons.

▼ Summary

This chapter is concerned primarily with computer vision, the field of AI that describes the automatic understanding of the structure and properties of the three-dimensional world from its two-dimensional images. The images are usually sampled in space and time, and the magnitudes of these samples are quantized so that they can be easily processed by a digital computer. In this text, we emphasize vision as the problem of deriving, from

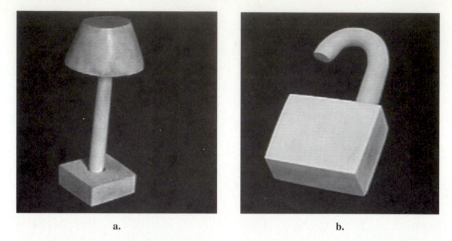

a.   **b.**

Figure 9.64   (a) Image of a table lamp. (b) Image of a lock. Both images are 256×256 pixels resolution. (From "3-D Shape Recovery Using Distributed Aspect Matching," S.J. Dickinson, A.P. Pentland, and A. Rosenfeld, IEEE PAMI, Vol. 14, No. 2, February 1992, pp. 174–198, ⓒ1992 IEEE.)

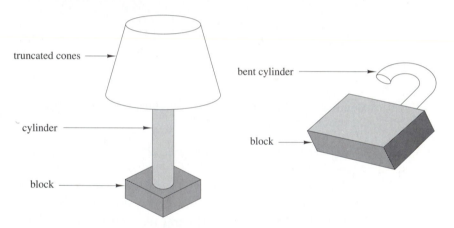

Figure 9.65   (a) Correct interpretation of the table lamp. (b) Correct interpretation of the lock. The labels indicate geons from Figure 9.63. (From "3-D Shape Recovery Using Distributed Aspect Matching," S.J. Dickinson, A.P. Pentland, and A. Rosenfeld, IEEE PAMI, Vol. 14, No. 2, February 1992, pp. 174–198, ⓒ1992 IEEE.)

one or more images of a scene, an accurate three-dimensional description of the objects in the scene appropriate for a given task.

We looked at the geometry and physics of image formation. In particular, we considered the pinhole camera as a simple model for describing the process of image formation. We described various mathematical projection models for analyzing images. Perspective projection was the most accurate model but complicated the mathematics. Orthographic projection was the simplest mathematically but was not sufficiently accurate. Paraperspective projection offered a compromise between accuracy and analytic tractability. We also considered simple optics for imaging with lenses that offer a more realistic model of image formation in both machines and animals.

To reduce the enormous amount of information in images, we considered methods for detecting edges and segmenting the images into homogeneous regions. We looked at operators to remove noise and detect changes in intensity that might indicate discontinuities in shape, depth, and other properties of the objects in a scene. We described various methods for recovering shape in terms of the orientation of small surface patches from shading, contour, and texture cues.

Stereo allows us two views of a scene at the same instant in time and can in some cases simplify the extraction of depth information. Stereo gives rise to the correspondence problem, which involves matching the image location of an object point in one image with the location of the object point in the other image. The stereo correspondence problem is generally addressed by methods that either match image intensities or match edges.

We can generalize from two views of a scene at a single point in time to multiple views of a possibly changing scene at different points in time. To extract motion from a sequence of images, we discussed the idea of a motion field that describes the image motion of each point in a scene. We considered methods to approximate the motion field by computing the optical flow field, a two-dimensional vector field describing image displacements.

We also considered briefly some of the issues raised in designing active observers that can move about and point their sensors to obtain different views. It turns out that several problems that are ill-posed in terms of a passive observer are well-posed for an active observer.

The primary focus of this chapter was on the theoretical principles of computational vision; several aspects related to complexity, color, architecture, and high-level concepts were left out. The problem of recognizing objects using prestored models, although extremely important, was not treated primarily because a common view on how visual recognition happens in artificial or biological systems does not exist. The conventional wisdom is shown in Figure 9.66 (page 474).

The study of vision is a difficult and exciting field, bringing together ideas from a multitude of disciplines such as artificial intelligence, engineering, mathematics, and biology. During the past ten years, the study of vision was separated from the study of artificial intelligence. This is reflected in the textbooks on the topic as well as the conferences and archival journals. This perhaps was necessary since the fields were in their infancy and needed some specialization in order to advance. Today, however, most fields of AI have reached a high level of sophistication, and specialists have started worrying about the next step in our effort to understand intelligence. This step is related to the problem of integration of the different AI fields that are described in this book.

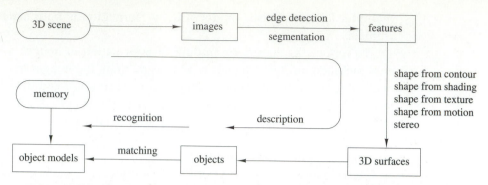

Figure 9.66   How recognition might be accomplished. Using the processes described in this chapter, we can arrive from images to object descriptions, which are then matched to models of object in memory to achieve recognition. Important issues have to do with what kinds of representations are needed for representing the objects and how is visual memory organized. See Levine [1985] for a detailed account of our understanding.

This chapter described a basic set of processes that need to be understood before we design systems with vision. Because of the nature of this book, we were constrained to describe only some fundamental operations. However, as we move to the next millenium, AI textbooks will be devoting more and more space to the study of perception.

● Background

Ballard and Brown [1982], Horn [1986], Nalwa [1993], and Rosenfeld and Kak [1982] are excellent general texts on computer vision. For more on active vision, see Aloimonos et al. [1988] and Bajcsy [1988].

Computer vision is related to a number of fields, the most important being *image processing, pattern recognition*, and *photogrammetry*. Image processing is a term for the processing of images to produce new images that have a desired property. The following tasks are examples of image processing (see Pratt [1991]). *Image enhancement* involves altering images to improve their appearance to humans. *Image restoration* aims to correct images for degradations due to noise. *Image compression* seeks to represent images in an economical way while maintaining image quality above some level. Figure 9.67 shows an example of image restoration.

Pattern recognition seeks to classify patterns into prespecified categories (see Duda and Hart [1973]). Pattern recognition has been a precursor of computer vision in the sense that the emphasis shifted to generating descriptions of 3D scenes—scenes that are not constrained to be instances of predetermined sets—for the purposes of recognition.

Finally, the field of photogrammetry [Wolf, 1974] seeks to develop the geometry of a 3D scene from several images of the scene. For example, from images of a scene like the one in Figure 9.68a and knowledge of the orientation of the cameras that collected the images as well as being able to find the same feature in all the images, a photogrammetric application can generate a relief map of the area (Figure 9.68b).

This chapter is primarily concerned with *what could be* inferred about the 3D world from its images. For research on and answers to the *empirical questions* (*what*

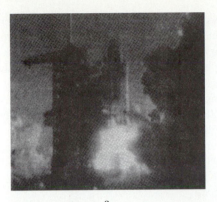 

a.   b.

Figure 9.67   (a) Original image. (b) Restored image produced by segmentation and fitting (see Section 9.5). (From "Segmentation Through Variable-Order Surface Fitting," P.J. Besl and R.C. Jain, IEEE PAMI, Vol. 10, No. 2, March 1988, pp. 167–192. ©1988 IEEE.)

is, that is, how existing biological vision systems work), see the special issue of *Scientific American* on "Mind and Brain," September 1992. Regarding the *normative questions* (*what should be*, that is, how organisms or robots should be designed in an optimal manner for achieving a set of tasks), see Aloimonos [1993].

See Gregory [1970] for a survey of research on animal vision from the perspectives of neurophysiology, psychology, and psychophysics. The Hough transform has a broad spectrum of applications besides edge aggregation. For additional applications of the Hough transform, see Ballard and Brown [1982].

 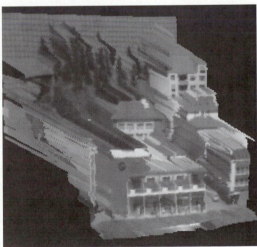

a.   b.

Figure 9.68   (a) One of the images collected. (b) Perspective view of the recovered scene depth. (From "A Stereo Matching Algorithm With an Adaptive Window: Theory and Experiment," T. Kanade and M. Okutami, Proc. 1991 Int'l Conf. on Robotics and Automation, April 9–11, 1991, Sacramento, CA, pp. 1088–1095. ©1991 IEEE.)

Aloimonos and Shulman [1989] provide an extended discussion of deterministic and probabilistic relaxation processes. Techniques of splitting and merging have received some attention but have had limited success [Horowitz and Pavlidis, 1976]. The taxonomy for labeling edges in a line drawing, which is described in the text, is due to Huffman [1971].

For more on recovering surface orientation from gray-level variations (called shape from shading) as well as a comprehensive discussion of reflectance maps for a variety of surface and light source conditions, see Horn [1986].

For more on the problem of recovering the orientation of a planar surface from texture, see Aloimonos [1988], Gibson [1979], and Witkin [1981]. See Terzopoulos [1986] and Grimson [1981] for more on edge-based matching techniques for estimating depth.

See Fermüller [1993] and Singh [1990] for further discussion of optical flow. Longuet-Higgins and Prazdny [1980] and Waxman and Ullman [1985] describe additional methods for approximating the surface patch in the scene around the optical axis using either a planar or a quadratic function. See Maxwell and Shafer [1993] for more on physics-based scene analysis.

Besides the ambitious goal of creating machines with visual capabilities comparable to human ones, computer vision has many applications [Brady, 1982]. These include automation on the assembly line, remote sensing, document understanding systems, generating maps of terrains, recognizing particular patterns, human–computer interaction, teleconferencing, inspection, aids for the handicapped, photointerpretation, virtual reality, and autonomously navigating systems.

■ Exercises

9.1 **a)** Show that the perspective image of an ellipse lying on a plane, not necessarily parallel to the image plane, is also an ellipse.
   b) Show that the image of a sphere is an ellipse whose major axis passes through the origin of the image.

9.2 The homogeneous coordinates are a representation that allows linearization of the nonlinear perspective projection (equation 9.1). Suppose we map each point (x, y, z) in 3D space to a line (wx, wy, wz, w) in four-dimensional space. The new coordinates (wx, wy, wz, w) are called homogeneous coordinates. A point (X, Y, Z, W), $W \neq 0$ in 4D space corresponds to a unique point $\left(\frac{X}{W}, \frac{Y}{W}, \frac{Z}{W}\right)$ in 3D space. Perspective projection can be expressed as follows:

$$[X_I, Y_I, Z_I, W_I]^T = P[X_W, Y_W, Z_W, W_W]^T$$

where $[X_W, Y_W, Z_W, W_W]^T$, $[X_I, Y_I, Z_I, W_I]^T$ are the homogeneous coordinates of a point and its image and

$$P = \begin{bmatrix} f & 0 & 0 & 0 \\ 0 & f & 0 & 0 \\ 0 & 0 & f & 0 \\ 0 & 0 & 1 & 0 \end{bmatrix}$$

the 4×4 perspective transformation matrix.
   a) Using homogeneous coordinates, express as linear transformations the following transformations: rotation around the x axis, rotation around any axis, scaling, skewing, and translation.

b) Before we use image information to derive properties of the 3D scene, we must determine the parameters that relate the position of a scene point to its image. This problem is known as geometric camera calibration. The parameters to be determined are the *six extrinsic* camera parameters and the four intrinsic camera parameters. Of the six extrinsic parameters, three are for the position of the center of projection and three for the orientation of the image coordinate system. Of the four intrinsic parameters, two are for the position of the origin of the image coordinate system and two for the scale factors of the axes of this frame. Given the perspective images of six known points in the scene, use homogeneous coordinates to derive closed form solutions to the calibration parameters.

Hint: The perspective mapping along with image scaling along any direction in the image are both linear transformations in homogeneous coordinates. Therefore, the complete mapping can be expressed as a multiplicative matrix in homogeneous coordinates. First derive this matrix [Ballard and Brown, 1982], and then use it to derive closed form solutions to the calibration parameters [Ganapathy, 1984].

9.3 Show that the paraperspective projection is an affine transformation, and derive its matrix [Aloimonos, 1990].

9.4 In the case of paraperspective projection, the auxiliary plane passed from the center of mass under consideration and was parallel to the image plane. If we change the orientation of the auxiliary plane, we can obtain a different approximation of the perspective. If the auxiliary plane is perpendicular to the line connecting the focal point of the camera and the mass center of the 3D planar patch under consideration, then this kind of paraperspective is called *orthoperspective*. Use the orthoperspective projection approximation to solve the three-point perspective problem: Given the images p_0, p_1, p_2 of three points in space P_0, P_1, P_2 with known relative positions but unknown positions along their lines of sight, estimate the orientation of the triangle $P_0 P_1 P_2$. How many solutions are possible [DeMenthon and Davis, 1989]?

9.5 Consider two planes P_1 and P_2 in a scene intersecting at a line e and their orthographic image. Let E be the edge representing the image of e. Show that the line connecting the gradients G_1 and G_2 of planes P_1 and P_2 in gradient space is perpendicular to the edge E in image space. The relative position of G_1 and G_2 is related to the convexity or concavity of the edge between the surfaces [Shafer et al. 1983].

9.6 Figure 9.69 (page 478) shows four classical optical illusions. In each of the drawings, geometric facts appear untrue. In the Zöllner illusion, the diagonals are parallel but appear otherwise. In the Müller–Lyer illusion, the horizontal line with reversed arrowheads appears longer than the line with the normal arrowheads although both lines have the same length. In the Hering and Wundt illusions, the two horizontal and parallel straight lines appear bowed. Explain each of the illusions by assuming that the observer attempts to give every drawing a 3D interpretation (see Gregory [1970]).

9.7 Consider the orthographic image of a trihedral vertex of a rectangular polyhedron as in Figure 9.70 (page 478), where the angles θ_1, θ_2, and θ_3 are known. Determine the orientation of the polyhedron in space.

9.8 For a line drawing consisting of straight-line segments to be realizable by trihedral vertex polyhedra, it is necessary, but not sufficient, to be able to assign to each

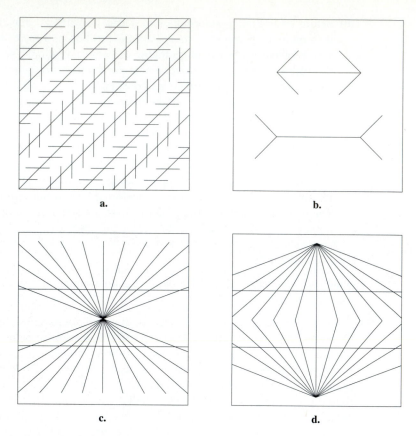

Figure 9.69 Optical illusions: (a) the Zöllner illusion. (b) The Müller–Lyer illusion. (c) The Hering illusion. (d) The Wundt illusion.

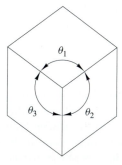

Figure 9.70 Orthographic image of a trihedral vertex of a rectangular polyhedron

straight-line segment in the drawing a single label (from among $+$, $-$, $\uparrow$) such that the line labels across each junction are consistent with the catalog of Figure 9.35. For each drawing in Figure 9.71, determine whether or not it is physically realizable.

9.9 The Lisp implementation at the end of this chapter provides code for interpreting line drawings of polyhedral scenes. The code filters the set of possible interpretations for a given line drawing and outputs a set of constraints that all legal interpretations

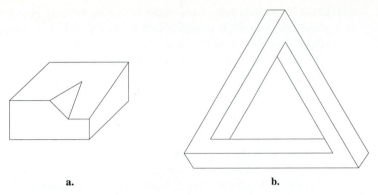

a.   b.

Figure 9.71   Line drawings

must adhere to. This filter may not identify a single interpretation if the line drawing has a unique interpretation or find a particular interpretation if the line drawing is ambigous. Write a search algorithm that takes as input the output of the filter and generates the set of all interpretations consistent with the constraints.

9.10 Assume that we have in an image a set of edge points, each point with an assigned tangent, belonging to a circle whose parameters we wish to determine. Describe how to determine the parameters of the circle (center and radius) using the Hough transform.

9.11 Suppose that through some shape-from-X method we have calculated a discrete surface normal map $\{(p_{ij}, q_{ij})\}$, $(i, j) \in$ Image. We now wish to recover the surface Z_{ij}. Develop a program that estimates the depth Z_{ij} (up to a constant factor) by minimizing the quantity

$$\sum_{i,j \in \text{Image}} \sum (Z_x - p_{ij})^2 + (Z_y - q_{ij})^2$$

where Z_x, Z_y denote derivatives of the depth function $Z(x, y)$.

9.12 The techniques for shape from shading developed in Section 9.7 do not require that the surface to be recovered satisfies the integrability constraint, that is, $\frac{\partial^2 Z}{\partial x \partial y} = \frac{\partial^2 Z}{\partial y \partial x}$ or $p_y = q_x$. Develop a shape-from-shading algorithm that takes into account the integrability constraint [Horn, 1986].

9.13 Many surfaces have the property that through every point on the surface there passes at least one straight line lying entirely on the surface. Such a surface is called a ruled surface, and the straight line lying entirely on the surface is called a ruling. If a ruled surface has the additional property that all points on a given rule have the same tangent plane, then the surface is called developable. Show that for developable surfaces the Hessian matrix can be determined locally from image intensity. In particular, show that

$$H = \begin{bmatrix} \cos a & -\sin a \\ \sin a & \cos a \end{bmatrix} \begin{bmatrix} \lambda & 0 \\ 0 & 0 \end{bmatrix} \begin{bmatrix} \cos a & \sin a \\ -\sin a & \cos a \end{bmatrix}$$

where

$$\lambda = \frac{\sqrt{I_x^2 + I_y^2}}{R_p \cos a + R_q \sin a}$$

and $\tan a = \frac{I_y}{I_x}$ [Woodham, 1981].

9.14 Consider a circle lying on a plane Π and its orthographic projection on the image plane. Show that the direction of the tilt of plane Π is along the minor axis of the elliptical projection of the circle and the slant of Π is the inverse cosine of the ratio of the minor to major axes of the elliptical projection of the circle.

9.15 Assuming that the orientations of the edge elements on a textured plane in 3D are equally likely, independent of each other, and of the surface orientation, develop a method for estimating the orientation of a planar surface from texture.

Hint: See Witkin [1981].

9.16 A simple algorithm can be formulated [Marr and Poggio, 1976] that computes disparity from random dot stereograms. Assuming that nearby points have similar disparities, develop a relaxation algorithm that computes depth.

Hint: Consider a matrix $C(x, y, d)$, where point (x, y, d) corresponds to a particular match between point (x_1, y_1) in the right image and (x_2, y_2) in the left (d is the disparity). Your algorithm should iteratively produce a series of matrices C_n that converge to a correct solution. For example,

$$C_{n+1} = \left\{ \sum_{x', y', d' \in S} C_n(x', y', d') - \sum_{x', y', d' \in \theta} C_n(x', y', d') + C_0(x, y, d) \right\}$$

where $\{t\} = \begin{cases} 1, & \text{if } t > T \text{ (threshold)} \\ 0 & \text{otherwise} \end{cases}$

$$S = \text{set of points } x', y', d' : \|x - x'\| \leq 1 \& d = d'$$
$$\theta = \text{set of points } x', y', d' : \|x - x'\| \leq 1 \& |d - d'| = 1$$

For some intuition, consider the following algorithm for a one-dimensional image (Figure 9.72a). The figure can be viewed as a binary network where each possible match is represented by a binary state. Matches have value 1 and nonmatches 0. Figure 9.72b shows an expanded version of Figure 9.72a. The connections of alternative matches for a point inhibit each other, and connections between matches of equal depth reinforce each other.

9.17 Very often we need to relate 3D coordinates determined by a stereo system. Consider four points P_1, P_2, P_3, and P_4 in 3D and $\vec{r}_{L_i} = (x_{L_i}, y_{L_i}, z_{L_i})$, $\vec{r}_{R_i} = (x_{R_i}, y_{R_i}, z_{R_i})$, the positions of point P_i measured in the left and right coordinate systems, respectively. The transformation between the two coordinate systems is a rotation R and a translation T. Given $\vec{r}_{L_i}, \vec{r}_{R_i}, i = 1, 2, 3, 4$, determine R and T [Horn, 1986].

9.18 Solve the problem of Exercise 9.17 assuming that we do not know the points $\vec{r}_{L_i}, \vec{r}_{R_i}$, but do know their projections. Also assume that you have available the correspondence of any number of points.

Hint: This problem is basically equivalent to the 3D motion determination problem in the discrete case. The translation can be estimated up to a constant factor [Tsai and Huang, 1984].

9.19 Consider a stereo system with baseline B, and assume that the lines from the left and right cameras center to a point P in 3D form angles θ and ϕ with the baseline. How does the accuracy of stereo degrade with distance?

Hint: Estimate the distance d of point P from the baseline B ($d = \beta \sin \theta \sin \phi / \sin(\phi - \theta)$), and estimate the variance of d assuming the variances of θ and ϕ are known.

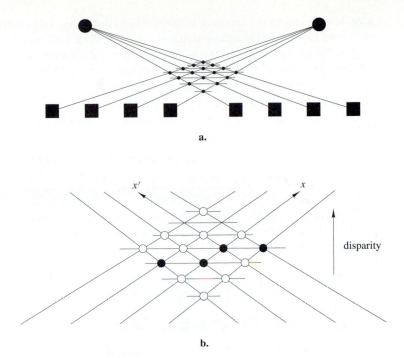

a.

b.

Figure 9.72 (a) Matching one-dimensional images of four points. (b) Expanded version of (a) in which ● indicates a match between x and x', slanted lines indicate inhibitory connections, and horizontal lines indicate exitatory connections.

9.20 In a stereo system, if a single continuous surface is imaged, show that corresponding points have to be in the same order in the two images. Determine under what circumstances a reversal occurs.

9.21 A camera is translating along its optical axis. Assume that the normal flow v_n is known at every image point (x, y). Estimate the time to contact, that is, the time that it will take for every point in the scene to hit the image plane.

9.22 Assume that an observer moves with rigid motion that is constant during the time interval $[t_1, t_2]$. Assume also that the motion filed is known at two time instances in $[t_1, t_2]$. Develop a closed-form solution for the rotation and the translational direction of the observer.

9.23 Visual search is a categorization task in which a subject must distinguish between at least two classes of signals: goals signals and target signals. Unbounded visual search is the case where the target either is not known explicitly or is not used in the execution of the search. Bounded visual search is the case where the target is explicitly known. Show that the unbounded visual search problem is NP-complete. Does the same result apply in the case of bounded visual search?

   Hint: Formulate an instance of the search problem assuming the following entities: a test image I, a target image T, a difference function $D(x)$, where x is an integer, a correlation function $C(x)$, where x is an integer, and two thresholds d and c, both positive integers. The problem of unbounded visual search can be formulated as does there exist $I' \subseteq I$ such that $\sum_{x \in I'} D(x) \leq d$ and $\sum_{x \in I'} C(x) \geq c$? Reduce the Knapsack problem to this one [Tsotsos, 1989].

9.24 Implement, in the language of your choice, the Canny edge detector [Canny, 1986]. Like the Marr–Hildreth operator, it also uses Gaussian smoothing. It detects edges at the zero-crossings of the second directional derivative of the smoothed image in the direction of the gradient where the gradient magnitude is above some threshold. That is, conditional on the magnitude of the gradient of the smoothed image being greater than some threshold, it looks for zero-crossings of $\frac{\partial^2 (G*I)}{\partial n^2} = \frac{\partial([\partial G/\partial n]*I)}{\partial n}$, where I is the image, G is a Gaussian, $*$ denotes convolution, and n is the direction of the gradient of the smoothed image.

9.25 If a surface $Z = Z(X, Y)$ is imaged under perspective projection, show that

$$\frac{\partial Z}{\partial X} = \frac{Z \frac{\partial Z}{\partial x}}{f - x \frac{\partial Z}{\partial x} - y \frac{\partial Z}{\partial y}} \quad \text{and} \quad \frac{\partial Z}{\partial Y} = \frac{Z \frac{\partial Z}{\partial y}}{f - x \frac{\partial Z}{\partial x} - y \frac{\partial Z}{\partial y}}$$

where f is the focal length, and x and y are retinal coordinates ($x = fX/Z$, $y = fY/Z$). From this, conclude that knowledge of shape under perspective implies knowledge of depth ratios.

▶ LISP IMPLEMENTATION

Labeling Polyhedral Scenes

Building computer vision systems is a complex engineering task. Such systems generally include cameras, robotic positioning devices, special-purpose computing hardware, and diverse software. Experimental software often combines prototype code written in Lisp or C and libraries of specialized routines written in highly optimized Lisp, C, or even assembly code. Many of these specialized subroutines implement *filters* that are used to process images for subsequent analysis.

For example, different filters are associated with each of the Sobel, Prewitt, and Roberts operators described in Section 9.5. These filters apply the operator to each pixel in the image to obtain a new *filtered* image. If you have access to Adobe Photoshop™ or other commercial image processing software, you can use the various filter options to experiment with the operators described in this text.

Without libraries of image processing code and appropriate hardware to create and manipulate images, it is difficult to do much low-level image understanding. In this section, we consider a relatively high-level image understanding task involving the qualitative analysis of line drawings of polyhedral scenes as described in Section 9.6. We restrict our attention to *trihedral* scenes in which each vertex has at most three incident edges. We assume that low-level image processing has identified lines and vertices in an image and we are interested in understanding the resulting lines and vertices in three-dimensional geometric terms.

In analyzing a line drawing, we are given a description of the vertices in the scene often with the background (for example, floor, sky) identified and asked to determine for each line in the drawing whether it is concave or convex in the case of a line where two physical surfaces meet or which side of the line the occluding surface is on for a line that is occluding another surface. Such a determination is called an *interpretation* of the line drawing and constitutes a semantic (geometric) analysis of the scene.

In some cases, there are a many possible interpretations given the visual cues available in the scene. In such cases, the drawing is said to be *ambiguous*. In other cases, there may be errors in the line drawing introduced by low-level image processing. In these cases, there may be no possible interpretations that make sense given the geometric constraints on real three-dimensional objects. We are interested in quickly determining whether or not a possible interpretation exists and, if so, finding one or more such interpretations.

The underlying search space for this problem of finding interpretations is quite large. In this section, we investigate a high-level symbolic filter that (at least in many cases) quickly reduces the search space to manageable size. We begin our discussion with the relevant abstract data types.

Abstract Data Types

A vertex consists of a name, a type (one of ELL, FORK, ARROW, or TEE), a list of neighboring vertices, and a list of labelings, where a labeling is a list of labels, and a label is one of +, -, LEFT, or RIGHT.

```lisp
(defun make-VERTEX (name type labelings)
  (list name type nil labelings))
(defun VERTEX-name (v) (first v))
(defun VERTEX-type (v) (second v))
(defun VERTEX-neighbors (v) (third v))
(defun VERTEX-labelings (v) (fourth v))
(defun VERTEX-number-of-labelings (v)
  (length (VERTEX-labelings v)))
(defun set-VERTEX-neighbors (v neighbors) (setf (third v) neighbors))
(defun set-VERTEX-labelings (v labelings) (setf (fourth v) labelings))
(defun copy-VERTEX (v) (copy-list v))
```

A diagram is just a list of vertices used to encode the information from the line drawing. Lines are implicit in the list of vertices and the information regarding neighboring vertices. The function copy-DIAGRAM allows us to make multiple copies of the same diagram to generate multiple interpretations of an ambiguous line drawing.

```lisp
(defun make-DIAGRAM (vertices) (list vertices))
(defun DIAGRAM-vertices (d) (first d))
(defun copy-DIAGRAM (d)
  (let ((new (make-diagram (mapcar #'copy-VERTEX
                                   (DIAGRAM-vertices d)))))
  ;; Install the neighbors for the new vertex copies.
  (mapc #'(lambda (vertex)
            (set-VERTEX-neighbors
              vertex
              (mapcar #'(lambda (neighbor)
                          (find-vertex (VERTEX-name neighbor) new))
                      (VERTEX-neighbors vertex))))
        (DIAGRAM-vertices new))
  new))
```

Constructing Diagrams from Vertex Descriptors

A vertex descriptor is a list consisting of a name and type for a vertex along with two additional vertex names for an ELL type or three additional vertex names for ARROW, FORK, or TEE types. For example, (A ARROW B C D) is a vertex descriptor for a vertex named A of type ARROW connected to vertices named B, C, and D. As another example, (E ELL F G) is a vertex descriptor for a vertex named E of type ELL connected to vertices named F and G. The function construct-VERTEX constructs a new vertex from a given vertex descriptor.

```
(defun construct-VERTEX (vertex-descriptor)
  (make-vertex (first vertex-descriptor)
               (second vertex-descriptor)
               (possible-labelings (second vertex-descriptor)))))
```

The function construct-DIAGRAM constructs a new diagram given a list of vertex descriptors.

```
(defun construct-DIAGRAM (vertex-descriptors)
  (let ((diagram (make-diagram (mapcar #'construct-VERTEX
                                       vertex-descriptors))))
    ;; Install the neighbors for the new vertices.
    (mapc #'(lambda (d)
              (set-VERTEX-neighbors
               (find-vertex (first d) diagram)
               (mapcar #'(lambda (n)
                           (find-vertex n diagram))
                       (v-d-neighbors d))))
          vertex-descriptors)
    diagram))
```

Given a vertex descriptor, the following function returns a list of the names of neighboring vertices.

```
(defun v-d-neighbors (vertex-descriptor)
  (rest (rest vertex-descriptor)))
```

The function find-vertex finds the vertex in the given diagram with the given name.

```
(defun find-vertex (name diagram)
  (find name (DIAGRAM-vertices diagram) :key #'VERTEX-name))
```

The function ground is used to indicate that the line between the two vertices is adjacent to the ground (floor) by labeling the line - (thereby indicating that the line is concave).

```
(defun ground (diagram vertex-a vertex-b)
  (let ((v (find-vertex vertex-a diagram))
        (u (find-vertex vertex-b diagram)) i)
    (setq i (index u (VERTEX-neighbors v)))
    (set-VERTEX-labelings v
      (mapcan #'(lambda (l) (and (eq (nth i l) '-) (list l)))
              (VERTEX-labelings v)))
    diagram))
```

Use index to compute the zero-based index of an item in a list.

```
(defun index (item list)
  (aux-index item list 0))
(defun aux-index (item list index)
  (if (null list) (princ "Item not in list!")
```

```
(if (eq item (first list)) index
    (aux-index item (rest list) (+ 1 index)))))
```

Manipulating Labelings

Four vertex types in the trihedral-vertex blocks world are used in the examples in this section: ELL, FORK, TEE, and ARROW. There are two labels for nonoccluding lines in the trihedral-vertex blocks world: + indicates a nonoccluding convex line, and – indicates a nonoccluding concave line. Occluding lines are labeled with respect to a vertex. RIGHT indicates an occluding line with the occluding matter to the right of the line as you face outward from the vertex. LEFT indicates an occluding line with the occluding matter to the left of the line as you face outward from the vertex. If a line is labeled RIGHT with respect to the vertex at one end of the line, then it is labeled LEFT with respect to the vertex at the other end of the line.

The function possible-labelings returns a list of the possible labelings in the junction catalog for a given vertex type.

```
(defun possible-labelings (vertex-type)
  (cond ((eq vertex-type 'ELL)
         ;; There are six possible labelings for an ELL type.
         '((RIGHT LEFT) (LEFT RIGHT) (+ RIGHT) (LEFT +) (- LEFT) (RIGHT -)))
        ((eq vertex-type 'FORK)
         ;; There are five possible labelings for a FORK type.
         '((+ + +) (- - -) (LEFT RIGHT -) (- LEFT RIGHT) (RIGHT - LEFT)))
        ((eq vertex-type 'TEE)
         ;; There are four possible labelings for a TEE type.
         '((RIGHT LEFT +) (RIGHT LEFT -) (RIGHT LEFT LEFT) (RIGHT LEFT RIGHT)))
        ((eq vertex-type 'ARROW)
         ;; There are three possible labelings for an ARROW type.
         '((LEFT RIGHT +) (- - +) (+ + -)))
        (t (princ "Unfamiliar vertex type!"))))
```

The function impossible-vertex returns t if the vertex has no possible labeling left, and nil otherwise.

```
(defun impossible-vertex (vertex)
  (null (vertex-labelings vertex)))
```

Waltz Filtering

In general, computing a consistent labeling for a polyhedral scene is computationally hard. In some cases, however, we can eliminate a large number of impossible labelings, thereby reducing the amount of search required to find a consistent labeling. The following algorithm, due to Waltz [1975], provides a very efficient filter on the set of possible labelings for a polyhedral scene.

The algorithm works as follows. We keep a list of the possible list of labelings for each vertex stored with the vertex. For each vertex, we consider for each possible labeling if that labeling is consistent with the possible labelings at neighboring vertices. A labeling is consistent with the possible labelings at neighboring vertices if there is some way that we can assign the labels in the labeling given the labelings at the neighboring vertices. If the labeling is not consistent, then we eliminate the labeling from the possible labelings stored with the vertex. If we eliminate at least one labeling, then the algorithm applies itself recursively to the neighboring vertices. If the algorithm ever finds a vertex that has no possible labelings, then it halts; otherwise, it continues to make recursive calls until no more labelings can be eliminated.

If there are n vertices and at most L labelings for each vertex type, then the Waltz filtering algorithm will terminate in at most $n \times L$ steps. Each consistent assignment of labelings to vertices constitutes a possible interpretation of the polyhedral scene. In the case of the cube shown in Figure 9.34, if we ignore the fact that it is resting on the ground, we begin with 29,160 possible interpretations, and Waltz filtering reduces the number to 216. If we account for the fact that the cube is resting on the ground, then there are 4,860 possible interpretations, and Waltz filtering reduces the number to a single interpretation. It still may be necessary to perform some additional search to find a consistent labeling. In Exercise 9.9, you are asked to write code to perform this additional search.

The function `filter` is just the top-level function for invoking the Waltz filter and displaying the results.

```
(defun filter (diagram)
  (format t "~%The initial diagram is:")
  (show-DIAGRAM diagram)
  (mapc #'waltz (DIAGRAM-vertices diagram))
  (format t "~%After filtering the diagram is:")
  (show-DIAGRAM diagram))
```

The function `waltz-filter` reduces the labelings on a vertex by considering the labeling of its neighbors. If it reduces the number of labelings at a vertex, then it applies itself recursively to its neighbors. It returns nil only if it encounters a vertex with no possible labelings.

```
(defun waltz (vertex)
  (let ((old-num (VERTEX-number-of-labelings vertex)))
    (set-VERTEX-labelings vertex (consistent-labelings vertex))
    (if (impossible-vertex vertex) nil
      (or (not (< (VERTEX-number-of-labelings vertex) old-num))
          (every #'waltz (VERTEX-neighbors vertex))))))
```

The function `consistent-labelings` returns the set of all labelings for a vertex consistent with the neighbors of the vertex.

```
(defun consistent-labelings (vertex)
  (let ((neighbor-labels
          (mapcar #'(lambda (neighbor) (labels-for neighbor vertex))
                  (VERTEX-neighbors vertex))))
    ;; Eliminate labelings that don't have all lines consistent
    ;; with the corresponding line's label from the neighbor.
    ;; Account for LEFT - RIGHT perspective change with reverse-label.
    (mapcan #'(lambda (labeling)
                (and (every #'member
                            (mapcar #'reverse-label labeling)
                            neighbor-labels)
                     (list labeling)))
            (VERTEX-labelings vertex))))
```

Return all the labels for the line going to vertex.

```
(defun labels-for (vertex from)
  (let ((i (index from (VERTEX-neighbors vertex))))
    (mapcar #'(lambda (labeling) (nth i labeling))
            (VERTEX-labelings vertex))))
```

The function reverse-label accounts for the fact that one vertex's RIGHT is an adjacent vertex's LEFT.

```
(defun reverse-label (label)
  (if (eq label 'LEFT) 'RIGHT
      (if (eq label 'RIGHT) 'LEFT label)))
```

Displaying Diagrams and Vertices

Display a vertex indicating the name, type, number of labelings, and the possible label assignments to neighboring vertices.

```
(defun show-VERTEX (vertex)
  (format t "~%  ~a/~d ~d:"
          (VERTEX-name vertex)
          (VERTEX-number-of-labelings vertex)
          (VERTEX-type vertex))
  (mapc #'(lambda (neighbor labels)
            (format t "  ~a~a=[~~a~]"
                    (VERTEX-name vertex)
                    (VERTEX-name neighbor) labels))
        (VERTEX-neighbors vertex)
        (matrix-transpose (VERTEX-labelings vertex))))
```

The following function turns a matrix on its side. For example, matrix-transpose turns ((1 2) (3 4))) into ((1 3) (2 4)).

```
(defun matrix-transpose (matrix)
  (if matrix (apply #'mapcar #'list matrix)))
```

Display a diagram by displaying all the vertices and indicating the total number of possible interpretations given the current labelings.

```
(defun show-DIAGRAM (diagram)
  (mapc #'show-VERTEX
        (DIAGRAM-vertices diagram))
  (format t "~%For ~:d interpretation(s)."
          (reduce #'* (mapcar #'VERTEX-number-of-labelings
                              (DIAGRAM-vertices diagram)))))
```

Here is a test function for the polyhedral scene shown in Figure 9.34. The first invocation of the filtering algorithm ignores the fact that the cube is sitting on the ground. The second invocation accounts for this fact.

```
(let ((cube (construct-DIAGRAM '((A FORK B C D)   (E ELL C B)
                                 (B ARROW G E A)   (F ELL D C)
                                 (C ARROW E F A)   (G ELL B D)
                                 (D ARROW F G A)))))
  (defun test ()
    (filter (copy-DIAGRAM cube))
    (filter (ground (copy-DIAGRAM cube) 'G 'D))))
```

CHAPTER 10

Natural Language Processing

The study of natural language has been an important area of artificial intelligence almost since the beginning of the field. Two main goals motivate AI work on natural language. One is the theoretical goal, and close to that of the linguist, namely, to discover how we use language to communicate. The other is a technological goal, namely, to enable the intelligent computer interfaces of the future, where natural language becomes an important means for man–machine interaction. Luckily, progress toward one of these goals often is progress toward the other—a better theoretical understanding leads to more robust systems, and a better understanding of processing issues in actual applications suggests new goals and techniques of theoretical interest. The ultimate solution to language understanding must wait until we can effectively model almost all aspects of human intelligence. Many applications, however, do not require full conversational capabilities or encyclopedic knowledge. For instance, a natural language interface that serves as a query language to a database need only focus on questions and can limit the language it understands to concepts that arise in the database. Here are a few examples of applications where you will probably see an impact in the next decade.

Spelling and grammar checkers   Though already provided in many word processing applications, are quite limited and more sophisticated tools are needed.

Spoken language control systems   Such as an automatic telephone service for inquiring about bills, bank accounts, and ordering merchandise.

Automatic message understanding and classification systems   Can search for news stories on particular topics, say stock transactions, and prepare summaries in a database format.

Machine translation tools   Can prepare initial rough translations that can then be edited by a human translator.

Some of these applications require speech recognition capabilities, whereas others involve processing text. Traditionally, speech recognition and natural language understanding have been pursued independently by different groups of researchers. Only recently has there been a significant effort to integrate speech recognition systems with natural language systems. Although, this is now a rapidly growing area, we will not have the space to deal with speech recognition issues in this book. We will assume we start with the words in text form. The same techniques, however, can be used for processing spoken language. In studying something as complex as language, it is worthwhile to subdivide the problem into parts and then work on each part separately. The study of language is typically divided into the following problem areas, each of which has its own substantial literature:

Phonology and phonetics   The study of the structure of the sounds of language, how words are realized as speech.

Morphology   The study of the structure of words, how words are formed from prefixes and suffixes and other components.

Syntax   The study of the structure of sentences, how words combine into phrases, and how these phrases combine into sentences.

Semantics   The study of meaning, how to represent the meaning of words and sentences, and how to derive the meaning of complex phrases from the meanings of its subparts.

Pragmatics   The study of the use of language, how are sentences used to convey information, make requests, and so on.

Discourse   The study of the structure of extended (multiple sentence) language, such as in text or in dialogs.

We primarily study syntactic and semantic processing here and have space for only a general discussion of the issues in most of the other areas. We begin with a brief outline of the basic structure of English sentences concentrating on words and phrases. Then we consider context-free grammars as a representation of syntax and explore some simple strategies for extracting the syntactic structure of sentences. We develop an augmented context-free formalism, using features, that is more convenient than basic context-free grammars for capturing natural language. We then look at some issues in building effective systems for extracting the syntactic structure of sentences. We then consider semantics and show how the meaning of a sentence can be derived while its structure is being analyzed. We look at issues in using language in applications and present an example of a simple natural interface to a database management system. Finally, we consider a few other problems that we were not able to address in detail earlier.

10.1 Components of Language

With a little study, you will find that there is considerable structure to language. Let us start by examining the nature of words. Words can be categorized along several different dimensions, which leads us to classify them in different general classes. The main criteria to consider are

- what syntactic structures can they participate in,
- what function do they play in the sentence, and
- what intuitively do the words describe.

Content and Function Words

Words fall into two major groups: the *content words*, which serve to identify objects, relationships, properties, actions, and events in the world, and the *function words*, which serve a more structural role in putting words together to form sentences. There are four general classes of content words, based on what the words tend to describe. In this chapter, we use slanted text to distinguish examples of words, sentences, and sentence fragments from the rest of the text.

- **Nouns** describe classes of objects, events, substances, and so on (for example, *ball*, *man*, *sand*, and *idea*)
- **Adjectives** describe properties of objects (for example, *red*, *tall*, and *special*)
- **Verbs** describe relationships between objects, activities, and occurrences (for example, *seems*, *ate*, *believes*, and *laughing*)
- **Adverbs** describe properties of relationships or other properties (for example, *very* and *slowly*)

The function words tend to define how the content words are to be used in the sentence, and how they relate to each other. Some common classes of function words are described in the following.

- **Determiners** indicate that a specific object is being identified (for example, *a*, *the*, *this*, and *that*)
- **Quantifiers** indicate how many of a set of objects are being identified (for example, *all, many, some,* and *none*)
- **Prepositions** signal a specific relationship between phrases (for example, *in, onto, by,* and *through*)
- **Connectives** indicate relationships between sentences and phrases (for example, *and, but,* and *while*)

English often allows a word in one class to be converted into a word in another class fairly freely by adding suffixes or by its particular use in a sentence. For instance, the word *sugar* is a noun, but like many nouns it can be used as a verb (for example, *He sugared the coffee*) or as an adjective (for example, *It was too sugary for me*). This is why morphology is so important in any theory of language. We will assume throughout, however, that all the uses of a particular word will be defined in advance in a structure called the *lexicon*.

Structure of Phrases

Words combine together to form phrases. Each phrase is based on a particular word, called the *head* of the phrase. The four classes of content words thus introduce four broad classes of phrases: *noun phrases, adjective phrases, verb phrases,* and *adverbial phrases*. Each of these phrases has a similar overall structure: The phrase starts with an optional function word or phrase called the *specifier*, this is followed by optional *prehead modifiers*, followed by the head, followed by the arguments to the head word, called the *complement* of the head, and finally followed by *posthead modifiers*. Figure 10.1 shows some examples of some simple phrases in each class.

Class	Prehead	Head	Complement	Posthead
Noun	the	man		in the corner
Phrase	this	picture	of Mary	over here
Adjective	very	angry		
Phrase		happy	to be here	
Verb		ate	the pizza	in the corner
Phrase		gave	the prize to the boy	without hesitation
	almost	ran	into the wall	
Adverb	too	quickly		
Phrase		regularly		during the game

Figure 10.1   This table illustrates the general structure of phrases. Prehead components are optional and include specifier words or phrases and modifiers. Complements are optional and serve as arguments to the head word. Posthead components are also optional and generally take the form of modifiers.

The distinction between complements and other postmodifiers lies in the closeness of the relationship to the head word. Some head words require certain complements. For instance, you cannot use the verb *put* in a sentence without a complement consisting of a noun phrase and a location phrase, as in

He put the book on the shelf

I put the book here

Note that you cannot say *I put*, or *He put the book*, or *He put on the shelf*. Postmodifiers, on the other hand, are always optional and seem less connected to the head word. The prepositional phrase *in the corner*, for instance, can occur in many noun or verb phrases to indicate the general location of the object or event. The complement structures of head words play a major role in restricting the structure of the sentences in which they occur. In fact, some theories of grammar base almost the entire structural analysis on the constraints that the head words impose on the sentence.

10.2 Context-Free Grammars

To examine the structure of natural language, you must have some formalism in which to state the structural constraints. In this section, we examine a set of formalisms called *rewrite systems* that have been used to describe a wide range of languages, from the formal languages such as Lisp and mathematical logic, to the natural languages such as English. The basic idea of a rewrite system is that one can specify a set of rewrite rules of the form

$$lhs_1 \ldots lhs_n \rightarrow rhs_1 \ldots rhs_m$$

such that whenever one has a sequence of symbols that matches the left-hand side of the rule, $lhs_1 \ldots lhs_n$, then one can replace these symbols with the symbols on the right-hand side of the rule, $rhs_1 \ldots rhs_m$.

For instance, the rewrite rule

$$X\ Y \rightarrow Y\ X$$

would allow us to transform a sequence A X Y B into the sequence A Y X B. A collection of rewrite rules is called a *grammar*, and grammars can define the set of legal sentences in a language as follows: A start symbol, say S, is defined such that every legal sentence in the language can be derived from S using the rewrite rules, and every derivation from S using rewrite rules produces a legal sentence. This is best illustrated by an example. Say we want to define the syntax of simple arithmetic expressions in a programming language, such as (3 + X) and ((Y + Z) * 3). A symbol EXPR is chosen to represent arithmetic expressions, and it is defined by the following rewrite rules.

1. EXPR $\rightarrow$ NUMBER
2. EXPR $\rightarrow$ VARIABLE
3. EXPR $\rightarrow$ (EXPR + EXPR)
4. EXPR $\rightarrow$ (EXPR * EXPR)

▲ AI IN PRACTICE

Air Travel Information Systems

The Air Travel Information Systems (ATIS) domain involves answering spoken questions using a database of airline flights between 50 cities in the United States. Each year, an evaluation is performed on systems built at different research sites worldwide. The systems are tested on a set of queries that have not been seen before and are evaluated on their word recognition rate and their ability to generate correct answers to the queries. The test data consists of recordings using high-quality microphones of actual interactions between a person not involved in the research and one of the systems. No constraints are placed on the person regarding how he or she speaks or what language he or she can use, except that the queries should be relevant to the domain. Typical utterances are

> *Show me the flights from Atlanta to Boston on Friday*
> *Do any of those flights serve a meal?*
> *What is the cheapest fare?*

All utterances collected are used, even those where the speakers misspeak or correct themselves, as in

> *Show me the flights from Boston—ah*
> *no—from Chicago to Boston*

It turns out that good coverage of this domain involves a vocabulary of about 1,500 different words. In the 1994 tests, the best systems could correctly identify more than 95% of the words spoken and answer 90% of the queries correctly.

The symbols NUMBER and VARIABLE would be defined by other rules that build them out of sequences of numbers or characters, respectively. We can now show that ((Y + Z) * 3) is a legal expression by showing that it can be derived from the symbol EXPR using the preceding grammar.

EXPR	*the start symbol*
(EXPR * EXPR)	*using rewrite Rule 4*
((EXPR + EXPR) * EXPR)	*using rewrite Rule 3*
((VARIABLE + EXPR) * EXPR)	*using rewrite Rule 2*

((VARIABLE + VARIABLE) * EXPR)   *using rewrite Rule 2*
((VARIABLE + VARIABLE) * NUMBER) *using rewrite Rule 1*
((Y + Z) * 3)   *using rules for* VARIABLE *and* NUMBER

Parsing

Thus ((Y + Z) * 3) is a legal expression according to the grammar. Note also that (3 5 * X) is not a legal expression according to this grammar since no sequence of rewrites from EXPR could derive such a sequence of symbols. In this way, the grammar defines a language of simple arithmetic expressions. The sequence of rewrite rules used to derive a sentence in this language reveals the structure of the sentence, and extracting this structure is called *parsing* the sentence. We can view the derivation of the expression graphically by drawing a *parse tree*, which shows how each symbol is rewritten until the expression is derived at the bottom of the tree. The parse tree for the derivation is shown in Figure 10.2.

The grammar presented here has an interesting property. All the rules have only a single symbol on the left-hand side. A grammar consisting solely of rules of this form is called a *context-free grammar*. The reason it is called context free is the symbol on the left-hand side, symbol X, can be rewritten whenever it appears in a string. There is no way to restrict the rewriting of X, say to cases when it occurs between symbols Y and Z. Such a rule is possible with a *context-sensitive grammar*, which allows a rule such as the following that states X can be replaced by A when it occurs between Y and Z:

$$Y\ X\ Z \rightarrow Y\ A\ Z$$

Most programming languages are designed so that they have a syntax definable by a context-free grammar. The reason for this is that there are efficient algorithms for parsing languages defined by context-free grammars. There are no fast algorithms for languages that must be described by context-sensitive grammars. Since the grammar is used to interpret and compile the programming language, it is important to have the context-free property.

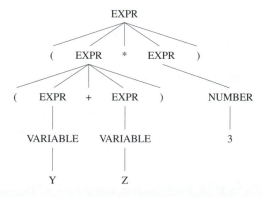

Figure 10.2   A parse tree for the expression ((Y + Z) * 3)

Since programming languages are designed by people, we can ensure that the language has the right properties to make it a context-free language.

We do not have the luxury of defining natural languages, however. They must be studied in the form in which they naturally occur. Thus, there is a pressing question about whether the structure of natural languages can be described by a context-free grammar. This has been a subject of much controversy for over three decades, and the general opinion of researchers has shifted dramatically. At first, researchers were mostly in agreement that natural languages were not context free. In the early 1980s, a new perspective on the role of grammars was developed and the issue arose again. After much further debate, the consensus now is that natural languages are almost context free. In other words, some slight extensions to the context-free grammar formalism are necessary, but one does not need to move all the way to context-sensitive grammars. More important, these extensions may not dramatically affect the complexity of the parsing algorithms so that the techniques developed for pure context-free grammars may be generalized to these richer formalisms.

10.3   Parsing Context-Free Grammars

To examine parsing strategies, consider the grammar for a small fragment of English shown in Figure 10.3. There are two basic strategies in parsing. *Top-down* parsing starts with the S symbol and uses the grammar to build the parse tree down to the sentence. It would rewrite the S to NP VP, then rewrite the NP, and so on until the sentence is generated. *Bottom-up* parsing starts with the sentence and uses the grammar to build the parse tree from the bottom leaves up to the root S symbol. It would start with a word sequence such as *the cat saw Sue*, rewrite the word *the* to ART and *cat* to N, and then rewrite the sequence ART N to NP, and so on until the symbol S is derived.

Consider building a top-down recognizer. This is an algorithm that, given a grammar and a sentence, returns true if the grammar can generate the sentence. We will formalize parsing as a search process as described in Chapter 4. To do this, we need to define what the states are and how to generate successor states. Once we have functions to generate successor states and recognize the goal state, we can use any of the search strategies described in Chapter 4. The state will contain a sequence of symbols that has been generated by the rewrite rules starting from the S symbol. This

1. S → NP VP	5. ART → a | the
2. VP → V NP	6. V → ate | saw
3. NP → NAME	7. N → cat | mouse
4. NP → ART N	8. NAME → Sue | Zak

Figure 10.3   A small context-free grammar. The vertical bar indicates disjunction, so the rule NAME → Sue | Zak represents two rules, NAME → Sue and NAME → Zak.

symbol list could be the entire definition of the state, and we could define the goal state as the sequence that is equal to the sentence. But this would be very inefficient since the input is not considered until an entire parse tree is generated. A better algorithm checks the input as soon as possible. When we have generated a sequence that matches the initial part of the input, we can simply remove the parts that match and focus on accounting for the rest of the input. Thus the parse state consists of two parts,

1. the sequence of symbols sought (to be rewritten or checked against the input), and
2. the input that has not yet been accounted for.

For example, in the state

        ((S) (the cat ate a mouse))

we are looking for an S and the input is the sentence *The cat ate a mouse.* As another example, in the state

        ((N VP) (cat ate a mouse))

we are looking for an N followed by a VP and the input is *cat ate a mouse.*
    The successor states are generated as follows. If the first symbol is identical to the first word in the sentence, then we can remove them both from their respective lists to generate the next state. For example, given the state

        ((the N) (the mouse))

the successor state is simply

        ((N) (mouse))

If the first symbol does not equal the first word in the input, then we must search the grammar for ways to rewrite the first symbol. Each applicable rule in the grammar generates a new state. For example, given a state

        ((NP) (the mouse))

and the grammar in Figure 10.3, one successor state, derived from Rule 3, would be

        ((NAME) (the mouse))

and the other, derived from Rule 4,

        ((ART N) (the mouse))

The goal state is simply (nil nil), that is, the state where all the rewritten symbols have matched successfully against the input and no input is left to be matched. The algorithm for generating the successor states is given as follows. Given a state of the form

$$((symbol_1 \ldots symbol_n) (word_1 \ldots word_m))$$

```
((S) (the mouse saw Sue))
    ((NP VP) (the mouse saw Sue))
        ((NAME VP) (the mouse saw Sue))
            ((Sue VP) (the mouse saw Sue))   no successors
            ((Zak VP) (the mouse saw Sue))   no successors
        ((ART N VP) (the mouse saw Sue))
            ((a N VP) (the mouse saw Sue))   no successors
            ((the N VP) (the mouse saw Sue))
                ((N VP) (mouse saw Sue))
                    ((cat VP) (mouse saw Sue))   no successors
                    ((mouse VP) (mouse saw Sue))
                        ((VP) (saw Sue))
                            ((V NP) (saw Sue))
                                ((ate NP) (saw Sue))   no successors
                                ((saw NP) (saw Sue))
                                    ((NP) (Sue))
                                        ((NAME) (Sue))
                                            ((Sue) (Sue))
                                                (NIL NIL) Success!
```

Figure 10.4   A trace of the states considered parsing *The mouse saw Sue*

the successor states are generated as follows:

1 If $symbol_1 = word_1$, there is one successor state,

$$((symbol_2 \dots symbol_n) (word_2 \dots word_m))$$

2 Otherwise, for each rule in the grammar of the form

$$symbol_1 \rightarrow symbol_1' \dots symbol_k'$$

generate a successor state

$$((symbol_1' \dots symbol_k' symbol_2 \dots symbol_n) (word_1 \dots word_m))$$

With this method of generating next states, the standard search algorithms described in Chapter 4 can be used.

Consider the trace of a depth-first search of the input *The mouse saw Sue* shown in Figure 10.4. The algorithm systematically rewrites the leftmost symbol in the symbol list until it matches the first word in the remaining input. When a symbol is rewritten incorrectly, the system eventually reaches a state that generates no successors, and a backup state is selected (based on the depth-first strategy). Figure 10.5 shows a trace of the parser running on the ill-formed input *The Sue saw*, which tries all possible rewrites but cannot find a state that matches *Sue* in the second position.

Exploiting the Lexicon

There are some efficiency problems with this parsing algorithm as it stands. In particular, consider what would happen if 1,000 nouns were in the lexicon. The current algorithm would systematically search through all 1,000

```
((S) (the Sue saw))
    ((NP VP) (the Sue saw))
        ((NAME VP) (the Sue saw))
            ((Sue VP) (the Sue saw))   no successors
            ((Zak VP) (the Sue saw))   no successors
        ((ART N VP) (the Sue saw ))
            ((a N VP) (the Sue saw))   no successors
            ((the N VP) (the Sue saw))
                ((N VP) (Sue saw))
                    ((cat VP) (Sue saw))   no successors
                    ((mouse VP) (Sue saw)) Failure!
```

Figure 10.5   A trace of a failed parse for *The Sue saw*

nouns checking if one were equal to *Sue*, and then fail. But this work could have been avoided if it had just checked whether *Sue* could be a noun. Because of this, parsing systems use a two-layered approach: The grammar is rewritten so that symbols like N and V are the terminal symbols (no rules are defined to rewrite them), and a second layer, the lexicon, provides a mapping from these terminal symbols to the words in the language. To implement this technique, the parsing algorithm needs to be modified in one place: Rather than checking for equality between the first symbol and the first word in the first step of the simple parsing algorithm described earlier, it now calls the lexicon to check if the word falls in the category named by the first symbol. Figure 10.6 shows a new trace of the parser using a lexicon on the input *The mouse saw Sue*. If you compare the size of the trace here with the trace in Figure 10.4, you see the savings. The difference would be much greater with a larger lexicon size.

Building a Parse Tree

To make this into a useful parser, it would have to return the structure of the sentence. One way to do this is to extend the definition of a state so that it keeps track of what rules are used. This can be done by defining a new data structure called an *arc*, which represents a partially completed rule, and then modifying the notion of a parse state to use arcs. An arc records

```
((S) (the mouse saw Sue))
    ((NP VP) (the mouse saw Sue))
        ((NAME VP) (the mouse saw Sue))   no successors
        ((ART N VP) (the mouse saw Sue))
            ((N VP) (mouse saw Sue))
                ((VP) (saw Sue))
                    ((V NP) (saw Sue))
                        ((NP) (Sue))
                            ((NAME) (Sue))
                                (NIL NIL)   Success!
```

Figure 10.6   A trace of the parse of *The mouse saw Sue* using a lexicon

two things: what parts of the rule have been completed so far and what parts remain to be found. For instance, consider a state in a parse where the rule NP → ART N is being used but no input has matched against ART yet. This might be summarized by an arc of the form

    (Seen: (NP) Seeking: (ART N))

In other words, nothing has been found so far in the NP structure, and we are looking for an ART followed by an N. A new operation is introduced called *extending the arc*. This operation takes a symbol that matches the first symbol being sought and inserts it into the list of symbols seen. It also removes the first symbol from the list of symbols being sought because this symbol has now been accounted for. For example, extending the arc with the article *a* would produce the new arc

    (Seen: (NP (ART a)) Seeking: (N))

In other words, we have seen an ART for the NP and are looking for an N. Extending this arc with the noun *mouse* would produce a completed arc

    (Seen: (NP (ART a) (N mouse)) Seeking: ())

We have seen an NP consisting of an ART and an N, and need no further input for the NP. A completed arc captures the structure of a particular subcomponent of the entire sentence. The representation of a subcomponent is called a *constituent*. A parse state consists of a list of arcs capturing the present state of the derivation and a specification of the remaining input. For example, consider a state that would arise once the symbol S is rewritten with Rule 1 and then the NP has been rewritten with Rule 3, but no input has been used yet.

    Arcs: ((Seen: (NP) Seeking: (ART N))
          (Seen: (S) Seeking: (NP VP)))
    Input: (A mouse saw Sue)

Here, the parser is trying to build a constituent of type NP by looking for the constituent sequence ART N, in order to build a constituent of type S, which is seeking the constituent sequence NP VP. The input is the sentence A mouse saw Sue. Once the top arc is completed to form an NP constituent, this constituent can be used to extend the S arc below it. More specifically, the new algorithm to generate successor states is described as follows. Given a parse state of the form

$$(\text{Arcs}: (arc_1 \ldots arc_n) \text{ Input}: (word_1 \ldots word_m))$$

where each arc_i is of the form

$$(\text{Seen}: constituent_i \text{ Seeking}: (symbol_1^i \ldots symbol_k^i))$$

The successor states are generated as follows:

1. If arc_1 is completed, remove it from the state and use $constituent_1$ to extend arc_2.

2 Otherwise,

    a) If $word_1$ is in the category $symbol_1$, extend arc_1 with $word_1$.

    b) Otherwise, for each rule in the grammar of the form

$$symbol_1^1 \rightarrow symbol_1' \ldots symbol_h'$$

generate a new parse state by adding a new arc to the old state, of the form

$$(\text{Seen} : constituent' \ \text{Seeking} : (symbol_1' \ldots symbol_h'))$$

where

$$constituent' = (symbol_1^1)$$

For example, consider the first few steps of the algorithm using a depth-first search strategy on the input *A mouse saw Sue*. The initial state of the parse is

```
Arcs: ((Seen: (S) Seeking: (NP VP)))
Input: (A mouse saw Sue)
```

Using step 2b in the algorithm, there are two successor states, namely,

```
Arcs: ((Seen: (NP) Seeking: (NAME))
       (Seen: (S) Seeking: (NP VP)))
Input: (A mouse saw Sue)
```

and

```
Arcs: ((Seen: (NP) Seeking: (ART N))
       (Seen: (S) Seeking: (NP VP)))
Input: (A mouse saw Sue)
```

The first state generates no successors because the word *a* cannot be a NAME. The second state, which requires an ART, can be extended with the word *a* to produce the new state:

```
Arcs: ((Seen: (NP (ART a)) Seeking: (N))
       (Seen: (S) Seeking: (NP VP)))
Input: (mouse saw Sue)
```

Step 2a is used again to extend the arc with the word mouse, producing the new state

```
Arcs: ((Seen: (NP (ART a) (N mouse)) Seeking: ())
       (Seen: (S) Seeking: (NP VP)))
Input: (saw Sue)
```

Since the first arc is now completed, it is used to extend the second arc (step 1), producing the state:

```
Arcs: ((Seen: (S (NP (ART a) (N mouse))) Seeking: (VP)))
Input: (saw Sue)
```

```
Seen:                                       Seeking:
(S (NP (ART A) (N mouse)))                  (VP)
Input: (saw Sue)


Seen:                                       Seeking:
(VP)                                        (V NP)
(S (NP (ART A) (N mouse)))                  (VP)
Input: (saw Sue)


Seen:                                       Seeking:
(VP (V saw))                                (NP)
(S (NP (ART A) (N mouse)))                  (VP)
Input: (Sue)


Seen:                                       Seeking:
(NP)                                        (ART N)
(VP (V saw))                                (NP)
(S (NP (ART A) (N mouse)))                  (VP)
Input: (Sue)


Seen:                                       Seeking:
(NP (NAME Sue))                             ()
(VP (V saw))                                (NP)
(S (NP (ART A) (N mouse)))                  (VP)
Input: ()


Seen:                                       Seeking:
(VP (V saw) (NP (NAME Sue)))                ()
(S (NP (ART A) (N mouse)))                  (VP)
Input: ()


Seen:                                       Seeking:
(S (NP (ART A) (N mouse))
   (VP (V saw) (NP (NAME Sue))))            ()
Input: ()
```

Figure 10.7   The remainder of the trace of the parse of *A mouse saw Sue*

The parse continues in the same manner, as shown in Figure 10.7. The arcs are shown in table form to make the trace easier to follow. The result of this parse is the constituent

(S (NP (ART a) (N mouse)) (VP (V saw) (NP (NAME Sue))))

This new algorithm generates the parse tree as it parses the sentence.

10.4   Grammars Involving Features

With an appropriate lexicon, the grammar consisting of the first four rules in Figure 10.3 would correctly parse sentences such as

The man ate the pizza

Jack is a man

Unfortunately, it would also accept many ill-formed sentences such as the following:

1. *The boys sees the idea
2. *A boys saw the pizza
3. *I is a man
4. *Sue sighed the pizza

where the (*) is used to indicate that the sentence is ill-formed. These ill-formed examples illustrate several different aspects of natural languages that make them complicated. Sentence (1) shows that the subject and verb phrase must agree in number, that is, they must both be singular or both plural. Sentence (2) shows that the article and noun in a noun phrase must also agree in number. Sentence (3) is ill-formed because subjects and verbs must also agree in person, and *I* is first person, whereas the verb form *is* is third person. Sentence (4) is ill-formed because the verb *sigh* cannot take an NP complement like *the pizza*.

These examples show that a lot is going on that is not captured by a word's basic category. Besides being a noun, a word may be singular or plural; first, second, or third person; nominative, accusative, or reflexive; and so on. Besides being a verb, a word may be in one of the five verb forms and may restrict the form of its complement. If there is a finite number of such distinctions, it would be possible to generate a context-free grammar by simply creating a new category for each combination. Thus, considering number and person, we might have categories such as N-SING-3rd and N-PLUR-3rd, which would be combined with articles in the classes ART-SING-3rd and ART-SING-3rd to form categories such as NP-SING-3rd and NP-PLUR-3rd. There would be a similar, but even more complex, breakdown of categories for the verbs based on their form and the restrictions they place on their complement. But we would never want to have to write down such a grammar since it would be unmanageably large and clearly would miss some important generalities about language. Clearly, some better formalism needs to be developed.

One way to generalize the formalism is to introduce features. A constituent is represented by a category, for example, N, V, ART, NP, VP, and a set of features that encode number and person information, verb form information, restrictions on the complement, and so on. Here are a few useful features:

AGR   The agreement feature, which takes a value that represents a number-person combination, 1s for first person singular, 2s for second person singular, and so on with the values 3s, 1p, 2p, and 3p.

VFORM   The verb form feature, which takes a value that represents the verb form: base, the base form (for example, *go*); pres, the present form (for example, *go*, *goes*); past, the past form (for example, *went*); prespart, the present participle (for example, *going*); and pastpart, the part participle (for example, *gone*).

Verb	SUBCAT value	Restriction on the complement	Example sentence
sleep	none	no complement	Jack slept
find	np	allows an NP	Jack found a ball
give	np-np	allows two NPs	Jack gave the man the ball
put	np-pp	allows an NP and PP	Jack put the ball in the corner
try	vp:inf	allows VP in infinitive form	Jack tried to open the door
regret	s:that	allows S with *that*	Jack regrets that he must leave

Figure 10.8 Some common SUBCAT restrictions for verbs

SUBCAT   The restrictions on the form of the complement. In principle, this could be an arbitrary list of restrictions on the constituents that can follow the verb. Grammars often have about 40 different forms for English verbs. Some common restrictions for verbs are shown in Figure 10.8.

For instance, a noun phrase NP1 with an AGR feature of 3s and a ROOT feature of *dog* would be represented by the list

NP1: (NP (AGR 3s) (ROOT dog))

Consider how to extend the grammar developed in the last section to allow features. In the old system, the rule

$$S \rightarrow NP\ VP$$

could be used to build an S from any NP and VP, leading to problems in accounting for agreement restrictions and so on. Specifically, the NP and VP must agree on the AGR feature. We generalize rules to allow features as well as the basic categories. In addition, variables are allowed as feature values so that agreement restrictions can be expressed. As usual, a variable is represented as a two-element list whose first element is a question mark. Thus the new S rule might be:

$$(S) \rightarrow (NP\ (AGR\ (?\ a)))\ (VP\ (AGR\ (?\ a)))$$

that is, an S constituent can be built from an NP constituent followed by a VP constituent if they both have the same AGR feature value. To use rules like this in a parser, we need to be able to compare constituents to see if they match. A constituent c matches a pattern constituent p if there is an instantiation of the variables in p and c such that the instantiated feature-value pairs of p are a subset of the instantiated feature-value pairs of c. For instance, constituent NP1 defined previously will match the constituent pattern

    NP2: (NP (AGR (? a)))

because there is an instantiation of the variable (? a), namely, 3s that makes
the features of the pattern, namely, ((AGR 3s)) a subset of the features of
NP1, namely, ((AGR 3s) (ROOT dog)). On the other hand, the constituent NP1 will
not match the pattern NP3, which involves a new feature POSS representing
whether or not NP is a possessive form.

    NP3: (NP (AGR (? a)) (POSS YES))

since there is no way to make these features match a subset of the NP1's
features.

Matching with Features

A general function can be defined to match two constituents by individually
checking each feature value defined in the pattern and using the unification
algorithm to handle variables. The algorithm to match constituent feature
list *features*(c) against pattern feature list *features*(p) is summarized as follows:

1. If *features*(p) is empty, then return success.
2. Let *f* be the first feature in *features*(p), and let its value be *v*, and let
   u be the value of the *f* feature in *features*(c). If *u* and *v* unify, then
   recursively match the remaining features in *features*(p) after substituting
   in the variable bindings.

Figure 10.9 shows the results of several matches. As with the unification
algorithm, the result returned is a list of bindings that make the match succeed. The value ((match t)) indicates a successful match with no variable
bindings required.

Pattern features	Constituent features	Result of match
((AGR (? a)) (VFORM inf))	((AGR 3s) (VFORM (? v)))	(((? a) 3s) ((? v) inf))
((AGR 3s))	((AGR (? a)) (VFORM inf))	((? a) 3s)
((AGR 3s))	((AGR 3p))	fail
((AGR 3s))	((AGR 3s) (VFORM inf))	((match t))
((AGR (? a)) (VFORM inf))	((AGR 3s))	fail

Figure 10.9 Results of matching various feature lists

The other use that we will make of features is to record the subconstituents so that details about the parse trees can be recorded. These will be stored in special feature values indicated by numbers: 1 for the first subconstituent, 2 for the second, and so on, with as many as needed. For example, here is an NP built from the phrase *the man*.

```
(NP (AGR 3s)
    (1 (ART (ROOT the) (AGR 3s)))
    (2 (N (ROOT man) (AGR 3s))))
```

Before we build a new parser using this new representation, Figure 10.10 shows a simple grammar and lexicon that would accept sentences such as

> *The dog saw the pizza*
>
> *The dog barks*

but not

> *∗The dog barks the pizza*
>
> *∗The dogs barks*
>
> *∗The dog saw*

The same basic top-down parsing algorithm as before can be used. The main difference is that constituents must be matched and variables instantiated. So, wherever the old parser checked to see if two symbols were equal, the new parser matches the two constituents together. The match returns a binding list that can be used to update the rule. For example, Rule 2 in Figure 10.10 would be used by the parser to build the following arc, which says that the parser is trying to build a constituent of the form (NP (AGR (? a))) and is looking for an ART and an N:

```
(Seen: (NP (AGR (? a)))
 Seeking: ((ART (AGR (? a))) (N (AGR (? a)))))
```

If the input word is *a*, with lexicon entry (ART (AGR 3s) (ROOT a)), then this will match the pattern based on the first constituent being sought, namely,

```
1. (S (AGR (? a)))  →  (NP (AGR (? a))) (VP (AGR (? a)))
2. (NP (AGR (? a)))  →  (ART (AGR (? a))) (N (AGR (? a)))
3. (VP (AGR (? a)) (VFORM (? vf)))  →
            (V (AGR (? a)) (VFORM (? vf)) (SUBCAT none))
4. (VP (AGR (? a)) (VFORM (? vf)))  →
            (V (AGR (? a)) (VFORM (? vf) (SUBCAT np)) (NP))


a:      (ART (AGR 3s) (ROOT a))
barks:  (V (AGR 3s) (VFORM pres) (SUBCAT none) (ROOT bark))
dog:    (N (AGR 3s) (ROOT dog))
dogs:   (N (AGR 3p) (ROOT dog))
pizza:  (N (AGR 3s) (ROOT pizza))
saw:    (V (AGR (? a)) (VFORM past) (SUBCAT np) (ROOT see))
```

Figure 10.10   A sample grammar and lexicon with features

(ART (AGR (? a))). The binding list returned from this match would be ((? a) 3s), and this information is used to build a new arc, which is of the form:

```
(Seen: (NP (AGR 3s) (1 (ART (AGR 3s) (ROOT a))))
 Seeking: ((N (AGR 3s))))
```

Note that the variable (? a) is replaced throughout the arc with its value 3s and that the ART subconstituent is now the value of the feature named 1. Figure 10.11 (page 508) shows a trace of the feature-based parser running on the sentence *The dog barks*. The final S constituent built by the parser is

```
(S (AGR 3s)
   (1 (NP (AGR 3s)
         (1 (ART (AGR 3s) (ROOT a)))
         (2 (N (AGR 3s) (ROOT dog)))))
   (2 (VP (AGR 3s)
         (1 (V (AGR 3s) (VFORM pres)
               (SUBCAT none) (ROOT bark))))))
```

This is an S with an AGR feature value 3s, and two subconstituents: an NP with AGR feature 3s consisting of an ART and an N, and a VP with AGR 3s consisting of a V.

10.5   Efficient Parsing with Charts

The top-down feature-based parser developed in the last section turns out to be too inefficient to use on large grammars. This is because all the constituents that are built while trying the unsuccessful paths are discarded when the parser backtracks during the search. If another rule used later in the search needs exactly the same constituent in the same place, it must rebuild it from scratch. In practice, any large-scale grammar will contain many rules for which this would happen, causing the parser to rebuild the same constituents over and over again. The standard solution to this problem is to store all constituents that are built during the parse in a data structure called a *chart*. The chart built for the sentence *The dog saw the pizza* is shown in Figure 10.12 (page 509). The constituent positions are indicated graphically. The parsing algorithm is then modified to always check the chart before attempting to use rules to derive a constituent so that it can avoid performing unnecessary work if the constituent has already been built. A parsing algorithm using a chart can be guaranteed to build every possible constituent only once.

Ambiguous Sentences

Charts are particularly useful when the parser is required to find many possible parses rather than stop at the first one it finds. To do this, you simply modify the stopping condition on the search so that it continues until the entire parse stack is empty. Every time a complete interpretation is found,

```
Seen:                                  Seeking:
(S (AGR (? a)))                        ((NP (AGR (? a))) (VP (AGR (? a))))
Input: (THE DOG BARKS)


Seen:                                  Seeking:
(NP (AGR (? a)))                       ((ART (AGR (? a))) (N (AGR (? a))))
(S (AGR (? a)))                        ((NP (AGR (? a))) (VP (AGR (? a))))
Input: (THE DOG BARKS)


Seen:                                  Seeking:
(NP (AGR 3S) (1 (ART ...)))            ((N (AGR 3S)))
(S (AGR (? a)))                        ((NP (AGR (? a))) (VP (AGR (? a))))
Input: (DOG BARKS)


Seen:                                  Seeking:
(NP (AGR 3S) (1 (ART ...))
             (2 (N ...)))              ()
(S (AGR (? a)))                        ((NP (AGR (? a))) (VP (AGR (? a))))
Input: (BARKS)


Seen:                                  Seeking:
(S (AGR 3S) (1 (NP ...)))              ((VP (AGR 3S)))
Input: (BARKS)


Seen:                                  Seeking:
(VP (AGR 3S) (VFORM (? v)))            ((V (AGR 3S) (VFORM (? v))
                                           (SUBCAT NONE)))
(S (AGR 3S) (1 (NP ...)))              ((VP (AGR 3S)))
Input: (BARKS)


Seen:                                  Seeking:
(VP (AGR 3S) (VFORM PRES)
    (1 (V ...)))                       ()
(S (AGR 3S) (1 (NP ...)))              ((VP (AGR 3S)))
Input: ()


Seen:                                  Seeking:
(S (AGR 3S) (1 (NP ...))
            (2 (VP ...)))              ()
Input: ()
```

Figure 10.11   A trace of the parse of *The dog barks*

the structure will be recorded in the chart, and the search continues. When
the parser terminates, you simply extract all the possible interpretations
from the chart. The chart structure allows for the efficient encoding on the
multiple interpretations because subconstituents common to different interpretations will be shared. For example, consider the grammar in Figure 10.13
that allows for PP modification of noun phrases and verb phrases.

With this grammar, a sentence such as *The woman saw the man in the
corner with a telescope* is five ways ambiguous, depending on what each of

S414: 1 NP407 2 VP413 AGR 3S				
VP413: 1 V409 2 NP412 VFORM PAST AGR (1S 2S 3S 1P 2P 3P)				
NP407: 1 ART 405 2 N406 AGR 3S			NP412: 1 ART 410 2 N 411 AGR 3S	
ART405: ROOT THE AGR (3S 3P)	N406: ROOT DOG AGR 3S	V409: ROOT SEE VFORM PAST SUBCAT NP AGR (1S...3P)	ART410: ROOT THE AGR (3S 3P)	N411: AGR 3S ROOT PIZZA
The	*dog*	*saw*	*the*	*pizza*

Figure 10.12   The complete chart for *The dog saw the pizza*

the prepositional phrases modifies. The five different interpretations of the verb phrase are shown in Figure 10.14 (page 510). In contrast, Figure 10.15 (page 510) shows the same five interpretations represented in the chart. The chart representation allows many of the constituents common to both interpretations to be shared. Rather than the 53 nodes required to represent the 5 different parse trees, the chart captures the same information using only 20 nodes. The savings are even greater with larger grammars that produce larger numbers of interpretations.

This technique not only saves space. Parsing algorithms using charts are substantially faster than those using pure top-down search. In fact, a chart parser can find all interpretations in Kn^3 steps, where n is the number of words in the sentence, and K is a constant determined by the algorithm and the size of the grammar. In contrast, the pure top-down search has an exponential time, C^n, where C is a constant determined by the algorithm and the size of the grammar. Even when K is much larger than C, the chart algorithm is substantially more efficient.

The chart representation also supports efficient bottom-up parsing algorithms as well as top-down. This makes it useful in applications where

1. S → NP VP
2. NP → ART N
3. VP → V NP
4. NP → NP PP
5. VP → VP PP

Figure 10.13   A small grammar allowing prepositional phrases

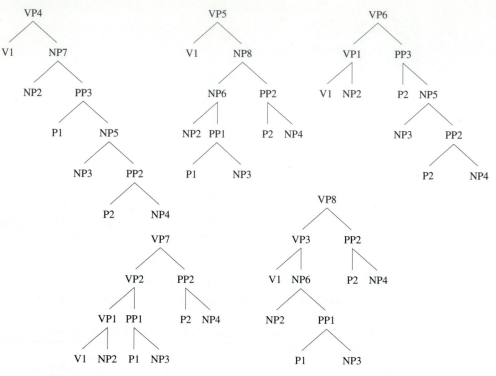

Figure 10.14   Five interpretations of the sentence fragment *saw the man in the corner with the telescope*

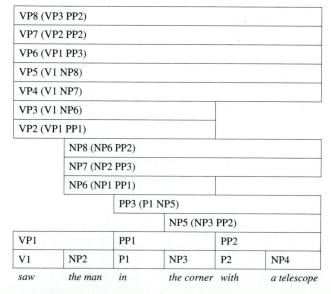

Figure 10.15   The chart for the sentence fragment *saw the man in the corner with a telescope*

you may have to process ill-formed sentences since it can capture what is known of the structure of a sentence even if no full S interpretation can be found. It might, for instance, be able to identify the major noun phrases, prepositional phrases, and the possible verbs, even if a complete coherent interpretation cannot be found. This a considerable advantage for applications like speech recognition, where the chances of ill-formed sentences, either because the speaker said something ill-formed or because the speech recognizer made an error, are quite considerable.

10.6 Semantic Interpretation

Although the meaning of logical expressions can be reduced to computing denotation and truth with respect to models, the meaning of natural language appears considerably more complex. For one thing, the truth of a sentence does not seem easily defined for many sentences. For example, questions do not naturally have a truth value—we do not talk of a question such as *Who came to the party?* as being true or false. Likewise, a request such as *Please open the door* is not easily analyzed in terms of truth values. Rather, sentences said in context are best viewed as actions, and we can consider whether they were successful, appropriate, and so on, but not whether they are true or false.

But truth conditions still play a major role in natural language semantics. This is because we typically separate the speech act performed by a sentence from its *propositional content*. The propositional content is that part of the meaning of the sentence that can have a truth conditional interpretation. Sentences may have a propositional content even if they do not make any claim about the world. For instance, the following two sentences both involve the same propositional content.

> *Jack ate the pizza yesterday*
> *Did Jack eat the pizza yesterday?*

The first sentence typically asserts the proposition, whereas the second typically asks whether the proposition is true. Computing this propositional content is the focus of this section.

Natural language meaning is highly dependent on context. It contains indexical expressions such as the pronouns and terms like *here* and *yesterday*, which obtain meaning only from the context of the utterance. For instance, the pronoun *I* refers to the person saying the sentence, whereas *yesterday* refers to a time relative to the time the sentence was uttered. In addition, natural language contains definite descriptions, such as *the man in the yellow hat*, which refer to objects that can be identified only in context. In particular, there may be many men in yellow hats in the world, but only one is relevant in context when this noun phrase is used successfully.

And perhaps the biggest problem of all, natural language expressions may be highly ambiguous even once a specific syntactic analysis has been identified. Several major sources of ambiguity need to be handled, including the following two sources:

Word-sense ambiguity   Even within a single syntactic category, words are semantically ambiguous. The verb *go*, for instance, has at least 40 different senses in most dictionaries.

Scope ambiguity   Even within a single syntactic analysis, a sentence such as *Every boy loves a dog* is ambiguous between there being one dog that every boy loves or there being a possibly different dog that is loved by each boy.

Starting from our intuitions drawn from predicate logic, we now develop a *logical-form language* that is suitable for representing the meaning of many natural language sentences.

Word Senses

The different meanings of a word are called its *senses*. These senses are the primitive building blocks of the logical-form language and fall into several different classes according to what syntactic category the word belongs to. Many classes have corresponding constructs in logic. Proper names, for instance, have senses that refer to particular objects in the word, just like the constants in logic. For example, the word *John* might have a sense JOHN1, which denotes a particular object in the world. Common nouns, such as *man*, *house*, and *idea*, have senses that denote sets of objects—the set of objects that are men, houses, and ideas, respectively. These correspond to unary predicates in logic. Verb senses correspond to predicates, where the arity of the predicate corresponds to the number of arguments the verb takes (that is, the subject and however many constituents in its complement). Figure 10.16 summarizes the treatment of the major classes of words in English.

Word senses are combined to form propositions. For example, the logical form of the sentence *Sue laughs* would combine the sense SUE1 with the verb sense LAUGHS1 in a simple proposition (LAUGHS1 SUE1). Natural language provides a much richer set of quantifiers than found in logic, and to handle them requires an extension of the language. Specifically, quantification in natural language is relative to specified sets of objects. These are captured using generalized quantifiers, which take an additional argument that indicates the set over which the quantifier ranges. For example, the sentence *Most dogs bark* would be defined by an expression

    (MOST x1 : (DOG1 x1) (BARKS x1))

This asserts that most of the objects that satisfy the predicate DOGS1 also satisfy the predicate BARKS. Note that this has a very different meaning than the logical form

    (MOST x1 : (BARKS x1) (DOG1 x1))

which is true if most objects that bark are dogs. The logical-form language

Syntactic category	Examples	Corresponding logical construct
NAME	John, New York Times	constants
N	man, house, idea	unary predicate name
V (intransitive)	laugh	unary predicate name
V (transitive)	find	binary predicate name
V (stative)	believe, know, want	modal operators
CONJ	and, but	logical operators
ART	the, a, this	quantifiers
QUANT	all, every, some, none	quantifiers
ADJ	red, heavy	unary predicate
P	in, on, above	binary predicate

Figure 10.16 Approximate correspondences between natural language and logic

can now be defined as follows. A term in the logical-form language is either

- A semantic marker (for example, a variable in the logical-form language) (for example, x1, y1)
- The sense of a proper name (for example, JOHN1, NYTIMES2)
- The sense of a function term applied to its arguments (for example, (FATHER JOHN1))

A proposition in the logical-form language is either

- An n-ary predicate sense with n terms as arguments (for example, (SAD1 JOHN1), (READ7 x NYTIMES2))
- A logical operator sense with proposition arguments (for example, (NOT (SAD1 JOHN1)), (AND (DOG1 x) (BARK2 x)))
- A modal operator sense with terms or propositions as arguments (for example, (BELIEVE1 JOHN1 (READ7 SUE1 NYTIMES2)))
- A generalized quantifier form (for example, (MANY x : (PERSON1 x) (READ7 x NYTIMES2)))

The logical-form language includes a special construct for encoding quantifier scope ambiguity. We saw that the scoping of quantifiers in natural language is not fully determined by the syntactic structure, and thus

▲ AI IN PRACTICE

Message Understanding Conference

Each year, there is a Message Understanding Conference (MUC) where researchers may evaluate their systems in a message understanding task. This task involves developing a system that can process news stories and reports, identify articles on a particular topic, and then fill in a preset template with information extracted from the article. For example, if the topic area is takeover attempts of companies, the systems would have to scan newspaper articles to find ones that describe takeover attempts, and then identify information such as who is trying to takeover whom, how much is offered, whether the takeover is hostile or friendly, and whether it was successful. The domain changes every year so that highly domain-specific approaches are discouraged. Sometime before the evaluation, the topic area is announced and data are released that give sample articles and filled-in templates that define the correct answer. The researchers have a short time to adapt their system to the new domain, and then the systems are evaluated on a set of stories not seen before. There are two principal evaluation measures in processing relevant stories: the recall rate—how much of the correct answer does the system identify—and precision of the information identified—how much is part of the correct answer. For instance, if a system extracted no information, it would have a recall rate of 0, but a precision rate of 100 since it made no mistakes. In 1993, the best systems had a recall rate of about 60%, with a precision of about 55%. This means that it identified 60% of the information in the perfect answers, but only 55% of the information it found was correct.

the sentence *Every boy loves a dog* is ambiguous between

```
(EVERY b1 : (BOY1 b1)
        (A d1 : (DOG1 d1) (LOVES1 b1 d1)))
```

and

```
(A d1 : (DOG d1)
       (EVERY b1 : (BOY b1) (LOVES b1 d1)))
```

A sentence with 3 quantifiers will have 6 possible scopings, and one with 4 will have 24. Clearly, some technique must be used to encode these possibilities. This is handled in the ambiguous logical-form language by allowing unscoped quantifiers. These can occur wherever a term is allowed and are of the same form as the first three parts of the generalized quantifier structure. To indicate these terms' special status, they will be written using angle brackets. For example, the unscoped form of *Every boy loves a dog* is

> (LOVES1 ⟨EVERY b1 (BOY b1)⟩ ⟨A d1 (DOG d1)⟩)

This ambiguous logical form concisely captures the common parts of the two interpretations and leaves the scoping unresolved.

Semantic Interpretation Using Features

The goal of semantic interpretation is to compute the logical forms (or ambiguous logical forms) for a sentence. The logical form for a constituent is stored in a special feature called SEM. Consider the sentence *Fido barked*. This is an S composed of an NP (*Fido*) and a VP (*barked*). The NP *Fido*, as a proper name, will map to a sense that denotes an individual, say FIDO1. The VP *barks*, on the other hand, will denote a unary predicate, say BARKS1, true of any object that barks. The SEM of the sentence is constructed simply by putting the two SEMs together to form the proposition

> (BARKS1 FIDO1)

This style of analysis will be used for every form of NP and VP that combine to form an S. But many verb phrases are more complex than this. For instance, what is the SEM of the verb phrase *saw Mary*? Following the same reasoning, it should be a unary predicate that is true of x only if (SEE1 x MARY1). Such expressions can be adapted for use in the grammar by using variables to specify each part of the formula. For example, the rule for transitive verbs would be

```
(VP (SEM ((? sem-v) (? subj) (? sem-np))) (SUBJ (? subj)))  →
        (V (SEM (? sem-v)) (SUBCAT np))
        (NP (SEM (? sem-np)))
```

In other words, the SEM of the new VP is a formula consisting of the SEM of the verb (? sem-v), followed by the SEM of the subject (? subj), followed by the SEM of the NP filling the object role in the verb complement (? sem-np).

Figure 10.17 (page 516) shows a simple grammar and lexicon that includes the SEM features. As you can see, each word defines a SEM feature that gives the sense of the word, and the rules use variables to specify how to build the SEM of larger constituents out of the SEM of its subconstituents. The * symbol in Rule 2 indicates that the parser should construct

```
1. (S (SEM (? sem-vp)) (AGR (? a)))  →
            (NP (SEM (? sem-np)) (AGR (? a)))
            (VP (SUBJ (? sem-np)) (SEM (? sem-vp)) (AGR (? a)))
2. (NP (SEM ((? sem-art) * ((? sem-n) *))) (AGR (? a)))  →
            (ART (SEM (? sem-art)) (AGR (? a)))
            (N (SEM (? sem-n)) (AGR (? a)))
3. (VP (SEM ((? sem-v) (? subj))) (SUBJ (? subj))
       (AGR (? a)))  →
            (V (SEM (? sem-v)) (AGR (? a)) (SUBCAT none))
4. (VP (SEM (? sem-v) (? subj) (? sem-np)) (SUBJ (? subj))
       (AGR (? a)))  →
            (V (SEM (? sem-v)) (AGR (? a)) (SUBCAT np))
            (NP (SEM (? sem-np)))


barks: (V (SEM BARKS1) (AGR 3s)
           (VFORM pres) (SUBCAT none) (ROOT bark)))
dog:   (N (SEM DOG1) (AGR 3s) (ROOT dog)))
dogs:  (N (SEM DOGS1) (AGR 3p) (ROOT dog)))
pizza: (N (SEM PIZZA1) (AGR 3s) (ROOT pizza)))
saw:   (V (SEM SEES1) (AGR (? a))
           (VFORM past) (SUBCAT np) (ROOT see)))
the:   (ART (SEM THE) (AGR 3s) (ROOT the)))
```

Figure 10.17   A grammar and lexicon with semantic features

a new constant and substitute the constant for the * every time the rule is used. This generates new semantic markers as needed during interpretation.

Consider some of the operations that occur while parsing *The dog barks*. Rule 1 first applies to produce the parse state

```
Seen: (S (SEM  (? sem-vp1)) (AGR (? a1)))
Seeking: ((NP (SEM (? sem-np1)) (AGR (? a1)))
         (VP (SEM (? sem-vp1)) (SUBJ (? sem-np1)) (AGR (? a1))))
Input: The dog barks
```

Rule 2 then applies, adding a new arc to the parse state

```
Seen: (NP (SEM ((? sem-art2) sv86 ((? sem-n2) sv86)))
           (AGR (? a2)))
Seeking: ((ART (SEM (? sem-art2)) (AGR (? a2)))
          (N (SEM (? sem-n2)) AGR (? a2)))
```

Note that the * in the rule has been replaced by a new constant sv86. Using the lexicon entry for *the*, this arc can then be extended and the variable (? sem-art2) is unified with the constant THE. The new arc resulting from this extension is

```
Seen: (NP (SEM (THE sv86 ((? sem-n2) sv86)))
           (AGR 3s) (1 (ART ...)))
Seeking: ((N (SEM (? sem-n2)) AGR (? a2)))
```

Extending this arc with the lexicon entry for *dog* will bind the variable (? sem-n) to DOG1 producing the arc

```
Seen: (NP (SEM (THE sv86 (DOG1 sv86)))
          (AGR 3s) (1 (ART ...)) (2 (N ...)))
Seeking: ()
```

Thus, the complete logical form for the noun phrase *the dog* has been constructed by the unification of features. This is then used to extend the original S arc, binding (? sem-np1) and producing the arc

```
    Seen: (S (SEM (? sem-vp1)) (AGR 3s)
             (1 (NP (SEM (THE sv86 (DOG1 sv86)))
                    (AGR 3s))))
Seeking: ((VP (SEM (? sem-vp1))
              (SUBJ (THE sv86 (DOG1 sv86)))
              (AGR 3s)))
```

Note that the value of the SUBJ feature in the VP is now set. Rule 3 in the grammar applies for this VP and produces the new arc

```
    Seen: (VP (SEM ((? sem-v1) (THE sv86 (DOG1 sv86))))
              (SUBJ (THE sv86 (DOG1 sv86)))
              (AGR 3s))
Seeking: ((V (SEM (? sem-v1)) (AGR 3s) (SUBCAT none)))
```

This arc can be extended by the lexical entry for *barks*, producing the completed arc

```
    Seen: (VP (SEM (BARKS1 (THE sv86 (DOG1 sv86))))
              (SUBJ (THE sv86 (DOG1 sv86)))
              (AGR 3s)
              (1 (V (SEM BARKS1) (AGR 3s) (SUBCAT none))))
Seeking: ()
```

When this VP is used to complete the S arc, the final constituent built is

```
(S (SEM (BARKS1 (THE sv86 (DOG1 sv86))))
   (AGR 3s)
   (1 (NP ...))
   (2 (VP ...)))
```

The final meaning of the sentence is (BARKS1 (THE sv86 (DOG1 sv86))). Any of the parsing techniques discussed earlier can be used with this grammar to construct a meaning of the sentence as it is parsed.

Disambiguating Word Senses

Although the techniques discussed here will compute a logical form for a sentence, they did not address the problem of ambiguity resolution. As a result, many semantically nonsensical logical forms would be produced that used impossible word senses in impossible combinations. For example, consider the sentence *The ruler likes the house*. The word *ruler* is ambiguous between sense RULING-PERSON, a person who rules, and sense RULER-TOOL, the instrument used to measure short distances. As a result, the parser could construct a nonsensical logical form in which an inanimate object (RULER-TOOL) likes houses. To eliminate such interpretations, a system must have some rudimentary knowledge of the world. Most systems encode restrictions on combinations of word senses using two sources of knowledge: a *word-sense hierarchy* and a set of *selectional restrictions*. The word-sense hierarchy indicates subclass (superclass) relations between different word senses. This would encode that the sense RULER-PERSON is a subclass of the class PERSON, which in turn is a subclass of ANIMATE objects. Likewise, the sense RULER-TOOL describes a small tool, which is an INANIMATE object. A simple type hierarchy is shown in Figure 10.18.

The selectional restrictions indicate possible combinations of word senses. For example, the word *like* would take two arguments: The first must be animate, and the second may be any object. This could be summarized by a pattern (LIKES1 ANIMATE OBJECT). There could also be other patterns defined for LIKES1 as well if it displays a different behavior in different circumstances. Once a set of patterns is defined, however, this set defines the possible formulas involving LIKES1 that are semantically well-formed. Similar selectional restriction patterns can be defined for all predicate types. The adjective *happy*, for instance, would map to a predicate HAPPY1, which is restricted to apply to animate objects. With the type hierarchy and the selectional restrictions defined, the parser could be modified so that it checks each semantic formula it constructs to see if it satisfies the selectional restrictions. If the restrictions are not satisfied, then the constituent is ill-formed and is not added to the chart. For instance, consider the sentence *The ruler likes the house*, where the word *ruler* has the two senses RULER-PERSON and RULER-TOOL. When the parser constructs the S structure for this sentence, it would generate two possible logical forms:

```
(LIKES1 ⟨THE r1 RULER-PERSON⟩ ⟨THE f1 HOUSE⟩)
(LIKES1 ⟨THE r1 RULER-TOOL⟩ ⟨THE f1 HOUSE⟩)
```

The selectional restrictions would eliminate the second interpretation because the type triple derived from the logical form, namely, (LIKES1 RULER-TOOL

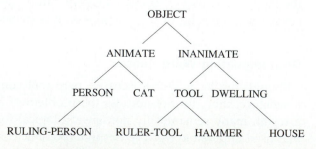

Figure 10.18   A small type hierarchy

HOUSE) does not match any selectional restriction for LIKES1. The first interpretation, with type triple (LIKES RULER-PERSON HOUSE), is acceptable because it will match the restriction (LIKES ANIMATE OBJECT) since RULER-PERSON is a subclass of ANIMATE and HOUSE is a subclass of OBJECT.

Many other techniques can be used in addition to selectional restrictions in order to effectively disambiguate natural language. But type hierarchies and selectional restrictions provide the backbone for most implemented systems.

10.7 Generating Natural Language

The same grammatical formalism described here can be used to generate sentences given a logical form as input. This is often called the *realization of a logical form* in language. This section briefly considers a simple realization algorithm.

Conceptually, realization is straightforward. You search for a parse tree that has the desired logical form. But, just as with parsing, an undirected search would be far too inefficient in practice. A variant of the basic top-down parsing algorithm, however, can be used for generation. Just as with the top-down parser, the algorithm maintains a list of constituents and updates the state by rewriting one of these constituents. But rather than rewriting in a pure left-to-right manner, it first rewrites constituents that have the SEM feature bound. Consider an example using the grammar and lexicon specified in Figure 10.17 and trying to realize the logical form (BARKS1 (THE sv86 (DOG1 sv86))). The initial constituent is

(S (SEM (BARKS1 (THE sv86 (DOG1 sv86)) (AGR (? a1)))))

Only Rule 1 in the grammar can rewrite the S constituent, producing the constituents

    (NP (SEM (? sem-np1)) (AGR (? a1)))
    (VP (SEM (BARKS1 (THE sv86 (DOG1 sv86))))
        (SUBJ (? sem-np1))
        (AGR (? a1)))

The SEM of the NP is unconstrained, so there is no way to effectively generate the subject at this point. So the algorithm attempts to rewrite the VP, which has its SEM specified. In using Rule 3 in the grammar of Figure 10.17, the VP is matched against

    (VP (SEM ((? sem-v) (? subj)))
        (SUBJ (? subj))
        (AGR (? a)))

Thus, the expression ((? sem-v) (? subj)) is matched against (BARKS1 (THE sv86 (DOG1 sv86))), and the variable (? sem-v) is bound to BARKS1, and (? subj) is bound to (THE sv86 (DOG1 sv86). The variable (? sem-np1), the value of the SUBJ

▲ AI IN PRACTICE

Machine Translation Systems

Perfect machine translation is difficult for humans to achieve, so it does not seem realistic to expect perfect translations by machine. It is possible to build effective machine translation aides, however. These tools are especially effective when the domain is constrained, say to the task of translating user manuals for products into different languages. A constrained domain helps minimize the effect of ambiguity. In such applications, many sentences are fairly simple to translate automatically using pattern matching techniques. As a result, one effective method used involves running the automatic translation system first and then having a human translator go over the output and correct it. This dramatically improves the overall rate of translation because the human spends almost no time on the simple sentences that are easily translated. In the worst case, the human translator has to retranslate a problematic sentence from scratch, and the automatic system yields no savings.

Another strategy is to hire a human to translate a document written in one language, say English, into a simple form of English in which, for example, all the pronoun references have been resolved. A computer then translates from simple English to, say, simple French, and a human then translates from simple French to more colloquial French. The advantage of this strategy is that it does not require a bilingual interpreter, and the computer's translation job is made much simpler by having humans resolve the ambiguities in the original input. Automatic translation systems improve the speed of translation while reducing the overall cost, so many large companies now use automatic translation tools in their translation activities.

feature, is also matched against (? subj), and so is also bound to the value (THE sv86 (DOG1 sv86)) as well. Thus, the resulting constituent list after rewriting the VP is

```
(NP (SEM (THE sv86 (DOG1 sv86))) (AGR (? a1)))
(V (SEM BARKS1) (AGR (? a1)) (SUBCAT none))
```

Note that the variable (? sem-np1) in the NP is now set, so we can rewrite the NP with Rule 2 to produce the constituent list

```
(ART (SEM THE) (AGR (? a1)))
(N (SEM DOG1) (AGR (? a1)))
(V (SEM BARKS1) (AGR (? a1)) (SUBCAT none))
```

It is a simple process now to select the items from the lexicon that can realize these constituents as the sentence *The dog barks*.

Note that the realization process is only a small part of the complete generation problem. It does not address, for instance, how a system would choose the logical form that should be generated in any particular situation. We discuss some issues relevant to this problem in the next section.

10.8 Natural Language in Context

So far, we have considered how to extract the syntactic structure and semantic content of sentences but have not considered how language is used in context. In a particular setting, language is used to refer to various objects, make claims about them, ask questions about them, and so on. Language also is used to convey hopes and goals, and to influence what others believe. This section considers a few simple cases of the use of language. After discussing some general issues, we develop an application that implements a simple natural language interface to a database system.

Speech Acts

As mentioned earlier, there is a distinction between what language is used for and the propositional content it conveys. A person might claim that a proposition P is true, deny that it is true, query whether P is true, suggest that P might be true, or state that it is unfortunate that P is true. All these different acts that a speaker can perform are called *speech acts*. Most speech acts are named by a verb that can be used to describe the act. For example, common speech acts are INFORM, REQUEST, ASK, DENY, SUGGEST, and so on. Each speech act reflects a different set of beliefs and intentions of the speaker. For example, when a speaker performs an INFORM act, you know that the speaker wants the hearer to believe the proposition, whereas when a speaker performs an ASK act, you know that the speaker wants the hearer to tell the speaker whether the proposition is true or not.

The relationship between the structure of a sentence and the speech act performed is complex. For example, a declarative mood sentence such as *It's midnight* would most likely be said as part of an INFORM act. But with the correct intonation, it could be a question (and written as *It's midnight?*). In other cases, it could be a reminder that it is late and a suggestion that it is time to leave a party. So though declarative mood sentences often correspond to INFORMs, they may be used for other acts as well. An interrogative mood

sentence often indicates a yes-or-no question, but this is not the usual interpretation of the sentence *Do you know the time?*, which is typically a request
that the hearer tell the speaker the time. Note also that in the right circumstances, it can also be an offer to tell the hearer the time rather than
a request!

To correctly identify the speech act, you need to consider both the structure of the sentence and the situation in which the sentence is used. By considering which speech act interpretations will yield appropriate intentions
given the context, the appropriate interpretation can be derived. Figure 10.19
considers the most likely interpretation of *Do you know the time?* in six different settings depending on whether the speaker knows the time or not
and whether the speaker believes that the hearer knows the time.

In order to handle speech act interpretation in a general fashion, a system must be able to represent the beliefs of different agents and use this
information to filter the possible interpretations. For instance, for an agent
to mean the sentence *Do you know the time?* as an offer, that agent must
know what the time is. On the other hand, to say it as a request, the agent
must not know the time. By checking such applicability conditions on each
act, many interpretations that are inappropriate in the current context can
be eliminated. Systems often view speech act interpretation as an application of plan recognition. The system attempts to identify the speaker's plan
that motivated the sentence, and the speech act interpretation that entails a
goal that fits into this plan is chosen as the intended interpretation.

Establishing Reference

Another problem involves connecting the sentence to objects in the domain
of discussion. The most obvious form of this occurs with noun phrase interpretation. We assume that the system has some *knowledge base* of facts representing the application domain. This knowledge base contains constants
and predicates assembled into formulas to represent facts about the domain.
The *reference problem* in such applications involves identifying which con-

Context	Speaker knows time	Speaker does not know time
Speaker believes hearer knows time	REQUEST that the hearer tell speaker the time	REQUEST that hearer tell speaker the time
Speaker believes hearer does not know time	OFFER to tell hearer the time	Speaker appears to be wasting his or her time
Speaker does not know if hearer knows time	YES–NO QUESTION or conditional OFFER	YES–NO QUESTION or conditional REQUEST

Figure 10.19 Different interpretations of *Do you know the time?*

stant in the knowledge base represents the object referred to by the noun phrase. Four basic classes of noun phrases require attention: proper names, pronouns, definite descriptions, and indefinite noun phrases.

Proper names are generally handled very simply. It is usually assumed that the system has knowledge about what object in the domain corresponds to each name. Thus, to interpret a proper name, the system simply uses a table lookup.

Pronouns typically refer to objects that have recently been mentioned in the preceding discourse. The simplest technique for handling pronouns is to keep a *history list*, a list of all objects mentioned in the interaction so far. These objects are ordered so that the most recently mentioned objects are considered first. One simple strategy for handling pronouns is to look through the history list for the first object that matches the features of the pronoun. This often is the correct answer. For example, consider the following three sentences in a conversation:

1a. *Jack went to the store yesterday*

1b. *The manager was very rude to the customers*

1c. *He insulted them*

The pronoun *he* in sentence (1c) should refer to an object on the history list that is singular (not a set such as the customers) and male. It most likely refers to the manager mentioned in sentence (1b), even though Jack is also a possible referent, since the manager was mentioned most recently. The pronoun *them*, on the other hand, refers to the customers as you would expect. Definite descriptions also often refer to objects on the history list. This allows them to successfully refer even though the description itself does not uniquely describe an object in the world. Consider the conversation

2a. *I bought a pencil and a pen at the store*

2b. *The pen did not work*

In sentence (2b), the definite description *the pen* refers to the pen mentioned in (2a), even when many other pens are in the knowledge base. In other cases, definite descriptions refer to objects that have not been mentioned previously but that are unique in the knowledge base.

Indefinite descriptions (for example, *a pen*) typically serve to introduce new objects into the conversation. These are handled by creating a new constant in the knowledge base and asserting the information known about it in the description. Thus, given the indefinite description *a pen*, the system creates a new constant, say X33, and then adds (PEN X33) to the database and the history list. This object can later be referred to by a definite description, as seen in sentence (2b). Indefinite descriptions act differently in questions, however. Consider the question

3. *Does Jack own a pencil?*

in a setting where the knowledge base contains the assertions (OWNS JACK1 PENCIL1) and (PENCIL PENCIL1). Assuming the preceding treatment of indefinite descriptions, a new constant X34 would be created and (PENCIL X34) would be added. Then, the query would be (OWNS JACK1 X34), which fails because it is not known that Jack owns X34. This is a similar problem to one found when skolemizing existential quantifiers in logic. When being asserted, skolemizing is the right approach, but when querying, the existential must map to a variable. The appropriate representation of (3) should be

(OWNS JACK1 (? x) (PENCIL (? x)))

Handling Database Assertions and Queries

We will use some of the techniques described to build a very simple database management system that uses a natural language interface for both assertions and queries. The database system provides two functions: Assert adds a list of formulas to the database, and Query searches the database and returns all possible sets of bindings that would make the queries present in the database. Figure 10.20 shows some typical database interactions.

A simple natural language interface to this database can be constructed out of the parser described earlier and some new code to handle the reference issues and the overall interaction. To simplify the development, we assume a direct correspondence between the different syntactic forms and the different speech acts, which is not true in general but is a reasonable start for the database application. An expanded grammar and lexicon for handling simple assertions and queries is shown in Figures 10.21 and 10.22. Given this grammar and lexicon, the parser computes semantic forms that include a speech act operator.

The next stage is to convert the descriptions into a usable form. The definite descriptions (the forms using THE) are handled by first checking for the objects on the history list that satisfy the description. If there is exactly one answer, then that object is used to replace the definite description in the logical form. If there is no object, then the database is queried for all objects

```
Assert (P A B)
        adds (P A B) to the database
Assert (P A C)
        adds (P A C) to the database
Assert (Q C)
        adds (Q C) to the database
Query (P A (? x))
        returns two answers, one with (? x) bound to A,
        and the other with (? x) bound to C
Query (AND (P A ?x) (Q (? x)))
        returns one answer, with (? x) bound to C
```

Figure 10.20   Some simple database interactions

```
1. (S (SEM (assert-prop (? sem-vp))) (AGR (? a)))  →
            (NP (SEM (? sem-np)) (AGR (? a)))
            (VP (SEM (? sem-vp)) (SUBJ (? sem-np)) (AGR (? a)))
2. (S (SEM (y-n-query (? sem-vp))) (AGR (? a)))  →
            (AUX (SEM (? sem-aux)))
            (NP (SEM (? sem-np)) (AGR (? a)))
            (VP (SEM (? sem-vp)) (SUBJ (? sem-np)) (AGR (? a)) (VFORM base))
3. (NP (SEM ((? sem-art) * ((? sem-n) *))) (AGR (? a)))  →
            (ART (SEM (? sem-art)) (AGR (? a)))
            (N (SEM (? sem-n)) (AGR (? a)))
4. (NP (SEM ((? sem-art) * ((? sem-n) *) ((? sem-adj) *)))
         (AGR (? a)))  →
            (ART (SEM (? sem-art)) (AGR (? a)))
            (ADJ (SEM (? sem-adj)))
            (N (SEM (? sem-n)) (AGR (? a)))
5. (NP (SEM (PRO * ((? sem-pro) *))) (AGR (? a)))  →
            (PRO (SEM (? sem-pro)) (AGR (? a)))
6. (VP (SEM ((? sem-v) (? s)))
       (SUBJ (? s)) (AGR (? a)) (VFORM (? v)))  →
            (V (SEM (? sem-v)) (AGR (? a)) (VFORM (? v)) (SUBCAT none))
7. (VP (SEM ((? sem-v) (? s) (? sem-np)))
       (SUBJ (? s)) (AGR (? a)) (VFORM (? v)))  →
            (V (SEM (? sem-v)) (AGR (? a)) (VFORM (? v)) (SUBCAT np))
            (NP (SEM (? sem-np)))
```

Figure 10.21   Expanded grammar for handling assertions and queries

that satisfy the description. Again, if there is exactly one answer, then this is used to replace the definite description. If there are no answers, or more than one, the sentence is consider defective. Pronouns are treated similarly except that they check only the history list. The history list is checked for the most recent object that satisfies the restrictions defined for the pronoun (for example, the antecedent of *she* must be singular and female). Indefinite descriptions will be allowed only in assertions (but see Exercise 10.9).

```
a:      (ART (SEM A) (AGR 3s) (ROOT a))
bark:   (V (SEM BARK1) AGR 3s) (VFORM base) (SUBCAT none) (ROOT bark))
barks:  (V (SEM BARKS1) (AGR 3s) (VFORM pres) (SUBCAT none) (ROOT bark))
did:    (AUX (SEM DID1))
dog:    (N (SEM DOG1) (AGR 3s) (ROOT dog))
dogs:   (N (SEM DOGS1) (AGR 3p) (ROOT dog))
it:     (PRO (SEM IT1) (AGR 3s))
large:  (ADJ (SEM LARGE1))
man:    (N (SEM MAN1) (AGR 3s) (ROOT man))
pizza:  (N (SEM PIZZA1) (AGR 3s) (ROOT pizza))
saw:    (V (SEM SEES1) (AGR (? a)) (VFORM past) (SUBCAT np) (ROOT see))
see:    (V (SEM SEES1) (AGR (? a)) (VFORM base) (SUBCAT np) (ROOT see))
small:  (ADJ (SEM SMALL1))
the:    (ART (SEM THE) (AGR 3s) (ROOT the))
```

Figure 10.22   Expanded lexicon for handling assertions and queries

In assertions, a new constant is added to the database with the declared properties.

The following algorithm is used for handling definite and indefinite descriptions, and pronouns. Given the logical form for a definite description (THE x (P x)),

1 Find most recent object on the history list satisfying (P (? x)). If one is found, return it as the answer.

2 Let ANS be the objects returned from querying the database for all (? x) such that (P (? x)) is true.

3 If ANS contains one answer, then update the history list and return it as the value.

4 Otherwise, fail (either no reference or ambiguous referents).

Given the logical form for an indefinite description (A x (P x)),

1 If the expression occurs in an assertion, then create a new object X and assert (P X) in the database. Update the history list, and return X as the value.

Given the logical form for a pronoun (PRO x (P x)), where P is a predicate determined by the pronoun,

1 Find most recent object O on history list such that (P O) is true.

With these functions defined, it is simple to define a function that traverses a logical form and resolves each noun phrase. The following description shows the top-level interaction manager, which calls the parser, then calls the reference function, and finally does the database interaction indicated by the speech act. Given a sentence S:

1 Parse the sentence, and extract the SEM value.

2 Replace all noun phrases in the SEM with their referents as described earlier.

3 If step 2 succeeded, then execute the SEM as a function call.

Consider this algorithm operating the interaction shown in Figure 10.23, where the initial database contains the propositions (DOG1 D9) and (DOG1 D10). The first sentence is *The dog barked*. Since several dogs are in the database, the system cannot find a unique reference for the noun phrase *the dog*, and so fails on the sentence giving an error message. The next sentence is *A dog saw a pizza*. In this case, both indefinite noun phrases introduce new objects into the database, a new dog D11 and a new pizza P11.

These are also added to the history list, and the assertion (SAW1 D11 P11) is added to the database. The next sentence is the same as the first, *The dog barked*. Although many dogs are in the database, only one is on the history list, namely, D11. This is taken as the referent of the noun phrase *the dog*,

```
Original database: (DOG1 D9) (DOG D10)


Input: The dog barked
SEM: (ASSERT-PROP (BARK1 (THE1 d1 (DOG1 d1))))
Result: Reference Failure: Cannot find referent of d1 since
                                two dogs are in the database.


Input: A dog saw a pizza
SEM: (ASSERT-PROP (SAW1 (A d1 (DOG1 d1)) (A p1 (PIZZA1 p1))))
SEM After Ref: (ASSERT-PROP (SEES1 D11 P11))
New Objects Defined: (DOG1 D11) (PIZZA1 P11)
New History List: (D11 P11)
Result: Adds (SAW1 D11 P11) to the database


Input: The dog barked
SEM: (ASSERT-PROP (BARKED1 (THE d2 (DOG1 d2))))
SEM After Ref: (ASSERT-PROP (BARKED1 D11))
      D11 is unique dog on history list.
New Objects Defined: none
New History List: (D11 P11)
Result: Adds (BARKED1 D11) to database


Input: A large dog saw the dog
SEM: (ASSERT-PROP (SAW1 (A d3 (LARGE d3) (DOG1 d3))
                        (THE d4 (DOG1 d4))))
SEM After Ref: (ASSERT-PROP (SAW1 D12 D11))
New Objects Defined: (LARGE1 D12) (DOG1 D12)
New History List: (D12 D11 P11)
Result: Adds (SAW1 D12 D11) to the database


Input: The dog barked
SEM: (ASSERT-PROP (BARKED1 (THE1 d4 (DOG1 d4))))
Result: Reference Failure: Cannot find referent of d4 since
                                two dogs are on the history list.


Input: The large dog barked
SEM: (ASSERT-PROP (BARKED1 (THE1 d5 (DOG1 d5) (LARGE1 d5))))
SEM After Ref: (ASSERT-PROP (BARKED1 D12))
New Objects Defined: none
New History List: (D12 D11 P11)
Result: Adds (BARKED D12) to the database
```

Figure 10.23 A dialog showing referential processing

and the sentence is processed appropriately. The assertion (BARKED1 D11) is added to the database. The next sentence is *A large dog saw the dog.* In this case, the indefinite noun phrase creates a new dog, D12, and the definite noun phrase is resolved to D11 as in the last sentence. The information on D12 is added to the database, and the assertion (SAW1 D12 D11) is added as the effect of the sentence. The next sentence is again the same as the first, *The dog barked.* This time, it causes a reference failure since no unique dog is on the history list. The noun phrase could refer to either D11 or D12. The final sentence, *The large dog barked* is fine, however, since exactly one object is on the history list that is a large dog.

To use the database, the system must also handle questions, such as the yes–no questions allowed by the grammar in Figure 10.21. For instance, given the database constructed in the dialog in Figure 10.23, the question *Did the large dog see the pizza?* should be answered no, whereas the question *Did the large dog bark?* should be answered yes. The existing system already handles such queries assuming that the act Y-N-QUERY is defined to appropriately query the database and return the result. Figure 10.24 shows two interactions assuming the question-answering starts a new session so that there is no initial history list. Note that the history list is used in the second query to correctly identify the referent of the pronoun *it* as D12. Without this context, the query would not be answerable since many dogs are in the database.

Of course, a useful database query system would also have to handle WH-questions as well such as *Which dogs saw the large pizza.* To implement such queries, the grammar would have to be expanded. Handling WH-questions in general is complex because the term corresponds to an argument position somewhere else in the sentence. For instance, in the question *Who did Jill see?* the object being queried is the object of the verb *see.* In *Who did Jill give the book to by the river?* the object queried is the object of the preposition *to.* Most systems handle such questions by using special features in which the queried term can be stored until the appropriate location for it can be found later in the parse. Here we consider the one simple question form in which the queried term is the subject of the sentence, as in *Who did Jill see?* The WH-terms will be handled by introducing a new quantifier WH, and the particular

```
Input: Did the large dog see the pizza?
SEM: (Y-N-QUERY (SAW1 (THE d6 (DOG1 d6) (LARGE d6))
                        (THE p1 (PIZZA1 p1))))
SEM After Ref: (ASSERT-PROP (SAW1 D12 P11))
New Objects Defined: none
New History List: (D12 P11)
Result: Queries (SAW1 D12 P11) in the database and returns NO

Input: Did it bark?
SEM: (Y-N-QUERY (BARKED1 (PRO d7 (IT1 d7))))
SEM After Ref: (Y-N-QUERY (BARKED1 D12))
New Objects Defined: none
New History List: (D12 P11)
Result: Queries (BARKED1 D12) in the database and returns YES
```

Figure 10.24   A short dialog involving questions

properties of the queried term become the restrictions in the quantifier. Thus the sentence *Who did Jill see?* will have the logical form (SAW1 (WH w1 (PERSON w1))(NAME j1 Jill)). To answer such a query, the WH-term would be mapped into a variable in the database query. For example, the database query from this sentence might be (AND (SEE1 (? w) JILL1) (PERSON (? w))). The system could then use the realization algorithm to generate an answer such as *Jill saw Jack.*

10.9   Quantifier Scoping

Many other issues would need to be addressed in order to construct a reasonable natural language interface. For instance, we have not discussed the treatment of quantifiers. Queries involving quantifiers are very common in database query applications and would need to be handled. For instance, consider the query *What did each dog eat?* This appears to be a request to list what each dog ate. Given a suitable database, a reasonable answer might be a list indicating what each dog ate. A query with a similar structure but a different interpretation would be *What did all dogs eat?*, which seems to be asking for a single object (or type of food) that every dog ate.

These two interpretations differ in terms of the preferred quantifier scoping. If we treat WH as a quantifier, then the two readings would be

(EACH d : (DOG1 d) (WH o : (Object o) (EATS1 d o)))

for the first, and

(WH o : (Object o) (ALL d : (DOG1 d) (EATS1 d o)))

for the second. Of course, the logical form produced by the parser does not indicate the scoping, and for each would produce a structure of the form

(EATS1 〈 EACH d (DOG1 d) 〉 〈 WH o (OBJECT o) 〉)
(EATS1 〈 ALL d (DOG1 d) 〉 〈 WH o (OBJECT o) 〉)

Considerable research has been done into scoping preferences, and it appears that no strategy based solely on structural properties is infallible. There do seem to be some heuristics based on the following preferences that work much of the time:

- Prefer a scoping order that reflects the syntactic position in the sentence (that is, the first NP, typically the subject, tends to take widest scope).
- Prefer readings in which EACH outscopes WH, which outscopes EVERY, which outscopes other quantifiers.

Of course, sometimes these preferences will conflict, and different systems use different strategies to resolve conflicting preferences.

Quantifier scoping also affects the interpretation of indefinite descriptions. For instance, in the sentence *Each man ate a pizza*, most likely many pizzas are eaten, one by each man. Thus, introducing a single new object for a pizza would not work. In this case, since a pizza is within the scope of each man, a Skolem function would need to be defined that given a man, stands for the pizza that the man ate. When an indefinite occurs within the scope of a universal, it produces a set in the history list for subsequent reference. Thus, you can say the following:

4a. *Each man ate a pizza*

4b. *They bought them at Mario's*

But (4a) could not be followed by *They bought it at Mario's* without forcing a reinterpretation of (4a) to involve a single pizza.

▼ Summary

This chapter focused on techniques for processing natural language. The problems break down into three main areas: identifying the structure of sentences (syntax), determining the surface meaning of sentences (semantics), and interpreting language in context. The most common approach to syntax uses context-free grammars extended with features. These extended context-free grammars are used as a compromise between having efficient parsing algorithms and having sufficient expressive power to describe natural language. Specifically, the parsing algorithms for pure context-free grammars can be adapted to these richer formalisms. One of the most useful structures in parsing is the chart. Using a chart as the central data structure, a wide variety of parsing algorithms can be explored and developed. The chart allows the sharing of common structures across different interpretations with great gains in time and space efficiency.

The idea behind most work in semantics is to represent the meaning of sentences in a formal language like logic. Handling natural language requires moving beyond simple first-order logics, however, and requires the introduction of modal operators, generalized quantifiers, and other complexities. Many natural language systems perform an initial semantic interpretation while parsing, computing a logical form for sentences in the features specified in the grammar. This logical form must then be interpreted in context to produce the final meaning of the sentence. Contextual processing requires general knowledge of the world, specific knowledge of discourse context, and some method to identify the intended use of each sentence. This chapter considered some simple techniques for resolving definite reference in language, and showed how to build a natural language interface to a simple database management application.

● Background

There is a wide literature in natural language processing. Allen [1994] provides a comprehensive overview of the field, with good coverage of syntax, semantics, and interpretation in context. Gazdar and Mellish [1989] is also a good introductory text and provides detailed descriptions of programs for natural language processing. Winograd [1983] addresses syntactic parsing in depth, although it is somewhat outdated now.

Much of the research in the field is reported first at the annual meetings of the Association for Computational Linguistics (ACL), and more mature work is reported in the journal *Computational Linguistics*. An excellent collection of papers covering the field can be found in Grosz et al. [1986].

Exercises

10.1 Identify the part of speech for each word in the following sentences. In addition, identify all noun phrases and verb phrases in the most intuitive reading of each sentence, and mark each head word and its complement (if any).

> *Every boy from my class went to the store yesterday*
> *I should have known that Jack would leak the report*
> *I put the ball in a box by the stove*
> *I saw John in the park before I went to the store*

10.2 Extend the context-free grammar for arithmetic expressions so that it allows subtraction and division and allows expressions where the parentheses have been dropped, such as (7 - 2 * 3). Draw the parse tree for this example based on your grammar. What would the value of this expression be given the structure that you assign to it?

10.3 Modify the parser specified in the Lisp Implementation so that it can use any one of the three basic search strategies: depth-first, breadth-first, or iterative-deepening. Using the grammar shown in Figure 10.13 and a suitable lexicon, perform some timing tests on each search strategy to determine which seems more efficient. To get accurate timings, test using a series of inputs of varying lengths. Does any one strategy seem uniformly better than the others? If so, explain why. If not, why not?

10.4 Extend the grammar in Figure 10.10 so that it accepts verb phrases that involve auxiliaries. You need consider only the third-person forms of the verbs *be* and *have*, and the modal *will*. Your grammar should at least accept the sentences

> *He has seen the dog*
> *He was barking*
> *He had been barking*
> *He will be barking*
> *He will have been barking*
> *He will have barked*

Make sure that your grammar does not accept illegal forms such as

> *∗He has see the dog*
> *∗He is seen the dog*
> *∗He was had barked*
> *∗He is will bark*
> *∗He will been barking*

Give two more structurally different examples of correct sentences that your grammar accepts and two more illegal forms that it rejects. Either draw out the parse trees for each acceptable sentence shown or test your grammar on all these examples using the parser described in the text.

10.5 Write a program that takes derived word forms that are not in the lexicon and produces lexicon entries based on its suffixes. For instance, if the lexicon has the following entry for *pizza*:

```
(pizza (N (AGR 3s) (ROOT pizza)))
```

your program could analyze the word *pizzas* and produce the lexical entry

```
(pizzas (N (AGR 3p) (ROOT pizza)))
```

Your program should similarly recognize the suffix *-s* on verbs and produce verb entries with the AGR feature 3p. Try to include some information about spelling to extend the capabilities of your program. For example, your program should recognize the word *cities* as the plural form of *city*. Integrate your program into the parser described in the text, and test the entire system on a range of input demonstrating your program's capabilities.

10.6 Modify the parser in the Lisp Implementation section so that it uses a chart structure to record each constituent as it is built. The resulting parser should be substantially faster than the one provided since it will only ever build each constituent once. Compare the performance of your new system with the old one on a sample of inputs, including ill-formed sentences. You may want to use the grammar defined in Figure 10.13 or specify a larger grammar since the performance difference should become greater as the grammar becomes more complex.

10.7 Specify a plausible logical form for each of the following sentences. In cases where there is a quantifier ambiguity, give the most likely interpretation. Discuss any problems that arise and the assumptions you made to overcome them.
Each boy ran to the park
Many people in each company did not come to the picnic
The cat ate the pizzas before we arrived
Many people believe that I won the lottery

10.8 Extend the grammar in Figure 10.21 so that it correctly parses and semantically analyses noun phrases that allow PP modifiers that describe locations. The general form of the rule should be NP $\rightarrow$ NP PP, and a noun phrase such as *The man in the park* would have a SEM of

```
(THE1 sv44 (MAN1 sv44) (IN1 sv44 (THE1 sv45 PARK1)))
```

Specify the lexical entry for the preposition *in*, and draw the parse tree for the noun phrase showing the SEM of each subconstituent. Does your solution support nested constructs such as *The man in the park with a green hat* where both *in the park* and *with a green hat* modify *the man*? Discuss any problems that arise in writing a rule to do this.

10.9 Extend the reference function in the database retrieval system so that it properly handles indefinite descriptions in queries. This is more complicated than it looks since it is hard to place the appropriate restrictions on the new variable into an appropriate place in the logical form. Document your solution carefully, and demonstrate its use in a sample set of interactions.

► LISP IMPLEMENTATION

Simple Parser

This Lisp Implementation section develops the code for a simple parser as described in the text. We start by defining the abstract data types that we will need in the implementation. A feature consists of an attribute and a value.

```
(defun make-FEATURE (attribute value) (list attribute value))
(defun FEATURE-attribute (feature) (first feature))
(defun FEATURE-value (feature) (second feature))
```

A constituent consists of a category and zero or more features.

```
(defun make-CONSTITUENT (category features) (cons category features))
(defun CONSTITUENT-category (constituent) (first constituent))
(defun CONSTITUENT-features (constituent) (rest constituent))
```

Here is the abstract data type for grammatical rules. The left-hand side of a rule is a constituent, and the right-hand side of a rule is a list of constituents.

```
(defun make-RULE (lhs rhs) (cons lhs (cons '-> rhs)))
(defun RULE-lhs (rule) (first rule))
(defun RULE-rhs (rule) (rest (rest rule)))
```

Here are functions for creating and testing variables repeated from Chapter 3.

```
(defun make-VAR (var) (list '? var))
(defun is-VAR (x) (and (consp x) (eq (first x) '?)))
```

A binding consists of a variable and a value.

```
(defun make-BDG (variable value) (list variable value))
(defun BDG-variable (bdg) (first bdg))
(defun BDG-value (bdg) (second bdg))
```

The following function is a utility for making substitutions given a list of bindings.

```
(defun subst-bdgs (expr bdgs)
  (if (null bdgs) expr
    (if (equal (first bdgs) '(match t))
        (subst-bdgs expr (rest bdgs))
      (subst-bdgs (subst (BDG-value (first bdgs))
                         (BDG-variable (first bdgs)) expr :test #'equal)
                  (rest bdgs)))))
```

A state consists of a list of arcs and a list of words.

```
(defun make-STATE (arcs words) (list arcs words))
(defun STATE-arcs (state) (first state))
(defun STATE-words (state) (second state))
```

An arc consists of a list of constituents already accounted for (the "seen" part), a list of constituents that need to be accounted for (the "seeking part"), and an integer number for the next subconstituent.

```
(defun make-ARC (seen seek number) (list seen seek number))
(defun ARC-seen (arc) (first arc))
(defun ARC-seek (arc) (second arc))
(defun ARC-number (arc) (third arc))
```

An arc is extended with a given constituent by creating a new arc in which the first unaccounted-for constituent is now accounted for by the given constituent and the rest of the unaccounted-for constituents still need to be accounted for. Substitutions are made where appropriate, and the new arc is given a subconstituent number corresponding to 1 plus the number of the original arc's subconstituent number.

```
(defun ARC-extend (arc constituent bdgs)
  (make-ARC (subst-bdgs (append (ARC-seen arc)
                                (list (list (ARC-number arc)
                                            constituent)))
                        bdgs)
            (subst-bdgs (rest (ARC-seek arc)) bdgs)
            (+ (ARC-number arc) 1)))
```

An arc is complete if it has no constituents left to account for.

```
(defun complete (arc) (null (ARC-seek arc)))
```

Matching Constituents

The next three functions implement a special-purpose matching algorithm for constituents and patterns. One of the key parts of this implementation is the code to match a constituent pattern to a constituent. This is developed as follows. Constituents are represented as a list of the form (category $(f_1 \; v_1) \ldots (f_n \; v_n)$). Like the unification algorithm discussed in Chapter 3, constituent-match returns a list of bindings. If it succeeds but no variables are bound, it returns the value ((match t)). Constituent-match checks that the categories are identical and then calls feature-match to match the features.

```
(defun constituent-match (pattern constituent)
  (if (eq (CONSTITUENT-category pattern)
          (CONSTITUENT-category constituent))
      (feature-match (CONSTITUENT-features pattern)
                     (CONSTITUENT-features constituent))))
```

Feature-match matches the feature lists for constituent-match. It handles the pattern features one at a time, ensuring a match before handling the rest of the pattern features using recursion.

```
(defun feature-match (pfeatures cfeatures)
  (if (null pfeatures) '((match t))
    (let ((bdgs (value-match
                  (FEATURE-value (first pfeatures))
                  (FEATURE-value (assoc (FEATURE-attribute (first pfeatures))
                                        cfeatures)))))
      (if bdgs
          (let ((result (feature-match (subst-bdgs (rest pfeatures) bdgs)
                                       (subst-bdgs cfeatures bdgs))))
            (if result (append bdgs result)))))))
```

Value-match compares two values and returns a binding list. If both values are variables, the pattern variable is bound to the other.

```
(defun value-match (pvalue value)
  (cond ((eq pvalue value) '((match t)))
        ;; If either argument is a variable, create new bindings.
        ((is-VAR pvalue) (list (make-BDG pvalue value)))
        ((is-VAR value) (list (make-BDG value pvalue)))
        (t nil)))
```

The Parser

The parser is defined by two functions that can be used with the search strategies discussed in Chapter 4. The function parse-found returns non-nil if the state consists of a completed S arc and no input is left.

```
(defun parse-found (state)
 (and (null (STATE-words state))
      (eq (length (STATE-arcs state)) 1)
      (complete (first (STATE-arcs state)))))
```

The function next-states generates the successors to a state depending on the state given.

```
(defun next-states (state)
  (let ((words (STATE-words state)) (arcs (STATE-arcs state)) constituent)
    (setq constituent (first (ARC-seek (first arcs))))
    (cond ((null (first arcs)) nil) ;; If no arc, then no successors.
          ;; If first arc is complete, use it to extend the second arc.
          ((and (complete (first arcs)) (second arcs))
           (list (build-parse-state (ARC-seen (first arcs))
                                    (second arcs)
                                    (rest (rest arcs))
                                    words)))
          ;; If the first symbol sought is a lexical category, look
          ;; it up, otherwise, create a new arc for the first symbol.
          ((and constituent
                (lexical-category (CONSTITUENT-category constituent)))
           (let ((lexicon-entries (lexicon-lookup (first words))))
             (if lexicon-entries
                 (mapcar #'(lambda (e)
                             (build-parse-state e (first arcs)
                                                (rest arcs) (rest words)))
                         lexicon-entries))))
          (constituent
           (make-states-for-constituent constituent arcs words)))))
```

The function build-parse-state uses a constituent to extend the top arc and returns a new parse state.

```
(defun build-parse-state (constituent arc rest-arcs words)
  (let ((bdgs (constituent-match (first (ARC-seek arc)) constituent)))
    (if bdgs
        (make-STATE (cons (ARC-extend arc constituent bdgs)
                          rest-arcs)
                    words))))
```

The function `make-states-for-constituent` finds possible rules from the grammar for a constituent and constructs an arc for each one found.

```
(defun make-states-for-constituent (constituent arcs words)
  (mapcar #'(lambda (rule)
              (make-STATE (cons (make-ARC (RULE-lhs rule)
                                          (RULE-rhs rule) 1)
                                arcs)
                          words))
          (get-rules constituent)))
```

Finally, here is a parse function that uses the standard depth-first search procedure defined in Chapter 4.

```
(defun parse (expr)
  (let ((result (dfs (make-states-for-constituent '(s) nil expr)
                     #'parse-found
                     #'next-states)))
    (and result (ARC-seen (first (STATE-arcs result))))))
```

Here is the depth-first search procedure repeated from Chapter 4.

```
(defun dfs (nodes goalp next)
  (cond ((null nodes) nil)
        ((funcall goalp (first nodes)) (first nodes))
        (t (dfs (append (funcall next (first nodes))
                        (rest nodes))
                goalp
                next))))
```

Grammar and Lexicon Access

All that is left is to define the functions that access the grammar and the lexicon. These are fairly straightforward, and the only complication arises in making a copy of each rule so that the variables are uniquely defined each time a rule is used. Here is the function for looking up words in the lexicon. It returns a list of constituents that could have generated the specified word. It also replaces any * in the rule with a new constant.

```
(let ((lexicon
       '((dog (n (agr 3s) (root dog)))
         (dogs (n (agr 3p) (root dog)))
         (pizza (n (agr 3s) (root pizza)))
         (saw (v (agr (? x)) (vform past) (subcat np) (root see)))
         (barks (v (agr 3s) (vform pres) (subcat none) (root bark)))
         (the (art (agr 3s) (root the))))))
  (defun lexicon-lookup (word)
    (mapcar #'(lambda (e) (subst (gensym) '* (second e)))
            (mapcan #'(lambda (x) (if (eq (first x) word) (list x)))
                    lexicon))))
```

Here is the function to find rules in the grammar whose left-hand side matches a specified constituent. Variables in the rule either are new copies or are bound to values based on the match against the constituent.

```
(let ((grammar
       '(((s (agr (? a))) ->
          (np (agr (? a))) (vp (agr (? a))))
         ((np (agr (? a))) ->
          (art (agr (? a))) (n (agr (? a))))
         ((vp (agr (? a)) (vform (? v))) ->
          (v (agr (? a)) (vform (? v)) (subcat none)))
         ((vp (agr (? a)) (vform (? v))) ->
          (v (agr (? a)) (vform (? v)) (subcat np)) (np)))))
  (defun get-rules (constituent)
    (let ((new-rules nil))
      (mapc #'(lambda (x)
                (let ((bdgs (constituent-match constituent (RULE-lhs x))))
                  (if bdgs
                      (setq new-rules (cons (cons bdgs x) new-rules)))))
            grammar)
      (reverse (mapcar #'gen-new-varnames new-rules)))))
```

We also need a function to recognize legal lexical categories.

```
(let ((categories '(n v p art adj adv aux)))
  (defun lexical-category (x) (member x categories)))
```

The function gen-new-varnames in conjunction with gen-varbindings renames all variables in a rule to make sure they are unique.

```
(defun gen-new-varnames (rule-bdgs-pair)
  (subst (gensym) '*
         (subst-bdgs (rest rule-bdgs-pair)
                     (gen-varbindings (rest rule-bdgs-pair)
                                      (first rule-bdgs-pair)))))

(defun gen-varbindings (expr bdgs)
 (cond ((atom expr) bdgs)
       ((is-VAR expr)
        ;; If already bound, then we don't need a new variable.
        (if (assoc expr bdgs :test #'equal)
            bdgs
          (cons (make-BDG expr (make-VAR (gensym))) bdgs)))
       (t (gen-varbindings (rest expr)
                           (gen-varbindings (first expr) bdgs)))))
```

Here is a simple test function to demonstrate the parser.

```
(defun test () (parse '(the dog saw the pizza)))
```

BIBLIOGRAPHY

[Aarup *et al.* 1987] Aarup, M.; Arentoft, M. M.; Parrod, Y.; Stader, J.; Stokes, I.; and Vadon, H. 1987. OPTIMUM-AIV: A knowledge based planning and scheduling system for space-craft AIV. In Fox, M. and Zweben, M., editors 1987, *Knowledge Based Scheduling*. Morgan Kaufmann.

[Abelson and Sussman 1985] Abelson, Harold and Sussman, Gerald Jay 1985. *Structure and Interpretation of Computer Programs*. MIT Press, Cambridge, Massachusetts.

[Agre and Chapman 1987] Agre, Philip E. and Chapman, David 1987. Pengi: An implementation of a theory of activity. In *Proceedings AAAI-87*. AAAI. 268–272.

[Allen *et al.* 1990] Allen, James F.; Hendler, James; and Tate, Austin, editors 1990. *Readings in Planning*. Morgan Kaufmann, San Mateo, California.

[Allen 1983] Allen, James F. 1983. Maintaining knowledge about temporal intervals. *Communications of the ACM* 26:832–843.

[Allen 1984] Allen, James F. 1984. Towards a general theory of action and time. *Artificial Intelligence* 23:123–154.

[Allen 1994] Allen, James F. 1994. *Natural Language Understanding, Second Edition*. Benjamin-Cummings, Redwood City, California.

[Aloimonos and Shulman 1989] Aloimonos, Y. and Shulman, D. 1989. *Integration of Visual Modules*. Academic Press, New York.

[Aloimonos *et al.* 1988] Aloimonos, J.; Weiss, I.; and Bandopadhyay, A. 1988. Active vision. *International Journal of Computer Vision* 2.

[Aloimonos 1988] Aloimonos, J. 1988. Shape from texture. *Biological Cybernetics* 58:345–360.

[Aloimonos 1990] Aloimonos, Y. 1990. Perspective approximations. *Image and Vision Computing* 8(3):179–193.

[Aloimonos 1993] Aloimonos, Y., editor 1993. *Active Perception*. Lawrence Erlbaum, Hillsdale, New Jersey.

[Alterman 1986] Alterman, Richard 1986. An adaptive planner. In *Proceedings AAAI-86*. AAAI. 65–69.

[Andreassen *et al.* 1987] Andreassen, S.; Woldbye, M.; Falck, B.; and Andersen, S. 1987. Munin: A causal probabilistic network for interpretion of electromygraphic findings. In *Proceedings AAAI-87*. AAAI. 121–124.

[Angluin 1987] Angluin, Dana 1987. Learning regular sets from queries and counterexamples. *Information and Computation* 75:87–106.

[Appel and Haken 1976] Appel, K. I. and Haken, W. 1976. Every planar map is four colorable. *Bulletin of the American Mathematical Society* 82:711–712.

[Bajcsy 1988] Bajcsy, R. 1988. Active perception. *Proceedings of the IEEE* 76(8):996–1005.

[Ballard and Brown 1982] Ballard, D.H. and Brown, C.M. 1982. *Computer Vision*. Prentice-Hall, Englewood Cliffs, New Jersey.

[Barker and O'Connor 1989] Barker, Virginia E. and O'Connor, Dennis E. 1989. Expert systems for configuration at digital: Xcon and beyond. *Communications of the ACM* 32(3):298–319.

[Barto *et al.* 1990] Barto, Andrew G.; Sutton, Richard S.; and Watkins, Christopher J. C. H. 1990. Learning and sequential decision making. In Gabriel, Michael and Moore, John, editors 1990, *Learning and Computational Neuroscience: Foundations of Adaptive Networks*. MIT Press, Cambridge, Massachusetts.

[Basye *et al.* 1995] Basye, Kenneth; Dean, Thomas; and Kaelbling, Leslie 1995. Learning dynamics: System identification for perceptually challenged agents. *Artificial Intelligence*.

[Biederman 1985] Biederman, I. 1985. Human image understanding: Recent research and a theory. *Computer Vision Graphics Image Processing* 32:29–73.

[Blumer *et al.* 1987] Blumer, Anselm; Ehrenfeucht, Andrzej; Haussler, David; and Warmuth, Manfred K. 1987. Occam's razor. *Information Processing Letters* 24:377–380.

[Blumer *et al.* 1989] Blumer, Anselm; Ehrenfeucht, Andrzej; Haussler, David; and Warmuth, Manfred K. 1989. Learnability and the vapnik-chervonenkis dimension. *Journal of the ACM*.

[Boddy and Dean 1994] Boddy, Mark and Dean, Thomas 1994. Decision-theoretic deliberation scheduling for problem solving in time-constrained environments. *Artificial Intelligence* 67(2):245–286.

[Brady 1982] Brady, M. 1982. Computational approaches to image understanding. *ACM Computing Surveys* 14:3–71.

[Bratko 1986] Bratko, Ivan 1986. *Prolog Programming for Artificial Intelligence*. Addison-Wesley, Reading, Massachusetts.

[Breiman *et al.* 1984] Breiman, L.; Friedman, J. H.; Olshen, R. A.; and Stone, C. J. 1984. *Classification and Regression Trees*. Wadsworth and Brooks, Monterey, California.

[Brooks 1981] Brooks, Rodney A. 1981. Symbolic reasoning among 3-d models and 2-d images. *Artificial Intelligence* 17:285–348.

[Brooks 1986] Brooks, Rodney A. 1986. A robust layered control system for a mobile robot. *IEEE Journal of Robotics and Automation* 2:14–23.

[Canny 1986] Canny, J. 1986. A computational approach to edge detection. *IEEE Transactions on Pattern Analysis and Machine Intelligence* 8:679–698.

[Chang and Lee 1973] Chang, Chin-Liang and Lee, Richard Char-Tung 1973. *Symbolic Logic and Mechanical Theorem Proving*. Academic Press, New York.

[Chapman 1987] Chapman, David 1987. Planning for conjunctive goals. *Artificial Intelligence* 32:333–377.

[Charniak and Goldman 1991] Charniak, Eugene and Goldman, Robert 1991. A probabilistic model for plan recognition. In *Proceedings AAAI-91*. AAAI. 160–165.

[Charniak and McDermott 1985] Charniak, Eugene and McDermott, Drew V. 1985. *Introduction to Artificial Intelligence*. Addison-Wesley, Reading, Massachusetts.

[Charniak *et al.* 1987] Charniak, Eugene; Riesbeck, Christopher K.; McDermott, Drew V.; and Meehan, James R. 1987. *Artificial Intelligence Programming, Second Edition*. Lawrence Erlbaum Associates, Hillsdale, New Jersey.

[Charniak 1991] Charniak, Eugene 1991. Bayesian networks without tears. *AI Magazine* Winter:51–63.

[Charniak 1993] Charniak, Eugene 1993. *Statistical Language Learning*. MIT Press, Cambridge, Massachusetts.

[Church and Patil 1982] Church, Kenneth and Patil, Ramesh 1982. Coping with syntactic ambiguity or how to put a block in the box on the table. *American Journal of Computational Linguistics* 8(3-4):139–149.

[Clocksin and Mellish 1987] Clocksin, W. F. and Mellish, C. S. 1987. *Programming in Prolog, Third Edition*. Springer-Verlag, New York.

[Collins and Pryor 1992] Collins, Gregg and Pryor, Louise 1992. Achieving the functionality of filter conditions in a partial order planner. In *Proceedings AAAI-92*. AAAI. 375–380.

[Cooper 1987] Cooper, Gregory F. 1987. Probabilistic inference using belief networks is NP-Hard. Technical Report KSL-87-27, Stanford Knowledge Systems Laboratory.

[Cornsweet 1970] Cornsweet, T.N. 1970. *Visual Perception*. Academic Press, New York.

[Dagum and Luby 1993] Dagum, P. and Luby, M. 1993. Approximating probabilistic inference in bayesian belief networks is NP-hard. *Artificial Intelligence* 60:141–153.

[Davis 1982] Davis, Randall 1982. Teiresias: Applications of meta-level knowledge. In Davis, Randall and Lenat, Douglas B., editors 1982, *Knowledge-Based Systems in Artificial Intelligence*. McGraw-Hill International Book Company. 227–490.

[Davis 1986] Davis, Ernest 1986. *Representing and Acquiring Geographic Knowledge*. Morgan-Kaufmann, Los Altos, California.

[Davis 1990] Davis, Ernest 1990. *Representations of Commonsense Knowledge*. Morgan-Kaufmann, Los Altos, California.

[de Dombal *et al.* 1974] Dombal, F.de; Leaper, D.; Horrocks, J.; Staniland, J.; and McCann, A. 1974. Human and computer-aided diagnosis of abdominal pain: Further report with emphasis on performance. *British Medical Journal* 1:376–380.

[Dean and Boddy 1988a] Dean, Thomas and Boddy, Mark 1988a. An analysis of time-dependent planning. In *Proceedings AAAI-88*. AAAI. 49–54.

[Dean and Boddy 1988b] Dean, Thomas and Boddy, Mark 1988b. Reasoning about partially ordered events. *Artificial Intelligence* 36(3):375–399.

[Dean and Kanazawa 1988] Dean, Thomas and Kanazawa, Keiji 1988. Probabilistic temporal reasoning. In *Proceedings AAAI-88*. AAAI. 524–528.

[Dean and Kanazawa 1989] Dean, Thomas and Kanazawa, Keiji 1989. A model for reasoning about persistence and causation. *Computational Intelligence* 5(3):142–150.

[Dean and McDermott 1987] Dean, Thomas and McDermott, Drew V. 1987. Temporal data base management. *Artificial Intelligence* 32(1):1–55.

[Dean and Wellman 1991] Dean, Thomas and Wellman, Michael 1991. *Planning and Control*. Morgan Kaufmann, San Mateo, California.

[Dean *et al.* 1988] Dean, Thomas L.; Firby, R. James; and Miller, David P. 1988. Hierarchical planning involving deadlines, travel time and resources. *Computational Intelligence* 4(4):381–398.

[Dean 1985] Dean, Thomas 1985. Temporal imagery: An approach to reasoning about time for planning and problem solving. Technical Report 433, Yale University Computer Science Department.

[DeMenthon and Davis 1989] DeMenthon, D. and Davis, L.S. 1989. New exact and approximate solutions of the three-point perspective problem. Technical Report CAR-TR-471, Center for Automation Research, University of Maryland, College Park, Maryland.

[Dickinson *et al.* 1992] Dickinson, S.J.; Pentland, A.P.; and Rosenfeld, A. 1992. 3-d shape recovery using distributed aspect matching. *IEEE Transactions on Pattern Analysis and Machine Intelligence* 14:174–198.

[Dieterrich 1990] Dieterrich, Thomas G. 1990. Machine learning. In *Annual Review of Computer Science, Volume 4*. Annual Review Inc.

[Duda and Hart 1973] Duda, R. O. and Hart, P. E. 1973. *Pattern Classification and Scene Analysis.* John Wiley and Sons, New York.

[Duda *et al.* 1981] Duda, R. O.; Hart, P. E.; and Nilsson, N. J. 1981. Subjective bayesian methods for rule-based inference systems. In Webber, B.W. and Nilsson, N.J., editors 1981, *Readings in Artificial Intelligence*. Tioga, Palo Alto, California.

[Dzierzanowski *et al.* 1992] Dzierzanowski, James; Hestenes, Eric; and Lawson, Susan 1992. The credit assistant: The second leg in the knowledge highway for american express. In *Proceedings of the Conference on Innovative Applications of Artificial Intelligence*. 127–134.

[Earley 1970] Earley, J. 1970. An efficient context-free parsing algorithm. *Communications of the ACM* 13(2):94–102.

[Ernst *et al.* 1969] Ernst, G.; Newell, Allen; and Simon, Herbert 1969. *GPS: A Case Study in Generality and Problem Solving*. Academic Press, New York.

[Etzioni *et al.* 1992] Etzioni, Oren; Hanks, Steve; Weld, Daniel; Draper, Denise; Lesh, Neal; and Williamson, Mike 1992. An approach to planning with incomplete information. In *Proceedings of the 1992 International Conference on Principles of Knowledge Representation and Reasoning*, Los Altos, California. Morgan-Kaufmann.

[Fagin *et al.* 1994] Fagin, Ronald; Y., Halpern Joseph; Moses, Yoram; and Vardi, Moshe Y. 1994. *Reasoning about Knowledge*. MIT Press.

[Farah 1990] Farah, M.J. 1990. *Visual Agnosia*. MIT Press, Cambridge, Massachusetts.

[Feldman 1985] Feldman, J.A. 1985. Four frames suffice: A provisional model of vision and space. *Behavioral and Brain Sciences* 8:265–313.

[Fermüller 1993] Fermüller, C. 1993. Basic visual capabilities. Technical Report CAR-TR-668, Center for Automation Research Technical Report, University of Maryland, College Park, Maryland.

[Fikes and Nilsson 1971] Fikes, Richard and Nilsson, Nils J. 1971. Strips: A new approach to the application of theorem proving to problem solving. *Artificial Intelligence* 2:189–208.

[Fikes *et al.* 1972] Fikes, Richard E.; Hart, Peter E.; and Nilsson, Nils J. 1972. Learning and executing generalized robot plans. *Artificial Intelligence* 3:251–288.

[Firby 1987] Firby, R. James 1987. An investigation in reactive planning in complex domains. In *Proceedings AAAI-87*. AAAI. 202–206.

[Fischler and Firschein 1987] Fischler, Martin and Firschein, Oscar 1987. *Intelligence: The Eye, the Brain, and the Computer*. Addison-Wesley, Reading, Massachusetts.

[Forbus and de Kleer 1994] Forbus, Ken and Kleer, Johande, editors 1994. *Building Problem Solvers*. MIT Press, Cambridge, Massachusetts.

[Ganapathy 1984] Ganapathy, S. 1984. Decomposition of transformation matrices for robot vision. *Pattern Recognition Letters* 2:401–412.

[Garey and Johnson 1979] Garey, Michael R. and Johnson, David S. 1979. *Computers and Intractibility: A Guide to the Theory of NP-Completeness*. W. H. Freeman and Company, New York.

[Gazdar and Mellish 1989] Gazdar, Gerald and Mellish, Chris 1989. *Natural Language Processing in LISP*. Addison-Wesley, Reading, Massachusetts.

[Genesereth and Nilsson 1987] Genesereth, Michael R. and Nilsson, Nils J. 1987. *Logical Foundations of Artificial Intelligence*. Morgan-Kaufmann, Los Altos, California.

[Georgeff and Lansky 1987] Georgeff, Michael P. and Lansky, Amy L. 1987. Reactive reasoning and planning. In *Proceedings AAAI-87*. AAAI. 677–682.

[Gibson 1950] Gibson, J.J. 1950. *The Perception of the Visual World*. Houghton-Mifflin, Boston, Massachusetts.

[Gibson 1979] Gibson, J.J. 1979. *The Ecological Approach to Visual Perception*. Houghton-Mifflin, Boston, Massachusetts.

[Ginsberg 1993] Ginsberg, Matthew L. 1993. *Essentials of Artificial Intelligence*. Morgan Kaufmann, San Mateo, California.

[Goldberg 1989] Goldberg, David E. 1989. *Genetic Algorithms in Search, Optimization, and Machine Learning*. Addison-Wesley, Reading, Massachusetts.

[Green 1969] Green, Cordell C. 1969. Application of theorem proving to problem solving. In *Proceedings IJCAI 1*. IJCAII. 219–239.

[Gregory 1970] Gregory, R.L. 1970. *The Intelligent Eye*. McGraw-Hill, New York.

[Grimson 1981] Grimson, W.E.L. 1981. A computer implementation of a theory of human stereo vision. *Philosophical Transactions of the Royal Society of London* Series B 292:217–253.

[Grosz *et al.* 1986] Grosz, Barbara; Sparck Jones, Karen; and Webber, Bonnie, editors 1986. *Readings in Natural Language Processing*. Morgan Kaufmann, San Mateo, California.

[Halpern and Moses 1985] Halpern, Joseph and Moses, Yoram 1985. A guide to the modal logics of knowledge and belief. In *Proceedings IJCAI 9*. IJCAII. 480–490.

[Halpern 1986] Halpern, Joseph Y., editor 1986. *Theoretical Aspects of Reasoning About Knowledge: Proceedings of the 1986 Conference*. Morgan Kaufmann.

[Hammond 1989] Hammond, Kristian J. 1989. *Case-Based Planning*. Academic Press, New York.

[Hanks and McDermott 1987] Hanks, Steve and McDermott, Drew V. 1987. Nonmonotonic logic and temporal projection. *Artificial Intelligence* 33:379–412.

[Hanks and Weld 1992] Hanks, Steven and Weld, Daniel S. 1992. Systematic adaptation for case-based planning. In *Proceedings of the First International Conference on Artificial Intelligence Planning Systems*. 96–105.

[Hart *et al.* 1968] Hart, Peter E.; Nilsson, Nils J.; and Raphael, B. 1968. A formal basis for the heuristic determination of minimum cost paths. *IEEE Transactions on Systems Science and Cybernetics* 4.

[Haugeland 1985] Haugeland, John 1985. *Artificial Intelligence: The Very Idea*. MIT Press, Cambridge, Massachusetts.

[Haussler 1988] Haussler, David 1988. Quantifying inductive bias: Ai learning algorithms and valiant's learning framework. *Artificial Intelligence* 38:177–221.

[Heckerman *et al.* 1992] Heckerman, D.; Horvitz, E.; and Nathwani, B. 1992. Toward normative expert systems: Part I. The Pathfinder project. *Methods of Information in Medicine* 31:90–105.

[Henrion *et al.* 1991] Henrion, Max; Breese, John S.; and Horvitz, Eric J. 1991. Decision analysis and expert systems. *AI Magazine* Winter:64–91.

[Henrion 1988] Henrion, Max 1988. Propagating uncertainty by logic sampling in Bayes networks. In Lemmer, John F. and Kanal, Laveen F., editors 1988, *Uncertainty in Artificial Intelligence 2*. North-Holland. 149–163.

[Hertz *et al.* 1991] Hertz, John; Krogh, Anders; and Palmer, Richard G. 1991. *Introduction to the Theory of Neural Computation*. Addison Wesley, Redwood City, California.

[Hobbs and Moore 1985] Hobbs, Jerry E. and Moore, Robert C., editors 1985. *Formal Theories of the Common Sense World*. Ablex, Norwood, New Jersey.

[Holland *et al.* 1987] Holland, John H.; Holyoak, Keith J.; Nisbett, Richard E.; and Thagard, Paul R. 1987. *Induction: Processes of Inference, Learning, and Discovery*. MIT Press, Cambridge, Massachusetts.

[Holland 1975] Holland, John H. 1975. *Adaptation in Natural and Artificial Systems*. University of Michigan Press, Ann Arbor, Michigan.

[Horn and Schunck 1981] Horn, B.K.P. and Schunck, B.G. 1981. Determining optical flow. *Artificial Intelligence* 17:185–203.

[Horn 1986] Horn, B.K.P. 1986. *Robot Vision*. McGraw-Hill, New York.

[Horowitz and Pavlidis 1976] Horowitz, S.L. and Pavlidis, T. 1976. Picture segmentation by a tree traversal algorithm. *Journal of the Association for Computing Machinery* 23:368–388.

[Howard and Matheson 1984] Howard, Ronald A. and Matheson, James E. 1984. Influence diagrams. In Howard, Ronald A. and Matheson, James E., editors 1984, *The Principles and Applications of Decision Analysis*. Strategic Decisions Group, Menlo Park, CA 94025.

[Howard 1960] Howard, Ronald A. 1960. *Dynamic Programming and Markov Processes*. MIT Press, Cambridge, Massachusetts.

[Hubel 1988] Hubel, D.H. 1988. *Eye, Brain, and Vision*. W.H. Freeman and Company, New York.

[Hueckel 1973] Hueckel, M.H. 1973. A local visual operator which recognizes edges and lines. *Journal of the Association for Computing Machinery* 20:634–647.

[Huffman 1971] Huffman, D.A. 1971. Impossible objects as nonsense sentences. In Meltzer, B. and Michie, D., editors 1971, *Machine Intelligence 6*. American Elsevier, New York. 295–323.

[Hunter 1973] Hunter, Geoffrey 1973. *Metalogic: an introdiction to the metatheory of standard first order logic*. University of California Press, Berkeley, California.

["I lied about the trees" or and in Knowledge Representation 1985] or, Defaults"I lied about the trees" and Knowledge Representation, Definitionsin 1985. Brachman, ronald j. *AI Magazine* 6(3):80–93.

[Jackson 1990] Jackson, Peter 1990. *Introduction to Expert Systems*. Addison-Wesley, Reading, Massachusetts.

[Jensen *et al.* 1990] Jensen, F.V.; Lauritzen, S.L.; and Olesen, K.G. 1990. Bayesian updating in recursive graphical models by local computations. *Computational Statisticals Quarterly* 4:269–282.

[Kaelbling 1992] Kaelbling, Leslie Pack 1992. *Learning in Embedded Systems*. MIT Press, Cambridge, Massachusetts.

[Kambhampati and Hendler 1992] Kambhampati, Subbarao and Hendler, James 1992. A validation structure based theory of plan modification and reuse. *Artificial Intelligence* 55(2-3):193–258.

[Kanizsa 1979] Kanizsa, G. 1979. *Organization in Vision: Essays on Gestalt Perception*. Praeger, New York.

[Karp 1972] Karp, Richard M. 1972. Reducibility among combinatorial problems. In Miller, R. E. and Thatcher, J. W., editors 1972, *Complexity of Computer Computations*. Plenum. 85–103.

[Kautz 1986] Kautz, Henry 1986. The logic of persistence. In *Proceedings AAAI-86*. AAAI. 401–405.

[Kirkpatrick *et al.* 1983] Kirkpatrick, S.; Gelatt, C. D.; and Vecchi, M. P. 1983. Optimization by simulated annealing. *Science* 220:671–680.

[Knoblock 1991] Knoblock, Craig A. 1991. Search reduction in hierarchical problem solving. In *Proceedings AAAI-91*. AAAI. 686–691.

[Korf 1985] Korf, Richard 1985. Depth-first iterative deepening: an optimal admissible tree search. *Artificial Intelligence* 29:97–109.

[Korf 1987] Korf, Richard 1987. Planning as search: A quantitative approach. *Artificial Intelligence* 33(1):65–88.

[Kowalski 1979] Kowalski, Robert 1979. *A Logic for Problem Solving*. North-Holland, New York.

[Krebsbach *et al.* 1992] Krebsbach, K.; Olawsky, D.; and Gini, M. 1992. An empirical studing of sensing and defaulting in planning. In *Proceedings of the First International Conference on Artificial Intelligence Planning Systems*. 136–144.

[Kripke 1971] Kripke, Saul A. 1971. *Semantical Considerations on Modal Logic*. Oxford University Press.

[Kuipers 1978] Kuipers, Benjamin 1978. Modeling spatial knowledge. *Cognitive Science* 2:129–153.

[Latombe 1990] Latombe, Jean-Claude 1990. *Robot Motion Planning*. Kluwer, Boston, Massachusetts.

[Lauritzen and Spiegelhalter 1988] Lauritzen, Steffen L. and Spiegelhalter, David J. 1988. Local computations with probabilities on graphical structures and their application to expert systems. *Journal of the Royal Statistical Society* 50(2):157–194.

[Levesque 1986] Levesque, Hector J. 1986. Making believers out of computers. *Artificial Intelligence* 30:81–108.

[Levine 1985] Levine, M.D. 1985. *Vision in Man and Machine*. McGraw-Hill, New York.

[Lifschitz 1987] Lifschitz, Vladimir 1987. Formal theories of action. In *Proceedings of the 1987 Workshop on the Frame Problem in Artificial Intelligence*.

[Lin and Kernighan 1973] Lin, S. and Kernighan, B. W. 1973. An effective heuristic for the travelling salesman problem. *Operations Research* 21:498–516.

[Lin and Shoham 1991] Lin, Fangzhen and Shoham, Yoav 1991. Provably correct theories of action. In *Proceedings AAAI-91*. AAAI. 349–354.

[Lin and Vitter 1992] Lin, Jyh-Han and Vitter, Jeffery Scott 1992. ϵ-approximations with minimum packing constraint violation. In *Proceedings of the 24th Annual ACM Symposium on Theory of Computing*.

[Lindley 1980] Lindley, D. V. 1980. *Introduction to Probability and Statistics*. Cambridge University Press.

[Longuet-Higgins and Prazdny 1980] Longuet-Higgins, H.C. and Prazdny, K. 1980. The interpretation of a moving retinal image. *Proceedings of the Royal Society of London* Series B 208:385–397.

[Lozano-Pérez 1983] Lozano-Pérez, Tomás 1983. Spatial planning: A configuration space approach. *IEEE Transactions on Computers* 32:108–120.

[Mackworth 1977] Mackworth, A. K. 1977. How to see a a simple world: An exegesis of some computer programs for scene analysis. In *Machine Intelligence*, 8, E. W. Elcock and D. Michie (Eds.), Ellis Horwood, Chichester, United Kingdom. 510–537.

[Manna and Waldinger 1983] Manna, Zohar and Waldinger, Richard 1983. *The Logical Basis for Computer Programming, Volume 1: Deductive Reasoning*. Addison-Wesley, Reading, Massachusetts.

[Marr and Hildreth 1980] Marr, D. and Hildreth, E. 1980. Theory of edge detection. *Proceedings of the Royal Society of London* Series B 207:187–217.

[Marr and Poggio 1976] Marr, D. and Poggio, T. 1976. Cooperative computation of stereo disparity. *Science* 194:283–287.

[Marr 1982] Marr, D. 1982. *Vision*. W. H. Freeman and Company, San Francisco, California.

[Maxwell and Shafer 1993] Maxwell, B.A. and Shafer, S.A. 1993. A framework for segmentation using physical models of image formation. Technical Report CMU-RI-TR-93-29, Robotics Institute, Carnegie Mellon University, Pittsburgh, Pennsylvania.

[McAllester and Rosenblitt 1991] McAllester, David A. and Rosenblitt, David 1991. Systematic nonlinear planning. In *Proceedings AAAI-91*. AAAI. 634–639.

[McCarthy and Hayes 1969] McCarthy, John and Hayes, Patrick J. 1969. Some philosophical problems from the standpoint of artificial intelligence. *Machine Intelligence* 4:463–502.

[McCarthy 1960] McCarthy, John 1960. Recursive functions of symbolic expressions and their computation by machine. *Communications of the ACM* 7:184–195.

[McCarthy 1963] McCarthy, John 1963. Situations, actions, and causal laws. Memo No. 2, Stanford University Artificial Intelligence Project.

[McCarthy 1980] McCarthy, John 1980. Circumscription - a form of nonmonotonic reasoning. *Artificial Intelligence* 13:295–323.

[McCorduck 1979] McCorduck, Pamela 1979. *Machines Who Think*. W. H. Freeman and Company, New York.

[McCulloch and Pitts 1943] McCulloch, W. S. and Pitts, W. H. 1943. A logical calculus of ideas immanent in nervous activity. *Bulletin of Mathematical Biophysics* 5:115–133.

[McDermott and Davis 1982] McDermott, Drew V. and Davis, Ernest 1982. Planning routes through uncertain territory. *Artificial Intelligence* 22:107–156.

[McDermott and Doyle 1980] McDermott, Drew V. and Doyle, Jon 1980. Non-monotonic logic I. *Artificial Intelligence* 13:41–72.

[McDermott 1978] McDermott, Drew V. 1978. Planning and acting. *Cognitive Science* 2:71–109.

[McDermott 1982] McDermott, Drew V. 1982. A temporal logic for reasoning about processes and plans. *Cognitive Science* 6:101–155.

[Mendelson 1979] Mendelson, Elliot 1979. *Introduction to Mathematical Logic*. D. Van Nostrand, New York.

[Michalski *et al.* 1983] Michalski, R. S.; Carbonell, J. G.; and Mitchell, T. M., editors 1983. *Machine Learning: an Artificial Intelligence Approach*. Tioga.

[Minsky and Papert 1969] Minsky, Marvin and Papert, Seymour 1969. *Perceptrons*. MIT Press, Cambridge, Massachusetts.

[Minsky 1975] Minsky, Marvin 1975. A framework for representing knowledge. In Winston, Patrick, editor 1975, *The Psychology of Computer Vision*. McGraw-Hill. 211–277.

[Minton *et al.* 1989] Minton, Steven; Carbonell, Jaime G.; Knoblock, Craig A.; Kuokka, Daniel R.; Etzioni, Oren; and Gil, Yolanda 1989. Explanation-based learning: A problem solving perspective. *Artificial Intelligence* 40:63–118.

[Minton 1988] Minton, Steven 1988. *Learning Search Control Knowledge: An Explanation-Based Approach*. Kluwer, Boston, Massachusetts.

[Mitchell 1977] Mitchell, Thomas M. 1977. Version spaces: An approach to concept learning. Ph.D. Thesis, Stanford University.

[Mitchell 1982] Mitchell, Thomas M. 1982. Generalization as search. *Artificial Intelligence* 18:203–226.

[Moore 1956] Moore, Edward F. 1956. Gedanken-experiments on sequential machines. In *Automata Studies*. Princeton University Press, Princeton, New Jersey. 129–153.

[Moore 1980] Moore, Robert C. 1980. Reasoning about knowledge and action. Technical Report Technical Note 191, SRI International.

[Morgan 1993] Morgan, M. Granger 1993. Risk analysis and management. *Scientific American* July:32–41.

[Morgenstern and Stein 1988] Morgenstern, Leora and Stein, Lynn Andrea 1988. Why things go wrong: A formal theory of causal reasoning. In *Proceedings AAAI-88*. AAAI. 518–523.

[Morgenstern 1986] Morgenstern, Leora 1986. A first order theory of planning, knowledge, and action. In Halpern [TARK86]. 83–98.

[Nalwa 1993] Nalwa, V.S. 1993. *A Guided Tour of Computer Vision*. Addison-Wesley, Reading, Massachusetts.

[Neapolitan 1990] Neapolitan, Richard E. 1990. *Probabilistic Reasoning in Expert Systems: Theory and Algorithms*. John Wiley and Sons, New York.

[Nelson and Aloimonos 1988] Nelson, R.C. and Aloimonos, J. 1988. Finding motion parameters from spherical motion fields. *Biological Cybernetics* 58:261–273.

[Nilsson 1965] Nilsson, Nils 1965. *Learning Machines*. McGraw-Hill, New York.

[Nilsson 1980] Nilsson, Nils J. 1980. *Principles of Artificial Intelligence*. Tioga Publishing Company, Palo Alto, California.

[Papadimitrio and Steiglitz 1982] Papadimitrio, Christos H. and Steiglitz, Kenneth 1982. *Combinatorial Optimization: Algorithms and Complexity*. Prentice-Hall, Englewood Cliffs, New Jersey.

[Pearl 1982] Pearl, Judea 1982. A solution for the branching factor of the alpha-beta pruning algorithm and its optimality. *Communications of the ACM* 25(8):559–564.

[Pearl 1985] Pearl, Judea 1985. *Heuristics*. Addison-Wesley, Reading, Massachusetts.

[Pearl 1988] Pearl, Judea 1988. *Probabilistic Reasoning in Intelligent Systems: Networks of Plausible Inference*. Morgan-Kaufmann, Los Altos, California.

[Pednault 1988] Pednault, Edwin P. D. 1988. Synthesizing plans that contain actions with context-dependent effects. *Computational Intelligence* 4(4):356–372.

[Penberthy and Weld 1992] Penberthy, J. S. and Weld, Daniel S. 1992. UCPOP: A sound, complete, partial order planner for ADL. In *Proceedings of the 1992 International Conference on Principles of Knowledge Representation and Reasoning*, Los Altos, California. Morgan-Kaufmann. 103–114.

[Peot and Shachter 1991] Peot, Mark and Shachter, Ross 1991. Fusion and propagation with multiple observations in belief networks. *Artificial Intelligence* 48(3):299–318.

[Peot and Smith 1992] Peot, Mark A. and Smith, David E. 1992. Conditional nonlinear planning. In *Proceedings of the First International Conference on Artificial Intelligence Planning Systems*. 189–197.

[Poggio and Girosi 1989] Poggio, Tomaso and Girosi, Federico 1989. A theory of networks for approximation and learning. Technical Report AI Memo No. 1140, MIT AI Laboratory.

[Pomerleau 1989] Pomerleau, Dean A. 1989. Alvinn: An autonomous land vehicle in a neural network. In Touretsky, David, editor 1989, *Advances in Neural Information Processing 1*. Morgan-Kaufmann, Los Altos, California.

[Pomerleau 1991] Pomerleau, Dean A. 1991. Rapidly adapting artificial neural network for autonomonus navgation. In Lippmann, R. P.; Moody, J. E.; and Touretsky, D. S., editors 1991, *Advances in Neural Information Processing 3*. Morgan-Kaufmann, Los Altos, California.

[Pratt 1991] Pratt, W.K. 1991. *Digital Image Processing, Second Edition*. John Wiley and Sons, New York.

[Quinlan 1986] Quinlan, J. R. 1986. Induction of decision trees. *Machine Learning* 1(1):81–106.

[Raiffa 1968] Raiffa, Howard 1968. *Decision Analysis: Introductory Lectures on Choices Under Uncertainty*. Addison-Wesley, Reading, Massachusetts.

[Reiter 1980] Reiter, Raymond 1980. A logic for default reasoning. *Artificial Intelligence* 13:81–132.

[Rich and Knight 1991] Rich, Elaine and Knight, Kevin 1991. *Artificial Intelligence*. McGraw-Hill, New York.

[Rivest and Schapire 1987] Rivest, Ronald L. and Schapire, Robert E. 1987. Diversity-based inference of finite automata. In *Proceedings of the Twenty Eighth Annual Symposium on Foundations of Computer Science*. 78–87.

[Robinson 1965] Robinson, J. A. 1965. A machine-oriented logic based on the resolution principle. *Journal of the ACM* 12:23–41.

[Rodieck 1973] Rodieck, R.W. 1973. *The Vertebrate Retina: Principles of Structure and Function*. W. H. Freeman and Company, San Francisco, California.

[Rosenblatt 1961] Rosenblatt, F. 1961. *Principles of Neurodynamics: Perceptrons and the Theory of Brain Mechanisms*. Spartan Books, Washington, D.C.

[Rosenfeld and Kak 1982] Rosenfeld, A. and Kak, A.C. 1982. *Digital Picture Processing, Second Edition*, volume 1-2. Academic Press, New York.

[Rosenschein and Kaelbling 1986] Rosenschein, Stan and Kaelbling, Leslie Pack 1986. The synthesis of digital machines with provable epistemic properties. In Halpern [TARK86]. 83–98.

[Rumelhart *et al.* 1986] Rumelhart, D. E.; Hinton, G. E.; and Williams, R. J. 1986. Learning internal representations by error propagation. In Rumelhart, D. E. and McClelland, J. L., editors 1986, *Parallel Distributed Processing: Explorations in the Microstructure of Cognition, Volume I: Foundations*. MIT Press, Cambridge, Massachusetts.

[Sacerdoti 1974] Sacerdoti, Earl 1974. Planning in a hierarchy of abstraction spaces. *Artificial Intelligence* 7:231–272.

[Sacerdoti 1977] Sacerdoti, Earl 1977. *A Structure for Plans and Behavior*. American Elsevier, New York.

[Sandewall 1989] Sandewall, Erik 1989. Filter preferential entailment for the logic of action in almost continuous worlds. In *Proceedings IJCAI 11*. IJCAII.

[Savage 1972] Savage, Leonard J. 1972. *The Foundations of Statistics, Second Edition*. Dover Publications, New York.

[Schagrin *et al.* 1985] Schagrin, Morton L.; Rapaport, William J.; and Dipert, Randall R. 1985. *Logic: A Computer Approach*. McGraw-Hill, New York.

[Schank and Abelson 1977] Schank, Roger C. and Abelson, Robert P. 1977. *Scripts, Plans, Goals and Understanding: An Inquiry into Human Knowledge Structures*. Lawrence Erlbaum, Hillsdale, New Jersey.

[Schoppers 1987] Schoppers, Marcel J. 1987. Universal plans for reactive robots in unpredictable environments. In *Proceedings IJCAI 10*. IJCAII. 1039–1046.

[Schorr and Rappaport 1989] Schorr, Herbert and Rappaport, Alain, editors 1989. *Innovative Applications of Artificial Intelligence*. MIT Press, Cambridge, Massachusetts.

[Sejnowski and Rosenberg 1987] Sejnowski, T. J. and Rosenberg, C. R. 1987. Parallel networks that learn to pronounce english text. *Complex Systems* 1.

[Selman *et al.* 1992] Selman, Bart; Levesque, Hector; and Mitchell, David 1992. A new method for solving hard satisfiability problems. In *Proceedings AAAI-92*. AAAI. 440–446.

[Shachter 1986] Shachter, Ross D. 1986. Evaluating influence diagrams. *Operations Research* 34(6):871–882.

[Shafer *et al.* 1983] Shafer, S.; Kanade, T.; and Kender, J. 1983. Gradient space under orthography and perspective. *Computer Vision, Graphic, Image Processing* 24:182–199.

[Shavlik and Dietterich 1990] Shavlik, Jude W. and Dietterich, Thomas G., editors 1990. *Readings in Machine Learning*. Morgan-Kaufmann, Los Altos, California.

[Shoham 1986] Shoham, Yoav 1986. Chronological ignorance: Time, nonmonotonicity, necessity, and causal theories. In *Proceedings AAAI-86*. AAAI. 389–393.

[Shoham 1988] Shoham, Yoav 1988. *Reasoning About Change: Time and Causation from the Standpoint of Artificial Intelligence*. MIT Press, Cambridge, Massachusetts.

[Shoham 1994] Shoham, Yoav 1994. *Artificial Intelligence Techniques in Prolog*. Morgan-Kaufmann, Los Altos, California.

[Shortliffe 1976] Shortliffe, E. H. 1976. *Computer-Based Medical Consultations: MYCIN*. American Elsevier, New York.

[Simmons and Davis 1987] Simmons, Reid and Davis, Randall 1987. Generate, test and debug: Combining associational rules and causal models. In *Proceedings IJCAI 10*. IJCAII. 1071–1078.

[Simon 1981] Simon, Herbert A. 1981. *The Sciences of the Artificial*. MIT Press, Cambridge, Massachusetts.

[Singh 1990] Singh, A. 1990. *Optic flow computation: A unified perspective*. Ph.D. Dissertation, Department of Computer Science, Columbia University, New York.

[Slate and Atkin 1977] Slate, D. J. and Atkin, L. R. 1977. *Chess 4.5: The Northwestern University Chess Program*. Springer-Verlag, New York.

[Steele Jr. 1990] Steele Jr., Guy L. 1990. *Common Lisp: The Language, Second Edition*. Digital Press, Billerica, Massachusetts.

[Stefik 1981] Stefik, Mark J. 1981. Planning with constraints. *Artificial Intelligence* 16:111–140.

[Sterling and Shapiro 1986] Sterling, Leon and Shapiro, Ehud 1986. *Qualitative Reasoning and Physical Systems*. MIT Press, Cambridge, Massachusetts.

[Sussman 1975] Sussman, Gerald J. 1975. *A Computer Model of Skill Acquisition*. American Elsevier, New York.

[Sutton 1988] Sutton, Richard S. 1988. Learning to predict by the methods of temporal differences. *Machine Learning* 3:9–44.

[Szolovits 1982] Szolovits, Peter 1982. Artificial intelligence in medicine. In Szolovits, Peter, editor 1982, *Artificial Intelligence in Medicine*. Westview, Boulder, Colorado. 1–19.

[Tate 1977] Tate, Austin 1977. Generating project networks. In *Proceedings IJCAI 5*. IJCAII. 888–893.

[Terzopoulos 1986] Terzopoulos, D. 1986. Image analysis using multigrid relaxation methods. *IEEE Transactions on Pattern Analysis and Machine Intelligence* 8:129–139.

[Tesauro and Sejnowski 1987] Tesauro, G and Sejnowski, T. J. 1987. A neural network that learns to play backgammon. In Anderson, D. Z., editor 1987, *Neural Information Processing Systems*. American Institute of Physics, New York.

[Tesauro 1992] Tesauro, Gerald 1992. Practial issues in temporal difference learning. *Machine Learning* 8.

[Touretsky 1984] Touretsky, David 1984. *LISP, A Gentle Introduction to Symbolic Computation*. Harper and Row, New York.

[Tsai and Huang 1984] Tsai, R.Y. and Huang, T.S. 1984. Uniqueness and estimation of three-dimensional motion parameters of rigid objects with curved surfaces. *IEEE Transactions on Pattern Analysis and Machine Intelligence* 6:13–27.

[Tsotsos 1989] Tsotsos, J. 1989. The complexity of perceptual search tasks. In *Proceedings of IJCAI 11.* IJCAII. 1517–1577.

[Turing 1950] Turing, Alan 1950. Computing machinery and intelligence. *Mind* 59:434–460.

[Ullman 1981] Ullman, Shimon 1981. Analysis of visual motion by biological and computer systems. *Computer* 14(8):57–69.

[Valiant 1984] Valiant, L. G. 1984. A theory of the learnable. *Communications of the ACM* 27:1134–1142.

[Waltz 1975] Waltz, D. 1975. Understanding line drawings of scenes with shadows. In Winston, P.H., editor 1975, *The Psychology of Computer Vision.* McGraw-Hill, New York. 19–91.

[Warren 1974] Warren, David 1974. Warplan: A system for generating plans. Technical Report Memo 76, Department of Computational Logic, University of Edinburgh.

[Waterman and Hayes-Roth 1978] Waterman, D. A. and Hayes-Roth, Frederick 1978. *Pattern-Directed Inference Systems.* Academic Press, New York.

[Waxman and Ullman 1985] Waxman, A.M. and Ullman, S. 1985. Surface structure and three-dimensional motion from image flow kinematics. *International Journal of Robotics Research* 4:72–94.

[Weld 1994] Weld, Daniel S. 1994. An introduction to partial-order planning. *AI Magazine* Fall.

[Wellman 1990] Wellman, Michael P. 1990. *Formulation of Tradeoffs in Planning Under Uncertainty.* Pitman, London.

[Werbos 1974] Werbos, P.J. 1974. Beyond regression: New tools for prediction and analysis in the behavioral sciences. Ph.D. Thesis, Harvard University.

[Widrow and Hoff 1960] Widrow, B. and Hoff, M. E. 1960. Adaptive switching circuits. In *1960 WESCON Convention Record Part IV, (Reprinted in J. A. Anderson and E. Rosenfeld,* Neurocomputing: Foundations of Research, *The MIT Press, Cambridge, MA, 1988).* 96–104.

[Wilensky 1983] Wilensky, Robert 1983. *Planning and Understanding.* Addison-Wesley, Reading, Massachusetts.

[Wilensky 1986] Wilensky, Robert 1986. *Common Lisp Craft.* Norton, New York.

[Wilkins 1988] Wilkins, David E. 1988. *Practical Planning: Extending the Classical AI Planning Paradigm.* Morgan-Kaufmann, Los Altos, California.

[Winograd 1983] Winograd, Terry 1983. *Language as a Cognitive Process, Volume 1: Syntax.* Addison-Wesley, Reading, Massachusetts.

[Winston 1992] Winston, Patrick H. 1992. *Artificial Intelligence, Third Edition.* Addison-Wesley, Reading, Massachusetts.

[Witkin 1981] Witkin, A.P. 1981. Recovering surface shape and orientation from texture. *Artificial Intelligence* 17:17–45.

[Wolf 1974] Wolf, P.R. 1974. *Elements of Photogrammetry.* McGraw-Hill, New York.

[Woodham 1980] Woodham, R.J. 1980. Photometric method for determining surface orientation from multiple images. *Optical Engineering* 19:139–144.

[Woodham 1981] Woodham, R.J. 1981. Analyzing images of curved surfaces. *Artificial Intelligence* 17:117–141.

[Wos et al. 1984] Wos, Larry; Overbeek, Ross; Lusk, Ewing; and Boyle, Jim 1984. *Automated Reasoning: Introduction and Applications.* Prentice-Hall, Englewood Cliffs, N.J.

VOCABULARY INDEX

CODE INDEX